Lecture Notes in Computer Science 6584

Commenced Publication in 1973
Founding and Former Series Editors:
Gerhard Goos, Juris Hartmanis, and Jan van Leeuwen

Xuejia Lai   Moti Yung   Dongdai Lin (Eds.)

Information Security and Cryptology

6th International Conference, Inscrypt 2010
Shanghai, China, October 20-24, 2010
Revised Selected Papers

 Springer

Volume Editors

Xuejia Lai
Shanghai Jiaotong University, Department of Computer Science and Engineering
Dongchuan Road 800, Shanghai 200240, China
E-mail: lai-xj@cs.sjtu.edu.cn

Moti Yung
Google Inc. and Columbia University, Computer Science Department
S.W. Mudd Building, New York, NY 10027, USA
E-mail: moti@cs.columbia.edu

Dongdai Lin
SKLOIS, Chinese Academy of Sciences, Institute of Software
Beijing 100190, China
E-mail: ddlin@is.iscas.ac.cn

ISSN 0302-9743   e-ISSN 1611-3349
ISBN 978-3-642-21517-9   e-ISBN 978-3-642-21518-6
DOI 10.1007/978-3-642-21518-6
Springer Heidelberg Dordrecht London New York

Library of Congress Control Number: 2011928934

CR Subject Classification (1998): C.2, K.6.5, E.3, D.4.6, J.1, K.4.4

LNCS Sublibrary: SL 4 – Security and Cryptology

Typesetting: Camera-ready by author, data conversion by Scientific Publishing Services, Chennai, India

Printed on acid-free paper

Springer is part of Springer Science+Business Media (www.springer.com)

Preface

The 6th China International Conference on Information Security and Cryptology (Inscrypt 2010) was held in Shanghai, China, during October 20–23, 2010. The conference is a leading annual international event in the area of cryptography and information security taking place in China. Inscrypt continues to get the support of the entire international community, reflecting the fact that the research areas covered by the conference are important to modern computing, where increased security, trust, safety and reliability are required.

Inscrypt 2010 was co-organized by the State Key Laboratory of Information Security and by the Chinese Association for Cryptologic Research, in cooperation with Shanghai Jiaotong Univeristy and the International Association for Cryptologic Research (IACR). The conference was further sponsored by the Institute of Software, the Graduate University of the Chinese Academy of Science and the National Natural Science Foundations of China.

The scientific program of the conference covered all areas of current research in cryptography and security, with sessions on central subjects of cryptographic research and on some important subjects of information security. The international Program Committee of Inscrypt 2010 received a total of 125 submissions from more than 29 countries and regions, from which only 35 submissions were selected for presentation in the regular papers track and 13 submissions in the short papers track. Regular track papers appear in these proceedings volume. All anonymous submissions were reviewed by experts in the relevant areas and based on their ranking, technical remarks and strict selection criteria the papers were chosen to the various tracks. The selection to both tracks was a highly competitive process. We further note that due to the conference format, many good papers were regrettably not accepted. Besides the contributed papers, the program also included two invited presentations by Bart Preneel and Moti Yung.

Inscrypt 2010 was made possible by a joint effort of numerous people and organizations worldwide. We take this opportunity to thank the Program Committee members and the external experts they employed for their invaluable help in producing the conference program. We further thank the conference Organizing Committee, the various sponsors, and the conference attendees. Last but not least, we express our great gratitude to all the authors who submitted papers to the conference, the invited speakers, and the session Chairs.

December 2010

Xuejia Lai
Moti Yung

Inscrypt 2010

6th China International Conference on Information Security and Cryptology

Shanghai, China
October 20–23, 2010

Sponsored and organized by

State Key Laboratory of Information Security
(Chinese Academy of Sciences)
Chinese Association for Cryptologic Research

in cooperation with

Shanghai Jiaotong University
International Association for Cryptologic Research

Steering Committee

Dengguo Feng	SKLOIS, Chinese Academy of Sciences, China
Dongdai Lin	SKLOIS, Chinese Academy of Sciences, China
Moti Yung	Google Inc. and Columbia University, USA
Chuankun Wu	SKLOIS, Chinese Academy of Sciences, China

General Chair

Dengguo Feng	SKLOIS, Chinese Academy of Sciences, China

Program Committee

Co-chairs

Xuejia Lai	Shanghai Jiaotong University, China
Moti Yung	Google Inc. and Columbia University, USA

Members

Vladimir Anashin	Moscow State University, Russia
Frederik Armknecht	Institute for Computer Science at the University of Mannheim, Germany
Rana Barua	Indian Statistical Institute, Kolkata, India
Zhenfu Cao	Shanghai Jiaotong University, China
Claude Carlet	Université Paris 8, France

Proceedings Co-editors

Xuejia Lai	Shanghai Jiaotong University, China
Moti Yung	Google Inc. and Columbia University, USA
Dongdai Lin	SKLOIS, Chinese Academy of Sciences, China

Organizing Committee

Co-chairs

Kefei Chen	Shanghai Jiaotong University, China
Chuankun Wu	SKLOIS, Chinese Academy of Sciences, China

Members

Feng Liu	Institute of Software, CAS, China
Yanfei Zheng	Shanghai Jiaotong University, China
Xianping Mao	Shanghai Jiaotong University, China

Publication Chair

Dongdai Lin   SKLOIS, Chinese Academy of Sciences, China

WEB Master

Jinyuan Tang   Institute of Software, CAS, China

Conference Secretary

Yi Qin   Institute of Software, CAS, China

Table of Contents

Hash Functions

Key Management

Digital Signatures

Privacy and Algebraic Cryptanalysis

Hashing and Authentication

Hardware and Software Issues

New Constructions of Public-Key Encryption Schemes from Conjugacy Search Problems

Lihua Wang[1], Licheng Wang[2,1], Zhenfu Cao[3], Eiji Okamoto[4], and Jun Shao[5]

[1] Information Security Research Center, National Institute of Information and Communications Technology, Tokyo 184-8795, Japan
[2] Information Security Center, State Key Laboratory of Networking and Switching Technology, Beijing University of Posts and Telecommunications Beijing, 100876, P.R. China
[3] Trusted Digital Technology Laboratory, Shanghai Jiao Tong University Shanghai, 200240, P.R. China
[4] Graduate School of Systems and Information Engineering, University of Tsukuba, Tsukuba 305-8573, Japan
[5] College of Computer and Information Engineering, Zhejiang Gongshang University Hangzhou, 310018, P.R. China

Abstract. We propose new public-key encryption schemes based on the conjugacy search problems (CSP) over noncommutative monoids. Under the newly developed cryptographic assumptions, our basic construction is proven IND-CPA secure in the standard model. Then, we describe two extensions: The first is proven IND-CCA secure in the random oracle model, while the second achieves the IND-CCA security in the standard model. Finally, our proposal is instantiated by using the monoid of matrices over truncated multivariable polynomials over rings. Meanwhile, we also give a discussion on the possibility to instantiate our schemes with braid groups.

Keywords: public-key encryption, conjugacy search problems, truncated multivariable polynomials over rings, braid groups.

1 Introduction

Most public-key cryptosystems that remain unbroken are based on the perceived difficulty of solving certain problems in large finite (abelian) groups. The theoretical foundations of these cryptosystems are related to the intractability of problems that are *closer to* number theory *than to* group theory [23]. In a quantum computer, most of these problems on number theory can be efficiently solved by using algorithms developed by Shor [27], Kitaev [17] and Proos-Zalka [26]. Although the quantum computation is still in its infancy, the knowledge regarding their potential will soon create distrust in the current cryptographic methods [21]. In order to enrich cryptography and not to put all eggs in one basket [21], many attempts have been made to develop alternative public-key cryptography (PKC) based on different kinds of problems [2,19,21,23].

X. Lai, M. Yung, and D. Lin (Eds.): Inscrypt 2010, LNCS 6584, pp. 1–17, 2011.

Under this background, some noncommutative groups have been attracted considerable attentions. One of the most popular groups in this category is the braid group. In 1999, Anshel et al. [2] proposed an algebraic method for PKC. Shortly afterward, Ko et al. [19] published a fully fledged encryption scheme using braid groups. In these schemes, the conjugacy search problem (CSP) (i.e., given two braids a and xax^{-1}, output the braid x) and its variants play a core role. Although there is no deterministic polynomial algorithms that can solve the CSP problem over braid groups [28] till now, many heuristic attacks, such as length-based attacks, linear representation attacks, have obtained remarkable success in attacking braid-based cryptosytems and lowered the initial enthusiasm on this subject. Naturally, two crucial questions arise: (1) Can we find some concrete platforms in which the CSP problems are intractable? If so, then many braid-based schemes can be transplanted into the new platforms; (2) Under the intractability assumption of certain platforms, how to design secure cryptographic schemes? Most recently, Grigoriev and Shpilrain [15] gave an informal analysis on the intractability of the CSP problem in the monoid of $n \times n$ matrices over truncated multivariable polynomials over a ring. This can be viewed as a potential answer for the first question. In this paper, we mainly focus on the second question.

We at first develop some cryptographic assumptions related to the CSP problem over noncommutative monoids, and then propose new public-key encryption schemes based on these assumptions. Under a stronger assumption, i.e., the CSP-DDH assumption, the ciphertext of our basic construction is proven indistinguishable against chosen plaintext attacks (IND-CPA) in the standard model. Then, two extended schemes that achieve the IND-CCA security are described. Finally, we instantiate our proposal by using the monoid of matrices over truncated multivariable polynomials over a ring [15]. Meanwhile, if the problem of sampling hard CSP instances from braid groups is solved, our proposal can also be instantiated with braid groups.

The rest of contents are organized as follows: In Section 2, we at first give a review on the CSP problem and left self-distributive system; and then we prove some properties for the CSP-based left self-distributive (Conj-LD) system; more fledged cryptographic assumptions over the Conj-LD system are developed in Section 3; based on these newly developed assumptions, a Diffie-Hellman-like key agreement protocol, an ElGamal-like encryption scheme and its hashed extension, as well as a Cramer-Shoup-like encryption scheme are proposed in Section 4; meanwhile, possible implementations on our proposal are addressed. Concluding remarks are given in Section 5.

2   Conjugacy Search Problem and Conj-LD System

At first, let us recall the definition of the conjugacy search problem and the so-called left self-distributive system [9].

Let $(G, \circ, 1)$ be a noncommutative monoid with identity 1. For $a \in G$, if there exists an element $b \in G$ so that $a \circ b = 1 = b \circ a$, then we say that a is *invertible*, and call b *an inverse of* a; the inverses of a, if they exist, are unique, and thus denoted by a^{-1}. *Note that not all elements in G are invertible.* In a monoid, one can define positive integer powers of an element a: $a^1 = a$, and $a^n = \underbrace{a \circ \cdots \circ a}_{n \text{ times}}$

for $n > 1$; if b is inverse of a, one can also define negative powers of a by setting $a^{-1} = b$ and $a^{-n} = \underbrace{b \circ \cdots \circ b}_{n \text{ times}}$ for $n > 1$. In addition, let us denote $a^0 = 1$ for

each element $a \in G$.

Throughout this paper, let G^{-1} be the set of all invertible elements belonging to G, i.e.,

$$G^{-1} \triangleq \{a \in G : \exists b \in G \text{ so that } a \circ b = 1 = b \circ a\}. \tag{1}$$

In fact, $(G^{-1}, \circ, 1)$ forms a group. For clarity, we omit "$\circ$" in the following presentation, i.e., writing $a \circ b$ as ab directly.

The conjugacy problem is extensively studied in *group theory*. But is this paper, we would like to use the conjugacy concept in *the context of monoid* by a similar manner: Given a monoid G with elements $a \in G$ and $x \in G^{-1}$, there must be an element $b \in G$ which is a similarity transformation of a, $b = xax^{-1}$ so we say that a and b are *conjugate* with respect to x [12].

Definition 1 (Conjugacy Search Problem, CSP). *Let G be a noncommutative monoid. Given two elements $a, b \in G$ so that $b = xax^{-1}$ for some unknown element $x \in G^{-1}$, the objective of the conjugacy search problem in G is to find $x' \in G^{-1}$ such that $b = x'ax'^{-1}$ holds. Here, x' is not required to be equivalent to x.*

Definition 2 (Left self-distributive system, LD[9]). *Suppose that S is a non-empty set, $F : S \times S \to S$ is a well-defined function and let us denote $F(a, b)$ by $F_a(b)$. If the following rewrite formula holds,*

$$F_r(F_s(p)) = F_{F_r(s)}(F_r(p)), \quad (\forall p, r, s \in S) \tag{2}$$

then, we call $F.(\cdot)$ a left self-distributive system, abbreviated as LD system.

The terminology "left self-distributive" arises from the following analogical observation: If we consider $F_r(s)$ as a binary operation $r * s$, then the formula (2) becomes

$$r * (s * p) = (r * s) * (r * p), \tag{3}$$

i.e., the operation "$*$" is left distributive with respect to itself [9].

Then, combining the above two concepts together, one can define the following LD system, named as Conj-LD system, which means an abbreviation of left self-distributive system defined by conjugate operations.

Definition 3 (Conj-LD System). *Let G be a noncommutative monoid. The binary function F given by the following conjugate operation*

$$F : G^{-1} \times G \to G, \quad (a, b) \mapsto aba^{-1}. \tag{4}$$

is an LD system, abbreviated as Conj-LD.

Proof. It is easy to see that F caters to the rewrite formula (2). Thus, $F_a(b)$ is an LD system.   □

To proceed, we prove some properties of the Conj-LD system. These properties are considerable simple, but very useful from the cryptographic viewpoint, providing that the related hardness assumptions hold.

Proposition 1. *Let G be a noncommutative monoid and F be a Conj-LD system defined over a noncommutative monoid G. For given $a \in G^{-1}$ and $b, c \in G$, we have that*

(i) F is idempotent in the sense of $F_a(a) = a$;
(ii) F is mutual inverse in the sense of $F_a(b) = c \Leftrightarrow F_{a^{-1}}(c) = b$;
(iii) F is homomorphic in the sense of $F_a(bc) = F_a(b)F_a(c)$.

Proof. See Appendix A.

Proposition 2 (Power Law). *Let G be a noncommutative monoid and F be a Conj-LD system defined over a noncommutative monoid G. Suppose that $a \in G^{-1}$ and $b \in G$ are given and fixed. Then, for arbitrary three positive integers m, s, t such that $m = s + t$, we have that*

$$F_a(b^m) = F_a(b^s)F_a(b^t) = F_a^m(b) \quad and \quad F_{a^m}(b) = F_{a^s}(F_{a^t}(b)). \quad (5)$$

Proof. It is easy to obtain by combining the property (iii) in Proposition 1, and the definition of the Conj-LD system given by the formula (4).

Remark 1. Careful readers might find that the above properties are essentially irrelevant for the so-called left self-distributiveness. However, for the following reasons we would like to use the term of left self-distributive system:

- First, the binary function defined by the formula (4) *does* satisfy the left self-distributiveness defined by the formula (2). Thus, we have no serious reason to refute referring it as a LD system. In addition, it is more convenient to use $F_a(b)$ than to user aba^{-1} in the sequel presentation, especially when some additional operations are exerted on a and a^{-1} simultaneously from both sides.
- Second, our originality is enlightened by Dehornoy's previous work on left self-distributive systems. In 2006, Dehorney [9] proposed an authentication scheme based on left self-distributive systems in braid groups. Although some cryptanalysis on Dehorney's authentication scheme were reported [22], we find that Dehorney's work is still meaningful at least in the following two aspects: (1) self-distributive systems can be defined over arbitrary non-commutative monoids, rather than braid groups only; (2) self-distributive systems have the potential for building variety of cryptographic schemes, rather than authentication schemes only. Therefore, in this paper, we would like to use the terminology of (left) self-distributive system with the purpose to give Dehornoy the credit for his pioneering work.

Now, using the notation of $F.(\cdot)$, the intractability assumption of the CSP problem in G can be re-formulated as follows: It is hard to retrieve a' from the given pair $(a, F_a(b))$ such that $F_a(b) = F_{a'}(b)$. We must take care of the relationship between the intractability assumption of CSP and the hardness CSP instances. The CSP problem is defined here as a *worst-case* problem, whereas from the cryptographic viewpoint, one needs *average-case* hardness for CSP instances. Therefore, we need a practical sample algorithm that can produce hard instances of CSP over G. For a generic noncommutative monoid G without explicit definition or presentation, it is difficult to discuss whether we can sample hard CSP instances from G. As for possible platforms on which our proposal is instantiated, we will address this issue in detail later(See Section 4.3). In sequel, the CSP instances used in our proposal are always assumed to be hard.

3 New Cryptographic Assumptions over Conj-LD Systems

Let G be a noncommutative monoid. Given a Conj-LD system F over a non-commutative monoid G (cf. Definition 3). For given $a \in G^{-1}$, let G_a denote the subgroup generated by $\{a, a^{-1}\}$, i.e., $G_a \triangleq \langle a, a^{-1} \rangle$. Now, for given $a \in G^{-1}$ and $b \in G$, let us define the following notations and use them in sequel without further explanation:

- $\mathbb{T} \triangleq \{1, \cdots, n\}$ is a *finite* subset of $\mathbb{Z}$, where n is the order of G_a.[1]
- The symbols "$\in \mathbb{T}$" and "$\xleftarrow{\$} \mathbb{T}$" always indicate sampling procedures that pick random integers uniformly from $\mathbb{T}$.
- $\mathcal{K}_{[a,b]} \triangleq \{F_{a^i}(b) : i \in \mathbb{T}\}$ is a *finite* subset of G.

Note that in cryptographic applications, a, b should be chosen appropriately so that n as well as $\mathcal{K}_{[a,b]}$ are large enough to resist exhaustive attacks.

Definition 4 (CSP-based Computational Diffie-Hellman: CSP-CDH).
Let G be a noncommutative monoid. Suppose F be a Conj-LD system over a noncommutative monoid G and let $\mathcal{A}$ be an adversary. For given $a \in G^{-1}$ and $b \in G$, consider the following experiment

$$\text{experiment } \mathbf{Exp}_{F,\mathcal{A}}^{csp-cdh}$$
$$i \xleftarrow{\$} \mathbb{T}; X \leftarrow F_{a^i}(b);$$
$$j \xleftarrow{\$} \mathbb{T}; Y \leftarrow F_{a^j}(b);$$
$$Z \leftarrow \mathcal{A}(X, Y);$$
$$\text{if } Z = F_{a^{i+j}}(b) \text{ then } b \leftarrow 1 \text{ else } b \leftarrow 0;$$
$$\text{return } b.$$

---

[1] In case of G_a is *infinite*, we can set n as a fixed integer that is large enough to resist exhaustive attacks, say 2^{160}. Furthermore, with the purpose to ensure the randomness of sampling from $\mathcal{K}_{[a,b]}$, n should be the order of a factor-group of G_a modulo the centralizer of b in G_a.

Now define the advantage *of $\mathcal{A}$ in violating the CSP-based computational Diffie-Hellman assumption as*

$$\mathbf{Adv}_{F,\mathcal{A}}^{csp-cdh} = \Pr[\mathbf{Exp}_{F,\mathcal{A}}^{csp-cdh} = 1]. \tag{6}$$

The CSP-CDH assumption states, roughly, that given $F_{a^i}(b)$ and $F_{a^j}(b)$, where i, j were drawn at random from $\mathbb{T}$, it is hard to compute $F_{a^{i+j}}(b)$. Under the CSP-CDH assumption it might well be possible for the adversary to compute something interesting about $F_{a^{i+j}}(b)$ given $F_{a^i}(b)$ and $F_{a^j}(b)$; for example, the adversary might be able to compute the most significant bit, or even half of the bits. This makes the assumption too weak to directly use in typical applications. Thus, we need the following stronger variants.

Definition 5 (CSP-based Decisional Diffie-Hellman: CSP-DDH). *Let G be a noncommutative monoid. Suppose F be a Conj-LD system over a noncommutative monoid G and let $\mathcal{A}$ be an adversary. For given $a \in G^{-1}$ and $b \in G$, consider the following two experiments in a paralleled manner*

experiment $\mathbf{Exp}_{F,\mathcal{A}}^{csp-ddh-real}$	experiment $\mathbf{Exp}_{F,\mathcal{A}}^{csp-ddh-rand}$
$i \xleftarrow{\$} \mathbb{T}; X \leftarrow F_{a^i}(b);$	$i \xleftarrow{\$} \mathbb{T}; X \leftarrow F_{a^i}(b);$
$j \xleftarrow{\$} \mathbb{T}; Y \leftarrow F_{a^j}(b);$	$j \xleftarrow{\$} \mathbb{T}; Y \leftarrow F_{a^j}(b);$
$Z \leftarrow F_{a^{i+j}}(b);$	$\ell \xleftarrow{\$} \mathbb{T}; Z \leftarrow F_{a^\ell}(b);$
$b \leftarrow \mathcal{A}(X, Y, Z);$	$b \leftarrow \mathcal{A}(X, Y, Z);$
return b.	*return* b.

Now define the advantage *of $\mathcal{A}$ in violating the CSP-based decisional Diffie-Hellman assumption as*

$$\mathbf{Adv}_{F,\mathcal{A}}^{csp-ddh} = |\Pr[\mathbf{Exp}_{F,\mathcal{A}}^{csp-ddh-real} = 1] - \Pr[\mathbf{Exp}_{F,\mathcal{A}}^{csp-ddh-rand} = 1]|. \tag{7}$$

In other words, the CSP-DDH assumption states, roughly, that the distributions $(F_{a^i}(b), F_{a^j}(b), F_{a^{i+j}}(b))$ and $(F_{a^i}(b), F_{a^j}(b), F_{a^\ell}(b))$ are computationally indistinguishable when i, j, ℓ are drawn at random from $\mathbb{T}$.

We now move on to another assumption that will be used in our proposal. Here, the adversary is allowed to access a restricted CSP-DDH oracle $\mathcal{O}_v(\cdot, \cdot)$, which behaves as follows:

$$\mathcal{O}_v(X, U) = \begin{cases} 1, \text{if } U = F_v(X); \\ 0, \text{otherwise.} \end{cases} \tag{8}$$

That is, the oracle tells whether the second argument equal to conjugating the first argument by v. This oracle can be seen as a restricted form a CSP-DDH oracle for which we fix one of its arguments as being $F_v(b)$.

Definition 6 (CSP-based Strong Diffie-Hellman: CSP-SDH). *Let G be a noncommutative monoid. Suppose F be a Conj-LD system over a noncommutative monoid G and let $\mathcal{A}$ be an adversary. For given $a \in G^{-1}$ and $b \in G$, consider the following experiment*

$$experiment\ \mathbf{Exp}_{F,\mathcal{A}}^{csp-sdh}$$

$$i \overset{\$}{\leftarrow} \mathbb{T}; X \leftarrow F_{a^i}(b);$$

$$j \overset{\$}{\leftarrow} \mathbb{T}; Y \leftarrow F_{a^j}(b);$$

$$\mathcal{O}_v(X, U) \overset{def}{=} (U = F_v(X));$$

$$Z \leftarrow \mathcal{A}^{\mathcal{O}_v(\cdot,\cdot)}(X, Y);$$

$$if\ Z = F_{a^{i+j}}(b)\ then\ b \leftarrow 1\ else\ b \leftarrow 0;$$

$$return\ b.$$

Now define the advantage *of $\mathcal{A}$ in violating the CSP-based strong Diffie-Hellman assumption as*

$$\mathbf{Adv}_{F,\mathcal{A}}^{csp-sdh} = \Pr[\mathbf{Exp}_{F,\mathcal{A}}^{csp-sdh} = 1]. \tag{9}$$

The intuition behind the CSP-SDH assumption is that the restricted CSP-DDH oracle is useless because the adversary already "knows" the answer to almost any query it will ask. Similar to [6], it is also worth mentioning that the CSP-SDH assumption is different from (and weaker than) the so-called *gap CSP-CDH assumption* where an adversary gets access to a *full* CSP-DDH desicion oracle.

Remark 2. At present, it is unclear whether the CSP-DDH problem is actually hard or not. Intuitively, we cannot solve the CSP-DDH problem without solving the CSP problem if G is modeled as a generic monoid model. In fact, the CSP problem and the CSP-DDH problem over Conj-LD systems over a noncommutative monoids are direct analogies of the DLP problem and the DDH problem over finite fileds, respectively. According to [24], we know that the DLP problem and the DDH problem are polynomially equivalent in a generic cyclic group. Therefore, by an analogical manner, we speculate that the CSP problem and the CSP-DDH problem in a generic noncommutative monoid are polynomially equivalent.

4 Cryptosystems from CSP-Based Left Self-distributive Systems

In this section, we always assume that G is a noncommutative monoid and F is a Conj-LD system defined over a noncommutative monoid G, while $a \in G^{-1}$ and $b \in G$ are two fixed elements.

4.1 Constructions

As a warmup step, let us at first describe a Diffie-Hellman-like key agreement protocol [10] by using the CSP-DDH assumption over a noncommutative monoid G. Assume that Alice and Bob want to negotiate a common session key. Then, Alice (resp. Bob) picks $s \in \mathbb{T}$ (resp. $t \in \mathbb{T}$) and then sends $F_{a^s}(b)$ (resp. $F_{a^t}(b)$) to Bob (resp. Alice). Finally, both of them can extract $F_{a^{s+t}}(b)$, by which a session key can be defined as

$$K_{session} = Kdf(F_{a^{s+t}}(b)), \tag{10}$$

where $Kdf(\cdot)$ is a key derivation function, such as KDF1 defined in IEEE Std 1363-2000.

The above protocol[2] immediately implies the following ElGamal-like construction.

The Basic Scheme—CSP-ElG. Our basic construction, which is an analogy of the ElGamal cryptosystem [11] and thus denoted by CSP-ElG, consists of the following three algorithms:

- **Key-generation.** Suppose that k is the security parameter, $\mathcal{M} = \{0,1\}^k$ is the message space, and $\mathcal{C} = \mathcal{K}_{[a,b]} \times \mathcal{M}$ is the ciphertext space. In addition, we need a cryptographic hash function $H : \mathcal{K}_{[a,b]} \to \mathcal{M}$. A user at first picks $s \in \mathbb{T}$, and then publishes $pk = F_{a^s}(b)$ as his public key, while keeps his secret key $sk = s$ unrevealed.
- **Encryption.** Given the public-key $pk \in \mathcal{K}_{[a,b]}$ and a message $m \in \mathcal{M}$, one picks $t \in \mathbb{T}$, and then constructs a ciphertext as follows:

$$c = (F_{a^t}(b), \ m \oplus H(F_{a^t}(pk))) \tag{11}$$

- **Decryption.** Given the secret key $s \in \mathbb{T}$ and a ciphertext $c = (c_1, c_2) \in \mathcal{K}_{[a,b]} \times \mathcal{M}$, one can extract a plaintext as follows:

$$m = c_2 \oplus H(F_{a^s}(c_1)) \tag{12}$$

The consistency of the CSP-ElG scheme is directly implied by the power law of the Conj-LD system, while the security of the CSP-ElG scheme is captured by the follow theorem.

Theorem 1 (IND-CPA of CSP-ElG). *Based on the CSP-DDH assumption, the ciphertexts of the encryption scheme CSP-ElG are indistinguishable under chosen plaintext attacks in the standard model.*

Proof. See Appendix B.

Based on the above scheme, it is not difficult to derive a CCA secure encryption scheme by employing the Fujisaki-Okamoto transformation [13]. Here, we would like to give two different extensions that are enlightened by [6,1,20,7]. The first extension is called the hashed ElGamal variant that is IND-CCA secure in the random oracle model, while the second is called the Cramer-Shoup-like variant that is IND-CCA secure even in the standard model.

---

[2] This protocol cannot resist the so-called man-in-the-middle attack. But in this study we don't pay attention to how to remedy it.

The First Extended Scheme—CSP-hElG. Our first extension is the hashed version of the above CSP-ElG scheme and thus denoted by CSP-hElG. The CSP-hElG scheme consists of the following three algorithms:

- **Key-generation.** Suppose that k is the security parameter, $\mathcal{M} = \{0,1\}^k$ is the message space, and $\mathcal{C} = \mathcal{K}_{[a,b]} \times \mathcal{M}$ is the ciphertext space. In addition, we need a symmetric cipher $\Pi = (E, D)$ with the key space $\mathcal{K}$ and a hash function $H : \mathcal{K}_{[a,b]}^2 \to \mathcal{K}$. A user at first picks an integer $s \in \mathbb{T}$, and then publishes $pk = F_{a^s}(b)$ as his public key, while keeps his secret key $sk = s$ unrevealed.
- **Encryption.** Given the public-key $pk \in \mathcal{K}_{[a,b]}$ and a message $m \in \mathcal{M}$, one picks an integer $t \in \mathbb{T}$, and then constructs a ciphertext $c = (c_1, c_2)$ as follows:

$$c_1 := F_{a^t}(b), \ T := F_{a^t}(pk), \ K := H(c_1, T), \ c_2 := E_K(m) \qquad (13)$$

- **Decryption.** Given the secret key $s \in \mathbb{T}$ and a ciphertext $c = (c_1, c_2) \in \mathcal{K}_{[a,b]} \times \mathcal{M}$, one can extract a plaintext as follows:

$$Z := F_{a^s}(c_1), \ K := H(c_1, Z), \ m := D_K(c_2) \qquad (14)$$

The consistency of the CSP-hElG scheme can also be easily verified according to the power law of the Conj-LD system, while the security of the CSP-ElG scheme is formulated by the follow theorem.

Theorem 2 (IND-CCA of CSP-hElG). *If H is modeled as a random oracle, and the underlying symmetric cipher Π is itself secure against chosen ciphertext attacks, then the hashed ElGamal encryption scheme CSP-hElG is secure against chosen ciphertext attacks under the strong CSP-CDH assumption.*

Proof. Analogically implied by Theorem 2 in [1] and Theorem 1 in [20], as well as the improvement of DHIES given in Section 5.1 of [20]. □

The Second Extended Scheme—CSP-CS. Our second extension, denoted by CSP-CS, is an analogy of the well-known cryptosystem due to Cramer and Shoup [7]. The CSP-CS scheme consists of the following three algorithms:

- **Key-generation.** Suppose that k is the security parameter, $\mathcal{M} = \{0,1\}^k$ is the message space, and $\mathcal{C} = \mathcal{K}_{[a,b]}^2 \times \widetilde{\mathcal{K}_{[a,b]}} \times \mathcal{M}$ is the ciphertext space, where $\widetilde{\mathcal{K}_{[a,b]}}$ is defined as

$$\widetilde{\mathcal{K}_{[a,b]}} \triangleq \{F_{a^i}(F_{a^{j_1}}(b)F_{a^{j_2}}(b)) : i, j_1, j_2 \in \mathbb{T}\}. \qquad (15)$$

In addition, we need a symmetric cipher $\Pi = (E, D)$ with the key space $\mathcal{K}$ and two hash functions $H : \mathcal{K}_{[a,b]}^2 \to \mathbb{T}$, and $H_1 : \mathcal{K}_{[a,b]} \to \mathcal{K}$. A user at first picks $x_1, x_2, x_3, x_4 \in \mathbb{T}$, and then publishes $pk = (X_1, X_2, X_3, X_4)$ as his public key, while keeps his secret key $sk = (x_1, x_2, x_3, x_4)$ unrevealed, where $X_i = F_{a^{x_i}}(b)$ for $i = 1, 2, 3, 4$.

- **Encryption.** Given the public-key $pk = (X_1, X_2, X_3, X_4) \in \mathcal{K}_{[a,b]}^4$ and a message $m \in \mathcal{M}$, one picks $t \in \mathbb{T}$, and then constructs a ciphertext $c = (c_1, c_2, c_3, c_4)$ as follows:

$$c_1 := F_{a^t}(b), \quad c_2 := F_{a^t}(X_1), \quad c_3 := F_{a^t}(F_{a^h}(X_2)X_3), \quad c_4 := E_K(m), \quad (16)$$

where $h := H(c_1, c_2)$ and $K := H_1(F_{a^t}(X_4))$.

- **Decryption.** Given the secret key $(x_1, x_2, x_3, x_4) \in \mathbb{T}^4$ and a ciphertext $c = (c_1, c_2, c_3, c_4) \in \mathcal{K}_{[a,b]}^2 \times \widetilde{\mathcal{K}_{[a,b]}} \times \mathcal{M}$, one at first computes $h := H(c_1, c_2)$ and then tests if

$$F_{a^{x_1}}(c_1) \overset{?}{=} c_2 \text{ and } F_{a^{h+x_2}}(c_1)F_{a^{x_3}}(c_1) \overset{?}{=} c_3.$$

If not, outputs $\perp$ indicating an invalid ciphertext. Otherwise, computes $K := H_1(F_{a^{x_4}}(c_1))$ and outputs $m := D_K(c_4)$.

The consistency and the security of the CSP-CS scheme are formulated by the follow theorems, respectively.

Theorem 3 (Consistency of CSP-CS). *The CSP-CS scheme is consistent.*

Proof. See Appendix C.

Theorem 4 (IND-CCA of CSP-CS). *Suppose H is a target collision resistant hash function. Further, suppose the CSP-DDH assumption holds, and the symmetric cipher $\Pi = (E, D)$ is secure against chosen ciphertext attack. Then CSP-CS is secure against chosen ciphertext attack.*

Proof. Analogically implied by Theorem 13 in [6].

4.2 Security and Efficiency Issues About $F_{a^t}(b)$

For computing $F_{a^t}(b)$, we should at first compute a^t, and then plus one inversion and two multiplications in the underlying noncommutative monoid G. When t is large, say several hundreds of digits, rather than to multiply a for t times, a similar "successive doubling" method should be employed, and thus a factor of $\log t$ would be taken into consideration in performance evaluations. At present, it is enough to set t as an integer with 160 bits to resist exhaustive attacks.

It is necessary to assume that the basic monoid operations (i.e., multiplication and inversion) can be finished efficiently. This assumption implies that the lengths of the representations of all elements in G, including a, b, a^t and $F_{a^t}(b)$, should be polynomial in the system security parameters, since the results have to be output bit-by-bit by using classical computers.

Moreover, we require that there is a *secure efficient canonical form* for representing elements in G. This means that

(C-1) By using this form, the representation of an element in G is unique. Otherwise, the proposed schemes cannot work.

(C-2) The transformation from an element in G to its canonical form can be finished efficiently. Otherwise, the proposed schemes are impractical.

(C-3) By using this form, the length of an element $F_{a^t}(b)$ does not reveal any information about a^t. Otherwise, the developed assumptions could suffers from the so-called length-based attacks [16].

4.3 Possible Implementations

Now, let us proceed to discuss possible implementations on our proposal.

The monoid of matrices over truncated multivariable polynomials. The first promising platform that have generically hard CSP problem is, introduced by Grigoriev and Shpilrain's [15] recently, the monoid of $\mu \times \mu$ matrices over λ-truncated κ-variable polynomials over a ring R. According to [15], we can choose the parameters as follows: $\mu = 3$, $\lambda = 1000$ and $\kappa = 10$, while the ring R is instantiated with $\mathbb{Z}_{12}$. Given a polynomial

$$f = \sum_{i_1, \cdots, i_\kappa} f_{i_1, \cdots, i_\kappa} x_1^{i_1} \cdots x_\kappa^{i_\kappa} \in \mathbb{Z}_{12}[x_1, \cdots, x_\kappa] \tag{17}$$

in $\kappa > 1$ variables, we let $\deg 0 = -1$ and define the *degree of f* by

$$\deg f = \max\{i_1 + \cdots + i_\kappa : f_{i_1, \cdots, i_\kappa} \neq 0\}. \tag{18}$$

Now, let us define [3]

$$\hat{R}_{\lambda, \kappa} \triangleq \{f \in \mathbb{Z}_{12}[x_1, \cdots, x_\kappa] : \deg(f) < \lambda\}. \tag{19}$$

Then, for $f, g \in \hat{R}_{\lambda, \kappa}$, the product of $f \circledast g$ will merely keep the term

$$(f_{i_1, \cdots, i_\kappa} x_1^{i_1} \cdots x_\kappa^{i_\kappa}) \cdot (g_{j_1, \cdots, j_\kappa} x_1^{j_1} \cdots x_\kappa^{j_\kappa}) \tag{20}$$

if $i_1 + j_1 + \cdots + i_\kappa + j_\kappa < \lambda$. Now, let us define

$$G \triangleq \mathbf{Mat}_\mu(\hat{R}_{\lambda, \kappa}), \tag{21}$$

(i.e., the set of $\mu \times \mu$ square matrices over $\hat{R}_{\lambda, \kappa}$) and for two matrices $A = (a_{ij})_{\mu \times \mu} \in G$ and $B = (b_{ij})_{\mu \times \mu} \in G$, the monoid operation is defined by

$$AB \triangleq C = (c_{ij})_{\mu \times \mu} \in G, \tag{22}$$

where

$$c_{ij} = \left(\sum_{\ell=1}^{\mu} a_{i\ell} \circledast b_{\ell j}\right). \tag{23}$$

---

[3] In a more rigorous manner, $\hat{R}_{\lambda, \kappa}$ should be defined as a quotient of the algebra of κ-variable polynomials by the ideal generated by all monomials of degree λ. But for simplicity, we would like to follow the formulation given in [14], where Gastineau gave a detailed introduction on the operations about truncated multivariate polynomials, especially from a perspective of complexity.

In our proposal, $\mathcal{K}_{[A,B]} \subset G$ is specified by two specified matrices $A, B \in G$. Here, the matrix B is not required to be invertible and easy to generate, while the matrix A should be invertible and can be generated as a random product of ν ($\mu^3 \leq \nu \leq 2\mu^3$) elementary matrices. Here, a square matrix is called *elementary* if it differs from the identity matrix by exactly one non-zero element outside the diagonal [15]. In other words, A can be specified by ν random triples $\{(i, j, u)\} \in \{1, \cdots, \mu\}^2 \times \hat{R}_{\lambda,\kappa}$: Each triple (i, j, u) indicates an elementary matrix that has a non-zero entry $u \neq 0$ in the (i, j)th place ($i \neq j$) and A is the product of all these ν elementary matrices.

According to [15], by using the above sample technique, the CSP problem over G seems intractable. According to the best of our knowledge, finding the matrix $A \in G$ from given $(B, ABA^{-1}) \in G^2$, one has to solve a system of μ^2 linear equations and μ^2 quadratic equations, with $2\mu^2$ unknowns, over $\hat{R}_{\lambda,\kappa}$. The adversary can further translate this into a system of linear equations over $\mathbb{Z}_{12}$ if she collects coefficients at similar monomials, but this system is going to be huge: as explained in [15], it is going to have more than 10^{20} equations (by the number of monomials). As far as we know, this monoid G seems to be the first serious candidate for the platforms that have generically hard CSP problem [15].

Moreover, it is not difficult to see that this platform satisfies the additional requirements (C-1), (C-2) and (C-3) mentioned in Section 4.2. Therefore, it can be used to define the Conj-LD system and then give an instantiation for our proposal.

The braid group. Is the braid group B_n qualified as a secure platform for supporting our proposal? Instead of giving a hasty negative answer, we would like to address this issue from the following aspects.

Is the CSP problem over braid groups intractable? For most instances, the answer is negative. But at present, finding a thorough solution for the CSP problem over braid groups is still out of reach.

On the one hand, Birman, Gebhardt and González-Meneses launched a project, referred as BGGM project, to find polynomial algorithms for solving the CSP problem over Garside groups, including braid groups [3,4,5]. The BGGM project might be the strongest known efforts for solving the CSP problem over braid groups in polynomial-time (w.r.t. the input size). Up to now, the BGGM project has already made a great progress: Except for rigid pseudo-Anosov braids, the CSP instances over other braids can be solved in polynomial time [5].

On the other hand, some researchers still keep on finding hard instances of the CSP problem in braid groups. For examples, in 2007, Ko et al. [18] proposed some ideas on generating hard instances for braid cryptography, and in 2009, Prasolov [25] constructed some small braids with large ultra summit set (USS). Prasolov's result means a frustration toward the BGGM project, but an encouragement toward the intractability assumption of the CSP problem over braid groups.

Does the braid group satisfy the condition (C-1), (C-2) and (C-3)? The answer is affirmative for (C-1) and (C-2), but partially negative for (C-3).

According to [8], if p and s are random braids, then the length of sps^{-1} is, with a high probability, about the length of p plus the double of the length of s. This is the reason why the length-based attacks work. This also suggests that one can defeat the length-based attacks by requiring that the length of sps^{-1} is closer to the length of p. This in turn requires that p should lie in its super summit set (SSS) [8]. We know that $USS \subset SSS$. Therefore, if we can work with the braids suggested by Prasolov, then not only the CSP instances are hard, but also the condition (C-3) holds. If so, we reach the point to instantiate our proposal with braid groups in a secure manner.

5   Conclusion

New public-key encryption schemes were constructed from the Conj-LD systems over generic noncommutative monoids with intractable CSP problems. A promising instantiation of our proposal is to use the monoid of matrices over truncated multivariable polynomials over rings. Meanwhile, if the problem of sampling hard CSP instances from braid groups is solved, our proposal can also be instantiated with braid groups. It is worth mentioning that even if the CSP problems in the above mentioned platforms were proven easy in future, our proposal is still realizable in other noncommutative algebraic systems in which the CSP problem is intractable.

Acknowledgements. The authors are grateful to Prof. Akihiro Yamamura and the anonymous referees for their valuable comments. The work is supported by the Japan NICT International Exchange Program (No. 2009-002), and the second author is also partially supported by the China National Natural Science Foundation Programs under grant numbers 90718001 and 60973159.

References

1. Abdalla, M., Bellare, M., Rogaway, P.: The oracle diffie-hellman assumptions and an analysis of DHIES. In: Naccache, D. (ed.) CT-RSA 2001. LNCS, vol. 2020, pp. 143–158. Springer, Heidelberg (2001)
2. Anshel, I., Anshel, M., Goldfeld, D.: An algebraic method for public key cryptography. Math. Research Letters (6), 287–291 (1999)
3. Birman, J.S., Gebhardt, V., González-Meneses, J.: Conjugacy in garside groups I: Cyclings, powers, and rigidity. Groups, Geometry and Dynamics 1(3), 221–279 (2007)
4. Birman, J.S., Gebhardt, V., González-Meneses, J.: Conjugacy in garside groups III: periodic braids. J. Algebra 316(2), 746–776 (2007)
5. Birman, J.S., Gebhardt, V., González-Meneses, J.: Conjugacy in garside groups II: Structure of the ultra summit set. Groups, Geometry and Dynamics 2(1), 16–31 (2008)
6. Cash, D.M., Kiltz, E., Shoup, V.: The twin diffie-hellman problem and applications. In: Smart, N.P. (ed.) EUROCRYPT 2008. LNCS, vol. 4965, pp. 127–145. Springer, Heidelberg (2008)

7. Cramer, R., Shoup, V.: Design and analysis of practical public-key encryption schemes secure against chosen ciphertext attack. SIAM Journal on Computing 33(1), 167–226 (2003)
8. Dehornoy, P.: Braid-based cryptography. Contemp. Math. 360, 5–33 (2004)
9. Dehornoy, P.: Using shifted conjugacy in braid-based cryptography. Contemporary Mathematics 418, 65–74 (2006)
10. Diffie, W., Hellman, M.E.: New directions in cryptography. IEEE Transactions on Information Theory 22(5), 644–654 (1976)
11. ElGamal, T.: A public key cryptosystem and a signature scheme based on discrete logarithms. IEEE Transactions on Information Theory 31(4), 469–472 (1985)
12. Eric, W.: Conjugate Element,
    http://mathworld.wolfram.com/ConjugateElement.html
13. Fujisaki, E., Okamoto, T.: How to enhance the security of public-key encryption at minimum cost. In: Imai, H., Zheng, Y. (eds.) PKC 1999. LNCS, vol. 1560, pp. 53–68. Springer, Heidelberg (1999)
14. Gastineau, M.: Multiplication of polynomials. Technique Report at Advanced School on Specific Algebraic Manipulators, ASD/IMCCE/CNRS, France (2007)
15. Grigoriev, D., Shpilrain, V.: Authentication from matrix conjugation. Groups, Complexity and Cryptology 1(2), 199–205 (2009)
16. Hughes, J.: The LeftSSS attack on Ko-Lee-Cheon-Han-Kang-Park Key Agreement Protocol in B45. In: Rump Session Crypto 2000 (2000)
17. Kitaev, A.: Quantum measurements and the abelian stabilizer problem. Electronic Colloquium on Computational Complexity (ECCC) 3(3), 1–22 (1996)
18. Ko, K.H., Lee, J., Thomas, T.: Towards generating secure keys for braid. Designs, Codes and Cryptography 45(3), 317–333 (2007)
19. Ko, K.H., Lee, S.J., Cheon, J.H., Han, J.W.: New public-key cryptosystem using braid groups. In: Bellare, M. (ed.) CRYPTO 2000. LNCS, vol. 1880, pp. 166–183. Springer, Heidelberg (2000)
20. Kurosawa, K., Matsuo, T.: How to remove MAC from DHIES. In: Wang, H., Pieprzyk, J., Varadharajan, V. (eds.) ACISP 2004. LNCS, vol. 3108, pp. 236–247. Springer, Heidelberg (2004)
21. Lee, E.: Braig groups in cryptography. IEICE Trans. Fundamentals E87-A(5), 986–992 (2004)
22. Longrigg, J., Ushakov, A.: Cryptanalysis of shifted conjugacy authentication protocol. Journal of Math. Cryptology (2), 107–114 (2008)
23. Magliveras, S.S., Stinson, D.R., Trung, T.: New approaches to designing public key cryptosystems using one-way functions and trapdoors in finite groups. Journal of Cryptography 15, 285–297 (2002)
24. Maurer, U.M.: Abstract models of computation in cryptography. In: Smart, N.P. (ed.) Cryptography and Coding 2005. LNCS, vol. 3796, pp. 1–12. Springer, Heidelberg (2005)
25. Prasolov, M.: Small braids having a big ultra summit set, http://arxiv.org/abs/0906.0076
26. Proos, J., Zalka, C.: Shor's discrete logarithm quantum algorithm for elliptic curves. Quantum Information and Computation 3, 317–344 (2003)
27. Shor, P.: Polynomail-time algorithms for prime factorization and discrete logarithms on a quantum computer. SIAM J. Comput. 5, 1484–1509 (1997)
28. Shpilrain, V., Ushakov, A.: An authentication scheme based on the twisted conjugacy problem. In: Bellovin, S.M., Gennaro, R., Keromytis, A.D., Yung, M. (eds.) ACNS 2008. LNCS, vol. 5037, pp. 366–372. Springer, Heidelberg (2008)

A Proof of Proposition 1

Proof. Suppose F is a Conj-LD system defined over noncommutative group G. Then, for given $a, b, c \in G$, we have that

- Property (i): Idempotent. Since $aaa^{-1} = a$, i.e., a will remain unchanged when it conjugates to itself. By using the notation as in the formula (2), we have $F_a(a) = a$.
- Property (ii): Mutual inverse. According to the definition of F (cf. (4)), we have

$$F_a(b) = c \Leftrightarrow c = aba^{-1} \Leftrightarrow a^{-1}ca = b \Leftrightarrow F_{a^{-1}}(c) = b.$$

- Property (iii): Homomorphic.

$$F_a(bc) = a(bc)a^{-1} = (aba^{-1})(aca^{-1}) = F_a(b)F_a(c).$$

This concludes the proposition.   □

B Proof of Theorem 1

Proof. Assume that the CSP-DDH assumption holds for the underlying noncommutative monoid G. We will prove by contradiction that CSP-ElG is IND-CPA. Suppose that CSP-ElG is not IND-CPA, and let $\mathcal{A}$ be an algorithm which, on the system parameters $a \in G^{-1}$, $b \in G$ and a random public key $pk \in \mathcal{K}_{[a,b]}$, has probability non-negligibly greater than $1/2$ of distinguishing random encryptions $Enc(m_0)$ and $Enc(m_1)$ of two messages m_0, m_1 of its choice. Let $Z = (F_{a^s}(b), F_{a^t}(b), F_{a^u}(b)) \in \mathcal{K}^3_{[a,b]}$ be either a random CSP-DDH triple or a random triple, with equal probability. We will produce an algorithm $\mathcal{B}$ which can distinguish between the two cases, using $\mathcal{A}$ as an oracle, with high probability.

The algorithm $\mathcal{B}$ who interacts with the algorithm $\mathcal{A}$ can be defined as follows:

1. $\mathcal{B}$ at first picks a random integer $v \in \mathbb{T}$ and sets the public-key as $pk = F_{a^{s+v}}(b) \in \mathcal{K}_{[a,b]}$, which is then sent to $\mathcal{A}$.
2. Upon receiving the public-key pk, $\mathcal{A}$ selects two messages $m_0, m_1 \in \mathcal{M}$ with equal length as the challenge messages, which is then sent to $\mathcal{B}$.
3. Upon receiving the challenge messages pair (m_0, m_1), $\mathcal{B}$ randomly picks another integer $w \in \mathbb{T}$, flips a coin $\beta \in \{0,1\}$ and then replies $\mathcal{A}$ with the challenge ciphertext as follows:

$$c^*_\beta = (F_{a^{t+w}}(b), m_\beta \oplus H(F_{a^{u+v+w}}(b))).$$

4. Upon receiving the challenge ciphertext c_β^*, $\mathcal{A}$ replies $\mathcal{B}$ with $\hat{\beta} \in \{0, 1\}$, i.e., $\mathcal{A}$'s guess on β.
5. Upon receiving $\hat{\beta} \in \{0, 1\}$, i.e., $\mathcal{A}$'s guess on β, $\mathcal{B}$ checks whether $\mathcal{A}$'s guess is correct, i.e., whether $\hat{\beta} = \beta$ holds.
6. By repeating the above process with several different choices of random integers v, w, the algorithm $\mathcal{B}$ can determine with high probability whether or not $\mathcal{A}$ can determine the value of β. Based on the detailed analysis given below, $\mathcal{B}$ can, in this way, determine whether or not Z is a CSP-DDH triple, thus violating the CSP-DDH assumption for G.

In detail, there are now two cases to consider for a single executing the above interactive process between $\mathcal{B}$ and $\mathcal{A}$.

- Suppose that $u = s + t$ holds. Then $u + v + w = (s + v) + (t + w)$, so Z is a CSP-DDH triple in $\mathcal{K}_{[a,b]}^3$. Moreover, all possible CSP-DDH triples w.r.t. (a, b) are equally likely to occur as Z, since v and w are random. Therefore c_β^* is a valid random encryption of m_β (random since $F_{a^{t+w}}(b)$ is random in $\mathcal{K}_{[a,b]}$). Under these conditions, the algorithm $\mathcal{A}$ by hypothesis will succeed in outputting β with probability exceeding $1/2$ by a non-negligible quantity.
- Suppose that u is random. Then Z is a random triple in $\mathcal{K}_{[a,b]}^3$, and all possible triples belonging to $\mathcal{K}_{[a,b]}^3$ occur with equal probability. In this situation, the probability distribution of c_0^* is *identical* to that of c_1^*, over all possible random choices of v and w. It follows that the algorithm $\mathcal{A}$ cannot exhibit different behavior for $\beta = 0$ and $\beta = 1$. Note that we can arrive at this conclusion even though the expression c_β^* is an invalid encryption of m_β — that is, even though we have no information about how $\mathcal{A}$ behaves on invalid inputs, we know for certain that $\mathcal{A}$ cannot behave differently depending on the value of β.

The above analysis reveals that if Z is a CSP-DDH triple then $\mathcal{A}$ with non-negligible probability exhibits different behavior depending on whether $\beta = 0$ or $\beta = 1$, whereas if Z is not a CSP-DDH triple then $\mathcal{A}$ must behave identically regardless of the value of β.   □

C   Proof of Theorem 3

Proof. Suppose that $c = (c_1, c_2, c_3, c_4)$ is a well-formed ciphertext on the message m. Then, there exists some integer $t \in \mathbb{T}$ such that

$$c_1 := F_{a^t}(b), \quad c_2 := F_{a^t}(X_1), \quad c_3 := F_{a^t}(F_{a^h}(X_2)X_3), \quad c_4 := E_K(m),$$

where $h := H(c_1, c_2)$ and $K := H_1(F_{a^t}(X_4))$. Since $X_i = F_{a^{x_i}}(b)$ for $i = 1, 2, 3, 4$, we have that

$$c_2 = F_{a^t}(F_{a^{x_1}}(b))$$
$$= F_{a^{x_1+t}}(b) \quad (\because \text{power law})$$
$$= F_{a^{x_1}}(F_{a^t}(b)) \quad (\because \text{power law})$$
$$= F_{a^{x_1}}(c_1), \tag{24}$$
$$c_3 = F_{a^t}(F_{a^h}(F_{a^{x_2}}(b))F_{a^{x_3}}(b))$$
$$= F_{a^t}(F_{a^{h+x_2}}(b)F_{a^{x_3}}(b)) \quad (\because \text{power law})$$
$$= F_{a^t}(F_{a^{h+x_2}}(b))F_{a^t}(F_{a^{x_3}}(b)) \quad (\because \text{property (iii)})$$
$$= F_{a^{t+h+x_2}}(b)F_{a^{t+x_3}}(b) \quad (\because \text{power law})$$
$$= F_{a^{h+x_2}}(F_{a^t}(b))F_{a^{x_3}}(F_{a^t}(b)) \quad (\because \text{power law})$$
$$= F_{a^{h+x_2}}(c_1)F_{a^{x_3}}(c_1), \quad (\because \text{power law}) \quad \text{and} \tag{25}$$
$$K = H_1(F_{a^t}(F_{a^{x_4}}(b)))$$
$$= H_1(F_{a^{t+x_4}}(b) \quad (\because \text{power law}))$$
$$= H_1(F_{a^{x_4}}(F_{a^t}(b)) \quad (\because \text{power law}))$$
$$= H_1(F_{a^{x_4}}(c_1)). \tag{26}$$

That is, the ciphertext c can stand the validation and the value of K used in encryption $c_4 = E_K(m)$ is exactly the value of K used in decryption $m = D_K(c_4)$. Since $\Pi = (E, D)$ is symmetric, the output m of the decryption is exactly the input m of the encryption. Therefore, the CSP-CS scheme is consistent. $\qquad\square$

On the CCA1-Security of Elgamal and Damgård's Elgamal

Helger Lipmaa

Cybernetica AS, Estonia
Tallinn University, Estonia

Abstract. It is known that there exists a reduction from the CCA1-security of Damgård's Elgamal (DEG) cryptosystem to what we call the ddh^{dsdh} assumption. We show that ddh^{dsdh} is unnecessary for DEG-CCA1, while DDH is insufficient for DEG-CCA1. We also show that CCA1-security of the Elgamal cryptosystem is equivalent to another assumption ddh^{csdh}, while we show that ddh^{dsdh} is insufficient for Elgamal's CCA1-security. Finally, we prove a generic-group model lower bound $\Omega(\sqrt[3]{q})$ for the hardest considered assumption ddh^{csdh}, where q is the largest prime factor of the group order.

Keywords: CCA1-security, DEG cryptosystem, Elgamal cryptosystem, generic group model, irreduction.

1 Introduction

Of the common security notions of public-key cryptosystems, CPA-security (security against chosen plaintext attacks) is not sufficient in many real-life applications. On the other hand, CCA2-security (security against adaptive chosen ciphertext attacks) is often too strong since it does forbid homomorphic properties that are necessary to efficiently implement many cryptographic protocols. CCA2-secure cryptosystems are also typically less efficient than CPA-secure cryptosystems. CCA1-security (security against nonadaptive chosen ciphertext attacks), a notion that is strictly stronger than CPA-security but does not yet forbid the cryptosystem to be homomorphic, seems to be a reasonable compromise.

In particular, CCA1-secure cryptosystems can be used instead of CPA-secure cryptosystems in many cryptographic protocols (say, e-voting) to achieve better security without any loss in efficiency. For example, one might be able to design an e-voting protocol where a vote cannot be decrypted even by an adversary who can *non-adaptively* (say, before the e-voting period starts) decrypt any ciphertexts of her choosing. We emphasize that while designing such cryptographic protocols, one should still recall that CCA1-security is a strictly weaker assumption than CCA2-security.

Unfortunately, CCA1-security itself has received very little study, and in particular not much is known about CCA1-security of most of the commonly used cryptosystems. As a concrete (and important) example, while the Elgamal cryptosystem [7] is one of the best-known and most efficient (number-theory based)

X. Lai, M. Yung, and D. Lin (Eds.): Inscrypt 2010, LNCS 6584, pp. 18–35, 2011.

public-key cryptosystems, results on its security have been slow to come. Only in 1998, it was proven that Elgamal is CPA-secure [14]. On the other hand, the Elgamal cryptosystem is clearly not CCA2-secure, because it is homomorphic. However, Elgamal's CCA1-security is a well-known open problem.

In 1991, Damgård proposed what we will call the DEG (Damgård's Elgamal) cryptosystem [4]. DEG is a relatively straightforward modification of Elgamal that employs an additional exponentiation to reject "incorrect" ciphertexts. Damgård proved DEG to be CCA1-secure under a nonfalsifiable [11] knowledge-of-the-exponent assumption. Only in 2006, Gjøsteen [8] proved that DEG is CCA1-secure under a more standard assumption that we will call ddh^{dsdh}: it basically states that DDH remains secure when the adversary is given a nonadaptive access to the Decisional Static Diffie-Hellman (DSDH) oracle [2]. Gjøsteen's security reduction consisted of a relatively long chain of games. Recently, in an unpublished preprint, Wu and Stinson [15] presented two alternative proofs of the CCA1-security of the DEG cryptosystem. First, they showed that DEG is CCA1-secure if both the DDH assumption and a weaker version of the knowledge-of-exponent assumption (see [15] for precise statement) hold. Second, they presented an alternative proof that it is CCA1-secure under the ddh^{dsdh} assumption, which is simpler than Gjøsteen's original proof.

Our contributions. In this paper, we establish the complete complexity landscape of CCA1-security of the Elgamal and the DEG cryptosystems. We establish precise security assumptions under which these cryptosystems are CCA1-secure. To be able to do so, we need to introduce several assumptions where the adversary has a nonadaptive oracle access to an oracle solving a more primitive assumption. Denote by X^Y the assumption that no adversary, given a *nonadaptive* oracle access to the Y oracle, can break the assumption X. Here, since Y is usually a static security assumption [2], it will be assumed that the fixed parameters of Y will be the same as the corresponding parameters in X. As an example, in the ddh^{dsdh} assumption, the adversary for the ddh problem has four inputs: a generator g and three group elements h_1, h_2, h_3. The DSDH problem is defined with respect to two fixed group elements g' and h'_1, and the adversary obtains two random group elements h'_2 and h'_3. We will assume that in the ddh^{dsdh} assumption, $g' = g$ and $h'_1 = h_1$. For the sake of clarity, we will give full definitions of all three used X^Y-type assumptions later.

All our reductions can be seen as simple hybrid arguments following the general guideline "if $X \Rightarrow X'$ and $Y' \Rightarrow Y$, then $X^Y \Rightarrow (X')^{Y'}$".(Here and in what follows, $X \Rightarrow Y$ means that the assumption Y can be reduced to the assumption X.) Thus all our reductions consist of at most two game hops. Our proof technique, albeit simple, may be a contribution by itself.

Regarding DEG, we first give a simple proof that DEG is CCA1-secure if and only if the ddeg^{csdeg} assumption holds, where both csdeg and ddeg are new but standard-looking (falsifiable) assumptions; we will give the precise definition of ddeg^{csdeg} in Sect. 3. This result is a tautology which is mainly useful to simplify further results. As for Elgamal, we show that Elgamal is CCA1-secure iff the ddh^{csdh} assumption holds, that is, if ddh is secure given nonadaptive access to a Computational Static Diffie-Hellman (csdh, [2]) oracle. This result is also a tautology. While ddh^{csdh} is a new assumption, it is again standard-looking (and falsifiable). We emphasize once more that it is the first known positive result about the CCA1-security of Elgamal at all.

We then concentrate on showing that the used assumptions are all (potentially) different. For this we construct several irreductions [3,1]. However, due to the nature of the studied problems, our irreductions are not ideally strong, and thus only of (somewhat) indicative nature. Briefly, the problem is that the CCA1-security is a static assumption, where the decryption oracle queries are limited to use the same secret key that is later used for encryption. For this reason, not only the underlying assumptions (like ddh^{dsdh}) inherit the same property, but also reductions and irreductions. On the one hand, for the underlying assumptions and reductions, this is good: for assumptions, since such static assumptions are weaker than non-static assumptions; for reductions, since static reductions are weaker than non-static reductions. On the other hand, for the irreductions this is bad, since static irreductions are weaker than non-static irreductions (i.e., they only show the nonexistence of static reductions and not all possible reductions). A possible solution here is to strengthen the CCA1-security assumption by allowing the decryption oracle to decrypt with a secret key that corresponds to any public key. This would solve the mentioned problem. However, since such a strengthened version of CCA1-security is nonstandard, we leave its study to a followup work.

We present (static) irreductions showing that ddh cannot be reduced to ddeg^{csdeg} (unless ddh is easy), ddeg^{csdeg} cannot be reduced to ddh^{dsdh} (unless ddeg^{csdeg} is easy) and ddh^{dsdh} cannot be reduced to the ddh^{csdh} (unless ddh^{dsdh} is easy). All those irreductions are optimal in the sense that they show that if assumption X can be reduced to Y in polynomial time, then X has to be solvable in polynomial time itself and thus *both* assumptions are broken.

Intuitively, the new irreductions show that DEG is CCA1-secure under an assumption that is strictly stronger than DDH (and thus there is no hope to prove that it is CCA1-secure just under the DDH assumption) and strictly weaker than ddh^{dsdh}, the assumption under which its CCA1-security was known before. Thus means that the CCA1-security of DEG can be rightfully seen as an independent (and plausible) security assumption, which is a new and possibly surprising result. Moreover, the CCA1-security of Elgamal is based on an assumption that is strictly stronger than the assumption that underlies the CCA1-security of DEG. In a nutshell, this means that while being somewhat less efficient than Elgamal, DEG is "more CCA1-secure" in a well-defined sense.

Finally, we show in the generic group model that the hardest considered assumption, ddh^{csdh} (that is, the CCA1-security of Elgamal), is secure in the generic group model [13]. More precisely, we show that any generic group algorithm that breaks ddh^{csdh} must take $\Omega(\sqrt[3]{q})$ steps, where q is the largest prime factor of the group order. We prove this lower bound in the generic group model by using the formalization of Maurer [10], but due to the use of *nonadaptive* oracle in our assumption, the proof of lower bound is more involved than any of the proofs in [10]. This can be compared to the known exact lower bound $\Omega(\sqrt{q})$ for ddh (that is, the CPA-security of Elgamal) [13], and shows that $\mathrm{ddh}^{\mathrm{csdh}}$ is likely to be secure (in generic group model) while the defined irreductions are likely to be meaningful due to the different lower bound.

To summarize, we prove that:

$$\boxed{\text{Elgamal-CCA1}} \overset{\Leftarrow}{\underset{\Rightarrow}{}} \boxed{\mathrm{ddh}^{\mathrm{csdh}}} \overset{\Leftarrow}{\underset{\not\Rightarrow \;\star}{}} \boxed{\mathrm{ddh}^{\mathrm{dsdh}}} \overset{\Leftarrow}{\underset{\not\Rightarrow \;\star}{}} \boxed{\mathrm{ddeg}^{\mathrm{csdeg}}} \overset{\Leftarrow}{\underset{\Rightarrow}{}} \boxed{\text{DEG-CCA1}} \overset{\Leftarrow}{\underset{\not\Rightarrow \;\star}{}} \boxed{\mathrm{ddh}}$$

Here, we have denoted with a star ($\star$) the new (ir)reductions that are most important in our opinion. We use theorems to prove the starred (ir)reductions, and lemmas to prove other reductions.

Therefore, we give a complete map of the related security reductions and irreductions between these security assumptions. We stress that irreductions are not yet commonly used, and we hope that the current paper provides an insight to their significance. (And shows, that they are often *not* difficult to construct.)

Recent Related Work. First, a number of recent papers [6,5,9] have studied the CCA1/CCA2-security of *hybrid* versions of the DEG cryptosystem. Such versions use additional cryptographic primitives like symmetric encryption and MAC. Compared to them, nonhybrid versions studied in this paper are both better known and simpler. Moreover, the study of nonhybrid versions is important because they are homomorphic and thus widely usable in cryptographic protocols. Second, in an unpublished preprint [15], Wu and Stinson also show that the Elgamal cryptosystem is one-way (under nonadaptive chosen ciphertext attacks) under two different conditions. They did *not* study the CCA1-security of Elgamal.

2   Preliminaries

2.1   Assumptions

Let the value of the predicate $[a \overset{?}{=} b]$ be 1, if $a = b$, and 0 otherwise. In the case of any security assumption X, we let the public variables $(X_1, \ldots, X_m)$ be all variables seen by the adversary (in a fixed order implicit in the definition). In the cases that we study in this paper, the first public variables are system parameters (like a generator of the underlying group), then the public key and finally the variables sent to the adversary during the security game.

Denote

$$\mathrm{cdh}(g, g^x, g^y) := g^{xy} \ , \quad \mathrm{ddh}(g, g^x, g^y, g^z) := [g^z \overset{?}{=} \mathrm{cdh}(g, g^x, g^y)] \ .$$

Based on these standard cdh and ddh oracles, we also define the Computational and Decisional Static Diffie-Hellman oracles [2]:

$$\mathrm{csdh}_{(g,g^x)}(g^y) := \mathrm{cdh}(g, g^x, g^y) = g^{xy} \ ,$$

$$\mathrm{dsdh}_{(g,g^x)}(g^y, g^z) := \mathrm{ddh}(g, g^x, g^y, g^z) = [g^z \overset{?}{=} \mathrm{cdh}(g, g^x, g^y)] \ .$$

Note that cdh and csdh are essentially the same functions, but as oracles they behave differently since (g, g^x) have been hardcoded in csdh and thus cannot be chosen by the adversary. The same comment is true for ddh and dsdh.

Fix a group $\mathbb{G} = \langle g \rangle$ of order q. The *ddh game* is defined as follows:

Setup phase. Challenger sets sk $\leftarrow \mathbb{Z}_q$, pk $\leftarrow g^{\text{sk}}$. He sends pk to adversary $\mathcal{A}$.
Challenge phase. Challenger sets $b_{\mathcal{A}} \leftarrow \{0,1\}$, $y^* \leftarrow \mathbb{Z}_q$, $z^* \leftarrow \mathbb{Z}_q$, $h_1^* \leftarrow g^{y^*}$.
   He sets $h_2^* \leftarrow g^{z^*}$ if $b_{\mathcal{A}} = 0$ and $h_2^* = \text{pk}^{y^*}$ if $b_{\mathcal{A}} = 1$. Challenger sends (h_1^*, h_2^*) to $\mathcal{A}$.
Guess phase. $\mathcal{A}$ returns a bit $b'_{\mathcal{A}} \in \{0,1\}$. $\mathcal{A}$ wins if $b'_{\mathcal{A}} = b_{\mathcal{A}}$, that is, if $b'_{\mathcal{A}} = \text{ddh}(g, \text{pk}, h_1^*, h_2^*)$.

Group $\mathbb{G}$ is a (τ, ε)-*ddh group* if for any adversary $\mathcal{A}$ working in time τ, $\Pr[\mathcal{A} \text{ wins in the ddh game}] \leq \frac{1}{2} + \varepsilon$. Note that the public variables are $\text{ddh}_1 = g$, $\text{ddh}_2 = \text{pk}$, $\text{ddh}_3 = h_1^*$, $\text{ddh}_4 = h_2^*$.

For comparison, we now give a complete description of a static game, csdh. Fix a group $\mathbb{G} = \langle g \rangle$ of order q, a generator g of group $\mathbb{G}$, and a random pk $\leftarrow \mathbb{G}$. The *csdh$_{(g,\text{pk})}$ game* is defined as follows:

Challenge phase. Challenger sets $x_{\mathcal{A}} \leftarrow \mathbb{Z}_q$. He sets $h \leftarrow g^{x_{\mathcal{A}}}$. Challenger sends h to $\mathcal{A}$.
Guess phase. $\mathcal{A}$ returns a group element $h'_{\mathcal{A}} \in \mathbb{G}$. $\mathcal{A}$ wins if $h'_{\mathcal{A}} = \text{csdh}_{g,\text{pk}}(h) = \text{pk}^{x_{\mathcal{A}}}$.

Group $\mathbb{G}$ is a (τ, ε)-*csdh group* if for any g, pk and any adversary $\mathcal{A}$ working in time τ, $\Pr[\mathcal{A} \text{ wins in the csdh game}] \leq \frac{1}{q} + \varepsilon$.

Based on arbitrary assumptions X and Y we define a new assumption X^Y. In the X^Y game, an adversary has *nonadaptive* oracle access to an oracle solving assumption Y, and she has to break a random instance of the X assumption. In our case, the Y assumption is always a static assumption, that is, it is defined with respect to some public parameters that come from the instance that the adversary for X^Y has to solve. Note that if Y is static, then we have to always fix the public parameters in the definition of X and Y. Clearly, $X^Y \Rightarrow (X')^{Y'}$ when $X \Rightarrow X'$ and $Y' \Rightarrow Y$. This can be proven by using a hybrid argument, showing say that $X^Y \Rightarrow X^{Y'}$, that $X^{Y'} \Rightarrow (X')^{Y'}$, etc. A group is (τ, ε)-X^Y *group* if for any adversary $\mathcal{A}$ working in time τ, $\Pr[\mathcal{A} \text{ wins in the } X^Y \text{ game}] \leq \delta + \varepsilon$, where $\delta = \frac{1}{2}$ in a decisional assumption, and $\delta = \frac{1}{q}$ in a computational assumption.

For the sake of clarity, we now give a precise definition of the ddh^{dsdh} game, and we state its relation to some of the existing assumptions. Similarly, we will later define all other used assumptions. Fix a group $\mathbb{G} = \langle g \rangle$ of order q. The ddh^{dsdh} *game* is defined as follows:

Setup phase. Challenger sets sk $\leftarrow \mathbb{Z}_q$, pk $\leftarrow g^{\text{sk}}$. He sends pk to adversary $\mathcal{A}$.
Query phase. $\mathcal{A}$ has a (nonadaptive) access to oracle dsdh$_{(g,\text{pk})}(\cdot, \cdot)$.
Challenge phase. Challenger sets $b_{\mathcal{A}} \leftarrow \{0,1\}$, $y^*, z^* \leftarrow \mathbb{Z}_q$, $h_1^* \leftarrow g^{y^*}$. He sets $h_2^* \leftarrow g^{z^*}$ if $b_{\mathcal{A}} = 0$ and $h_2^* \leftarrow \text{pk}^{y^*} = \text{csdh}_{(g,\text{pk})}(h_1^*)$ if $b_{\mathcal{A}} = 1$. Challenger sends (h_1^*, h_2^*) to $\mathcal{A}$.

Guess phase. $\mathcal{A}$ returns a bit $b'_\mathcal{A} \in \{0, 1\}$. $\mathcal{A}$ wins if $b'_\mathcal{A} = b_\mathcal{A}$, that is, if $b'_\mathcal{A} = \mathrm{ddh}(g, \mathrm{pk}, h_1^*, h_2^*)$.

Group $\mathbb{G}$ is a (τ, ε)-ddh^{dsdh} *group* if for any adversary $\mathcal{A}$ working in time τ, $\Pr[\mathcal{A}$ wins in the ddh^{dsdh} game$] \leq \frac{1}{2} + \varepsilon$. Here, the 2 variables are g and pk are shared by the ddh oracle invoked in the query phase and by the instance the adversary is trying to solve.

Several versions of the X^Y game for different values of X and Y, have been used before. ddh^{dsdh} assumption has been used before say in [8]. The gap DH assumption of [12] is similar to cdh^{dsdh} (defined later), except that there the adversary gets access to the oracle also after seeing the challenge. Some other papers deal with the so called *one-more DDH* assumption, where $\mathcal{A}$ has to answer correctly to $t + 1$ DDH challenges after making only t DDH queries. See, for example, [3].

2.2 Reductions and Irreductions

We say that security assumption Y can be reduced to assumption X, $X \Rightarrow Y$, if there exists a *reduction* $\mathcal{R}$, such that: for every adversary $\mathcal{A}$ that breaks assumption X, $\mathcal{R}$ can break assumption Y by using $\mathcal{A}$ as an oracle. More precisely, in an $X \Rightarrow Y$ reduction game, the challenger $\mathcal{C}$ generates for $\mathcal{R}$ the public parameters of an Y instance. Then, the challenger sends to $\mathcal{R}$ a challenge of the game Y that $\mathcal{R}$ has to solve. $\mathcal{R}$ can use $\mathcal{A}$ as an oracle.

Following [3], we call an algorithm $\mathcal{I}$ an *irreduction* $Z \not\Rightarrow_Y X$, if it can, given as an oracle an arbitrary reduction algorithm $Z \Rightarrow X$, solve problem Y. If $Y = X$, then we say that $\mathcal{I}$ is an *optimal irreduction* algorithm and write $Z \not\Rightarrow_! X$. More precisely, in a $Z \not\Rightarrow_Y X$ irreduction game, the challenger $\mathcal{C}$ generates for $\mathcal{I}$ the public parameters of an Y instance. Then, the challenger sends to $\mathcal{I}$ a challenge of the game Y that $\mathcal{I}$ has to solve. $\mathcal{I}$ can use a reduction $\mathcal{R}$ of the game $Z \Rightarrow X$ as an oracle.

Now, in our case, most of the assumptions are static in nature. That is, we either have an assumption X_α with some externally given variables α, or an assumption $X_{\alpha, \beta'}^{Y_{\alpha, \beta}}$, where variables α of the X's instance are fixed in the invocation of the oracle for Y. (To simplify the notation, we will usually not write down α, β and β', but define them while defining the static assumption X^Y.) Analogously, in a *static* reduction $X^Y \Rightarrow (X')^{Y'}$ game, the adversary in the $X^Y \Rightarrow (X')^{Y'}$ game (1) has to know how to answer the Y queries only when some variables are fixed, and (2) can only query the oracle that solves X^Y or Y' under some fixed variables. Analogously, an adversary in the irreduction $X^Y \not\Rightarrow_Z (X')^{Y'}$ game has similar restrictions.

Briefly, the problem is that the CCA1-security is a static assumption, where the decryption oracle queries are limited to use the same secret key that is later used for encryption. For this reason, not only the underlying assumptions (like ddh^{dsdh}) inherit the same property, but also reductions and irreductions. This is since in the reduction and irreduction games, some of the oracles are equal to the decryption oracle (or to some other static oracle). On the one hand, for the underlying assumptions and reductions, this is good: for assumptions, since such static assumptions are weaker than non-static assumptions; for reductions, since static reductions are weaker than non-static reductions. On the other hand, for the irreductions this is bad, since static irreductions are weaker than non-static irreductions (i.e., they only show the nonexistence of static reductions and not all possible reductions).

Thus, In our (ir)reductions, it is important to see which variables are fixed in all X, Y, and Z. For example, in an reduction $X \Rightarrow Z$, both instances X and Z may depend on some public generator g and public key pk. In all our reductions, the reduction algorithm only uses the oracle $\mathcal{A}$ with all public parameters and public keys being fixed. We say that such a reduction is *static*. Analogously, we say that an irreduction $Z \not\Rightarrow_Y X$ is *static*, if its oracle reduction algorithm is static. To make this completely clear, we state the names of fixed parameters in all of our results. We refer to the beginning of Sec. 5 for further discussion.

Finally, when we show the existence of a reduction (resp., irreduction), we construct a reduction $\mathcal{R}$ (resp., irreduction $\mathcal{I}$) that simulates the challenger $\mathcal{C}$ to adversary $\mathcal{A}$ (resp., reduction $\mathcal{R}$). In the case of an irreduction, $\mathcal{I}$ also simulates $\mathcal{A}$ to $\mathcal{R}$. If a party $\mathcal{X}$ simulates party $\mathcal{Y}$, then we denote $\mathcal{X}$ as $\mathcal{X}[\mathcal{Y}]$ for the sake of clarity.

2.3 Cryptosystems

A *public-key cryptosystem* Π is a triple of efficient algorithms (G, E, D), where $G(1^k)$ outputs a key pair (sk, pk), $E_{\text{pk}}(m; r)$ returns a ciphertext and $D_{\text{sk}}(c)$ returns a plaintext, so that $D_{\text{sk}}(E_{\text{pk}}(m; r)) = m$ for any $(\text{sk}, \text{pk}) \in G(1^k)$. Here, k is a security parameter that we will just handle as a constant.

Fix a cyclic group $\mathbb{G} = \langle g \rangle$ of order q. The *Elgamal cryptosystem* [7] in group $\mathbb{G}$ is defined as follows:

Key generation $G(1^k)$. Select a random sk $\leftarrow \mathbb{Z}_q$, set pk $\leftarrow g^{\text{sk}}$. Publish pk.
Encryption $E_{\text{pk}}(m; \cdot)$. Return $\perp$ if $m \notin \mathbb{G}$. Otherwise, select a random $r \leftarrow \mathbb{Z}_q$,
    set $E_{\text{pk}}(m; r) \leftarrow (g^r, m \cdot \text{pk}^r)$.
Decryption $D_{\text{sk}}(c)$. Parse $c = (c_1, c_2)$, return $\perp$ if $c_i \notin \mathbb{G}$ for some i. Otherwise,
    return $D_{\text{sk}}(c) \leftarrow c_2 / c_1^{\text{sk}}$.

Fix a group $\mathbb{G} = \langle g \rangle$ of order q. The *Damgård's Elgamal (DEG) cryptosystem [4]* in group $\mathbb{G}$ is defined as follows:

Key generation $G(1^k)$. Select random $\text{sk}_1, \text{sk}_2 \leftarrow \mathbb{Z}_q$, set $\text{pk}_1 \leftarrow g^{\text{sk}_1}, \text{pk}_2 \leftarrow g^{\text{sk}_2}$. Publish pk $\leftarrow (\text{pk}_1, \text{pk}_2)$, set sk $\leftarrow (\text{sk}_1, \text{sk}_2)$.
Encryption $E_{\text{pk}}(m; \cdot)$. Return $\perp$ if $m \notin \mathbb{G}$. Otherwise, select a random $r \leftarrow \mathbb{Z}_q$,
    set $E_{\text{pk}}(m; r) \leftarrow (g^r, \text{pk}_1^r, m \cdot \text{pk}_2^r)$.
Decryption $D_{\text{sk}}(c)$. Parse $c = (c_1, c_2, c_3)$, return $\perp$ if $c_i \notin \mathbb{G}$ for some i. Return
    $\perp$ if $c_2 \neq c_1^{\text{sk}_1}$. Otherwise, return $D_{sk}(c) \leftarrow c_3 / c_1^{\text{sk}_2}$.

Let $\Pi = (G, E, D)$ be a public-key cryptosystem. The *CCA1-game* for Π is defined as follows:

Setup phase. Challenger chooses $(\text{sk}, \text{pk}) \leftarrow G(1^k)$ and sends pk to adversary $\mathcal{A}$.

Query phase. $\mathcal{A}$ has access to an oracle $D_{\text{sk}}(\cdot)$.

Challenge phase. $\mathcal{A}$ submits (m_0, m_1) to the challenger, who picks a random bit $b_{\mathcal{A}} \leftarrow \{0, 1\}$ and a random $r \leftarrow \mathbb{Z}_q$, and returns $E_{\text{pk}}(m_{b_{\mathcal{A}}}; r)$.

Guess phase. $\mathcal{A}$ returns a bit $b'_{\mathcal{A}} \in \{0, 1\}$. $\mathcal{A}$ wins if $b'_{\mathcal{A}} = b_{\mathcal{A}}$.

A public-key cryptosystem is $(\tau, \gamma, \varepsilon)$-*CCA1-secure* if for any adversary $\mathcal{A}$ working in time τ and making γ queries, $\Pr[\mathcal{A} \text{ wins in the CCA1-game}] \leq \frac{1}{2} + \varepsilon$. A $(\tau, 0, \varepsilon)$-CCA1-secure cryptosystem is also said to be (τ, ε)-*CPA-secure*. Note that CCA1-security is an explicitly static assumption, since the adversary can only access the decryption oracle with respect to a fixed secret key.

The DEG cryptosystem was proven to be CCA1-secure under the ddh^{dsdh} assumption in [8]. More precisely, Gjøsten proved the CCA1-security of a (hash-proof based) generalization of the DEG cryptosystem under a generalization of the ddh^{dsdh} assumption. Elgamal's cryptosystem is known to be CPA-secure [14] but not known to be CCA1-secure for $\gamma = \text{poly}(k)$.

3   CCA1-Security of DEG

In this section we investigate the CCA1-security of DEG.

3.1   DEG Is CCA1-Secure $\Leftrightarrow$ ddeg^{csdeg}

First, we prove that the security of DEG is equivalent to a new but standard-looking assumption ddeg^{csdeg}. This result itself is not so interesting, but combined with the result from the next subsection it will provide a reduction of the CCA1-security of DEG to the more standard (but as we will also see later, a likely stronger) ddh^{dsdh} assumption.

The ddeg^{csdeg} Assumption. We first define the new assumption. For implicitly defined $g, \text{pk}_1, \text{pk}_2$, let $\mathcal{DEG}_0 := \{(g^y, \text{pk}_1^y, \text{pk}_2^z) : y, z \leftarrow \mathbb{Z}_q\}$ and $\mathcal{DEG}_1 := \{(g^y, \text{pk}_1^y, \text{pk}_2^y) : y \leftarrow \mathbb{Z}_q\}$. Define the next oracles csdeg$_{(\cdot, \cdot, \cdot)}$ and ddeg:

- csdeg$_{(g, \text{pk}_1, \text{pk}_2)}(h_1, h_2)$ first checks if ddh$(g, \text{pk}_1, h_1, h_2) = 1$. If this is not true, it returns $\perp$. Otherwise, it returns $h_3 \leftarrow \text{cdh}(g, \text{pk}_2, h_1)$.
- ddeg$(g, \text{pk}_1, \text{pk}_2, h_1, h_2, h_3)$ has to distinguish between $\mathcal{DEG}_0$ and $\mathcal{DEG}_1$. That is, on the promise that ddh$(g, \text{pk}_1, h_1, h_2) = 1$, ddeg$(g, \text{pk}_1, \text{pk}_2, h_1, h_2, h_3) \leftarrow [\text{ddh}(g, \text{pk}_2, h_1, h_3) \overset{?}{=} 1]$. The oracle is not required to output anything if ddh$(g, \text{pk}_1, h_1, h_2) = 0$.

Fix a group $\mathbb{G} = \langle g \rangle$ of order q. The *ddeg^{csdeg} game* in group $\mathbb{G}$ is defined as follows:

Setup phase. Challenger sets $\text{sk}_1, \text{sk}_2 \leftarrow \mathbb{Z}_q$, $\text{pk}_1 \leftarrow g^{\text{sk}_1}$, $\text{pk}_2 \leftarrow g^{\text{sk}_2}$. He sends $\text{pk} \leftarrow (\text{pk}_1, \text{pk}_2)$ to adversary $\mathcal{A}$, and sets $\text{sk} \leftarrow (\text{sk}_1, \text{sk}_2)$.

Query phase. $\mathcal{A}$ has access to the oracle csdeg$_{(g, \text{pk}_1, \text{pk}_2)}(\cdot, \cdot)$.

Challenge phase. Challenger sets $b_{\mathcal{A}} \leftarrow \{0,1\}$, $y^*, z^* \leftarrow \mathbb{Z}_q$, $h_1^* \leftarrow g^{y^*}$, and $h_2^* \leftarrow \mathrm{pk}_1^{y^*}$. If $b_{\mathcal{A}} = 0$, then $h_3^* \leftarrow \mathbb{G}$. If $b_{\mathcal{A}} = 1$, then $h_3^* \leftarrow \mathrm{pk}_2^{y^*}$. Challenger sends (h_1^*, h_2^*, h_3^*) to $\mathcal{A}$.

Guess phase. $\mathcal{A}$ returns a bit $b_{\mathcal{A}}' \in \{0,1\}$. $\mathcal{A}$ wins if $b_{\mathcal{A}}' = b_{\mathcal{A}}$.

Group $\mathbb{G}$ is a $(\tau, \gamma, \varepsilon)$-$ddeg^{csdeg}$ group if for any adversary $\mathcal{A}$ working in time τ and making γ queries, $\Pr[\mathcal{A} \text{ wins}] \leq \frac{1}{2} + \varepsilon$. Note that this definition does directly follow from the definition of the $csdeg_{(\cdot, \cdot, \cdot)}$ and ddeg oracles.

Security Results. In all next results, small denotes some unspecified small value (usually $O(1)$ group operations) that is dominated by some other addend in the same formula. The next lemma is basically a tautology, and useful mostly to simplify further proofs.

Lemma 1 (DEG-CCA1 $\Leftrightarrow$ ddeg^{csdeg}). *Fix a group $\mathbb{G} = \langle g \rangle$ of order q.*
(1) Assume that $\mathbb{G}$ is a $(\tau, \gamma, \varepsilon)$-$ddeg^{csdeg}$ group. Then DEG is $(\tau - \gamma \cdot (\tau_{csdeg} + \mathsf{small}) - \mathsf{small}, \gamma, 2\varepsilon)$-CCA1-secure where τ_{csdeg} is the working time of the $csdeg_{(\cdot, \cdot, \cdot)}$ oracle.
(2) Assume that DEG is $(\tau, \gamma, \varepsilon)$-CCA1-secure. Then $\mathbb{G}$ is a $(\tau - \gamma \cdot (\tau_D + \mathsf{small}) - \mathsf{small}, \gamma, \varepsilon)$-$ddeg^{csdeg}$ group, where τ_D is the working time of the decryption oracle D.

Proof. 1) **First direction (DEG-CCA1 $\Rightarrow$ ddeg^{csdeg} with fixed $(g, \mathrm{pk}_1, \mathrm{pk}_2)$):** Assume $\mathcal{A}$ is an adversary who can $(\tau', \gamma', \varepsilon')$-break the CCA1-security of DEG with probability ε' and in time τ', making γ' queries. Construct the next reduction $\mathcal{R}$ that aims to break ddeg^{csdeg}:

- Challenger generates new sk $\leftarrow (\mathrm{sk}_1, \mathrm{sk}_2) \leftarrow \mathbb{Z}_q^2$, $\mathrm{pk}_1 \leftarrow g^{\mathrm{sk}_1}$, $\mathrm{pk}_2 \leftarrow g^{\mathrm{sk}_2}$ and sends pk $\leftarrow (\mathrm{pk}_1, \mathrm{pk}_2)$ to $\mathcal{R}$. $\mathcal{R}$ forwards pk to $\mathcal{A}$.
- In the query phase, whenever $\mathcal{A}$ asks a decryption D_{sk} query (c_1, c_2, c_3) from $D_{\mathrm{sk}}(\cdot, \cdot, \cdot)$, $\mathcal{R}$ rejects if either c_1, c_2 or c_3 is not a valid group element. Otherwise $\mathcal{R}$ makes a $csdeg_{(g, \mathrm{pk}_1, \mathrm{pk}_2)}(c_1, c_2)$ query. $\mathcal{R}$ receives a c' such that $c' \leftarrow \bot$, if $c_2 \neq c_1^{\mathrm{sk}_1}$, and $c' \leftarrow c_1^{\mathrm{sk}_2}$ otherwise. $\mathcal{R}$ returns $\bot$ in the first case, and c_3/c' in the second case.
- In the challenge phase, whenever $\mathcal{A}$ submits her challenge (m_0^*, m_1^*), $\mathcal{R}$ asks the challenger for his own challenge. The challenger sets $b_{\mathcal{R}} \leftarrow \{0,1\}$, $y^* \leftarrow \mathbb{Z}_q$, $h_1^* \leftarrow g^{y^*}$, $h_2^* \leftarrow \mathrm{pk}_1^{y^*}$. If $b_{\mathcal{R}} = 0$, then he sets $h_3^* \leftarrow \mathbb{G}$, otherwise $h_3^* \leftarrow \mathrm{pk}_2^{y^*}$. $\mathcal{R}$ picks a random bit $b_{\mathcal{A}} \leftarrow \{0,1\}$, and sends $(h_1^*, h_2^*, m_{b_{\mathcal{A}}}^* \cdot h_3^*)$ to $\mathcal{A}$. $\mathcal{A}$ returns a bit $b_{\mathcal{A}}'$.
- In the guess phase, if $b_{\mathcal{A}}' = b_{\mathcal{A}}$, then $\mathcal{R}$ returns $b_{\mathcal{R}}' \leftarrow 1$, otherwise $\mathcal{R}$ returns $b_{\mathcal{R}}' \leftarrow 0$.

Now, $\Pr[\mathcal{R} \text{ wins}] = \Pr[b_{\mathcal{R}}' = b_{\mathcal{R}}] = \Pr[\mathcal{A} \text{ wins}|b_{\mathcal{R}} = 1] \cdot \Pr[b_{\mathcal{R}} = 1] + \Pr[\mathcal{A} \text{ wins}|b_{\mathcal{R}} = 0] \cdot \Pr[b_{\mathcal{R}} = 0] = \left(\frac{1}{2} + \varepsilon'\right) \cdot \frac{1}{2} + \frac{1}{2} \cdot \frac{1}{2} = \frac{1}{2} + \frac{\varepsilon'}{2}$. Clearly $\mathcal{R}$ works in time $\tau = \tau' + \gamma \cdot (\tau_{csdeg} + \mathsf{small}) + \mathsf{small}$. $\square$

2) **Second direction (ddeg^{csdeg} $\Rightarrow$ DEG-CCA1 with fixed $(g, \text{pk}_1, \text{pk}_2)$):**
Assume $\mathcal{A}$ is an adversary who can $(\tau', \gamma', \varepsilon')$-break the ddeg^{csdeg} assumption. Construct the next reduction $\mathcal{R}$ that aims to break the CCA1-security of the DEG cryptosystem:

- Challenger generates new sk $\leftarrow (\text{sk}_1, \text{sk}_2) \leftarrow \mathbb{Z}_q^2$, $\text{pk}_1 \leftarrow g^{\text{sk}_1}$, $\text{pk}_2 \leftarrow g^{\text{sk}_2}$, and sends pk $= (\text{pk}_1, \text{pk}_2)$ to $\mathcal{R}$. $\mathcal{R}$ forwards pk to $\mathcal{A}$.
- In the query phase, whenever $\mathcal{A}$ asks a query $\text{csdeg}_{(g, \text{pk}_1, \text{pk}_2)}(h_1, h_2)$, $\mathcal{R}$ makes a decryption D_{sk} query $(h_1, h_2, 1)$, and receives back either $\bot$ or $k \leftarrow h_1^{-\text{sk}_2}$. $\mathcal{R}$ returns $h_3 \leftarrow \bot$ in the first case, and $h_3 \leftarrow k^{-1}$ in the second case.
- In the challenge phase, whenever $\mathcal{A}$ asks for a challenge, $\mathcal{R}$ sends his challenge pair $(m_0^*, m_1^*) \leftarrow (g^{r_1^*}, 1)$, for $r_1^* \leftarrow \mathbb{Z}_q$, to the challenger. Challenger picks a random bit $b_{\mathcal{R}} \leftarrow \{0, 1\}$ and a random $r_2^* \leftarrow \mathbb{Z}_q$, and sends $(c_1^*, c_2^*, c_3^*) \leftarrow (g^{r_2^*}, \text{pk}_1^{r_2^*}, g^{r_1^*(1-b_{\mathcal{R}})} \cdot \text{pk}_2^{r_2^*})$ to $\mathcal{R}$. $\mathcal{R}$ forwards (c_1^*, c_2^*, c_3^*) to $\mathcal{A}$, who returns a guess $b_{\mathcal{A}}'$.
- In the guess phase, $\mathcal{R}$ returns $b_{\mathcal{R}}' \leftarrow b_{\mathcal{A}}'$ to challenger.

Now, $\Pr[\mathcal{R} \text{ wins}] = \Pr[b_{\mathcal{R}}' = b_{\mathcal{R}}] = \Pr[\mathcal{A} \text{ wins}] = \varepsilon'$. Clearly $\mathcal{R}$ works in time $\tau' + \gamma \cdot (\tau_D + \text{small}) + \text{small}$. $\qquad \square$

Lemma 2 (DEG-CCA1 $\Rightarrow$ ddh^{dsdh} with fixed $(g, \text{pk} = \text{pk}_1)$).
(1) Assume that $\mathbb{G} = \langle g \rangle$ is a $(\tau, \gamma, \varepsilon)$-ddh^{dsdh} group. Then the DEG cryptosystem is CCA1-secure in group $\mathbb{G}$.
(2) Any ddh^{dsdh} group $\mathbb{G} = \langle g \rangle$ is also a ddeg^{csdeg} group.

Proof. Proof of the first claim is given in [8,15]. The second claim follows from the first claim and Lem. 1. $\qquad \square$

By following a very similar proof, a variant of the DEG cryptosystem where the decryption, given an invalid ciphertext, returns a random plaintext instead of $\bot$, is CCA1-secure under the ddh assumption.

Relation with ddh. It is obviously important to establish the relationships of the new assumptions with the well-known assumptions like ddh. Here we construct a static reduction ddh $\Rightarrow$ ddeg^{csdeg} and in Thm. 1, we construct a static irreduction ddh$^{\text{csdeg}} \not\Rightarrow_! $ ddh. As a careful reader will observe, in fact both the reduction and the irreduction will be to the static version of ddh, where the first three inputs $(g, \text{pk}_1, \text{pk}_2)$ are fixed, and the adversary can only choose the four inputs. This static version of ddh is clearly at least as strong as ddh since anybody who can break the static version can also break the ddh.

Lemma 3 (ddh $\Rightarrow$ ddeg^{csdeg} with fixed $(g, \text{pk}_1, \text{pk}_2)$). *Any $(\tau, \gamma, \varepsilon)$-ddeg^{csdeg} group $\mathbb{G} = \langle g \rangle$ is also a $(\tau - \text{small}, \varepsilon)$-ddh group.*

Proof. Fix a group $\mathbb{G} = \langle g \rangle$ of order q. Assume $\mathcal{A}$ is an adversary who can $(\tau', \gamma', \varepsilon')$-break the ddh assumption. Construct the next reduction $\mathcal{R}$ that aims to break ddeg^{csdeg} in the same group:

- Challenger generates new $(\mathrm{sk}_1 \leftarrow \mathbb{Z}_q, \mathrm{sk}_2 \leftarrow \mathbb{Z}_q, \mathrm{pk}_1 \leftarrow g^{\mathrm{sk}_1}, \mathrm{pk}_2 \leftarrow g^{\mathrm{sk}_2})$ and sends $\mathrm{pk} = (\mathrm{pk}_1, \mathrm{pk}_2)$ to $\mathcal{R}$. $\mathcal{R}$ forwards (g, pk_2) to $\mathcal{A}$ as her system parameters.
- In the challenge phase, if $\mathcal{A}$ asks for a challenge, then $\mathcal{R}$ asks for a challenge. Challenger sets $b_{\mathcal{R}} \leftarrow \{0, 1\}$, $y^* \leftarrow \mathbb{Z}_q$, $h_1^* \leftarrow g^{y^*}$, $h_2^* \leftarrow \mathrm{pk}_1^{y^*}$. If $b_{\mathcal{R}} = 0$, then he sets $h_3^* \leftarrow \mathbb{G}$, otherwise $h_3^* \leftarrow \mathrm{pk}_2^{y^*}$. He sends (h_1^*, h_2^*, h_3^*) to $\mathcal{R}$. $\mathcal{R}$ sends (h_1^*, h_3^*) to $\mathcal{A}$. $\mathcal{A}$ returns a bit $b'_{\mathcal{A}}$. $\mathcal{R}$ returns $b'_{\mathcal{R}} \leftarrow b'_{\mathcal{A}}$ to the challenger.

Clearly, $\mathcal{R}$ wins if and only if $\mathcal{A}$ wins. $\qquad\square$

4   CCA1-Security of ElGamal

To prove the security of ElGamal we need the next assumption. As we will see from the security proofs, this assumption basically just asserts that Elgamal is CCA1-secure.

Fix a group $\mathbb{G} = \langle g \rangle$ of order q. The ddh^{csdh} game is defined as follows:

Setup phase. Challenger sets $\mathrm{sk} \leftarrow \mathbb{Z}_q$, $\mathrm{pk} \leftarrow g^{\mathrm{sk}}$. He sends pk to adversary $\mathcal{A}$.
Query phase. $\mathcal{A}$ has access to oracle $\mathrm{csdh}_{(g,\mathrm{pk})}(\cdot)$, that is, $\mathrm{csdh}_{(g,\mathrm{pk})}(h) := h^{\mathrm{sk}}$.
Challenge phase. Challenger sets $b_{\mathcal{A}} \leftarrow \{0, 1\}$, $y^* \leftarrow \mathbb{Z}_q$, $h_1^* \leftarrow g^{y^*}$. He sets $h_2^* \leftarrow \mathbb{G}$ if $b_{\mathcal{A}} = 0$ and $h_2^* \leftarrow \mathrm{pk}^{y^*} = \mathrm{csdh}_{(g,\mathrm{pk})}(h_1^*)$ if $b_{\mathcal{A}} = 1$. Challenger sends (h_1^*, h_2^*) to $\mathcal{A}$.
Guess phase. $\mathcal{A}$ returns a bit $b'_{\mathcal{A}} \in \{0, 1\}$. $\mathcal{A}$ wins if $b'_{\mathcal{A}} = b_{\mathcal{A}}$, that is, if $b_{\mathcal{A}} = \mathrm{ddh}(g, \mathrm{pk}, h_1^*, h_2^*)$.

Group $\mathbb{G}$ is a $(\tau, \gamma, \varepsilon)$-$ddh^{csdh}$ group if for any adversary $\mathcal{A}$ working in time τ and making γ queries, $\Pr[\mathcal{A} \text{ wins in the ddh}^{\mathrm{csdh}} \text{ game}] \leq \frac{1}{2} + \varepsilon$.

Lemma 4 (Elgamal-CCA1 $\Leftrightarrow$ ddh^{csdh} with fixed (g, pk)). *Fix a group* $\mathbb{G} = \langle g \rangle$ *of order* q.
(1) Assume that $\mathbb{G}$ *is a* $(\tau, \gamma, \varepsilon)$-$ddh^{csdh}$ *group. Then ElGamal is* $(\tau - \gamma \cdot (\tau_{\mathrm{csdh}} + \mathsf{small}) - \mathsf{small}, \gamma, 2\varepsilon)$-*CCA1-secure, where* τ_{csdh} *is the working time of the* $\mathrm{csdh}_{(g,\mathrm{pk})}(\cdot)$ *oracle.*
(2) Assume that ElGamal is $(\tau, \gamma, \varepsilon)$-*CCA1-secure. Then* $\mathbb{G}$ *is a* $(\tau - \gamma \cdot (\tau_D + \mathsf{small}) - \mathsf{small}, \gamma, \varepsilon)$-$ddh^{csdh}$ *group, where* τ_D *is the working time of the* D *oracle.*

Proof. 1) **First direction (Elgamal-CCA1 $\Rightarrow$ ddh^{csdh} with fixed (g, pk)):** Assume $\mathcal{A}$ is an adversary who can $(\tau', \gamma', \varepsilon')$-break the CCA1-security of Elgamal in group $\mathbb{G}$ with probability ε' and in time τ', making γ' queries. Construct the next reduction $\mathcal{R}$ that aims to break ddh^{csdh} in group $\mathbb{G}$:

– Challenger generates a new keypair $(\mathrm{sk} \leftarrow \mathbb{Z}_q, \mathrm{pk} \leftarrow g^{\mathrm{sk}})$ and sends pk to $\mathcal{R}$. $\mathcal{R}$ forwards pk to $\mathcal{A}$.

– In the query phase, whenever $\mathcal{A}$ asks a decryption D_{sk} query (c_1, c_2), $\mathcal{R}$ rejects if either c_1 or c_2 is not a valid group element. Otherwise $\mathcal{R}$ asks a CSDH query $c_3 \leftarrow \mathrm{csdh}_{(g,\mathrm{pk})}(c_1)$. $\mathcal{R}$ returns c_2/c_3.

– In the challenge phase, whenever $\mathcal{A}$ gives a pair (m_0^*, m_1^*) of messages, $\mathcal{R}$ asks his challenge from the challenger. The challenger sets $b_{\mathcal{R}} \leftarrow \{0,1\}$, $y^* \leftarrow \mathbb{Z}_q$, $h_1^* \leftarrow g^{y^*}$. If $b_{\mathcal{R}} = 0$, then he sets $h_2^* \leftarrow \mathbb{G}$, otherwise $h_2^* \leftarrow \mathrm{pk}^{y^*}$. $\mathcal{R}$ picks a random bit $b_{\mathcal{A}} \leftarrow \{0,1\}$ and sends $(h_1, m_{b_{\mathcal{A}}} \cdot h_2)$ to $\mathcal{A}$. $\mathcal{A}$ returns a bit $b_{\mathcal{A}}'$.

– In the guess phase, if $b_{\mathcal{A}}' = b_{\mathcal{A}}$, then $\mathcal{R}$ returns $b_{\mathcal{R}}' = 1$, otherwise $\mathcal{R}$ returns $b_{\mathcal{R}}' = 0$.

Now, $\Pr[\mathcal{R} \text{ wins in the } \mathrm{ddh}^{\mathrm{csdh}} \text{ game}] = \Pr[b_{\mathcal{R}}' = b_{\mathcal{R}}] = \Pr[\mathcal{A} \text{ wins}|b_{\mathcal{R}} = 1] \cdot \Pr[b_{\mathcal{R}} = 1] + \Pr[\mathcal{A} \text{ wins}|b_{\mathcal{R}} = 0] \cdot \Pr[b_{\mathcal{R}} = 0] = (\frac{1}{2} + \varepsilon') \cdot \frac{1}{2} + \frac{1}{2} \cdot \frac{1}{2} = \frac{1}{2} + \frac{\varepsilon'}{2}$. Clearly $\mathcal{R}$ works in time $\tau' + \gamma \cdot (\tau_{\mathrm{csdh}} + \mathsf{small}) + \mathsf{small}$. $\square$

2) **Second direction ($\mathrm{ddh}^{\mathrm{csdh}} \Rightarrow$ Elgamal-CCA1 with fixed (g, pk)):** Assume $\mathcal{A}$ is an adversary who can $(\tau', \gamma', \varepsilon')$-break the $\mathrm{ddh}^{\mathrm{csdh}}$ assumption in group $\mathbb{G}$. Construct the next reduction $\mathcal{R}$ that aims to break the CCA1-security of Elgamal:

– Challenger generates a new keypair $(\mathrm{sk} \leftarrow \mathbb{Z}_q, \mathrm{pk} \leftarrow g^{\mathrm{sk}})$ and sends pk to $\mathcal{R}$. $\mathcal{R}$ forwards pk to $\mathcal{A}$.

– In the query phase, whenever $\mathcal{A}$ asks a CSDH query $\mathrm{csdh}_{(g,\mathrm{pk})}(h)$, $\mathcal{R}$ asks a decryption D_{sk} query $(h, 1)$, and receives back $c \leftarrow h^{-\mathrm{sk}}$. $\mathcal{R}$ returns c^{-1} to $\mathcal{A}$.

– In the challenge phase, whenever $\mathcal{A}$ asks for a challenge, $\mathcal{R}$ sends his message pair $(m_0^*, m_1^*) \leftarrow (g^r, 1)$ to challenger, where $r \leftarrow \mathbb{Z}_q$. Challenger picks a random bit $b_{\mathcal{R}} \leftarrow \{0,1\}$ and a random $r^* \leftarrow \mathbb{Z}_q$, and sends $(c_1^*, c_2^*) \leftarrow (g^{r^*}, g^{r(1-b_{\mathcal{R}})} \cdot \mathrm{pk}^{r^*})$ to $\mathcal{R}$. $\mathcal{R}$ forwards (c_1^*, c_2^*) to $\mathcal{A}$, who returns a guess $b_{\mathcal{A}}'$. $\mathcal{R}$ returns $b_{\mathcal{R}}' \leftarrow b_{\mathcal{A}}'$ to challenger.

Now, $\Pr[\mathcal{R} \text{ wins}] = \Pr[b_{\mathcal{R}}' = b_{\mathcal{R}}] = \Pr[\mathcal{A} \text{ wins}] = \varepsilon$. Clearly $\mathcal{R}$ works in time $\tau' + \gamma \cdot (\tau_D + \mathsf{small}) + \mathsf{small}$. $\square$

It is straightforward to prove the next lemma.

Lemma 5 ($\mathrm{ddh}^{\mathrm{dsdh}} \Rightarrow \mathrm{ddh}^{\mathrm{csdh}}$). *If ddh^{csdh} holds, then ddh^{dsdh} holds.*

Proof (Sketch). Build a wrapper that uses the oracle that solves the CDH problem to solve the DDH problem. $\square$

5 Irreductions

We will now show irreductions between the main security assumptions of this paper. We emphasize, see Sect. 2.2, that the irreductions will be somewhat limited by fixing some of the parameters. For example, Lem.3 stated that there does exist a reduction that solves $\text{ddeg}^{\text{csdeg}}$ on some input $(g, \text{pk}_1, \text{pk}_2, h_1^*, h_2^*, h_3^*)$ (with pk_1, pk_2) being randomly generated) given an access to a $\text{dsdh}_{(g, \text{pk}_2)}$ oracle with inputs $(\cdot, \cdot)$, i.e., with (g, pk_2) being fixed. As an example, the next Thm. 1 shows that there does not exist a reduction that solves dsdh on some input $(g, \text{pk}, h_1^*, h_2^*)$ (with pk being randomly generated) given an access to a $\text{ddeg}^{\text{csdeg}}$ oracle with inputs $(g, \text{pk}, \cdot, \cdot, \cdot)$, i.e., again with two inputs being fixed. Other irreductions are similar. Thus, the next irreductions are somewhat limited, since they do exclude the existence of reductions with arbitrary oracle queries. Nevertheless, they are still important, since all (known to us) reductions between similar problems in fact have limited oracle access.

In what follows, we will not state the concrete security parameters in the theorems, however, they are easy to calculate and one can verify that all following theorems provide exact (ir)reductions.

Theorem 1 ($\text{ddeg}^{\text{csdeg}} \not\Rightarrow_! \text{ddh}$). *If there exists a static reduction $\mathcal{R}$ that reduces ddh to $\text{ddeg}^{\text{csdeg}}$, then there exists an efficient static irreduction $\mathcal{I}$ that, given $\mathcal{R}$ as an oracle and with fixed (g, pk), solves ddh.*

Proof. Fix a cyclic group $\mathbb{G} = \langle g \rangle$ of prime order q. Assume that $\mathcal{R} = \mathcal{R}^{\mathcal{A}}$ is an arbitrary reduction that uses $\mathcal{A}$ as an oracle to solve ddh. Here, $\mathcal{A}$ is an arbitrary algorithm that solves $\text{ddeg}^{\text{csdeg}}$. Equivalently, $\mathcal{A} = \mathcal{A}^{\text{csdeg}_{(g, \text{pk}_1, \text{pk}_2)}(\cdot, \cdot)}$ solves ddeg. In particular, $\mathcal{A}$ can have an access to a $\text{csdeg}_{(g, \text{pk}_1, \text{pk}_2)}$ oracle provided to her by $\mathcal{R}$. We now construct the next oracle machine $\mathcal{I} = \mathcal{I}^{\mathcal{R}}$ to solve ddh in time and with success probability comparable with those of $\mathcal{R}$. Note that $\mathcal{I}$ simulates the oracle $\mathcal{A}$ to $\mathcal{R}$, and therefore has access to the oracle $\text{csdeg}_{(g, \text{pk}_1, \text{pk}_2)}(\cdot, \cdot)$. Moreover, $\mathcal{I}$ simulates the challenger $\mathcal{C}_2$ of the internal $\text{ddeg}^{\text{csdeg}} \Rightarrow \text{ddh}$ game to $\mathcal{R}$.

- The challenger $\mathcal{C}_1$ of the $\text{ddeg}^{\text{csdeg}} \not\Rightarrow_! \text{ddh}$ game sets $\text{sk} \leftarrow \mathbb{Z}_q$ and $\text{pk} \leftarrow g^{\text{sk}}$. He sends pk to $\mathcal{I}$ as the public key in the $\text{ddeg}^{\text{csdeg}} \not\Rightarrow_! \text{ddh}$ game.
- $\mathcal{I}$ simulates the challenger $\mathcal{C}_2$ to $\mathcal{R}$ in the $\text{ddeg}^{\text{csdeg}} \Rightarrow \text{ddh}$ game as follows:
  - **Setup phase:** $\mathcal{I}[\mathcal{C}_2]$ forwards $\text{pk}_1 \leftarrow \text{pk}$, as the public parameter of the $\text{ddeg}^{\text{csdeg}} \Rightarrow \text{ddh}$ game, to $\mathcal{R}$. $\mathcal{R}$ generates $\text{pk}_2 \leftarrow \mathbb{G}$.
  - **Query phase:** If $\mathcal{R}$ asks a $\text{ddeg}^{\text{csdeg}_{(g, \text{pk}_1, \text{pk}_2)}}$ query (h_1, h_2, h_3) from $\mathcal{A}$, then $\mathcal{I}[\mathcal{A}]$ simulates $\mathcal{A}$ as follows:
    1. $\mathcal{I}$ sends the query (h_1, h_2) to her $\text{csdeg}_{(g, \text{pk}_1, \text{pk}_2)}(\cdot, \cdot)$ oracle in the $\text{ddeg}^{\text{csdeg}}$ game. The oracle replies with some h_3'.
    2. If $h_3' = h_3$, then $\mathcal{I}$ sets $b_{\mathcal{A}}' \leftarrow 1$, otherwise $\mathcal{I}$ sets $b_{\mathcal{A}}' \leftarrow 0$.
    3. $\mathcal{I}$ replies with $b_{\mathcal{A}}'$ as her answer to the $\text{ddeg}^{\text{csdeg}}$ challenge.
  - **Challenge phase:** If $\mathcal{R}$ asks $\mathcal{C}_2$ for his challenge in the $\text{ddeg}^{\text{csdeg}} \Rightarrow$ ddh game, then $\mathcal{I}[\mathcal{C}_2]$ simulates $\mathcal{C}_2$ as follows. She asks the challenger $\mathcal{C}_1$ for her challenge (h_1^*, h_2^*) in the irreduction game. $\mathcal{I}[\mathcal{A}]$ forwards (h_1^*, h_2^*) to $\mathcal{R}$ as his challenge.
  - **Guess phase:** $\mathcal{R}$ outputs a bit $b_{\mathcal{R}}'$.
- **Guess phase (of irreduction game):** $\mathcal{I}$ returns $b_{\mathcal{R}}'$.

Clearly, $\mathcal{I}$ emulates $\mathcal{A}$ correctly. Thus, $\Pr[\mathcal{I} \text{ wins}] = \Pr[\mathcal{R} \text{ wins}]$, and $\mathcal{I}$ spends marginally more time than $\mathcal{R}$.   □

Theorem 2 (ddh^{dsdh} $\not\Rightarrow_!$ ddeg^{csdeg} for static reductions with fixed $(g, \text{pk}_1, \text{pk}_2)$). *If there is a static reduction $\mathcal{R}$ that reduces ddeg^{csdeg} to ddh^{dsdh}, then there is an efficient static irreduction $\mathcal{I}$ that, given $\mathcal{R}$ as an oracle and with fixed $(g, \text{pk}_1, \text{pk}_2)$, solves ddeg^{csdeg}.*

Proof. Fix a cyclic group $\mathbb{G} = \langle g \rangle$ of prime order q. Let $\mathcal{A}$ be an arbitrary algorithm that solves ddh^{dsdh}. Equivalently, $\mathcal{A}^{\text{ddh}(g,\text{pk},\cdot,\cdot)}$ solves ddh. Assume that $\mathcal{R} = \mathcal{R}^{\mathcal{A}}$ is an efficient algorithm that uses $\mathcal{A}$ as an oracle to solve ddeg^{csdeg}. Equivalently, $\mathcal{R} = \mathcal{R}^{\mathcal{A}, \text{csdeg}_{(g,\text{pk}_1,\text{pk}_2)}(\cdot,\cdot)}$ is an efficient algorithm that solves ddeg. Construct now the next oracle machine $\mathcal{I} = \mathcal{I}^{\mathcal{R}, \text{csdeg}(\cdot,\cdot,\cdot)}$ to solve ddeg with the help of $\mathcal{R}$ and $\text{csdeg}_{(g,\text{pk}_1,\text{pk}_2)}(\cdot,\cdot)$ as oracles, in time and with success probability comparable with those of $\mathcal{R}$.

- **Setup phase:** The challenger $\mathcal{C}_1$ of the ddh^{dsdh} $\not\Rightarrow_!$ ddeg^{csdeg} game sets $\text{sk}_1, \text{sk}_2 \in \mathbb{Z}_q$ and $\text{pk} \leftarrow (\text{pk}_1 \leftarrow g^{\text{sk}_1}, \text{pk}_2 \leftarrow g^{\text{sk}_2})$. He sends pk to $\mathcal{I}$ as the public key in the ddh^{dsdh} $\not\Rightarrow_!$ ddeg^{csdeg} game.
- $\mathcal{I}$ simulates both the challenger $\mathcal{C}_2$ and $\mathcal{A}$ to $\mathcal{R}$ in the ddh^{dsdh} $\Rightarrow$ ddeg^{csdeg} game as follows:
  - **Setup phase:** $\mathcal{I}[\mathcal{C}_2]$ forwards pk to $\mathcal{R}$ as $\mathcal{R}$'s public key in the ddh^{dsdh} $\Rightarrow$ ddeg^{csdeg} game.
  - **Query phase:**
    * If $\mathcal{R}$ asks a $\text{csdeg}_{(g,\text{pk}_1,\text{pk}_2)}(\cdot,\cdot)$ query (h_1, h_2) from $\mathcal{A}$, then $\mathcal{I}[\mathcal{A}]$ forwards it to her own $\text{csdeg}_{(g,\text{pk}_1,\text{pk}_2)}$ oracle.
    * If $\mathcal{R}$ asks a ddh^{dsdh} query (h_1, h_2) from $\mathcal{A}$, then $\mathcal{I}[\mathcal{A}]$ forwards it to her $\text{csdeg}_{(g,\text{pk}_1,\text{pk}_2)}(\cdot,\cdot)$ oracle. If the oracle returns $\bot$, then $\mathcal{I}$ returns 0. Otherwise, $\mathcal{I}$ returns 1. (Note that $\mathcal{I}$ does not need to use a ddh oracle of the ddh^{dsdh} game here.)
  - **Challenge phase:** If $\mathcal{R}$ asks for a ddeg challenge from $\mathcal{C}_2$, then $\mathcal{I}[\mathcal{C}_2]$ simulates $\mathcal{C}_2$ as follows:
    1. $\mathcal{I}$ asks challenger $\mathcal{C}_1$ for her challenge in the ddh game. $\mathcal{C}_1$ sets $b_{\mathcal{I}} \leftarrow \{0,1\}$ and $y^* \leftarrow \mathbb{Z}_q$. He sets $h_1^* \leftarrow g^{y^*}$ and $h_2^* \leftarrow \text{pk}_1^{y^*}$. If $b_{\mathcal{I}} = 0$ then he sets $h_3^* \leftarrow \mathbb{G}$, otherwise he sets $h_3^* \leftarrow \text{pk}_2^{y^*}$. $\mathcal{C}_1$ sends (h_1^*, h_2^*, h_3^*) to $\mathcal{I}$ as a challenge.
    2. $\mathcal{I}[\mathcal{C}_2]$ forwards (h_1^*, h_2^*, h_3^*) to $\mathcal{R}$ as his challenge.
  - **Guess phase:** $\mathcal{R}$ outputs a bit $b_{\mathcal{R}}'$.
- **Guess phase (of the irreduction game):** $\mathcal{I}$ returns $b_{\mathcal{I}}' \leftarrow b_{\mathcal{R}}'$.

First, $\mathcal{I}$ emulates the queries correctly. Thus if $\mathcal{R}$ responds with a correct answer to the ddh query, then $\mathcal{I}$ responds with a correct answer to the ddh^{dsdh} query. Thus $\Pr[\mathcal{I} \text{ wins}] = \Pr[\mathcal{R} \text{ wins}]$, and $\mathcal{I}$ works in time $\tau + \gamma_{\text{ddeg}} \cdot (\tau_{\text{ddeg}} + \text{small}) + \gamma_{\mathcal{A}} \cdot \text{small} + \text{small}$, where τ is the working time of $\mathcal{R}$, τ_{ddeg} is the working time of the ddeg oracle, γ_{ddeg} is the number of queries to the ddeg oracle, $\gamma_{\mathcal{A}}$ is the number of queries to $\mathcal{A}$.   □

Theorem 3 (ddh^{csdh} $\not\Rightarrow_!$ ddh^{dsdh} for static reductions with fixed (g, pk)). *If there is a static reduction $\mathcal{R}$ that reduces ddh^{dsdh} to ddh^{csdh}, then there is an efficient static irreduction $\mathcal{I}$ that, given $\mathcal{R}$ as an oracle and with fixed (g, pk), solves ddh^{dsdh}.*

Proof. Fix a cyclic group $\mathbb{G} = \langle g \rangle$ of prime order q. Let $\mathcal{A}$ be an arbitrary algorithm that solves ddh^{csdh}. Equivalently, $\mathcal{A} = \mathcal{A}^{\mathrm{csdh}_{(g, \mathrm{pk}_1)}(\cdot)}$ solves ddh. Assume that $\mathcal{R} = \mathcal{R}^{\mathcal{A}}$ is an efficient algorithm that uses $\mathcal{A}$ as an oracle to solve ddh^{dsdh}. Equivalently, $\mathcal{R} = \mathcal{R}^{\mathcal{A},\mathrm{dsdh}_{(g,\mathrm{pk})}(\cdot)}$ is an efficient algorithm that solves ddh. Construct now the next oracle machine $\mathcal{I} = \mathcal{I}^{\mathcal{R},\mathrm{ddh}}$ to solve ddh with the help of $\mathcal{R}$ and $\mathrm{dsdh}_{(g,\mathrm{pk})}(\cdot)$ as oracles, in time and with success probability comparable with those of $\mathcal{R}$.

- Challenger $\mathcal{C}_1$ of the ddh^{csdh} $\not\Rightarrow_!$ ddh^{dsdh} game sets sk $\in \mathbb{Z}_q$ and pk $\leftarrow g^{\mathrm{sk}}$. He sends pk to $\mathcal{I}$ as the public key.
- $\mathcal{I}$ simulates the challenger $\mathcal{C}_2$ of the ddh^{csdh} $\Rightarrow$ ddh^{dsdh} game to $\mathcal{R}$:
  - **Setup phase:** $\mathcal{I}$ forwards pk to $\mathcal{R}$ as his public key in the ddh^{csdh} $\Rightarrow$ ddh^{dsdh} game. $\mathcal{R}$ forwards pk as the public key to $\mathcal{A}$ in the ddh^{csdh} game.
  - **Query phase:**
    * If $\mathcal{R}$ asks a $\mathrm{dsdh}_{(g,\mathrm{pk})}(\cdot, \cdot)$ query (h_1, h_2) from $\mathcal{A}$, then $\mathcal{I}[\mathcal{A}]$ forwards it to her dsdh oracle.
    * If $\mathcal{R}$ asks a ddh^{csdh} query (h_1, h_2) from $\mathcal{A}$, then $\mathcal{I}[\mathcal{A}]$ forwards h_1 to her $\mathrm{csdh}_{(g,\mathrm{pk})}(\cdot)$ oracle, getting back some value h'. If $h' = h_2$ then $\mathcal{I}$ returns 1, otherwise $\mathcal{I}$ returns 0.
  - **Challenge phase:** When $\mathcal{R}$ asks his challenge from $\mathcal{I}[\mathcal{C}_2]$, then $\mathcal{I}[\mathcal{C}_2]$ asks her challenge from $\mathcal{C}_1$. $\mathcal{C}_1$ sets $b_{\mathcal{I}} \leftarrow \{0, 1\}$ and $y^* \leftarrow \mathbb{Z}_q$. He sets $h_1^* \leftarrow g^{y^*}$. If $b_{\mathcal{I}} = 0$ then he sets $h_2^* \leftarrow \mathbb{G}$, otherwise he sets $h_2^* \leftarrow \mathrm{pk}^{y^*} = \mathrm{cdh}(g, \mathrm{pk}, h_1^*)$. $\mathcal{C}_1$ sends (h_1^*, h_2^*) to $\mathcal{I}$ as a challenge. $\mathcal{I}$ forwards (h_1^*, h_2^*) to $\mathcal{R}$ as his challenge.
  - **Guess phase:** $\mathcal{R}$ outputs a bit $b'_{\mathcal{R}}$.
- **Guess phase (of the irreduction game):** $\mathcal{I}$ returns $b'_{\mathcal{I}} \leftarrow b'_{\mathcal{R}}$.

First, $\mathcal{I}$ emulates the queries correctly. Thus if $\mathcal{R}$ responds with a correct answer to the cdh query, then $\mathcal{I}$ responds with a correct answer to the ddh^{csdh} query. Thus $\Pr[\mathcal{I} \text{ wins}] = \Pr[\mathcal{R} \text{ wins}]$, and $\mathcal{I}$ works in time $\tau + \gamma_{\mathrm{ddh}} \cdot (\tau_{\mathrm{ddh}} + \mathsf{small}) + \gamma_{\mathcal{A}} \cdot \mathsf{small} + \mathsf{small}$, where τ is the working time of $\mathcal{R}$, τ_{ddh} is the working time of the ddh oracle, γ_{ddh} is the number of queries to the ddh oracle, $\gamma_{\mathcal{A}}$ is the number of queries to $\mathcal{A}$. $\square$

6   Hardness in Generic Group Model

Maurer's Formalization of Generic Group Model. In this section, we show that ddh^{csdh} is hard in the generic group model [13]. To do this, we use the abstraction of generic group model from [10]. Namely, we assume that **B** is a black-box that can store values from a certain ring $\mathbb{R}$ in internal state variables $V_1, V_2, \ldots, V_m$. The storage capacity m is in our case unbounded. The initial state consists of the values of $V^d := [V_1, \ldots, V_d]$ for some $d < m$, which are set according to some probability distribution P_{V^d}. The black-box $\mathbf{B}$ allows two types of operations, computation operations on internal state variables, and queries about the internal state. No other interaction with $\mathbf{B}$ is possible. Formally, for a set Π of operations on $\mathbb{R}$, a computation operation consists of selecting a (say) t-ary operation $f \in \Pi$ and indices $i_1 \ldots, i_{t+1} \leq m$. Then $\mathbf{B}$ computes $f(V_{i_1}, \ldots, V_{i_t})$ and stores the result in $V_{i_{t+1}}$. Since m is unbounded, we can always assume that i_{t+1} is a unique index. We also assume that no computation operation $(f, V_{i_1}, \ldots, V_{i_t})$ is repeated. As for queries, for a set Σ of relations on $\mathbb{R}$, a query consits of selecting a (say) t-ary relation $\sigma \in \Sigma$ and indices $i_1 \ldots, i_t \leq m$. The query is replied by $\sigma(V_{i_1}, \ldots, V_{i_t})$.

In the case of proving lower bounds for a decisional problem, the task is to distinguish between two black boxes $\mathbf{B}$ and $\mathbf{B}'$ of the same type with different distributions of the initial state V^d. The success probability of an algorithm is taken over the choice of the initial state V^d, and of the randomness of the algorithm.

Let $\mathcal{C}$ denote the set of constant operations on $\mathbb{R}$. Let $\mathcal{L}$ denote the set of linear functions (of the form of $a_1 V_1 + \cdots + a_d V_d$) on the initial state V^d. For a given set Π of operations, let $\overline{\Pi}$ be the set of functions on the initial state that can be computed using operations in Π. See [10] for more details.

We also use the following lemma from [13].

Lemma 6 (Shoup [13]). *The fraction of solutions $(x_1, \ldots, x_k) \in \mathbb{Z}_n$ of the multivariate polynomial equation $p(x_1, \ldots, x_k) \equiv 0 \pmod{n}$ of degree d is at most d/q, where q is the largest prime factor of n.*

Hardness of ddh^{csdh} in Generic Group Model. Recall that the hardest assumption of this paper is ddh^{csdh}, which is equivalent to the assumption that Elgamal is CCA1-secure. To motivate that ddh^{csdh} is a reasonable assumption, we now prove its security in the generic group model. We note here that differently from [10], the adversary here has a *nonadaptive* access to a multiplication operator in $\mathbb{R}$. This will add another level of complication to the proof.

Theorem 4. *Let $\mathbb{R} = \mathbb{Z}_n$, where p is the smallest prime factor of n and q is the largest prime factor of n. For $\Pi = \mathcal{C} \cup \{+\}$ and $\Sigma = \{=\}$, the advantage of every k-step adversary, $k \geq 1$, that has access to a nonadaptive oracle for multiplication with x, for distinguishing a random triple (x, y, z) from a triple $(x, y, x \cdot y)$ is upper bounded by $(4k^3 - (3 + \sqrt{3})k^2 - k + 2)/(54q)$.*

Proof. As in [10], the basic strategy of the proof is to consider two black boxes, one of which has initial state (x, y, z), and another one has initial state $(x, y, x \cdot y)$. For either of the black boxes, we assume that the adversary has been successful if it has found a collision between two different elements V_i and V_j. The distinguishing probability is upperbounded by the maximum of those two collision-finding probabilities.

We only analyze the case where the initial state is $(x, y, x \cdot y)$. Let Q be the number of queries made by the adversary to the nonadaptive oracle (thus the adversary obtains values $x, \ldots, x^Q$), P the number of degree $\leq Q$ polynomials computed by the adversary before the challenge phase starts, and R be the number of polynomials computed after the challenge phase. For simplicity, we assume that when x^i are already given, any degree ℓ polynomial can be computed in 1 step. (The precise bound depends crucially on this. For example, if it took ℓ steps to compute a single polynomial, we would get upper bound $(k^2 - k)/(2q)$.) Due to this,

$$Q + P + R \leq k . \tag{1}$$

Due to the presence of the nonadaptive oracle, the adversary first asks the black-box to compute P different polynomials

$$f_i(x, y) := \sum_{j=0}^{Q} f_{ij} x^j + c_i y + d_i xy \tag{2}$$

for $i \in \{0, \ldots, P-1\}$. Since neither y or $x \cdot y$ is available yet, $c_i = d_i = 0$. Thus, after the query phase, **B**'s state is equal to $(x, y, x \cdot y, f_0(x, y), \ldots, f_{P-1}(x, y))$.

After the challenge phase, the adversary can ask the black-box to compute R functions $f_i(x, y) := \sum_{j=0}^{Q} a_{ij} f_j(x) + b_i x + c_i y + d_i xy + e_i = \sum_{t=0}^{Q} \left(\sum_{j=0}^{P-1} a_{ij} f_{jt} \right) x^t + b_i x + c_i y + d_i xy + e_i$ for $i \in \{P, \ldots, P + R - 1\}$. Clearly, each $f_i(x, y)$ for $i \geq P$ can be also written in form Eq. (2) though not with c_i and d_i necessarily being equal to 0. Here we assume that $f_i \neq f_j$ as a polynomial.

Now, any $f_i(x, y)$ is a degree $\leq Q$ polynomial. According to Lem. 6, the probability that any two of the $P + R$ functions $f_i \neq f_j$ have a common root is Q/q, and thus the *total* probability of finding a collision is bounded by

$$\frac{Q \cdot \binom{P+R}{2}}{q} . \tag{3}$$

Let $k' = \sqrt{k^2 - k + 1}$. Note that $\frac{\sqrt{3}}{2} \cdot k \leq k' \leq k$ for $k \geq 1$. Observe that, under the inequality Eq. (1), Eq. (3) is largest if $Q = (2k - k' - 1)/3$ and $P + R = (k + k' + 1)/3$. Then for $k \geq 1$,

$$Q \cdot \binom{P+R}{2} = \frac{2k^3 + 2k^2 k' - 3k^2 - 2kk' - 3k + 2k' + 2}{54}$$

$$\leq \frac{4k^3 - (3 + \sqrt{3})k^2 - k + 2}{54} .$$

In particular, constant success probability requires $k = \Omega(\sqrt[3]{q})$ steps.   □

Acknowledgments. The author was supported by Estonian Science Foundation, grant #8058, and European Union through the European Regional Development Fund. We thank Daniel Brown for discussions.

References

1. Bresson, E., Monnerat, J., Vergnaud, D.: Separation Results on the "One-More" Computational Problems. In: Malkin, T. (ed.) CT-RSA 2008. LNCS, vol. 4964, pp. 71–87. Springer, Heidelberg (2008)
2. Brown, D., Gallant, R.: The Static Diffie-Hellman Problem. Tech. Rep. 2004/306, International Association for Cryptologic Research (2004), http://eprint.iacr.org/2004/306, http://eprint.iacr.org/2004/306
3. Brown, D.R.L.: Irreducibility to the One-More Evaluation Problems: More May Be Less. Tech. Rep. 2008/435, International Association for Cryptologic Research (2007), http://eprint.iacr.org/2007/435
4. Damgård, I.: Towards Practical Public Key Systems Secure against Chosen Ciphertext Attacks. In: Feigenbaum, J. (ed.) CRYPTO 1991. LNCS, vol. 576, pp. 445–456. Springer, Heidelberg (1992)
5. Desmedt, Y., Lipmaa, H., Phan, D.H.: Hybrid Damgård Is CCA1-Secure under the DDH Assumption. In: Franklin, M.K., Hui, L.C.K., Wong, D.S. (eds.) CANS 2008. LNCS, vol. 5339, pp. 18–30. Springer, Heidelberg (2008)
6. Desmedt, Y., Phan, D.H.: A CCA Secure Hybrid Damgård's ElGamal Encryption. In: Baek, J., Bao, F., Chen, K., Lai, X. (eds.) ProvSec 2008. LNCS, vol. 5324, pp. 68–82. Springer, Heidelberg (2008)
7. Elgamal, T.: A Public Key Cryptosystem and a Signature Scheme Based on Discrete Logarithms. IEEE Transactions on Information Theory 31(4), 469–472 (1985)
8. Gjøsteen, K.: A New Security Proof for Damgård's ElGamal. In: Pointcheval, D. (ed.) CT-RSA 2006. LNCS, vol. 3860, pp. 150–158. Springer, Heidelberg (2006)
9. Kiltz, E., Pietrzak, K., Stam, M., Yung, M.: A New Randomness Extraction Paradigm for Hybrid Encryption. In: Joux, A. (ed.) EUROCRYPT 2009. LNCS, vol. 5479, pp. 590–609. Springer, Heidelberg (2009)
10. Maurer, U.M.: Abstract Models of Computation in Cryptography. In: Smart, N.P. (ed.) WCC 2005. LNCS, vol. 3796, pp. 1–12. Springer, Heidelberg (2005)
11. Naor, M.: On Cryptographic Assumptions and Challenges. In: Boneh, D. (ed.) CRYPTO 2003. LNCS, vol. 2729, pp. 96–109. Springer, Heidelberg (2003)
12. Okamoto, T., Pointcheval, D.: The Gap-Problems: A New Class of Problems for the Security of Cryptographic Schemes. In: Kim, K.-c. (ed.) PKC 2001. LNCS, vol. 1992, pp. 104–118. Springer, Heidelberg (2001)
13. Shoup, V.: Lower Bounds for Discrete Logarithms and Related Problems. In: Fumy, W. (ed.) EUROCRYPT 1997. LNCS, vol. 1233, pp. 256–266. Springer, Heidelberg (1997)
14. Tsiounis, Y., Yung, M.: On the Security of ElGamal Based Encryption. In: Imai, H., Zheng, Y. (eds.) PKC 1998. LNCS, vol. 1431, pp. 117–134. Springer, Heidelberg (1998)
15. Wu, J., Stinson, D.R.: On the Security of the ElGamal Encryption Scheme and Damgård's Variant. Tech. Rep. 2008/200, International Association for Cryptologic Research (2008), http://eprint.iacr.org/2008/200

Online/Offline Identity-Based Signcryption Revisited[*]

Joseph K. Liu, Joonsang Baek, and Jianying Zhou

Cryptography and Security Department
Institute for Infocomm Research (I²R), Singapore
{ksliu,jsbaek,jyzhou}@i2r.a-star.edu.sg

Abstract. In this paper, we redefine a cryptographic notion called *Online/Offline Identity-Based Signcryption*. It is an "online/offline" version of identity-based signcryption, where most of the computations are carried out offline while the online part does not require any heavy computations such as pairings or multiplications on elliptic curve. It is particularly suitable for power-constrained devices such as smart cards. We give a concrete implementation of online/offline identity-based signcryption, which is very efficient and flexible. Unlike all the previous schemes in the literature, our scheme does *not* require the knowledge of receiver's information (either public key or identity) in the offline stage. The receiver's identity and the message to be signcrypted are only needed in the online stage. This feature provides a great flexibility to our scheme and makes it practical to use in real-world applications. To our knowledge, our scheme is the *first* one in the literature to provide this kind of feature. We prove that the proposed scheme meets strong security requirements in the random oracle model, assuming the Strong Diffie-Hellman (SDH) and Bilinear Diffie-Hellman Inversion (BDHI) are computationally hard.

1 Introduction

1.1 Motivation

Providing efficient mechanisms for authentication and confidentiality is probably the most important requirement in electronic transactions, especially in mobile devices or smart cards. Since attackers can easily access the physical layer and launch some potential attacks in such devices, inclusion of cryptographic protection as a countermeasure should be very effective. However, due to the power-constrained nature of these devices, only light operations are allowed to be implemented. For this reason, efficiency becomes the main concern in the design of cryptographic algorithm for such environment.

IDENTITY-BASED CRYPTOGRAPHY. Identity (ID)-based Cryptography, introduced by Shamir [18], eliminates the need for checking the validity of certificates in traditional public key infrastructure (PKI). In an ID-based cryptography, public key of each user is easily computable from an arbitrary string corresponding

---

[*] This work is funded by the A*STAR project SEDS-0721330047.

X. Lai, M. Yung, and D. Lin (Eds.): Inscrypt 2010, LNCS 6584, pp. 36–51, 2011.

to this user's identity (e.g. an email address, a telephone number, and etc.). Using its master key, the private key generator (PKG) then computes a private key for each user. This property avoids the requirement of using digital certificates (which contain Certificate Authority (CA)'s signature on each user's public key) and associates implicitly a public key (i.e. user identity) to each user within the system. One only needs to know the recipient's identity in order to send an encrypted message to him. It avoids the complicated and costly certificate (chain) verification for the authentication purpose. In the case of signature schemes, verification takes only the identity together with the message and a signature pair as input and executes the algorithm directly. In contrast, the traditional PKI needs an additional certification verification process, which is in fact equivalent to the computation of *two* signature verifications.

We argue that ID-based cryptography is particularly suitable for smart cards. The most important reason is that it eliminates the costly certificate verification process and the storage of the lengthy certificate. In addition, when there is a new card issued, other terminals or payment gateways do not need to have its certificate verified in order to communicate in a secure and authenticated way. This can greatly reduce communication overhead and computation cost.

SIGNCRYPTION. Signcryption, whose concept was introduced by Zheng [23], is a cryptographic primitive aiming to provide unforgeability and confidentiality simultaneously as typical signature-then-encryption technique does but with less computational complexity and lower communication cost. Due to the efficiency one can obtain, signcryption is suitable for many applications which require secure and authenticated message delivery using resource-constrained devices.

The idea of ID-based signcryption was first proposed by Malone-Lee [16]. It was further improved in [7,13,2,8] for efficiency and security.

ONLINE/OFFLINE SIGNATURE. Online/Offline Signature was first introduced by Even, Goldreich and Micali [9]. The main idea is to perform signature generation in two phases. The first phase is performed offline (before the message to be signed is given) and the second phase is performed online (after the message to be signed is given). Online/offline signature schemes are useful, since in many applications the signer has a very limited response time once the message is presented, but he can carry out costly computations between consecutive signing requests. We note that smart card applications may take full advantages of online/offline signature schemes: The offline phase is implemented during the card manufacturing process, while the online phase uses the stored result of the offline phase to sign actual messages. The online phase is typically very fast, and hence can be executed efficiently even on a weak processor.

ONLINE/OFFLINE SIGNCRYPTION. The notion of online/offline signcryption was first introduced by An, Dodis and Rabin [1]. As in the case of online/offline signature schemes, online/offline signcryption schemes should satisfy a basic property that online computation should be performed very efficiently. All expensive operations such as exponentiation or pairing computation should be conducted offline in the first phase of the scheme. Similar to online/offline signature, it is also reasonable to assume that the offline operations are independent of the particular message to be signed and encrypted, since the message only becomes available at a later stage. The second phase is performed online, once the message is presented.

An, Dodis and Rabin [1] did not give any concrete construction of online/offline signcryption, but focused mainly on establishing formal security model for signcryption and analysis of some generic constructions. The first concrete online/offline signcryption scheme was given by Zhang, Mu and Susilo [22], and it requires an additional symmetric key encryption scheme to achieve confidentiality. Another scheme can be found in [21]. However, its practicality is dubious since the scheme requires every user to execute a key exchange protocol with the remaining users in the system. Moreover, both of them are in the PKI (non ID-based) setting. The first ID-based online/offline signcryption scheme was given by Sun, Mu and Susilo [19] in a semi-generic setting, from any ID-based signature scheme.

1.2   Limitation of Existing Schemes

All of the schemes mentioned above have a restriction which renders them impractical in many situations: They require the receiver's public key / identity to be known in the offline phase, which can result in serious performance degradation. Smartcard is one of the examples. Suppose there are some sensitive data stored in a smartcard, which has only very limited computation power. In order to send the sensitive data to a recipient in a secure and authenticated way, it should be encrypted using the recipient's public key and signed with the card owner's private key. To ensure timely and efficient delivery, it would be much better if part of the signcryption process could be done *prior* to know the data to be encrypted *and* the recipient's public key. Wireless sensor network (WSN) or mobile devices can be another example. Similar to smartcard, wireless sensors or mobile devices such as PDA or smart phone have only limited resources. It may take very long time, or even impossible to execute heavy computations on those tiny devices. Yet the data they process may be sensitive which is necessary to be encrypted and authenticated before sending off to the terminal stations. By using online/offline signcryption, the offline part (containing all heavy computation) can be done by a third party at the setup or manufacturing stage or when external power is connected. However, it is obvious that the data to be processed and the receiver's information is unknown at this stage.

In the above examples, the previous online/offline signcryption schemes (such as [1,22]) cannot be used, since they require the receiver's public key in the offline stage. This maybe one of the very important reasons that previous online/offline signcryption schemes are not practical to be used in daily life applications.

1.3   Our Contributions

In this paper, we make the following contributions.

1. We reformulate the notion of *online/offline signcryption in the ID-based setting*. We argue that it would be the best solution to provide authentication

and confidentiality to smart cards or mobile devices for the following reasons. First, it combines the separate process of *sign* and *encrypt* into one *"signcryption"*. Second, it even splits the signcryption process into *online* and *offline* stages, so that all the heavy computations can be performed in the offline stage, leaving only light operations such as hashing or integer multiplication to be done on tiny devices when the signcrypted message is known. Third, it is in the identity-based setting which gets rid of the costly process of certificate verification.

2. We present a concrete online/offline ID-based signcryption scheme, which does not require any heavy computation (such as pairing or elliptic curve multiplication) in the online stage. The security is proven using two assumptions, namely the Strong Diffie-Hellman (SDH) and Bilinear Diffie-Hellman Inversion (BDHI) assumptions in the random oracle model.

3. More importantly, unlike all other previous schemes[1], our proposed scheme does <u>not</u> require the receiver's information (in our case, the identity) in the offline stage. The receiver's identity, together with the message to be signcrypted, are needed only in the online stage. This feature greatly increases the practicality of online/offline signcryption scheme. Our scheme is the first in the literature to allow this kind of flexibility.

4. When compared to the combination of online/offline ID-based encryption and online/offline ID-based signature, although the combination may achieve the same features as our scheme, efficiency is far more behind. Our scheme is about $30\% - 50\%$ more efficient than any combination of the state of the art online/offline ID-based encryption and signature schemes.

1.4 Organization

The rest of the paper are organized as follows. We review some definitions in Section 2. It is followed by our proposed scheme in Section 3. We analyze the performance of our scheme in Section 4. Our paper is concluded in Section 5.

2 Definitions

2.1 Pairings

We briefly review the bilinear pairing. Let $\mathbb{G}$ and $\mathbb{G}_T$ be two multiplicative cyclic groups of prime order q. Let g be a generator of $\mathbb{G}$, and e be a bilinear map such that $e : \mathbb{G} \times \mathbb{G} \to \mathbb{G}_T$ with the following properties:

---

[1] Very recently, another identity-based online/offline signcryption scheme was proposed [17] in eprint. They have some comments to the preliminary version of our scheme [14] in eprint. However, the comments are not true in the current version. We also note that although the authors in [17] claimed that they are the first to propose such an ID-based online/offline signcryption with similar features as our scheme, it is not accurate. Our preliminary version [14] appeared before their scheme. It is, at most to say, two schemes with the same features were proposed almost at the same time. In addition, they do not contain any proof in the eprint version. We do not include their scheme for comparison.

1. *Bilinearity:* For all $u, v \in \mathbb{G}$, and $a, b \in \mathbb{Z}$, $e(u^a, v^b) = e(u, v)^{ab}$.
2. *Non-degeneracy:* $e(g, g) \neq 1$.
3. *Computability:* It is efficient to compute $e(u, v)$ for all $u, v \in \mathbb{G}$.

2.2   Intractability Assumption

Definition 1 (ℓ-Strong Diffie-Hellman Assumption (ℓ-SDH)). *[4] The ℓ-Strong Diffie-Hellman (ℓ-SDH) problem in $\mathbb{G}$ is defined as follow: On input a $(\ell + 1)$-tuple $(g, g^\alpha, g^{\alpha^2}, \cdots, g^{\alpha^\ell}) \in \mathbb{G}^{\ell+1}$, output a pair $(g^{\frac{1}{\alpha+c}}, c)$ where $c \in \mathbb{Z}_q^*$. We say that the (t, ϵ, ℓ)-SDH assumption holds in $\mathbb{G}$ if no t-time algorithm has advantage at least ϵ in solving the ℓ-SDH problem in $\mathbb{G}$.*

Definition 2 (ℓ-Bilinear   Diffie-Hellman   Inversion   Assumption (ℓ-BDHI)). *[3] The ℓ- Diffie-Hellman (ℓ-BDHI) problem in $\mathbb{G}$ is defined as follow: On input a $(\ell + 1)$-tuple $(g, g^\alpha, g^{\alpha^2}, \cdots, g^{\alpha^\ell}) \in \mathbb{G}^{\ell+1}$, output $e(g, g)^{\frac{1}{\alpha}} \in \mathbb{G}_T$. We say that the (t, ϵ, ℓ)-BDHI assumption holds in $\mathbb{G}$ if no t-time algorithm has advantage at least ϵ in solving the ℓ-BDHI problem in $\mathbb{G}$.*

2.3   Definition of Signcryption

An ID-based online/offline signcryption scheme consists of the following six probabilistic polynomial time (PPT) algorithms:

- $(param, msk) \leftarrow \mathsf{Setup}(1^k)$ takes a security parameter $k \in \mathbb{N}$ and generates $param$ the global public parameters and msk the master secret key of the PKG.
- $D_{ID} \leftarrow \mathsf{Extract}(1^k, param, msk, ID)$ takes a security parameter k, a global parameters $param$, a master secret key msk and an identity ID to generate a secret key D_{ID} corresponding to this identity.
- $\bar{\phi} \leftarrow \mathsf{Offline\text{-}Signcrypt}(1^k, param, D_{ID_s})$ takes a security parameter k, a global parameters $param$, a secret key of the sender D_{ID_s}, to generate an offline ciphertext $\bar{\phi}$.
- $\phi \leftarrow \mathsf{Online\text{-}Signcrypt}(1^k, param, m, \bar{\phi}, ID_r)$ takes a security parameter k, a global parameters $param$, a message m, an identity of the receiver ID_r where $ID_s \neq ID_r$, an offline ciphertext $\bar{\phi}$ to generate a ciphertext ϕ.
- $(m, \sigma)/ \perp \leftarrow \mathsf{De\text{-}Signcrypt}(1^k, param, \phi, D_{ID_r})$ takes a security parameter k, a global parameters $param$, a ciphertext ϕ, a secret key of the receiver D_{ID_r} to generate a message m and a signature σ, or $\perp$ which indicates the failure of de-signcryption.
- valid$/ \perp \leftarrow \mathsf{Verify}(1^k, param, m, \sigma, ID_s)$ takes a security parameter k, a global parameters $param$, a message m, a signature σ, an identity ID_s to output valid of $\perp$ for an invalid signature.

For simplicity, we omit the notation of 1^k and $param$ from the input arguments of the above algorithms in the rest of this paper. For correctness, if

$$\bar{\phi} \leftarrow \mathsf{Offline\text{-}Signcrypt}(D_{ID_s})$$
$$\phi \leftarrow \mathsf{Online\text{-}Signcrypt}(m, \bar{\phi}, ID_r)$$
$$(\tilde{m}, \tilde{\sigma}) \leftarrow \mathsf{De\text{-}Signcrypt}(\phi, D_{ID_r})$$

we require that

$$\tilde{m} = m$$
$$\mathsf{valid} \leftarrow \mathsf{Verify}(\tilde{m}, \tilde{\sigma}, \tilde{ID}_s)$$

Note that our definition differs from the one in [19] in the way where the offline signcrypt stage does *not* require the receiver's identity as input. In our definition, the receiver's identity is only required in the online signcrypt stage.

2.4 Security of Signcryption

Definition 3 (Confidentiality). *An ID-based online/offline signcryption scheme is semantically secure against chosen ciphertext insider attack (SC-IND-CCA) if no PPT adversary has a non-negligible advantage in the following game:*

1. *The challenger runs* **Setup** *and gives the resulting param to adversary* $\mathcal{A}$. *It keeps msk secret.*
2. *In the first stage,* $\mathcal{A}$ *makes a number of queries to the following oracles which are simulated by the challenger:*
   (a) **Extraction oracle:** $\mathcal{A}$ *submits an identity ID to the extraction oracle for the result of* **Extract**(*msk, ID*).
   (b) **Signcryption oracle:** $\mathcal{A}$ *submits a sender identity* ID_s, *a receiver identity* ID_r *and a message m to the signcryption oracle for the result of* **Online-Signcrypt**(*m,* **Offline-Signcrypt**(D_{ID_s}), ID_r).
   (c) **De-signcryption oracle:** $\mathcal{A}$ *submits a ciphertext* ϕ *and a receiver identity* ID_r *to the oracle for the result of* **De-Signcrypt**(ϕ, D_{ID_r}). *The result is made of a message and a signature if the de-signcryption is successful and the signature is valid under the sender's identity. Otherwise, a symbol* $\perp$ *is returned for rejection.*

   These queries can be asked adaptively. That is, each query may depend on the answers of previous ones.
3. $\mathcal{A}$ *produces two messages* m_0, m_1, *two identities* ID_s^*, ID_r^* *and a valid secret key* $D_{ID_s^*}$ *corresponding to* ID_s^*. *The challenger chooses a random bit* $b \in \{0,1\}$ *and computes a signcryption ciphertext* $\phi^* = $ **Online-Signcrypt**($m_b,$ **Offline-Signcrypt**($D_{ID_s^*}$), ID_r^*). ϕ^* *is sent to* $\mathcal{A}$.
4. $\mathcal{A}$ *makes a number of new queries as in the first stage with the restriction that it cannot query the de-signcryption oracle with* (ϕ^*, ID_r^*) *and the extraction oracle with* ID_r^*.
5. *At the end of the game,* $\mathcal{A}$ *outputs a bit* b' *and wins if* $b' = b$.

$\mathcal{A}$*'s advantage is defined as* $\boldsymbol{Adv}^{IND-CCA}(\mathcal{A}) = |\Pr[b' = b] - \frac{1}{2}|$.

Definition 4 (Unforgeability). *A signcryption scheme is existentially unforgeable against chosen-message insider attack (SC-EUF-CMA) if no PPT adversary has a non-negligible advantage in the following game:*

1. *The challenger runs* **Setup** *and gives the resulting param to adversary* $\mathcal{A}$. *It keeps msk secret.*
2. $\mathcal{A}$ *makes a number of queries to the following oracles which are simulated by the challenger:*
   (a) **Extraction oracle:** $\mathcal{A}$ *submits an identity* ID *to the extraction oracle for the result of* **Extract**(msk, ID).
   (b) **Signcryption oracle:** $\mathcal{A}$ *submits a sender identity* ID_s, *a receiver identity* ID_r *and a message* m *to the signcryption oracle for the result of* **Online-Signcrypt**$(m,$ **Offline-Signcrypt**$(D_{ID_s}),\ ID_r)$.
   (c) **De-signcryption oracle:** $\mathcal{A}$ *submits a ciphertext* ϕ *and a receiver identity* ID_r *to the oracle for the result of* **De-Signcrypt**(ϕ, D_{ID_r}). *The result is made of a message and a signature if the de-signcryption is successful and the signature is valid under the sender's identity. Otherwise, a symbol* $\perp$ *is returned for rejection.*

   These queries can be asked adaptively. That is, each query may depend on the answers of previous ones.
3. $\mathcal{A}$ *produces a signcryption ciphertext* ϕ^* *and two identity* ID_r^*, ID_s^*. $\mathcal{A}$ *wins if*
   (a) **De-Signcrypt**$(\phi^*, D_{ID_r^*})$ *returns a tuple* (m^*, σ^*) *such that* valid $\leftarrow$ Verify (m^*, σ^*, ID_s^*);
   (b) *No output of the signcryption oracle decrypts to* (m^*, σ^*) *such that* valid $\leftarrow$ Verify(m^*, σ^*, ID_s^*); *and*
   (c) *No extraction query was made on* ID_s^*.

$\mathcal{A}$'s *advantage is defined as* $\mathbf{Adv}^{EUF-CMA}(\mathcal{A}) = \Pr[\mathcal{A}\ wins\ ]$.

3   The Proposed Online/Offline ID-Based Signcryption Scheme

3.1   Construction

Let $\mathbb{G}$ and $\mathbb{G}_T$ be groups of prime-order q, and let $e : \mathbb{G} \times \mathbb{G} \to \mathbb{G}_T$ be the bilinear pairing. We use a multiplicative notation for the operation in $\mathbb{G}$ and $\mathbb{G}_T$.

<u>Setup:</u> The PKG selects a generator $g \in \mathbb{G}$ and randomly chooses $s \in_R \mathbb{Z}_q^*$. It sets $g_1 = g^s$ and $g_2 = g_1^s$. Define $\mathcal{M}$ to be the message space. Let $n_M = |\mathcal{M}|$. Also let n_d be the length of an identity, $H_1 : \{0,1\}^{n_d} \to \mathbb{Z}_q^*$, $H_2 : \{0,1\}^* \times \mathbb{G}_T \to \mathbb{Z}_q^*$ and $H_3 : \{0,1\}^* \to \{0,1\}^{n_M}$ be some cryptographic hash functions. The public parameters $param$ and master secret key msk are given by

$$param = (\mathbb{G}, \mathbb{G}_T, q, g, g_1, g_2, \mathcal{M}, H_1, H_2, H_3) \qquad msk = s$$

<u>Extract:</u> To generate a secret key for a user with identity $ID \in \{0,1\}^{n_d}$, the PKG computes:

$$d_{ID} \leftarrow g^{\frac{1}{H_1(ID)+s}}$$

The user also computes and stores $\overline{G_{ID}} = e(g^{H_1(ID)}g_1, g)$ for future use.

Offline-Signcrypt: The user with identity $ID_s \in \{0,1\}^{n_d}$, with secret key d_{ID_s}, at the offline stage first randomly generates $u, x, \alpha, \beta, \gamma, \delta \in_R \mathbb{Z}_q^*$ and computes:

$$U \leftarrow d_{ID_s} g^{-u} \qquad R \leftarrow (\overline{G_{ID_s}})^x$$

$$T_0 \leftarrow \left(g^{\alpha H_1(ID_s)} g_1^{H_1(ID_s)+\gamma} g_2\right)^x$$

$$T_1 \leftarrow g^{x\beta^{-1}H_1(ID_s)} \qquad T_2 \leftarrow g_1^{x\delta^{-1}}$$

Outputs the offline ciphertext $\bar{\phi} = (U, R, x, u, T_0, T_1, T_2, \alpha, \beta, \gamma, \delta)$.

Online-Signcrypt: At the online stage, to encrypt a message $m \in \mathcal{M}$ to a user with identity $ID_r \in \{0,1\}^{n_d}$ computes:

$$t_1' \leftarrow \beta\Big(H_1(ID_r) - \alpha\Big) \bmod q \qquad t_2' \leftarrow \delta\Big(H_1(ID_r) - \gamma\Big) \bmod q$$

$$t \leftarrow h_2 x + u \bmod q \qquad c \leftarrow h_3 \oplus m$$

where $h_2 = H_2(m, ID_s, R, T_0, T_1, T_2, t_1', t_2', U)$ and $h_3 = H_3(R, T_1, T_2, U)$. Outputs the ciphertext $\phi = (U, t, c, T_0, T_1, T_2, t_1', t_2')$.

De-Signcrypt: To de-signcrypt ϕ using secret key D_{ID_r}, computes

$$R \leftarrow e(T_0 T_1^{t_1'} T_2^{t_2'}, d_{ID_r}) \qquad m \leftarrow c \oplus H_3(R, T_1, T_2, U)$$

and outputs (m, σ, ID_s) where $\sigma = \{R, t, U, T_0, T_1, T_2, t_1', t_2'\}$.

Verify: Computes $h_2 = H_2(m, ID_s, R, T_0, T_1, T_2, t_1', t_2', U)$ and checks whether

$$R^{h_2} \stackrel{?}{=} e\big(g^t U, g^{H_1(ID_s)} g_1\big) \cdot e(g, g)^{-1} \tag{1}$$

Outputs valid if it is equal. Otherwise outputs $\perp$.

We note that the term $e(g, g)^{-1}$ can be pre-computed or published as part of the public parameter by the PKG. Thus the number of pairing required in the whole de-signcryption process is just 2, while there is no pairing required in either offline signcrypt or online signcrypt stage.

3.2 Security Analysis

Theorem 1 (Confidentiality). *If there is a SC-IND-CCA adversary $\mathcal{A}$ of the proposed scheme in Section 3 that succeeds with probability ϵ, then there is a simulator $\mathcal{B}$ running in polynomial time that solves the $(\ell + 1)$-BDHI problem with probability at least*

$$\epsilon \cdot \frac{1}{q_1}\left(1 - q_s\frac{q_s + q_2}{q}\right)\left(1 - \frac{q_d}{q}\right)$$

where q_1, q_2, q_3, q_s, q_d are the number of queries allowed to the random oracle H_1, H_2, H_3, signcryption oracle and de-signcryption oracle respectively and we assume $q_1 = \ell$.

Proof. <u>Setup</u>: Suppose $\mathcal{B}$ is given a random instance of the $(\ell+1)$-BDHI problem $(g, g^{\alpha}, g^{\alpha^2}, \ldots, g^{\alpha^{\ell}}, g^{\alpha^{\ell+1}})$, $\mathcal{B}$ runs $\mathcal{A}$ as a subroutine to output $e(g,g)^{\frac{1}{\alpha}}$. $\mathcal{B}$ sets up a simulated environment for $\mathcal{A}$ as follow.

$\mathcal{B}$ first randomly selects $\pi \in_R \{1, \ldots, q_1\}$, $I_{\pi} \in_R \mathbb{Z}_q^*$ and $w_1, \ldots, w_{\pi-1}$, $w_{\pi+1}, \ldots, w_{\ell} \in_R \mathbb{Z}_q^*$. For $i \in \{1, \ldots, \ell\} \setminus \{\pi\}$, it computes $I_i = I_{\pi} - w_i$. Construct a polynomial with degree $\ell - 1$ as

$$f(z) = \prod_{i=1, i \neq \pi}^{\ell} (z + w_i)$$

to obtain $c_0, \ldots, c_{\ell-1} \in \mathbb{Z}_q^*$ such that $f(z) = \sum_{i=0}^{\ell-1} c_i z^i$. Then it sets generator $\hat{g} = g^{\sum_{i=0}^{\ell-1} c_i \alpha^i} = g^{f(\alpha)}$.

For $i \in \{1, \ldots, \ell\} \setminus \{\pi\}$, $\mathcal{B}$ expands $f_i(z) = \frac{f(z)}{(z + w_i)} = \sum_{j=0}^{\ell-2} d_{i,j} z^j$ to obtain $d_{i,1}, \ldots, d_{i,\ell-2} \in \mathbb{Z}_q^*$ and sets

$$\tilde{H}_i = g^{\sum_{j=0}^{\ell-2} d_{i,j} \alpha^j} = g^{f_i(\alpha)} = g^{\frac{f(\alpha)}{\alpha + w_i}} = \hat{g}^{\frac{1}{\alpha + w_i}}$$

It computes the public key g_1 and g_2 as

$$g_1 = \hat{g}^{-\alpha} \hat{g}^{-I_{\pi}} = \hat{g}^{-\alpha - I_{\pi}} \qquad g_2 = \hat{g}^{\alpha^2} \hat{g}^{2I_{\pi}\alpha} \hat{g}^{I_{\pi}^2} = \hat{g}^{(\alpha + I_{\pi})^2}$$

where $\hat{g}^{\alpha} = g^{\sum_{i=0}^{\ell-1} c_i \alpha^{i+1}}$ and $\hat{g}^{\alpha^2} = g^{\sum_{i=0}^{\ell-1} c_i \alpha^{i+2}}$ so that its unknown private key is implicitly set to $x = -\alpha - I_{\pi} \in \mathbb{Z}_q^*$. For all $i \in \{1, \ldots, \ell\} \setminus \{\pi\}$, we have $(I_i, -\tilde{H}_i) = (I_i, \hat{g}^{\frac{1}{I_i + x}})$.

<u>Oracle Simulation</u>: $\mathcal{B}$ first initializes a counter ν to 1 and starts $\mathcal{A}$. Throughout the game, we assume that H_1-queries are distinct, that the target identity ID_r^* is submitted to H_1 at some point.

1. *Random Oracle:* For H_1-queries (we denote ID_{ν} the input of the νth one of such queries), $\mathcal{B}$ answers I_{ν} and increments ν.
   For H_2-queries on input $(m, ID_s, R, T_0, T_1, T_2, t_1', t_2', U)$ and H_3-queries on input (R, T_1, T_2, U), $\mathcal{B}$ returns the defined value if it exists and a randomly chosen $h_2 \in_R \mathbb{Z}_q^*$ for H_2 and $h_3 \in_R \{0,1\}^{n_M}$ for H_3 respectively, otherwise. $\mathcal{B}$ stores the information $\{h_2, (m, ID_s, R, T_0, T_1, T_2, t_1', t_2', U, \gamma)\}$ in L_2, where $\gamma = R^{h_2} \cdot e(\hat{g}, \hat{g})$, and $\{h_3, (R, T_1, T_2, U)\}$ in L_3.
2. *Extraction Oracle:* On input ID_{ν}, if $\nu = \pi$, $\mathcal{B}$ aborts. Otherwise, it knows that $H_1(ID_{\nu}) = I_{\nu}$ and returns $-\tilde{H}_{\nu} = \hat{g}^{1/(I_{\nu}+x)}$.
3. *Signcryption Oracle:* On input a plaintext m and identities $(ID_s, ID_r) = (ID_{\mu}, ID_{\nu})$ for $\mu, \nu \in \{1, \ldots, q_1\}$, we observe that if $\mu \neq \pi$, $\mathcal{B}$ knows the sender's private key $d_{ID_{\mu}} = -\tilde{H}_{\mu}$ and can answer the query according to the specification of the algorithm. We thus assume $\mu = \pi$ and hence $\nu \neq \pi$. Also observe that $\mathcal{B}$ knows the receiver's private key $d_{ID_{\nu}} = -\tilde{H}_{\nu}$. The remaining task is to find a triple $(U, t, T_0, T_1, T_2, t_1', t_2', h)$ such that

$$e(T, d_{ID_{\nu}})^h = e(\hat{g}^t U, g_{ID_{\pi}}) \cdot e(\hat{g}, \hat{g})^{-1}$$

where $T = T_0 T_1^{t_1'} T_2^{t_2'}$, $g_{ID_\pi} = \hat{g}^{I_\pi} g_1$. To do so, $\mathcal{B}$ randomly generates t, t', h, t_1', $t_2', \tilde{t}_1, \tilde{t}_2 \in_R \mathbb{Z}_q^*$, computes

$$U = d_{ID_\nu}^{\ t'+t_1'\tilde{t}_1+t_2'\tilde{t}_2} \hat{g}^{-t} \qquad R = e(T, d_{ID_\nu})$$

$$T_0 = g_{ID_\pi}^{\ \frac{t'}{h}} g_{ID_\nu}^{\ -\frac{1}{h}} \qquad T_1 = g_{ID_\pi}^{\ \frac{\tilde{t}_1}{h}} \qquad T_2 = g_{ID_\pi}^{\ \frac{\tilde{t}_2}{h}}$$

where $g_{ID_\nu} = \hat{g}^{I_\nu} g_1$, and back patching the hash value $H_2(m, ID_\pi, R, T_0, T_1,$ $T_2, t_1', t_2', U)$ to h. These values satisfy equation (1) as

$$\begin{aligned} R^h &= e(T_0 T_1^{t_1'} T_2^{t_2'}, d_{ID_\nu})^h \\ &= e(g_{ID_\pi}^{\ t'+t_1'\tilde{t}_1+t_2'\tilde{t}_2} g_{ID_\nu}^{\ -1}, d_{ID_\nu}) \\ &= e(g_{ID_\pi}, d_{ID_\nu})^{t'+t_1'\tilde{t}_1+t_2'\tilde{t}_2} \cdot e(\hat{g}, \hat{g})^{-1} \\ &= e(U\hat{g}^t, g_{ID_\pi}) \cdot e(\hat{g}, \hat{g})^{-1} \end{aligned}$$

and they are valid ciphertext tuples as the distribution of the simulated ciphertexts is the same as the one in the real protocol. The ciphertext $\phi = (U, T_0, T_1, T_2, t_1', t_2', t, m \oplus H_3(R, T_1, T_2, U))$ is returned.

4. *De-signcryption Oracle:* On input a ciphertext $\phi = (U, T_0, T_1, T_2, t_1', t_2', t, c)$ for identity (receiver) $ID_r = ID_\nu$, we assume that $\nu = \pi$ because otherwise $\mathcal{B}$ knows the receiver's private key $d_{ID_\nu} = -\tilde{H}_\nu$ and can normally run the decryption algorithm.

First, we note the following fact. Let $\tilde{x} \in \mathbb{Z}_q$ such that

$$\begin{aligned} d_{ID_\mu}^{\ \tilde{x}} &= \hat{g}^t U d_{ID_\mu}^{\ -1} \\ (\hat{g}^{\frac{1}{I_\mu+x}})^{\tilde{x}} &= \hat{g}^t U \hat{g}^{\frac{-1}{I_\mu+x}} \\ \hat{g}^{\tilde{x}} &= (\hat{g}^t U)^{I_\mu+x} \hat{g}^{-1} \end{aligned} \qquad (2)$$

Also let $T = T_0 T_1^{t_1'} T_2^{t_2'}$, $g_{ID_\nu} = \hat{g}^{I_\nu} g_1$, and $h = H_2(m, ID_\mu, R, \cdots)$ (which is yet unknown to $\mathcal{B}$ at this moment). As all valid ciphertext satisfies

$$\begin{aligned} R^h &= e(\hat{g}^t U, \hat{g}^{I_\mu+x}) \cdot e(\hat{g}, \hat{g})^{-1} \\ e(T^h, \hat{g}^{\frac{1}{I_\nu+x}}) &= e((\hat{g}^t U)^{I_\mu+x}, \hat{g}) \cdot e(\hat{g}^{-1}, \hat{g}) \\ e(T^{\frac{h}{I_\nu+x}}, \hat{g}) &= e((\hat{g}^t U)^{I_\mu+x} \hat{g}^{-1}, \hat{g}) \\ &\Rightarrow T^{\frac{h}{I_\nu+x}} = (\hat{g}^t U)^{I_\mu+x} \hat{g}^{-1} \end{aligned} \qquad (3)$$

Let $\tilde{x}' \in \mathbb{Z}_q$ such that

$$\begin{aligned} g_{ID_\nu}^{\ \tilde{x}'} &= T^h \\ \hat{g}^{\tilde{x}'(I_\nu+x)} &= T^h \\ \hat{g}^{\tilde{x}'} &= T^{\frac{h}{I_\nu+x}} \end{aligned}$$

$$= (\hat{g}^t U)^{I_\mu + x} \hat{g}^{-1} \text{ (from equation(3))}$$
$$= \hat{g}^{\tilde{x}} \text{ (from equation(2))}$$
$$\Rightarrow \tilde{x}' = \tilde{x}$$
$$\Rightarrow \log_{d_{ID_\mu}} (\hat{g}^t U d_{ID_\mu}^{-1}) = \log_{g_{ID_\nu}} (T^h) \tag{4}$$

From equation (4), we have

$$e(T^h, d_{ID_\mu}) = e(g_{ID_\nu}, S \cdot d_{ID_\mu}^{-1}) \tag{5}$$

where $S = \hat{g}^t U$, which yields $e(T^h, d_{ID_\mu}) = e(g_{ID_\nu}, S) \cdot e(g_{ID_\nu}, d_{ID_\mu})^{-1}$.

The query is handled by computing $\gamma = e(S, \hat{g}^{I_\mu} g_1)$, and search through the list L_2 for entries of the form $(m_i, R_i, h_{2,i}, \cdots, \gamma)$ indexed by $i \in \{1, \ldots, q_2\}$. If none is found, ϕ is rejected. Otherwise, each one of them is further examined: for the corresponding indexes, $\mathcal{B}$ checks if

$$\frac{e(T, d_{ID_\mu})^{h_{2,i}}}{e(S, g_{ID_\nu})} = e(g_{ID_\nu}, d_{ID_\mu})^{-1} \tag{6}$$

meaning that equation (5) is satisfied. If the unique $i \in \{1, \ldots, q_2\}$ satisfying equation (6) is detected, the matching pair $(m_i, h_{2,i}, S)$ is returned. Otherwise ϕ is rejected.

Challenge: $\mathcal{A}$ outputs messages (m_0, m_1) and identities ID^* for which it never obtained ID^*'s private key. If $ID^* \neq ID_\pi$, $\mathcal{B}$ aborts. Otherwise it randomly selects $t, t'_1, t'_2, \tilde{t}_0, \tilde{t}_1, \tilde{t}_2 \in_R \mathbb{Z}_q^*$, $c \in_R \{0,1\}^{n_m}$ and $U \in_R \mathbb{G}$. Computes $T_0 = \hat{g}^{\tilde{t}_0}, T_1 = \hat{g}^{\tilde{t}_1}, T_2 = \hat{g}^{\tilde{t}_2}$ to return the challenge ciphertext $\phi^* = (U, t, T_0, T_1, T_2, t'_1, t'_2, c)$. Let $\xi = \tilde{t}_0 + t'_1 \tilde{t}_1 + t'_2 \tilde{t}_2$ and $T = \hat{g}^{-\xi}$. Since $x = -\alpha - I_\pi$, we let $\rho = \frac{\xi}{\alpha(I_\mu - \alpha - I_\pi)} = -\frac{\xi}{(I_\pi + x)(I_\mu + x)}$, we can check that

$$T = \hat{g}^{-\xi} = \hat{g}^{-\alpha(I_\mu - \alpha - I_\pi)\rho}$$
$$= \hat{g}^{(I_\pi + x)(I_\mu + x)\rho}$$
$$= \hat{g}^{(I_\pi I_\mu + (I_\mu + I_\pi)x + x^2)\rho}$$

$\mathcal{A}$ cannot recognize that ϕ^* is not a proper ciphertext unless it queries H_2 or H_3 on $e(\hat{g}^{I_\mu} g_1, \hat{g})^\rho$. Along the guess stage, its view is simulated as before and its output is ignored. Standard arguments can show that a successful $\mathcal{A}$ is very likely to query H_2 or H_3 on the input $e(g_{ID_\mu}, \hat{g})^\rho$ if the simulation is indistinguishable from a real attack environment.

Output Calculation: $\mathcal{B}$ fetches a random entry $(m, R, T_0, T_1, T_2, t'_1, t'_2, U, h_2)$ or $(R, T_1, T_2, U, \cdot)$ from the lists L_2 or L_3. With probability $1/(2q_2 + q_3)$, the chosen entry will contain the right element

$$R = e(g_{ID_\mu}, \hat{g})^\rho = e(\hat{g}, \hat{g})^{-\xi/(I_\pi + x)} = e(g, g)^{f(\alpha)^2 \xi/\alpha}$$

where $f(z) = \sum_{i=0}^{\ell-1} c_i z^i$ is the polynomial for which $\hat{g} = g^{f(\alpha)}$. The $(\ell+1)$-BDHI solution can be extracted by computing

$$
\left(\frac{R^{1/\xi}}{e\left(g^{\sum_{i=0}^{\ell-2} c_{i+1}\alpha^i}, g^{c_0}\right) e\left(g^{\sum_{j=0}^{\ell-2} c_{j+1}\alpha^j}, \hat{g}\right)} \right)^{1/c_0^2}
$$

$$
= \left(\frac{e(g,g)^{f(\alpha)^2/\alpha}}{e(g,g)^{c_0(c_1+c_2\alpha+c_3\alpha^2+\ldots c_{\ell-1}\alpha^{\ell-2})} e(g,g)^{f(\alpha)(c_1+c_2\alpha+c_3\alpha^2+\ldots c_{\ell-1}\alpha^{\ell-2})}} \right)^{1/c_0^2}
$$

$$
= \left(\frac{e(g,g)^{f(\alpha)^2/\alpha}}{e(g,g)^{\frac{c_0(c_1\alpha+c_2\alpha^2+\ldots c_{\ell-1}\alpha^{\ell-1})+f(\alpha)(c_1\alpha+c_2\alpha^2+\ldots c_{\ell-1}\alpha^{\ell-1})}{\alpha}}} \right)^{1/c_0^2}
$$

$$
= e(g,g)^{\frac{f(\alpha)^2 - (c_1\alpha+c_2\alpha^2+\ldots c_{\ell-1}\alpha^{\ell-1})(c_0+f(\alpha))}{c_0^2\alpha}}
$$

$$
= e(g,g)^{\frac{c_0^2}{c_0^2\alpha}}
$$

$$
= e(g,g)^{1/\alpha}
$$

Probability Analysis: $\mathcal{B}$ only fails in providing a consistent simulation because one of the following independent events happen:

- E_1 : $\mathcal{A}$ does not choose to be challenged on ID_π.
- E_2 : A key extraction query is made on ID_π.
- E_3 : $\mathcal{B}$ aborts in a Signcryption query because of a collision on H_2.
- E_4 : $\mathcal{B}$ rejects a valid ciphertext at some point of the game.

We have $\Pr[\neg E_1] = 1/q_1$ and $\neg E_1$ implies $\neg E_2$. Also observe that $\Pr[E_3] \leq q_s(q_s + q_2)/q$ and $\Pr[E_4] \leq q_d/q$. Combining together, the overall successful probability $\Pr[\neg E_1 \wedge \neg E_3 \wedge \neg E_4]$ is at least

$$
\frac{1}{q_1}\left(1 - q_s\frac{q_s + q_2}{q}\right)\left(1 - \frac{q_d}{q}\right)
$$

$\square$

Theorem 2 (Unforgeability). *If there is an SC-UEF-CMA adversary $\mathcal{A}$ of the proposed scheme in Section 3 that succeeds with probability ϵ, then there is a simulator $\mathcal{B}$ running in polynomial time that solves the $\ell + 1$-SDH problem with probability at least*

$$
\epsilon^2 \cdot \frac{1}{q_1 q_2}\left(1 - q_s\frac{q_s + q_2}{q}\right)\left(1 - \frac{q_d}{q}\right)
$$

where q_1, q_2, q_3, q_s, q_d are the number of queries allowed to the random oracle H_1, H_2, H_3, signcryption oracle and de-signcryption oracle respectively and we assume $q_1 = \ell$.

Proof. <u>Setup:</u> Suppose $\mathcal{B}$ is given a random instance of the $(\ell+1)$-SDH problem $(g, g^\alpha, g^{\alpha^2}, \ldots, g^{\alpha^\ell}, g^{\alpha^{\ell+1}})$, $\mathcal{B}$ runs $\mathcal{A}$ as a subroutine to output $(c, g^{\frac{1}{c+\alpha}})$. $\mathcal{B}$ sets up a simulated environment for $\mathcal{A}$ as follow.

$\mathcal{B}$ first randomly selects $\pi \in_R \{1, \ldots, q_1\}$, $I_\pi \in_R \mathbb{Z}_q^*$ and $w_1, \ldots, w_{\pi-1},$ $w_{\pi+1}, \ldots, w_\ell \in_R \mathbb{Z}_q^*$. Construct a polynomial with degree $\ell - 1$ as

$$f(z) = \prod_{i=1, i\neq\pi}^{\ell} (z + w_i)$$

to obtain $c_0, \ldots, c_{\ell-1} \in \mathbb{Z}_q^*$ such that $f(z) = \sum_{i=0}^{\ell-1} c_i z^i$. Then it sets generator $\hat{g} = g^{\sum_{i=0}^{\ell-1} c_i \alpha^i} = g^{f(\alpha)}$.

For $i \in \{1, \ldots, \ell\} \setminus \{\pi\}$, $\mathcal{B}$ expands $f_i(z) = f(z)/(z + w_i) = \sum_{j=0}^{\ell-2} d_{i,j} z^j$ to obtain $d_{i,1}, \ldots, d_{i,\ell-2} \in \mathbb{Z}_q^*$ and sets

$$\tilde{H}_i = g^{\sum_{j=0}^{\ell-2} d_{i,j}\alpha^j} = g^{f_i(\alpha)} = g^{\frac{f(\alpha)}{\alpha+w_i}} = \hat{g}^{\frac{1}{\alpha+w_i}}$$

It computes the public key g_1 and g_2 as

$$g_1 = \hat{g}^\alpha \qquad g_2 = \hat{g}^{\alpha^2}$$

where $\hat{g}^\alpha = g^{\sum_{i=0}^{\ell-1} c_i \alpha^{i+1}}$ and $\hat{g}^{\alpha^2} = g^{\sum_{i=0}^{\ell-1} c_i \alpha^{i+2}}$ so that its unknown private key is implicitly set to $x = \alpha$. For all $i \in \{1, \ldots, \ell\} \setminus \{\pi\}$, we have $(I_i, \tilde{H}_i) = (w_i, \hat{g}^{\frac{1}{w_i+\alpha}})$.

<u>Oracle Queries</u> are answered in the same way as in Theorem 1.

<u>Output Calculation:</u> $\mathcal{A}$ has produced a forged ciphertext $(U, T_0, T_1, T_2, t_1', t_2', t_1, c)$, a sender identity ID_s and a receiver identity ID_r. If $ID_s \neq ID_\pi$, $\mathcal{B}$ aborts. Otherwise $\mathcal{B}$ uses D_{ID_r} to decrypt and gets R and m^*.

We denote h_1 for the reply of the H_2 query on $(m^*, ID_\pi, R, T_0, T_1, T_2, t_1', t_2', U)$. $\mathcal{B}$ rewinded to the point just before making this particular query. This time $\mathcal{B}$ supplies to a different value $h_2 \neq h_1$ to this query. $\mathcal{A}$ produced another forged ciphertext $(U, \hat{T}_0, T_1, T_2, \hat{t_1'}, \hat{t_2'}, \hat{t}, \hat{c})$ based on h_2. Note that (U, T_1, T_2) are the same in both ciphertext as they are inputs to the H_2 query. R and m^* are also the same, as they are also one of the inputs to the H_2 query. By rewinding to the point just before making this particular query does not change the input values, but only the output values. If both forgeries satisfy equation (1), we obtain the relations

$$e(S_1, g_{ID_\pi})^{\frac{1}{h_1}} e(\hat{g}, \hat{g})^{-\frac{1}{h_1}} = e(S_2, g_{ID_\pi})^{\frac{1}{h_2}} e(\hat{g}, \hat{g})^{-\frac{1}{h_2}}$$

where $S_1 = \hat{g}^t U$, $S_2 = \hat{g}^{\hat{t}} U$ and $g_{ID_\pi} = \hat{g}^{H_1(ID_\pi)} g_1 = \hat{g}^{I_\pi + \alpha}$. Then, it comes that

$$e\left(S_1^{\frac{h_2}{h_2-h_1}} S_2^{-\frac{h_1}{h_2-h_1}}, g_{ID_\pi}\right) = e(\hat{g}, \hat{g})$$

Let $\tilde{T} = S_1^{\frac{h_2}{h_2 - h_1}} S_2^{-\frac{h_1}{h_2 - h_1}} = \hat{g}^{\frac{1}{I_\pi + \alpha}}$. From $\tilde{T}$, $\mathcal{B}$ can proceed as in [4] to extract $\sigma^* = g^{\frac{1}{I_\pi + \alpha}}$: it first obtains $\gamma_{-1}, \gamma_0, \ldots, \gamma_{q-2} \in \mathbb{Z}_q^*$ for which $f(z)/(z + I_\pi) = \frac{\gamma_{-1}}{z + I_\pi} + \sum_{i=1}^{\ell-2} \gamma_i z^*$ and computes

$$\sigma^* = \left(\tilde{T} g^{-\sum_{i=0}^{\ell-2} \gamma_i \alpha^i} \right)^{\frac{1}{\gamma_{-1}}} = g^{\frac{1}{I_\pi + \alpha}}$$

and returns the pair (I_π, σ^*) as a result.

Probability Analysis is similar to the one in Theorem 1. In addition, there is a rewind here, with successful probability ϵ/q_2. Combine together, the overall successful probability is at least

$$\epsilon^2 \cdot \frac{1}{q_1 q_2} \left(1 - q_s \frac{q_s + q_2}{q} \right) \left(1 - \frac{q_d}{q} \right) \qquad \square$$

4   Performance Analysis

The performance of our scheme is comparable to previous non-identity based online/offline signcryption scheme, such as [1,22]. Yet they need to fix the receiver's public key in the offline stage but we allow it to be known only in the online stage.

In terms of functionality, our scheme can be replaced by an online/offline identity-based encryption (OOIBE) (such as [11,15]) plus an online/offline identity-based signature (OOIBS) (such as [10]) to obtain the same features. However, the efficiency of our scheme highly surpasses the combination of an OOIBE and OOIBS. The advantages are shown in the following table. In the comparison, we assume that $|\mathbb{G}| = 160$ bits, $|q| = 160$ bits, $|\mathbb{G}_T| = 1024$ bits and $|\mathcal{M}| = |q| = 160$ bits. We denote by E the point multiplication in $\mathbb{G}$ or $\mathbb{G}_T$, ME the multi-point multiplication in $\mathbb{G}$ or $\mathbb{G}_T$ (which costs about 1.3 times more than a single point multiplication), M the point addition in $\mathbb{G}$ or $\mathbb{G}_T$ and m_c the modular computation in $\mathbb{Z}_q$.

Table 1. Comparison of computation cost and size

	GMC-1 + OOIBS	GMC-2 + OOIBS	LZ + OOIBS	Our scheme
Offline computation	$6E + 2ME$	$5E + 2ME$	$5E + 1ME$	$4E + 1ME$
Online computation	$1M + 3m_c$	$1M + 3m_c$	$4m_c$	$3m_c$
Offline storage (bits)	2944	5376	2944	2624
Ciphertext length (bits)	3104	7424	2080	1280
Number of pairing for decryption + verification	9	4	5	2
Security model	selective ID	standard	random oracle	random oracle

Currently there are just 3 OOIBE schemes that allow the intended receiver's identity to be unknown in the offline stage. We use GMC-1 and GMC-2 to denote the first two in [11] and LZ to denote the one in [15]. For OOIBS, there is only one concrete scheme by Xu *et al.* [20]. However it was proven insecure by Li *et al.* [12] later. We use the generic construction by Galindo *et al.* [10]. The generic construction requires one public key based signature scheme and one online/offline signature scheme. The underlying signature schemes we use are from [6] (random oracle) and [4] (without random oracle) and the underlying online/offline signature scheme we use is from [5]. All these signature schemes are the most efficient one in the state of the art within their respective security model.

From the above table, we can see that our scheme achieves the least computation and the smallest size in both offline and online stage, when compare to the combinations of OOIBE and OOIBS.

5   Conclusion

In this paper, we redefined the notion "online/offline ID-based signcryption" and provided a scheme that realizes it. Our construction is very efficient in a sense that it does not require any pairing operation in offline and online signcryption stages. Furthermore, we do *not* require the receiver's information (in our case, identity) in the offline signcryption stage. It is the first in the literature to remove such requirement. Without this restriction, our scheme is more flexible and practical. Our scheme is particularly suitable to provide authentication and confidentiality to power-constrained communication devices. We believe our proposed scheme may provide a practical solution in secure and authenticated transaction for smart cards or mobile devices such as smart phone.

References

1. An, J.H., Dodis, Y., Rabin, T.: On the Security of Joint Signature and Encryption. In: Knudsen, L.R. (ed.) EUROCRYPT 2002. LNCS, vol. 2332, pp. 83–107. Springer, Heidelberg (2002)
2. Barreto, P.S.L.M., Libert, B., McCullagh, N., Quisquater, J.-J.: Efficient and provably-secure identity-based signatures and signcryption from bilinear maps. In: Roy, B. (ed.) ASIACRYPT 2005. LNCS, vol. 3788, pp. 515–532. Springer, Heidelberg (2005)
3. Boneh, D., Boyen, X.: Efficient Selective-ID Secure Identity-Based Encryption Without Random Oracles. In: Cachin, C., Camenisch, J.L. (eds.) EUROCRYPT 2004. LNCS, vol. 3027, pp. 223–238. Springer, Heidelberg (2004)
4. Boneh, D., Boyen, X.: Short Signatures Without Random Oracles. In: Cachin, C., Camenisch, J.L. (eds.) EUROCRYPT 2004. LNCS, vol. 3027, pp. 56–73. Springer, Heidelberg (2004)
5. Boneh, D., Boyen, X.: Short signatures without random oracles and the sdh assumption in bilinear groups. J. Cryptology 21(2), 149–177 (2008)

6. Boneh, D., Lynn, B., Shacham, H.: Short Signatures from the Weil Pairing. In: Boyd, C. (ed.) ASIACRYPT 2001. LNCS, vol. 2248, pp. 514–532. Springer, Heidelberg (2001)
7. Boyen, X.: Multipurpose Identity-Based Signcryption (A Swiss Army Knife for Identity-Based Cryptography). In: Boneh, D. (ed.) CRYPTO 2003. LNCS, vol. 2729, pp. 383–399. Springer, Heidelberg (2003)
8. Chen, L., Malone-Lee, J.: Improved Identity-Based Signcryption. In: Vaudenay, S. (ed.) PKC 2005. LNCS, vol. 3386, pp. 362–379. Springer, Heidelberg (2005)
9. Even, S., Goldreich, O., Micali, S.: On-line/Off-line digital signatures. In: Brassard, G. (ed.) CRYPTO 1989. LNCS, vol. 435, pp. 263–275. Springer, Heidelberg (1990)
10. Galindo, D., Herranz, J., Kiltz, E.: On the generic construction of identity-based signatures with additional properties. In: Lai, X., Chen, K. (eds.) ASIACRYPT 2006. LNCS, vol. 4284, pp. 178–193. Springer, Heidelberg (2006)
11. Guo, F., Mu, Y., Chen, Z.: Identity-Based Online/Offline Encryption. In: Tsudik, G. (ed.) FC 2008. LNCS, vol. 5143, pp. 247–261. Springer, Heidelberg (2008)
12. Li, F., Shirase, M., Takagi, T.: On the security of online/offline signatures and multisignatures from acisp'06. In: Franklin, M.K., Hui, L.C.K., Wong, D.S. (eds.) CANS 2008. LNCS, vol. 5339, pp. 108–119. Springer, Heidelberg (2008)
13. Libert, B., Quisquater, J.-J.: New Identity Based Signcryption Schemes from Pairings. In: IEEE Information Theory Workshop 2003, pp. 155–158 (2003)
14. Liu, J.K., Baek, J., Zhou, J.: Online/offline identity-based signcryption re-visited. Cryptology ePrint Archive, Report 2010/274 (2010), http://eprint.iacr.org/
15. Liu, J.K., Zhou, J.: An efficient identity-based online/offline encryption scheme. In: Abdalla, M., Pointcheval, D., Fouque, P.-A., Vergnaud, D. (eds.) ACNS 2009. LNCS, vol. 5536, pp. 156–167. Springer, Heidelberg (2009)
16. Malone-Lee, J.: Identity-Based Signcryption. Cryptology ePrint Archive, Report 2002/098 (2002), http://eprint.iacr.org/
17. Selvi, S.S.D., Vivek, S.S., Rangan, C.P.: Identity based online/offline signcryption scheme. Cryptology ePrint Archive, Report 2010/376 (2010), http://eprint.iacr.org/
18. Shamir, A.: Identity-Based Cryptosystems and Signature Schemes. In: Blakely, G.R., Chaum, D. (eds.) CRYPTO 1984. LNCS, vol. 196, pp. 47–53. Springer, Heidelberg (1985)
19. Sun, D., Mu, Y., Susilo, W.: A generic construction of identity-based online/offline signcryption. In: ISPA, pp. 707–712. IEEE, Los Alamitos (2008)
20. Xu, S., Mu, Y., Susilo, W.: Online/offline signatures and multisignatures for AVOD and DSR routing security. In: Batten, L.M., Safavi-Naini, R. (eds.) ACISP 2006. LNCS, vol. 4058, pp. 99–110. Springer, Heidelberg (2006)
21. Xu, Z., Dai, G., Yang, D.: An efficient online/offline signcryption scheme for MANET. In: AINA Workshop 2007, pp. 171–176. IEEE Computer Society, Los Alamitos (2007)
22. Zhang, F., Mu, Y., Susilo, W.: Reducing security overhead for mobile networks. In: AINA Workshop 2005, pp. 398–403. IEEE Computer Society, Los Alamitos (2005)
23. Zheng, Y.: Digital Signcryption or How to Achieve Cost (Signature & Encryption) << Cost(Signature) + Cost(Encryption). In: Kaliski Jr., B.S. (ed.) CRYPTO 1997. LNCS, vol. 1294, pp. 165–179. Springer, Heidelberg (1997)

Error-free, Multi-bit Non-committing Encryption with Constant Round Complexity

Huafei Zhu and Feng Bao

Institute for Infocomm Research, Singapore

Abstract. This paper studies error-free, multi-bit non-committing encryptions in the universally composable (UC) framework with constant round complexity. Previous efficient protocols such as the Beaver's protocol and the Damgard-Nielsen's protocol cause errors with certain probability, and require restarting the channel setup procedures if an error happens. This causes the main problem of UC-security of a non-committing protocol with error. The proposed error-free, l-bit non-committing encryption is fixed 4-round and it is as efficient as l-instance of the Beaver's protocol running in parallel. We show that the proposed scheme realizes the UC-security in the presence of adaptive adversary assuming that the decisional Diffie-Hellman problem is hard.

Keywords. Adaptive security, non-committing encryptions, universal composability.

1 Introduction

Non-committing encryption introduced and formalized by Canetti, Feige, Goldreich and Naor [9] is a key to realize adaptive security. The known protocols with error during the course of the channel setup such as the Beaver's protocol [1], the Damgård and Nielsen's protocol [12] (based on the general notion of oblivious public key encryption scheme), the Lei, Chen and Chen's scheme [15] (based on the quadratic residue problem) and Zhu and Bao's scheme [18] (based on the notion of oblivious public-key encryptions instantiated by the DDH problem) and Zhu, Araragi, Nishide and Sakurai [20] (based on the notion of the oblivious transfer protocols) consist of two stages: a channel setup stage and a message transfer stage, where the channel setup stage essentially needs rewinding. This is because when an error occurs two parties (a sender and a receiver involved in a non-committing encryption scheme with error) have to rewind to the beginning of this channel setup stage until agreeing on a common coin tossing result. The parties might try the channel setup many times.

To prove a coin-tossing protocol causing error with certain probability in the UC-security, Backes, Müller-Quade and Unruh [3], and Backes and Unruh [4] have mentioned that one must consider the tries before agreeing on the coin-tossing result. However, the ideal adversary only considers the current try and simulates the internal states of adaptively corrupted parties accordingly and the previous tries are neglected. Thus, the internal states of corrupt parties in previous tries are also neglected. This causes the main problem of UC-security of a protocol with error.

X. Lai, M. Yung, and D. Lin (Eds.): Inscrypt 2010, LNCS 6584, pp. 52–61, 2011.
© Springer-Verlag Berlin Heidelberg 2011

1.1   Error-free, Single-bit Non-committing Encryptions

Canetti, Feige, Goldreich and Naor [9] have proposed the first error free non-committing encryptions based on so called common-domain permutations in the stand-alone, simulation-based framework. To encrypt 1 bit, $\Theta(k^2)$ public key bits are communicated.

At Asiacrypt'09, Soled, Malkin and Wee [11] have presented a new implementation of non-committing encryptions based on a weaker notion called trapdoor simulatable cryptosystems in the simulation-based framework. To encrypt a bit $b \in \{0, 1\}$, the sender sends $4k$ ciphertexts of which k ciphertexts are encrypted b and the remaining $3k$ ones are obliviously sampled. The non-committing encryption scheme in [11] achieves the UC-security in the presence of adaptively semi-honest adversaries but is at the expense of higher computation and communication than the Damgård and Nielsen's protocol [12]. The CSMW protocol nevertheless is of interest since it is an error-free non-committing encryption.

Very recently, Zhu, Araragi, Nishide and Sakurai [19] have presented an new implementation of error-free, single-bit non-committing encryption. The idea is to use a pair of Diffie-Hellman and non-Diffie-Hellman quadruples as a 1-bit one-sided non-committing encryption and let the receiver to select the one-time one-bit key for every transmission of 1 bit. The proposed scheme realizes the UC-security in the presence of adaptive adversary assuming that the decisional Diffie-Hellman problem is hard.

1.2   This Work

This paper studies error-free, multi-bit non-committing encryptions in the universally composable framework of Canetti [5,6]. There are known error-free, single-bit non-committing encryptions [9,12,11,19], but there has not been any work that extends the single-bit non-committing encryption to the multi-bit setting so far. Although the universal composability ensures that an l-bit non-committing encryption can be implemented trivially by invoking an adaptive and composable, error-free, single-bit non-committing encryption scheme l times, the round complexity of the resulting l-bit non-committing encryption scheme is linear with l. A challenging task now is to construct error-free, multi-bit non-committing encryption schemes with constant round complexity.

The Technique. The idea behind our construction is that the sender generates l-pair of random Diffie-Hellman and non-Diffie-Hellman quadruples $\{S_{\alpha_i}^i, S_{\overline{\alpha_i}}^i\}_{i=1}^l$ in parallel. Similarly, the receiver randomly generates l-pair of random Diffie-Hellman and non-Diffie-Hellman quadruples $\{R_{\beta_i}^i, R_{\overline{\beta_i}}^i\}_{i=1}^l$ in parallel indexed by an l-bit string $(\beta_1, \ldots, \beta_l)$ serving as a session key. A Diffie-Hellman randomizer (say, the Naor-Pinkas randomizer, see Section 2 for more details) now is applied to the Diffie-Hellman quadruple $S_{\beta_i}^i$ to generate a response $(u_{S^i,\beta_i}, v_{S^i,\beta_i})$ while an oblivious sampling algorithm (say, the Canetti-Fischlin's oblivious sampling algorithm, see Section 2 for more details) is applied to $S_{\overline{\beta_i}}^i$ to generate a random response $(u_{S^i,\overline{\beta_i}}, v_{S^i,\overline{\beta_i}})$. Since the sender holds the auxiliary strings sk_{S^i} that has been used to generate the Diffie-Hellman quadruple $S_{\alpha_i}^i$, it follows that the sender is able to distinguish whether $(u_{S^i,\alpha_i}, v_{S^i,\alpha_i})$ is a random response or not from which the sender retrieves the session key specified by the receiver. At this point, a secure channel has been established between the parties. We refer to the reader Section 3 for more details.

The Proof of Security. We claim that the proposed error-free, multiple bits non-committing encryption scheme realizes the UC-security in the presence of adaptive adversary assuming that the decisional Diffie-Hellman problem is hard. To prove the security, a simulator first generates $2l$ random Diffie-Hellman quadruples $\{S^i_{\alpha_i}, S^i_{\overline{\alpha_i}}\}^l_{i=1}$ in parallel for the sender and then generates $2l$ random Diffie-Hellman quadruples $\{R^i_{\alpha_i}, R^i_{\overline{\alpha_i}}\}^l_{i=1}$ in parallel for the receiver. The simulator also generates $2l$ response messages $\{(u_{S^i,\beta_i}, v_{S^i,\beta_i}), (u_{S^i,\overline{\beta_i}}, v_{S^i,\overline{\beta_i}})\}^l_{i=1}$, where each response message $(u_{S^i,\gamma_i}, v_{S^i,\gamma_i})$ is generated by the Naor-Pinkas randomizer with auxiliary string $(x_{R^i,\gamma_i}, y_{R^i,\gamma_i}) \in Z_q \times Z_q$ which is chosen randomly and independently. If a corruption occurs, the simulator $\mathcal{S}$ invokes the Canetti-Fischlin's faking algorithm to generate randomness that will be revealed to the adversary $\mathcal{A}$ such that the view of environment $\mathcal{Z}$ in the real-world when it interacts with the adversary $\mathcal{A}$ is computationally indistinguishable from that when the environment $\mathcal{Z}$ interacts with the simulator $\mathcal{S}$ in the ideal-world. This technique is crucial for proving the security of multi-bit non-committing encryption scheme.

The Computation, Communication and Round Complexity. The total communication for encrypting l-bit message requires to generate $2l$ Diffie-Hellman quadruples and $2l$ two random quadruples, together with $2l$ Naor-Pinkas randomizers and $2l$ oblivious randomizers. Thus, our non-committing encryption protocol is as efficient as l-instance of Beaver's protocol running in parallel (in [1], the probability that a failure occurs during the course of one bit communication is 1/2. This stand-alone, non-committing encryption scheme is possibly the most efficient implementation of single-bit non-committing encryptions with error so far). Furthermore, the proposed l-bit non-committing encryption is fixed 4-round, a significant feature of our protocol.

RoadMap: The rest of this paper is organized as follows: The functionality and security definition of non-committing encryption protocols and the building blocks are presented in Section 2. In Section 3, a new implementation of error-free, string non-committing encryption scheme is proposed and we show that the proposed scheme realizes the UC-security in the presence of adaptive adversaries. We conclude our work in Section 4.

2   Non-committing Encryptions: Functionality, Security Definition and Building Blocks

We assume that the reader is familiar with the universally composable framework [5,6] and thus the detailed description of real-world vs. ideal-world framework is omitted.

2.1   Functionality of Non-commitment Encryptions

The functionality of a non-committing encryption scheme depicted in **Fig. 1** (in terms of secure message transmission) is due to Canetti [5]

Definition 1. *We call the functionality $\mathcal{F}^{\mathcal{N}}_{\text{NCE}}$ a secure message transmission channel. A real-world protocol π which realizes $\mathcal{F}^{\mathcal{N}}_{\text{NCE}}$ is called a secure non-committing encryption protocol.*

Functionality $\mathcal{F}_{\mathrm{NCE}}^{\mathcal{N}}$

$\mathcal{F}_{\mathrm{NCE}}^{\mathcal{N}}$ proceeds as follows, when parameterized by leakage function $\mathcal{N} \colon \{0,1\}^* \to \{0,1\}^*$

1. Upon receiving an input (send, sid, m), do: If $sid = (S, R, sid')$ for some R then send (send, $sid, \mathcal{N}(m)$) to the adversary, generate a private delayed output (send, sid, m) to R and halt. Else, ignore the input.
2. Upon receiving (corrupt, sid, P) from the adversary, where $P \in \{S, R\}$, disclose m to the adversary. Next, if the adversary provides a value m', and $P = S$, and no output has been yet written to R, then output (send, sid, m') to R and halt.

Fig. 1. The non-committing encryption functionality parameterized by leakage function $\mathcal{N}$.

2.2 Building Blocks

In this section, we sketch the building blocks for constructing non-committing encryptions.

The Naor-Pinkas randomizer. Let $p = 2q + 1$ and p, q be large prime numbers. Let $G \subseteq Z_p^*$ be a cyclic group of order q. Let g be a random generator of G. For any $0 \neq x \in Z_q$, we define $\mathsf{DLog}_G(x) = \{(g, g^x) : g \in G\}$. On input $(g_1, h_1) \in \mathsf{DLog}_G(x_1)$, and $(g_2, h_2) \in \mathsf{DLog}_G(x_2)$, a mapping ϕ called Naor-Pinkas randomizer is defined below:

$$\phi((g_1, g_2, h_1, h_2) \times (s, t)) = (g_1^s g_2^t \bmod p, \ h_1^s h_2^t \bmod p)$$

where $s, t \in_U Z_q$

Denote $u = g_1^s g_2^t \bmod p$ and $v = h_1^s h_2^t \bmod p$. Naor and Pinkas [17] have shown that

- if $x_1 = x_2 \ (= x)$, then (u, v) is uniformly random in $\mathsf{DLog}_G(x)$;
- if $x_1 \neq x_2$, then (u, v) is uniformly random in G^2.

The oblivious sampling and faking algorithms. The oblivious sampling and faking algorithms described below are due to Canetti and Fischlin [8].

Oblivious sampling algorithm: Let $p = wq + 1$ for some w not divisible by q, and G is a cyclic group of order q in Z_p^*. The Canetti-Fischlin oblivious sampling algorithm **sample** takes $r \in \{0,1\}^{2|p|}$ as input and outputs an element $r_G \in G$ via the following computations

- the sampling algorithm **sample** chooses a string $r \in \{0,1\}^{2|p|}$ uniformly at random, where $|p|$ be the bit length of the prime number p.
- Let $r_p = r \bmod p$ and $r_G = r_p^w \bmod p$.

Lemma 1. *(due to [8]) Let* $X = [X = x : x \in_U G]$, *and* $Y = [Y = y : y \leftarrow$ **sample**$(r), r \in_U \{0,1\}^{2|p|}]$, *then the distributions between two random variables X and Y are statistically indistinguishable.*

Oblivious faking algorithm: Let $p = wq + 1$ for some w not divisible by q, and G is a cyclic group of order q in Z_p^*. The Canetti-Fischlin oblivious faking algorithm **fake** takes a random element $h \in G$ as input and outputs $r_h \in \{0,1\}^{2|p|}$ via the following computations

- On input $h \in G$, the faking algorithm **fake** picks a random integer $i \in Z_w$. Let $h_p = h^x g^{iq} \bmod p$, where $xw \equiv 1 \bmod q$;
- **fake** randomly selects $j \in Z_p$ and let $r_h = \text{Len}(jp + h_p)$, where $\text{Len}(x)$ denotes the bit length of an integer x.

Lemma 2. *(due to [8]) Let* $X = [X = x : x \in_U \{0,1\}^{2|p|}]$, *and* $Y = [Y = y : y \leftarrow \textbf{fake}(g), g \in_U G]$, *then the distributions between two random variables X and Y are statistically indistinguishable.*

3   Universally Composable Non-Committing Encryptions

In this section, a new error-free, multiple bits non-committing encryption is described and analyzed. We show that the proposed scheme realizes the UC-security in the presence of adaptive adversaries.

3.1   The Description of Non-Committing Encryptions

INITIALIZATION. The environment $\mathcal{Z}$ takes security parameter k as input and outputs (p, q, G), where p is a large safe prime number (i.e., $p = 2q + 1$, q is a prime number) and G is a cyclic group with order q. Let $pk = (p, q, G)$. The environment $\mathcal{Z}$ then provides a description **des** of algorithm **sample** defined over G. Let $gpk = (pk, \textbf{des})$ (the global key for all participants). Finally, the environment provides input message $m \in \{0,1\}^l$ to the sender S.

CHANNEL SETUP. The error-free, multiple bits channel setup phase comprises the following four steps in parallel

STEP 1 On input 1^k, the sender S performs the following computations for $i = 1, \ldots, l$

- S selects $\alpha_i \in \{0,1\}$ uniformly at random;
- S randomly generates a Diffie-Hellman quadruple $(S_{\alpha_i,1}^i, S_{\alpha_i,2}^i, S_{\alpha_i,3}^i, S_{\alpha_i,4}^i)$ such that $\log_{S_{\alpha_i,1}^i}(S_{\alpha_i,3}^i) = \log_{S_{\alpha_i,2}^i}(S_{\alpha_i,4}^i)$. Let $S_{\alpha_i}^i = (S_{\alpha_i,1}^i, S_{\alpha_i,2}^i, S_{\alpha_i,3}^i, S_{\alpha_i,4}^i)$ and $sk_{S^i} = \log_{S_{\alpha_i,1}^i}(S_{\alpha_i,3}^i) = (\log_{S_{\alpha_i,2}^i}(S_{\alpha_i,4}^i))$;
- S invokes **sample** to obliviously generate a random quadruple $(S_{\overline{\alpha_i},1}^i, S_{\overline{\alpha_i},2}^i, S_{\overline{\alpha_i},3}^i, S_{\overline{\alpha_i},4}^i)$. Let $S_{\overline{\alpha_i}}^i = (S_{\overline{\alpha_i},1}^i, S_{\overline{\alpha_i},2}^i, S_{\overline{\alpha_i},3}^i, S_{\overline{\alpha_i},4}^i)$, where $\overline{\alpha_i} = 1 - \alpha_i$;
- Let $sk_S = (sk_{S^1}, \ldots, sk_{S^l})$. S keeps sk_S secret and sends $\{(S_0^i, S_1^i)\}_{[l]}$ to R, where $[l] = \{1, \ldots, l\}$;

STEP 2 upon receiving $\{(S_0^i, S_1^i)\}_{[l]}$, the receiver R performs the following computations for $j = 1, \ldots, l$

- R selects a bit $\beta_j \in \{0, 1\}$ uniformly at random;
- R randomly generates a Diffie-Hellman quadruple $(R^j_{\beta_j,1},\ R^j_{\beta_j,2},\ R^j_{\beta_j,3},\ R^j_{\beta_j,4})$ such that $\log_{R^j_{\beta_j,1}}(R^j_{\beta_j,3}) = \log_{R^j_{\beta_j,2}}(R^j_{\beta_j,4})$. Let $R^j_{\beta_j} = (R^j_{\beta_j,1},\ R^j_{\beta_j,2},\ R^j_{\beta_j,3},$ $R^j_{\beta_j,4})$ and $sk_{R^j} = \log_{R^j_{\beta_j,1}}(R^j_{\beta_j,3}) = (\log_{R^j_{\beta_j,2}}(R^j_{\beta_j,4}))$;
- R invokes **sample** to obliviously generate a random quadruple $(R^j_{\overline{\beta_j},1}, R^j_{\overline{\beta_j},2}, R^j_{\overline{\beta_j},3},$ $R^j_{\overline{\beta_j},4})$; Let $R^j_{\overline{\beta_j}} = (R^j_{\overline{\beta_j},1},\ R^j_{\overline{\beta_j},2},\ R^j_{\overline{\beta_j},3},\ R^j_{\overline{\beta_j},4})$;
- R invokes the Naor-Pinkas randomizer with the randomness $x_{R^j} \in Z_q$ and $y_{R^j} \in Z_q$ to generate $u_{S^j,\beta_j} = S^j_{\beta_j,1}{}^{x_{R^j}} S^j_{\beta_j,2}{}^{y_{R^j}}$ and $v_{S^j,\beta_j} = S^j_{\beta_j,3}{}^{x_{R^j}} S^j_{\beta_j,4}{}^{y_{R^j}}$ for the given quadruple $S^j_{\beta_j}$. Let $w_{S^j,\beta_j} = (u_{S^j,\beta_j}, v_{S^j,\beta_j})$.
- R invokes **sample** to output two random strings $u_{S^j,\overline{\beta_j}} \in Z_p^*$ and $v_{S^j,\overline{\beta_j}} \in Z_p^*$ for the given quadruple $S^j_{\overline{\beta_j}}$. Let $w_{S^j,\overline{\beta_j}} = (u_{S^j,\overline{\beta_j}}, v_{S^j,\overline{\beta_j}})$.
- Let $sk_R = (sk_{R^1}, \dots, sk_{R^l})$. R keeps sk_R secret and sends $\{(R^j_0, R^j_1)\}_{[l]}$ and $\{(w_{S^j,0}, w_{S^j,1})\}_{[l]}$ to S;

STEP 3 upon receiving $\{(R^j_0, R^j_1)\}_{[l]}$ and $\{(w_{S^j,0}, w_{S^j,1})\}_{[l]}$ from R, the sender S performs the following computations for $i = 1, \dots, l$

- parsing w_{S^i,α_i} as $(u_{S^i,\alpha_i}, v_{S^i,\alpha_i})$, S checks $v_{S^i,\alpha_i} \overset{?}{=} u_{S^i,\alpha_i}^{sk_{S^i}}$:
  - if the check is valid, S selects $x_{S^i} \in Z_q$ and $y_{S^i} \in Z_q$ uniformly at random, and then invokes the Naor-Pinkas randomizer to generate $u_{R^i,\alpha_i} = R^i_{\alpha_i,1}{}^{x_{S^i}} R^i_{\alpha_i,2}{}^{y_{S^i}}$ and $v_{R^i,\alpha_i} = R^i_{\alpha_i,3}{}^{x_{S^i}} R^i_{\alpha_i,4}{}^{y_{S^i}}$. S then invokes **sample** to output random elements $(u_{R^i,\overline{\alpha_i}}, v_{R^i,\overline{\alpha_i}}) \in G^2$; Let $\gamma_i = \alpha_i$ and let $w_{R^i,\alpha_i} = (u_{R^i,\alpha_i}, v_{R^i,\alpha_i})$ and $w_{R^i,\overline{\alpha_i}} = (u_{R^i,\overline{\alpha_i}}, v_{R^i,\overline{\alpha_i}})$;
  - otherwise, S selects $(x_{S^i}, y_{S^i}) \in (Z_q)^2$ uniformly at random, and then invokes the Naor-Pinkas randomizer to generate $u_{R^i,\overline{\alpha_i}} = R^i_{\overline{\alpha_i},1}{}^{x_{S^i}} R^i_{\overline{\alpha_i},2}{}^{y_{S^i}}$ and $v_{R^i,\overline{\alpha_i}} = R^i_{\overline{\alpha_i},3}{}^{x_{S^i}} R^i_{\overline{\alpha_i},4}{}^{y_{S^i}}$; S then invokes **sample** to output random elements $(u_{R^i,\alpha_i}, v_{R^i,\alpha_i}) \in G^2$; Let $\gamma_i = 1 - \alpha_i$ and let $w_{R^i,\alpha_i} = (u_{R^i,\alpha_i}, v_{R^i,\alpha_i})$ and $w_{R^i,\overline{\alpha_i}} = (u_{R^i,\overline{\alpha_i}}, v_{R^i,\overline{\alpha_i}})$;
- Let $\gamma = (\gamma_1, \dots, \gamma_l)$. S then sends $\{(w_{R^i,0}, w_{R^i,1})\}_{[l]}$ to R and outputs γ;

STEP 4 upon receiving $\{(w_{R^i,0}, w_{R^i,1})\}_{[l]}$, the receiver R performs the following computations for $j = 1, \dots, l$

- parsing w_{R^j,β_j} as $(u_{R^j,\beta_j}, v_{R^j,\beta_j})$, R checks $v_{R^j,\beta_j} \overset{?}{=} u_{R^j,\beta_j}^{sk_{R^j}}$;
  - if the check is valid, let $\gamma_i = \beta_i$ and outputs γ_i;
  - otherwise, output $\bot$ (notice that the probability that the honest party R outputs $\bot$ is negligible in case that the sender is honest).

MESSAGE TRANSFER On input $m \in \{0, 1\}^l$ and $\gamma \in \{0, 1\}^l$, S computes $m \oplus \gamma$. Let $c = m \oplus \gamma$. S then sends the ciphertext c to R. Upon receiving a ciphertext c, R obtains m by computing $c \oplus \gamma$.

This ends the description of the protocol π.

3.2 The Proof of Security

Theorem 1. *The protocol π realizes the UC-security in the presence of adaptive adversary in the authenticated channel assuming that the decisional Diffie-Hellman problem is hard.*

Proof. Same as that presented in the initial procedure in the real-world protocol, the environment $\mathcal{Z}$ first takes security parameter k as input and outputs $gpk =(pk, \mathbf{des})$, the global key for all participants. The environment $\mathcal{Z}$ then provides input message $m \in \{0,1\}^l$ to the sender S. We assume the channel between the sender S and the receiver R is authenticated and consider the following cases

1. the first corruption occurs after a ciphertext c has been received successfully by the receiver R;
2. the first corruption occurs after a secure channel has been setup but before a ciphertext c is generated;
3. the first corruption occurs during the course of a channel setup phase.

CASE 1: Upon receiving $(corrupt, sid, P)$, where $P \in \{S, R\}$, the simulator S performs the following computations on behalf of the honest sender S (simulating views of the environment $\mathcal{Z}$ from Step 1 to Step 4)

- generates two random Diffie-Hellman quadruples $(S_{0,1}^i, S_{0,2}^i, S_{0,3}^i, S_{0,4}^i)$ and $(S_{1,1}^i,$ $S_{1,2}^i, S_{1,3}^i, S_{1,4}^i)$ such that $\log_{S_{0,1}^i}(S_{0,3}^i) = \log_{S_{0,2}^i}(S_{0,4}^i)$ $(=: sk_{S_0^i})$ and $\log_{S_{1,1}^i}(S_{1,3}^i)$ $= \log_{S_{1,2}^i}(S_{1,4}^i)$ $(=: sk_{S_1^i})$.
  Let $S_{\alpha_i}^i = (S_{\alpha_i,1}^i, S_{\alpha_i,2}^i, S_{\alpha_i,3}^j, S_{\alpha_i,4}^j)$ and $S_{\overline{\alpha_i}}^i = (S_{\overline{\alpha_i},1}^i, S_{\overline{\alpha_i},2}^j, S_{\overline{\alpha_i},3}^i, S_{\overline{\alpha_i},4}^j)$. Let $sk_{S^i} = (sk_{S_0^i}, sk_{S_1^i})$. The simulator S keeps the trapdoor string sk_{S^i} secret for $i = 1, \ldots, l$.
- selects $(x_{R^i,\alpha_i}, y_{R^i,\alpha_i}) \in Z_q \times Z_q$ and $(x_{R^i,\overline{\alpha_i}}, y_{R^i,\overline{\alpha_i}}) \in Z_q \times Z_q$ uniformly at random;
- invokes the Naor-Pinkas randomizer to generate $u_{S^i,\alpha_i} = S_{\alpha_i,1}^i{}^{x_{R^i,\alpha_i}} S_{\alpha_i,2}^i{}^{y_{R^i,\alpha_i}}$ and $v_{S^i,\alpha_i} = S_{\alpha_i,3}^i{}^{x_{R^i,\alpha_i}} S_{\alpha_i,4}^i{}^{y_{R^i,\alpha_i}}$ for each Diffie-Hellman quadruple $S_{\alpha_i}^i$ also, invokes the Naor-Pinkas randomizer to generate $u_{S^i,\overline{\alpha_i}} = S_{\overline{\alpha_i},1}^i{}^{x_{R^i,\overline{\alpha_i}}} S_{\overline{\alpha_i},2}^i{}^{y_{R^i,\overline{\alpha_i}}}$ and $v_{S^i,\overline{\alpha_i}} = S_{\overline{\alpha_i},3}^i{}^{x_{R^i,\overline{\alpha_i}}} S_{\overline{\alpha_i},4}^i{}^{y_{R^i,\overline{\alpha_i}}}$ for each Diffie-Hellman quadruple $S_{\overline{\alpha_i}}^i$.
  Let $w_{S^i,\alpha_i} = (u_{S^i,\alpha_i}, v_{S^i,\alpha_i})$, $w_{S^i,\overline{\alpha_i}} = (u_{S^i,\overline{\alpha_i}}, v_{S^i,\overline{\alpha_i}})$ and $w_{S^i} = (w_{S^i,0}, w_{S^i,1})$.

Similarly, S performs the following computations on behalf of the honest receiver R (simulating views of the environment $\mathcal{Z}$ from Step 1 to Step 4)

- generates two random Diffie-Hellman quadruples $(R_{0,1}^j, R_{0,2}^j, R_{0,3}^j, R_{0,4}^j)$ and $(R_{1,1}^j, R_{1,2}^j, R_{1,3}^j, R_{1,4}^j)$ such that $\log_{R_{0,1}^j}(R_{0,3}^j) = \log_{R_{0,2}^j}(R_{0,4}^j)$ $(=: sk_{R_0^j})$ and $\log_{R_{1,1}^j}(R_{1,3}^j) = \log_{R_{1,2}^j}(R_{1,4}^j)$ $(=: sk_{R_1^j})$.
  Let $R_{\beta_j}^j = (R_{\beta_j,1}^j, R_{\beta_j,2}^j, R_{\beta_j,3}^j, R_{\beta_j,4}^j)$ and $R_{\overline{\beta_j}}^j = (R_{\overline{\beta_j},1}^j, R_{\overline{\beta_j},2}^j, R_{\overline{\beta_j},3}^j, R_{\overline{\beta_j},4}^j)$.
  Let $sk_{R^j} = (sk_{R_0^j}, sk_{R_1^j})$. The simulator S keeps the trapdoor string sk_{R^j} secret for $j = 1, \ldots, l$;

- selects $(x_{R^j,\beta_j}, y_{R^j,\beta_j}) \in Z_q \times Z_q$ and $(x_{R^j,\overline{\beta_j}}, y_{R^j,\overline{\beta_j}}) \in Z_q \times Z_q$ uniformly at random;
- invokes the Naor-Pinkas randomizer to generate $u_{S^j,\beta_j} = S_{\beta_j,1}^j{}^{x_{R^j,\beta_j}} S_{\beta_j,2}^j{}^{y_{R^j,\beta_j}}$ and $v_{S^j,\beta_j} = S_{\beta_j,3}^j{}^{x_{R^j,\beta_j}} S_{\beta_j,4}^j{}^{y_{R^j,\beta_j}}$ for each Diffie-Hellman quadruple $S_{\beta_j}^j$; also, invokes the Naor-Pinkas randomizer to generate $u_{S^j,\overline{\beta_j}} = S_{\overline{\beta_j},1}^j{}^{x_{R^j,\overline{\beta_j}}} S_{\overline{\beta_j},2}^j{}^{y_{R^j,\overline{\beta_j}}}$ and $v_{S^j,\overline{\beta_j}} = S_{\overline{\beta_j},3}^j{}^{x_{R^j,\overline{\beta_j}}} S_{\overline{\beta_j},4}^j{}^{y_{R^j,\overline{\beta_j}}}$ for the each Diffie-Hellman quadruple $S_{\overline{\beta_j}}^j$;

  Let $w_{S^j,\beta_j} = (u_{S^j,\beta_j}, v_{S^j,\beta_j})$, $w_{S^j,\overline{\beta_j}} = (u_{S^j,\overline{\beta_j}}, v_{S^j,\overline{\beta_j}})$ and $w_{S^j} = (w_{S^j,0}, w_{S^j,1})$.

Let $P \in \{S, R\}$ be the first corrupted party after a ciphertext c has been received by R. The simulator S corrupts the corresponding dummy party $\widetilde{P} \in \{\widetilde{S}, \widetilde{R}\}$ in the ideal world and learns m from the functionality $\mathcal{F}_{NCE}^N$. Let $\gamma \leftarrow c \oplus m$ and $(\gamma_1, \ldots, \gamma_l) \leftarrow \gamma$. The simulator S now invokes **fake** to interpret $R_{\overline{\gamma_i}}^i$ as a random non-Diffie-Hellman quadruple and interprets $R_{\gamma_i}^i$ as a random Diffie-Hellman quadruple. That is, for $i = 1, \ldots, l$, the simulator performs the following computations:

- extracting the randomness $(r_{R_{\overline{\gamma_i}}^i,1}, r_{R_{\overline{\gamma_i}}^i,2}, r_{R_{\overline{\gamma_i}}^i,3}, r_{R_{\overline{\gamma_i}}^i,4})$ used to generate $R_{\overline{\gamma_i}}^i$ (via the Canetti-Fischlin's faking algorithm). Let $r_{R_{\overline{\gamma_i}}^i} = (r_{R_{\overline{\gamma_i}}^i,1}, r_{R_{\overline{\gamma_i}}^i,2}, r_{R_{\overline{\gamma_i}}^i,3}, r_{R_{\overline{\gamma_i}}^i,4})$ and reveals $r_{R_{\overline{\gamma_i}}^i}$ to the adversary $\mathcal{A}$;
- extracting the randomness $(r_{R_{\gamma_i}^i,1}, r_{R_{\gamma_i}^i,2}, r_{R_{\gamma_i}^i,3}, r_{R_{\gamma_i}^i,4})$ used to generate $R_{\gamma_i}^i$ and $sk_{R_{\gamma_i}^i}$. Let $r_{R_{\gamma_i}^i} = (r_{R_{\gamma_i}^i,1}, r_{R_{\gamma_i}^i,2}, r_{R_{\gamma_i}^i,3}, r_{R_{\gamma_i}^i,4})$ and reveals $r_{R_{\gamma_i}^i}$ and $sk_{R_{\gamma_i}^i}$ to the adversary $\mathcal{A}$.

Similarly, S interprets $(u_{S^i,\gamma_i}, v_{S^i,\gamma_i})$ as randomness $(r_{u_{S^i,\gamma_i}}, r_{v_{S^i,\gamma_i}})$ generated by the Naor-Pinkas randomizer with the auxiliary string $(x_{R^i,\gamma_i}, y_{R^i,\gamma_i})$ and interprets $(u_{S^i,\overline{\gamma_i}}, v_{S^i,\overline{\gamma_i}})$ as randomness $(r_{u_{S^i,\overline{\gamma_i}}}, r_{v_{S^i,\overline{\gamma_i}}})$ generated by **fake**. The simulator reveals the randomness $(r_{u_{S^i,\gamma_i}}, r_{v_{S^i,\gamma_i}})$, $(r_{u_{S^i,\overline{\gamma_i}}}, r_{v_{S^i,\overline{\gamma_i}}})$ and $(x_{R^i,\gamma_i}, y_{R^i,\gamma_i})$ to $\mathcal{A}$. S then interprets $(u_{R^i,\overline{\gamma_i}}, v_{R^i,\overline{\gamma_i}})$ as randomness $(r_{u_{R^i,\overline{\gamma_i}}}, r_{v_{R^i,\overline{\gamma_i}}})$ generated by **fake** and interprets $(u_{R^i,\gamma_i}, v_{R^i,\gamma_i})$ as randomness $(r_{u_{R^i,\gamma_i}}, r_{v_{R^i,\gamma_i}})$ generated by the Naor-Pinkas randomizer with the auxiliary string $(x_{S^i,\gamma_i}, y_{S^i,\gamma_i})$. All these randomness are revealed to $\mathcal{A}$. Finally, the simulator S then randomly selects a bit $b_i \in \{0,1\}$ and interprets $S_{b_i}^i$ as a random Diffie-Hellman quadruple and interprets $S_{\overline{b_i}}^i$ as a random quadruple and reveals all these randomness $(r_{S_{b_i}^i}, r_{S_{\overline{b_i}}^i})$ together with sk_{S^i,b_i} to the adversary $\mathcal{A}$.

Assuming the hardness of the DDH problem, one can check that the view of environment $\mathcal{Z}$ in the real-world when it interacts with the adversary $\mathcal{A}$ is computationally indistinguishable from that when the environment $\mathcal{Z}$ interacts with the simulator S in the ideal-world, i.e., $\text{REAL}_{\pi,\mathcal{A},\mathcal{Z}} \approx \text{IDEAL}_{\mathcal{F},S,\mathcal{Z}}$.

CASE 2: The first corruption occurs after a secure channel has been set up but before a ciphertext c is generated; Upon receiving $(corrupt, sid, P)$ from the environment $\mathcal{Z}$, where $P \in \{S, R\}$, the simulator randomly selects l-bit string $\gamma \in \{0,1\}^l$ uniformly at random as a random string selected by the receiver R. The specified l-bit string γ is then shared between the sender S and the receiver R. The rest work of the simulator is same as that described in CASE 1 and the details are thus omitted.

CASE 3: The first corruption occurs during the course of the channel setup phase. Upon receiving (corrupt, sid, P) from the environment $\mathcal{Z}$, where $P \in \{S, R\}$, the ideal world adversary simulates the following two cases for $i = 1, \ldots, l$:

- if the receiver R gets corrupted at first, then the simulator $\mathcal{S}$ parses w_{S^i, α_i} as $(u_{S^i, \alpha_i}, v_{S^i, \alpha_i})$, S checks $v_{S^i, \alpha_i} \stackrel{?}{=} u_{S^i, \alpha_i}^{sk_{S^i, \alpha_i}}$ (all these values are generated as that interpreted in CASE 1); If yes, the simulator $\mathcal{S}$ sets $\gamma_i = \alpha_i$; otherwise, the simulator $\mathcal{S}$ sets $\gamma_i = 1 - \alpha_i$. The rest of the simulation is same as that described in CASE 1 and the details are thus omitted.
- if the sender S gets corrupted at first, then the simulator randomly selects a bit β_i. The simulator then provides a simulation session key β_i same as that described in CASE 1 and the details are thus omitted. □

4 Conclusion

In this paper, an error-free, multi-bit non-committing encryption scheme has been presented and analyzed. Interestingly, our protocol is fixed 4-round and thus independent the length of session key. We have shown that the proposed non-committing scheme realizes the UC-security in the presence of adaptive adversary assuming that the decisional Diffie-Hellman problem is hard.

References

1. Beaver, D.: Plug and play encryption. In: Kaliski Jr., B.S. (ed.) CRYPTO 1997. LNCS, vol. 1294, pp. 75–89. Springer, Heidelberg (1997)
2. Ben-Or, M., Goldwasser, S., Wigderson, A.: Completeness Theorems for Non-Cryptographic Fault-Tolerant Distributed Computation (Extended Abstract). In: STOC 1988, pp. 1–10 (1988)
3. Backes, M., Müller-Quade, J., Unruh, D.: On the Necessity of Rewinding in Secure Multiparty Computation. In: Vadhan, S.P. (ed.) TCC 2007. LNCS, vol. 4392, pp. 157–173. Springer, Heidelberg (2007)
4. Backes, M., Unruh, D.: Limits of Constructive Security Proofs. In: Pieprzyk, J. (ed.) ASIACRYPT 2008. LNCS, vol. 5350, pp. 290–307. Springer, Heidelberg (2008)
5. Canetti, R.: Universally Composable Security: A New Paradigm for Cryptographic Protocols, Cryptology ePrint Archive: Report 2000/067
6. Canetti, R.: A new paradigm for cryptographic protocols. In: FOCS 2001, pp. 136–145 (2001)
7. Chaum, D., Crépeau, C., Damgård, I.: Multiparty Unconditionally Secure Protocols (Extended Abstract). In: STOC 1988, pp. 11–19 (1988)
8. Canetti, R., Fischlin, M.: Universally Composable Commitments. In: Kilian, J. (ed.) CRYPTO 2001. LNCS, vol. 2139, pp. 19–40. Springer, Heidelberg (2001)
9. Canetti, R., Feige, U., Goldreich, O., Naor, M.: Adaptively Secure Multi-Party Computation. In: STOC 1996, pp. 639–648 (1996)

10. Canetti, R., Krawczyk, H.: Universally Composable Notions of Key Exchange and Secure Channels. In: Knudsen, L.R. (ed.) EUROCRYPT 2002. LNCS, vol. 2332, pp. 337–351. Springer, Heidelberg (2002)
11. Choi, S.G., Dachman-Soled, D., Malkin, T., Wee, H.: Improved non-committing encryption with applications to adaptively secure protocols. In: Matsui, M. (ed.) ASIACRYPT 2009. LNCS, vol. 5912, pp. 287–302. Springer, Heidelberg (2009)
12. Damgård, I.B., Nielsen, J.B.: Improved Non-committing Encryption Schemes Based on a General Complexity Assumption. In: Bellare, M. (ed.) CRYPTO 2000. LNCS, vol. 1880, pp. 432–450. Springer, Heidelberg (2000)
13. Goldreich, O., Micali, S., Wigderson, A.: Proofs that Yield Nothing But their Validity and a Methodology of Cryptographic Protocol Design (Extended Abstract). In: FOCS 1986, pp. 174–187 (1986)
14. Goldreich, O., Micali, S., Wigderson, A.: How to Play any Mental Game or A Completeness Theorem for Protocols with Honest Majority. In: STOC 1987, pp. 218–229 (1987)
15. Lei, F., Chen, W., Chen, K.: A non-committing encryption scheme based on quadratic residue. In: Levi, A., Savaş, E., Yenigün, H., Balcısoy, S., Saygın, Y. (eds.) ISCIS 2006. LNCS, vol. 4263, pp. 972–980. Springer, Heidelberg (2006)
16. Nielsen, J.B.: Separating Random Oracle Proofs from Complexity Theoretic Proofs: The Non-committing Encryption Case. In: Yung, M. (ed.) CRYPTO 2002. LNCS, vol. 2442, pp. 111–126. Springer, Heidelberg (2002)
17. Naor, M., Pinkas, B.: Efficient oblivious transfer protocols. In: SODA 2001, pp. 448–457 (2001)
18. Zhu, H., Bao, F.: Non-committing Encryptions Based on Oblivious Naor-Pinkas Cryptosystems. In: Roy, B., Sendrier, N. (eds.) INDOCRYPT 2009. LNCS, vol. 5922, pp. 418–429. Springer, Heidelberg (2009)
19. Zhu, H., Araragi, T., Nishide, T., Sakurai, K.: Adaptive and composable non-committing encryptions. In: Steinfeld, R., Hawkes, P. (eds.) ACISP 2010. LNCS, vol. 6168, pp. 135–144. Springer, Heidelberg (2010)
20. Zhu, H., Araragi, T., Nishide, T., Sakurai, K.: Universally Composable Non-committing Encryptions in the Presence of Adaptive Adversaries. In: SECRYPT 2010 (2010)

A New Practical Key Recovery Attack on the Stream Cipher RC4 under Related-Key Model

Jiageng Chen* and Atsuko Miyaji**

School of Information Science,
Japan Advanced Institute of Science and Technology,
1-1 Asahidai, Nomi, Ishikawa 923-1292, Japan
{jg-chen,miyaji}@jaist.ac.jp

Abstract. A new key recovery attack under related-key model on RC4 is presented in this paper. This novel attack is based on the property that RC4 can generate a large amount of colliding key pairs. By making use of this property, we are able to recover any random key in practical time when the length of the key is large under a new proposed related key model. Differing from the attack against WEP, neither the knowledge of the IVs nor the keystream outputs are required. Also compared with some recent key recovery attacks, which assume that the attacker knows the S-Box after KSA algorithm and can only recover very short keys (5 bytes) efficiently, our attack works very well for keys with larger size. We give the theoretical proof for the complexity of our attack which matches with the experimental result very well. An 86-byte random secret key can be recovered in about 21.2 hours time by using a standard desktop PC. This novel attack provides us with another theoretical approach to attack WPA and WEP. Remark that our model can be used for more efficient key recovering if any new key collisions can be further discovered in the future.

Keywords: RC4, KSA, Related Keys, Key Collisions, Key Recovery.

1 Introduction

The stream cipher RC4 is one of the most famous ciphers widely used in real world applications such as Microsoft Office, Secure Socket Layer (SSL), Wired Equivalent Privacy (WEP), etc. Due to its popularity and simplicity, RC4 has become a hot cryptanalysis target since its specification was made public on the Internet in 1994 [5]. More than twenty-year study on RC4 has revealed a lot of weaknesses of this cipher and a lot different attacks have been proposed since then. Generally speaking, all these attacks can be categorized into two kinds, namely, distinguishing attack and key recovery attack. This paper focuses on key recovery attack. In a distinguishing attack, the attacker tries to distinguish between an output stream generated by PRGA and a random stream [7,8,9].

* This author is supported by the Graduate Research Program.
** This work is supported by Grant-in-Aid for Scientific Research (B), 20300003.

X. Lai, M. Yung, and D. Lin (Eds.): Inscrypt 2010, LNCS 6584, pp. 62–76, 2011.

Other various general weaknesses of RC4 have been discovered in the previous works [6,10,11], etc. We first briefly summarize the previous key recovery attack against RC4.

The first class of this kind of attack applies to the WEP environment, where RC4 is used with a session key which is derived from a shared secret key and an Initial Value (IV). The secret key is concatenated after the IV which is transmitted unencrypted. First chosen IV attack was shown in [12]. By observing the first many keystream outputs, they recovered the secret key with high probability. Another statistical bias between the keystream output and the value of $S[j]$ was discovered in [13] and [14]. By using this bias, they can also recover the entire key in practical time, which was then improved by reducing the dependency when recovering the key bytes later in [15]. The above attacks assume that the attacker has the knowledge of the IVs and the keystream outputs.

Another kind of key recovery approach is just by observing the final S-Box after KSA algorithm [17,18,19]. The basic idea is that the first few bytes of the S-Box is obviously biased, which indicates a connection to the secret key. By creating equations which hold with certain probability, they try to recover the whole keys. This kind of attack works only when the key has a very small size (5 byte), and the successful probability will drop dramatically to impractical level when the key size is larger than 16 bytes.

We propose yet another approach to launch a practical key recovery attack against RC4. Our attack is based on the property that RC4 has a large amount of colliding key pairs [2,4] especially when the key size is very large. Since the colliding key pairs of RC4 follow some specific patterns, some key information will leak if the attacker knows under which pattern the two unknown keys can achieve a collision. In our attack, the attacker is allowed to query key differentials to the KSA Oracle, which will return the S-Box differences to the attacker. If KSA Oracle returns with a (near) collision, then the attacker is able to recover some information of this tweaked key pair according to the key collision properties. And since the attacker knows the key differentials he submitted to the Oracle, he thus can trace back to recover the key based on the key differentials and the leaked key information from the tweaked key pair. Compared with the attacks against WEP, neither the knowledge of the IVs nor the keystream outputs are required. If the first hundreds keystream output bytes are discarded, which is the usual way to fix this weak point, the first kind of attack will not work while our attack will still be available. Compared with the attacks that require the knowledge of the final S-Box, our attack works efficiently for any random keys having large size with probability one, which can be seen as a complement to the second kind of previous attack.

Structure of the paper. In Section 2, we briefly describe the RC4 algorithm followed by the key collision techniques which are needed for the attack in Section 3. Section 4 describes the detailed attack starting with the description of the related key model, and then followed by the detailed techniques to recover full length keys as well as the short keys. Section 5 gives the comparison between our attack and some of the previous attacks in complexity and probability, and also the experimental results are shown in this section. Finally, we give the conclusion in Section 6.

2   The RC4 Stream Cipher and Notations

2.1   RC4

The internal state of RC4 consists of a permutation S of the numbers $0, ..., N-1$ and two indices $i, j \in \{0, ..., N-1\}$. The index i is determined and known to the public, while j and permutation S remain secret. RC4 consists of two algorithms: The Key Scheduling Algorithm (KSA) and the Pseudo Random Generator Algorithm (PRGA). The KSA generates an initial state from a random key K of k bytes as described in Algorithm 1. It starts with an array $\{0, 1, ..., N-1\}$ where $N = 256$ by default. At the end, we obtain the initial state S_{N-1}.

Once the initial state is created, it is used by PRGA. The purpose of PRGA is to generate a keystream of bytes which will be XORed with the plaintext to generate the ciphertext. PRGA is described in Algorithm 2. In this paper, we mainly focus on KSA.

Algorithm 1. KSA	Algorithm 2. PRGA
1: **for** $i = 0$ **to** $N-1$ **do**	1: $i \leftarrow 0$
2: $S[i] \leftarrow i$	2: $j \leftarrow 0$
3: **end for**	3: **loop**
4: $j \leftarrow 0$	4: $i \leftarrow i + 1$
5: **for** $i = 0$ **to** $N-1$ **do**	5: $j \leftarrow j + S[i]$
6: $j \leftarrow j + S[i] + K[i \bmod l]$	6: swap($S[i], S[j]$)
7: swap($S[i], S[j]$)	7: keystream byte $z_i = S[S[i] + S[j]]$
8: **end for**	8: **end loop**

2.2   Notations

The following are the notations used in this paper.

- K: target random secret key.
- K_1, K_2: two secret keys related in some pattern, which will be described in the next section.
- $\Delta K_1^t[i] (\Delta K_2^t[i])$: Differential between target key K and K_1 (K_2) at index i at attacking step t.
- $j_{1,i}(j_{2,i})$: internal state j at step i for $K_{1,t}$ ($K_{2,t}$) respectively.
- $S_{1,i}(S_{2,i})$: the S-Box at step i for $K_{1,t}$ ($K_{2,t}$) before the swap operation.
- d: the first key difference index.
- k: the lengths (bytes) of the secret keys.
- n: the number of times the differences of the keys appear during KSA. $n = \lfloor \frac{256+k-1-d}{k} \rfloor$.

3   Key Collisions of RC4

This novel attack is based on the fact that RC4 can generate a large amount of (near) colliding key pairs. Before going into detail of the attack, we briefly describe the key collision techniques here.

We call a key pair K_1 and K_2 ($K_1 \neq K_2$) a colliding key pair if after KSA, the two corresponding S-Boxes are equal to each other ($S_{1,255} = S_{2,255}$). A near colliding key pair is only different at that the final two S-Boxes need not to be totally the same. The corresponding procedures are called key collisions and near key collisions. The previous researches showed that key collisions or near key collisions can be achieved under some specific key pattern with some probability.

The key collision of RC4 has been first studied back in 2000 in [1]. They pointed out the existence of the near collisions for large size keys. First key collisions with the pattern that two keys differ at one position from each other were found in [2], where we say that those key pairs have hamming distance one. In [3], key collisions with another pattern which has hamming distance three was confirmed, and later in [4], formalized key collisions have been studied and generalized RC4 collision patterns were demonstrated in the paper. Our attack is divided into two categories based on the key collision properties, namely, key collision for full length 256-byte keys, and short keys. We describe the two key collision techniques below.

3.1   Key Collisions for Full Length 256-byte Keys

The previous researches have demonstrated that the probability for a key pair following some certain pattern to form a colliding key pair will drop as the key size gets shorter and the hamming distance gets larger. Thus for a full length key pair with length 256 bytes, it is very easy to achieve a collision under some specific pattern. We describe one here that will be used in the later attack.

Key Pattern: $K_2[d] = K_1[d]+1, K_2[d+1] = K_1[d+1]-1, K_2[d+2] = K_1[d+2]+1$

The following extra conditions during KSA are necessary for two keys with the above pattern to achieve a collision.

1. When i touches index d, we require $S_{1,d}[d+1] = S_{1,d}[d] + 1$ ($S_{2,d}[d+1] = S_{2,d}[d] + 1$).
2. At step $i = d$ after the swap, we require $j_{1,d} = d$ ($j_{2,d} = d+1$).
3. At step $i = d+1$ after the swap, we require $j_{1,d+1} = d+1$ ($j_{2,d+1} = d$).

Table 1 illustrates how it works when $d = 0$. The S-Box part of the internal state shown in Table 1 demonstrates the S-Box state after the swap operation at each step of KSA.

Table 1 shows that for a key pair, which follows the previous pattern (differing from each other at indices 0, 1 and 2 in this example), will achieve a collision after round 2 (The internal states j and S-Box become the same again after round 2).

Table 1. Collisions for 256-byte full length keys when $d = 0$

Internal State							Difference
i	$K_1[i]/K_2[i]$	$j_{1,i}/j_{2,i}$	0 1	2		3 4	
0	0	0	0 1	2		3 4	$K_2[0] = K_1[0] + 1$
	1	1	1 0	2		3 4	$j_{2,0} = j_{1,0} + 1, S_1 \neq S_2$
1	0	1	0 1	2		3 4	$K_2[1] = K_1[1] - 1$
	255	0	0 1	2		3 4	$j_{2,1} = j_{1,1} - 1, S_1 = S_2$
2	X	$X+3$	0 1	$S[X+3]$	3 4		$K_2[2] = K_1[2] + 1$
	$X+1$	$X+3$	0 1	$S[X+3]$	3 4		$j_{1,2} = j_{2,2}, S_1 = S_2$

3.2 (Near) Key Collisions for Short Keys

To recover random keys with shorter size using the above collision pattern will result in a relatively high complexity time. Here we introduce another collision pattern which was first discovered in [2] and later generalized in [4].

In this pattern, two keys can differ from each other at h places, which is called to have hamming distance h. We will only use $h = 1$ in our attack. The general idea is that when i touches the different index d, two consecutive S-Box differences are expected to be generated, and one of them will be swapped to the later key difference indices. And the differences will be absorbed when i touches the last key difference in the KSA.

Key Pattern: $K_2[d] = K_1[d] + 1$

The following extra conditions during KSA are necessary for two keys with the above relations to achieve a collision.

1. When i touches index d, we require $S_{1,d}[d + 1] = S_{1,d}[d] + 1$ ($S_{2,d}[d + 1] = S_{2,d}[d] + 1$).
2. At step $i = d$ after the swap, we require $j_{1,d} = d$ ($j_{2,d} = d + 1$).
3. At step $i = d + 1$, we require $j_{1,d+1} = j_{2,d+1} = d + k$.
4. During steps $i = d + 2$ to $i = d + k$, we require $j_{1,i} \neq d + k$.
5. At step $i = d + p \times k$, $p = 1, ..., n - 2$, we require $j_{1,i} = j_{2,i} = i + k$.
6. During steps $i = d + p \times k + 1$ to $i = d + (p + 1) \times k$, we require $j_{1,i} \neq i + k$.
7. At step $i = d + (n - 1) \times k - 2$, we require the two S-Box differences to be at indices $d + (n - 1) \times k - 2$ and $d + (n - 1) \times k - 1$.
8. At step $i = d + (n - 1) \times k - 1$, we require $j_{1,i} = i - 1$ ($j_{2,i} = i$).

Table 2 illustrates how it works when $d = 0, k = 128$.

Notice that we can achieve a near collision if we replace the conditions 7 and 8 with the condition: At step $i = d + (n - 1)k$, we require $j_{1,i} \leq i$ ($j_{2,i} < i$). Namely, we will have two S-Boxes with three differences between them since i will never touch those differences again.

Table 2. Collisions for short keys when $d = 0, k = 128$

	Internal State			Difference
i	$K_1[i]/K_2[i]$	$j_{1,i}/j_{2,i}$	0 1 2 3 ... 126 127 128	
0	$K_1[0] = 0$	0	0 1	$j, S\text{-Box}$
	$K_2[0] = K_1[0] + 1 = 1$	1	1 0	
1	$K_1[1] = 127$	128	0 1	$S\text{-Box}$
	$K_2[1] = 127$	128	1 0	
126	$K_1[126]$	0	0 1	$S\text{-Box}$
	$K_2[126] = K_1[126]$	0	1 0	
127	$K_1[127]$	127	0 1	$j, S\text{-BoX}$
	$K_2[127] = K_1[127]$	126	0 1	
128	$K_1[0] = 0$	$S_{1,127}[128] + 127$	0 1	Same
	$K_2[0] = K_1[0] + 1 = 1$	$S_{2,127}[128] + 127$	0 1	

4 New Key Recovery Attacks

4.1 Related-Key Model

First, we define the related-key model under which the attack is carried. In this model, the attacker's goal is to recover a random secret key K and the attacker has no prior information about it. We assume that there is a KSA Oracle service which can be queried by the attacker. The attacker has the power to do the following things. He can specify key differential sets $\Delta K_1[i]$ and $\Delta K_2[i]$ for $i \in [0, 255]$ and send them to the KSA Oracle. Then the KSA Oracle will run the KSA algorithm under the new key pair $K_1 = K + \Delta K_1[i]$ and $K_2 = K_1 + \Delta K_2[i]$ and send back the S-Box differential information, namely, whether $\Delta S = 0$ to the attacker (key relations is shown in Figure 1). Repeat the previous procedure many times. The attacker tries to recover the target key K from the submitted key differentials and the corresponding S-Box differentials. Key recovery attack under the related-key model is described in Figure 2. Although recovering full size 256-byte key is different from recovering short size key, the procedure of the algorithm is the same. There are three blocks we need to explain specifically, namely the querying differentials block, observing the S-Box differentials block and recovering two key bytes block.

Querying Differentials Block. In this block, the attacker tries to query the KSA Oracle a key differential set ΔK and expecting the KSA Oracle to send back the two S-Box differentials. The attacker tries to recover two consecutive key bytes at one time and starts from the beginning of the key to the end in turn. For two target consecutive key bytes, the attacker will submit the corresponding designed key differentials.

Observing the S-Box differentials Block. In this block, the KSA Oracle will return the corresponding S-Box differentials (ΔS) to the attacker. Here the ΔS specifically means how many indices the two S-Boxes differ from each other. The attacker needs not to know the detailed values of the S-Boxes nor the

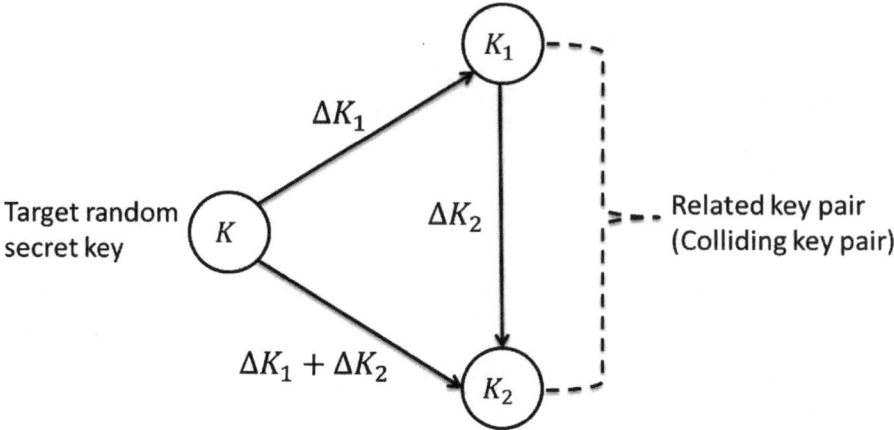

Fig. 1. Related Key Model

differentials. The attacker will decide whether to submit new key differentials to the KSA Oracle again depending on the ΔS.

Recovering two key bytes Block. In this block, the attacker has already gotten the expected ΔS after querying the key differentials several times. He will check the corresponding key collision patterns described previously to search for clues of the target key bytes. After he recovered the two key bytes successfully, go to the querying differentials block to repeat the previous procedures until the key is fully recovered.

4.2   Recovering the Full Length Random 256-byte Key

The querying differentials block for recovering 256-byte key is shown in Figure 3.

   The attacker's goal is to recover a 256-byte secret key K in turn, namely, from $K[0]$ to $K[255]$, two consecutive key bytes can be recovered at one time as illustrated in Figure 1. The attacker first queries two differentials $\Delta K_1^1[0]$ and $\Delta K_1^1[1]$ to the KSA Oracle, and ask it to run the KSA algorithm under two keys K_1 and K_2 which satisfy $K_1[0] = K[0] + \Delta K_1^1[0], K_1[1] = K[1] + \Delta K_1^1[1], K_1[i] = K[i]$ for $i \neq 0, 1$ and $K_2[0] = K_1[0] + 1, K_2[1] = K_1[1] - 1, K_2[2] = K_1[2] + 1, K_2[i] = K_1[i]$ for $i \neq 0, 1, 2$ respectively. If he is lucky enough, he will observe a collision. Recall the previous collision requirements that a collision means that $j_{1,0} = i = 0$ $(j_{2,0} = i + 1 = 1)$ and $j_{1,1} = i = 1$ $(j_{1,2} = i - 1 = 0)$. This gives $K_1[0] = 0 - S_{1,0}[0] = 0$ $(K_2[0] = 1)$ and $K_1[1] = 1 - 0 - S_{1,1}[1] = 0$ $(K_2[1] = 255)$. Then the attacker can easily recover $K[0]$ and $K[1]$ by computing $K[0] = K_1[0] - \Delta K_1^1[0]$ and $K[1] = K_{1,1}[1] - \Delta K_1^1[1]$ with the two known differentials. We call this two differentials $(\Delta K_1^1[0], \Delta K_1^1[1])$ a right differential pair, and $(K_{1,1}, K_{1,2})$ a right related key pair at step one. The worst case to the attacker is that he won't be able to get the right differential pair until he queries all the 256 possible values for one differential, namely, 256^2 time queries in total.

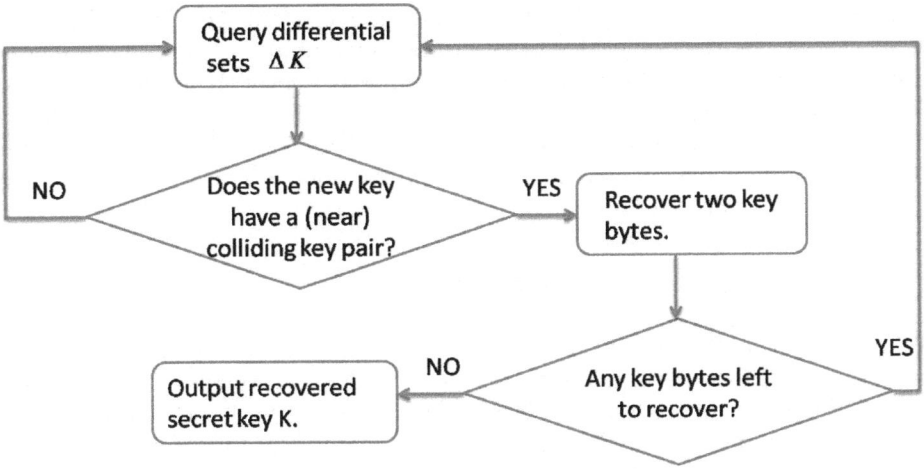

Fig. 2. New Key Recovery Algorithm

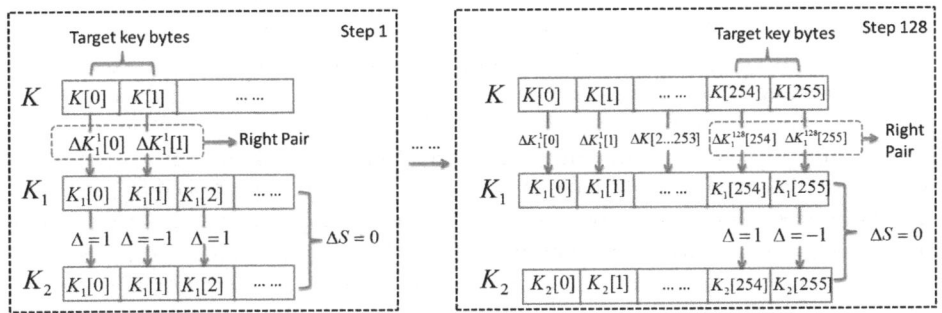

Fig. 3. Querying Differentials Block for recovering 256-byte keys

Now the attacker has successfully recovered $K[0]$ and $K[1]$. To recover the next two bytes $K[2]$ and $K[3]$, the attacker tries to query two differentials $\Delta K_1^2[2]$ and $\Delta K_2^2[3]$, hoping it to be a right differential pair, also along with the previous right pair $(\Delta K_1^1[0], \Delta K_2^1[1])$. The KSA Oracle will run the KSA algorithm under two keys K_1 and K_2 which satisfy $K_1[0] = K[0] + \Delta K_1^1[0], K_1[1] = K[1] + \Delta K_1^1[1], K_{1,2}[2] = K[2] + \Delta K_1^2[2], K_{1,2}[3] = K[3] + \Delta K_1^2[3], K_{1,2}[i] = K[i]$ for $i \neq 0, 1, 2, 3$ and $K_2[2] = K_1[2] + 1, K_2[3] = K_1[3] - 1, K_2[4] = K_1[4] + 1, K_2[i] = K_1[i]$ for $i \neq 2, 3, 4$ respectively, and sends back the information whether a collision happens or not. If he is unlucky, query differentials $\Delta K_1^2[2]$ and $\Delta K_2^2[3]$ again until it is a right pair (collision happens). Notice that the differential pair $(\Delta K_1^1[0], \Delta K_1^1[1])$ need not be changed since it is the right pair results from the previous stage and we need it there to satisfy the first collision condition for the second stage attack.

Each time when the attacker successfully recovers two key bytes $K[i]$ and $K[i+1]$, he has the knowledge of the right differential pair, and with all the previous known right differential pairs, he is able to recover the future key bytes. The complexity of the attack can be computed from the worst case in which the attacker has to try 256^2 times before he can find the right pair to recover two bytes key. Thus the total complexity time in the worst case is $O(128 \times 256^2) = O(2^{23})$ with probability 1.

4.3   Recovering the Random Short Keys

When recovering the full size 256-byte keys, the attacker at each step only need to query key differentials at the two target key indices. Because he knows that due to the collision pattern, he will observe a collision no later than the worst case. However, in case of short keys, only changing the target key bytes will not grantee a collision even in the worst case. It is straightforward because the worst case in querying key differentials at two target key bytes involves 256^2 operations, since the probability for the collision may be smaller than $\frac{1}{256^2}$, in other words, we may need to query also some other key bytes to ensure a (near) collision observation. We illustrate how many key bytes differentials we need to query by computing the collision probability in Figure 4. It is an example of 64-byte key and difference is at index 0.

Recall that for a key pair to achieve a collision in short key pattern, we need $j_{1,0} = 0$ and j touches 64, 128 and 192 when i touches 1, 64 and 128 respectively. And when i is between $[1, 63]$, $[65, 127]$ or $[129, 191]$, j is not allowed to touch the later bound. Finally, when i touches 192, if j is less or equal than 192, it will result in a near collision with two different indices. We assume the internal variable j behaves randomly, which is a reasonable assumption in most of the cases, we get the probability for the collision of a 64-byte key: $(\frac{1}{256})^4 (\frac{255}{256})^{62+63+63} \frac{193}{256} \approx 8.5 \times 10^{-11}$. In other words, we'll need to query $\frac{log_2(8.5 \times 10^{-11})^{-1}}{8} \approx 4$ bytes each time, two extra indices except the two target key bytes. By generalizing this analysis, we can get the following theorem.

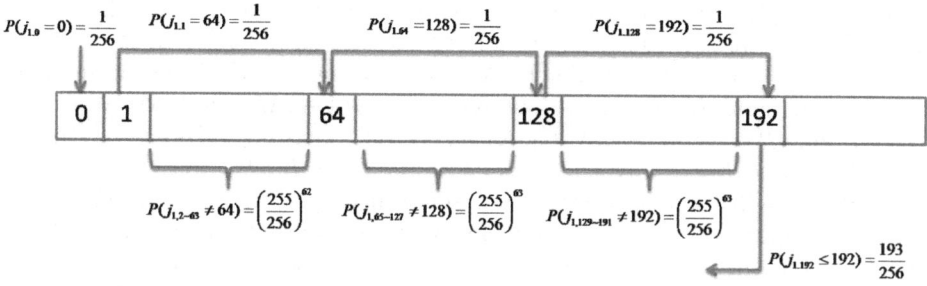

Fig. 4. Determine the number of differentials to query

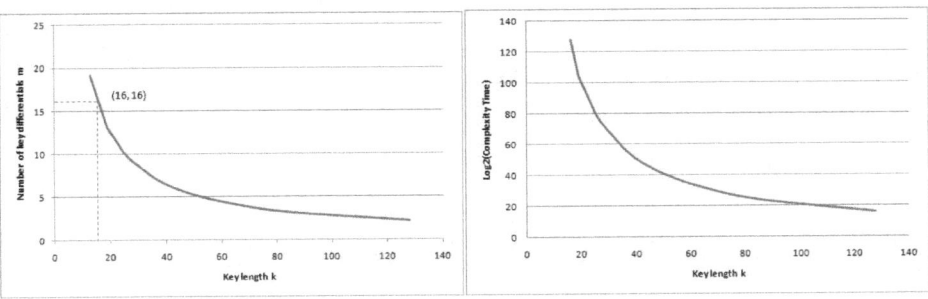

(a) Relations between m and k   (b) Complexity for recovering two key bytes

Fig. 5. Theorem 1

Theorem 1. *To construct a related key K_1 which has a colliding key pair under the short key collision pattern from the target key K, the attacker has to query m key differential bytes at two target key bytes indices and $m - 2$ other indices. m is given below:*

$$m = log_2 \left(\left(\frac{1}{256} \right)^n \times \left(\frac{255}{256} \right)^{k-2+(k-1)(n-2)} \times \frac{(n-1)k+d}{256} \right)^{-1} / 8$$

Here, k is the key length, n is the number of times the differences of the keys appear during KSA, and d denotes the first key difference index.

Figure 5(a) is the direct visualization of the Theorem 1. From the figure, we know that for key size smaller than 16 bytes, the attacker has to query more than 16 bytes in order to observe a collision, thus makes the attack impossible. We give the theoretical bound of the complexity time for the attack in Figure 5(b). We can conclude that for keys with length larger than 40 bytes, they will fall into our practical attack area.

After the attacker knows how many bytes he should query, he is ready to launch the attack. The querying differentials block for short keys is illustrated in Figure 6.

Suppose the target key has length k and will repeat n times during KSA. Again the attacker tries to recover the key one by one starting from the beginning. His first two target key bytes is $K[0]$ and $K[1]$. According to Theorem 1, he can compute m, thus besides indices 0 and 1, he can randomly choose other $m - 2$ indices and submit the differential queries $\Delta K_1^1[0], \Delta K_1^1[1], \Delta K_1^1[i], ..., \Delta K_1^1[i + m-2]$. To ease the explanation, we assume the $m-2$ indices to be the consecutive ones. The KSA Oracle will return the differential information of two S-Boxes under K_1 and K_2 which differs from K_1 at index 0 by value 1. If he observes that $\Delta S = 2$, then he confirms that a near collision has happened. According to the short key collision pattern, $j_{1,0} = i = 0$ ($j_{2,0} = i + 1 = 1$) and $j_{1,1} = j_{2,1} = i + k = k + 1$. Thus, $K_1[0] = 0 - S_{1,0}[0] = 0(K_2[0] = 1)$, and $K_1[1] =$

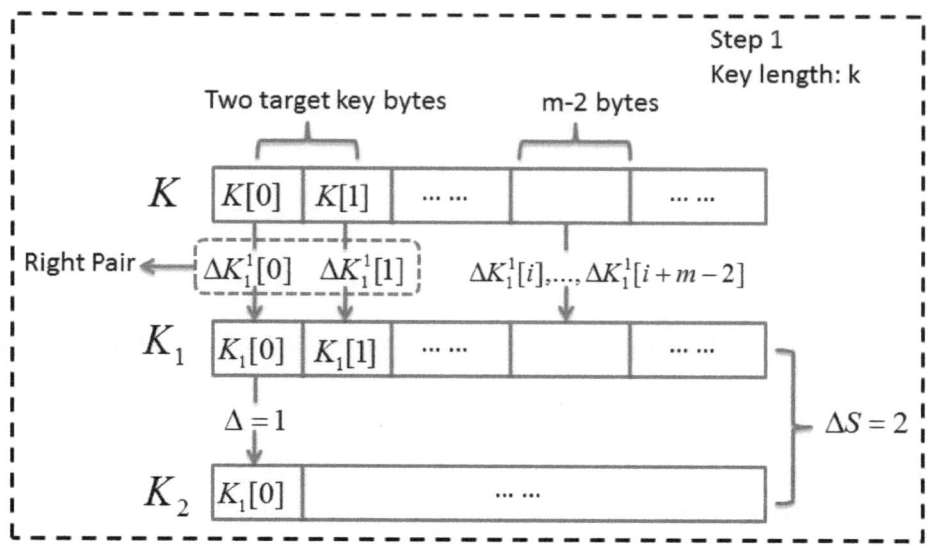

Fig. 6. Querying Differentials Block for Recovering Short keys

$K_2 = k + 1 - 1 = k$. Then the attacker can recover $K[0]$ and $K[1]$ by computing $K[0] = K_1[0] - \Delta K_1^1[0]$ and $K[1] = K_1[1] - \Delta K_1^1[1]$. Store the right differential pair $\Delta K_1^1[0]$ and $\Delta K_1^1[1]$ to recover the next two target key bytes, repeat the procedure until the whole key is recovered.

5   Experiment and Comparison

5.1   Implementation

The following table illustrates the implementation details we used to recover the short keys. Each time two consecutive bytes of key are recovered once a near collision ($\Delta S = 2$) is found.

Table 3 illustrates the experimental results of key recovery by using our new algorithm. We show the data of recovering three random secret key with length 256, 128 and 86 bytes. Actually, this three random key represents three classes of keys with parameter n equals to 1, 2 and 3, respectively. The experiment is performed by randomly choosing many target keys and the average data is shown in the table. For key length 256 and 128, 100 times were performed, but due to the long time period, only 3 times were done for the key length 86. We list the number of bytes (m) we need to query in order to recovery two key bytes. For 256-byte full length key, we only need to query two key bytes, and can be recovered in a very short time (0.038 seconds). For 128-byte key, 55% of the key bytes need querying two bytes in order to be recovered, and rest 45% of the key need to query three key bytes in order to be recovered. The number of query bytes increased to four when we try to recover 86-byte key. About 63% of the key requires to query four bytes in order to be recovered. The experimental value of

---

Short Key Recovery Implementation

Input:

1. Target key length (bytes) of target secret key K: k.

2. S-Box difference: ΔS.

3. Key differentials: ΔK_1(randomly chosen) and $\Delta K_2 = 1$ (fixed).

Output:

Target secret key K.

Procedures:

1. Set target key index byte $d = 0$.

    1-1. Set the number of query bytes $m = 2$.

    1-2. Prepare the differentials $\Delta K_1 = (\Delta K_1[d], \Delta K[d+1], ..., \Delta K[d+m-1])$ and
    $\Delta K_1 + \Delta K_2 = (\Delta K_1[d] + 1, \Delta K[d+1], ..., \Delta K[d+m-1])$, and run the
    KSA under the related keys $K_1 = K + \Delta K_1$ and $K_2 = K + \Delta K_1 + \Delta K_2$.

    1-3. If $\Delta S \neq 2$ after running KSA with 256^m related key pairs, $m = m + 1$, goto 1-2.

    1-4. If $\Delta S \neq 2$ before running KSA with 256^m related key pairs, goto 1-2.

    1-5. If $\Delta S = 2$, then recover two bytes $K[d]$ and $K[d+1]$, $d = d + 2$, goto 1-1.

---

m is very close to the theoretical value which can be calculated from Theorem 1. The experiment is done on an i7 CPU desktop PC with Windows XP system (parallel computing is not involved).

Table 3. Experimental Results of the New Key Recovery Algorithm

n	Key Length	Number of Query Bytes					Time
		$m = 2$	$m = 3$	$m = 4$	**Exp Value**	**Theo Value**	
1	256	128(100%)	0	0	2	2	0.038s
2	128	35(55%)	29(45%)	0	2.42	2.21	287s
3	86	0	16(37%)	27(63%)	3.63	3.19	76323s (21.2h)

5.2 Comparison and Other Applications

We summarize all the key recovery attacks on RC4 in Table 4. Compared with the previous works, our main contribution is that we can attack long keys within practical complexity time. And also, due to various biases discovered at the beginning of PRGA, it is the usual case that the implementation will discard the first hundreds output bytes of the keystream, which make the attacks such as by taking advantage of the weak IVs impossible. Our attack can survive this kind of remedies because discarding the first hundreds output keystream bytes

Table 4. Comparison of the Key Recovery Attacks

Paper	Resources available to the attacker	Key Length	Complexity	Probability
[12,13,14,15]	IV, Keystream output	All keys	Practical	1
[17]		$k = 5$	2^{20}	0.86
[18]	S-Box	$k = 16$	2^{64}	0.005
		$k \gg 16$	Impractical	Impractical
		$k = 5$	2^{24}	0.998
[19]	S-Box	$k = 16$	2^{35}	0.075
		$k \gg 16$	Impractical	Impractical
		$k = 256$	2^{23}	1
Ours	$\Delta K, \Delta S$	$k > 40$	$< 2^{48}$	1
		$k < 16$	Impractical	Impractical

will not affect the observation of the output differences, especially when the total key collisions are achieved. Early in [15], the authors proposed a new way to attack WEP and pointed out that their passive attack can be theoretically adapted to WPA, although no further detailed explanation was given. Here we give another theoretical way to attack WPA. Recall the pattern we use to recover the full 256-byte key, where two keys differ from each other at three indices. Here treat the first one as IV, by changing its value so that let the second and third key differences step through the whole key. Once a collision or a near collision is observed, the attacker can recover the key at the second and third difference indices. Similarly, we can also use the transitional pattern to recover. The main difficulty is that all the currently known key collision patterns have a high complexity when the key is short, and in WPA as well as in WEP settings, only 16-byte key is used. This makes our attack impractical in such environments. However, we cannot rule out the existence of other kinds of colliding key pairs with short key size and low complexity. If that is possible, than the attack is not theoretical any more.

6   Conclusion

In this paper, we presented a new approach to recover secret keys of RC4 in practical time in a related-key model by making use the property that RC4 can generate a large mount of colliding key pairs. Our main contribution is that our attack can recover large keys efficiently with probability 1 while some the previous researches can only recover very short keys with small probability. Although the attack against WEP can efficiently recover the secret keys within practical time, it requires the knowledge of IVs and the keystream outputs. It will not work if the first hundreds keystream outputs are discarded, while our attack is not affected by this remedy. Thus our method shows another way to attack the applications which use the IV setting, especially when the key size is large. Theoretically speaking, our method can also be adapted to attack WPA if colliding key pairs with shorter key size (lower complexity) can be found.

References

1. Grosul, A.L., Wallach, D.S.: A Related-Key Cryptanalysis of RC4. Technical Report TR-00-358, Department of Computer Science, Rice University (2000), http://cohesion.rice.edu/engineering/computerscience/tr/TRDownload.cfm?SDID=126
2. Matsui, M.: Key Collisions of the RC4 Stream Cipher. In: Dunkelman, O. (ed.) FSE 2009. LNCS, vol. 5665, pp. 38–50. Springer, Heidelberg (2009)
3. Chen, J., Miyaji, A.: A New Class of RC4 Colliding Key Pairs With Greater Hamming Distance. In: Kwak, J., Deng, R.H., Won, Y., Wang, G. (eds.) ISPEC 2010. LNCS, vol. 6047, pp. 30–44. Springer, Heidelberg (2010)
4. Chen, J., Miyaji, A.: Generalized RC4 Key Collisions and Hash Collisions. In: Garay, J.A., De Prisco, R. (eds.) SCN 2010. LNCS, vol. 6280, pp. 73–87. Springer, Heidelberg (2010)
5. Anonymous: RC4 Source Code. CypherPunks mailing list (September 9, 1994), http://cypherpunks.venona.com/date/1994/09/msg00304.html, http://groups.google.com/group/sci.crypt/msg/10a300c9d21afca0
6. Roos, A.: A Class of Weak Keys in the RC4 Stream Cipher (1995), http://marcel.wanda.ch/Archive/WeakKeys
7. Fluhrer, S.R., McGrew, D.A.: Statistical Analysis of the Alleged RC4 Keystream Generator. In: Schneier, B. (ed.) FSE 2000. LNCS, vol. 1978, pp. 19–30. Springer, Heidelberg (2001)
8. Golić, J.D.: Linear Statistical Weakness of Alleged RC4 Keystream Generator. In: Fumy, W. (ed.) EUROCRYPT 1997. LNCS, vol. 1233, pp. 226–238. Springer, Heidelberg (1997)
9. Mantin, I.: Predicting and Distinguishing Attacks on RC4 Keystream Generator. In: Cramer, R. (ed.) EUROCRYPT 2005. LNCS, vol. 3494, pp. 491–506. Springer, Heidelberg (2005)
10. Mantin, I., Shamir, A.: A Practical Attack on Broadcast RC4. In: Matsui, M. (ed.) FSE 2001. LNCS, vol. 2355, pp. 152–164. Springer, Heidelberg (2002)
11. Paul, S., Preneel, B.: A New Weakness in the RC4 Keystream Generator and an Approach to Improve the Security of the Cipher. In: Roy, B., Meier, W. (eds.) FSE 2004. LNCS, vol. 3017, pp. 245–259. Springer, Heidelberg (2004)
12. Fluhrer, S., Mantin, I., Shamir, A.: Weaknesses in the Key Scheduling Algorithm of RC4. In: Vaudenay, S., Youssef, A.M. (eds.) SAC 2001. LNCS, vol. 2259, pp. 1–24. Springer, Heidelberg (2001)
13. Klein, A.: Attacks on the RC4 Stream Cipher. Designs, Codes and Cryptography 48(3), 269–286 (2008)
14. Tews, E., Weinmann, R.-P., Pyshkin, A.: Breaking 104 Bit WEP in Less Than 60 Seconds. In: Kim, S., Yung, M., Lee, H.-W. (eds.) WISA 2007. LNCS, vol. 4867, pp. 188–202. Springer, Heidelberg (2008)
15. Vaudenay, S., Vuagnoux, M.: Passive–Only Key Recovery Attacks on RC4. In: Adams, C., Miri, A., Wiener, M. (eds.) SAC 2007. LNCS, vol. 4876, pp. 344–359. Springer, Heidelberg (2007)

16. Finney, H.: An RC4 cycle that can't happen. Newsgroup post in sci.crypt (September 1994)
17. Paul, G., Maitra, S.: Permutation After RC4 Key Scheduling Reveals the Secret Key. In: Adams, C., Miri, A., Wiener, M. (eds.) SAC 2007. LNCS, vol. 4876, pp. 360–377. Springer, Heidelberg (2007)
18. Biham, E., Carmeli, Y.: Efficient Reconstruction of RC4 Keys from Internal States. In: Nyberg, K. (ed.) FSE 2008. LNCS, vol. 5086, pp. 270–288. Springer, Heidelberg (2008)
19. Akgün, M., Kavak, P., Demirci, H.: New Results on the Key Scheduling Algorithm of RC4. In: Chowdhury, D.R., Rijmen, V., Das, A. (eds.) INDOCRYPT 2008. LNCS, vol. 5365, pp. 40–52. Springer, Heidelberg (2008)

An Efficient, Parameterized and Scalable S-box for Stream Ciphers

Sourav Das[1,2] and Dipanwita RoyChowdhury[1]

[1] Dept. of CSE, Indian Institute of Technology, Kharagpur, India
drc@cse.iitkgp.ernet.in
[2] Also affiliated to: Alcatel-Lucent India Limited, Bangalore, India
sourav10101976@gmail.com

Abstract. In stream ciphers, the ratio of performance to the security is the most important issue. However, the S-boxes used in a stream cipher can become a bottleneck of speed due to use of large memory, difficulty in hardware realization and more processing. This paper proposes an S-box construction that is easy to implement both in hardware and software. The proposed S-box is efficient in speed, parameterized and scalable with excellent security properties. It also provides a designer with the flexibility to trade-off among speed, area and the security properties. The security analysis has been performed on the S-box. The security properties are found to be comparable with the existing standards.

Keywords: Cellular Automata, S-box, Stream Cipher, Security Properties.

1 Introduction

Stream Ciphers provide ultra-fast encryption that can be used in communication channels. In search of a good stream cipher ESTREAM [24] project has been launched. S-boxes are integral part of most of the cryptographic algorithms and provide the non-linearity that is essential for all cryptographic algorithms. At the same time, the S-boxes can also become a bottleneck for speed and source of attacks. Since, there is no standard S-box for stream ciphers, every algorithm either has to devise a new S-box or use the S-boxes used in block ciphers. Some of the contemporary stream ciphers like Trivium [6], Salsa [3] and RC4 do not use S-boxes but use other methods for non-linearity. Using an S-box of a block cipher directly in a stream cipher may not be a good idea as there are basic differences in the requirements of the block ciphers and stream ciphers.

First, the block ciphers go through multiple rounds of processing of plaintext and key before producing the ciphertext. In stream cipher, the plaintext is just XORed with the pseudo-random key that is generated from the key stream generation algorithm. So, in a stream cipher, S-box must be large enough to hide the key information completely. That is why Rabbit [5], HC-256[25] use 32 bit S-box. Next, the speed of the S-box must be very high in the stream cipher as that is the main intention of a stream cipher, so it should not use large

X. Lai, M. Yung, and D. Lin (Eds.): Inscrypt 2010, LNCS 6584, pp. 77–94, 2011.

look-up tables. Next, the S-box of the stream cipher should be easily scalable in terms of security and size as stream ciphers are prone to attacks; so that even if the stream cipher is attacked, the security properties of the stream ciphers can be preserved by an easy upgrade. Finally, nowadays most of the encryption functions are performed in hardware to have a greater speed. Also, there is a need for implementation of cryptographic primitives on small micro-chips in applications like PDAs which have limited memory and power. So, the hardware realization of the S-box must be easy along with an efficient way for software implementation.

Keeping all the above conflicting requirements in mind, we have proposed an S-box that is scalable, parameterized and which has a flexible design option to optimize speed vs area in hardware implementation. For ease of hardware implementation, we have used Cellular Automata (CA) which display locality and topological regularity that are important attribute for VLSI implementation. In [8], the authors have shown that CA provide better performance than LFSR, which have been used traditionally in hardware oriented stream ciphers, while not consuming much more area. Also, the length of the CA can easily be increased without redesigning the circuit, which can provide scalability to the application. The proposed S-box is scalable not only in terms of size but also in terms of its security properties. The parameterizations of the S-box will aid to the setting and modification of Initial Value of the stream ciphers. This can also provide key dependent S-boxes which can be very useful tool for cipher design.

In the S-box proposed in this paper, first we vary the number of cycles depending on input in a maximum length CA with a constant seed to get the output. That is, input to the mapping decides the number of cycles to be run in a maximum length CA with a constant seed. For a CA with small number of cells (say, four, five or six) it gives a good value of non-linearity with acceptable number of cycles. The high non-linearity generated from a small length of CA can be utilized as a non-linear primitive in a large CA. In this paper, we propose a scheme where these primitives are utilized to generate highly non-linear, scalable boolean mappings having seeds as parameters. These mappings can be used as S-boxes and hence we use the terms *S-box* and *non-linear mapping* interchangeably. Note that, there are other S-box construction methods that are present in literature [18], [21]. All of them can execute in polynomial time. There are two advantages of the S-box described here over those constructions. First, this method of generating S-boxes runs in linear time helping in scalability and second, it provides key dependent S-boxes unlike others. Both these facts will aid to the design of the stream ciphers and other cryptographic algorithms. In [22] and [23], the authors propose S-box construction based on non-linear CA rules and running for few cycles. In the current S-box, the non-linearity is derived from varying the number of clock cycles, whereas in those S-boxes the non-linearity is derived using non-linear rules. In addition to the above advantages, the advantages of the current S-box over those CA based S-boxes are more efficiency, less hardware and coverage of complete state space.

This paper begins with an introduction of CA in section 1.1. In section 1.2, it introduces the generation of non-linear CA mappings by varying the number of cycles with respect to input. Section 2 shows how to generate scalable S-boxes from the mappings. A few sample S-boxes generated in this fashion are also shown in section 2. Section 3 presents the hardware implementation of the proposed S-boxes and a pseudo-code for the software implementation. Section 4 provides the security analysis of the proposed S-boxes. In section 5, it compares the proposed S-boxes with non-linear blocks used in contemporary stream ciphers. Finally, we give a schematic of a new stream cipher, based on the S-boxes designed in this paper, to concretize the motivation of designing such S-boxes in section 6. In the next subsection, we provide an introduction to Cellular Automata.

1.1   Cellular Automata (CA)

The CA structure can be viewed as a lattice of cells where every cell can take values either 0 or 1 [20]. The cells evolve in each time step depending on some combinational logic on itself and its neighbors. The combinational logic is called the *rule* of the CA. Two of the common rules used are Rule 90 which is the XOR of left neighbor and right neighbor; and the Rule 150 which is the XOR of left neighbor, self and right neighbor.

The characteristic matrix of a CA operating over $GF(2)$ is a matrix that describes the behavior of the CA with linear rules. We can calculate the next state of the CA by multiplying the characteristic matrix by the present state of the CA. A characteristic matrix is constructed as:

$T[i,j] = 1$, if the next state of the ith cell depends on jth cell
$\quad\quad = 0$, otherwise

If $S(t)$ represents the state of the CA at the ith instant of time then the state at the next time instant can be represented as:
$S(t+1) = [T]S(t)$ and $S(t+2) = [T]^2 S(t)$ and so on. So we can write:
$S(t+p) = [T]^p S(t)$
The following subsection describes how to generate the Non-linearity using CA.

1.2   A Highly Non-linear Boolean Mapping Using CA

Cellular Automata take two input parameters; one is the seed of the CA and the other one is the number of cycles that needs to be run. The relationship between the input seed and the output is completely linear, if the CA rules are linear. However, we have studied and observed that, the relationship between the number of cycles and the output is highly non-linear even if the linear rules are used in the CA. If n denotes the seed, m denotes the number of cycles and y denotes the output of a CA transformation, then, any CA transformation can be expressed as:
$y = T^m n$, where T is the characteristic matrix of the CA.

If we keep the seed constant and vary the number of cycles based on input x, the CA transformation becomes:

$$y = T^{(x)}n \qquad (1)$$

Hence the output varies exponentially with input giving rise to Non-linearity. The above construction can also be viewed as $O = S(cycles, seed)$, where the output varies non-linearly in terms of number of cycles and linearly in terms of seed. The seed can be used as a parameter in a key dependent S-box.

Note that varying the clock rate is also a common way to achieve non-linearity in LFSR based stream ciphers (to combine one or more LFSRs, to obtain a nonlinear construction, e.g.,self-shrinking generator in stream ciphers, and the use of majority clocking in A5/1). However, unlike LFSR we can achieve parallel non-linear transformations by this method.

2   The Proposed Scalable, Parameterized S-box

The S-box, that is described in this paper, has been generated using Cellular Automata (CA). For the non-linear primitive, we have used a Maximum Length Linear Hybrid CA, but the non-linearity is achieved by governing the number of cycles of the CA based the input to the mapping. Then a mixing between the non-linear primitives are achieved using a bigger Linear Hybrid CA whose length is equal to the S-box size. The Khazad S-box uses a similar idea by putting simple permutation. However, scaling up Khazad S-boxes requires additional layers of costly look-up tables. This S-box can be scaled up in size without any additional layers. The next subsection describes the construction of large, non-linear boolean mappings using these non-linear primitives.

2.1   Design of a Scalable, Non-linear Boolean Mapping

Since, there is a latency involved for varying the number of cycles with respect to input, the method described in section 1.2 will not scale very well with the length of the cellular automata. But for a small length of CA, this construction can be used as a non-linear primitive which can be placed in a large length of CA application to achieve maximum non-linearity. For example, a four cell CA may be used where the worst case complexity is sixteen cycles if run sequentially. Such a small non-linear primitive can also be implemented using a look-up table or combinational logic with a complexity of only one cycle.

The detail schematic of such a CA based non-linear mapping (S-box) is shown in figure 1. This S-box takes n bits constants (parameters) to be used as seeds in the non-linear layer and one n bits input variable that is transformed to output. For each different value of this constant (used as seed), a different S-box will be generated. Internally, the S-box has a layered architecture. For an $n \times n$ bits transformation, the first layer consists of a series of four bits non-linear CA transformations as described in section 1.2. For simplicity, we show and describe the non-linear layer consisting of only four cell maximum length CAs.

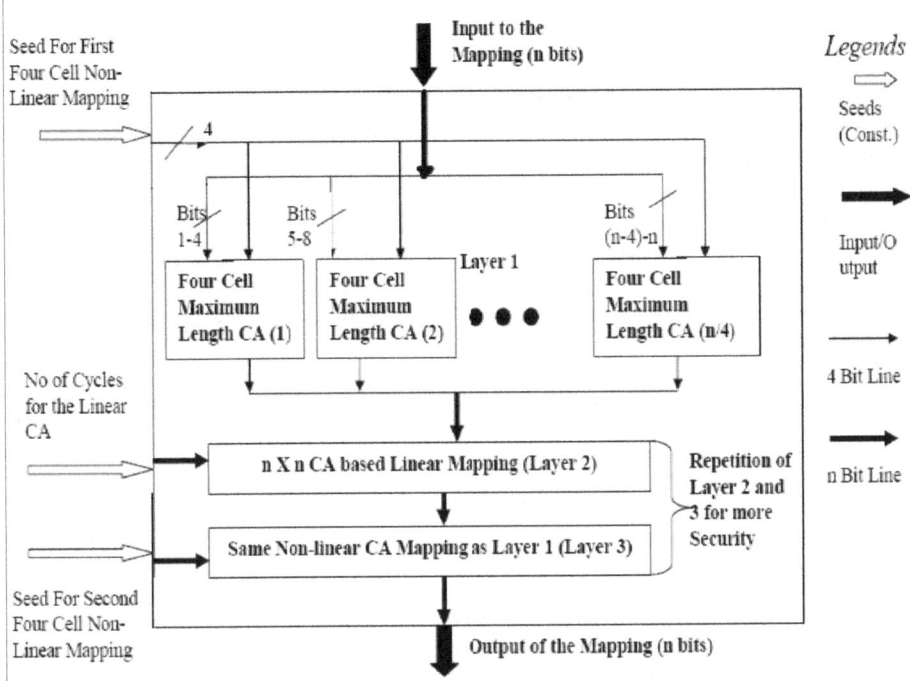

Fig. 1. Processing of the Non-linear Mapping

However, there can be a combination of four, five and six cell maximum length CAs in the non-linear layer, the total number of input bits should be distributed among them accordingly. There are a total of $n/4$ such transformations running in parallel. The input bits are divided into $n/4$ groups where each group being of size four bits. These four bits determine the number of cycles to be run for each of the four cell CAs. This can also be an asymmetric four, five and six cells CA running in the same fashion. The output of those transformations are simply concatenated to provide the input to an n bit maximum length linear CA run with a fixed number of cycles. The output of the layer 2 (the linear CA) is again fed to a series of four bits non-linear CA transformations (layer 3) similar to the first layer. The output of the layer 3 is again simply concatenated to produce the output to the mappings (S-box). These layers are the basic layers of the S-box. Layer 2 and 3, that are linear CA and the CA based non-linear operation, can be repeated after layer 3 so that better security properties can be achieved. At the minimum two non-linear layers and one linear layer are required.

2.2 Analytical Framework

The theoretical basis for the above construction is as follows. At the end of the first non-linear layer each intermediate output bit depends on the input bits for the non-linear CA element (that it is a part of) in an exponential manner.

$$y_1 = T^{(x_k)} * n \qquad (2)$$

where y_1 denotes the intermediate output of the first non-linear layer and x_k denotes the input bits of the kth non-linear element in non-linear layer for which individual intermediate output bit is involved. This has a theoretical similarity with the finite field exponentiation done in Magenta S-boxes [14]. In Magenta, the look-up table is the main option for implementation, but this CA based variable clock method provides sequential implementation and also parameterized.

If we design the linear layer such that each output bit of the linear transformation depends on all the input bits, then the output of the linear transformation layer (denoting y_2) becomes:

$$y_2 = \sum a_i y_{1i} = \sum a_i (T^{(x_k)} * n) \qquad (3)$$

where $a_i \in 0, 1$.

In the third non-linear layer, the output (denoting it as y_3) becomes,

$$y_3 = T^{(y_{2k})} * n = T^{(\sum a_i(T^{(x_k)} * n))} * n = T^{f(x)} * n \qquad (4)$$

The net effect of the above equation is exponentiation and multiplication with respect to the input bits. y_3 can be extracted directly to give the final output. We can add more layers to have a better mixing and better exponentiation giving rise to more non-linearity.

2.3   Sample S-boxes

Using the schema described in section 2.1, different S-boxes can be generated. In this section, we take some specific examples and show how different S-boxes can be generated using some specific values of the parameters. We also show the security properties of few of them in the next section.

8×8 **S-box:** We have implemented the non-linear mapping (S-box) for 8×8 bits using one linear and two non-linear layers. Similarly, we have implemented the S-box using three nonlinear layers and two linear layers in between them. Table 1 shows the output of the S-box implemented with seeds 0101 for all the four cell CAs.

16×16 **S-box:** We have also implemented 16×16 S-box using a few different ways. Instead of using four cell maximum length CA for non-linearity, we have also used a combination of four, five and six cell maximum length CA in the non-linear layer in bigger S-boxes. The combination gives even better security properties. The following are the few different ways to design the 16×16 S-box.

Case1: In this case, we have implemented the 16×16 S-box using two non-linear layers with four 4-cell maximum length CA and one sixteen cell linear CA running a constant twelve cycles.

Case2: In this case, we have generated 16×16 S-box using three non-linear layers with four 4-cell maximum length CA and two sixteen cell linear CA running a constant six cycles.

Table 1. The S-box Output

0	7a	d4	be	ed	29	74	64	ba	5	85	a3	6a	75	eb	d0
87	6d	e8	4d	c8	59	17	c2	8e	df	89	8c	8a	a	81	3b
5f	2d	ee	47	28	58	c	79	40	61	a1	16	49	af	27	c7
b0	7e	bd	e9	d9	2c	68	bf	d8	80	2a	c0	45	2e	9d	da
98	22	6	e0	1b	f1	f4	5d	b7	7c	4c	9c	2b	f8	88	37
9	fc	c9	42	bb	1e	7f	aa	2f	c5	ec	d	dd	34	57	94
b	d7	91	a2	3c	1d	99	46	6f	93	3d	33	d1	8f	8	f9
4a	72	e	4b	c4	66	e2	a6	48	c6	6e	13	ef	67	4	a7
11	35	71	2	63	7	36	db	ce	69	cc	24	1c	55	5e	60
18	15	38	10	e4	31	78	f6	e6	83	44	e7	d6	84	30	f0
fb	fe	9e	ff	26	b3	9b	52	cf	cd	32	a8	fa	7b	b6	1
82	e1	43	4f	a9	70	51	ae	de	56	f7	1f	d3	fd	97	ad
12	b5	90	3f	e5	3e	ea	e3	b2	d5	9a	a5	1a	f	39	4e
23	b9	cb	92	f5	ca	73	6b	ab	21	3	f3	d2	54	c3	5b
8d	3a	b4	14	19	41	f2	7d	b8	65	50	b1	5c	62	20	bc
95	96	25	5a	76	c1	9f	ac	a0	86	53	8b	a4	6c	77	dc

Case3: In this case, we bring in asymmetry in the non-linear layer. Here the non-linear layers consist of a five cell maximum length CA, followed by a six cell maximum cell CA which is again followed by a five cell maximum length CA.

Case4: In this case, we bring more asymmetry to the non-linear layer. Here the first non-linear layer consists of five, six and five cell maximum length CA respectively in parallel. The second non-linear layer consists of six, four and six cell maximum length CA respectively in parallel.

Case5: This case is similar to case 4 as described above. The difference is, we have added one more non-linear layer. The third non-linear layer consisted of a symmetric four 4-cell CA as in case 1 and case 2. Obviously, we achieved the best result in this configuration, and the results are shown in the analysis section.

32 × 32 S-box: We have also implemented 32 × 32 S-box using four 5-cell CAs with three 4-cell CAs in between them in the first non-linear layer. For the linear layer, we used 32-cell maximum length CA. Finally, in the third non-linear layer, we have used one four cell CA in the extreme left and one in extreme right, one four cell CA in the middle and two five cell CA each in between them.

3   Implementation and Performance

In this section, we describe specifics of implementation both in hardware and software. First we describe the complexity of the S-box (boolean mapping).

3.1   The Complexity of the Mapping

The main advantage of the mapping is that it scales very well as the size of the transformation (n) increases. The number of cycles required for the mapping increases only linearly with the size of the non-linear mapping. In the first layer, the total number of cycles remains constant irrespective of the size, n, of the mapping. Similarly, in the third layer also, the number of cycles doesn't vary with the size of the input. All the CA transformations in both layer one and layer three will be run in parallel. In the second layer (linear transformation), the number of cycles required to achieve the mixing of the CA is less than n. The time complexity of this mapping is $O(n)$ only. We can add more layers to have better security margins and better non-linearity. In that case also the number of cycles required increases linearly.

Since CA based transformations can also be viewed as multiplication of powers of T matrices, the full construction can be implemented using combinational logic of hardware. In that case the whole S-box can be implemented using a single cycle. This would require additional hardware. So this construction gives the designer the flexibility to trade-off between the area and speed.

We recommend to take a combined approach of combinational and sequential logic where the non-linear layer should be implemented using combinational logic and the linear layer should be implemented using sequential logic. The non-linear elements can be implemented using small look-up tables. The purpose of the linear layer is to mix the bits between different non-linear elements. Since each non-linear element mixes the bits very well within itself, running 3 cycles on the linear layer should be enough to achieve the mixing for an 8×8 S Box.

So far as hardware complexity is concerned, a four bit counter for each of the four bit maximum length CA and three layers of CAs each of complexity n are required, if implemented using sequential logic. For a combinational implementation, a small look-up table and a few AND-XOR gates are required to implement the whole construction. Since the layers are in serial, the hardware complexity does not increase with the number of additional layers. In fact, the first and the third layers can be realized with a single layer of four cell CAs with a switch to toggle between the first non-linear layer and the second non-linear layer. This necessitates only two layers (for hardware realization) of CA with complexity n for linear and non-linear transformation.

We can also have more layers to have better security properties with no additional hardware complexity. This is because the non-linear layer and the linear layer can be reused as many times as required with a simple switch to toggle between the successive layers. So this S-box is scalable in terms of security margin without any additional hardware complexity.

3.2   Hardware Implementation

The hardware implementation of the mapping is simple. The re-usable non-linear component can be implemented in three different ways.

Using Look-up Table: A simple look-up table can be synthesized by its reduced boolean equation without using any memory.

Using ROM: The non-linear CA can also be implemented using a ROM, for example, for a 4-Cell CA, a 16×4 bit ROM i.e. 4 bit address and 4 bit data can be used.

Using Sequential Logic: Using a pure sequential logic, the non-linear primitive can be implemented using a CA, a counter and a comparator.

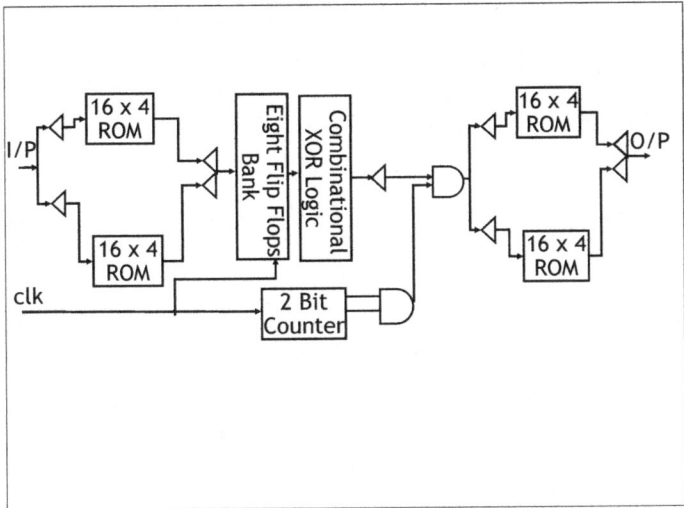

Fig. 2. Hardware Architecture of the S-box

The linear layer is implemented with a series of flip-flops with neighboring combinational logic using XOR gates as in normal Cellular Automata. The clock signal is fed into the structure and it is controlled by a $lg(n)$ bit counter. Since the S-Box has a modular architecture, the architecture diagram in figure 1 can be directly translated into hardware implementation using one of the above schemes. The hardware architecture using ROM for 8×8 S-box is shown in figure 2.

We have implemented the 8×8 S-box in FPGA using Xilinx Synthesis Tool. Four 16×4 bit ROMs were used for the two non-linear layers. The linear transformation was implemented using an eight cell maximum length CA running for four times. Overall this construction required one two bit up-counter, eight 1-bit registers, one 8-bit latch, five 2-input XOR and three 3-input XOR gate when implemented using Xilinx ISE v7.1i on Spartan 3 xc3s5000-4-fg900 device. The speed of execution was 313 MHz and number of slices was 23. When three non-linear layers were used with two linear layers in between running for 2 cycles, the area estimates were 41 slices and speed estimation was 314 MHz. For a 16×16 S-box using two non-linear layers, with the linear layer running for 12 cycles, the area estimation was 47 slices and the speed estimation was 312 MHz. Finally, for a 16×16 S-box using three non-linear layers, with two linear layers running for 6 cycles, the area estimation was 84 slices and the speed estimation was 313 MHz. It can be easily seen that in each of the above cases the throughput is in the order of magnitude of giga-bits per second.

3.3   Software Implementation

The software implementation consists of three 16, 32 and 64 element re-usable arrays for the non-linear layers and a linear layer. The implementation of a 32×32

Table 2. The C Code Snippet for the S-box

```
1 #define Rule 0x4609BBD5
2 int fourCellCA[16] = /* Initialize with pre − computed output */;
3 int fiveCellCA[32] = /* Initialize with pre − computed output */;

4 temp1 = fiveCellCA[input & 0x1F] + fourCellCA[(input ≫ 5) & 0xF] ≪ 5 +
  fiveCellCA[(input ≫ 9) & 0x1F] ≪ 9 + fourCellCA[(input ≫ 14) & 0xF] ≪ 14
  +fiveCellCA[(input ≫ 18) & 0x1F] ≪ 18 + fourCellCA[(input ≫ 23) & 0xF] ≪ 23
  + fiveCellCA[(input ≫ 27) & 0x1F] ≪ 27;

5 for(i = 0; i < LINCYCLES; i + +) /* LINCYCLES = No of Cycles in Lin Layer.*/
  temp1 = (temp1 ≪ 1) ⊕ (temp1&Rule) ⊕ (temp1 ≫ 1);

6 output = fourCellCA[temp1 & 0xF] + fiveCellCA[(temp1 ≫ 4) & 0x1F] ≪ 4+
  fiveCellCA[(temp1 ≫ 9)& 0x1F] ≪ 9 + fourCellCA[(temp1 ≫ 14)& 0xF] ≪ 14+
  fiveCellCA[(temp1 ≫ 18)& 0x1F] ≪ 18 + fiveCellCA[(temp1 ≫ 23)& 0x1F] ≪ 23
  + fourCellCA[(temp1 ≫ 28) & 0xF] ≪ 28;
```

element S-box was described before. A pseudo-code for a 32×32 element S-box is given in table 2 which can be used as a reference in other implementations. The variable *input* denotes the input to the S-box and the variable *output* stores the output of the S-box.

The above function, with both three non-linear layers and two non-linear layers, was run on HP rp3440-4core server with OS HP-UX B.11.23 and PA8900 CPU (999MHz). Also the same program was run on Windows XP SP2 OS, Intel(R) Core(TM) Duo CPU T2500 @2.00GHz. The time taken in nano-seconds (ns) is shown in the table 3. HP-UX took more time because the CPU speed is less. Since these measurements are for 32 bits S-box, we can see that the per-bit substitution took in the order of 10^{-9} seconds on average for these S-boxes.

Table 3. Software Performance

Parameters	HP-UX	Windows	Parameters	HP-UX	Windows
LINCYCLES=32, 2 NL layers	426ns	255ns	LINCYCLES=24, 2 NL layers	351ns	198ns
LINCYCLES=10, 3 NL layers	351ns	178ns	LINCYCLES=12, 3 NL layers	396ns	208ns

4   Security Analysis

From equation 4, we can see that each output bit depends on the input in an exponential manner. Hence, if we expand, we can easily observe that the S-box will have a strong algebraic immunity. The non-linearity of an $n \times n$ S-box is given by [7], [21]:

$N_f = 2^{n-1} - 0.5max \mid \sum_{u,v,x \in V_n} (-1)^{v \cdot f(x) \oplus u \cdot x} \mid$, where V_n denotes a vector space of n tuples in GF(2).

If we substitute $f(x)$, with equation 4, we get:

$$N_f = 2^{n-1} - 0.5max \mid \sum_{u,v,x\in V_n} (-1)^{v \cdot T^{f(x)} \oplus u \cdot x} \mid \qquad (5)$$

From equation 5, $v \cdot T^{f(x)}$ will not be equal to $u \cdot x$ in most of the cases for $u, v \in V_n$ giving rise to the high non-linearity of the proposed S-box. This is because $v \cdot T^{f(x)}$ varies exponentially with x whereas $u \cdot x$ varies linearly with x.

Another important property of any boolean function is its *balancedness*. A boolean function is said to be *balanced*, if its output has equal number of zeros and ones for all possible inputs. Since, we are using maximum length CA for all the CAs in this S-box construction, the period of the S-box is the maximum possible. This automatically guarantees the balancedness for the proposed S-box.

We experimentally determined the security properties of the proposed S-box described in section 2. We show the results for 8 × 8 S-box with two non-linear layers (*SBOX1*) and with three non-linear layers (*SBOX2*). We chose all the seeds to be alternating ones and zeros starting with one. The results are comparable with AES S-box. The main advantage of these S-boxes over AES S-box is the scalability in terms of size with linear increase of hardware and cycles. In addition, the security of the proposed S-box can be increased with very little extra hardware and linear increase of cycles.

4.1 Algebraic Normal Form

The algebraic normal form for all the output bits in terms of input bits is calculated. We found that each output bit depends complexly on all the input bits. The algebraic degree of each of the output bit is six for *SBOX1*. For *SBOX2* the algebraic degree is seven which is equivalent to AES S-box.

For a random Boolean function in 8 variables, the average total number of monomials is $2^7 = 128$. Table 4 shows the number of monomials for both *SBOX1* and *SBOX2* and compared with AES S-box. It can be seen that *SBOX2* is comparable with AES; for bits 4 to 7 the number of terms are more than AES, while for bits 0 to 3 they are less. Table 5 shows the degree distribution for each of the output bits of both *SBOX1* and *SBOX2*. That shows the proximity towards the random boolean functions. We also considered the overlap between the monomials in the expression of the output bit. The number of monomials not occurring at all in any of the output bit expression is 33 and the number of terms occurring only once is 14 for *SBOX1*. The number of monomials not occurring at all is 4 and the number of monomials occurring only once is 11 in all the output bits of *SBOX2*. To compare, for the AES S-box, the number of monomials not occurring at all is 2 and the number of monomials occurring only once is 13. Hence, *SBOX2* is competitive with AES S-box in this aspect. These tables also show how the security properties are scaled up in *SBOX2* compared to *SBOX1*.

4.2 Linear and Differential Cryptanalysis

The maximum linear probability bias [16] for both the S-boxes, *SBOX1* and *SBOX2*, is 2^{-3} which is good for an 8 × 8 S-box. The *robustness* parameter, as

Table 4. Number of Monomials in the Algebraic Normal Form

Output Bit	0	1	2	3	4	5	6	7
SBOX1	122	101	108	108	99	100	97	90
SBOX2	115	137	115	127	123	129	132	119
AES	131	132	145	136	131	113	111	110

Table 5. The Distribution of Algebraic Degree in the Algebraic Normal Form

SBOX1	1	2	3	4	5	6	*SBOX2*	1	2	3	4	5	6	7
Bit 0	5	15	31	34	27	10	Bit 0	4	16	28	31	23	8	5
Bit 1	3	10	23	35	22	8	Bit 1	5	16	29	41	30	11	5
Bit 2	2	12	26	38	22	8	Bit 2	4	14	18	29	33	14	3
Bit 3	5	12	26	33	20	12	Bit 3	4	12	26	42	26	15	2
Bit 4	2	12	26	30	22	7	Bit 4	2	11	27	36	31	12	4
Bit 5	4	10	26	31	20	9	Bit 5	4	16	34	30	33	8	4
Bit 6	3	13	24	29	20	8	Bit 6	6	13	34	31	31	13	4
Bit 7	5	7	15	29	25	9	Bit 7	3	15	21	32	24	18	6

defined in [21], measures the immunity from differential cryptanalysis [4]. The maximum value of any entry in the difference distribution table was found to be 16 for *SBOX1*. The robustness against differential cryptanalysis was found to be 0.9375 for *SBOX1*. For SBOX2, the maximum entry was 10 and the corresponding robustness value was found to be 0.953125. We compare the robustness of DES S-boxes and AES S-box with our S-box in the table 6, where S1 to S8 are DES S-boxes. We can see that the robustness of the proposed S-box is as good as the S-boxes proposed by Sebbary [21] (Seb1, Seb2 and Seb3 in the table) and AES; it is approximately three times more than the DES S-boxes.

Table 6. Robustness Comparison

S1	S2	S3	S4	S5	S6	S7	S8	Seb1	Seb2	Seb3	AES	*SBOX1*	*SBOX2*
0.316	0.363	0.316	0.469	0.387	0.367	0.340	0.328	0.875	0.969	0.992	0.984	0.938	0.961

4.3   Non-linearity

The theoretical maximum non-linearity for an 8×8 S-box is $2^{8-1} - 2^{.5(8-1)} = 116$. The maximum non-linearity for the *SBOX1* was found to be 108 and minimum was 100. The maximum non-linearity for the *SBOX2* was found to be 110 and the minimum was 102. For AES S-box, the maximum non-linearity is 114 and the minimum is 112, which are comparable with the S-boxes generated in this paper.

4.4   Strict Avalanche Criterion

We did see an equal number of zeros and ones for each of the input bit flipping and then XORing the output differences except for very few cases. For the mapping *SBOX1*, after flipping each input bits, the maximum value of number of ones was seen to be 160 and minimum value as 88. For *SBOX2*,the maximum value was 152 and the minimum value was 96, thereby scaling up the security properties of SBOX1. For AES S Box, maximum SAC value is 144 and the minimum is 116. Although, AES S-boxes are better in terms of SAC properties, the main advantage of these S-boxes over AES S-boxes is the scalability to an extent that the whole non-linear block of a stream cipher can be generated using this method. Multiplicative inverse, as employed by AES S-boxes, is undoubtedly one of the most secure cryptographic primitives, but it is difficult to scale up (increased complexity of implementation) beyond a certain size and the only variability of multiplicative inverse is the choice of the primitive polynomial. The intention of the comparison is to show that, we can generate scalable and key-dependent S-boxes with comparable (better in some cases and worse in some cases) security properties using the method described in this paper.

4.5   Effect of Parameter on Security

Since this S-box is parameterized, we have evaluated the effect of the parameter (i.e. seed of the non-linear layer) on the security properties. Note that, the parameter is the variable n in equation 4. The table 7 shows some of the key security properties after varying the seed (parameter). These properties were calculated for the construction with three non-linear layers, with two linear layers in between them, in an 8×8 S-box. It can be seen that the security properties do not vary much with the change in parameter (seed). However, the security properties reduced for the penultimate row (with seed 11110000). The reason being, with this seed, the second non-linear CA does not run at all (having 0000 as seed). In this case, the input is directly returned to the output in the code. Hence care should be taken while selecting the parameter so that it does not make any of the non-linear elements not run at all. The same seed has been used for each non-linear layer except for the last row, where, the seeds 10101010, 11111111 and 01010101 were used for the three non-linear layers. Here also the security properties did not vary much.

4.6   Security Analysis for 16×16 S-box

Similar security analysis was performed for 16×16 S-box (the case5 in the previous section). Table 8 summarizes the results obtained. The maximum differential value was found to be 22 with the robustness value as 0.9996. Hence differential attack is difficult for this S-box. The maximum value in linear distribution table was 33396 and minimum was 32110. For zero probability bias (in an ideal case) it should be 32768. Hence there were not much variation from the ideal one in linear distribution table. The algebraic degree was maximum possible for all the output bits. Number of terms not occurring at all in algebraic normal form was

Table 7. Parameter Effect on Security Properties

Seed	Mx Term	Mn Term	Mx Deg	Mn Deg	Mx Diff	Mx Bias	Mx SAC	Mn SAC	Mx NL	Mn NL
10101010	137	115	7	7	10	-3	152	96	110	102
01010101	140	109	7	7	12	-2.76	152	112	108	98
00110011	139	115	7	7	12	-2.68	152	108	108	98
00011000	141	115	7	7	12	-2.92	152	104	110	102
00010001	131	118	7	7	12	-2.83	152	104	110	102
11111111	131	115	7	7	10	-3	152	108	108	100
11110000	133	61	7	5	64	-2	160	64	104	96
Mixed	147	123	7	7	10	-2.92	152	104	108	98

Table 8. Security Properties for 16×16 S-box

Mx ANF Term	Mn ANF Term	Mx Deg	Mn Deg	Mx Diff	Mx SAC	Mn SAC	Mx NL	Mn NL	Robustness
32985	32633	15	15	22	33556	32192	32268	32204	0.9996

4 and the number of terms occurring only once in algebraic normal form of all the output bits was 13. The non-linearity for each of the output bit was also quite close to the theoretical maximum value 32586 of non-linearity for 16 bits. Finally, the SAC table also showed the values near the ideal value of 32768.

4.7   Statistical Properties

To evaluate the statistical properties of the proposed construction, NIST [19] test suit was run for each individual output bit and the overall S-box output. Among the tests, the Approximate Entropy, Block Frequency, Cumulative Sum, FFT, Frequency, Linear Complexity, Longest Run, Non-overlapping templates, Overlapping template, Rank, Runs and Serial tests were passed for each individual output bit as well as all output bits. The tests Universal, Random Excursion and Random Excursion Variant were run and passed for all output bits in 16×16 S-box only as the sample size was in-sufficient for the other cases.

5   Comparison with Existing Stream Cipher

In the proposed S-box, the whole 2^n state space of the n bit S-box can be utilized. Hence, after scaling up the S-box in terms of size, this can directly be used as a non-linear block in a stream cipher. This maximum period is not guaranteed in any of the non-linear blocks used in current finalists of ESTREAM stream ciphers e.g. Trivium's [6] strong non-linear state transitions; Grain's [13] non-linear feedback shift registers and Micky's [1] irregular clocking. Also, due to parallel transformation in CA, the speed will be much better compared to any of the non-linear blocks in those stream ciphers. However, the hardware requirement for the proposed method will be more than the non-linear blocks of those three ciphers.

Since the proposed S-box can also be implemented in software, we compare this S-box with Rabbit's [5] G function. Rabbit's G function is difficult to realize in hardware as it involves square function, however the proposed S-box in this paper is easy to implement in hardware. The security properties claimed in Rabbit G function are achievable by the current S-box as it is flexible in terms of enhancement of security properties. The Rabbit G function of 32 variables has an algebraic degree of at least 31. In the current S-box also the maximum algebraic degree is achievable in a large S-box by the asymmetric design. For example, for the 16×16 S-box shown in the previous sections, the algebraic degree came out to be 15. The average number of monomials in a random boolean function of n bits is 2^{n-1}. For Rabbit 32 bits G functions it ranged from $2^{24.5}$ to $2^{30.9}$ whereas in this construction the number of monomials were seen to be nearing the random boolean function. The overlap of monomials is also better in the proposed S-box as compared to rabbit G function. In Rabbit the number of monomials that do not occur at all is $2^{26.2}$ and monomials occurring only once is $2^{26.03}$, whereas for a random function it should average to 1. Our construction also nears the random function as seen for the 16 bit and 8 bit S-boxes.

6   Application

An obvious application for these S-boxes is design of a stream cipher. We introduce one schema for a new stream cipher here. We acknowledge that a new stream cipher requires complete security analysis and performance evaluation. But, since the scope of this paper is an S-box and due to page limitation, we keep

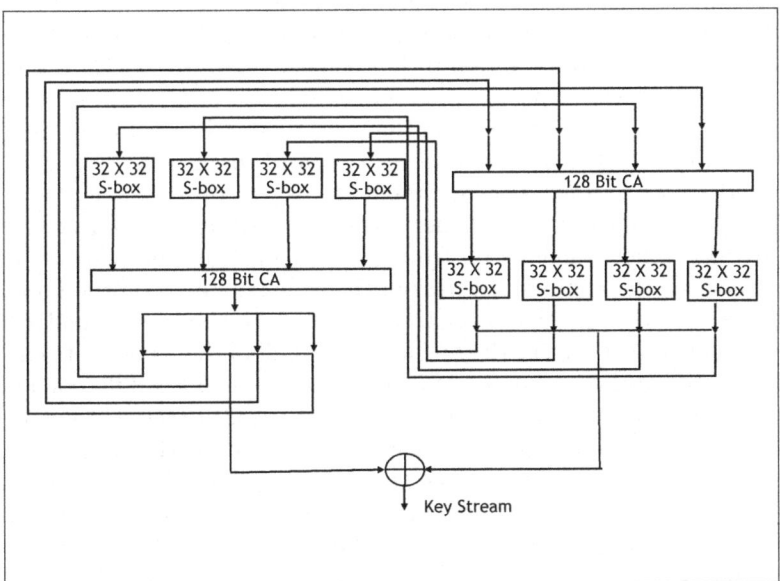

Fig. 3. An Application of the S-boxes in Stream Cipher Construction

the detailed security analysis and performance evaluation of the stream cipher as a future work. However, we justify why we believe the proposed steam cipher should work and worth giving future attention.

Figure 3 shows the proposed application of the S-boxes in a stream cipher. The key stream generation process is shown here. The outputs of two non-linear blocks are XORed to produce the key streams. The left hand side non-linear block contains four 32-bits S-boxes followed by a 128 bits CA which are run equal number of cycles that the 32-bits S-boxes would require. The right hand side non-linear block contains a 128 bits CA running same number of cycles that the 32-bits S-box would require; followed by a layer of four 32-bits S-boxes. At each round the state bits of each side are updated with a simple 32 bit permutation of the output of the other side. Basically, the first, second, third and fourth 32 bits blocks of each side update the third, fourth, first and second 32 bits blocks of the other side.

This stream cipher uses a non-linear combiner model. Unlike NFSR based non-linear combiners which output one bit as a key stream at every cycle, this design performs a block-wise non-linear combination. Traditionally, NFSR based non-linear combiners have been subjected to correlation attacks [15], [17] and algebraic attacks [9], [10]. Even non-linear combiners with non-linear filters have been attacked [2]. During the initial key-stream generations the NFSR based stream ciphers do not provide enough algebraic immunity. This however increases with the number of key stream produced. The attacks exploit the algebraic weakness of the initial key stream bits. Hence, if there is a non-linear combiner whose constituents produce parallel bits in a highly non-linear manner, attacks such as correlation or distinguishing attacks would not be possible. In order to produce highly non-linear block generators, the S-boxes that are described in this paper are very useful. It has been shown that [11] the reported attacks on Grain stream cipher can be prevented with parallel transformation of CA by replacing the LFSR with CA. Moreover, these S-boxes are key dependent, hence this will aid to the good initialization algorithm of such stream ciphers to prevent slide-re-synchronization or chosen IV attacks on stream ciphers. Again, NFSRs are known for low period whereas each constituent non-linear generators in this stream cipher is maximum length by design. Questions can be raised on power attacks as the number of cycles in the S-box depends on the input. However, please note that in each layer the 32×32 S-box contains smaller S-boxes whose outputs are not sent to the linear layer till all of them complete execution, which would average out the power or cycles consumed for different inputs. It will be easy to show that time/memory/data tradeoff attack will not be possible with maximum sampling resistance. As far as the performance estimation is concerned, it is possible to get two to four bits per clock cycles even though there is a latency involved in the S-boxes without compromising on security. Finally, an optimized hardware implementation is possible by reusing the same 128 bits CA and 32-bits S-box layer. The construction will aid to efficient software implementation as all permutations are with 32 bits that can fit into integers.

7   Conclusions

This paper devices a method for generating scalable, parameterized S-boxes that are very well suited for the stream ciphers. The S-boxes are realized with cellular automata and hence are easy to implement using hardware. This paper also evaluates some specific S-boxes in terms of security and shows that all these S-boxes can give very good security properties. As an application, a new stream cipher can be proposed with these S-boxes.

References

1. Babbage, S., Dodd, M.: The stream cipher MICKEY 2.0, http://www.ecrypt.eu. org/stream/mickeyp3.html
2. Berbain, C., Gilbert, H., Joux, A.: Algebraic and Correlation Attacks against Linearly Filtered Non Linear Feedback Shift Registers. In: Avanzi, R.M., Keliher, L., Sica, F. (eds.) SAC 2008. LNCS, vol. 5381, pp. 184–198. Springer, Heidelberg (2009)
3. Bernstein, D.J.: Salsa 20 Specification, http://www.ecrypt.eu.org/stream/ salsa20p3.html
4. Biham, E., Shamir, A.: Differential Cryptanalysis of DES-like Cryptosystems. Journal of Cryptology 4(1), 3–72 (1991)
5. Boesgaard, M., Vesterager, M., Pedersen, T., Christiansen, J., Scavenius, O.: Rabbit: A New High-Performance Stream Cipher. In: Johansson, T. (ed.) FSE 2003. LNCS, vol. 2887, pp. 307–329. Springer, Heidelberg (2003)
6. De Canniere, C., Preneel, B.: Trivium Specification, http://www.ecrypt.eu.org/ stream/triviump3.html
7. Chabaud, F., Vaudenay, S.: Links between differential and linear cryptanalysis. In: De Santis, A. (ed.) EUROCRYPT 1994. LNCS, vol. 950, pp. 356–365. Springer, Heidelberg (1995)
8. Cardoso, P.S., Strum, M., Amazonas, J.R.d.A., Chau, W.J.: Comparison between Quasi-Uniform Linear Cellular Automata and Linear Feedback Shift Registers as Test Pattern Generators for Built-in Self-Test Applications. In: XII Brazilian Symposium on Integrated Circuits and Systems Design, sbcci, p. 0198 (1999)
9. Courtois, N.T.: Fast algebraic attacks on stream ciphers with linear feedback. In: Boneh, D. (ed.) CRYPTO 2003. LNCS, vol. 2729, pp. 176–194. Springer, Heidelberg (2003)
10. Courtois, N., Meier, W.: Algebraic Attacks on Stream Ciphers with Linear Feedback. In: Biham, E. (ed.) EUROCRYPT 2003. LNCS, vol. 2656, pp. 345–359. Springer, Heidelberg (2003)
11. Das, S., Roychowdhury, D.: Prevention of Attacks on Grain Using Cellular Automata. Presented in Inscrypt 2009, Beijing, China (2009)
12. Hawkes, P., Paddon, M., Rose, G.G., de Vries, M.W.: Primitive Specification for NLSv2, http://www.ecrypt.eu.org/stream/nlsp3.html
13. Hell, M., Johansson, T., Meier, W.: Grain - A Stream Cipher for Constrained Environments, http://www.ecrypt.eu.org/stream/grainp3.html
14. Jacobson, M.J., Hubery, K., Ag, D.T.: The MAGENTA Block Cipher Algorithm. NIST AES Proposal (1998)

15. Johansson, T., Jonsson, F.: Improved fast correlation attacks on stream ciphers via convolutional codes. In: Stern, J. (ed.) EUROCRYPT 1999. LNCS, vol. 1592, pp. 347–362. Springer, Heidelberg (1999)
16. Matsui, M.: Linear cryptanalysis method for DES cipher. In: Helleseth, T. (ed.) EUROCRYPT 1993. LNCS, vol. 765, pp. 386–397. Springer, Heidelberg (1994)
17. Meier, W., Staffelbach, O.: Fast correlation attacks on stream ciphers. In: Gunther, C.G. (ed.) EUROCRYPT 1988. LNCS, vol. 330, pp. 301–314. Springer, Heidelberg (1988)
18. Nyberg, K.: Differentially uniform mappings for cryptography. In: Helleseth, T. (ed.) EUROCRYPT 1993. LNCS, vol. 765, pp. 55–64. Springer, Heidelberg (1994)
19. NIST Statistical Test Suit, http://csrc.nist.gov/rng/
20. Pal Chaudhury, P., Roy Chowdhury, D., Nandi, S., Chattopadhay, S.: Additive Cellular Automata Theory and Application, vol. 1. IEEE Computer Society Press, Los Alamitos
21. Seberry, J., Zhang, X.-M., Zheng, Y.: Systematic Generation Cryptographically Robust S-boxes. In: 1st Conference Computer and Communication Security, VA, USA, pp. 171–182 (1993)
22. Szaban, M., Seredynski, F.: Application of cellular automata to create S-box functions. In: IPDPS 2008, pp. 1–7 (2008)
23. Szaban, M., Seredynski, F.: Cryptographically Strong S-Boxes Based on Cellular Automata. In: Umeo, H., Morishita, S., Nishinari, K., Komatsuzaki, T., Bandini, S. (eds.) ACRI 2008. LNCS, vol. 5191, pp. 478–485. Springer, Heidelberg (2008)
24. The Estream Project, http://www.ecrypt.eu.org/stream/
25. Wu, H.: The Stream Cipher HC-128, http://www.ecrypt.eu.org/stream/p3ciphers/hc/hc128$_p$3.pdf

A Family of Binary Threshold Sequences Constructed by Using the Multiplicative Inverse

Zhixiong Chen[1], Xiangguo Cheng[2], and Chenhuang Wu[1]

[1] Key Laboratory of Applied Mathematics, Putian University, Fujian 351100, China
{ptczx,wuchenhuang2008}@126.com
[2] College of Information Engineering, Qingdao University, Qingdao, Shandong
266071, P.R. China
chengxg@qdu.edu.cn

Abstract. We point out that a family of pseudorandom binary lattices, which were constructed by using the multiplicative inverse, can be generated as binary threshold sequences. Hence we can estimate the well-distribution measure and the correlation measure of order ℓ of the binary lattices in terms of discrepancy bounds on corresponding pseudorandom numbers in the interval $[0,1)$. We also consider the modified well-distribution measure and the modified correlation measure of order ℓ, which were introduced by Sárközy and Winterhof, for the binary lattices.

Keywords: Pseudorandom sequences, binary lattices, binary threshold sequences, correlation measure, well-distribution measure, discrepancy, exponential sums.
MSC(2010): 11K45, 94A60, 94A55.

1 Introduction

In a series of papers starting from [9], Mauduit and Sárközy (partly with further coauthors) studied finite binary pseudorandom sequences. They introduced certain measures of pseudorandomness for finite pseudorandom binary sequences

$$E_T = \{e_0, \ldots, e_{T-1}\} \in \{-1, +1\}^T.$$

The *well-distribution measure* of E_T is defined by

$$W(E_T) = \max_{a,b,t} \left| \sum_{j=0}^{t-1} e_{a+bj} \right|,$$

where the maximum is taken over all $a \in \mathbb{N} \cup \{0\}$, $b, t \in \mathbb{N}$ such that $0 \leq a \leq a + b(t-1) \leq T - 1$, and the *correlation measure of order ℓ* of E_T is defined as

$$C_\ell(E_T) = \max_{M,D} \left| \sum_{n=0}^{M-1} e_{n+d_1} e_{n+d_2} \cdots e_{n+d_\ell} \right|,$$

X. Lai, M. Yung, and D. Lin (Eds.): Inscrypt 2010, LNCS 6584, pp. 95–104, 2011.

where the maximum is taken over all $D = (d_1, \ldots, d_\ell)$ and M such that $0 \le d_1 < \cdots < d_\ell \le T - M$.

It was shown in [2] that for a "truly random" sequence both $W(E_T)$ and $C_\ell(E_T)$ are "small". More precisely, a binary sequence E_T can be considered as a "good" pseudorandom sequence if both $W(E_T)$ and $C_\ell(E_T)$ (for "small" ℓ) are ideally greater than $T^{1/2}$ only by at most a power of $\log T$.

In [6] Hubert, Mauduit and Sárközy extended the constructive theory of pseudorandomness of binary sequences to *several dimensions* called binary lattice. A *binary lattice* (or an *r-dimensional binary T-lattice*) is a function of the type

$$\eta(x) : I_T^r \to \{+1, -1\},$$

where $I_T^r = \{x = (x_1, \ldots, x_r) | x_1, \ldots, x_r \in \{0, 1, \ldots, T-1\}\}$. The *pseudorandom measure of order ℓ of dimension r* of $\eta(x)$ is defined by

$$Q_\ell(\eta) = \max_{\overline{B}, d_1, \cdots, d_\ell, \overline{T}} \left| \sum_{j_1=0}^{t_1} \cdots \sum_{j_r=0}^{t_r} \eta \left(\sum_{m=1}^{r} j_m b_m \overline{u_m} + d_1 \right) \cdots \eta \left(\sum_{m=1}^{r} j_m b_m \overline{u_m} + d_\ell \right) \right|$$

where $\overline{u_m} (m = 1, \ldots, r)$ denotes the r-dimensional unit vector whose m-th coordinate is 1 and the other coordinates are 0 and the maximum is taken over all r-dimensional vectors $\overline{B} = (b_1, \ldots, b_r), d_1, \ldots, d_\ell, \overline{T} = (t_1, \ldots, t_r)$ such that their coordinates are non-negative integers, $b_1, \ldots, b_r$ are non-zero, $d_1, \ldots, d_\ell$ are distinct, and all the points $\sum_{m=1}^{r} j_m b_m \overline{u_m} + d_i$ occurring in the multiple sum belong to I_T^r.

An r-dimensional binary T-lattice η is considered as a "good" pseudorandom binary lattice if $Q_\ell(\eta)$ is "small" and ideally greater than $T^{r/2}$ only by at most a power of $\log T^r$, see [6]. Some constructions of binary lattices were presented in [6,11] by using the *quadratic character* of a finite field $\mathbb{F}_q$, $q = p^r$, an extension field of the prime field $\mathbb{F}_p$.

This paper contributes to estimating the well-distribution measure and the correlation measure of order ℓ of a family of binary lattices, which were constructed by using the *multiplicative inverse* of the finite field $\mathbb{F}_q$ in [12], in terms of discrepancy bounds on pseudorandom numbers in the interval $[0, 1)$. We also consider the modified measures (the *modified well-distribution measure* and the *modified correlation measure of order ℓ*, see Section 4 for the definitions), which were introduced by Sárközy and Winterhof in [16]. Finally a lower bound on the linear complexity profile of the binary lattices is derived from the correlation measure of order ℓ in Section 5.

2   Binary Lattice and Binary Threshold Sequence

Now we review the construction of binary lattices studied in [12]. For an ordered basis $\{\gamma_1, \ldots, \gamma_r\}$ of $\mathbb{F}_q$ over $\mathbb{F}_p$, we order the elements of $\mathbb{F}_q = \{\xi_0, \xi_1, \ldots, \xi_{q-1}\}$ as

$$\xi_n = n_1 \gamma_1 + n_2 \gamma_2 + \cdots + n_r \gamma_r, \quad 0 \le n < q$$

if
$$n = n_1 + n_2 p + \cdots + n_r p^{r-1}, \ 0 \leq n_i < p, \quad i = 1, \ldots, r.$$

For $n \geq 0$ we define $\xi_{n+q} = \xi_n$. Define the boxes $A_1, A_2, \ldots, A_r$ by

$$A_1 = \left\{ \sum_{l=1}^{r} a_l \gamma_l : 0 \leq a_1 \leq \tfrac{p-3}{2}, a_2, \ldots, a_r \in \mathbb{F}_p \right\}$$

$$A_2 = \left\{ \sum_{l=1}^{r} a_l \gamma_l : a_1 = \tfrac{p-1}{2}, 0 \leq a_2 \leq \tfrac{p-3}{2}, a_3, \ldots, a_r \in \mathbb{F}_p \right\}$$

$$\ldots\ldots$$

$$A_r = \left\{ \sum_{l=1}^{r} a_l \gamma_l : a_1 = a_2 = \ldots = a_{r-1} = \tfrac{p-1}{2}, 0 \leq a_r \leq \tfrac{p-3}{2} \right\}$$

and write
$$\mathcal{A} = \cup_{l=1}^{r} A_l.$$

Then for distinct elements $\alpha_1, \ldots, \alpha_k \in \mathbb{F}_q$ and

$$f(x) = (x + \alpha_1)(x + \alpha_2) \cdots (x + \alpha_k) \in \mathbb{F}_q[x], \tag{1}$$

the binary lattice is defined by

$$\eta(n) = \eta(n_1, \cdots, n_r) = \begin{cases} +1, \text{if } f(\xi_n) \neq 0 \text{ and } f(\xi_n)^{-1} \in \mathcal{A}, \\ -1, \text{otherwise.} \end{cases} \tag{2}$$

It was shown in [12] that $Q_\ell(\eta)$ is "small" for the binary lattice (2) above

$$Q_\ell(\eta) < (2^{\ell+3} + 1) k \ell r^\ell q^{1/2} (2 + \log p)^{r+\ell},$$

where $k, \ell < p$, $k + \ell \leq p + 1$ and $k\ell \leq q/2$.

Now we define a binary threshold sequence using the multiplicative inverse. Let
$$f(\xi_n)^{-1} = c_{n,1}\gamma_1 + c_{n,2}\gamma_2 + \cdots + c_{n,r}\gamma_r, \quad 0 \leq n \leq q - 1$$

with all $c_{n,i} \in \mathbb{F}_p = \{0, 1, \ldots, p-1\}$ for $1 \leq i \leq r$. If $f(\xi_n) = 0$ we set $c_{n,i} = 0$ for $1 \leq i \leq r$. We obtain a sequence $\{y_0, y_1, \ldots, y_{q-1}\}$ of numbers in the interval $[0, 1)$ by defining

$$y_n = \sum_{j=1}^{r} c_{n,j} p^{-j}. \tag{3}$$

Then we obtain the *binary threshold sequence* $E_q = \{e_0, e_1, \ldots, e_{q-1}\}$ by defining

$$e_n = \begin{cases} +1, \text{if } 0 \leq y_n < \tfrac{1}{2}, \\ -1, \text{if } \tfrac{1}{2} \leq y_n < 1. \end{cases} \tag{4}$$

Indeed, the binary threshold sequence E_q is almost the same as the binary lattice (2) except $n = (\tfrac{p-1}{2}, \ldots, \tfrac{p-1}{2})$ and those n (only k many such n) with $f(\xi_n) = 0$. We note that this difference will not influence the properties considered in this article.

In particular, E_q extends a construction of binary sequences studied in our work [3,4]. As a finite binary sequence, it seems that we can't estimate the well-distribution measure $W(E_q)$ and the correlation measure $C_\ell(E_q)$ of order ℓ for E_q according to $Q_\ell(\eta)$. So we will apply another technique (see [8]) to estimating $W(E_q)$ and $C_\ell(E_q)$.

Note that in some references actually the sequences $\{e'_0, e'_1, \ldots, e'_{T-1}\} \in \{0,1\}^T$ with $e_i = (-1)^{e'_i}$, $0 \le i \le T - 1$, and the corresponding definitions of the well-distribution measure and the correlation measure are considered.

The implied constants in the symbols 'O' and '$\ll$' are absolute. We recall that the notations $U = O(V)$ and $U \ll V$ are both equivalent to the assertion that the inequality $|U| \le cV$ holds for some constant $c > 0$.

3   Classical Measures

Given a sequence Γ of N points

$$\Gamma = \left\{ (\omega_{n,0}, \ldots, \omega_{n,s-1})_{n=1}^N \right\}$$

in the s-dimensional unit cube $[0,1)^s$, the *discrepancy* $\Delta(\Gamma)$ is defined by

$$\Delta(\Gamma) = \sup_{B \subseteq [0,1)^s} \left| \frac{T_\Gamma(B)}{N} - |B| \right|,$$

where $T_\Gamma(B)$ is the number of points of Γ inside the box

$$B = [0, \beta_0) \times \cdots \times [0, \beta_{s-1}) \subseteq [0,1)^s$$

and the supremum is taken over all such boxes, see [14, Definition 2.1].

Mauduit, Niederreiter and Sárközy [8] developed a technique to estimate the well-distribution measure $W(E_q)$ and the correlation measure $C_\ell(E_q)$ of order ℓ for E_q by using discrepancy bounds on the sequences

$$\{y_a, y_{a+b}, \ldots, y_{a+(t-1)b}\}, \quad a \in \mathbb{N} \cup \{0\}, b, t \in \mathbb{N}, 0 \le a \le a + b(t-1) \le q - 1$$

and

$$\{(y_{n+d_1}, y_{n+d_2}, \ldots, y_{n+d_\ell})\}, \quad 0 \le d_1 < \cdots < d_\ell < q, n \ge 0,$$

respectively. Below we present the corresponding discrepancy bounds. We will fix the notations $\deg(f) = k$ and $k, \ell < p$ with $k + \ell \le p + 1$ and $k\ell \le q/2$.

Lemma 1. *Let $\{y_n\}$ be numbers defined as in (3). For any integers $a \in \mathbb{N} \cup \{0\}$ and $b, t \in \mathbb{N}$ with $0 \le a \le a + b(t-1) \le q - 1$, the discrepancy $\Delta(t; a, b)$ of the sequence $\{y_a, y_{a+b}, \ldots, y_{a+(t-1)b}\}$ satisfies*

$$\Delta(t; a, b) \ll t^{-1} k p^{r-1/2} \log q (2 + \log p)^r,$$

where $k = \deg(f)$.

Proof. Let $e_p(z) = \exp(2\pi i z/p)$ for integers z. Let $\lambda_i \in \mathbb{F}_p$ $(1 \le i \le r)$ be not all zero and

$$S_t(\lambda_1, \ldots, \lambda_r) = \sum_{j=0}^{t-1} e_p \left(\sum_{i=1}^{r} \lambda_i c_{a+jb,i} \right),$$

where $f(\xi_{a+jb})^{-1} = c_{a+jb,1}\gamma_1 + c_{a+jb,2}\gamma_2 + \cdots + c_{a+jb,r}\gamma_r$. According to [14, Proposition 2.4, Theorem 3.12 and Lemma 3.13] we have

$$\Delta(t; a, b) \ll \frac{1}{t} \log q \max_{\lambda_1, \ldots, \lambda_r} |S_t(\lambda_1, \ldots, \lambda_r)|. \tag{5}$$

So we only consider $S_t(\lambda_1, \ldots, \lambda_r)$. Let $\{\gamma_1', \ldots, \gamma_r'\}$ be the dual basis of $\{\gamma_1, \ldots, \gamma_r\}$. Since $f(x)$ has at most k roots in $\mathbb{F}_q$, we have

$$\begin{aligned}
S_t(\lambda_1, \ldots, \lambda_r) &= \sum_{j=0}^{t-1} e_p \left(\sum_{i=1}^{r} \lambda_i \mathrm{Tr}_{q|p}(\gamma_j' f(\xi_{a+jb})^{-1}) \right) + O(k) \\
&= \sum_{j=0}^{t-1} e_p \left(\mathrm{Tr}_{q|p} \left(\sum_{i=1}^{r} \lambda_i \gamma_j' f(\xi_{a+jb})^{-1} \right) \right) + O(k) \\
&= \sum_{j=0}^{t-1} \psi \left(\lambda f(\xi_{a+jb})^{-1} \right) + O(k),
\end{aligned}$$

where ψ is the *additive canonical character* of $\mathbb{F}_q$ and $\lambda = \sum_{i=1}^{r} \lambda_i \gamma_j'$. Since $\lambda_i \in \mathbb{F}_p$ $(1 \le i \le r)$ are not all zero and $\{\gamma_1', \cdots, \gamma_r'\}$ is a basis of $\mathbb{F}_q$ over $\mathbb{F}_p$, we have $\lambda \ne 0$. Then exactly in the same way as in [16,4], we get

$$\left| \sum_{j=0}^{t-1} \psi \left(\lambda f(\xi_{a+jb})^{-1} \right) \right| \le 3(k+1)p^{r-1/2}(2 + \log p)^r.$$

We obtain the desired result.   □

Lemma 2. Let $\{y_n\}$ be numbers defined as in (3). For $\ell \in \mathbb{N}$, non-negative integers $d_1, \ldots, d_\ell$ with $0 \le d_1 < \cdots < d_\ell < q$ and an positive integer N with $1 \le N + d_\ell \le q$, the discrepancy $\Delta(N; d_1, \ldots, d_\ell)$ of N points

$$(y_{n+d_1}, y_{n+d_2}, \ldots, y_{n+d_\ell}) \in [0, 1)^\ell, \quad n = 0, 1, \ldots, N - 1$$

satisfies

$$\Delta(N; d_1, \ldots, d_\ell) \ll N^{-1} 2^{r+r\ell} r k \ell q^{1/2} (\log q)^\ell (2 + \log p)^r,$$

where $k = \deg(f)$.

Proof. Let $\lambda_{ij} \in \mathbb{F}_p$ $(1 \le i \le \ell, 1 \le j \le r)$ be not all zero and

$$S_N(\lambda_{11}, \ldots, \lambda_{\ell r}) = \sum_{n=0}^{N-1} e_p \left(\sum_{i=1}^{\ell} \sum_{j=1}^{r} \lambda_{ij} c_{n+d_i, j} \right),$$

where $f(\xi_{n+d_i})^{-1} = c_{n+d_i,1}\gamma_1 + c_{n+d_i,2}\gamma_2 + \cdots + c_{n+d_i,r}\gamma_r$. According to [14, Proposition 2.4, Theorem 3.12 and Lemma 3.13] we have

$$\Delta(N; d_1, \ldots, d_\ell) \ll 2^\ell (\log q)^\ell \frac{1}{N} \max_{\lambda_{11}, \ldots, \lambda_{\ell r}} |S_N(\lambda_{11}, \ldots, \lambda_{\ell r})|. \tag{6}$$

So it suffices to estimate $S_N(\lambda_{11}, \ldots, \lambda_{\ell r})$. Since $\{\gamma_1', \ldots, \gamma_r'\}$ is the dual basis of the ordered basis $\{\gamma_1, \ldots, \gamma_r\}$ of $\mathbb{F}_q$ over $\mathbb{F}_p$, we have

$$\begin{aligned}
S_N(\lambda_{11}, \ldots, \lambda_{\ell r}) &= \sum_{n=0}^{N-1} e_p\left(\sum_{i=1}^{\ell}\sum_{j=1}^{r} \lambda_{ij}\mathrm{Tr}_{q|p}(\gamma_j' f(\xi_{n+d_i})^{-1}\right) + O(k\ell) \\
&= \sum_{n=0}^{N-1} e_p\left(\mathrm{Tr}_{q|p}\left(\sum_{i=1}^{\ell}\sum_{j=1}^{r} \lambda_{ij}\gamma_j' f(\xi_{n+d_i})^{-1}\right)\right) + O(k\ell) \\
&= \sum_{n=0}^{N-1} \psi\left(\sum_{i=1}^{\ell} \mu_i f(\xi_{n+d_i})^{-1}\right) + O(k\ell),
\end{aligned}$$

where ψ is the additive canonical character of $\mathbb{F}_q$ as in Theorem 1 and

$$\mu_i = \sum_{j=1}^{r} \lambda_{ij}\gamma_j', \quad i = 1, \ldots, \ell.$$

Since $\lambda_{ij} \in \mathbb{F}_p$ ($1 \le i \le \ell, 1 \le j \le r$) are not all zero and $\{\gamma_1', \cdots, \gamma_r'\}$ is a basis of $\mathbb{F}_q$ over $\mathbb{F}_p$, it follows that $\mu_1, \ldots, \mu_\ell$ are not all zero.

Combining with the idea of [16,4], we get

$$\left|\sum_{n=0}^{N-1} \psi\left(\sum_{i=1}^{\ell} \mu_i f(\xi_{n+d_i})^{-1}\right)\right| \ll 2^{(r-1)\ell} 2^r r k\ell q^{1/2}(2 + \log p)^r.$$

Now by (6), we obtain the desired result.   □

By [8, Theorems 1 and 2], we bound the well-distribution measure $W(E_q)$ for E_q defined in (4) by

$$W(E_q) \le 2 \max_{1 \le t \le q-1}\left(t \max_{a+(t-1)b \le q-1} \Delta(t; a, b)\right)$$

and the correlation measure $C_\ell(E_q)$ of order ℓ by

$$C_\ell(E_q) \le 2^\ell \max_{\substack{M \in \mathbb{N} \\ 0 \le d_1 < \cdots < d_\ell < q-M}} M\Delta(M + d_\ell; d_1, \ldots, d_\ell).$$

So we get the following results.

Theorem 1. *Let E_q be the binary sequence of length $q = p^r$ defined as in (4) with $f(x)$ of degree k as in (1). If $k, \ell < p$, $k + \ell \le p + 1$ and $k\ell \le q/2$, then the well-distribution measure of E_q holds*

$$W(E_q) \ll k p^{r-1/2} \log q(2 + \log p)^r,$$

and the correlation measure of order ℓ of E_q holds

$$C_\ell(E_q) \ll 2^{r+r\ell+\ell} rk\ell q^{1/2} (\log q)^\ell (2 + \log p)^r.$$

Of course, one can use the inequality (see [10, Theorem 1])

$$W(E_q) \leq 3(q \cdot C_2(E_q))^{1/2}$$

to obtain an improved upper bound for $W(E_q)$.

4 Modified Measures

In [16], a slight modifications of the measures $W(E_q)$ and $C_\ell(E_q)$ were introduced for the sequence E_q in (4). For the ordering $\xi_n \in \mathbb{F}_q$, define

$$n \oplus d = m \quad \text{if and only if} \quad \xi_n + \xi_d = \xi_m, \quad 0 \leq n, d, m < q,$$

and

$$n \odot d = m \quad \text{if and only if} \quad \xi_n \cdot \xi_d = \xi_m, \quad 0 \leq n, d, m < q.$$

Then the *modified well-distribution measure* $W^\oplus(E_q)$ is defined by

$$W^\oplus(E_q) = \max_{\substack{0 \leq a < q, \ 1 \leq b < q \\ 1 \leq t \leq q}} \left| \sum_{j=0}^{t-1} e_{a \oplus (b \odot j)} \right|$$

and the *modified correlation measure of order ℓ* by

$$C_\ell^\oplus(E_q) = \max_{\substack{0 \leq d_1 < d_2 < \ldots < d_\ell < q \\ 1 \leq t \leq q}} \left| \sum_{n=0}^{t-1} e_{n \oplus d_1} \cdots e_{n \oplus d_\ell} \right|.$$

Theorem 2. *Let E_q be the binary sequence of length $q = p^r$ defined as in (4) with $f(x)$ of degree k as in (1). If $k, \ell < p$, $k + \ell \leq p + 1$ and $k\ell \leq q/2$, then we have*

$$W^\oplus(E_q) \ll kq^{1/2}(\log q)^2,$$

and

$$C_\ell^\oplus(E_q) \ll 2^\ell k\ell q^{1/2}(\log q)^{\ell+1}.$$

Similar to Theorem 1, the results follow from [8, Theorems 1 and 2]. So we only need to estimate the discrepancy bound $\Delta^\oplus(t; a, b)$ on the sequence

$$\{y_a, y_{a \oplus b}, \ldots, y_{a \oplus (t-1) \odot b}\}, \quad 0 \leq a < q, 1 \leq b < q, 1 \leq t \leq q$$

and the discrepancy bound $\Delta^\oplus(t; d_1, \ldots, d_\ell)$ on the points of ℓ-dimension

$$\{(y_{n \oplus d_1}, y_{n \oplus d_2}, \ldots, y_{n \oplus d_\ell})\}_{n=0}^{t-1}, \quad 0 \leq d_1 < \cdots < d_\ell < q, 1 \leq t \leq q.$$

As in the proofs of Lemmas 1 and 2, it suffices to consider the exponential sums

$$S_t^{\oplus}(\lambda_1,\ldots,\lambda_r) = \sum_{j=0}^{t-1} e_p\left(\sum_{i=1}^{r} \lambda_i c_{a\oplus j\odot b,i}\right)$$

and

$$S_t^{\oplus}(\lambda_{11},\ldots,\lambda_{\ell r}) = \sum_{n=0}^{t-1} e_p\left(\sum_{i=1}^{\ell}\sum_{j=1}^{r} \lambda_{ij} c_{n\oplus d_i,j}\right)$$

respectively. We first present a lemma, which is an extension of [17, Lemma 3.9].

Lemma 3. *Let* $S \subseteq \mathbb{F}_q$ *and* $g(x), h(x) \in \mathbb{F}_q[x]$. *Then*

$$\left|\sum_{z\in S} \psi\left(\frac{g(x)}{h(x)}\right)\right| \leq \frac{1}{q}\sum_{w\in\mathbb{F}_q^*}\left|\sum_{z\in S}\psi(wz)\right|\left|\sum_{x\in\mathbb{F}_q}\psi\left(\frac{g(x)}{h(x)} - wx\right)\right| + \frac{|S|}{q}\left|\sum_{x\in\mathbb{F}_q}\psi\left(\frac{g(x)}{h(x)}\right)\right|$$

Proof. We get the desired result by using the standard method for reducing incomplete exponential sums to complete ones [7, Chapter 12].   □

Now we return to prove Theorem 2. We also adopt the notations in the proofs of Lemmas 1 and 2.

$$\begin{aligned}
S_t^{\oplus}(\lambda_1,\ldots,\lambda_r) &= \sum_{j=0}^{t-1} e_p\left(\sum_{i=1}^{r} \lambda_i c_{a\oplus j\odot b,i}\right) \\
&= \sum_{j=0}^{t-1} e_p\left(\sum_{i=1}^{r} \lambda_i \mathrm{Tr}_{q|p}(\gamma_j' f(\xi_{a\oplus j\odot b})^{-1})\right) + O(k) \\
&= \sum_{j=0}^{t-1} \psi\left(\lambda f(\xi_{a\oplus j\odot b})^{-1}\right) + O(k) \\
&= \sum_{j=0}^{t-1} \psi\left(\lambda f(\xi_a + \xi_j \cdot \xi_b)^{-1}\right) + O(k),
\end{aligned}$$

where $\lambda = \sum_{i=1}^{r} \lambda_i \gamma_j'$. Then by Lemma 3, [15, Lemma 2], [15, Lemma 1] (which in turns comes from [13, Theorem 2]), and [17, Lemma 3.11], we obtain

$$S_t^{\oplus}(\lambda_1,\ldots,\lambda_r) \ll kq^{1/2}(1 + \log q)$$

Similarly, with

$$\mu_i = \sum_{j=1}^{r} \lambda_{ij}\gamma_j', \quad i = 1,\ldots,\ell$$

we obtain

$$S_t^{\oplus}(\lambda_{11},\ldots,\lambda_{\ell r}) = \sum_{n=0}^{t-1} \psi\left(\sum_{i=1}^{\ell} \mu_i f(\xi_n + \xi_{d_i})^{-1}\right) + O(k\ell)$$

$$\ll k\ell q^{1/2}(1 + \log q).$$

Now we use (5) and (6) with $S_t^{\oplus}(\lambda_1, \ldots, \lambda_r)$ and $S_N^{\oplus}(\lambda_{11}, \ldots, \lambda_{\ell r})$ to obtain

$$\Delta^{\oplus}(t; a, b) \ll \frac{1}{t} k q^{1/2} (\log q)^2$$

and

$$\Delta^{\oplus}(t; d_1, \ldots, d_\ell) \ll \frac{1}{t} k \ell q^{1/2} (\log q)^{\ell+1}.$$

Then by [8, Theorems 1 and 2] we obtain the desired results.   □

5   Linear Complexity Profile

The linear complexity profile is an important cryptographic characteristic of sequences and provides information on the predictability and thus suitability for cryptography.

The *linear complexity profile* of a sequence $E_T' = (e_0', e_1', \ldots, e_{T-1}') \in \{0,1\}^T$ over $\mathbb{F}_2$ is the smallest L, denoted by $L(E_T', N)$, such that a linear recurrence of order L over $\mathbb{F}_2$ can generate the first N terms of E_T', see, e.g. [5,18].

The linear complexity profile $L(E_T', N)$ of E_T' and the correlation measure $C_\ell(E_T)$ of order ℓ of $E_T = (e_0, e_1, \ldots, e_{T-1}) \in \{-1, +1\}^T$ defined by $e_n = (-1)^{e_n'}$ are related by the relation

$$L(E_T', N) \geq N - \max_{1 \leq \ell \leq L(E_T', N)+1} C_\ell(E_T), \quad 2 \leq N \leq T - 1,$$

see [1]. By Theorem 1, we have the following result.

Corollary 1. *Let E_q be the binary sequence of length $q = p^r$ defined as in (4). Then the linear complexity profile of $E_q' = (e_0', e_1', \ldots, e_{q-1}') \in \{0,1\}^q$ defined by $e_n = (-1)^{e_n'}$ satisfies*

$$L(E_q', N) = \Omega \left(\frac{\log(N q^{-1/2} 2^{-r} r^{-1} k^{-1} (2 + \log p)^{-r})}{r + \log \log q} \right), \quad 2 \leq N < q.$$

Acknowledgement

This work was partially supported by the Program for New Century Excellent Talents in Fujian Province University (No. JK2010047) and the National Natural Science Foundation of China (No. 61063041).

The authors wish to thank the reviewers for their valuable comments.

References

1. Brandstätter, N., Winterhof, A.: Linear complexity profile of binary sequences with small correlation measure. Periodica Mathematica Hungarica 52(2), 1–8 (2006)
2. Cassaigne, J., Mauduit, C., Sárközy, A.: On finite pseudorandom binary sequences, VII: the measures of pseudorandomness. Acta Arithmetica 103(2), 97–118 (2002)

3. Chen, Z.: Finite binary sequences constructed by explicit inversive methods. Finite Fields and Their Applications 14(3), 579–592 (2008)
4. Chen, Z., Gomez, D., Winterhof, A.: Distribution of digital explicit inversive pseudorandom numbers and their binary threshold sequence. In: L'Ecuyer, P., Owen, A.B. (eds.) Monte Carlo and Quasi-Monte Carlo Methods 2008, pp. 249–258. Springer, Heidelberg (2009)
5. Cusick, T.W., Ding, C.S., Renvall, A.: Stream Ciphers and Number Theory. North-Holland Mathematical Library, vol. 66. Elsevier Science B.V., Amsterdam (2004) (revised ed.)
6. Hubert, P., Mauduit, C., Sárközy, A.: On pseudorandom binary lattices. Acta Arithmetica 125, 51–62 (2006)
7. Iwaniec, H., Kowalski, E.: Analytic Number Theory. American Mathematical Society Colloquium Publications, vol. 53. American Mathematical Society, Providence (2004)
8. Mauduit, C., Niederreiter, H., Sárközy, A.: On pseudorandom [0, 1) and binary sequences. Publicationes Mathematicae Debrecen 71(3-4), 305–324 (2007)
9. Mauduit, C., Sárközy, A.: On finite pseudorandom binary sequences I: measures of pseudorandomness, the Legendre symbol. Acta Arithmetica 82, 365–377 (1997)
10. Mauduit, C., Sárközy, A.: On the measures of pseudorandomness of binary sequences. Discrete Mathematics 271, 195–207 (2003)
11. Mauduit, C., Sárközy, A.: On large families of pseudorandom binary lattices. Uniform Distribution Theory 2, 23–37 (2007)
12. Mauduit, C., Sárközy, A.: Construction of pseudorandom binary lattices by using the multiplicative inverse. Monatsh. Math. 153(3), 217–231 (2008)
13. Moreno, C.J., Moreno, O.: Exponential sums and Goppa codes. I. Proc. Amer. Math. Soc. 111, 523–531 (1991)
14. Niederreiter, H.: Random Number Generation and Quasi-Monte Carlo Methods. In: SIAM CBMSNSF Regional Conference Series in Applied Mathematics, vol. 63. SIAM, Philadelphia (1992)
15. Niederreiter, H., Winterhof, A.: Incomplete exponential sums over finite fields and their applications to new inversive pseudorandom number generators. Acta Arithmetica 93, 387–399 (2000)
16. Sárközy, A., Winterhof, A.: Measures of pseudorandomness for binary sequences constructed using finite fields. Discrete Mathematics 309, 1327–1333 (2009)
17. Winterhof, A.: Incomplete additive character sums and applications. In: Jungnickel, D., et al. (eds.) Proceedings of the 5th International Conference on Finite Fields and Applications, Augsburg, pp. 462–474. Springer, Heidelberg (2001)
18. Winterhof, A.: Linear complexity and related complexity measures. In: Selected Topics in Information and Coding Theory, pp. 3–40. World Scientific, Singapore (2010)

A Generalization of Verheul's Theorem for Some Ordinary Curves[*]

Zhi Hu[1,2], Maozhi Xu[1,**], and Zhenghua Zhou[1]

[1] LMAM, School of Mathematical Sciences, Peking University,
Beijing, 100871, P.R. China
[2] Department of Computer Science, University of Bristol,
Bristol, BS8 1UB, United Kingdom
{huzhi,mzxu}@math.pku.edu.cn, ttimezhou@yahoo.com.cn

Abstract. Verheul's theorem [20,21] on some certain supersingular elliptic curves is usually considered as an evidence for the difficulty of pairing inversion. Moody in [16] generalized it to some other supersingular curves. In this paper, we construct two types of ordinary elliptic curves with embedding degree $k = 1$, and give the corresponding distortion maps. Following their method, we generalize Verheul's theorem to our curves.

Keywords: Elliptic curve, Diffie-Hellman problem, pairing, distortion map.

1 Introduction

Bilinear pairings such as the Tate pairing and the Weil pairing on elliptic curves are very important in cryptography. Let E be an elliptic curve defined over a finite field $\mathbb{F}_q$, and let P be a base point with prime order n dividing $\#E(\mathbb{F}_q)$. Let k be the embedding degree of $E(\mathbb{F}_q)$, in other words, the smallest positive integer such that $n|q^k - 1$. It is proved by Menezes, Okamoto and Vanstone in [17] that the Weil pairing can reduce the discrete logarithm problem in the group $\langle P \rangle \subset E(\mathbb{F}_q)$ to the same problem in $\mathbb{F}_{q^k}^*$ (This method is called as MOV embedding). The Tate pairing was introduced into cryptography by Frey and Rück [4], and can similarly do as the Weil pairing does (also known as FR embedding). They also induces some varieties of bilinear pairings, and have even been used to construct numerous cryptosystems.

In 2001, Verheul in [20] proved that by using pairings, there was a computable homomorphism from certain supersingular elliptic curves to the group used in the XTR cryptosystems [13]. He also proved that if the map could be efficiently inverted, then the Difffie-Hellman problem would be efficiently solved in the certain finite fields. Verheul proved the following:

---

[*] Supported by the Natural Science Foundation of China (Grants No.10990011 and No.60763009). The author Zhi Hu was also supported by China Scholarship Council (Grant No.2009601236).
[**] Corresponding author.

X. Lai, M. Yung, and D. Lin (Eds.): Inscrypt 2010, LNCS 6584, pp. 105–114, 2011.

Theorem 1. *Let p be a prime $p \equiv 2 \bmod 3$, and n a prime number such that $n | (p^2 + p - 1)$. Let g be a generator of μ_n, the group of nth roots of unity in $\mathbb{F}_{p^6}^*$. Let P a point of order n on a supersingular curve E defined over $\mathbb{F}_{p^2}$ with $\#E(\mathbb{F}_{p^2}) = p^2 - p + 1$. If an efficiently computable homomorphism can be found from μ_n to $\langle P \rangle$, then the Diffie-Hellman problem can be efficiently solved in both μ_n and $\langle P \rangle$.*

This theorem can be generalized to some other classes of supersingular curves. Moody generalized it as

Theorem 2 ([16]). *Let $\mathbb{F}_q$ be an arbitrary finite field. Then there is an elliptic curve E over $\mathbb{F}_q$ such that the twisted curve $\tilde{E}(\mathbb{F}_{q^2})$ is a product of two cyclic groups of order $q-1$. Given such a curve, let P be a generator for one of the cyclic subgroups of order $q - 1$. Under the MOV embedding, we have an isomorphism from $\langle P \rangle$ to $\mathbb{F}_q^*$. If an efficiently computable isomorphism can be found from $\mathbb{F}_q^*$ to $\langle P \rangle$, then (assuming the Generalized Riemann Hypothesis) the Diffie Hellman problem can be efficiently solved in both $\mathbb{F}_q^*$ and $\langle P \rangle$.*

An open question is to generalize some form of Verheul's theorem to ordinary curves with low embedding degree. It would be interesting to find a way to construct distortion maps efficiently for ordinary curves with embedding degree $k = 1$, since Verheul proved that distortion maps for ordinary curves existed only in this case.

Our main contribution of this work is to answer the above question by two types of ordinary elliptic curves with $k = 1$. The paper is organized as follows. Section 2 introduces some basic notions for pairings and pairing inversion problems. We compare the supersingular curves and ordinary curves in some aspects in section 3. In section 4 we put our two types of ordinary curves with $k = 1$ and give the corresponding distortion maps. At last in section 5 we generalize the Verheul's theorem and estimate the cost of pairing computation in our cases.

2   Pairing and Pairing Inversion

2.1   Pairing

We consider cryptographic pairings in a formal way. Let G_1, G_2 and G_T be cyclic groups of prime order r. Supposing non-degenerate bilinear pairings of the form

$$e : G_1 \times G_2 \to G_T.$$

Galbraith, Paterson and Smart in [7] separated different possible pairings instantiations into three basic types:

Type 1: $G_1 = G_2$;
Type 2: $G_1 \neq G_2$ but there is an efficiently computable homomorphism $\phi :$ $G_1 \to G_2$;

Type 3: $G_1 \neq G_2$ and there are no efficiently computable homomorphisms between G_1 and G_2.

A Type 2 pairing is essentially a Type 1 pairing. Usually we call Type 1 & 2 pairings are symmetric pairings, while the Type 3 ones are called as asymmetric pairings.

The Weil and Tate pairings in some certain case (with the help of distortion maps) can be modified to symmetric ones.

2.2   Pairing Inversion

The approach to construct an efficiently computable homomorphism from $\mathbb{F}_{q^k}^*$ to $\langle P \rangle$ is to invert a pairing. Verheul's results are usually considered as evidence for the difficulty of pairing inversion.

Galbraith, Hess and Vercauteren in [6] defined some pairing inversion problems under consideration:

FAPI-1. (Fixed Argument Pairing Inversion 1) Problem: Given $g_1 \in G_1$ and $z \in G_T$, compute $g_2 \in G_2$ such that $e(g_1, g_2) = z$.
FAPI-2. (Fixed Argument Pairing Inversion 2) Problem: Given $g_2 \in G_2$ and $z \in G_T$, compute $g_1 \in G_1$ such that $e(g_1, g_2) = z$.
GPI. (Generalized Pairing Inversion) Problem: Given a pairing e and a value $z \in G_T$, find $g_1 \in G_1$ and $g_2 \in G_2$ with $e(g_1, g_2) = z$.

For pairing of Type 1 & 2, the FAPI-1,FAPI-2 problems are essentially the same. In the following, we focus on pairing of Type 1 & 2 (For convenience, we set $G_1 = G_2$).
We also consider the following problems:

BDHP. (bilinear Diffie-Hellman problem): Given $g, g^a, g^b, g^c \in G_1$, determine $e(g^a, g^b)^c$.
DHP. (Diffie-Hellman problem): Given $g, g^x, g^y \in G_1$ or G_T, determine g^{xy}.
DLP. (discrete logarithm problem): Given $g, g^x \in G_1$ or G_T, determine x.

We summarize the complexity relations between these problems in pairing based cryptography as (The arrow goes from a complexity assumption to a weaker one):

$$BDHP_{G_1} \diagup\begin{array}{c} DHP_{G_1} \\ \diagdown \\ DHP_{G_T} \end{array}\diagup GPI \to FAPI \diagup\begin{array}{c} DLP_{G_1} \\ \updownarrow \\ DLP_{G_T} \end{array}$$

3   Supersingular vs. Ordinary

Let E be an elliptic curve defined over $\mathbb{F}_q$ where q is a power of prime p. If $\#E(\mathbb{F}_q) \equiv 1 \bmod p$, the curve E is *supersingular*, otherwise E is said to be *ordinary*. There are several equivalent conditions for the definition of super-singular curves [18, Chapter V, Theorem 3.1]. We compare the supersingular elliptic curves and ordinary ones in some aspects:

3.1 The Torsion Group

Let $\mathbb{F}_q$ be a finite field of characteristic p and E be an elliptic curve over $\mathbb{F}_q$. Let $\overline{\mathbb{F}_q}$ be the algebraic closure of $\mathbb{F}_q$. Let $r \in \mathbb{Z}$, $r \neq 0$. Define

$$E(\overline{\mathbb{F}_q})[r] = \{P \in E(\overline{\mathbb{F}_q}) : [r]P = \mathcal{O}\}.$$

$E(\overline{\mathbb{F}_q})[r]$ is called as the r-torsion group of $E(\mathbb{F}_q)$. Recall that it is another notation for $Ker[r]$, the set of points of E having order r. It has the property [19]: If $(r, p) = 1$, then

$$E(\overline{\mathbb{F}_q})[r] \cong \mathbb{Z}/r\mathbb{Z} \oplus \mathbb{Z}/r\mathbb{Z}$$

If $r = p^e$, $e = 1, 2, 3, ...$, then

$$E(\overline{\mathbb{F}_q})[r] \cong \begin{cases} \{\mathcal{O}\} & \text{if } E \text{ is supersingular} \\ \mathbb{Z}/p^e\mathbb{Z} & \text{Otherwise.} \end{cases}$$

3.2 The Distortion Map

A distortion map ϕ (defined over $\mathbb{F}_{q^k}$) with respect to a cyclic subgroup $\langle P \rangle$ of order r is an endomorphism (defined over $\mathbb{F}_{q^k}$) of the curve that maps any non-zero point $Q \in \langle P \rangle$ to a point $\phi(Q)$ independent from Q [21]. Verheul proved that the distortion maps always exist on groups of points on supersingular elliptic curves [21, Theorem 5]. Verheul in [21, Theorem 6,7] and Charles in [2, Theorem 2.1] proved that distortion maps for ordinary curves exist only when the embedding degree $k = 1$ and under some certain conditions. Here we deduce an obvious conclusion.

Theorem 3. *Let E be a non-supersingular curve defined over $\mathbb{F}_q$ and let $P \in E(\mathbb{F}_q)$ of order r, where r is prime and coprime to q. If there exist a distortion map w.r.t. P, then the r-torsion group $E(\overline{\mathbb{F}_q})[r] \subset E(\mathbb{F}_q)$. Moreover, $r^2|\#E(\mathbb{F}_q)$ and $r|(q-1)$.*

Proof. This can be derived from [20, Theorem 11] and [19, Proposition 3.7]. ∎

3.3 The Embedding Degree

For supersingular elliptic curves the embedding degree is either $1, 2, 3, 4$ or 6. For ordinary ones the degree is various.

As far as we know, most papers concerned the embedding degree from the beginning that $k \geq 2$, few papers discussed the case $k = 1$. Let $t = q+1-\#E(\mathbb{F}_q)$ be the Frobenius trace. We briefly introduce the existent types of curves with $k = 1$.

Supersingular Curves. Supersingular curves with $k = 1$ exists only over finite field $\mathbb{F}_q$ where $q = p^s$ with s even [17]. In this case, we must have $t = \pm 2\sqrt{q}$, and thus $\#E(\mathbb{F}_q) = (\sqrt{q} \pm 1)^2$.

Ordinary Curves with Frobenius trace $t = 2$.

1. Joux et al. in [11,12] considered the elliptic curve $E(\mathbb{F}_q)$ with Frobenius trace $t = 2$, thus $\#E(\mathbb{F}_q) = q - 1$.
2. Koblitz and Menezes in [10] constructed a type of curves with $t = 2$ as follows. Let $q > 2$ be a prime of the form $A^2 + 1$. If $A \equiv 0 \bmod 4$, let $E : y^2 = x^3 - x$ be the elliptic curve defined over $\mathbb{F}_q$. If $A \equiv 2 \bmod 4$, then let $E : y^2 = x^3 - 4x$ be the curve. In both cases, $\#E(\mathbb{F}_q) = A^2$.
3. Freeman, Scott and Teske in [5] extended the above results and parameterized a complete family of elliptic curves with $k = 1$ and $t = 2$.

4 Our Ordinary Elliptic Curves

Motivated by Theorem 3, we construct two types of ordinary elliptic curves with embedding degree $k = 1$ in this section.

4.1 Type I

Let $\omega = \frac{-1+\sqrt{-3}}{2}$ represent the third root of unity in $\mathbb{C}$, as usual we have $\omega^2 = \overline{\omega}$. The ring $\mathbb{Z}[\omega] = \{c + d\omega | c, d \in \mathbb{Z}\}$ is known as the ring of Eisenstein integers, which is a principal ideal domain. The norm of $c + d\omega \in \mathbb{Z}[\omega]$ is given by $\mathbf{N}(c + d\omega) = (c + d\omega)(\overline{c + d\omega}) = (c^2 - cd + d^2)$.

Let $r \equiv 2 \bmod 3$ be an odd integer and set $R = r^2 + r + 1$. Apparently, $R \equiv 1 \bmod 3$. Let $\pi = \omega - r\overline{\omega}$, then $\pi \equiv 2 \bmod 3$, and thus we have the factorizations $R = \pi\overline{\pi}$. Denote $(\cdot)_6$ as the six residue symbol. Assume r, R are both primes, and $\left(\frac{4b}{\pi}\right)_6 = -\omega$, we consider the ordinary elliptic curve

$$E(\mathbb{F}_R) : y^2 = x^3 + b. \tag{1}$$

Note that $\left(\frac{4b}{\pi}\right)_6 = \left(\frac{b}{\pi}\right)_6 = -\omega$, thus b is neither a square nor a cube in $\mathbb{F}_R^*$. We claim that such b always exists in $\mathbb{F}_R^*$, since $R \equiv 1 \bmod 6$, only one third of the elements of $\mathbb{F}_R^*$ are cubes and only one half of the elements of $\mathbb{F}_R^*$ are squares. Moreover, if we find some β satisfying that polynomial $X^6 - \beta$ is irreducible over $\mathbb{F}_R[X]$, then b can be given by $b = \beta$ or $b = \beta^5$.

The action [3, §7.2.3 Example]

$$\omega : E(\mathbb{F}_R) \to E(\mathbb{F}_R)$$
$$(x, y) \mapsto (r \cdot x, y)$$
$$\mathcal{O} \mapsto \mathcal{O}$$

is an endomorphism of $E(\mathbb{F}_R)$. We note that the group $E(\mathbb{F}_R)$ can be viewed as a $\mathbb{Z}[\omega]$-module.

Lemma 1. $\#E(\mathbb{F}_R) = r^2$.

Proof. By [9, Chap. 18, § 3, Theorem 4], we have

$$\#E(\mathbb{F}_R) = R + 1 + (\frac{\overline{4b}}{\pi})_6 \pi + (\frac{4b}{\pi})_6 \overline{\pi} = R + 1 - (r + 2) = r^2.$$

$\square$

Since $r|R - 1$, we deduce that the embedding degree of $E(\mathbb{F}_R)$ is 1. Note that this type of curve is not some one with Frobenius trace $t = 2$.

Lemma 2. $E(\mathbb{F}_R) \cong \mathbb{Z}[\omega]/(r) \cong \mathbb{Z}/r\mathbb{Z} \oplus \mathbb{Z}/r\mathbb{Z}$.

Proof. Since $\mathbb{Z}[\omega]$ is a principal ideal domain and $E(\mathbb{F}_R)$ is a finite group and a finitely generated $\mathbb{Z}[\omega]$-module, then $E(\mathbb{F}_R)$ is isomorphic to the additive group:

$$\mathbb{Z}[\omega]/(\alpha_1) \oplus \mathbb{Z}[\omega]/(\alpha_2) \oplus \cdots \oplus \mathbb{Z}[\omega]/(\alpha_d)$$

for some $d \in \mathbb{N}$ and $\{\alpha_i\} \subset \mathbb{Z}[\omega]$, $\alpha_1|\alpha_2| \cdots |\alpha_d$. We can view each $\mathbb{Z}[\omega]/(\alpha_i)$ as a subgroup of $E(\mathbb{F}_R)$ and thus $\#\mathbb{Z}[\omega]/(\alpha_i) = \mathbf{N}(\alpha_i) = \alpha_i\overline{\alpha_i}$ divides $\#E(\mathbb{F}_R) = r^2$.

Since $r \equiv 2 \bmod 3$ is prime, then $(\frac{-3}{r}) = -1$, and hence polynomial $X^2 + 3$ is irreducible over $\mathbb{F}_r[X]$, which indicates that r is inert in $\mathbb{Z}[\omega]$ and (r) is the unique prime ideal in $\mathbb{Z}[\omega]$ with norm equal to a power of r. By uniqueness of factorization, we obtain that for each i there exists some n_i such that $(\alpha_i) = (r)^{n_i}$. At last, since $[r]$ is a degree r^2 endomorphism, which implies that $d = 1$.

$\square$

To generalize Verheuls theorem, we need to find distortion maps. We have the following result

Theorem 4. *The action ω is a distortion map on the group $E(\mathbb{F}_R)$.*

Proof. Let P be a point of $E(\mathbb{F}_R)$ with order r. We prove that ω is a distortion map on $\langle P \rangle$. If not, there exists some $\lambda \in \mathbb{Z}$ such that $\omega(P) = [\lambda]P$, then $\lambda^2 + \lambda + 1 \equiv 0 \bmod r$. Thus λ is a solution for the equation $x^2 + x + 1 \equiv 0 \bmod r$ and hence $(\frac{-3}{r}) = 1$, which contradicts to $r \equiv 2 \bmod 3$. So we have $\omega(P) \notin \langle P \rangle$.

$\square$

In fact, $\{P, \omega(P)\}$ generates $E(\mathbb{F}_R)[r]$, and we have

$$\omega \begin{pmatrix} P \\ \omega(P) \end{pmatrix} = \begin{bmatrix} 0 & 1 \\ -1 & -1 \end{bmatrix} \begin{pmatrix} P \\ \omega(P) \end{pmatrix}$$

4.2   Type II

Let $r \equiv 3 \bmod 4$ be an integer and set $R = 16r^2 + 1$. Apparently, $R \equiv 1 \bmod 4$. Setting $\pi = 1 + 4ri$, we have the factorizations $R = \pi\overline{\pi}$. Note that $\pi \equiv 1 \bmod (2 + 2i)$. Assume r and R are both primes, we consider the ordinary elliptic curve

$$E(\mathbb{F}_R) : y^2 = x^3 - x. \tag{2}$$

The action [3, §7.2.3 Example]

$$i : E(\mathbb{F}_p) \to E(\mathbb{F}_p)$$
$$(x, y) \mapsto (-x, 4r \cdot y)$$
$$\mathcal{O} \mapsto \mathcal{O}$$

is an endomorphism on the group $E(\mathbb{F}_R)$. We observe that the group $E(\mathbb{F}_R)$ can be viewed as a $\mathbb{Z}[i]$-module.

Lemma 3. $\#E(\mathbb{F}_R) = 16r^2$.

Proof. By [9, Chap. 18, § 4, Theorem 5], we have

$$\#E(\mathbb{F}_R) = R + 1 - (\frac{\overline{1}}{\pi})_4 \pi - (\frac{1}{\pi})_4 \overline{\pi} = R + 1 - 2 = 16r^2.$$

$\square$

Since $r|R - 1$, we deduce that the embedding degree $k = 1$.

Lemma 4. $E(\mathbb{F}_R) \cong \mathbb{Z}[i]/(4ri) \cong \mathbb{Z}/4r\mathbb{Z} \oplus \mathbb{Z}/4r\mathbb{Z}$.

Proof. The proof is similar to that for Lemma 2. Actually, as claimed in [10], since all $\mathbb{F}_R$-points on E are in the kernel of the endomorphism $\pi - 1 = 4ri$, the $\mathbb{Z}[i]$-module $E(\mathbb{F}_R)$ is isomorphic to $\mathbb{Z}[i]/(4ri) \cong \mathbb{Z}/4r\mathbb{Z} \oplus \mathbb{Z}/4r\mathbb{Z}$. $\square$

The corresponding distortion map is given by the following theorem

Theorem 5. *The action i is a distortion map on the group $E(\mathbb{F}_R)$.*

Proof. Note that $(\frac{-1}{r}) = -1$, the proof is similar to that for Theorem 3. $\square$

Our type II curve is a special case of Koblitz and Menezes's trace 2 curves in [10]. Let P be a point of $E(\mathbb{F}_R)$ with order r, $\{P, i(P)\}$ generates $E(\mathbb{F}_R)[r]$, and we have

$$i \begin{pmatrix} P \\ i(P) \end{pmatrix} = \begin{bmatrix} 0 & 1 \\ -1 & 0 \end{bmatrix} \begin{pmatrix} P \\ i(P) \end{pmatrix}$$

5 Applications

5.1 Generalized Verheul's Theorem

We would like to show that if the pairing inversion problem could be solved on our embedding degree $k = 1$ curves, then the DLP on the same curves is equivalent to (and not easier than) the DLP in $\mathbb{F}_R^*$. The result is put as follows:

Theorem 6. *Given an ordinary elliptic curve $E(\mathbb{F}_R)$ as Type I or II. Then $E(\mathbb{F}_R)[r]$ is a product of two cyclic groups of order r. Let P be a generator for one of the cyclic subgroups. Let μ_r be the group of rth roots of unity in $\mathbb{F}_R^*$. Under the MOV embedding, we have an isomorphism from $\langle P \rangle$ to μ_r. If an efficiently computable isomorphism can be found from μ_r to $\langle P \rangle$, then the DHP can be efficiently solved in both μ_r and $\langle P \rangle$.*

Proof. (Sketch) Denote by $I : \mu_r \to \langle P \rangle$ the isomorphism. Let ϕ be the corresponding distortion map on $E(\mathbb{F}_R)$ for P, then P and $\phi(P)$ are linearly independent. Let e be the Weil pairing. Set $\zeta = e(P, \phi(P))$, then ζ is a generator for μ_r. Suppose we are given $P, [a]P, [b]P$. If $I(\zeta) = [c]P$, then by the method of Verheul in [20,21], we compute $Q = [c^{-2}]P = [c^{r-3}]P$ as follows: Given $[c^i]P$ one can compute $[c^{i+1}]P = I(e(P, \phi([c^i]P)))$ and $[c^{2i+1}]P = I(e([c^i]P, \phi([c^i]P)))$. At last, we have $[ab]P = I(e(I(e(I(e([c^{-2}]P, \phi([a]P))), \phi([b]P))))$, which shows that the DHP in $\langle P \rangle$ can be efficiently solved. Moreover, it follows that the DHP in μ_r can also be efficiently solved. $\qquad\square$

5.2   Pairings on Our Curves

Let $f_{r,P}$ be the function whose divisor is $r(P) - r(\mathcal{O})$. For $P, Q \in E(\mathbb{F}_R)[r]$, $Q \notin \langle P \rangle$, the Weil pairing e and the Tate pairing t of P, Q are given by

$$e(P, Q) = f_{r,P}(Q)/f_{r,Q}(P), t(P, Q) = f_{r,P}(Q)^{(R-1)/r}.$$

The distortion map ϕ on our curve maps point $P(\neq \mathcal{O})$ to $\phi(P)$, which is linearly independent from P. As consequences, the Weil pairing e and the Tate pairing t of P and $\phi(P)$ are non-trival, thus we can modify both e and t of $P_1, P_2 \in \langle P \rangle$ as

$$\hat{e}(P_1, P_2) = e(P_1, \phi(P_2)), \hat{t}(P_1, P_2) = t(P_1, \phi(P_2))$$

which are non-degenerate type 1 pairings in Section 2.1, thus they satisfy all the required properties for realizing a single point tripartite Diffie-Hellman protocol in [11] and other type 1 pairing based protocols.

Since the pairings on our type I or II curves take values in the base prime field $\mathbb{F}_R$ over which the curves are defined, we do not need computation in any extension field. The Miller algorithm [14,15] has been widely used to compute the Weil and Tate pairings. It is convenient for us to use the Jacobian coordinates [1,8] on our curves. For elliptic curve $E : Y^2 Z = X^3 + aXZ^2 + bZ^3$ in Jacobian coordinates, a point (X, Y, Z) corresponds to the point (x, y) in affine coordinates with $x = X/Z^2, y = Y/Z^3$. Doubling a point $T = (X, Y, Z)$ as $[2]T = (X_2, Y_2, Z_2)$.

$$X_2 = (3X^2 + aZ^4)^2 - 8XY^2,$$
$$Y_2 = (3X^2 + aZ^4)(4XY^2 - X_2) - 8Y^4,$$
$$Z_2 = 2YZ.$$

We should also evaluate the iterative function

$$f_1 \leftarrow f_1^2 \cdot \iota_1 \upsilon_2;$$
$$f_2 \leftarrow f_2^2 \cdot \iota_2 \upsilon_1;$$
$$\iota(x, y) = \iota_1(x, y)/\iota_2$$
$$= (Z_2 Z^2 y - 2Y^2 - (3X^2 + aZ^4)(xZ^2 - X))/(Z_2 Z^2);$$
$$\upsilon(x) = \upsilon_1(x)/\upsilon_2 = (Z_2^2 x - X_2)/Z_2^2.$$

Let S denote squaring and M denote multiplying in $\mathbb{F}_R$. For each doubling step of Miller algorithm, the field operation count for computing Tate pairing on Type I curves is $8S + 12M$ (w.r.t. $9S + 12M$ on Type II curves). Since computing Weil pairing needs this procedure twice, each doubling step of Miller algorithm costs $16S + 24M$ for Weil pairing computation on Type I curves (w.r.t. $18S + 24M$ on Type II curves). The computation of Tate pairing also needs a extra final exponentiation which costs about $(B_R/B_r - 1)B_r S$, where B_x denotes the bit length of x.

Note that in our construction, if r has a low hamming weight, then so does R (Example curves are given in Appendix). Hence the cost of adds/substracts is negligible compared to that of doublings. Since $B_R/B_r \approx 2$ for Type I and II curves, and then $(B_R/B_r - 1)B_r S < B_r(8S + 12M)$, we point out that the computation of Tate pairing is usually faster than that of Weil pairing on our curves.

Acknowledgments. The authors would like to thank Prof. Nigel Smart for some suggestions on the pairing inversion problem, and thank the anonymous reviewers for their helpful comments and constructive suggestions on an earlier version of this paper.

References

1. Avanzi, R., Cohen, H., Doche, C., Frey, G., Lange, T., Nguyen, K., Vercauteren, F.: Handbook of Elliptic and Hyperelliptic Cryptography. Chapman and Hall/CRC (2006)
2. Charles, D.: On the Existence of Distortion Maps on Ordinary Elliptic Curves. Cryptology ePrint Archive Report 2006/128, http://eprint.iacr.org/2006/128/
3. Cohen, H.: A Course in Computational Algebraic Number Theory. Springer, Berlin (1996)
4. Frey, G., Rück, H.: A Remark Concerning m-divisibility and The Discrete Logarithm in The Divisor Class Group of Curves. Math. Comp. 62, 865–874 (1994)
5. Freeman, D., Scott, M., Teske, E.: A Taxonomy of Pairing-Friendly Elliptic Curves. J. Cryptology 23, 224–280 (2010)
6. Galbraith, S.D., Hess, F., Vercauteren, F.: Aspects of Pairing Inversion. IEEE Trans. Inform. Theory 12, 5719–5728 (2008)
7. Galbraith, S.D., Paterson, K.G., Smart, N.P.: Pairings for Cryptographers. Discrete Applied Mathematics 156, 3113–3121 (2008)
8. Hankerson, D., Menezes, A.J., Vanstone, S.: Guide to Elliptic Curve Cryptography. Springer, Heidelberg (2004)
9. Ireland, K., Rosen, M.: A Classical Introduction to Modern Number Theory, 2nd edn. Grad. Texts in Math., vol. 84. Springer, New York (1990)
10. Koblitz, N., Menezes, A.J.: Pairing-Based Cryptography at High Security Levels. In: Smart, N.P. (ed.) Cryptography and Coding 2005. LNCS, vol. 3796, pp. 13–36. Springer, Heidelberg (2005)
11. Joux, A.: A One Round Protocol for Tripartite Diffie-Hellman. J. Cryptology 17, 263–276 (2004)

12. Joux, A., Nguyen, K.: Separating Decision Diffie-Hellman from Computational Diffie-Hellman in Cryptographic Groups. J. Cryptology 16, 239–247 (2003)
13. Lenstra, A.K., Verheul, E.R.: The XTR Public Key System. In: Bellare, M. (ed.) CRYPTO 2000. LNCS, vol. 1880, pp. 1–19. Springer, Heidelberg (2000)
14. Miller, V.S.: Short Programs for Functions on Curves. Unpublished manuscript (1986)
15. Miller, V.S.: The Weil Pairing, and Its Efficient Calculation. J. Cryptology 17, 235–261 (2004)
16. Moody, D.: The Diffie-Hellman Problem and Generalization of Verheuls Theorem. Des. Codes Cryptogr. 52, 381–390 (2009)
17. Menezes, A.J., Okamoto, T., Vanstone, S.A.: Reducing Elliptic Curve Logarithms to Logarithms in a Finite Field. IEEE Trans. Inform. Theory 39(5), 1639–1646 (1993)
18. Silverman, J.: The Arithmetic of Elliptic Curves. Springer, New York (1986)
19. Schoof, R.: Nonsingular Plane Cubic Curves over Finite Fields. J. Combinatorial Theory, Series A 46(2), 183–208 (1987)
20. Verheul, E.R.: Evidence that XTR Is More Secure than Supersingular Elliptic Curve Cryptosystems. In: Pfitzmann, B. (ed.) EUROCRYPT 2001. LNCS, vol. 2045, pp. 195–210. Springer, Heidelberg (2001)
21. Verheul, R.: Evidence that XTR Is More Secure than Supersingular Elliptic Curve Cryptosystems. J. Cryptology 17, 277–296 (2004)

Appendix: Examples

Type I

80-bit security level:

$$r = 2^{160} + 29431, E(\mathbb{F}_R) : y^2 = x^3 + 97.$$

128-bit security level:

$$r = 2^{256} + 98545, E(\mathbb{F}_R) : y^2 = x^3 + 3.$$

256-bit security level:

$$r = 2^{512} + 436711, E(\mathbb{F}_R) : y^2 = x^3 + 29.$$

Type II

80-bit security level:

$$r = 2^{160} + 23923, E(\mathbb{F}_R) : y^2 = x^3 - x.$$

128-bit security level:

$$r = 2^{256} + 95203, E(\mathbb{F}_R) : y^2 = x^3 - x.$$

256-bit security level:

$$r = 2^{512} + 611515, E(\mathbb{F}_R) : y^2 = x^3 - x.$$

On the Combinatorial Approaches of Computing Upper Bounds on the Information Rate of Secret Sharing Schemes[*]

Zhanfei Zhou

State Key Laboratory of Information Security,
Graduate University of Chinese Academy of Sciences,
Beijing, China 100049

Abstract. Computing the information rate of access structures is an important part of the research of secret sharing schemes. In this paper, we investigate two combinatorial approaches of computing upper bounds on the information rate of access structures - the Csirmaz's polymatroid approach and the independent sequence approach. We prove that the Csirmaz's polymatroid approach is only a special variant of the independent sequence approach, and finding an independent sequence with respect to a graph-based access structure with maximum length is equivalent to finding a maximum alternating cycle-free matching in a bipartite graph, which is a NP hard problem.

Keywords: secret sharing scheme, graph-based access structure, independent sequence, alternating cycle-free matching of a bipartite graph.

1 Introduction

A secret sharing scheme (SSS) consists of a dealer p_0, a finite set P of participants and a collection $\mathcal{A}$ of subsets of P called the access structure. In a SSS realizing access structure $\mathcal{A}$, the dealer p_0 distributes shares of a secret to participants such that any qualified subset $A \in \mathcal{A}$ can reconstruct the secret from its shares, whereas any unqualified subset $A \notin \mathcal{A}$ can't reveal any partial information about the secret in information theoretic sense. SSS was firstly proposed for the threshold case by Blakley [1] and Shamir [15] in 1979, and generalized by Ito et al. [11] to general cases.

In a SSS, data expansion, i.e. the size of every share set is no less than that of the secret set [12], makes it difficult to manage shares. In order to measure it, the concept of information rate was introduced by Brickell et al. [6]. By information theoretic approach, Capocelli et al.[7] firstly gave upper bounds on the information rate of some access structures. Henceforward, the information rates of some access structures were given in [3–6, 9, 16].

---

[*] Supported by National Natural Science Foundation of China (Grant No. 60573004) and National Basic Research Program of China (973 Program, Grant No. 2007CB311202).

Computing the information rate of access structures consists of computing an upper bound on the information rate by information theoretic approach and computing a lower bound on the information rate by an approach called decomposition of access structures. When an upper bound and a lower bound on the information rate of an access structure are equal, the exact value of the information rate of the access structure is reached. However, the information theoretic approach is so technical and empirical that it seems very difficult to compute upper bound on the information rate of an access structure over a large set of participants. Up to date, the known upper bounds on the information rate of access structures are confined to that of some graph-based access structures [3–6, 9, 16] and that of some special access structures [8]. By submodularity of a polymatroid, a class of access structures with known upper bounds on the information rate is constructed by Csirmaz [8]. For the first time, this approach makes it possible to compute upper bounds on the information rate only by combinatorial property of access structures. Based on the previous works, Blundo et al. [2] introduced an approach called independent sequence. With the help of the Csirmaz's polymatroid approach and the independent sequence approach, researchers can compute upper bounds on the information rate of access structures from combinatorial point of view. However, few research works had been devoted to this area, the relationship between the Csirmaz's polymatroid approach and the independent sequence approach, and how to find an independent sequence with maximum length are still not known.

In this paper, the relationship between the Csirmaz's polymatroid approach and the independent sequence approach, and properties of independent sequences with respect to graph-based access structures have been investigated, and the problem of finding an independent sequence with respect to a graph-based access structure with maximum length has been reduced to that of finding a maximum alternating cycle-free matching in a bipartite graph. In Section 2, some basic notions and related results will be introduced. In Section 3, the relationship between the Csirmaz's polymatroid approach and the independent sequence approach will be discussed. Finally, properties of independent sequences with respect to graph-based access structures will be investigated.

2 Notions and Related Results

Let P be a set of participants, a collection of subsets $\mathcal{A} \subseteq 2^P$ is an access structure over P, if it is monotone, i.e. $A \in \mathcal{A}$ and $A \subseteq B \subseteq P$ implies $B \in \mathcal{A}$. Given an access structure $\mathcal{A}$ over P, let $\mathcal{A}_m = \{A \in \mathcal{A} : B \subset A \Rightarrow B \notin \mathcal{A}\}$. Let $\mathcal{A}$ be an access structure over P and $X \subseteq P$, the restriction of $\mathcal{A}$ to X is defined as $\mathcal{A}|_X = \{A \in \mathcal{A} : A \subseteq X\}$. Obviously, the restriction of access structure $\mathcal{A}$ to X is still an access structure, and $(\mathcal{A}|_X)_m = \mathcal{A}_m|_X$.

Firstly, let's introduce the formal definition of secret sharing schemes.

Definition 1. *Let $P = \{p_1, p_2, \cdots, p_n\}$ be a set of participants, $\mathcal{A} \subseteq 2^P$ be an access structure over P, and $S, S_1, \cdots, S_n$ be $n + 1$ finite sets. Suppose $\pi \subseteq S \times S_1 \times \cdots \times S_n$ is the probability space of random variables $(p_0, p_1, \cdots, p_n)$*

such that for any $\alpha \in \pi$, the probability $P(\alpha) > 0$. π is a secret sharing scheme (SSS) realizing access structure $\mathcal{A}$, if it satisfies the following conditions:

1. $\forall A \in \mathcal{A}$, $H(S|A) = 0$,
2. $\forall A \notin \mathcal{A}$, $H(S|A) = H(S)$,

where $H(\cdot)$ is the entropy function.

Let $P' = P \cup \{p_0\}$ and $A = \{p_{j_1}, p_{j_2}, \cdots, p_{j_k}\}$ be a subset of P', where $0 \leq j_1 \leq \cdots \leq j_k \leq n$. For $\alpha = (s, s_1, \cdots, s_n) \in \pi$, let $\alpha(A) = (s_{j_1}, s_{j_2}, \cdots, s_{j_k})$. $S' = \{\alpha(p_0) : \alpha \in \pi\}$ is the secret space of the SSS π, and $S'_j = \{\alpha(p_j) : \alpha \in \pi\}$ is the share space of the SSS π corresponding to p_j, where $1 \leq j \leq n$. For convenience, we still denote the secret space by S, and denote the share space corresponding to p_j by S_j.

Karnin et al.[12] proved that in a SSS, $H(S_i) \geq H(S), \forall 1 \leq i \leq n$. To measure data expansion in a SSS, Brickell et al. [6] introduced the concept of information rate.

Definition 2. *Let P be a set of participants, $\mathcal{A}$ be an access structure over P, and $PS(\mathcal{A})$ be a SSS realizing access structure $\mathcal{A}$. The information rate of SSS $PS(\mathcal{A})$ is defined as*

$$\rho(PS(\mathcal{A})) = \min_{p_i \in P} H(S)/H(S_i)$$

where S is the secret space and $S_i(1 \leq i \leq n)$ is the share space. $\rho(\mathcal{A}) = \sup\{\rho(PS(\mathcal{A}))\}$ is called the information rate of access structure $\mathcal{A}$.

To derive an upper bound on the information rate, computing a lower bound on the mutual information $I(A; B)$ between $A \subseteq P$ and $B \subseteq P$ is the key point[16]. To solve this problem, Csirmaz [8] used a polymatroid approach, and Blundo et al. [2] proposed the concept of independent sequence.

In the following, we will introduce the concept of polymatroid and its properties, please refer to [14, 17] for details.

Definition 3. *A polymatroid is a pair $\mathcal{S} = (Q, f)$ satisfying the following conditions, where $f : 2^Q \rightarrow \mathcal{R}$.*

1. $f(\emptyset) = 0$,
2. *monotone: if $X \subseteq Y \subseteq Q$, then $f(X) \leq f(Y)$,*
3. *submodular: if $X, Y \subseteq Q$, then $f(X) + f(Y) \geq f(X \cup Y) + f(X \cap Y)$.*

Let π be a SSS, and $A \subseteq P'$, define $f(A) = H(A)/H(S)$. It's easy to verify that (P', f) is a polymatroid, and satisfies the following conditions [8].

Proposition 1. *The function f defined above satisfies the following conditions:*

1. *if $A \subseteq B$, $A \notin \mathcal{A}$ and $B \in \mathcal{A}$, then $f(B) \geq f(A) + 1$,*
2. *if $A \in \mathcal{A}$, $B \in \mathcal{A}$ and $A \cap B \notin \mathcal{A}$, then $f(A) + f(B) \geq f(A \cup B) + f(A \cap B) + 1$.*

Based on the previous works, Blundo et al.[2] proposed an independent sequence approach.

Definition 4. *Let $\mathcal{A}$ be an access structure over P, and $A, B \subseteq P$, where $B \notin \mathcal{A}$. A sequence of pairs $(A_1, B_1), \cdots, (A_n, B_n)$ is an independent sequence of (A, B) with respect to access structure $\mathcal{A}$ with length $n - 1$, if $A_1, \cdots, A_n \subseteq A$, $B_1 \subseteq \cdots \subseteq B_n = B$ and the following conditions are satisfied.*

1. $\forall 1 \leq i \leq n$, $A_i \cup B_i \in \mathcal{A}$,
2. $\forall 1 \leq i \leq n - 1$, $A_{i+1} \cup B_i \notin \mathcal{A}$.

Given an independent sequence $(A_1, B_1), \cdots, (A_n, B_n)$, it can be proved

$$H(A|B_i) - H(A|B_{i+1}) \geq H(S), \ \forall 1 \leq i \leq n - 1.$$

By this property, lower bound on the conditional mutual information between A and B can be derived as follows:

$$\begin{aligned} I(A; B|B_1) &= H(A|B_1) - H(A|B_n) \\ &= \sum_{i=1}^{n-1}(H(A|B_i) - H(A|B_{i+1})) \\ &\geq (n-1)H(S) \end{aligned}$$

In this paper, we will investigate independent sequences with respect to graph-based access structures. Now, let's introduce some basic concepts of graph theory.

Let $G = (V, E)$ be a finite, undirected simple graph. A sequence $(v_1, v_2, \cdots, v_k)$ of distinct vertices forms a path in G, if for any $2 \leq i \leq k$, $\{v_{i-1}, v_i\} \in E$. A path $(v_1, v_2, \cdots, v_k)$ forms a cycle in G if $\{v_1, v_k\} \in E$. A graph $G = (V, E)$ is a bipartite graph, if there is a partition of V into two disjoint subsets X, Y such that every edge has its end in different sets. A bipartite graph is also denoted by (X, Y, E). A set $M \subseteq E$ of nonadjacent edges is a matching in G. For a given matching M, a cycle C is an alternating cycle if there is a numeration such that $C = (v_1, v_2, \cdots, v_{2k})$ and for any $i \in \{1, 2, \cdots, k\}$, $\{v_{2i-1}, v_{2i}\} \in M$. A matching M in G is alternating cycle-free if G has no alternating cycle with respect to M.

Given a graph G with the participants as its vertices, an access structure based on G consists of all subsets containing an edge of G.

3   On the Relationship between the Csirmaz's Polymatroid Approach and the Independent Sequence Approach

At first, let's summarize the Csirmaz's polymatroid approach as follows.

Definition 5. *Let $A_1, A_2, B_1, B_2 \subseteq P$, where $A_1 \cup B_2 = A_2$, $A_1 \cap B_2 = B_1$ and $A_1 \in \mathcal{A}, B_2 \notin \mathcal{A}$. $(A_1, B_1), (A_2, B_2)$ is a grid of (A_1, B_2) with respect to access structure $\mathcal{A}$, if there is $B_2 \subseteq Y \subseteq A_2$ such that $Y \in \mathcal{A}$ and $X = A_1 \cap Y \notin \mathcal{A}$. $(A_1, B_1), (A_2, B_2), \cdots, (A_n, B_n)$ is a sequence of grids of (A_1, B_n) with respect to access structure $\mathcal{A}$ with length $n - 1$, if for any $1 \leq i \leq n - 1$, $(A_i, B_i), (A_{i+1}, B_{i+1})$ is a grid with respect to access structure $\mathcal{A}$.*

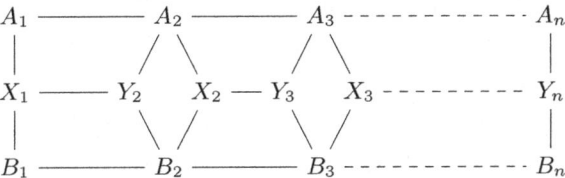

Fig. 1. A sequence of grids

Given a grid $(A_1, B_1), (A_2, B_2)$, it's obvious that $A_1 \cup Y = A_2$, $X \cup B_2 = Y$ and $X \cap B_2 = B_1$. And for a sequence of grids $(A_1, B_1), (A_2, B_2), \cdots, (A_n, B_n)$, it can be proved that $A_1 \cup B_n = A_n$ and $A_1 \cap B_n = B_1$. By submodularity of polymatroid and Proposition 1(2), we have

$$f(A_1) + f(Y) \geq f(A_2) + f(X) + 1$$
$$f(X) + f(B_2) \geq f(Y) + f(B_1)$$

Add the above inequalities, we get

$$f(A_1) - f(B_1) \geq f(A_2) - f(B_2) + 1$$

Then for a sequence $(A_1, B_1), (A_2, B_2), \cdots, (A_n, B_n)$ of grids,

$$f(A_i) - f(B_i) \geq f(A_{i+1}) - f(B_{i+1}) + 1, \quad \forall 1 \leq i \leq n - 1$$

Hence

$$f(A_1) - f(B_1) \geq f(A_n) - f(B_n) + (n - 1)$$

By definition of grid, we have $A_1 \cup B_n = A_n, A_1 \cap B_n = B_1$. By definition of function f in the polymatroid induced by a SSS, the following inequality can be deduced.

$$
\begin{aligned}
I(A_1; B_n | B_1) &= H(A_1 | B_1) - H(A_1 | B_n) \\
&= H(A_1) - H(B_1) - H(A_n) + H(B_n) \\
&= (f(A_1) - f(B_1) - f(A_n) + f(B_n))H(S) \\
&\geq (n - 1)H(S)
\end{aligned}
$$

Similar to that of the independent sequence approach, from the above inequality we can obtain an upper bound on the information rate of access structure $\mathcal{A}$.

Theorem 1. *There is a sequence of grids of (A, B) with respect to access structure $\mathcal{A}$ with length $n-1 \Leftrightarrow$ there is an independent sequence $(A'_1, B_1), \cdots, (A'_n, B_n)$ of (A, B) with respect to access structure $\mathcal{A}$ with length $n-1$ such that $A \cap B \subseteq B_1$.*

Proof: "$\Leftarrow$" Let $(A_1, B_1), \cdots, (A_n, B_n)$ be a sequence of grids of (A, B) with respect to access structure $\mathcal{A}$. By the definition of grid, for any $2 \leq i \leq n$, there is $B_i \subseteq Y_i \subseteq A_i$ such that $Y_i \in \mathcal{A}$ and $X_i = A_{i-1} \cap Y_i \notin \mathcal{A}$. Let $A_1' = A_1 \backslash B_1$ and $A_i' = Y_i \backslash B_i (2 \leq i \leq n)$. For any $2 \leq i \leq n$,

$$
\begin{aligned}
A_i' \cup B_{i-1} &= (Y_i \backslash B_i) \cup B_{i-1} \\
&= (X_{i-1} \backslash B_i) \cup B_{i-1} \qquad \text{(from the fact that } X_{i-1} \cup B_i = Y_i) \\
&= (X_{i-1} \backslash B_i) \cup (X_{i-1} \cap B_i) \text{ (from the fact that } X_{i-1} \cap B_i = B_{i-1}) \\
&= X_{i-1} \notin \mathcal{A}.
\end{aligned}
$$

For any $2 \leq i \leq n$,

$$
\begin{aligned}
A_i' &= Y_i \backslash B_i \\
&\subseteq A_i \backslash B_i \qquad \text{(from the definition of a grid)} \\
&= (A_1 \cup B_i) \backslash B_i \text{ (frome the fact that } A_1 \cup B_i = A_i) \\
&= A_1 \backslash B_i \\
&\subseteq A_1.
\end{aligned}
$$

Hence $(A_1', B_1), \cdots, (A_n', B_n)$ is an independent sequence of (A, B) with respect to access structure $\mathcal{A}$.

"$\Rightarrow$" Let $(A_1', B_1), \cdots, (A_n', B_n)$ be an independent sequence of (A, B) with respect to $\mathcal{A}$ such that $A \cap B \subseteq B_1$. For any $1 \leq i \leq n$, let $A_i = A \cup B_i$. Obviously, for $2 \leq i \leq n$, $A_{i-1} \cup B_i = (A \cup B_{i-1}) \cup B_i = A \cup B_i = A_i$, and since $A \cap B_i \subseteq A \cap B_n \subseteq B_1 \subseteq B_{i-1}$, $A_{i-1} \cap B_i = (A \cup B_{i-1}) \cap B_i = (A \cap B_i) \cup B_{i-1} = B_{i-1}$. Let $Y_i = A_i' \cup B_i$, and $X_i = A_{i-1} \cap Y_i$. By definition of independent sequence, $Y_i = A_i' \cup B_i \in \mathcal{A}$, $X_i = (A \cup B_{i-1}) \cap (A_i' \cup B_i) = A_i' \cup B_{i-1} \notin \mathcal{A}$. Hence $(A_1, B_1), \cdots, (A_n, B_n)$ is a sequence of grids of (A, B) with respect to access structure $\mathcal{A}$.

4 Independent Sequences with Respect to Graph-Based Access Structures

For convenience, we adopt the following definition of independent sequence, which is equivalent to Definition 4.

Definition 6. *Let $\mathcal{A}$ be an access structure over P. Given $A, B \subseteq P$, where $B \notin \mathcal{A}$. $(A_1, B_1), \cdots, (A_n, B_n)$ is an independent sequence of (A, B) with respect to access structure $\mathcal{A}$ with length $n - 1$, if it satisfies the following conditions, where $\forall 1 \leq i \leq n$, $A_i \subseteq A$ and $B_i \subseteq B$.*

1. $\forall 1 \leq i \leq n$, $A_i \cup B_i \in \mathcal{A}$,
2. $\forall 2 \leq i \leq n$, $A_i \cup (\bigcup_1^{i-1} B_j) \notin \mathcal{A}$.

Obviously, $(A_1, B_1), \cdots, (A_n, B_n)$ is an independent sequence of (A, B) with respect to access structure $\mathcal{A}$ if and only if $(A_1, B_1), \cdots, (A_n, B_n)$ is an independent sequence of (A, B) with respect to access structure $\mathcal{A}|_{A \cup B}$. Hence in this section, we always assume $P = A \cup B$.

An independent sequence $(A_1, B_1), \cdots, (A_n, B_n)$ of (A, B) with respect to access structure $\mathcal{A}$ is reduced, if for any $1 \leq i \leq n$, $A_i \cup B_i \in \mathcal{A}_m$ and $A_i \cap B_i = \emptyset$.

It can be verified that there is an independent sequence of (A, B) with respect to access structure $\mathcal{A}$ with length $n-1$ if and only if there is a reduced independent sequence of (A, B) with respect to access structure $\mathcal{A}$ with length $n - 1$. Unless specified definitely, we always assume the independent sequence in the following paper is reduced.

Let $\mathcal{A}^*$ be an access structure over P such that $(\mathcal{A}^*)_m = \mathcal{A}_m \backslash (\mathcal{A}|_{A \backslash B})_m$. Obviously, $\mathcal{A}^* \subseteq \mathcal{A}$.

Lemma 1. *Let $\mathcal{A}$ be a graph-based access structure over P, and $B \notin \mathcal{A}$. (A_1, B_1), $\cdots$, (A_n, B_n) is an independent sequence of (A, B) with respect to access structure $\mathcal{A}$, where $B_1 \neq \emptyset$ if and only if $(A_1, B_1), \cdots, (A_n, B_n)$ is an independent sequence of $(A \backslash B, B)$ with respect to access structure $\mathcal{A}^*$.*

Proof: "$\Leftarrow$" Let $(A_1, B_1), \cdots, (A_n, B_n)$ be an independent sequence of (A, B) with respect to access structure $\mathcal{A}$, and $B_1 \neq \emptyset$. Then for any $1 \leq i \leq n$, $B_i \neq \emptyset$. For any $1 \leq i \leq n$, since $\mathcal{A}$ is a graph-based access structure over P and $A_i \cup B_i \in \mathcal{A}_m$, then $|A_i \cup B_i| = 2$. In addition, since $B_i \neq \emptyset$, we have $|A_i| = 1$. Hence $A_i \subseteq A \backslash B$. From $A_i \cup B_i \nsubseteq A \backslash B$, we can deduce $A_i \cup B_i \notin (\mathcal{A}|_{A \backslash B})_m$. Hence $A_i \cup B_i \in \mathcal{A}_m^*$. For any $2 \leq i \leq n$, $A_i \cup (\bigcup_1^{i-1} B_j) \notin \mathcal{A}$ implies $A_i \cup (\bigcup_1^{i-1} B_j) \notin \mathcal{A}^*$.

"$\Rightarrow$" Let $(A_1, B_1), \cdots, (A_n, B_n)$ be an independent sequence of $(A \backslash B, B)$ with respect to access structure $\mathcal{A}^*$. Then $B_1 \neq \emptyset$. Now prove that $\forall 2 \leq i \leq n, A_i \cup (\bigcup_1^{i-1} B_j) \notin \mathcal{A}$. Assume that there exists $2 \leq i \leq n$ such that $A_i \cup (\bigcup_1^{i-1} B_j) \in \mathcal{A}$. Choose $X \subseteq A_i \cup (\bigcup_1^{i-1} B_j)$ arbitrarily such that $X \in \mathcal{A}_m$, then either $X \in (\mathcal{A}^*)_m$ or $X \in (\mathcal{A}|_{A \backslash B})_m$. Since $A_i \cup (\bigcup_1^{i-1} B_j) \notin \mathcal{A}^*$, then $X \notin (\mathcal{A}^*)_m$. If $X \in (\mathcal{A}|_{A \backslash B})_m$, then $X \subseteq A \backslash B$. Hence $X = X \backslash B \subseteq A_i$, contradicted with $A_i \notin \mathcal{A}$.

Lemma 2. *Let $\mathcal{A}$ be a graph-based access structure over P, and $B \notin \mathcal{A}$. If $A_1 \in \mathcal{A}_m$, $B_1 = \emptyset$ and $(A_2, B_2), \cdots, (A_n, B_n)$ is an independent sequence of (A, B) with respect to access structure $\mathcal{A}$, where $\forall 2 \leq i \leq n$, $B_i \neq \emptyset$, then $(A_1, B_1), \cdots, (A_n, B_n)$ is an independent sequence of (A, B) with respect to access structure $\mathcal{A}$.*

Proof: Since $B_2 \neq \emptyset$ and $A_2 \cup B_2 \in \mathcal{A}_m$, $A_2 \notin \mathcal{A}$. Hence $A_2 \cup B_1 = A_2 \notin \mathcal{A}$. On the other hand, $\forall 2 \leq i \leq n$, $A_i \cup (\bigcup_1^{i-1} B_j) = A_i \cup (\bigcup_2^{i-1} B_j) \notin \mathcal{A}$.

Proposition 2. *Let $\mathcal{A}$ be a graph-based access structure over P, and $A, B \notin \mathcal{A}$. $(A_1, B_1), \cdots,$ (A_n, B_n) is an independent sequence of (A, B) with respect to access structure $\mathcal{A}$ if and only if $(A_1, B_1), \cdots, (A_n, B_n)$ is an independent sequence of $(A \backslash B, B)$ with respect to access structure $\mathcal{A}^*$.*

Proof: Since $A \notin \mathcal{A}$, $B_1 \neq \emptyset$. By Lemma 1, this proposition can be proved.

Proposition 3. *Let $\mathcal{A}$ be a graph-based access structure over P, and $A \in \mathcal{A}, B \notin \mathcal{A}$. $(A_1, B_1), \cdots,$*

(A_n, B_n) *is an independent sequence of* (A, B) *with respect to access structure* $\mathcal{A}$ *with maximum length if and only if* $A_1 \in \mathcal{A}_m$, $B_1 = \emptyset$ *and* $(A_2, B_2), \cdots, (A_n, B_n)$ *is an independent sequence of* $(A \backslash B, B)$ *with respect to access structure* $\mathcal{A}^*$ *with maximum length.*

Proof: "$\Leftarrow$" Let $(A_1, B_1), \cdots, (A_n, B_n)$ be an independent sequence of (A, B) with respect to $\mathcal{A}$ with maximum length. Obviously, $\forall 2 \leq i \leq n$, $B_i \neq \emptyset$. Now prove $B_1 = \emptyset$. Assume $B_1 \neq \emptyset$. Choose $A_0 \subseteq A$, $B_0 = \emptyset$ arbitrarily such that $A_0 \in \mathcal{A}_m$. By Lemma 2, $(A_0, B_0), \cdots, (A_n, B_n)$ is an independent sequence of (A, B) with respect to access structure $\mathcal{A}$, contradiction. Assume $(A_2', B_2'), \cdots, (A_{n'}', B_{n'}')$ is an independent sequence of $(A \backslash B, B)$ with respect to access structure $\mathcal{A}^*$ (where $n' > n$). By Lemma 1, we have that $(A_2', B_2'), \cdots, (A_{n'}', B_{n'}')$ is an independent sequence of (A, B) with respect to access structure $\mathcal{A}$ and $B_2' \neq \emptyset$. By Lemma 2, $(A_1, B_1), (A_2', B_2'), \cdots, (A_{n'}', B_{n'}')$ is an independent sequence of (A, B) with respect to $\mathcal{A}$, contradiction.

"$\Rightarrow$" Let $A_1 \in \mathcal{A}_m$, $B_1 = \emptyset$, and $(A_2, B_2), \cdots, (A_n, B_n)$ is an independent sequence of $(A \backslash B, B)$ with respect to $\mathcal{A}^*$ with maximum length. By Lemma 1, $(A_2, B_2), \cdots, (A_n, B_n)$ is an independent sequence of (A, B) with respect to access structure $\mathcal{A}$ and $B_2 \neq \emptyset$. By Lemma 2, $(A_1, B_1), \cdots, (A_n, B_n)$ is an independent sequence of (A, B) with respect to $\mathcal{A}$. If there is an independent sequence $(A_1', B_1'), \cdots, (A_{n'}', B_{n'}')$ (where $n' > n$) of (A, B) with respect to $\mathcal{A}$, then $(A_2', B_2'), \cdots, (A_{n'}', B_{n'}')$ is an independent sequence of $(A \backslash B, B)$ with respect to access structure $\mathcal{A}^*$, contradiction.

From the above propositions, we can deduce that finding an independent sequence of (A, B) with respect to access structure $\mathcal{A}$ with maximum length is equivalent to finding an independent sequence of $(A \backslash B, B)$ with respect to $\mathcal{A}^*$ with maximum length. Since neither $A \backslash B$ nor B contains an element of graph-based access structure $\mathcal{A}^*$, $\mathcal{A}^*$ is a bipartite graph-based access structure. Consider an access structure $\mathcal{A}$ based on bipartite graph $G = (A, B, E)$. From the above proof, we know that if $(A_1, B_1), \cdots, (A_n, B_n)$ is an independent sequence of (A, B) with respect to the access structure $\mathcal{A}$, then $|A_i| = |B_i| = 1, \forall 1 \leq i \leq n$. For convenience, we denote an independent sequence of (A, B) with respect to the bipartite graph-based access structure $\mathcal{A}$ by $(a_1, b_1), \cdots, (a_n, b_n)$. It is easy to verify that $(a_1, b_1), \cdots, (a_n, b_n)$ is an independent sequence of (A, B) with respect to a bipartite graph-based access structure $\mathcal{A}$ if and only if $\{a_i, b_i\} \in \mathcal{A}_m$ and $\{a_i, b_j\} \notin \mathcal{A}_m, j < i$.

Theorem 2. *Let* $\mathcal{A}$ *be an access structure based on a bipartite graph* $G = (A, B, E)$. $(a_1, b_1), \cdots,$ (a_n, b_n) *is an independent sequence of* (A, B) *with respect to* $\mathcal{A}$ *if and only if* $\{\{a_1, b_1\}, \cdots, \{a_n, b_n\}\}$ *is an alternating cycle-free matching in the bipartite graph* G.

Proof: "$\Leftarrow$" Let $(a_1, b_1), \cdots, (a_n, b_n)$ be an independent sequence of (A, B) with respect to access structure $\mathcal{A}$. Given $(a_i, b_i), (a_j, b_j)$, where $i < j$, it's obvious that $a_i \neq a_j$ and $b_i \neq b_j$. Hence, $M = \{\{a_1, b_1\}, \cdots, \{a_n, b_n\}\}$ is a matching in the bipartite graph G. Assume that there is an alternating cycle C in the bipartite graph G. Suppose $C \cap M = \{\{a_{i_1}, b_{i_1}\}, \cdots, \{a_{i_k}, b_{i_k}\}\}$, where $i_1 \le i_2 \le \cdots \le i_k$. Since $(a_1, b_1), \cdots, (a_n, b_n)$ is an independent sequence, $(a_{i_1}, b_{i_1}), \cdots, (a_{i_k}, b_{i_k})$ is also an independent sequence. On the other hand, since C is a cycle, there is $i_j < i_k$ such that $\{a_{i_k}, b_{i_j}\} \in C \subseteq \mathcal{A}$, contradiction.

"$\Rightarrow$" Suppose $M = \{(a_1, b_1), \cdots, (a_n, b_n)\}$ is a matching in the bipartite graph G, and there is no alternating cycle in this graph, where $\forall 1 \le i \le n, a_i \in A$, and $b_i \in B$. Let $p(i) = \{j \ne i : \{a_j, b_i\} \in \mathcal{A}_m\}$. Let's prove firstly that for any $X \subset \{1, \cdots, n\}$, there is $i \in Y = \{1, \cdots, n\} \backslash X$ such that $p(i) \subseteq X$. Otherwise, assume there is $X \subseteq \{1, \cdots, n\}$ such that for any $i \in Y$, $p(i) \backslash X \ne \emptyset$. Choose arbitrarily $i_1 \in Y, i_2 \in p(i_1) \backslash X, \cdots, i_k \in p(i_{k-1}) \backslash X, \cdots$. It can be verified that for any $j < k$, $i_j \notin p(i_k)$. If not, assume that i_k is the first element such that $\{i_1, \cdots, i_{k-1}\} \cap p(i_k) \ne \emptyset$. Let $i_j \in \{i_1, \cdots, i_{k-1}\} \cap p(i_k)$. So we can obtain a cycle $C = (a_{i_j}, b_{i_j}, a_{i_{j+1}}, b_{i_{j+1}}, \cdots, a_{i_k}, b_{i_k})$, where $\{a_{i_j}, b_{i_j}\}, \cdots, \{a_{i_k}, b_{i_k}\} \in M$. Since M is a matching in the bipartite graph determined by $\mathcal{A}$, $\{a_{i_{j+1}}, b_{i_j}\}, \cdots, \{a_{i_k}, b_{i_{k-1}}\}, \{a_{i_j}, b_{i_k}\} \notin M$. Hence C is an alternating cycle of bipartite graph determined by $\mathcal{A}$, contradiction. Since $p(i_k) \subseteq \{1, \cdots, n\} \backslash \{i_1, \cdots, i_{k-1}\}$, $p(i_k) \backslash X \subseteq Y \backslash \{i_1, \cdots, i_{k-1}\}$. Since Y is finite, there is i_k such that $p(i_k) \backslash X = \emptyset$. By the above proof, we can arrange $1, \cdots, n$ as $i_1, \cdots, i_n$ such that $\forall 1 \le j \le n$, $p(i_j) \subseteq \{i_1, \cdots, i_{j-1}\}$. Obviously, $\forall 1 \le j \le n, \{a_{i_j}, b_{i_j}\} \in \mathcal{A}_m$. On the other hand, $\forall 1 \le k < j$, $p(i_k) \subseteq \{i_1, \cdots, i_{k-1}\}$ and $i_j \notin \{i_1, \cdots, i_{k-1}\}$, then $i_j \notin p(i_k)$, i.e. $\{a_{i_j}, b_{i_k}\} \notin \mathcal{A}_m$.

The above theorem shows that finding an independent sequence with respect to a bipartite graph-based access structure with maximum length is equivalent to finding a maximum alternating cycle-free matching in a bipartite graph. The problem of finding a maximum alternating cycle-free matching in a bipartite graph is NP hard, and there are some polynomial time algorithms to solve this problem only for some special bipartite graphs [10, 13].

References

1. Blakley, G.R.: Safeguarding cryptographic keys. In: Proc. AFIPS 1979 Nat. Computer Conf., vol. 48, pp. 313–317 (1979)
2. Blundo, C., De Santis, A., De Simone, R., Vaccaro, U.: Tight bounds on the information rate of secret sharing schemes. Designs, Codes and Cryptography 11(2), 107–110 (1997)
3. Blundo, C., De Santis, A., Gaggia, A.G., Vaccaro, U.: New bounds on the information rate of secret sharing schemes. IEEE Transactions on Information Theory IT-41(2), 549–554 (1995)
4. Blundo, C., De Santis, A., Gargano, L., Vaccaro, U.: On the information rate of secret sharing schemes. In: Brickell, E.F. (ed.) CRYPTO 1992. LNCS, vol. 740, pp. 148–167. Springer, Heidelberg (1993)
5. Blundo, C., De Santis, A., Stinson, D.R., Vaccaro, U.: Graph decompositions and secret sharing schemes. In: Rueppel, R.A. (ed.) EUROCRYPT 1992. LNCS, vol. 658, pp. 1–24. Springer, Heidelberg (1993)
6. Brickell, E.F., Stinson, D.R.: Some improved bounds on the information rate of perfect secret sharing schemes. Journal of Cryptology 5(3), 153–166 (1992)

7. Capocelli, R.M., De Santis, A., Gargano, L., Vaccaro, U.: On the size of shares for secret sharing schemes. Journal of Cryptology 6(3), 157–169 (1993)
8. Csirmaz, L.: The size of a share must be large. Journal of Cryptology 10(4), 223–231 (1997)
9. Csirmaz, L., Tardos, G.: Secret sharing on trees: problem solved. Cryptology ePrint Archive, Report 2009/071 (2009), http://eprint.iacr.org/
10. Dahlhaus, E.: The computation of the jump number of convex graphs. In: Bouchitté, V., Morvan, M. (eds.) ORDAL 1994. LNCS, vol. 831, pp. 176–185. Springer, Heidelberg (1994)
11. Ito, M., Saito, A., Nishizeki, T.: Secret sharing schemes realizing general access structure. In: Proc. IEEE Global Telecommunication Conf., Globecom 1987, pp. 99–102 (1987)
12. Karnin, E.D., Greene, J.W., Hellman, M.E.: On secret sharing systems. IEEE Transactions on Information Theory IT-29(1), 35–41 (1983)
13. Müller, H.: Alternating cycle-free matchings. Order 7(1), 11–21 (1990)
14. Oxley, J.G.: Matroid Theory. Oxford University Press, New York (1992)
15. Shamir, A.: How to share a secret. Communications of the ACM 22(11), 612–613 (1979)
16. van Dijk, M.: On the information rate of perfect secret sharing schemes. Designs, Codes and Cryptography 6(2), 143–169 (1995)
17. Welsh, D.J.A.: Matroid Theory. Academic, London (1976)

Building Oblivious Transfer on Channel Delays

Paolo Palmieri and Olivier Pereira

Université catholique de Louvain
UCL Crypto Group
Place du Levant 3, B-1348 Louvain-la-Neuve, Belgium
{paolo.palmieri,olivier.pereira}@uclouvain.be

Abstract. In the information-theoretic setting, where adversaries have unlimited computational power, the fundamental cryptographic primitive Oblivious Transfer (OT) cannot be securely achieved if the parties are communicating over a clear channel. To preserve secrecy and security, the players have to rely on noise in the communication. Noisy channels are therefore a useful tool to model noise behavior and build protocols implementing OT. This paper explores a source of errors that is inherently present in practically any transmission medium, but has been scarcely studied in this context: delays in the communication.

In order to have a model for the delays that is both general and comparable to the channels usually used for OT – such as the Binary Symmetric Channel (BSC) – we introduce a new noisy channel, the Binary Discrete-time Delaying Channel (BDDC). We show that such a channel realistically reproduces real-life communication scenarios where delays are hard to predict and we propose a protocol for achieving oblivious transfer over the BDDC. We analyze the security of our construction in the semi-honest setting, showing that our realization of OT substantially decreases the protocol sensitivity to the user's knowledge of the channel compared to solutions relying on other channel properties, and is very efficient for wide ranges of delay probabilities. The flexibility and generality of the model opens the way for future implementation in media where delays are a fundamental characteristic.

Keywords: Oblivious transfer, secure multi-party computation, information theoretic security, cryptography on noisy channels.

1   Introduction

The first uses of cryptography arose from the necessity of sending a secret message to some trusted correspondent in a way that only the intended receiver could learn the information. However, we may sometime be interested in communicating with someone we do not trust. Secure multi-party computation allows several parties to perform a shared computation while preserving the secrecy of their respective inputs and the correctness of the results [2].

In the case of two-party computation, where only two players are involved in the communication, a primitive of central importance is Oblivious Transfer (OT). In a protocol that realizes OT, a sender sends some information to a receiver,

X. Lai, M. Yung, and D. Lin (Eds.): Inscrypt 2010, LNCS 6584, pp. 125–138, 2011.

which is however able to learn only part of it, while the sender remains oblivious as to what is received. The relevance of OT is due to its universality: any other two-party computation can be achieved on top of it [10]. However, if we make no computational assumption, that is, if we assume adversaries have unlimited computational capabilities, such a fundamental primitive cannot be implemented with unconditional security over a standard, error-free communication medium. Thus is the importance of using noisy channels, where we can exploit errors in the communication to our advantage in order to implement oblivious transfer in an unconditionally secure fashion. In general, any non-trivial noisy channel can be used for this purpose [6,11].

The first protocol for OT was built on the Binary Symmetric Channel (BSC) [5,4], a noisy channel where bits have some fixed probability of being flipped during the transmission. Other models of communication channels have since been designed and studied, in respect of their property of being a good medium over which to build OT. Of the fair number of noisy channels proposed over the years, most are derived from the BSC itself. The Unfair Noisy Channel (UNC), a weaker and therefore less assuming noisy channel, was introduced by Damgård, Kilian and Salvail [8]. Instead of a fixed error probability, as in the case of a regular BSC, this channel allows for a known range of possible noise levels, and, to add more generality, it also let the potential attacker to be given the advantage of knowing exactly what the actual noise level is (from which the name "unfair" is derived). In [17], Wullschleger proposes a new set of noisy channels, called Weak Noisy Channels (WNC). In particular, he revised two common primitives redesigning them into a new fashion: the Weak Erasure Channel (WEC) and the Weak Binary Symmetric Channel (WBSC). The aim of this work is to define the channels not with a predefined set of functionalities, but only by a set of conditions that the channels must satisfy. In this way, the primitives allow the attacker some more freedom. For instance, it is taken into account the possibility for a malicious player to know, with a certain probability, if the bit received through the channel was in fact correct or not.

Despite the differences in the channels, the respective protocols designed to build OT usually follow the same scheme: the channel is used repeatedly by the parties, to benefit from privacy amplification, and error correcting codes (ECC) are used to ensure the correctness of the communication. Unfortunately, the use of ECC's also limits the flexibility of the construction by reducing the ranges of acceptable error probabilities, while applying privacy amplification techniques implies that a considerable amount of data needs to be transmitted through the channel for each single bit of private information we want to send. These factors, along with the strong requirements still imposed by current noisy channel models, prevent any real application of oblivious transfer protocols not based on computational assumptions.

1.1 Contribution

In order to decrease the sensitivity of OT protocols to the precise knowledge of channel characteristics and make actual implementation a more realistic prospect, we propose a new noisy channel primitive, called Binary Discrete-time Delaying Channel (BDDC). The BDDC preserves the basic characteristics of the BSC: it is a binary, discrete and memoryless channel; but it is based on a common but rarely used error source, the delays in communication. Delays happen in almost any telecommunication medium, both wired and wireless, but, to the best of our knowledge, have never been used in the design of oblivious transfer protocols in the information theoretic setting before.

To show how the channel can be used to achieve any secure two-party computation, we propose a protocol that implements oblivious transfer over the BDDC, and we provide a proof of the security of our realization in a scenario where players are honest-but-curious. The protocol design has two original features that largely increase its flexibility and efficiency compared to current constructions. First, the information sent by the sender through the channel is structured in a specific way in order to exploit the peculiarities of the channel and reduce the amount of communication required. Second, the protocol does not need error correcting codes to preserve the correctness of the communication. This allows for a much larger tolerance of variations in the error probability of the channel, even during the protocol execution.

The flexibility and generality of the model opens the way for future implementation, especially in media where delays are a fundamental characteristic, as in the case of wireless communication, or wired IP networks.

1.2   Outline of the Paper

In Section 2 we introduce a new noisy channel based on data transmission delays, and we show how it actually models realistic communication scenarios. In Section 3 we provide a security definition for oblivious transfer, as well as some other useful definitions and preliminary notions which will be needed. We also propose a protocol that implements oblivious transfer over the new channel. In Section 4 we prove the security in the semi-honest model and we show the efficiency of our construction.

2   Transmission Delays as a Source of Noise

Digital communications are almost always affected by delays in data transmission, a fundamental characteristic of wireless communication, but also a common problem in wired IP networks [14]. Reducing or limiting delays has always been one of the main challenges in the communication field. Delays are quite often difficult to predict and almost impossible to eliminate. Moreover, in real and non-isolated systems, they usually depend on external, uncontrollable factors. But what can be a daunting property in the field of communication, can turn out to be extremely useful in cryptography, where noisy channels have long been studied in order to achieve secure computation.

However, despite having these appealing characteristics, delays have not been systematically used as a source of noise in noise-demanding security applications. In particular, specific studies in the field of secure two-party computation against computationally unbounded adversaries are still missing. In this paper we address this by proving that oblivious transfer can be achieved on a channel whose only source of noise is transmission delays.

In order to obtain results as general and widely applicable as possible, we need a channel model that makes no unnecessary assumptions on the delay. At the same time, to be able to make meaningful comparisons, we want the channel to maintain the common features of the other channels currently used for oblivious transfer protocols in the information-theoretic setting – most notably the binary symmetric channel and its modifications. In information theory literature, there is an abundance of channel definitions that model most, if not all, forms of delay. However, those channels are designed around specific communication scenarios and for purposes different from those of cryptography. Therefore, we define a new noisy channel that is based on a small set of assumptions and is simple enough to allow for clear constructions and proofs, the Binary Discrete-time Delaying Channel (BDDC). In section 2.2 we show how the BDDC succeeds in modeling real-life communication scenarios.

2.1   Binary Discrete-Time Delaying Channel (BDDC)

Our model of communication channel is a box accepting binary strings and emitting each accepted string after a certain delay. The channel operates at discrete times, which means that it is not continuously accepting inputs and emitting outputs, but these actions can only occur at specific instants in time. For simplicity, we assume that the action of accepting or emitting a string is instantaneous, that is, it takes no time to be accomplished.

Definition 1. *A* Binary Discrete-time Delaying Channel *with delaying probability p consists of*

- *an input alphabet* $\{0,1\}^n$,
- *an output alphabet* $\{0,1\}^n$,
- *a set of consecutive input times* $T = \{t_0, t_1, \ldots\} \subseteq \mathbb{N}$,
- *a set of consecutive output times* $U = \{u_0, u_1, \ldots\} \subseteq \mathbb{N}$ *where* $\forall u_i \in U, t_i \in T, u_i \geq t_i$.

Each input admitted into the channel at input time $t_i \in T$ is output once by the channel, with probability of being output at time $u_j \in U$

$$\Pr[u_j] = p^{(j-i)} - p^{(j-i+1)} \ . \tag{1}$$

Example 1. The probability of a string x, admitted into the channel at t_0, to be emitted without delay at u_0 is

$$\Pr[u_0] = 1 - p \ .$$

The channel is memoryless. A string of symbols is delayed with probability p independent of the history of strings, symbols or delays. For instance, the probability for two strings sent at the same input time t_i of being both delayed while transmitted is p^2. Neither the sender nor the receiver gets any feedback about the transmission, i.e. they do not learn any information about whether or not a string sent or received was actually delayed.

Informally put, the channel models a non-instantaneous communication between two parties, where the transmission takes a standard time $(t_i - u_i)$. Some of the content transmitted suffers unpredictable delays, which are usually short, but can sometimes take much longer.

Remark 1. It should be noted that there is no strict requirement regarding the discrete output times in relation to the input ones. For example, while logically u_i cannot precede t_i on the time-line, it is perfectly acceptable for the purpose of the channel both having u_i and t_i happen simultaneously, or having u_i happening later, even after any number of t_j with $j > i$. The channel also makes no claim whether or not the distance between each input (or output) time has to be fixed, but for clarity's sake we assume that to be the case.

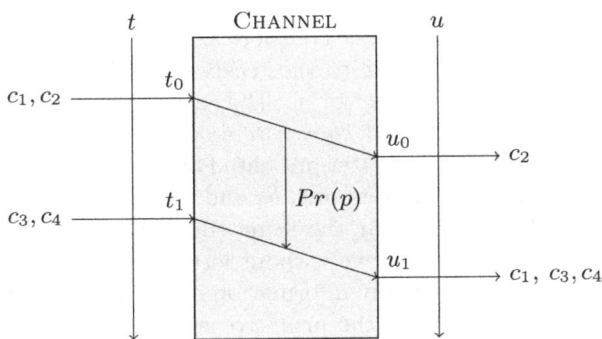

Fig. 1. A schematization representing a Binary Discrete-time Delaying Channel accepting two strings at time t_0, one of which gets delayed once, and two at time t_1, none of which gets delayed. This results in the channel emitting one string at time u_0 and three at u_1.

2.2   Real-World Communication Scenarios

While delays generally occur in most forms of telecommunication, a digital networking communication method that is particularly sensitive to them is packet switching. Packets moving through a shared network are usually delivered to destination passing by a variable number of nodes, routers and switches. At each hop a packet may be buffered and queued, building up a variable delay depending on the traffic load of the network. For a deliberate design choice, the Internet Protocol (IP) does not guarantee that packets are delivered in the same order in which they were originally sent. The behavior of a network resulting in out-of-order delivery of packets is known as *packet reordering*. A 2004 study by

Zhou and Van Mieghem found that, tracing sets composed of 50 100-byte UDP packets between 12 Internet test boxes, around 56% of the streams were subject to packet reordering [18], while Bellardo and Savage found in [1] that minium-sized TCP packets are reordered more than 10 percent of the time. Mesurements techniques are available to assess the impact of this phenomenon [1], and the analysis of the reordering caused by *multipath forwarding* (the choice of different routes for packets in the same stream) indicates that the current trend of increase in parallelism necessary to handle high speed links is also increasing the occurrence of packet reordering [12].

The binary discrete-time delaying channel is well suited to simulate the behavior of an IP network affected by packet reordering. The model approximates reality by introducing the requirement of discrete times for inputs and outputs, which allows for a remarkably more flexible and easier to study noisy channel. Generally, any packet switching network where a packet has some probability of being delayed during the transmissions can be modeled using a BDDC.

3   Building Oblivious Transfer over a BDDC

In the original concept of oblivious transfer, as presented by Rabin [15], the sender, Sam, sends his secret bit b to the receiver, Rachel. Rachel receives the bit with probability $\frac{1}{2}$ and, whether or not she receives it, she will not tell Sam. A variant of the primitive, named *chosen one-out-of-two oblivious transfer*, or simply 1-2 oblivious transfer, was later presented by Even, Goldreich and Lempel [9]. In this case Sam has two secrets bits, b_0 and b_1, and wants to communicate one of them to Rachel, without at the same time revealing the other. Rachel wants to choose which one to receive without letting Sam know her selection s, but should not be able to learn any information other than the secret bit b_s she has selected. The two versions of the primitive were shown to be equivalent by Crépeau [3]. We choose to focus on 1-2 oblivious transfer, and in the following, for simplicity, we refer to it simply as oblivious transfer.

3.1   A Security Definition for Oblivious Transfer

A protocol implements OT in a secure manner if three conditions are satisfied after a successful execution: Rachel learns the value of b_s (correctness); Rachel gains no further information about the value of b_{1-s} (security for Sam); Sam learns nothing about the value of s (security for Rachel) [5]. We give a formal definition of these security conditions by using the concept of *prediction advantage*. The prediction advantage is a measure of the advantage an adversary has in guessing a secret bit when using all the information available to her. We use the notation found in [16].

Definition 2. ([16]) *Let P_{XY} be a distribution over $\{0,1\} \times \mathcal{Y}$. The maximal bit prediction advantage of X from Y for a function f is*

$$\text{PredAdv}(X \mid Y) = 2 \cdot \max_f \Pr[f(Y) = X] - 1 \ . \tag{2}$$

We call *view* of a player all the information that the player obtains during an execution of the protocol. For each execution there are both a receiver's view and a sender's view. In the *semi-honest model*, the adversary is *passive*: she follows the protocol, but outputs her entire view [16].

When proving the security of our construction, we use the following definition of oblivious transfer.

Definition 3. *A protocol Π between a sender and a receiver, where the sender inputs $(b_0, b_1) \in \{0,1\}$ and outputs nothing, and the receiver inputs $s \in \{0,1\}$ and outputs S, securely computes 1-2 oblivious transfer with an error of at most ε, assuming that U and V represent the sender and receiver views respectively, if the following conditions are satisfied:*

- (Correctness) *If both players are honest, we have*

$$Pr\left[S = b_s\right] \geq 1 - \varepsilon \ . \tag{3}$$

- (Security for Sam) *For an honest sender and an honest (but curious) receiver we have*

$$\mathrm{PredAdv}\left(b_{1-s} \mid V, s\right) \leq \varepsilon \ . \tag{4}$$

- (Security for Rachel) *For an honest receiver and an honest (but curious) sender we have*

$$\mathrm{PredAdv}\left(s \mid U, b_0, b_1\right) \leq \varepsilon \ . \tag{5}$$

3.2 A Protocol for Oblivious Transfer over a BDDC

The protocol we introduce allows the construction of oblivious transfer over a BDDC. The protocol is composed of a first phase, during which the sender Sam transmits through the channel multiple times and the receiver Rachel listen, and a second phase, where communication happens on a clear channel and the parties exploit the noise introduced by the channel to achieve their goals of secrecy and security. Before any communication can actually begin, some introductory computation by the sending party is needed, in order to craft the strings that will be sent later on to the receiver through the channel.

This construction follows the basic concepts introduced by Crépeau and Kilian while describing for the first time how to build OT over the BSC [5].

Protocol 1. Before starting any communication, some preparatory computation needs to be completed. Sam selects two disjoints sets E and E' of n distinct binary strings of length l: $e_1, \ldots, e_n$ and $e'_1, \ldots, e'_n$.

Then, Sam builds the following sets:

- C, that contains the strings $c_1, \ldots, c_n$ defined as the concatenation $c_i := e_i \| i$;
- C', that contains the strings $c'_1, \ldots, c'_n$ defined as $c'_i := e'_i \| i$.

We call the i's *sequence numbers*, while the strings in $E \cup E'$ are used as *string identifiers*. The values n and l are shared between the parties. The players can communicate either using a binary discrete-time delaying channel with probability p, called p-BDDC, or a clear channel.

Completed these preliminary steps, the parties are ready to proceed with the protocol as follows:

1. Sam sends C to Rachel using the p-BDDC at instant t_0.
2. Sam sends the set C' to Rachel using the p-BDDC at instant t_1.
3. At instant u_0 Rachel receives over the p-BDDC all the strings in C that have not been delayed by the channel. If less than $\frac{n}{2}$ strings are received Rachel instructs Sam to abort the communication.
4. At instant u_1 Rachel receives over the p-BDDC the strings from C delayed once, plus the strings of set C' that have not been delayed. She keeps listening on the channel at instants $u_2, u_3, \ldots$ until all the delayed strings have been received.
5. Rachel selects a set of string identifiers I_s, where $s \in \{0,1\}$ is her selection bit, such that $|I_s| = \frac{n}{2}$ and so that every string $c \in C$ with $i \in I_s$ has been received for the first time at u_0. Then she puts the remaining i's in I_{1-s} and sends I_0 and I_1 to Sam over a clear channel.[1]
6. Sam receives I_0 and I_1, and chooses two universal hash functions f and f', whose output is 1-bit long for any input. Let $E_j \subset E$ be the set containing every $e_i \in E$ corresponding to an $i \in I_j$, such that

$$e_i \in E_j \Leftrightarrow i \in I_j \ . \tag{6}$$

For each set I_j, Sam computes the string g_j by concatenating each $e_k^j \in E_j$, ordering them for increasing binary value, so that

$$g_j = \left(e_1^j \| \ldots \| e_{\frac{n}{2}}^j \right) \quad \text{with } e_1^j, \ldots, e_{\frac{n}{2}}^j \in E_j \ . \tag{7}$$

The two strings g_0, g_1 are given in input to the hash functions f, f' to obtain the two values

$$h_0 = f(g_0) \ , \qquad h_1 = f'(g_1) \ . \tag{8}$$

When the computation is complete, Sam sends to Rachel the functions f, f' and the two values

$$i_0 = (h_0 \oplus b_0) \ , \qquad i_1 = (h_1 \oplus b_1) \ . \tag{9}$$

7. Rachel computes her guess for b_s, according to the formula

$$b_s = f^s(g_s) \oplus i_s \ . \tag{10}$$

Remark 2. It should be noted that the steps 2 and 3 of the protocol could also happen in the inverse order, or simultaneously. This is due to the fact that there is no explicit constraint regarding the chronological order of t_1 and u_0.

---

[1] Or Rachel can just send one of these two sets in order to save bandwidth as Sam can easily reconstruct the other.

Remark 3. Since the elements in $E \cup E'$ have to be distinct, we gather that

$$2^l \geq |E \cup E'| = 2n \ . \tag{11}$$

Remark 4. While in our constructions we use the sequence numbers i's, it should be noted that any set D of n distinct binary strings $d_1, \ldots, d_n$ might be used in their place in a setting where using unordered strings may be preferred.

4 Security in the Semi-honest Scenario

In the semi-honest setting, both parties are honest-but-curious, meaning that they follow the protocol, but try afterward to learn extra knowledge from their record of the conversation. In particular, Sam wants to guess which secret Rachel selected, while Rachel's aim is to get as much information as possible on the other secret.

Theorem 1. *The protocol described in Section 3.2, securely computes 1-2 oblivious transfer with error probability ε when it is executed on a p-BDDC with $0 < p < \frac{1}{2}$ and*

$$n > \max\left(\frac{-2\log(\varepsilon)}{(1-2p)^2}, \frac{\log\left(\frac{\varepsilon}{2}\right)}{\log\left(1-\frac{p}{2}\right)}\right) \ . \tag{12}$$

Proof. We prove the security of our construction by showing that each of the three conditions of Definition 3 hold.

Correctness. Rachel is able to compute the bit b_s when she receives, at step 3 of the protocol, a number of non-delayed strings that is greater than $\frac{n}{2}$. If we use X to denote the random variable counting this number, we see that $\Pr\left[X < \frac{n}{2}\right]$, that is, the probability that too many strings are delayed for the protocol to succeed, follows the cumulative distribution function of the binomial distribution. Using Hoeffding's inequality, we then observe that

$$\Pr\left[X < \frac{n}{2}\right] \leq \exp\left(-2n\left(\frac{1}{2}-p\right)^2\right) \ , \tag{13}$$

which shows that the correctness condition is satisfied by our protocol with overwhelming probability in n when $p < \frac{1}{2}$.[2] By extracting n in this inequality, we obtain the first argument of the maximum function in the theorem statement.

---

[2] Note that, for channels where $\frac{1}{2} \leq p < 1$, the correctness condition on p can be relaxed by requiring Rachel to build sets containing less than half of the strings, which would allow the protocol to succeed even if more than half of the strings are delayed.

Security for Sam. We evaluate the probability that Rachel is able to compute both b_s and b_{1-s} in a protocol session. In the semi-honest setting, which we consider here, this probability is upper-bounded by the probability that Rachel is able to compute b_{1-s}. Let us call this event Success.

Rachel has two ways to compute b_{1-s}: by evaluating the appropriate universal hash function on the correct inputs, as Sam does in Step 6 of the protocol (let us call GuessInputHash this event), or by not doing so. So, $\Pr[\mathsf{Success}] = \Pr[\mathsf{Success} \wedge \mathsf{GuessInputHash}] + \Pr[\mathsf{Success} \wedge \neg\mathsf{GuessInputHash}]$. The probability of the second alternative is upper-bounded by $\frac{1}{2}$, due to the properties of the universal hash function. The probability of the first alternative is in turn upper-bounded by $\Pr[\mathsf{GuessInputHash}]$. Let us now evaluate that probability.

For each pair of strings sharing the same sequence number i, four events can happen:

1. The first string of the pair is not delayed, which happens with probability $1 - p$.
2. The first string of the pair is delayed, but the two strings still reach Rachel in the same order they were sent. This happens with probability $\frac{p^2}{1+p}$.
3. Those two strings are delivered to Rachel in reverse order, which also happens with probability $\frac{p^2}{1+p}$.
4. The two strings are delivered to Rachel at the same time, which happens with probability $\frac{p(1-p)}{1+p}$.

When the first string is not delayed, Rachel can be sure of which was sent first. When the first string is delayed, and the two strings are delivered at different times, Rachel cannot guess with a probability better than $\frac{1}{2}$ whether the two strings are switched or delivered in the sending order: both events happen with the same probability. This is obviously also true when the two strings are delivered at the same time.

So, as soon as the first of the two strings is delayed, no strategy can provide a probability higher than $\frac{1}{2}$ to guess which string was sent first, meaning that Rachel is able to guess with probability $1 - \frac{p}{2}$ which one among any two strings with identical sequence number was sent first. Let us denote by GuessCorrectOrder the number of such correct guesses among n pairs of strings.

We have that $\Pr[\mathsf{GuessInputHash}] = \Pr[\mathsf{GuessInputHash} \wedge \mathsf{GuessCorrectOrder} = n] + \Pr[\mathsf{GuessInputHash} \wedge \mathsf{GuessCorrectOrder} < n]$. Let us now observe that the first term of this sum is upper bounded by:

$$\Pr\left[\mathsf{GuessCorrectOrder} = n\right] = \left(1 - \frac{p}{2}\right)^n , \tag{14}$$

which is negligible in n as soon as $p > 0$. Besides, since the input of the hash function is not correctly guessed when $\mathsf{GuessCorrectOrder} < n$, we have that the second term of the sum is null. This shows that:

$$\Pr\left[\mathsf{Success}\right] \le \frac{1}{2} + \left(1 - \frac{p}{2}\right)^n . \tag{15}$$

By using the definition of prediction advantage and extracting n in this inequality, we obtain the second argument of the maximum function in the theorem statement.

Security for Rachel. The only step in the protocol in which Rachel uses her selection s to generate messages to Sam is number 5, when she sends back I_0 and I_1. During any other step Rachel is not sending any information at all to Sam. A BDDC gives no feedback to the sender or the receiver about which strings are delayed: each string c is delayed at least once with probability p independent of c. Therefore, from Sam's point of view, the distribution (I_0, I_1) is independent of s, and Sam's prediction advantage on s given his view and his input bits is null.   □

Remark 5. We observe that the semi-honest assumption is only required for the sender, but not for the receiver. When acting as a malicious receiver, Rachel can either produce a malformed set I_{1-s} (reducing the number of strings included, or including non-delayed strings already present into I_s) in order to put only non-delayed strings into the set, or swap delayed strings with non-delayed ones between the sets I_s and I_{1-s}. In the first case, a simple additional check on the sender's side of the protocol will prevent any response to a malformed I_{1-s}. In the second case Rachel, by moving delayed strings from I_{1-s} to I_s, increases her probability to get the other bit b_{1-s} at the cost of lowering her probability to get the selected bit b_s. In fact, the number of delayed strings, which is also the total number of guesses needed by Rachel, remains the same. Therefore the probability of decoding both bits is the same whether she acts honestly or in a malicious way.

5   Conclusion

In this paper, we proposed using channel delays as a source of uncertainty to realize oblivious transfer. To this purpose, we introduced a new channel, called Binary Discrete-time Delaying Channel (BDDC), and propose an OT protocol built on this channel.

We believe that building OT on communication delays provides important benefits compared to the existing solutions. In particular, our protocol has a remarkably low sensitivity to the precise knowledge of the channel parameters, a factor that often constitutes one of the main inconveniences of cryptographic protocols relying on communication channel properties.

Figure 2 illustrates this little sensitivity by plotting the two curves of which the maximum is taken in the statement of Theorem 1, for a security parameter $\varepsilon = 10^{-9}$. The curve that grows when p tends to 0 shows that the number of strings to be sent must increase when p is small in order to ensure that Rachel is not able to decode both of the sender bits of the OT protocol. The curve that grows with p shows that the number of strings to be sent must increase when p tends to $\frac{1}{2}$ in order to ensure that Rachel gets one of the two sender bits.

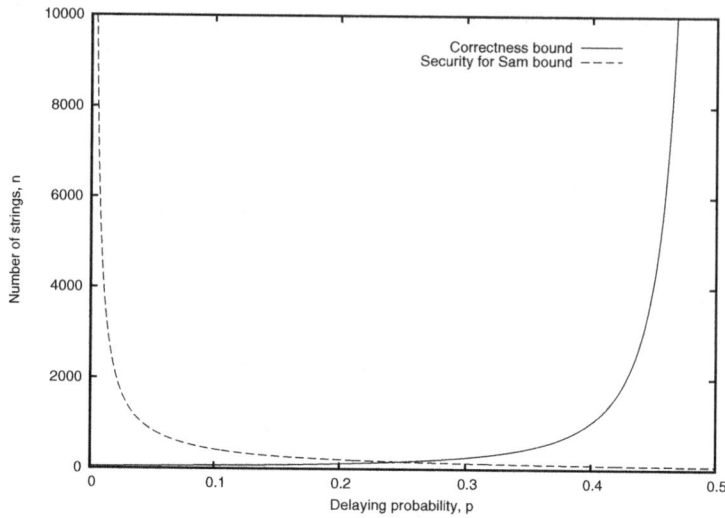

Fig. 2. n as a function of p for $\varepsilon = 10^{-9}$

This graph shows that our protocol is able to tolerate a very wide range of uncertainty on the channel parameters: the exchange of 1000 strings (that is, approximately 42000 bits transferred on the BDDC channel and less than 12000 bits sent on the noiseless channel) guarantees oblivious transfer with error $\varepsilon = 10^{-9}$ for values of p ranging from 0.05 to 0.4 approximately. This practically means that an active adversary able to set the probability to a desired level within this range does not reduce the security of the construction. The idea of letting the adversary choose the channel probability was first introduced with the Unfair Noisy Channel (UNC) [8], a binary symmetric channel where the error rate is only known to be in a certain interval $[\gamma \cdots \delta]$. This work shows that OT cannot be achieved as soon as the difference $\delta - \gamma$ becomes too large, namely, if $\delta \geq 2\gamma(1-\gamma)$. This interval has a maximum width equal to 0.125 when $\gamma = 0.25$ and $\delta = 0.375$, even though no protocol is known that can tolerate such a wide interval width on a UNC. Interval widths for which OT can be achieved on UNCs have also been studied [7], showing experimentally that OT can be built on a UNC for intervals of maximum width around 0.04.

We believe that these figures show a crucial benefit of exploiting delays on channels: delays provide the uncertainty that is needed to build security, but they also offer the possibility to be sure that some strings have been sent before others (if they are received before other strings are sent, for instance). This is not the case on other channels that have been considered until now, like the BSC channel and its variants, where one can never be sure that a string is delivered correctly, raising the need to precisely calibrate error correction mechanisms.

Our protocol also appears to be very efficient for important delay probability ranges: we observe that sending 250 pairs of strings on the p-BDDC channel, that is, around 8500 bits, is enough to realize OT for $0.17 \leq p \leq 0.29$ and

$\varepsilon = 10^{-9}$. We eventually observe that, in many practical applications, the protocol parameters might be adapted in order to influence the delaying probability if needed. For instance, it appears that packet size has an important impact on reordering occurrences in IP networks [1].

Acknowledgments

This research work was supported by the SCOOP Action de Recherche Concertées. Olivier Pereira is a Research Associate of the F.R.S.-FNRS. We also want to thank Abdellatif Zaidi and Luc Vandendorpe for interesting discussions on the subject.

References

1. Bellardo, J., Savage, S.: Measuring packet reordering. In: Internet Measurement Workshop, pp. 97–105. ACM, New York (2002)
2. Chaum, D., Damgård, I., van de Graaf, J.: Multiparty computations ensuring privacy of each party's input and correctness of the result. In: Pomerance [13], pp. 87–119
3. Crépeau, C.: Equivalence between two flavours of oblivious transfers. In: Pomerance [13], pp. 350–354
4. Crépeau, C.: Efficient cryptographic protocols based on noisy channels. In: Fumy, W. (ed.) EUROCRYPT 1997. LNCS, vol. 1233, pp. 306–317. Springer, Heidelberg (1997)
5. Crépeau, C., Kilian, J.: Achieving oblivious transfer using weakened security assumptions (extended abstract). In: FOCS, pp. 42–52. IEEE, Los Alamitos (1988)
6. Crépeau, C., Morozov, K., Wolf, S.: Efficient unconditional oblivious transfer from almost any noisy channel. In: Blundo, C., Cimato, S. (eds.) SCN 2004. LNCS, vol. 3352, pp. 47–59. Springer, Heidelberg (2005)
7. Damgård, I., Fehr, S., Morozov, K., Salvail, L.: Unfair noisy channels and oblivious transfer. In: Naor, M. (ed.) TCC 2004. LNCS, vol. 2951, pp. 355–373. Springer, Heidelberg (2004)
8. Damgård, I.B., Kilian, J., Salvail, L.: On the (Im)possibility of basing oblivious transfer and bit commitment on weakened security assumptions. In: Stern, J. (ed.) EUROCRYPT 1999. LNCS, vol. 1592, pp. 56–73. Springer, Heidelberg (1999)
9. Even, S., Goldreich, O., Lempel, A.: A randomized protocol for signing contracts. Commun. ACM 28(6), 637–647 (1985)
10. Kilian, J.: Founding cryptography on oblivious transfer. In: STOC, pp. 20–31. ACM, New York (1988)
11. Nascimento, A.C.A., Winter, A.: On the oblivious-transfer capacity of noisy resources. IEEE Transactions on Information Theory 54(6), 2572–2581 (2008)
12. Piratla, N.M., Jayasumana, A.P.: Reordering of packets due to multipath forwarding - an analysis. In: Proc. IEEE Int. Conf. on Communications (ICC 2006), pp. 28–36 (2006)
13. Pomerance, C. (ed.): CRYPTO 1987. LNCS, vol. 293. Springer, Heidelberg (1988)
14. Proakis, J.G.: Digital Communications, 4th edn. McGraw-Hill Science Engineering, New York (2000)

15. Rabin, M.O.: How to exchange secrets by oblivious transfer. Technical Report TR-81, Aiken Computation Laboratory, Harvard University (1981), manuscript
16. Wullschleger, J.: Oblivious-transfer amplification. In: Naor, M. (ed.) EUROCRYPT 2007. LNCS, vol. 4515, pp. 555–572. Springer, Heidelberg (2007)
17. Wullschleger, J.: Oblivious transfer from weak noisy channels. In: Reingold, O. (ed.) TCC 2009. LNCS, vol. 5444, pp. 332–349. Springer, Heidelberg (2009)
18. Zhou, X.M., Van Mieghem, P.: Reordering of IP packets in internet. In: Barakat, C., Pratt, I. (eds.) PAM 2004. LNCS, vol. 3015, pp. 237–246. Springer, Heidelberg (2004)

Variants of Multicollision Attacks on Iterated Hash Functions

Tuomas Kortelainen[1], Juha Kortelainen[2], and Kimmo Halunen[3]

[1] Mathematics Division, Department of Electrical and Information Engineering,
University of Oulu
[2] Department of Information Processing Science, University of Oulu
[3] Oulu University Secure Programming Group,
Department of Electrical and Information Engineering, University of Oulu

Abstract. We introduce a statistical experiment setting to carry out a multicollision attack on any iterated hash function. We develop a method for finding multicollisions that gives larger multicollision sets for the same amount of work as Joux's famous method i.e. with $2.5 \cdot k 2^{\frac{n}{2}}$ work one can find greater than 2^k-collisions for large k. Furthermore, if the message length is not restricted, we show that we can create arbitrarily large multicollisions by finding two cycles in the iterated hash function. This applies even when an ideal compression function is used.

1 Introduction

Hash functions are functions, which take as input arbitrary strings from a fixed alphabet (usually assumed to be the binary alphabet $\{0,1\}$) and return a (binary) string of fixed length as their output. These functions are used in various cryptographic protocols such as message authentication, digital signatures and electronic voting. In order to be useful in cryptographic context, hash functions need to have three properties, *preimage resistance, second preimage resistance* and *collision resistance.*

Merkle and Damgård [1,2] devised a method for constructing hash functions from compression functions (functions $f : \{0,1\}^m \rightarrow \{0,1\}^n, m > n$). In this method, the message to be hashed is divided into blocks and hash value is computed by the repeated use of the compression function to the message blocks and to the previous value of the computation. The value after the final computation is then defined as the hash value of the message. Both Merkle and Damgård were able to prove that if the length of the message is added to the end of the message and the resulting message is hashed in this iterative fashion using a collision resistant compression function, the resulting hash function is also collision resistant.

The iterative method for constructing hash functions has been found quite susceptible to multicollision attacks. Multicollisions are sets of distinct messages all giving the same hash value under the hash function. Joux [3] demonstrated that for iterated hash functions 2^k-multicollisions can be found with $O(k \cdot 2^{n/2})$ compression function operations. For an ideal hash function this would be much

X. Lai, M. Yung, and D. Lin (Eds.): Inscrypt 2010, LNCS 6584, pp. 139–154, 2011.

higher [4]. Further improvements have been made by Kelsey & Schneier [5] and Aumasson [6] where fixed points and memory are used to generate larger multi-collisions for $O(2^{n/2})$ work. These methods are discussed in more detail later.

There are also methods for finding multicollisions for generalized versions of iterated hash functions, where one may use the message blocks several times and in permuted order instead of just going through them once from beginning to end. Nandi & Stinson [7] have shown that when message blocks are used no more than two times in the iteration, multicollisions can still be found fairly easily. Hoch & Shamir [8] have generalized these results to cover the cases where message blocks can be used more than two times.

Multicollisions can be utilized in attacks against iterated hash functions, both particular hash functions and the iterative structure itself. For example many second preimage attacks use multicollisions as a starting point. Furthermore, the herding attack [9] uses multicollisions of a special type as a starting point for the attack. The herding attack has also been applied to the dithered variants of iterated hash functions successfully [10].

This paper is organized in the following way. In the next two sections, we give some necessary definitions and results on algebra and hash functions. The fourth section describes some of the earlier methods for finding multicollisions for iterated hash functions in more detail. The fifth section presents a variant on the attack proposed by Joux [3] and analyzes its complexity, memory consumption and shows that for large k the new method outperforms Joux's attack. The sixth section introduces an automata perspective of iterated hash functions. We show that by finding two cycles one can obtain arbitrarily large multicollisions if the length of the messages is not restricted. The final section contains conclusions and further research proposals.

2   Basics on Alphabets and Words

Denote by $\mathbb{N}_+$ the set of all *positive integers*, i.e., $\mathbb{N}_+ = \{1, 2, \ldots\}$. Then $\mathbb{N} = \mathbb{N}_+ \cup \{0\}$ is the set of all *natural numbers*. For each finite set S, let $|S|$ be the *cardinality* of S that is to say, the number of elements in S.

An *alphabet* is any finite, nonempty set of abstract symbols called *letters* or *symbols*. Let A be an alphabet. A *word* (over A) is any finite sequence of symbols (in A). Thus, assuming that w is a word over A, we can write $w = x_1 x_2 \cdots x_n$, where n is a nonnegative integer and $x_i \in A$ for $i = 1, 2, \ldots, n$. Above n is the *length* $|w|$ of w. Notice that n may be equal to zero; then w is the *empty word*, often denoted by ϵ, which contains no letters. The *catenation* of two words u and v in is the word uv obtained by writing u and v after one another. The *powers of the word* u are defined recursively as: $u^0 = \epsilon$, $u^1 = u$, and $u^{i+1} = u^i u$ for $i \in \mathbb{N}_+$.

For each $n \in \mathbb{N}_+$, denote by A^n the set of all words of length n over A. Then $A^+ = \bigcup_{n=1}^{\infty} A^n$ is the set of all nonempty words over A. Clearly catenation defines a binary operation $\cdot$ in A^+: $u \cdot v = uv$ for all $u, v \in A^+$. In algebraic terms $(A^+, \cdot)$ is a *free semigroup*.

Any subset of A^+, where A is an alphabet, is a *language* over A. Let L and T be languages over A. The *product* of L and T is the language $LT = \{uv \mid u \in L, v \in T\}$. The *powers of* L are defined recursively as: $L^0 = \{\epsilon\}$, $L^1 = L$, and $L^{i+1} = L^i L$ for $i \in \mathbb{N}_+$. Denote $L^+ = \cup_{i=1}^{\infty} L^i$ and $L^* = L^+ \cup \{\epsilon\}$. If L contains only one word, say u, we write respectively u^+ and u^* instead of L^+ and L^*.

3   Hash Functions and Collisions

Assume (without loss of generality) that all our messages are nonempty words over the (message block) alphabet A. Let $B = \{0, 1\}$ be the binary alphabet.

Definition 1. *A* hash function *(of length n, where $n \in \mathbb{N}_+$) is a mapping $g : A^+ \to B^n$.*

An ideal hash function g is a variable input length random oracle (VIL-RO): for each $x \in A^+$, the value $g(x) \in B^n$ is chosen uniformly at random.

Let $k \in \mathbb{N}_+$. A *k-collision* in the hash function g is a set $C \subseteq A^+$ such that $|C| = k$ and $g(x) = g(y)$ for all $x, y \in C$.

According to the (generalized) *birthday paradox*, a k-collision in g can be found (with probability approx. $\frac{1}{2}$) by hashing $(k!)^{\frac{1}{k}} 2^{\frac{n(k-1)}{k}}$ messages [4]. Two remarks can be made immediately:

- In the case $k = 2$ approximately $\sqrt{2} \cdot 2^{\frac{n}{2}}$ hashings are needed; intuitively most of us would expect the number to be around 2^{n-1}.
- For each k in $\mathbb{N}_+$, finding a $(k+1)$-collision consumes much more resources than finding a k-collision.

Joux proved in [3] that the latter property does not hold for the so called iterated hash functions which we rigorously introduce next.

Definition 2. *A* compression function *(of length n) is a mapping $f : B^n \times A \to B^n$ where A is an alphabet, $n \in \mathbb{N}_+$, and $|A| > 2^n$.*

Again, an ideal compression function f is a *fixed input length random oracle* (FIL-RO for short): for each $h \in B^n$ and $y \in A$, the value $f(h, y) \in B^n$ is chosen uniformly at random.

Let now f be as above; define the *iterated hash function* $f^+ : B^n \times A^+ \to B^n$ (based on f) inductively as follows. Let $h \in B^n$, $y_1 \in A$, and $y_2 \in A^+$. Then $f^+(h, y_1) = f(h, y_1)$ and $f^+(h, y_1 y_2) = f^+(f(h, y_1), y_2)$.

Given $k \in \mathbb{N}_+$ and $h_0 \in A$, a *k-collision (with initial value h_0) in the iterated hash function* f^+ is a set $C \subseteq A^+$ such that $|C| = k$ and for all $u, v \in C$, $|u| = |v|$ and $f^+(h_0, u) = f^+(h_0, v)$.

We assume that the attacker knows f (and thus f^+) only as a black box. She/he does not know anything about the internal structure of f, but can make *queries* on f and get the respective responses.

A *k-collision attack on a f^+* can loosely be defined to be a probabilistic process (often based on the birthday problem) that, given any initial value h_0, finds a

k-collision on f^+ with probability one. Moreover, it is assumed that the expected number of queries on f in the aforementioned probabilistic process remains the same with any initial value. The *complexity of a k-collision attack on* f^+ is then the expected number of queries on f required to get an k-collision. The attacks are realised in a stepwise manner; in each step a statistical experiment, often a birthday attack -like procedure, is carried out. The execution of the step is repeated until a collision is found.

4   Previous Work

In this section, we describe some of the previous methods for finding multicollisions. First of all, a basic brute force multicollision attack against any hash function has the complexity $O(k!^{\frac{1}{k}}2^{\frac{n(k-1)}{k}})$ for k colliding messages [4]. This was thought to be optimal also for iterated hash functions, until Joux's discovery. In the following, we denote by f the compression function used in the iterated hash function.

The Joux's method [3] for generating 2^k-collisions is of the (average) complexity $O(k2^{\frac{n}{2}})$. In this method, one can begin with any initial value h_0 and one finds two message blocks x_1 and x_1' such that $h_1 = f(h_0, x_1) = f(h_0, x_1')$. Now, continuing the same approach to h_1 and so on, one obtains a 2^k-collision after finding k collisions. In Joux's method there is no restriction on the initial values or the function f, which can be assumed to be a FIL-RO or any other compression function. Also the birthday attacks in each of the steps can be performed with the memoryless birthday attack described in [11] and [12].

Kelsey and Schneier describe a multicollision finding algorithm in their paper [5]. This algorithm is used to generate a second preimage attack against iterated hash functions and it has the complexity $O(2^{\frac{n}{2}})$ for arbitrarily large multicollisions. However, there are some assumptions on the underlying function f and the memory required by the attacker. The function f is assumed to have easily found fixed points, i.e. such values of f denoted by h and message blocks m for which $f(h, m) = h$. Also the attacker is assumed to have $O(2^{\frac{n}{2}})$ memory available for storing the intermediate values. There is also a variant which does not rely on fixed points and generates large multicollisions in $O(2^{n/2})$ time. These messages are too long to be used in practice.

Aumasson [6] has modified the above method in such a way that there is no need to assume any memory for the attacker and the complexity remains the same $O(2^{\frac{n}{2}})$ for arbitrarily large multicollisions. This method also assumes that fixed points are easily found for f and that the attacker can choose the initial value. After this, one only needs to find one fixed point collision and arbitrarily large multicollisions can be generated. Messages generated with this method are fairly short and could be used in practical attacks.

Multicollisions have been applied in recent attacks against iterated hash functions. Kelsey & Kohno [9] describe a generic chosen target forced prefix preimage attack and apply a special diamond structure multicollision in their attack.

This method has been applied to gain second preimage attacks on dithered hash functions [10].

5   A Variant of Joux's Attack

Next we present a variant of Joux's multicollision attack. The attack is a generalization of Joux's method and uses the information on messages and hash values gathered in previous steps of the attack.

5.1   Background Contemplations

Let us suppose that Joux's attack is carried out as a statistical experiment in the following way. In step k of the attack we create $2^{\frac{n}{2}}$ message blocks $m_{k,1}, m_{k,2}, \ldots, m_{k,2^{\frac{n}{2}}}$ and hash values $f(h_{k-1}, m_{k,i}) = h_{k,i}$ for all $i = 1, 2, \ldots,$ $2^{\frac{n}{2}}$. Then we look for a value $h_k = h_{k,i_k} = h_{k,j_k}$, where $j_k, i_k \in \{1, 2, \ldots, 2^{\frac{n}{2}}\}$ and $j_k \neq i_k$. In k steps this method creates a collision with size 2^k where the colliding messages are $m_1 m_2 \cdots m_k$, with $m_t \in \{m_{t,i_t}, m_{t,j_t}\}$ for $t = 1, 2, \ldots, k$.

In $2^{\frac{n}{2}}$ hash values we have $\binom{2^{\frac{n}{2}}}{2}$ pairs of hash values. Thus we assume, that in

$$\binom{2^{\frac{n}{2}}}{2} = 2^{n-1} - 2^{\frac{n}{2}-1}$$

possible pairs of messages there should be at least one pair with the same hash value thus providing an 2-collision. The probability for finding a 2−collision in $2^{\frac{n}{2}}$ messages is approximately 0.4 [13,7,4]. We repeat the procedure until a collision is found and the expected number of repetitions is 2.5. This implies that the expected complexity of creating a 2^k-collision with Joux attack as described above is approximately $2.5 \cdot k\, 2^{\frac{n}{2}}$. Note that the amount of memory needed is approximately $2^{\frac{n}{2}}$; having less memory increases the number of compression function calls [11].

The basic idea of our attack is to create smaller sets of message blocks and instead of searching for the collision only in the current set, we also compare the hash values of the current set with s previous ones. This gives us greater probability of finding collisions with less work. The downside is that we need more memory space to store the message blocks and hash values .

Let $s \in \mathbb{N}_+$. Suppose that we have enough memory to store the message blocks and the respective hash values produced during the previous s steps of the attack. Suppose furthermore that in each step approx. $\frac{1}{\sqrt{2s}} 2^{\frac{n}{2}}$ message blocks are generated and their respective hash values computed. The amount of memory needed here is approximately $\frac{s+1}{\sqrt{2s}} 2^{\frac{n}{2}}$.

Assume that we are in the $(k+1)$st step of the attack ($k \in \mathbb{N}$, $k \geq s$). Let M_j be the set of pairs of message blocks and respective hash values computed in the step $j = k-s+1, k-s+2, \ldots, k$. Next we generate $\frac{1}{\sqrt{2s}} 2^{\frac{n}{2}}$ new random messages and hash values. According to Theorem 2.1 in [7] the probability $p_1(s)$ of finding a collision within this new set through birthday paradox is approximately $1 - e^{-\frac{q(s)^2}{2^{n+1}}}$, where $q(s) = \frac{1}{\sqrt{2s}} 2^{\frac{n}{2}}$ and we get $p_1(s) \approx 1 - e^{-\frac{1}{4s}}$.

Let H_i be the set of hash values in step i, where $i = k - s + 1, k - s + 2, \ldots, k$. Denote by $p_2(s)$ the probability that a collision is found between the newest set and some of the previously generated s sets, i.e., that $H_{k+1} \cap H_i$ is nonempty for at least one $i \in \{k - s + 1, k - s + 2, \ldots, k\}$. Let us evaluate the value of $p_2(s)$. We can calculate the number of possible pairs h_1, h_2, where $h_1 \in H_{k+1}$, $h_2 \in H$, where $H = \cup_{i=k-s+1}^{k} H_i$ and get

$$|H_{k+1} \times H| \approx \frac{1}{\sqrt{2s}} 2^{\frac{n}{2}} \cdot \frac{s}{\sqrt{2s}} 2^{\frac{n}{2}} = 2^{n-1}$$

which is more pairs of hash values than $2^{n-1} - 2^{\frac{n}{2}-1}$ that is provided in each step of Joux's attack. Thus we can safely assume, that $p_2(s) \approx 0.4$.

Suppose now that $p_3(s)$ is the probability that either 1° there is a collision between hash values calculated in the $(k+1)$st step or that 2° there exists a common hash value in the sets H_{k+1} and H. Since the events in 1° and in 2° are clearly statistically independent, the equality $p_3(s) = p_1(s) + p_2(s) - p_1(s)p_2(s)$ holds. This means that

$$p_3(s) \approx 1 - e^{-\frac{1}{4s}} + \frac{2}{5} - (1 - e^{-\frac{1}{4s}})\frac{2}{5} = 1 - \frac{3}{5}e^{-\frac{1}{4s}}.$$

When we let s grow, $p_3(s)$ approaches from above the number 0.4, the collision probability of Joux's attack.

5.2   The (Probabilistic) Attack Algorithm

Let an iterated hash function $f^+ : B^n \times A^+ \to B^n$, an initial value $h_0 \in B^n$, and an integer $s \in \mathbb{N}_+$ be given. Denote $d = \frac{1}{\sqrt{2s}} 2^{\frac{n}{2}}$.

Initialization. Let $h := h_0$, $i := 1$, and $C_0 := \{\epsilon\}$. While $i < s + 1$ do the following.

Generate d random message blocks $m_1, m_2, \ldots, m_d$. Compute the respective compression function values $f(h, m_j)$ for $j = 1, 2, \ldots, d$. Let $(m_{i,j}, h_{i,j}) := (m_j, f(h, m_j))$ for $j = 1, 2, \ldots, d$, $M_i := \{(m_{i,j}, h_{i,j}) | j = 1, 2, \ldots, d\}$ and $H_i = \{h_{i,j} | j = 1, 2, \ldots, d\}$. Search for a collision in $h_{i,1}, h_{i,2} \ldots, h_{i,d}$.

A. Suppose that a collision is found. Let $j_1, j_2 \in \{1, 2, \ldots, d\}$, $j_1 \neq j_2$, be such that $h_{i,j_1} = h_{i,j_2}$. Then set $D := \{m_{i,j_1}, m_{i,j_2}\}$, $h := h_{i,j_1}$, and $C_i := C_{i-1} \cdot D$. Finally set $i := i + 1$.

B. Suppose that no collision is found in $h_{i,1}, h_{i,2}, \ldots, h_{i,d}$. If $i = 1$, set $h := h_{i,1}$, $C_1 := C_0 \cdot \{m_{i,1}\}$, and $i := i + 1$. Assume that $i > 1$. Search for a collision between the values in the set H_i and the values in the union $\cup_{j=1}^{i-1} H_j$.

1° Assume that a collison is found. Let $i_1 \in \{1, 2, \ldots, i - 1\}$ be the greatest number such that there exist $l_1, l_2 \in \{1, 2, \ldots, d\}$, $l_1 \neq l_2$, for which $h_{i,l_1} = h_{i_1,l_2}$. Set $C_i := C_{i-1} \cdot \{m_{i,l_1}\} \cup C_{i_1-1} \cdot \{m_{i_1,l_2}\}$, and $i := i + 1$.

$2°$ Assume that no collision between the values in the set H_i and the values in the union $\cup_{j=1}^{i-1} H_j$ is found. Then set $C_i := C_{i-1} \cdot \{m_{i_1}\}$ and $i := i + 1$.

We have now completed the initialization and are ready to describe the real attack. The procedure is exactly the same as before, except that if no collision is found, we shall repeat the generation of the set of random message blocks (and the execution of the step) until a collision is found.

Assumptions for the general step. Let $k \in \mathbb{N}_+$, $k \geq s$. Suppose that the sets $M_{k-i} := \{(m_{k-i,j}, h_{k-i,j}) | j = 1, 2, \ldots, d\}$ and $H_{k-i} = \{h_{k-i,j} | j = 1, 2, \ldots, d\}$ for $i = 0, 1, \ldots, s-1$ are created as well as the collision sets $C_{k-s}, C_{k-s+1}, \ldots, C_k$. Assume that h is given.

The general (k+1)st step. Generate d random message blocks $m_1, m_2, \ldots, m_d$. Compute the respective hash values $f(h, m_i)$ for $i = 1, 2, \ldots, d$. Set

$$(m_{k+1,j}, h_{k+1,j}) := (m_j, f(h, m_j))$$

for $j = 1, 2, \ldots, d$, $M_{k+1} := \{(m_{k+1,j}, h_j) | j = 1, 2, \ldots, d\}$ and $H_{k+1} = \{h_{k+1,j} | j = 1, 2, \ldots, d\}$. Search for collision in $h_{k+1,1}, h_{k+1,2}, \ldots, h_{k+1,d}$.

C. Suppose that a collision is found. Let $j_1, j_2 \in \{1, 2, \ldots, d\}$, $j_1 \neq j_2$ are such that $h_{i,j_1} = h_{i,j_2}$. Then set $D := \{m_{k+1,j_1}, m_{k+1,j_2}\}$ and $h := h_{k+1,j_1}$. Finally set $C_{k+1} := C_k \cdot D$.

D. Suppose that no collision is found in $h_{k+1,1}, h_{k+1,2} \ldots, h_{k+1,d}$. Search for a collision between the values in the set H_{k+1} and the values in the union $\cup_{j=k-s+1}^{k} H_j$.

$3°$ Assume that a collison is found. Let $i_1 \in \{k - s + 1, k - s + 2, \ldots, k\}$ be the greatest number such that there exist $l_1, l_2 \in \{1, 2, \ldots, d\}$, $l_1 \neq l_2$ for which $h_{k+1,l_1} = h_{i_1,l_2}$. Set $C_{k+1} := C_k \cdot \{m_{k+1,l_1}\} \cup C_{i_1-1} \cdot \{m_{i_1,l_2}\}$.

$4°$ Assume that no collision between the values in the set H_{k+1} and the values in the union $\cup_{j=k-s+1}^{k} H_j$ is found. Then repeat the execution of the $(k + 1)$st step.

Let us now assume that the $(k+1)$st step is carried out successfully and we have found a match. It is time to look at the size of the created multicollision. If there is a match between hash values $h_{k+1,1}, h_{k+1,2}, \ldots, h_{k+1,d}$, say $h_{k+1,i} = h_{k+1,j}$, $i \neq j$, then we have just doubled the size of our multicollision, because the last block of the colliding messages can be chosen to be $\{m_{k+1,i}, m_{k+1,j}\}$. This means that the value $|C_{k+1}| = 2|C_k|$. If this is not the case then $h_{k+1,l_1} = h_{i_1,l_2}$ for some $i_1 \in \{k - s + 1, k - s + 2, \ldots, k\}$ and $l_1, l_2 \in \{1, 2, \ldots, d\}$, $l_1 \neq l_2$. This means that almost certainly the equality $|C_{k+1}| = |C_k| + |C_{i_1-1}|$ holds.

Remark 1. Obviously all the messages in our collision set C_{k+1} are not of equal length, which at first seems to be a problem. We shall address this problem later.

5.3   Calculating the Expected Value

Let us now evaluate the size of the created multicollision in step $k + 1$, $k \geq s$. If there is a match in $h_{k+1,1}, h_{k+1,2}, \ldots, h_{k+1,d}$ the size of the created collision is $|C_{k+1}| = 2|C_k|$ and the probability for this is $\frac{p_1(s)}{p_3(s)}$. Otherwise the collision is between sets H_{k+1} and some set H_i, where $i_1 \in \{k - s + 1, k - s + 2, \cdots, k\}$ which means that $|C_{k+1}| = |C_k| + |C_{i_1 - 1}|$. We may assume that each of the sets $H_{k-s+1}, H_{k-s+2}, \ldots, H_k$ contains the matching hash value with equal likelihood; this probability is $\frac{p_3(s)-p_1(s)}{sp_3(s)}$ since the number of sets is s.

If we now mark the expected size of the multicollision in step i with E_i we get the equations

$$E_{k+s+1} = \frac{p_1(s)}{p_3(s)}(2E_{k+s}) + \frac{p_3(s) - p_1(s)}{p_3(s)}\left(E_{k+s} + \frac{1}{s}(E_{k+s-1} + E_{k+s-2} + \cdots + E_k)\right)$$

$$= \left(1 + \frac{p_1(s)}{p_3(s)}\right)(E_{k+s}) + \left(1 - \frac{p_1(s)}{p_3(s)}\right)\frac{1}{s}(E_{k+s-1} + E_{k+s-2} + \cdots + E_k) \quad (1)$$

for each $k \in \mathbb{N}$. From the definitions of $p_1(s)$ and $p_3(s)$, it is easy to see that when s is large $E_{k+s+1} \approx E_{k+s} + \frac{1}{s}(E_{k+s-1} + E_{k+s-2} + \cdots + E_k), k \in \mathbb{N}$.

Let us now assume that s is large and evaluate the size of the multicollision in step $k + s + 1$. We agree that the equation

$$E_{k+s+1} = E_{k+s} + \frac{1}{s}(E_{k+s-1} + E_{k+s-2} + \cdots + E_k)$$

holds when $k \in \mathbb{N}$. Moreover, we set $E_i = |C_i|$ for all $i = 1, 2, \ldots, s$, where $|C_1|, |C_2|, \ldots, |C_s|$ are the cardinalities of the sets determined in the initialization step of our attack. The above recursive equation has the characteristic polynomial $f_s(x) = x^{s+1} - x^s - \frac{1}{s}(x^{s-1} + x^{s-2} + \cdots + 1)$. The roots of this polynomial certainly determine the values of E_k, where $k > s$. For large values of k the root that has the greatest absolute value dominates the values of the sequence and gives us the ratio $\frac{E_{k+1}}{E_k}, k \in \mathbb{N}$.

The basic analysis shows that there exists exactly one positive real root x_s for $f_s(x)$, with $x_s \in]1 + \frac{1}{\sqrt{s+2}}, 1 + \frac{1}{\sqrt{s}}[$. When s is odd, there is also a negative real root y for $f(x)$, with $|y| < 1$. Also all the complex roots have absolute values strictly less than x_s. The rigorous mathematical proof of the last fact can be found in the appendix. Thus we have found the ratio $\frac{E_{k+1}}{E_k}$ for the large values of k. This means that by taking k steps where k is large we can create a multicollision with expected size x_s^k, where $x_s^k > (1 + \frac{1}{\sqrt{s+2}})^k$.

5.4   Comparing the Procedure to Joux's Attack

MD-strengthening means that the length of the message is added to the end of the original message before hashing. This forces all of the colliding messages in our method to have the same length. In Joux's attack, this is not a problem because all the messages have the same length. At first this might seem problematic to our attack, since the lengths of the created messages are not equal. However when the number of the steps taken is large, we can overcome this obstacle.

If we take k steps, then there are certainly fewer than k possible lengths for the messages. This means that the expected value for the largest set with the same length messages is at least

$$\frac{(1 + \frac{1}{\sqrt{s+2}})^k}{k}.$$

In reality the largest collision set with messages of the same length is of course much greater, but even this evaluation shows that when we are considering large values of k the length of the messages is not really a hindrance.

Let us now compare the complexity of our attack with the complexity of the Joux's attack. As we have stated before, with $2.5 \cdot k2^{\frac{n}{2}}$ work, we should get

$$0.4 \cdot \frac{2.5k2^{\frac{n}{2}}}{2^{\frac{n}{2}}} = k$$

successful steps in Joux's attack. Each step of Joux's attack multiplies the size of the multicollision by two and thus, k steps gives us a 2^k-collision.

With $2.5 \cdot k2^{\frac{n}{2}}$ work our method yields us

$$\frac{p_3(s) \cdot 2.5 \cdot k \cdot 2^{\frac{n}{2}}}{\frac{1}{\sqrt{2s}} \cdot 2^{\frac{n}{2}}} = p_3(s) \cdot 2.5 \cdot \sqrt{2s}k > \sqrt{2s}k$$

successful steps. In each step of our attack the size of the multicollision is multiplied by x_s. Thus, the expected size of the multicollision is greater than

$$\frac{x_s^{\sqrt{2sk}}}{\sqrt{2sk}} > \frac{1}{\sqrt{2sk}} \cdot (1 + \frac{1}{\sqrt{s+2}})^{\sqrt{2sk}}.$$

From this equation we get

$$\frac{1}{\sqrt{2sk}} \cdot ([1 + \frac{1}{\sqrt{s+2}}]^{\sqrt{2s}})^k$$

Thus, when $s \to \infty$

$$\left(1 + \frac{1}{\sqrt{s+2}}\right)^{\sqrt{2s}} = \left[\left(1 + \frac{1}{\sqrt{s+2}}\right)^{\sqrt{s}}\right]^{\sqrt{2}} \to e^{\sqrt{2}} \approx 4.113.$$

So, if we are creating large multicollisions (k is large) and using a large number of stored sets of message blocks (s is large), our attack creates a $\frac{1}{\sqrt{2sk}}(e^{\sqrt{2}})^k$-collision, whereas Joux's attack creates a 2^k-collision, with the same amount of compression function calls. This means that, assuming that s and k are large, while Joux's attack produces a 2^k-collision, our method (with the same amount of work), provides us with a multicollision of size approximately 2^{2k}.

Remark 2. Assume momentarily that fixed points for the compression function are easy to generate. Then the above attack can be initiated by generating a fixed point and, proceeding as presented above and applying the fixed point, adjust the lengths of the generated attack messages to be of equal length.

6 Special Cases with Small Values of s

In practice the amount of usable memory and the maximum length of the messages limit the use of our attack. However, even the small values of s give us quite nice results for large k. We can assume that the case $s = 0$ is the standard attack by Joux.

If we choose $s = 1$, the probability of succeeding in a step is $p_3(1) \approx 0.53272$ and by (1) the expected size of the created multicollision is

$$E_{k+2} = \left(1 + \frac{p_1(1)}{p_3(1)}\right)(E_{k+1}) + \left(1 - \frac{p_1(1)}{p_3(1)}\right)(E_k).$$

By using MAPLE or similar mathematical software, we may evaluate the positive real root of the characteristic polynomial $f_1(x)$ and obtain

$$x_1 = \frac{\left(1 + \frac{p_1(1)}{p_3(1)}\right) + \sqrt{\left(1 + \frac{p_1(1)}{p_3(1)}\right)^2 + 4\left(1 - \frac{p_1(1)}{p_3(1)}\right)}}{2} \approx 1.74948.$$

If we now call compression function $2.5\,k2^{\frac{n}{2}}$ times, we should get $p_3(1)\frac{2.5k2^{\frac{n}{2}}}{\frac{1}{\sqrt{2}}2^{\frac{n}{2}}} = \sqrt{2} \cdot 2.5\,p_3(1)k$ successful steps. Thus the expected value for multicollisions with equal length messages is approximately

$$\frac{1}{\sqrt{2k}}(1.74948)^{\sqrt{2}\cdot2.5p_3(1)k} \approx \frac{1}{\sqrt{2k}}(2.87)^k.$$

When $s = 2$ we get $p_3(2) \approx 0.47050$ and the positive real root of $f_2(x)$ is approximately 1.62322. Thus with $2.5 \cdot k2^{\frac{n}{2}}$ work, the number of successful steps should be $p_3(2)\frac{2.5k2^{\frac{n}{2}}}{0.5\cdot2^{\frac{n}{2}}} = 2 \cdot 2.5 \cdot p_3(2)k$. This means that our attack creates a multicollision with a total expected size of approximately $\frac{1}{2k}(3.13)^k$.

The last case we are able to solve simply by using a general formula (for the equation with power 4) is the case $s = 3$. Now we get $p_3(3) \approx 0.44797$ and the positive real root of $f_3(x)$ is approximately 1.54478. Thus with $2.5 \cdot k2^{\frac{n}{2}}$ work, the number of successful steps should be $p_3(3)\frac{2.5k2^{\frac{n}{2}}}{\frac{1}{\sqrt{6}}2^{\frac{n}{2}}} = \sqrt{6} \cdot 2.5 \cdot p_3(3)k$. Thus our attack creates a multicollision with a total expected size of approx. $\frac{1}{\sqrt{6k}}(3.30)^k$.

7 Borderline Considerations: Collisions Based either on Very Long Messages or Fixed Points of the Function f

Given a compression function $f : B^n \times A \to B^n$, we can interpret the functioning of f^+ as a (deterministic) *finite state automaton* (abbrev. *dfsa*) $\mathcal{A}_f$:

- locally in any (inner) state $h \in B^n$, the automaton $\mathcal{A}_f$ reads an arbitrary (input) symbol $a \in A$, changes its state to $f(h, a)$ and is ready to read a new symbol; and

- globally starting in the initial state (or value) $h_0 \in B^n$, after reading the word $a_1 a_2 \cdots a_m$, where $m \in \mathbb{N}_+$ in a stepwise manner described above, the automaton $\mathcal{A}_f$ is in the state $f^+(h, a_1 a_2 \cdots a_m)$.

7.1 Multicollisions Induced by the Cycle Structure of the Finite State Automaton $\mathcal{A}_f$

Fix $a \in A$ and, starting from the initial value h_0, generate the compression function values $h_i = f(h_{i-1}, a)$ for $i = 1, 2, 3, \ldots$. By the birthday paradox, there exists, with a probability approx. 0.4, a collision among the first $2^{\frac{n}{2}}$ values of the above sequence. As seen before, the expected number of queries required to find such a sequence is $2.5 \cdot 2^{\frac{n}{2}}$. Let $p, p' \in \{1, 2, \ldots 2^{\frac{n}{2}}\}$, $p < p'$, be such that $h_p = h_{p'}$. Denote $r = p' - p$. Obviously all the messages in the language $a^p(a^r)^*$ induce the same hash value h_p. The language $a^p(a^r)^*$, however, does not contain a proper multicollision set in f^+; all the messages in $a^p(a^r)^*$ are of different length. From automata-theoretic point of view, we have found a cycle

$$(h_p, a, h_{p+1})(h_{p+1}, a, h_{p+2}) \cdots (h_{p'-1}, a, h_p)$$

starting and ending in the state h_p in the set of computations of $\mathcal{A}_f$.

To solve the length problem, we proceed as follows. Let $b \in A \setminus \{a\}$, be a new symbol; starting from the hash value $l_0 = h_p$ generate the compression function values $l_i = f(l_{i-1}, b)$ for $i = 1, 2, 3, \ldots$ Again, with a significant probability, there exists a collision among the values $l_0, l_1, l_2 \ldots, l_{2^{n/2}}$. Let $q, q' \in \{1, 2, \ldots 2^{\frac{n}{2}}\}$, $q < q'$, be such that $l_q = l_{q'}$. Denote $s = q' - q$ and notice that all the messages in the language $a^p(a^r)^* b^q(b^s)^*$ have the same hash value. A second cycle

$$(l_q, b, l_{q+1})(l_{q+1}, b, l_{q+2}) \cdots (l_{q'-1}, b, l_q)$$

starting and ending in the state l_q among the computations of $\mathcal{A}_f$ has been located. It is also important to notice that there exist equal length messages in the above language. Our next task is to pick those up. Let d be the least common multiplier of the integers r and s. Since both r and s divide the positive integer d, the language $R = a^p(a^d)^* b^q(b^d)^*$ is a subset of $a^p(a^r)^* b^q(b^s)^*$. Thus $f^+(h_0, w) = l_q$ for all $w \in R$. Let $k \in \mathbb{N}_+$. Then

$$R_k = \{ a^p(a^d)^i b^q(b^d)^{k-1-i} \mid i \in \{0, 1, \ldots, k-1\} \}$$

is a k-multicollision set in f^+ with initial value h_0 since all its messages are of the same length ($= p + q + (k-1)d$) and have the same hash value ($= l_q$).

Some complexity remarks are now well justified.

1. To find the language $a^p(a^r)^* b^q(b^s)^*$, and thus a multicollision set R_k on f^+, in average $5 \cdot 2^{\frac{n}{2}}$ queries on f is required. The same symbols a and b of A and the same cycles of the automaton $\mathcal{A}_k$ can be exploited for all sets R_k, $k \in \mathbb{N}_+$.

2. The messages in the sets R_k can be very long. For randomly chosen positive integers i and j, the probability that the greatest common divisor of i and j is equal to one, is approximately $6/\pi^2$. Thus there is no reason to assume that the integers r and s in our construction possess a large common divisor. A reasonable upper bound for least common multiplier d of r and s is 2^n. The length of any message in R_k is thereby at most $2^{\frac{n}{2}+1} + (k-1) \cdot 2^n$, $k \in \mathbb{N}_+$. This makes these collision sets useless in practice.

3. Regardless of the huge length, the (information theory or Kolmogorov) complexity of messages in R_k, $k \in \mathbb{N}_+$, is very small. To present and store the multicollision set R_k, very little resources is required. In fact, one only needs to store the symbols a and b and the numbers p, r, q and s. Also the possibility to choose, instead of the symbols a and b, any messages x and y, $x \neq y$, should increase the flexibility of the collision set and the number of alternatives to create it.

As we have seen above, the cycle construction in $\mathcal{A}_f$ creates infinitely large multicollisions while the work we have to do remains constant. In the basic construction, the expected number of calls of the compression function f is $5 \cdot 2^{\frac{n}{2}}$. On the downside, the generated messages are extremely long, the length is in the order of magnitude $O(k \cdot 2^n)$ blocks. This is of course huge, when we compare it with the attack by Joux, which gives us 2^r-collision, where the messages size is r blocks.

The downside of the Joux attack is that we have to search for k 2-collisions to create a 2^k-collision. It is possible to combine our attack with that of Joux's and retain many properties from both of them.

Suppose that the attacker is capable of processing messages of length approximately $2^{\frac{n}{2}}$.

We start by generating the values $h_i = f(h_{i-1}, a)$ for $i = 1, 2, \ldots, 2^{\frac{n}{2}}$, where h_0 is an initial value and a a fixed symbol in A. Next we, applying Joux's method, search message block symbols b and c in A such that $b \neq c$ and $f(h_{2^{\frac{n}{2}}}, b) = f(h_{2^{\frac{n}{2}}}, c)$. Denote $l_0 = f(h_{2^{\frac{n}{2}}}, c)$. We continue by generating the values $l_i = f(l_{i-1}, a)$ for $i = 1, 2, \ldots, 2^{\frac{n}{2}}$. By the birthday paradox, with a significant probability, there exist $r, s \in \{1, 2, \ldots, 2^{\frac{n}{2}}\}$ such that $h_r = l_s$. Obviously all the messages in the language

$$T = a^r \{ a^{2^{\frac{n}{2}}-r} b\, a^s, a^{2^{\frac{n}{2}}-r} c\, a^s \}^*$$

have the same hash value l_s. To create T, on average $5.5 \cdot 2^{\frac{n}{2}}$ queries on f are required.

Let now $k \in \mathbb{N}_+$ and

$$T_k = a^r \{ a^{2^{\frac{n}{2}}-r} b\, a^s, a^{2^{\frac{n}{2}}-r} c\, a^s \}^k .$$

All the messages in T_k are of the same length ($= r + k(2^{\frac{n}{2}} - r + s)$) with the same hash value ($= l_s$), so T_k is a k-collision set on f^+ with initial value h_0.

We have to do more work than would be necessary for the normal cycle construction. Basically, the expected number of compression function calls is $5.5 \cdot 2^{n/2}$ times. On the other hand, the length of the messages for 2^k-collision is $r + k(2^{n/2} - r + 1 + s)$ blocks, which gives us messages the size of which is the order of magnitude $O(k\, 2^{n/2})$ blocks.

7.2 When Fixed Points of f Are Easily Constructed

A *fixed point* of the compression function f is a pair $(h, x) \in B^n \times A$ such that $f(h, x) = h$. Suppose for a while that fixed points of f can easily be found [5]. In our case, this means that there exists a *random fixed point generator* for f, i.e., a randomized algorithm $RFPG_f$ which, when requested, returns a random fixed point of f. Suppose furthermore that $RFPG_f$ works in constant time in the sense that the generation of $2^{\frac{n}{2}}$ fixed points of f requires only $O(2^{\frac{n}{2}})$ queries on f.

Multicollision sets in f^+ can now be generated as follows.

1. Given an initial value h_0, generate $2^{\frac{n}{2}}$ random messages a_i, $i = 1, 2, \ldots, 2^{\frac{n}{2}}$ and their respective compression function values $h_i = f(h_0, a_i)$, $i = 1, 2, \ldots, 2^{\frac{n}{2}}$.
2. Using $RFPG_f$, generate $2^{\frac{n}{2}}$ random fixed points $(k_1, b_1), (k_2, b_2) \ldots, (k_{2^{\frac{n}{2}}}, b_{2^{\frac{n}{2}}})$ of f.
3. Find $p, q \in \{1, 2, \ldots, 2^{\frac{n}{2}}\}$ such that $h_p = k_q$.
4. Let $l_0 = h_p$. Generate $2^{\frac{n}{2}}$ random messages c_i, $i = 1, 2, \ldots, 2^{\frac{n}{2}}$ and their respective compression function values $l_i = f(l_0, c_i)$, $i = 1, 2, \ldots, 2^{\frac{n}{2}}$.
5. Using the previously generated random fixed point sequence $(k_1, b_1), (k_2, b_2) \ldots, (k_{2^{\frac{n}{2}}}, b_{2^{\frac{n}{2}}})$ of f, find $r, s \in \{1, 2, \ldots, 2^{\frac{n}{2}}\}$ such that $l_r = k_s$.
6. Return the set $R = a_p b_q^* c_r b_s^*$.

We may assume that the probability that $b_q = c_r$ is negligible. Certainly $f(h_0, a_p) = f(h_p, b_q) = h_p$. On the other hand $f(l_0, c_r) = f(l_r, b_s) = l_r$. This means that each message in R has the same hash value $(= l_r)$. The construction of the set R can (with nonnegligible probability) be carried out with $2^{\frac{n}{2}}$ requests on f.

Let $k \in \mathbb{N}_+$ and $R_k = \{a_p b_q^i c_r b_s^{k-i} | i \in \{0, 1, \ldots, k-1\}\}$. Obviously each message in R_k is of length $k + 2$, so R_k is a k-collision set on f with initial value h_0.

We have proved that if we have $RFPG_f$ available, then by making $2^{\frac{n}{2}+1}$ queries on f plus $2^{\frac{n}{2}}$ requests on $RFPG_f$, one can construct a multicollison set from which any k-collision set, $k \in \mathbb{N}_+$, easily can be picked.

Remark 3. The above method is essentially the same as presented in [5].

Remark 4. In information sciences in general and in information security in particular it is a common habit to visualize iterated structures with (directed) graphs. It is well known that finite digraphs represent an equivalent notion to finite state automata. However, when the state space of a system grows large, graphs loose their power of expression. Also when it is necessary treat computations as rigorous mathematical objects, system description with automata substantially outweighs graph representation.

8   Conclusion

In this paper, we have demonstrated some generalizations of recent multicollision attacks on iterated hash functions. Our first method shows that by using some memory and computing several smaller sets of hash values for comparison we can achieve better performance than with Joux's method with the same amount of work. Although Joux's method can also be applied with the so called memoryless birthday attacks, it should be noted that in [11] the authors mention, that any available memory can be used to enhance the performance of the algorithm. Thus memoryless birthday attacks have large constant factors affecting their performance. Similarly our method can be applied with smaller memory than $2^{n/2}$, but then one must do a lot more calculations to gain the necessary collisions.

The second method shows a fundamental property of iterated hash functions, which has been previously used in multicollision finding algorithms with some added assumptions. We were able to show that when the length of the messages is not restricted, finding arbitrarily large multicollisions takes only the same amount of work as finding two collisions. This idea is only of theoretical interest, as the messages generated with our method are utterly impractical to be used with real iterated hash functions.

The results, however, raise some interesting research problems. As the results of Joux and this paper show, one can generate practical multicollisions for iterated hash functions, even when the underlying compression function would be a FIL-RO. This requires a logarithmic factor of the size of the multicollision to enter in to the complexity. On the other hand, the theoretical result in this paper shows that arbitrarily large multicollisions for an ideal iterated hash function can be constructed without the logarithmic factor, when the message length is not restricted. The most intriguing result would be to find a result, which states that this theoretical limit can be reached even with practical message lengths. Also finding that there is a trade-off between the message length and the complexity of a multicollision attack would be an interesting result. We believe that such a trade-off exists and that practical multicollisions cannot be found for ideal iterated hash functions without some factor of the multicollision size coming in to the complexity.

References

1. Merkle, R.C.: One way hash functions and DES. In: Brassard, G. (ed.) CRYPTO 1989. LNCS, vol. 435, pp. 428–446. Springer, Heidelberg (1990)
2. Damgård, I.B.: A design principle for hash functions. In: Brassard, G. (ed.) CRYPTO 1989. LNCS, vol. 435, pp. 416–427. Springer, Heidelberg (1990)
3. Joux, A.: Multicollisions in iterated hash functions. application to cascaded constructions. In: Franklin, M. (ed.) CRYPTO 2004. LNCS, vol. 3152, pp. 306–316. Springer, Heidelberg (2004)
4. Suzuki, K., Tonien, D., Kurosawa, K., Toyota, K.: Birthday paradox for multicollisions. IEICE Transactions 91-A(1), 39–45 (2008)

5. Kelsey, J., Schneier, B.: Second preimages on n-bit hash functions for much less than 2^n work. In: Cramer, R. (ed.) EUROCRYPT 2005. LNCS, vol. 3494, pp. 474–490. Springer, Heidelberg (2005)

6. Aumasson, J.-P.: Faster multicollisions. In: Chowdhury, D.R., Rijmen, V., Das, A. (eds.) INDOCRYPT 2008. LNCS, vol. 5365, pp. 67–77. Springer, Heidelberg (2008)

7. Nandi, M., Stinson, D.R.: Multicollision attacks on some generalized sequential hash functions. IEEE Transactions on Information Theory 53(2), 759–767 (2007)

8. Hoch, J.J., Shamir, A.: Breaking the ICE - finding multicollisions in iterated concatenated and expanded (ICE) hash functions. In: Robshaw, M.J.B. (ed.) FSE 2006. LNCS, vol. 4047, pp. 179–194. Springer, Heidelberg (2006)

9. Kelsey, J., Kohno, T.: Herding Hash Functions and the Nostradamus Attack. In: Vaudenay, S. (ed.) EUROCRYPT 2006. LNCS, vol. 4004, pp. 183–200. Springer, Heidelberg (2006)

10. Andreeva, E., Bouillaguet, C., Fouque, P.-A., Hoch, J.J., Kelsey, J., Shamir, A., Zimmer, S.: Second preimage attacks on dithered hash functions. In: Smart, N.P. (ed.) EUROCRYPT 2008. LNCS, vol. 4965, pp. 270–288. Springer, Heidelberg (2008)

11. Sedgewick, R., Szymanski, T.G., Yao, A.C.: The complexity of finding cycles in periodic functions. SICOMP: SIAM Journal on Computing 11, 376–390 (1982)

12. Quisquater, J.-J., Delescaille, J.-P.: How easy is collision search. New results and applications to DES. In: Brassard, G. (ed.) CRYPTO 1989. LNCS, vol. 435, pp. 408–413. Springer, Heidelberg (1990)

13. Menezes, A.J., van Oorschot, P.C., Vanstone, S.A. (eds.): Handbook of Applied Cryptography. CRC Press, Boca Raton (1996)

Appendix

Now we have to find the solution to equation $x^{s+1} - x^s - \frac{1}{s}(x^{s-1} + x^{s-2} + \cdots + 1) = 0$ with the greatest absolute value. It is easy to see, that $x = 0$ is not root for the equation and so it can be written in the form $1 = x^{-1} + \frac{1}{s}(x^{-2} + x^{-3} + \cdots + x^{-s-1})$. Clearly $x^{-1} + \frac{1}{s}(x^{-2} + x^{-3} + \cdots + x^{-s-1})$ is decreasing when $x \in \mathbb{R}_+$ and so our equation can have only one positive real root. Polynomial $x^{s+1} - x^s - \frac{1}{s}(x^{s-1} + x^{s-2} + \cdots + 1)$ is clearly increasing without limit, when the values of x are large enough. It follows that if $x \in \mathbb{R}_+$ the values of the polynomial will be neqative before this root value and positive after it. It is also obvious that $x \neq 1$ so the equation can be written as

$$x^s(x-1) - \frac{1}{s}(x^{s-1} + x^{s-2} + \cdots + 1)$$

$$= x^s(x-1) + \frac{1 - x^s}{s(x-1)} = \frac{x^s[s(1-x)^2 - 1] + 1}{s(x-1)} = 0.$$

Finding a general solution to such equation is a hard if not impossible task. However finding an approximation is relatively easy. Let us set $g(x) = x^s[s(1 - x)^2 - 1] + 1$. Now $g(1 + \frac{1}{\sqrt{s}}) = (1 + \frac{1}{\sqrt{s}})^s[s(\frac{1}{\sqrt{s}})^2 - 1] + 1 = 1 > 0$. On the other hand $g(1 + \frac{1}{\sqrt{s+2}}) = (1 + \frac{1}{\sqrt{s+2}})^s[s(\frac{1}{\sqrt{s+2}})^2 - 1] + 1 = (1 + \frac{1}{\sqrt{s+2}})^s \frac{(-2)}{s+2} + 1 = 1 - (1 + \frac{1}{\sqrt{s+2}})^s \frac{1}{\frac{s}{2}+1}$. It is easy to compute this value for all $s = 2, 3, \cdots, 19$ and see that in these cases $g(1 + \frac{1}{\sqrt{s+2}}) < 0$.

Now we can assume, that $s \geq 20$. In this case, we get

$$(1 + \frac{1}{\sqrt{s+2}})^s = 1 + \frac{s}{(s+2)^{\frac{1}{2}}} + \frac{s(s-1)}{2(s+2)^1} + \frac{s(s-1)(s-2)}{6(s+2)^{\frac{3}{2}}} + \sum_{i=4}^{s} \binom{s}{i} \frac{1}{\sqrt{s+2}^i}.$$

Now $\frac{s(s-1)(s-2)}{6(s+2)^{\frac{3}{2}}} = \frac{s}{6} \cdot \frac{s-1}{s+2} \cdot \frac{s-2}{\sqrt{s+2}}$. If $s = 20$, $\frac{s-1}{s+2} \cdot \frac{s-2}{\sqrt{s+2}} > 3$. Since $\frac{s-1}{s+2}$ and $\frac{s-2}{\sqrt{s+2}}$ are clearly increasing when $s \geq 20$ we get $\frac{s(s-1)(s-2)}{6(s+2)^{\frac{3}{2}}} > \frac{s}{2}$, when $s \geq 20$. Thus $(1 + \frac{1}{\sqrt{s+2}})^s > \frac{s}{2} + 1$ which in turn means that $g(1 + \frac{1}{\sqrt{s+2}}) < 0$ also for values $s = 20, 21, \cdots$.

We have now proven that there is a positive real root $x \in]1 + \frac{1}{\sqrt{s+2}}, 1 + \frac{1}{\sqrt{s}}[$ for $g(x)$. This root is also the only positive real root of our equation. We mark this root with x_1. Next we will prove that other roots will have smaller absolute values.

Our equation can also be written in the form

$$x^{s+1} = x^s + \frac{1}{s}(x^{s-1} + x^{s-2} + \cdots + 1).$$

Let us now assume, that y is the root of equation and $y \notin \mathbb{R}_+$. This means that $|y + 1| < |y| + 1$. It follows that $|y^{s+1}| < |y^s| + \frac{1}{s}(|y^{s-1}| + |y^{s-2}| + \cdots |y| + 1)$. This in turn means that

$$|y|^{s+1} - |y|^s - \frac{1}{s}(|y|^{s-1} + |y|^{s-2} + \cdots + 1) < 0.$$

Since this equation has only single root in $\mathbb{R}_+$ and $|y| \in \mathbb{R}_+$ we have $|y| < x_1 = |x_1|$.

Hyper-Sbox View of AES-like Permutations: A Generalized Distinguisher

Shuang Wu, Dengguo Feng, Wenling Wu, and Bozhan Su

State Key Lab of Information Security, Institute of Software
Chinese Academy of Sciences
Beijing 100190, China
{wushuang,feng,wwl,subozhan}@is.iscas.ac.cn

Abstract. Grøstl[1] is one of the second round candidates of the SHA-3 competition[2] hosted by NIST, which aims to find a new hash standard. In this paper, we studied equivalent expressions of the generalized AES-like permutation. We found that four rounds of the AES-like permutation can be regarded as a Hyper-Sbox. Then we further analyzed the differential properties of both Super-Sbox and Hyper-Sbox. Based on these observations, we give an 8-round truncated differential path of the generalized AES-like permutation, which can be used to construct a distinguisher of 8-round Grøstl-256 permutation with 2^{64} time and 2^{64} memory. This is the best known distinguisher of reduced-round Grøstl permutation.

Keywords: Super-Sbox, Hyper-Sbox, AES-like permutation, Distinguisher, Grøstl, SHA-3 candidates.

1 Introduction

In the last few years, the cryptanalysis of hash functions has been significantly improved. The attacks on widely used hash standards, such as MD5 [3,4] and SHA-1 [5,6], have become serious threats to the security of the cryptographic systems based on these standards. In 2007, NIST announced the SHA-3 competition calling for new hash function designs in order to find a replacement of SHA-2. Since then, many new hash function designs have been submitted to the competition and only 14 of them are selected by NIST as the second round candidates.

The AES-like permutation is a very popular building block used in the second round candidates, such as ECHO[7], Grøstl[1], JH[8], Luffa[8] and SHAvite-3[9]. Some designers proved that properties of their hash functions can be reduced to the properties of the underlying building blocks. Cryptanalysis of the AES-like permutations is of significant value since it helps us to improve our understanding of these designs.

In FSE 2009, Florian Mendel et al. proposed a new tool of "Rebound" technique [10], which works amazingly well on AES-like designs. Then following researches focused on how to use degrees of freedom more efficiently [11,12,13,14].

X. Lai, M. Yung, and D. Lin (Eds.): Inscrypt 2010, LNCS 6584, pp. 155–168, 2011.
© Springer-Verlag Berlin Heidelberg 2011

In FSE 2010, Henri Gilbert et al. introduced the Super-Sbox view of AES-like permutations [15]. A Super-Sbox consists of two Sbox layers with an MDS layer inserted in the middle. They found that two rounds of AES-like permutation can be considered as a Super-Sbox, which allows more efficient use of the degrees of freedom in a rebound attack. Improved distinguishers of AES, Grøstl and ECHO permutations are constructed based on their observation.

Our contributions. In this paper, we considered the equivalent expressions of AES-like permutation and find that four rounds of the permutation can be considered as a Hyper-Sbox. Then we studied differential properties of both Super-Sbox and Hyper-Sbox and analyzed the complexity to find solutions for them with given input and output truncated differences.

Based on these observations, we tried to construct distinguisher of a generalized permutation based on an 8-round truncated differential path. Then we found that this distinguisher only works on permutations with state size of $r \times r$ cells, where $r \geq 7$. Since $r = 8$ for Grøstl-256, this generalized distinguisher works on 8-round Grøstl-256 permutation. The distinguisher has a complexity of 2^{64} computations and 2^{64} memory. Comparison with the distinguishers proposed by others are listed in Table 1.

Distinguisher proposed by Thomas Peyrin taks advantages of the different constant additions between two permutations P and Q used in Grøstl. It is the best known distinguisher on Grøstl compression function. Our result is a generalized distinguisher on AES-like permutations, also the best distinguisher on Grøstl-256 permutation.

We also considered distinguisher for AES-like permutations with non-square states. We found that this kind of distinguisher does not exist for 8-round Grøstl-512 permutation, because of some impossible truncated differential characteristics implied by the shift vector.

Table 1. Comparison to previous works

type	target	rounds	computational complexity	memory requirement	source
distinguisher	Grøstl-256 compression function	7	2^{56}	-	[11]
		8	2^{112}	2^{64}	[15]
		8	2^{64}	2^{64}	this paper
		9	2^{80}	2^{64}	[16]
		10	2^{192}	2^{64}	[16]
	Grøstl-512 compression function	11	2^{640}	2^{64}	[16]
	Grøstl-256 permutation	7	2^{56}	-	[11]
		8	2^{112}	2^{64}	[15]
		8	2^{64}	2^{64}	this paper

2 Preliminary

2.1 The Generalized AES-like Permutation

In this paper, we consider the generalized AES-like permutation. The state of a generalized AES-like permutation is considered as a $r \times r$ matrix of c-bit cells. One round of the permutation is written as

$$R = MixColumns \circ ShiftRows \circ SubBytes \circ AddConstant.$$

The four transformations are defined as:

- **AddConstant:** The AddConstant operation XORs a round-dependent constant to the state.
- **SubBytes:** The SubBytes transformation applies an S-box to each cell of the state.
- **ShiftRows:** The ShiftRows transformation cyclically rotates the cells of the i-th row leftwards by i positions.
- **MixColumns:** In the MixColumns operation, each column of the matrix is multiplied by an MDS matrix.

We use AC, SB, SR and MC to denote these transformations for short. One round of AES-like permutation is illustrated is Figure 1.

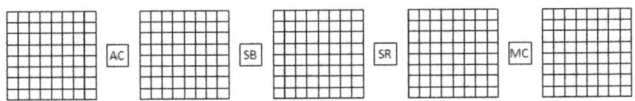

Fig. 1. One round of the generalized AES-like permutation

2.2 Specification of Grøstl Compression Function

The compression function f of Grøstl is constructed using two AES-like permutations P and Q: $f(h, m) = P(h \oplus m) \oplus Q(m) \oplus h$, as illustrated in Figure 2. The only difference between P and Q is that they use different round constants.

Grøstl-256 uses 10-round 512-bit permutations and Grøstl-512 uses 14-round 1024-bit permutations. State of the 512-bit permutation is processed as an 8×8 matrix of bytes. The 1024-bit permutation uses an 8×16 matrix of bytes. The 8-bit S-box used in Grøstl is the same as the one used in AES. ShiftRows transformations in the 512-bit and 1024-bit permutations use different shift vectors: $(0, 1, 2, 3, 4, 5, 6, 7)$ for the former one and $(0, 1, 2, 3, 4, 5, 6, 11)$ for the latter one. The MDS matrix used in the MC transformation is a circulant matrix $\mathcal{B} = circ(02, 02, 03, 04, 05, 03, 05, 07)$.

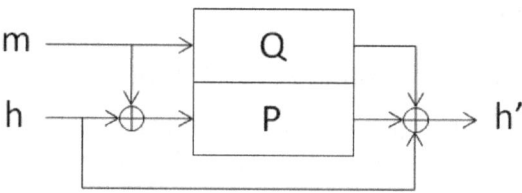

Fig. 2. Compression function of Grøstl

2.3   The Rebound Techniques and Properties of S-Boxes

The rebound techniques are proposed by Florian Mendel et al. at FSE 2009 [10]. The main idea is to solve the most expensive part of a truncated differential path and leave the cheaper part fulfilled by chance. In the intermediate part of the path, differences match with surprisingly high probability. The matching part of the attack takes advantage of differential properties of S-boxes.

For an c-bit S-box S, we say that its input difference $\triangle a$ and output difference $\triangle b$ match, if solutions exist for this equation $S[x] \oplus S[x \oplus \triangle a] = \triangle b$. In this paper, this fact is denoted as "$\triangle a \triangleright \triangle b$". The set of solutions to this equation is denoted as $D(\triangle a, \triangle b)$. Since S-box is a bijective function, we can immediately find that $0 \triangleright 0$, $\triangle c \not\triangleright 0$ and $0 \not\triangleright \triangle c$, where $\triangle c \neq 0$.

If x is a solution to this equation $S[x] \oplus S[x \oplus \triangle a] = \triangle b$, $x \oplus \triangle a \neq x$ is another solution. So, if $\triangle a \triangleright \triangle b$, at least two solutions can be found. For the 8-bit S-box used in AES and Grøstl, element numbers of $D(\triangle a, \triangle b)$ for all non-zero $\triangle a$ and $\triangle b$ are shown in Table 2, which proves another property: randomly chosen non-zero differences can match at the S-box with probability of about $1/2$.

Table 2. Solution numbers of the AES S-box for non-zero difference pair $(\triangle a, \triangle b)$

$|D(\triangle a, \triangle b)|$	Number of pair $(\triangle a, \triangle b)$
0	32640
2	32130
4	255
all	65025 in total

For $s \times t$ matrices M and N of c-bit cells, notation $\triangle M \triangleright \triangle N$ stands for the fact that differences in all cells of M and N at the same positions match. Namely, $\triangle M \triangleright \triangle N \Leftrightarrow \triangle M_{i,j} \triangleright \triangle N_{i,j}$ for $1 \leq i \leq s$ and $1 \leq j \leq t$.

3   Study of Super-Sbox and Hyper-Sbox

3.1   Super-Sbox and Hyper-Sbox View of AES-Like Permutations

The Super-Sbox view are independently discovered and used by two research groups [13,15],which can be used to increase one round of inbound steps in

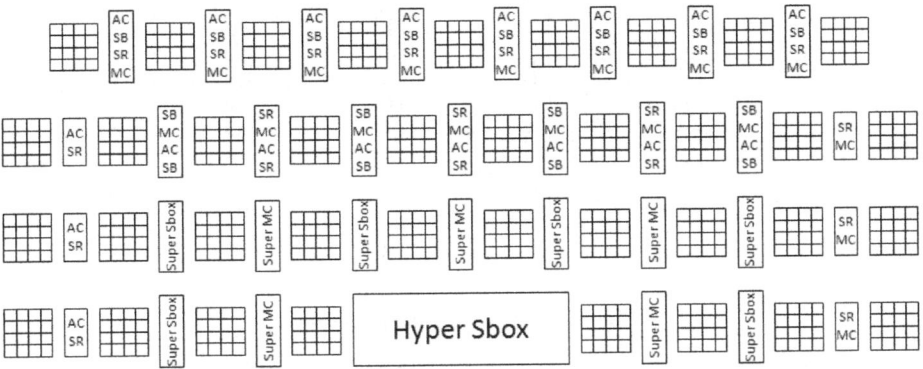

Fig. 3. Four equivalent expressions of 8-round AES-like permutation

a rebound attack. Since SubBytes and ShiftRows are exchangeable, namely $SB \circ SR() = SR \circ SB()$, there are several alternative expressions of AES-like permutations as illustrated in Figure 3. Two rounds of AES-like permutations can be regarded as Super-Sboxes, where

$$SuperSbox() = SB \circ AC \circ MC \circ SB(),$$

$$SuperMC() = SR \circ AC \circ MC \circ SR().$$

We will use the alternative expressions in the following sections, since the structure of our differential path can be described more clearly in the alternative expressions.

The Super-Sbox consists of two S-boxes, inserted by an MDS transformation in the middle, which can be considered as a $(r \times c)$-bit S-box. We can find a fact that the Super-MC transformation is an MDS transformation on $(r \times c)$-bit columns. Proof of this fact is described in appendix A. The branch number of Super-MC is also $r + 1$.

Now we try to combine two Super-Sboxes with a Super-MC in the middle, just like the inner structure of a Super-Sbox. We call the combination a "Hyper-Sbox", which is part of the equivalent expression of four-round AES-like permutations.

$$HyperSbox() = SuperSbox \circ SuperMC \circ SuperSbox().$$

Due to the similar inner structures of Super-Sbox and Hyper-Sbox, one may be inspired that they should have similar properties. We studied their differential properties and found something in common.

3.2 Differential Property of Super-Sbox

Now, consider a generalized Super-Sbox illustrated in Figure 4 with c-bit S-boxes and r cells in a column as input. Suppose there are n active cells in the input difference and m active cells in the output difference, where $m + n \geq r + 1$.

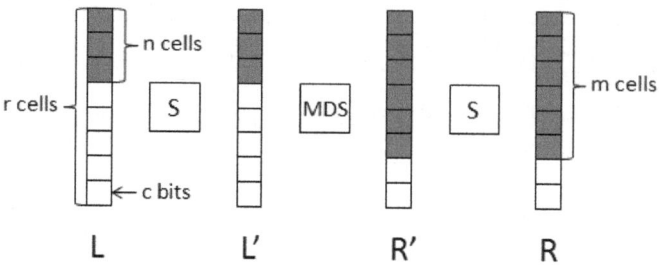

Fig. 4. A generalized Super-Sbox

Without loss of generality, we assume that $n \leq m$. Since if $n > m$, we can reverse the Super-Sbox and get an equivalent expression. In the following analysis, we name the four states in Figure 4 as L, L', R' and R. Now, the question is, given valid input and output difference pairs $(\triangle L, \triangle R)$, how many solutions exist? In a trivial case that $m = n = 0$, there are 2^{rc} solutions. In another trivial case that $m > 0$, $n > 0$ and $m + n \leq r$, no solution exists. The proposition below answers the question of non-trivial cases. We prove it using facts about S-boxes.

Proposition 1. *For random input and output difference pair $(\triangle L, \triangle R)$ of the generalized Super-Sbox(with $m \geq n$ active bytes, where $m + n \geq r + 1$), expected number of solutions is about 1.*

Proof. Let $\mathbb{C} = \{(\triangle L', \triangle R') | \triangle R' = MDS(\triangle L')\}$. Element number of $\mathbb{C}$ is:

$$|\mathbb{C}| = (2^c - 1)^{(m+n-r)} \approx 2^{(m+n-r)c}$$

Let $\mathbb{C}_{\triangleright} = \{(\triangle L', \triangle R') \in \mathbb{C} | \triangle L \triangleright \triangle L', \triangle R' \triangleright \triangle R\}$,

$$|\mathbb{C}_{\triangleright}| = |\mathbb{C}| \cdot 2^{-m-n} = 2^{(m+n)(c-1)-rc}$$

Let $S_{L'} = \{L' | S^{-1}[L'] \oplus S^{-1}[L' \oplus \triangle L'] = \triangle L\}, S_{R'} = \{R' | S[R'] \oplus S[R' \oplus \triangle R'] = \triangle R\}$. For each $(\triangle L', \triangle R') \in \mathbb{C}_{\triangleright}$,

$$|S_{L'}| = 2^n (2^c)^{r-n} = 2^{rc-(c-1)n}$$

$$|S_{R'}| = 2^m (2^c)^{r-m} = 2^{rc-(c-1)m}$$

This is a meet-in-the-middle setting for solutions from both sides. So we can find a common element of $S_{L'}$ and $S_{R'}$ with probability of

$$Pr = \frac{|S_{L'}| \cdot |S_{R'}|}{2^{rc}} = 2^{rc-(c-1)(m+n)}$$

Expected number of solutions we can find for one pair of $\triangle L$ and $\triangle R$ is:

$$|\mathbb{C}_{\triangleright}| \cdot Pr = 1,$$

which completes the proof.

Note that the meet-in-the-middle solution matching step can be done by solving a linear equation group. Since we can freely choose values of the non-active cells, one non-active cell can be considered as c variables in bits. For active cells, once the differences matched, there are two values fulfilling the differences of the active cell. We use one bit variable to indicate which value it is. So, the matching step becomes a linear equation group. Solutions to this equation group are the values fulfilling the input and output differences of the generalized Super-Sbox.

3.3 Differential Property of Hyper-Sbox

Proposition 2. *For random input and output difference pair* $(\triangle L, \triangle R)$ *(with* $m \geq n$ *active columns, where* $m + n \geq r + 1$*) of the generalized Hyper-Sbox, expected number of solutions is 1.*

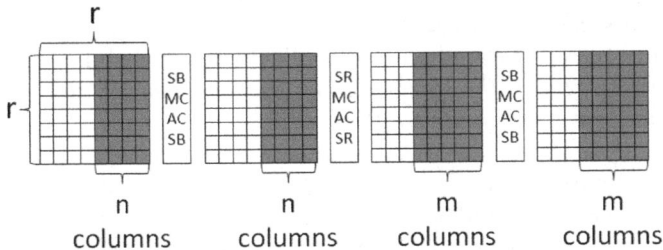

Fig. 5. A generalized active pattern for Hyper-Sbox

Proof. A generalized active pattern is shown in Figure 5. Since Super-Sbox behaves like a big S-box on each column and Super-MC is also an MDS transformation on columns with a branch number of $r + 1$.

We can easily adapt notations used in proof of Proposition 1 and prove Proposition 2. Since the difference between two proofs is minor, here we don't describe details of this proof.

4 Distinguisher of 8-Round Grøstl Permutation

4.1 A Generalized Differential Path

In this section, instead of considering a specific algorithm, we try to construct a differential path for the generalized AES-like permutation. An 8-round truncated differential path for the permutations with states of $r \times r$ c-bit cells is illustrated in Figure 6. Without loss of generality, let $n \leq m$. From property of MDS transformation, we have $m + n \geq r + 1$.

Now we consider the complexity to find one solution to this differential path and the complexity to find one pair fulfilling the input and output truncated differences of a random permutation.

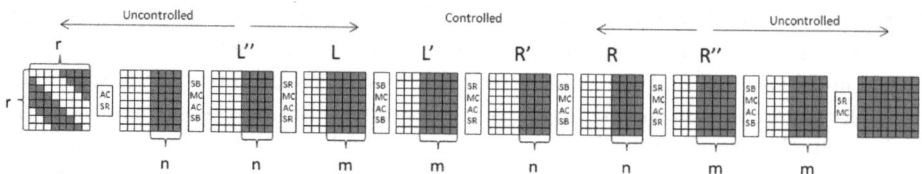

Fig. 6. 8-round truncated differential path for AES-like permutations

Claim (1). It takes $2^{(m+n-r)rc}$ computations and 2^{rc} memory to find one solution to Hyper-Sbox part of this generalized differential path.

Proof. Randomly choose $\triangle L''$ and $\triangle R''$ s.t. $\triangle L = SuperMC(\triangle L'')$ and $\triangle R = SuperMC^{-1}(\triangle R'')$ follow the truncated differential pattern in Figure 6. $\triangle L$ and $\triangle R$ are the input and output differences for the Hyper-Sbox. (About $2^{(m+n-r)rc}$ such differences exist for both sides.)

Since the uncontrolled rounds can be fulfilled with probability of 1. The problem is simplified: *What is the complexity to find one solution to the Hyper-Sbox, with given valid input and output differences?*

This problem can be solved in three steps:

1. Local pre-computations: For each active column $\triangle L_i$ of $\triangle L$, go through all 2^{rc} values of L_i, calculate and store $(L_i', \triangle L_i')$ with difference mask $\triangle L_i$. Do the same thing to $\triangle R$ in backward direction. This step requires 2^{rc} computations and 2^{rc} memory.

2. For all difference pairs $(\triangle L', \triangle R')$ s.t. $\triangle R' = SuperMC(\triangle L')$ ($2^{(m+n-r)rc}$ pairs in total), check if differences in their active columns are stored in the pre-computation tables of both sides. If we found one such difference pair, we obtain the solutions to the Super-Sboxes immediately from pre-computations tables and go to step 3, otherwise check another difference pair.

3. The matching problem of solutions can be solved with similar techniques used in cryptanalysis of Super-Sbox in Section 3.2: view this problem as solving a linear equation group, though in this case only one value can be selected for each active cell. The matching probability is $2^{(r-m-n)rc}$. We leave the details of the matching step explained in section 4.2. If not all inner pairs $(\triangle L', \triangle R')$ have been checked, go to step 2 and continue.

Since there are about $2^{(m+n-r)rc}$ intermediate pairs $(\triangle L', \triangle R')$, according to proposition 1, we expect to match the solutions $2^{(m+n-r)rc}$ times. So the total complexity is about $2^{(m+n-r)rc}$ computations and 2^{rc} memory. After we went through all the possible pairs $(\triangle L', \triangle R')$, we expect to find one solution to the Hyper-Sbox, according to proposition 2. Note that solution to the Hyper-Sbox part is also solution to this generalized differential path, since the uncontrolled rounds can be fulfilled with probability of 1.

Claim (2). It takes $2^{(r-m)rc/2}$ computations to find one pair of solution for a random permutation with n active columns and m active columns at prescribed positions of input and output states.

Proof. Consider the limited birthday problem discussed by Henri Gilbert et al. in section 4.1 of [15]. Our case has a setting of $i = (r - n)rc$ and $j = (r - m)rc$. With assumption that $m \geq n$, it's easy to see that $i \geq j$. Introduction to the limited birthday problem is illustrated in Appendix B.

Since $m + n \geq r + 1 \Rightarrow j < 2(r^2 c - i)$, the complexity is $2^{j/2} = 2^{(r-m)rc/2}$.

4.2   How to Match the Solutions

As illustrated in Figure 7, values of the active cells in L' and R' have been determined while values of the non-active cells are free to choose. We can match them in the inner states L''' and R''' column by column.

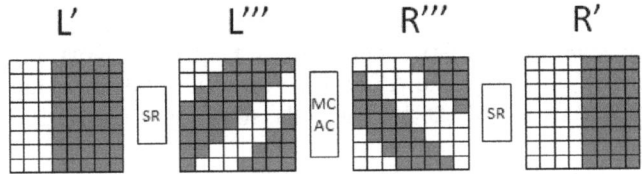

Fig. 7. Solution matching step with $r = 8, m = 5$ and $n = 4$

For example, considering the case of $r = 8, m = 5$ and $n = 4$, the first column of L''' and R''' can be matched by solving this linear equation group:

$$\mathcal{B} \cdot \begin{pmatrix} x_0 \\ x_1 \\ x_2 \\ c_0 \\ c_1 \\ c_2 \\ c_3 \\ c_4 \end{pmatrix} + \mathcal{C} = \begin{pmatrix} x_3 \\ c_5 \\ c_6 \\ c_7 \\ c_8 \\ x_4 \\ x_5 \\ x_6 \end{pmatrix}$$

where $\mathcal{B} = circ(02, 02, 03, 04, 05, 03, 05, 07)$ is the matrix used in MixBytes operation and $\mathcal{C}$ is the round constant used in AddRoundConstant operation. $c_0, c_1, ...c_8$ are the values of active bytes, which are also solutions we get from two Super-Sboxes. Because we can freely choose values of the non-active cells, and consider them as variables. So, there are 7 variables (non-active cells $x_0, x_1, ...x_6$) and 8 equations, the probability that we can find one solution of this equation group is 2^{-c} for each column.

In the generic case, there are $(r - m) + (r - n) = 2r - m - n$ variables (non-active cells) and r equations in one column. The probability that we can find one solution is $2^{(-c) \cdot (r - (2r - m - n))} = 2^{(r-m-n)c}$ for each column. So, for r columns, the matching probability is $2^{(r-m-n)rc}$.

4.3   Conclusion of the Distinguisher

If the complexity of finding one solution to our differential path is lower than the complexity of finding one solution to a random permutation, the fact can be considered as a distinguisher. For our distinguisher, we need $2^{(m+n-r)rc} < 2^{(r-m)rc/2}$, which is equivalent to

$$3r > 3m + 2n. \tag{1}$$

Since $m + n \geq r + 1$ and $m \geq n$, we have $m \geq r + 1 - [\frac{r+1}{2}]$. So,

$$3r > m + 2(m+n) \geq r + 1 - [\frac{r+1}{2}] + 2r + 2 \Rightarrow [\frac{r+1}{2}] > 3 \Rightarrow r \geq 7.$$

This means the generalized distinguisher doesn't work on algorithms with a state size smaller than 7×7 cells, like AES. Note that the ECHO permutation uses a structure with 4×4 state of 128-bit big cells, so our distinguisher does not work on ECHO, too.

From $m \geq n$ and equation 1, we have

$$3r > 3m + 2n \geq 5n \Rightarrow n \leq \frac{3}{5}r.$$

We also have $n \geq r + 1 - m$, then from equation 1,

$$3r > 3m + 2n \geq 3m + 2(r + 1 - m) \Rightarrow r > m + 2 \Rightarrow m \leq r - 3$$

Now we have the bounds of m and n:

$$r + 1 - [\frac{r+1}{2}] \leq m \leq r - 3,$$

$$r + 1 - m \leq n \leq \frac{3}{5}r.$$

For Grøstl permutation, $r = c = 8$.

$$r = 8 \Rightarrow 5 = 8 + 1 - [\frac{8+1}{2}] \leq m \leq 8 - 3 = 5 \Rightarrow m = 5.$$

Since

$$4 = 8 + 1 - 5 = r + 1 - m \leq n \leq \frac{3}{5}r = 4.8 \Rightarrow n = 4,$$

we have the only pattern $m = 5$ and $n = 4$ for the distinguisher of 8-round Grøstl permutation.

It takes 2^{64} computations and 2^{64} memory to find one solution of the differential path for Grøstl. For an ideal permutation, the complexity is 2^{96}. This fact distinguishes 8-round Grøstl permutation from an ideal permutation.

5 Considering Non-square States

In this section, we aim to find a similar distinguisher of 8-round Grøstl-512 permutation. First, we also consider a generalized permutation with a state of $r \times 2r$ cells. We use the same active pattern as in Figure 6, namely, m and n full active columns appearing alternately.

For the non-square state, shift vector could lead to impossible differentials for non-square states. In fact, we found that distinguishers with similar structure don't exist for Grøstl-512, due to such impossible differentials. We will talk about the details later. Now we assume that the $SuperMC$ transformation can turn m full active columns into n full active columns in the $(r \times 2r)$-sized state, where $m \geq n$.

In order to construct the distinguisher, we need some calculation first. Suppose that all columns of the input and output state of the intermediate MC of the $SuperMC$ are active, there are at least $r + 1$ active cells. So, at least $2r \times (r + 1)$ active cells exist in total. This fact implies an inequality $r(m + n) \geq 2r(r + 1)$, from which the first restriction on m and n can be derived:

$$m + n \geq 2(r + 1).$$

With similar techniques, we can calculate the complexity to find one solution of the differential path is $2^{(m+n-r)rc}$ computations and 2^{rc} memory. For a random permutation, the complexity to find one solution fulfilling the input and output truncated differential pattern is $2^{(2r-m)rc/2}$. The distinguisher requires that $2^{(m+n-r)rc} < 2^{(2r-m)rc/2}$, which can be simplified to:

$$6r > 3m + 2n.$$

$m + n \geq 2(r + 1)$ and $m \geq n$ implies that $m \geq r + 1$. So,

$$6r > 3m + 2n = m + 2(m + n) \geq m + 4r + 4 \geq 5r + 5 \Rightarrow r > 5$$

From this inequality, we know such distinguisher doesn't work on algorithms using $r \times 2r$ states with $r \leq 5$, like AES-256. In Grøstl-512 permutation, $r = 8$ and $c = 8$. It's easy to find all the solutions fulfilling both inequalities above: $m = n = 9$, $m = 10, n = 8$ and $m = 11, n = 7$.

We searched for the possible positions of active columns, but unfortunately, no possible differential patterns exist with the shift vector $(0, 1, 2, 3, 4, 5, 6, 7, 11)$. An impossible differential pattern is illustrated in Figure 8. All columns are valid except for the 9-th column, since there are only 8 active bytes in that column, which are indicated by the black cells.

Then we tried another shift vector from message expansion of Cheetah hash function[17]. As we know, this is the only AES-like permutation with 8×16 states except the one used in Grøstl-512. The shift vector used in message expansion of Cheetah is $(0, 1, 2, 3, 5, 6, 7, 8)$. Again, we found no possible differential pattern with $m = n = 9$, $m = 10, n = 8$ or $m = 11, n = 7$ for this shift vector.

Does such differential pattern exist for some shift vector? The answer is positive. We found that for the shift vector $(0, 1, 2, 3, 4, 5, 6, 15)$ a differential pattern

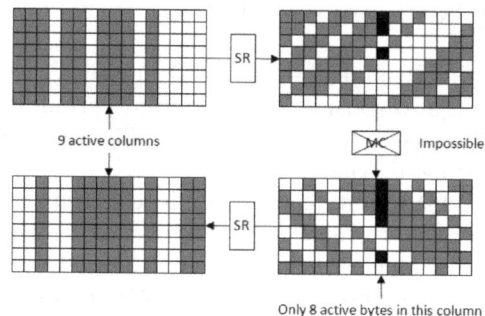

Fig. 8. An impossible differential pattern of Grøstl-512

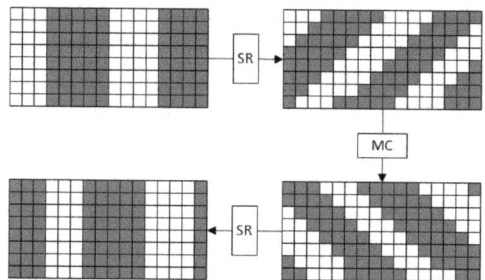

Fig. 9. A differential pattern with $m = n = 9$ for shift vector (0,1,2,3,4,5,6,15)

with $m = n = 9$ exists, which is illustrated in Figure 9. As we know, no algorithms use this shift vector. So, our attempts to construct similar distinguisher
for non-square states failed.

6   Conclusion

In this paper, we introduced the Hyper-Sbox view of AES-like permutations.
based on this observation, we studied the differential properties of Super-Sbox
and Hyper-Sbox and found their similarity. Then we proposed a new type of
distinguisher which works on 8-round AES-like permutations if the state size
is $r \times r$, where $r \geq 7$. This distinguisher can be applied directly on 8-round
Grøstl-256 permutation.

Though there is a better distinguisher on the full-round Grøstl-256 compression function, its application is restricted by the specific structure of Grøstl. Our
proposal is a generalized distinguisher and the best one of 8-round Grøstl-256
permutation with 2^{64} time and 2^{64} memory.

We also considered similar distinguisher on the non-square AES-like permutation. We found that if size of the state is $r \times 2r$, where $r < 6$, the distinguisher
doesn't work. We also found that this distinguisher doesn't work on Grøstl-512
permutation or any other known algorithm due to the shift vector.

Acknowledgements. This work is supported by the National Natural Science Foundation of China (No.60873259), and the Knowledge Innovation Project of The Chinese Academy of Sciences.

References

1. Gauravaram, P., Knudsen, L.R., Matusiewicz, K., Mendel, F., Rechberger, C., Schlæffer, M., Thomsen, S.S.: Grøstl – a SHA-3 candidate. Submission to NIST (2008)
2. National Institute of Standards and Technology: Announcing Request for Candidate Algorithm Nominations for a New Cryptographic Hash Algorithm (SHA-3) Family. Federal Register 27(212), 62212–62220 (November 2007), http://csrc.nist.gov/groups/ST/hash/documents/FR_Notice_Nov07.pdf (2008/10/17)
3. Wang, X., Yu, H.: How to Break MD5 and Other Hash Functions. In: Cramer, R. (ed.) EUROCRYPT 2005. LNCS, vol. 3494, pp. 19–35. Springer, Heidelberg (2005)
4. Stevens, M., Lenstra, A.K., de Weger, B.: Chosen-Prefix Collisions for MD5 and Colliding X.509 Certificates for Different Identities. In: Naor, M. (ed.) EURO-CRYPT 2007. LNCS, vol. 4515, pp. 1–22. Springer, Heidelberg (2007)
5. Wang, X., Yin, Y.L., Yu, H.: Finding Collisions in the Full SHA-1. In: Shoup, V. (ed.) CRYPTO 2005. LNCS, vol. 3621, pp. 17–36. Springer, Heidelberg (2005)
6. De Cannière, C., Mendel, F., Rechberger, C.: Collisions for 70-Step SHA-1: On the Full Cost of Collision Search. In: Adams, C., Miri, A., Wiener, M. (eds.) SAC 2007. LNCS, vol. 4876, pp. 56–73. Springer, Heidelberg (2007)
7. Benadjila, R., Billet, O., Gilbert, H., Macario-Rat, G., Peyrin, T., Robshaw, M., Seurin, Y.: SHA-3 Proposal: ECHO. Submission to NIST (updated) (2009)
8. Wu, H.: The Hash Function JH. Submission to NIST (updated) (2009)
9. Biham, E., Dunkelman, O.: The SHAvite-3 Hash Function. Submission to NIST (Round 2) (2009)
10. Mendel, F., Rechberger, C., Schläffer, M., Thomsen, S.S.: The Rebound Attack: Cryptanalysis of Reduced Whirlpool and Grøstl. In: Dunkelman, O. (ed.) FSE 2009. LNCS, vol. 5665, pp. 260–276. Springer, Heidelberg (2009)
11. Mendel, F., Peyrin, T., Rechberger, C., Schläffer, M.: Improved Cryptanalysis of the Reduced Grøstl Compression Function, ECHO Permutation and AES Block Cipher. In: [18], pp. 16–35 (2009)
12. Wu, S., Feng, D., Wu, W.: Cryptanalysis of the LANE Hash Function. In: [18], pp. 126–140
13. Lamberger, M., Mendel, F., Rechberger, C., Rijmen, V., Schläffer, M.: Rebound Distinguishers: Results on the Full Whirlpool Compression Function. In: [19], pp. 126–143
14. Matusiewicz, K., Naya-Plasencia, M., Nikolic, I., Sasaki, Y., Schläffer, M.: Rebound Attack on the Full Lane Compression Function. In: [19], pp. 106–125
15. Gilbert, H., Peyrin, T.: Super-Sbox Cryptanalysis: Improved Attacks for AES-Like Permutations. In: Hong, S., Iwata, T. (eds.) FSE 2010. LNCS, vol. 6147, pp. 365–383. Springer, Heidelberg (2010)
16. Peyrin, T.: Improved Differential Attacks for ECHO and Grøstl. Cryptology ePrint Archive, Report 2010/223 (2010), http://eprint.iacr.org/
17. Khovratovich, D., Biryukov, A., Nikolić, I.: The Hash Function Cheetah: Speciffication and Supporting Documentation. Submission to NIST (2008)
18. Jacobson Jr., M.J., Rijmen, V., Safavi-Naini, R. (eds.): SAC 2009. LNCS, vol. 5867. Springer, Heidelberg (2009)
19. Matsui, M. (ed.): ASIACRYPT 2009. LNCS, vol. 5912. Springer, Heidelberg (2009)

A   Proof of the Fact that Super-MC Is MDS

This proof is illustrated using Figure 7 again. Assume that the number of active bytes in the i-th column of L''' is m_i and the number of active bytes in the i-th column of R''' is n_i. Number of active columns in L' and R' are m and n. It's easy to find the relation: for any i, $m \geq m_i$ and $n \geq n_I$. Then we have

$$m \geq max_i\{m_i\},$$

$$n \geq max_i\{n_i\}.$$

Branch number of MC is $r + 1$, which means if the i-th column($1 \leq i \leq r$) of L''' is active,

$$m_i + n_i \geq r + 1.$$

Since at least one column in L''' is active, we have $max_i\{m_i + n_i\} \geq r + 1$. So,

$$m + n \geq max_i\{m_i\} + max_i\{n_i\} \geq max_i\{m_i + n_i\} \geq r + 1,$$

which completes the proof.

B   The Limited Birthday Problem

In [15], Henri Gilbert discussed the limited birthday problem: What is the generic attack complexity of finding a solution with i zero bits in prescribed positions of the input and j zero bits in prescribed positions of the output for an ideal(random) permutation?

Assume that $i \geq j$ and n is the bit size of the permutation. Due to the birthday paradox, each structure of 2^{n-i} input values with those i zero bits fixed allows to provide at most $2(n - i)$ zero bits in prescribed positions of the output value.

- if $j \leq 2(n - i)$, degrees of freedom is sufficient to achieve a collision on the j prescribed bit position. So, the complexity is $2^{j/2}$.
- if $j > 2(n - i)$, since on structure of 2^{n-i} input values can provide at most $2(n-i)$ collision bits, $j - 2(n - i)$ structures are required to achieve j collision bits. The complexity is $2^{n-i} \times 2^{j-2(n-i)} = 2^{i+j-n}$.

Preimage Attacks on Step-Reduced RIPEMD-128 and RIPEMD-160

Chiaki Ohtahara[1], Yu Sasaki[2], and Takeshi Shimoyama[3]

[1] Chuo-University
cohtahara@chao.ise.chuo-u.ac.jp
[2] NTT Corporation
sasaki.yu@lab.ntt.co.jp
[3] Fujitsu Laboratories Ltd.
shimo@labs.fujitsu.com

Abstract. This paper presents the first results on the preimage resistance of ISO standard hash functions RIPEMD-128 and RIPEMD-160. They were designed as strengthened versions of RIPEMD. While preimage attacks on the first 33 steps and intermediate 35 steps of RIPEMD (48 steps in total) are known, no preimage attack exists on RIPEMD-128 (64 steps) or RIPEMD-160 (80 steps). This paper shows three variations of attacks on RIPEMD-128; the first 33 steps, intermediate 35 steps, and the last 32 steps. It is interesting that the number of attacked steps for RIPEMD-128 reaches the same level as RIPEMD. We show that our approach can also be applied to RIPEMD-160, and present preimage attacks on the first 30 steps and the last 31 steps.

Keywords: RIPEMD-128, RIPEMD-160, hash, preimage, meet-in-the-middle.

1 Introduction

Cryptographic hash functions are one of the most basic primitives. For symmetric-key primitives, it is quite standard to evaluate their security by demonstrating cryptanalysis on them or weakened versions e.g. step-reduced versions. In fact, analysis on the step-reduced versions is useful to know the security margin.

Preimage resistance is an important security for hash functions. When digests are n-bits, the required security is usually n-bits e.g. the SHA-3 competition [1].

Since the collision resistance of MD5 and SHA-1 have been significantly broken [2,3], many hash functions with various designs such as RIPEMD, Tiger, Whirlpool, and FORK-256 have been pointed out to be vulnerable or non-ideal [4,5,6,7,8]. Meanwhile, no attack is known against (full specifications of) RIPEMD-128 and RIPEMD-160 [9] though they were designed more than ten years ago.

RIPEMD [10] is a double-branch hash function, where the compression function consists of two parallel copies of a compression function. In 1996, Dobbertin *et al.* designed RIPEMD-128 and RIPEMD-160 [9] as strengthened versions of RIPEMD. They are standardized in ISO/IEC 10118-3:2003 [11].

X. Lai, M. Yung, and D. Lin (Eds.): Inscrypt 2010, LNCS 6584, pp. 169–186, 2011.
© Springer-Verlag Berlin Heidelberg 2011

Table 1. Summary of attack results

Target	Steps	Method	Time for pseudo-preimage	Time for (2nd-)preimage	Mem.	Ref.
RIPEMD-128	first 33	IE	2^{119}	$2^{124.5}$	2^{12}	Ours
	middle 35	LC	2^{112}	2^{121}	2^{16}	Ours
	last 32	IE	$2^{122.4}$	$2^{126.2}$ †	2^{12}	Ours
RIPEMD-160	first 30	IE	2^{148}	2^{155} †	2^{16}	Ours
	last 31	IE	2^{148}	2^{155}	2^{17}	Ours

IE and LC represent the Initial-Exchange and Local-Collision approaches, respectively. Attacks with † can generate second-preimages but cannot generate preimages.

In 2005, Wang *et al.* showed a collision attack on full RIPEMD [4]. They used a property where two compression functions are identical but for the constant value and thus the same differential path can be used for both branches. Because RIPEMD-128 and -160 adopt different message expansion for two branches, the attack cannot be applied to them. For RIPEMD-128 and -160, only pseudo-(near-)collisions against step-reduced and modified versions are known [12].

On the preimage resistance, Wang *et al.* attacked the first 29 steps of RIPEMD [13]. Then, Sasaki *et al.* attacked more steps; the first 33 and intermediate 35 steps [14]. These attacks seem inefficient for RIPEMD-128 and -160 due to the different message expansion between two branches. In fact, as far as we know, no preimage attack exists on RIPEMD-128 and -160 even for step-reduced versions.

Saarinen [8] presented a preimage attack on a 4-branch hash function FORK-256 [15]. It uses several properties particular to FORK-256, and thus the same approach cannot be applied to RIPEMD, RIPEMD-128, or RIPEMD-160.

Our contributions. We present the first results on the preimage resistance of RIPEMD-128 and -160. Our attacks employ the meet-in-the-middle preimage attack [16]. Firstly, we devise *initial-exchange* technique, which exchanges a message-word position located in the first several steps for a branch with the one for the other branch. Secondly, we use a *local-collision* approach, which was first proposed by [14] to attack RIPEMD. The results are summarized in Table 1. Note that the approach of attacking the last few rounds was also taken by [17].

2   Specifications

RIPEMD-128. RIPEMD-128 [9] takes arbitrary and finite length messages as input and outputs 128-bit digest. It follows the Merkle-Damgård hash function mode (with standard length encoding). The input message is padded to be a multiple of 512 bits and is divided into 512-bit blocks M_i. Then, the hash value is computed as follows:

$$H_0 \leftarrow \text{IV}, \qquad H_{i+1} \leftarrow \text{CF}(H_i, M_i) \text{ for } i = 0, 1, \ldots, N-1$$

where IV is the initial value defined in the specification, H_N is the output hash value, and CF: $\{0,1\}^{128} \times \{0,1\}^{512} \to \{0,1\}^{128}$ is a compression function.

The compression function has a double-branch structure. Two compression functions $\text{CF}^L(H_i, M_i) : \{0,1\}^{128} \times \{0,1\}^{512} \to \{0,1\}^{128}$ and $\text{CF}^R(H_i, M_i) : \{0,1\}^{128} \times \{0,1\}^{512} \to \{0,1\}^{128}$ are computed and the output of the compression function is a mixture of (H_i, M_i), $\text{CF}^L(H_i, M_i)$, and $\text{CF}^R(H_i, M_i)$. Let $p_j^L, a_j^L, b_j^L, c_j^L, d_j^L$ be 128-bit, 32-bit, 32-bit, 32-bit, 32-bit variables, respectively, satisfying $p_j^L = a_j^L \| b_j^L \| c_j^L \| d_j^L$. Similarly, we define $p_j^R, a_j^R, b_j^R, c_j^R, d_j^R$. Details of the computation procedure is as follows.

1. M_i is divided into sixteen 32-bit message words m_j ($j = 0, 1, \ldots, 15$) and H_i is divided into four 32-bit chaining variables $H_i^a \| H_i^b \| H_i^c \| H_i^d$.
2. p_0^L and p_0^R are set to H_i (and thus $p_0^L = p_0^R$).
3. Compute $p_{j+1}^L \leftarrow R_j^L(p_j^L, m_{\pi^L(j)})$ and $p_{j+1}^R \leftarrow R_j^R(p_j^R, m_{\pi^R(j)})$ for $j = 0, 1, \ldots, 63$, where $R_j^L, m_{\pi^L(j)}, R_j^R$, and $m_{\pi^R(j)}$ will be explained later.
4. Compute the output value $H_{i+1} = (H_{i+1}^a \| H_{i+1}^b \| H_{i+1}^c \| H_{i+1}^d)$ as follows, where "+" denotes a 32-bit word-wise addition.

$$H_{i+1}^a = H_i^b + c_{64}^L + d_{64}^R, \qquad H_{i+1}^b = H_i^c + d_{64}^L + a_{64}^R,$$
$$H_{i+1}^c = H_i^d + a_{64}^L + b_{64}^R, \qquad H_{i+1}^d = H_i^a + b_{64}^L + c_{64}^R.$$

R_j^L and R_j^R are the step functions for Step j. $R_j^L(p_j^L, m_{\pi^L(j)})$ is defined as follows:

$$a_{j+1}^L = d_j^L, \qquad b_{j+1}^L = (a_j^L + \Phi_j^L(b_j^L, c_j^L, d_j^L) + m_{\pi^L(j)} + k_j^L) \lll s_j^L,$$
$$c_{j+1}^L = b_j^L, \qquad d_{j+1}^L = c_j^L,$$

where Φ_j^L, k_j^L, and $\lll s_j^L$ are Boolean function, constant, and left rotation defined in Table 2. $\pi^L(j)$ is the message expansion of CF^L. R_j^R is similarly defined.

RIPEMD-160. Each branch of RIPEMD-160 consists of 80 steps using 160-bit state. Let the chaining variables in step j of CF^L be $p_j^L = a_j^L \| b_j^L \| c_j^L \| d_j^L \| e_j^L$. Step function $R_j^L(p_j^L, m_{\pi^L(j)})$ is as follows. ($R_j^R(p_j^R, m_{\pi^R(j)})$ is similarly described.)

$$a_{j+1}^L = e_j^L, \quad c_{j+1}^L = b_j^L, \quad d_{j+1}^L = c_j^L \lll 10, \quad e_{j+1}^L = d_j^L,$$
$$b_{j+1}^L = ((a_j^L + \Phi_j^L(b_j^L, c_j^L, d_j^L) + m_{\pi^L(j)} + k_j^L) \lll s_j^L) + e_j^L.$$

$\pi(j), \Phi_j$, and $\lll s_j$ are shown in Table 2. Finally, the output value $H_{i+1} = (H_{i+1}^a \| H_{i+1}^b \| H_{i+1}^c \| H_{i+1}^d \| H_{i+1}^e)$ is computed as follows.

$$H_{i+1}^a = H_i^b + c_{80}^L + d_{80}^R, \quad H_{i+1}^b = H_i^c + d_{80}^L + e_{80}^R, \quad H_{i+1}^c = H_i^d + e_{80}^L + a_{80}^R,$$
$$H_{i+1}^d = H_i^e + a_{80}^L + b_{80}^R, \quad H_{i+1}^e = H_i^a + b_{80}^L + c_{80}^R.$$

Table 2. Detailed specifications of RIPEMD-128 and RIPEMD-160

r	$\pi^L(r), \pi^L(r+1), \ldots, \pi^L(r+15)$	$\pi^R(r), \pi^R(r+1), \ldots, \pi^R(r+15)$
0	0 1 2 3 4 5 6 7 8 9 10 11 12 13 14 15	5 14 7 0 9 2 11 4 13 6 15 8 1 10 3 12
16	7 4 13 1 10 6 15 3 12 0 9 5 2 14 11 8	6 11 3 7 0 13 5 10 14 15 8 12 4 9 1 2
32	3 10 14 4 9 15 8 1 2 7 0 6 13 11 5 12	15 5 1 3 7 14 6 9 11 8 12 2 10 0 4 13
48	1 9 11 10 0 8 12 4 13 3 7 15 14 5 6 2	8 6 4 1 3 11 15 0 5 12 2 13 9 7 10 14
64	4 0 5 9 7 12 2 10 14 1 3 8 11 6 15 13	12 15 10 4 1 5 8 7 6 2 13 14 0 3 9 11

j	$\Phi_j(X,Y,Z)$	Abbreviation
$0 \leq j \leq 15$	$X \oplus Y \oplus Z$	Φ_F
$16 \leq j \leq 31$	$(X \wedge Y) \vee (\neg X \wedge Z)$	Φ_G
$32 \leq j \leq 47$	$(X \vee \neg Y) \oplus Z$	Φ_H
$48 \leq j \leq 63$	$(X \wedge Z) \vee (Y \wedge \neg Z)$	Φ_I
$64 \leq j \leq 79$	$X \oplus (Y \vee \neg Z)$	Φ_J

For RIPEMD-128: $\Phi_j^L = \Phi_j$, $\Phi_j^R = \Phi_{63-j}$

For RIPEMD-160: $\Phi_j^L = \Phi_j$, $\Phi_j^R = \Phi_{79-j}$

r	$s_r^L, s_{r+1}^L, \ldots, s_{r+15}^L$	$s_r^R, s_{r+1}^R, \ldots, s_{r+15}^R$
0	11 14 15 12 5 8 7 9 11 13 14 15 6 7 9 8	8 9 9 11 13 15 15 5 7 7 8 11 14 14 12 6
16	7 6 8 13 11 9 7 15 7 12 15 9 11 7 13 12	9 13 15 7 12 8 9 11 7 7 12 7 6 15 13 11
32	11 13 6 7 14 9 13 15 14 8 13 6 5 12 7 5	9 7 15 11 8 6 6 14 12 13 5 14 13 13 7 5
48	11 12 14 15 14 15 9 8 9 14 5 6 8 6 5 12	15 5 8 11 14 14 6 14 6 9 12 9 12 5 15 8
64	9 15 5 11 6 8 13 12 5 12 13 14 11 8 5 6	8 5 12 9 12 5 14 6 8 13 6 5 15 13 11 11

3 Related Work

3.1 Converting Pseudo-Preimage Attack to Preimage Attack

Given a hash value H_N, a pseudo-preimage is a pair of (H_{N-1}, M_{N-1}) such that $CF(H_{N-1}, M_{N-1}) = H_N$, and $H_{N-1} \neq IV$. In n-bit narrow-pipe iterated hash functions, if pseudo-preimages with appropriate padding string can be generated with a complexity of 2^m, where $m < n - 2$, preimages can be generated with a complexity of $2^{\frac{m+n}{2}+1}$ [18, Fact9.99]. Leurent pointed out that constraints of the padding string can be ignored when we generate second preimages [19].

3.2 Meet-in-the-Middle Preimage Attack

Aoki *et al.* proposed a framework of the meet-in-the-middle preimage attack [16]. The attack divides the compression function into two *chunks* of steps so that each chunk includes independent message words, which are called *neutral words*. Then, pseudo-preimages are obtained by performing the meet-in-the-middle attack, namely, computing each chunk independently and matching the partially-computed intermediate chaining variables. The framework is illustrated in Figure 1. Please refer [16] for more details such as terminologies and procedure.

Assume that the first chunk has d_1 free bits and the second chunk has d_2 free bits, where $d_1 \leq d_2$. Also assume that each chunk computes d_3 bits of intermediate chaining variables used for the match, where $d_3 \geq min(d_1, d_2) = d_1$. In this framework, an attacker computes d_3 match bits of the first chunk for 2^{d_1} possible values and store the results in a table. The table is sorted with time 2^{d_1} (e.g. Bucket Sort) so that look-up can later be carried out with time 1. Then, for each of 2^{d_2} possible values, compute the d_3 match bits of the second chunk and

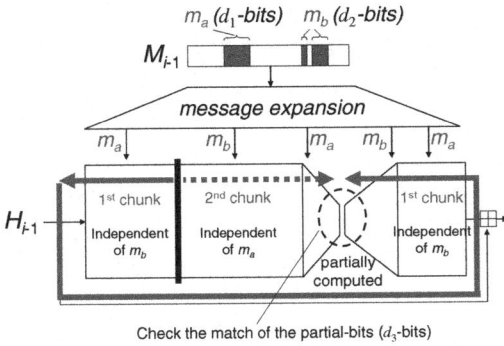

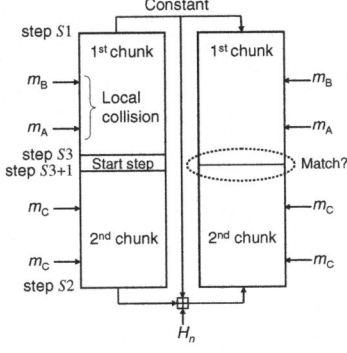

Fig. 1. Framework of the meet-in-the-middle preimage attack

Fig. 2. Local-collision approach by [14] against RIPEMD

check if they exist in the table. If exist, compute and check the match of the other $n - d_3$ bits with the matched message words, where n is the state size. Using the 2^{d_2} computations of the second chunk, $2^{d_1 + d_2 - d_3}$ pairs whose d_3 bits match are obtained. Finally, by iterating the procedure $2^{n-(d_1+d_2)}$ times, a pseudo-preimage will be obtained. The attack complexity is $(2^{d_1} + 2^{d_2}) \cdot 2^{n-(d_1+d_2)}$ in time, and 2^{d_1} in memory.

The *initial-structure* technique proposed by Sasaki *et al.*[20] is a technique for this attack framework, which exchanges the positions of two message words in neighbouring steps. This can increase the search space of neutral words.

3.3 Preimage Attacks on RIPEMD

Since the internal state size of RIPEMD is double of the digest size, a simple application of the meet-in-the-middle attack for RIPEMD does not give any advantage. Sasaki *et al.* proposed an approach using a local-collision to solve this problem [14], which is depicted in Figure 2. In this approach, the attack target (steps $S1$ to $S2$) is divided into two chunks; $S1$ to $S3$ are the first chunk and $S3 + 1$ to $S2$ are the second chunk. The independent computations start from the middle of CF^L and find a match in the middle of CF^R. However, because of the feed-forward operation, the second chunk cannot be computed independently of the first chunk in a straight-forward manner. To avoid this, [14] used local-collisions. Namely, the first chunk includes two neutral words, and the attacker chooses neutral words so that the impact of changing one neutral word is always cancelled by the other neutral word. This fixes the feed-forward value to a constant, and thus independent computations can be carried out.

4 New Analytic Tool: Initial-Exchange Technique

In this section, we explain the *initial-exchange* technique, which exchanges the message-word positions located in the top of the steps across the right and left

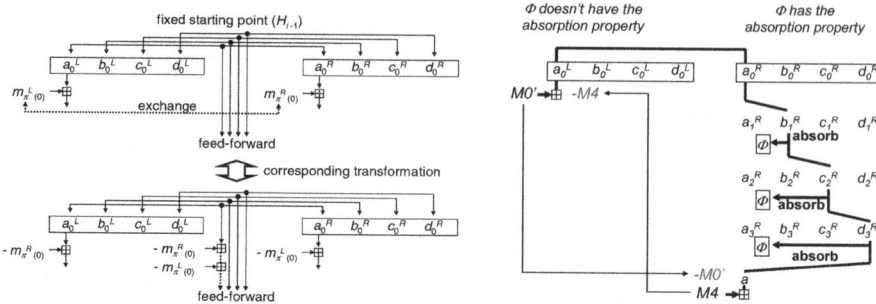

Fig. 3. Basic initial-exchange   **Fig. 4.** Extended initial-exchange 1

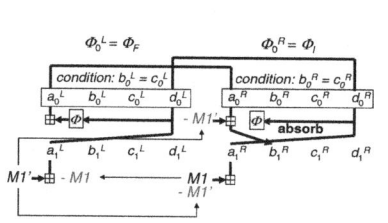

Fig. 5. Extended initial-exchange 2   **Fig. 6.** Exchanging addition positions over a rotation. Top is for the standard initial-exchange. Bottom is for the partial-bit initial-exchange.

branches. This technique can be applied to both of RIPEMD-128 and RIPEMD-160. In this section, we explain the technique based on RIPEMD-128. We introduce the basic concept in Sect. 4.1 and extend the idea in Sect. 4.2.

4.1 Basic Idea of the Initial-Exchange Technique

We explain the basic idea; how to exchange the positions of $m_{\pi^L(0)}$ and $m_{\pi^R(0)}$. The idea is illustrated in Figure 3. In the standard computation, the value of H_{i-1} is fixed, and we compute CF^L by using $m_{\pi^L(0)}$ and CF^R by using $m_{\pi^R(0)}$. We transform this computation by exchanging the order of additions so that the positions of $m_{\pi^L(0)}$ and $m_{\pi^R(0)}$ are exchanged (bottom of Figure 3). This enables us to compute CF^L and CF^R independently for more steps. Note that the value of H_i^a used in the feed-forward operation is affected by both of $m_{\pi^L(0)}$ and $m_{\pi^R(0)}$, and thus, we cannot fix it until we fix $m_{\pi^L(0)}$ and $m_{\pi^R(0)}$. However, we can still partially compute the feed-forward operation for other variables.

4.2 Extension of the Initial-Exchange Technique

The basic idea only exchanges the messages in the first steps. By considering absorption properties of Φ_j^L and Φ_j^R, we can exchange messages in various

Table 3. Summary of the initial-exchange technique for RIPEMD-128

Left (Φ_F)	Right (Φ_I)	FF effect	Conditions for M'_i	Conditions for M_i	comments
M'_0	M_0	H^a	—		
M'_0	M_1	H^a, H^d	—	$b_0 = c_0$	
M'_0	M_2	H^a, H^c	$d_1 = 0$	$d_0 = 1, b_1 = c_1$	partial bit condition
M'_0	M_3	H^a, H^b	$d_1 = 0, d_2 = 1$	$d_0 = 0, d_1 = 1, b_2 = c_2$	partial bit condition
M'_0	M_4	H^a	same as right	$d_1 = 0, d_2 = 1, b_3 = c_3$	
M'_0	M_8	H^a	same as right	$d_1 = 0, d_2 = 1, b_3 = c_3,$ $d_5 = 0, d_6 = 1, b_7 = c_7$	
M'_1	M_0	H^a, H^d	$b'_0 = c'_0$	—	
M'_1	M_1	H^a, H^d	$b'_0 = c'_0$	$b_0 = c_0$	same condition

On the 1st round (similar on the 4th round)

Left (Φ_H)	Right (Φ_G)	FF effect	Conditions for M'_i	Conditions for M_i	comments
M'_0	M_0	H^a	—		
M'_0	M_1	H^a, H^d	—	$b_0 = 1$	
M'_0	M_2	H^a, H^c	$c_1 = d_1$	$b_0 = 0, b_1 = 1$	partial bit condition
M'_0	M_3	H^a, H^b	$c_1 = d_1, b_2 = 0$	$c_0 = d_0, b_1 = 0, b_2 = 1$	partial bit condition
M'_0	M_4	H^a	same as right	$c_1 = d_1, d_2 = 0, b_3 = 1$	
M'_0	M_8	H^a	same as right	$c_1 = d_1, d_2 = 0, b_3 = 1,$ $c_5 = d_5, d_6 = 0, b_7 = 1$	
M'_1	M_0	H^a, H^d	$b'_0 = 0, c'_0 = 1$	—	
M'_1	M_1	H^a, H^d	$b'_0 = 0, c'_0 = 1$	$b_0 = 1$	partial bit condition

On the 3rd round (similar on the 2nd round)

positions. Note that the absorption property is the one where the output of $\Phi(X, Y, Z)$ can be independent of one input variable. For example, the output of $\Phi_I(X, Y, Z) = (X \wedge Z) \vee (Y \wedge \neg Z)$ can be independent of X by fixing Z to 0. It is well-known that Φ_G and Φ_I have absorption properties [2].

The first round of CF^R uses Φ_I, which has the absorption property. In such a case, messages words located in the second or latter step can be exchanged. Figure 4 shows an example where $M4$ and $M0'$ are exchanged. Mi is a message word $m_{\pi^R(i)}$ for a branch with the absorption property and Mi' is $m_{\pi^L(i)}$ for the other branch.

Moreover, even if Φ does not have the absorption property, we may exchange the message words in a few steps from the initial step. For example, we consider exchanging message words of the second steps, which is illustrated in Figure 5. Φ^L_j is Φ_F, which does not have the absorption property. Therefore, the impact of changing the value of $M1'$ always go through Φ^L_0. However, we still can apply the corresponding transformation by fixing Φ^L_0 as a simple function. In Figure 5, we guarantee that the output of Φ^L_0 is always $-M1'$ by setting the condition $b^L_0 = c^L_0$ and $d^L_0 = -M1'$. On the other hand, because the corresponding condition $b^R_0 = c^R_0$ also makes the absorption property for Φ^R_0, we can apply the corresponding transformation and thus can exchange the positions of these message words.

Note that when we exchange positions of message-word additions over a bit-rotation, we need to set conditions as shown in Figure 6 in order to avoid the uncontrolled carry. We confirmed all of our attacks could satisfy this restriction.

Besides the above two examples, many other extensions of initial-exchange are possible. Some of such extension, for example the case shown in Figure 8 which will be explained later, require more complicated analysis to exchange message words. In several steps of this example, two input variables to Φ are changed depending on different neutral words. It is known that Φ used in RIPEMD-128 cannot absorb independent changes of two different input variables, and thus the initial-exchange cannot be applied directly. To overcome this problem, we adopt a *partial-bit initial-exchange*, where only a part of bits in neutral words are changed so that the active-bit positions of two input chaining variables do not overlap each other. This enables us to use the *cross-absorption property* proposed by Sasaki *et al.*[20] to absorb the changes of two input variables of Φ. Finally, we can exchange message words even in such a complicated case.

Table 3 summarizes the initial-exchange technique applied to each round of RIPEMD-128. The first two columns show the message words where we exchange their positions. The third column shows feed-forward variables which cannot be fixed in advance. We denote by "FF effect" such an effect. The forth and fifth columns list the conditions to set up the absorption properties for Φ_F or Φ_H.

5   Attacks on RIPEMD-128

5.1   Attack on the First 33 Steps of RIPEMD-128

With the initial-exchange technique explained in Sect. 4, we attack the first 33 steps of RIPEMD-128. The chunk separation for the first 33 steps is shown in Figure 7. Note that for all attacks in this paper, we searched for the chunk separations by hand. In this attack, m_2 is a neutral word for computing CF^L and m_0 is for CF^R. The positions of $m_{\pi^L(0)}$ and $m_{\pi^R(5)}$ are exchanged with the initial-exchange technique, and the last 8 steps of CF^L and the last 2 steps of CF^R, in total 10 steps are skipped in the partial-matching phase.

Step	0	1	2	3	4	5	6	7	8	9	10	11	12	13	14	15
index L	**(0)** IE	1	**(2)**	3	4	5	6	7	8	9	10	11	12	13	14	15
			first chunk (depends on m_2)													
index R	5	14	7	**(0)**	9	**(2)** IE	11	4	13	6	15	8	1	10	3	12
						second chunk (depends on m_0)										

Step	16	17	18	19	20	21	22	23	24	25	26	27	28	29	30	31
index L	7	4	13	1	10	6	15	3	12	**(0)**	9	5	**(2)**	14	11	8
		first chunk (depends on m_2)										skip				
index R	6	11	3	7	**(0)**	13	5	10	14	15	8	12	4	9	1	**(2)**
				second chunk (depends on m_0)												skip

Step	32	33	34	35	36	37	38	39	40	41	42	43	44	45	46	47
index L	3 skip	10	14	4	9	15	8	1	**(2)**	7	**(0)**	6	13	11	5	12
						excluded										
index R	15 skip	5	1	3	7	14	6	9	11	8	12	**(2)**	10	**(0)**	4	13
						excluded										

"IE" represents that the message positions will be exchanged with the initial-exchange technique.

Fig. 7. Chunk separation for the first 33 steps of RIPEMD-128

Set up for the initial-exchange technique. Because this attack includes another neutral word $m_{\pi^R(3)}$ in the initial-exchange section, the construction, especially selection of the active-bit positions of neutral words is complicated. The details of the construction is shown in Figure 8. As a result of our by-hand analysis, we determine that 9 bits (bit positions 23–31) of m_2 and 9 bits (bit positions 2–10) of m_0 are active. This avoids the overlap of the active bit positions for Φ_j, and thus we can absorb the impact of changes of these bits with absorption or cross-absorption properties [20]. Please refer to Table 3 for conditions to achieve these properties. With this effort, the positions of $m_{\pi^L(0)} = m_0$ and $m_{\pi^R(5)} = m_2$ are exchanged, hence CF^L and CF^R can be computed independently by using 9 free bits of m_2 and m_0, respectively. Note that the active bits of m_0 make the 9 bits (bit positions 2–10) of a feed-forward value H_a^i unfixed. In other words, 23 bits (bit positions 0–1 and 11–31) of H_a^i are fixed. Similarly, m_2 makes 9 bits (bit positions 14–22) of a feed-forward value H_d^i unfixed and 23 bits (bit positions 0–13 and 23–31) of H_d^i are fixed.

Partial-matching phase. Computation for steps 25 to 32 of CF^L and 31 and 32 of CF^R are performed only partially. Because each neutral word has 9 active bits, we need to match at least 9 bits of results from each chunk. Details of the partial-computations are shown in Figure 9. We compute 23 bits of d_{28}^L, 23 bits of c_{28}^L, and 14 bits of b_{28}^L in the first chunk. We denote these partially computed bits in the first chunk by α. In the second chunk, we compute 4 bits of d_{28}^L, 11 bits of c_{28}^L, and 11 bits of b_{28}^L, which are denoted by β. Note that α and β include 15 bit positions in common (4 bits of d_{28}^L, 5 bits of c_{28}^L, and 6 bits of b_{28}^L).

In the computations of α and β, we often compute the modular additions without knowing the carry from the lower bit positions. For example in Figure 9, to compute the bit positions 0–13 and 23–31 of b_{26}^L, we compute the addition of

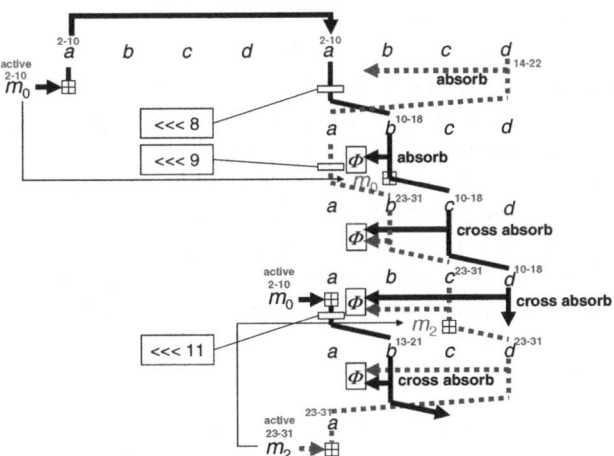

Fig. 8. Construction of the initial-exchange for the first 33 steps of RIPEMD-128

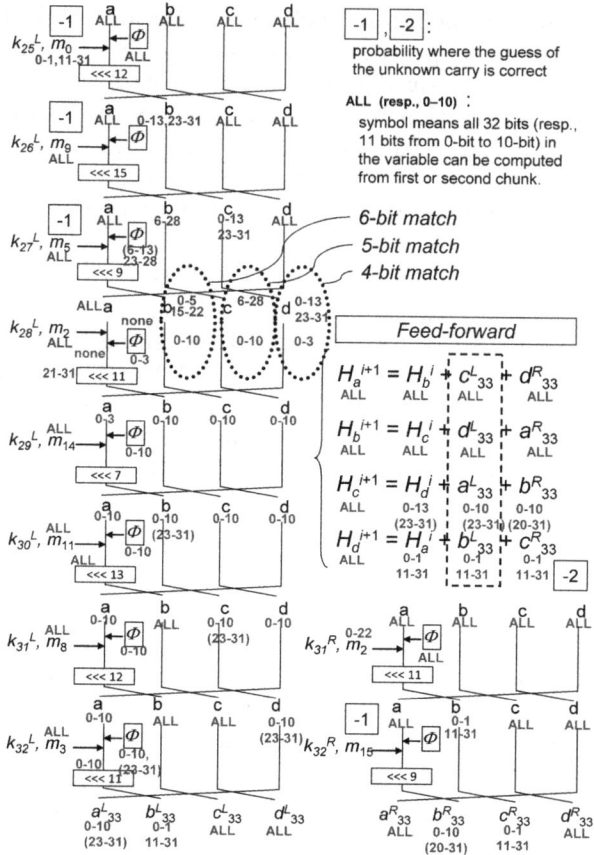

Fig. 9. Partial-match for the first 33 steps of RIPEMD-128

m_0 where only bit positions 0–1 and 11–31 are known. In this case, we obtain two candidates of bit positions 11–31 of the addition results, because we need to consider two carry patterns from bit positions 10 to 11. The computations of α and β require such a trick 3 times and 3 times respectively as marked in Figure 9. Hence, the number of pairs where we check the match will increase 2^6 times. To filter out these wrong candidates efficiently, we need to check the match of additional 6 bits of the results from each chunk. (9 bits for the standard meet-in-the-middle and 6 bits for filtering wrong candidates, in total 15 bits.) Because it can match 15 bits, our attack can filter out wrong candidates efficiently, and has the same efficiency as the standard meet-in-the-middle attack.

Attack procedure

1. Fix message words and chaining variables so that the set up for the initial-exchange technique and the padding for 2-block messages are satisfied. In the followings, every time we are short of freedom degrees, we go back to this step and restart the procedure by changing the values fixed in this step.

2. For 9 active bits (positions 23–31) of m_2, compute the first chunk. For each m_2, we obtain 2^3 candidates of α due to the unknown carry. Hence, we obtain $2^9 \cdot 2^3 = 2^{12}$ candidates of α. Store them in a table, and sort the table.

3. For each of 9 active bits (positions 2–10) of m_0, compute the second chunk to obtain β. For each of m_0, we obtain 2^3 candidates of β due to the unknown carry. For 2^9 values of m_0, we obtain $2^9 \cdot 2^3 = 2^{12}$ candidates of β.

4. For each β, check the match of 15 bits described in Figure 9 with all 'α's stored in the table.

5. If they match, with the corresponding m_0 and m_2, check the correctness of the carry assumptions step by step.

6. If all carry assumptions are correct, compute the remaining $128 - 15 = 113$ bits and check if all 113 bits will match or not.

7. If all bits match, the corresponding p_0 and message words are the pseudo-preimage of the given hash value.

Complexity evaluation. Steps 2 and 3 require 2^9 computations of the half of the compression function. Step 4 matches the 15 bits of $2^{12} \cdot 2^{12} = 2^{24}$ pairs and $2^{24} \cdot 2^{-15} = 2^9$ pairs will remain. In Step 5, a pair satisfies all the carry assumptions with a probability of 2^{-6}, hence 2^3 pairs will remain. So far, we obtain 2^3 pairs whose 15 bits match. Therefore, by iterating Step 6 2^{110} times, we will find a pair where all bits match, namely, a pseudo-preimage is obtained.

The complexity of the pseudo-preimage attack is $2^9 \cdot 2^{110} = 2^{119}$, and we need 2^{12} memory for Step 2. Note that Step 3 can be performed sequentially, and thus we do not need 2^{13} memory. Finally, this pseudo-preimage attack can be converted to a preimage attack with a complexity of $2^{\frac{119+128}{2}+1} = 2^{124.5}$ by using the conversion algorithm explained in Sect. 3.1.

5.2   Attack on Intermediate 35 Steps of RIPEMD-128

To attack intermediate steps, the local-collision approach [14] explained in Sect. 3.3 is more effective than the initial-exchange approach. The chunk separation for the intermediate 35 steps is shown in Figure 10, where neutral words are (m_0, m_6) and m_2. We make local collisions in Steps 21 to 25 of CF^L. For the partial-matching, we only activate bit positions 16 to 31 of m_0 and 5 to 20 of m_2.

Set up for the attack. Fix chaining variables between p_{21}^L and p_{26}^L as shown in Table 4, where $C_0, C_1, \ldots, C_4$ are arbitrary fixed values, **0** denotes 0 ($=$0x00000000), **1** denotes -1 ($=$0xffffffff), and $*$ denotes a variable that changes depending on the values of (m_0, m_6). Compute m_{15}, m_3, and m_{12} with a equation $m_{\pi^L(j)} \leftarrow (b_{j+1}^L \ggg s_j^L) - k_j^L - \Phi_j^L(b_j^L, c_j^L, d_j^L) - a_j^L$, so that the values fixed in Table 4 can be achieved. This equation can be computed without fixing the value of $*$ due to the absorption property. Now, every time we choose the value of m_6, we can make a local collision by adaptively choosing m_0 as follows:
$m_0 \leftarrow (b_{26}^L \ggg s_{25}^L) - k_{25}^L - \Phi_{25}^L(b_{25}^L, c_{25}^L, d_{25}^L) - ((a_{21}^L + \Phi_{21}^L(b_{21}^L, c_{21}^L, d_{21}^L) + m_6 +$

Step	0	1	2	3	4	5	6	7	8	9	10	11	12	13	14	15
index L	(0)	1	(2)	3	4	5	(6)	7	8	9	10	11	12	13	14	15
			excluded								fix					
index R	5	14	7	(0)	9	(2)	11	4	13	(6)	15	8	1	10	3	12
			excluded					fix			first chunk					

Step	16	17	18	19	20	21	22	23	24	25	26	27	28	29	30	31
index L	7	4	13	1	10	(6)	15	3	12	(0)	9	5	(2)	14	11	8
			fix				local-collision				fix		second chunk			
index R	(6)	11	3	7	(0)	13	5	10	14	15	8	12	4	9	1	(2)
					first chunk											skip

Step	32	33	34	35	36	37	38	39	40	41	42	43	44	45	46	47
index L	3	10	14	4	9	15	8	1	(2)	7	(0)	(6)	13	11	5	12
		second chunk										excluded				
index R	15	5	1	3	7	14	(6)	9	11	8	12	(2)	10	(0)	4	13
		skip						2nd chunk				excluded				

Fig. 10. Chunk separation for intermediate 35 steps of RIPEMD-128

Table 4. Set up for the local-collision

j	$m_{\pi^L(j)}$	$a_j^L\ b_j^L\ c_j^L\ d_j^L$
21	m_6	$C_0\ C_1\ C_1\ C_2$
22	m_{15}	$C_2\ *\ C_1\ C_1$
23	m_3	$C_1\ 0\ *\ C_1$
24	m_{12}	$C_1\ 1\ 0\ *$
25	m_0	$*\ C_3\ 1\ 0$
26		$0\ C_4\ C_3\ 1$

$k_{21}^L) \lll s_{21}^L)$. With this equation, fix the bit positions 0 to 15 of m_6 and compute the corresponding bits of m_0 so that local-collision can be formed. Then, fix the values of m_j, where $0 \leq j \leq 15, j \notin \{15, 3, 12, 0, 2, 6\}$, to randomly chosen values. Finally, compute the fixed part $(p_7^L, \ldots, p_{20}^L, p_{27}^L, p_{28}^L, p_8^R, p_9^R)$ of the attack target. Store the randomly chosen values and corresponding p_{28}^L and p_9^R.

Attack procedure

1. Carry out the set up procedure.
2. For all active bits (bit positions 16 to 31) of m_6, do as follows.
   (a) Compute the values of m_0 so that the local-collision can be formed.
   (b) Compute $p_{j+1}^R \leftarrow R_j^R(p_j^R, m_{\pi^R(j)})$ for $j = 9, 10, \ldots, 30$.
   (c) Compute the bit positions 0 to 15 of b_{32}^R by using $R_{31}^R(p_{31}^R, m_{\pi^R(31)})$ with fixed bits (bit positions 0 to 4 and 21 to 31) of $m_{\pi^R(31)} = m_2$.
   (d) Store the values of m_6, m_0, p_{31}^R and the lower half bits of b_{32}^R in a table.
3. For all active bits (bit positions 5 to 20) of m_2, do as follows.
   (a) Compute $p_{j+1}^L \leftarrow R_j^L(p_j^L, m_{\pi^L(j)})$ for $j = 28, 29, \ldots, 41$,
   (b) Compute p_{42}^R by using feed-forward equations.
   (c) Compute $p_j^R \leftarrow R_j^{R(-1)}(p_j^R, m_{\pi^R(j)})$ for $j = 41, 40,$ and, 39.

Step	32	33	34	35	36	37	38	39	40	41	42	43	44	45	46	47
index L	(3)	10	14	4	9	15	8	1	2	(7)	0	6	13	11	5	12
	IE				first chunk (depends on m_7)											
index R	15	5	1	(3)	(7)	14	6	9	11	8	12	2	10	0	4	13
					IE	second chunk (depends on m_3)										

Step	48	49	50	51	52	53	54	55	56	57	58	59	60	61	62	63
index L	1	9	11	10	0	8	12	4	13	(3)	(7)	15	14	5	6	2
	first chunk (depends on m_7)											skip				
index R	8	6	4	1	(3)	11	15	0	5	12	2	13	9	(7)	10	14
	second chunk (depends on m_3)													skip		

Fig. 11. Chunk separation for the last 32 steps of RIPEMD-128

(d) Compute bit positions 0 to 15 of b_{32}^R by using $R_j^{R(-1)}(p_{j+1}^R, m_{\pi^R(j)})$ for $j = 38, 37, \ldots, 32$ with fixed bits (positions 0 to 15) of $m_{\pi^R(38)} = m_6$.

(e) Check if the computed results (bit positions 0 to 15 of b_{32}^R) match the one of the values stored at Step 2d.

(f) If they match, compute all values of p_{32}^R from both chunks with the corresponding m_0, m_6, and m_2.

(g) If all bits match, the corresponding message words and p_7 are the pseudo-preimage of the given output value.

Complexity evaluation. Complexity for the set up part can be ignored because it is less often repeated. Complexity for Steps 2 and 3 are roughly 2^{16} computations of the half compression function, respectively. In the matching part, we check the match of 2^{16} items of 16 bits stored at Step 2d and 2^{16} items of 16 bits computed at Step 3d. Therefore, we obtain 2^{16} pairs where 16 bits of p_{32}^R are matched. Other 112 bits are randomly satisfied. Therefore, by repeating the above procedure $2^{112-16} = 2^{96}$ times, we will find a matched pair. The total complexity is $2^{16} \cdot 2^{96} = 2^{112}$ compression function computations. Note that for Step 2d, we need 2^{16} memory. Finally, this pseudo-preimage attack can be converted to a second-preimage attack with a complexity of $2^{\frac{112+128}{2}+1} = 2^{121}$.

Note that in the set up procedure using Table 4, we can make the freedom degrees for m_{15} instead of C_2. This enables us satisfy the padding string located in m_{13}, m_{14}, and m_{15}. Therefore, this attack can generate preimages.

5.3 Attack on the Last 32 Steps of RIPEMD-128

We use the initial-exchange technique to attack the last 32 steps of RIPEMD-128. The chunk separation is shown in Figure 11.

The form of the initial-exchange used in this attack is exactly the same as the one in Figure 4. Hence we omit the details. Different from the attack for the first 33 steps, we do not have to use the partial-bit initial-exchange. However, due to the large number of skipped steps in the partial-matching phase, many bits of neutral words need to be fixed. In this attack, we make 7 bits (positions 18–24) of m_3 and 9 bits (positions 0–3 and 27–31) of m_7 active. Then, in the partial-matching phase, we can match 14 bits as shown in Figure 12. Note that the partial-computation with unknown carry effect is performed 8 times.

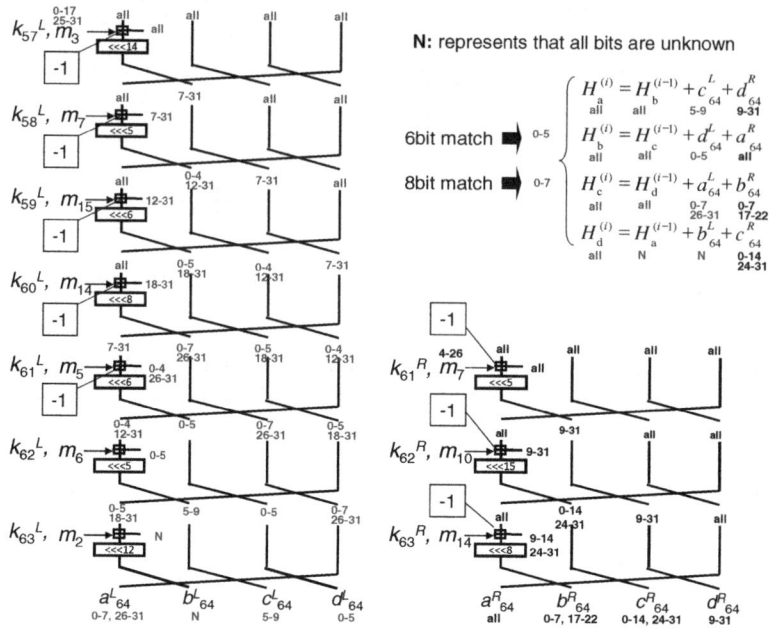

Fig. 12. Partial-match for the last 32 steps of RIPEMD-128

Attack summary. To avoid the redundancy, we omit the details of the attack procedure. In summary, the first and second chunks include 7 and 9 active bits, respectively. During the partial-computation, the number of candidates will increase 2^8 times, and we can match 14 bits of the results from two chunks. As a result, with a complexity of $2^7 + 2^9$ half compression function computations, we will obtain $2^{7+9+8-14} = 2^{10}$ matched pairs. Then, with a complexity of 2^{10}, we can check the correctness of the carry assumption and $2^{10-8} = 2^2$ pairs will remain. By iterating this procedure 2^{112} times, we will find a pseudo-preimage. The attack complexity is $(\frac{1}{2} \cdot 2^7 + \frac{1}{2} \cdot 2^9 + 2^{10}) \cdot 2^{112} \approx 2^{122.39}$ and we use 2^{12} memory (for 2^7 values of m_3, we obtain 2^5 candidates of α). In this attack, the value of m_{15} cannot be controlled because we need to fix it to a certain constant value in order to achieve the absorption property used in the initial-exchange technique. Therefore, with the conversion algorithm explained in Section 3.1, this can only be a second-preimage attack with a complexity of $2^{\frac{122.39+128}{2}+1} \approx 2^{126.20}$.

6 Attacks on RIPEMD-160

RIPEMD-160 follows the same structure as RIPEMD-128. However, several different characteristics give influence to the attack strategy. Specifically, the direct addition of e_j to update b_{j+1} increases the resistance against our attacks. In this section, we first summarize our observations particular to RIPEMD-160.

Step	0	1	2	3	4	5	6	7	8	9	10	11	12	13	14	15
index L	(0) IE	1	2	3	4	5	6	7	8	9	10	11	12	13	(14)	15
					first chunk (depends on m_{14})											
index R	5	(14) IE	7	(0)	9	2	11	4	13	6	15	8	1	10	3	12
					second chunk (depends on m_0)											

Step	16	17	18	19	20	21	22	23	24	25	26	27	28	29	30	31
index L	7	4	13	1	10	6	15	3	12	(0)	9	5	2	(14)	11	8
	first chunk (depends on m_{14})									skip					excluded	
index R	6	11	3	7	(0)	13	5	10	(14)	15	8	12	4	9	1	2
	2nd chunk (depends on m_0)									skip					excluded	

Fig. 13. Chunk separation for the first 30 steps of RIPEMD-160

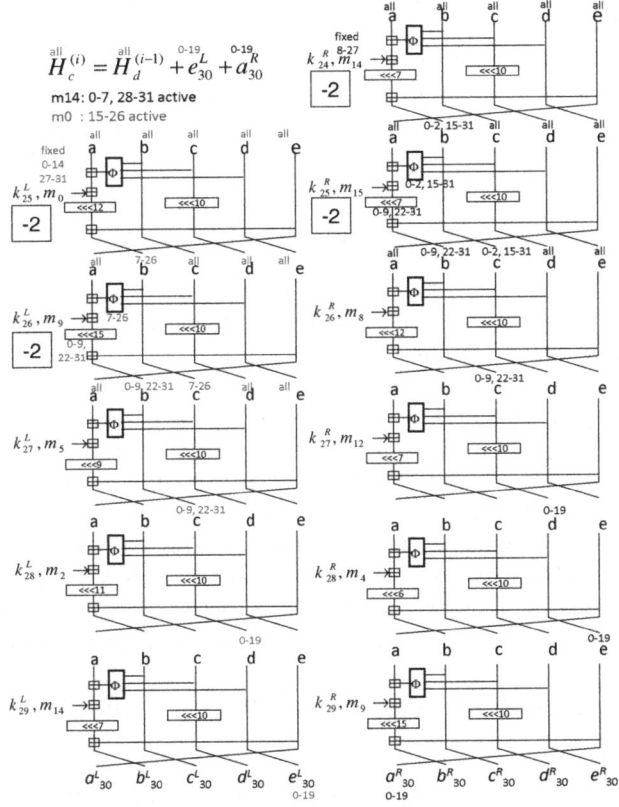

Fig. 14. Partial-match for the first 30 steps of RIPEMD-160

Step	48	49	50	51	52	53	54	55	56	57	58	59	60	61	62	63
index L	1	9	(11)	10	0	8	12	4	13	(3)	7	15	14	5	6	2
excluded			IE			first chunk (depends on m_3)										
index R	8	6	4	1	(3)	(11)	15	0	5	12	2	13	9	7	10	14
excluded					IE	second chunk (depends on m_{11})										

Step	64	65	66	67	68	69	70	71	72	73	74	75	76	77	78	79
index L	4	0	5	9	7	12	2	10	14	1	(3)	8	(11)	6	15	13
		first chunk (depends on m_3)											skip			
index R	12	15	10	4	1	5	8	7	6	2	13	14	0	(3)	9	(11)
		second chunk (depends on m_{11})												skip		

Fig. 15. Chunk separation for the last 31 steps of RIPEMD-160

- Due to the addition of e_j to b_{j+1}, 3 message words are necessary to form a local-collision. This makes the local-collision approach inefficient.
- Basic strategy of the initial-exchange technique can be applied to RIPEMD-160. However, the direct addition of e_j, which can be regarded as a function without the absorption property, makes its extension very hard.
- The number of chaining variables increases from RIPEMD-128. This enables attackers to skip more steps in the partial-matching phase.
- Φ in the first round do not have the absorption property in both sides. This makes the attack from the first steps harder than RIPEMD-128.

6.1 Attack on the First 30 Steps of RIPEMD-160

The chunk separation for the first 30 steps of RIPEMD-160 is shown in Figure 13. Due to the difficulties of applying the initial-exchange technique in the first round of RIPEMD-160, the positions where we can exchange the message words are limited. On the other hand, we can skip more steps in the partial-matching phase. As a result, the number of attacked steps reaches 30 steps. In this attack, we make 12 bits of m_{14} and 12 bits of m_0 active. In the partial-matching phase, we consider unknown carry effects 8 times and match the results in 20 bits, which results in the same efficiency as the standard meet-in-the-middle attack. Details of the partial-matching phase is described in Figure 14. Finally, the pseudo-preimages can be found with a complexity of 2^{148} and with a memory of 2^{16}. Note that we cannot satisfy the padding because m_{14} is a neutral word. Finally, this attack is converted to a second preimage attack with a complexity of 2^{155}.

6.2 Attack on the Last 31 Steps of RIPEMD-160

The chunk separation for the last 31 steps is shown in Figure 15. We make 12 bits of m_3 and 12 bits of m_{11} active. The initial-exchange construction is depicted in Figure 16. In the partial-matching phase, we consider the match of $15 + 8 = 23$ bits in the feed-forward equation with 5 unknown carry effects. Note that increasing match bits is possible by considering more unknown carry effects. However, because this does not impact to the final complexity, we simply match only 23 bits. Details of the partial-matching phase is described in Figure 17.

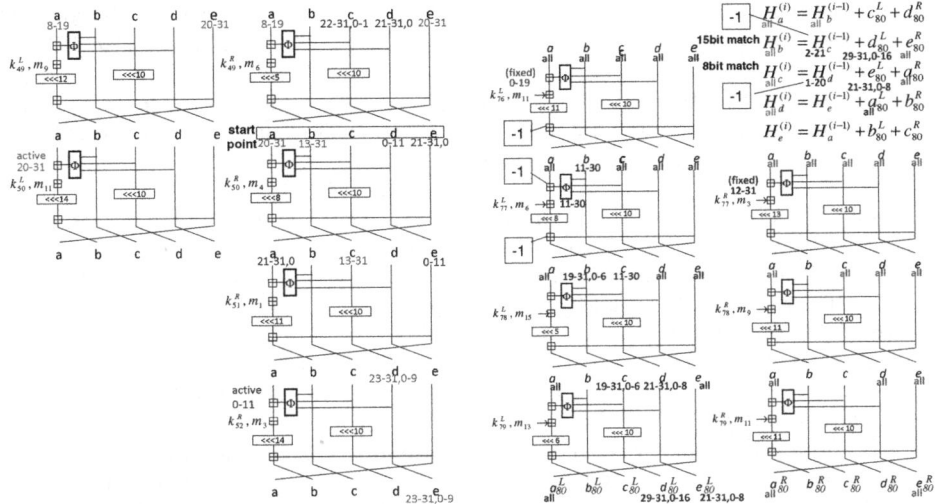

Fig. 16. Initial-exchange for last 31 steps   **Fig. 17.** Partial-match for the last 31 steps

Pseudo-preimages can be found with a complexity of 2^{148} and 2^{17} memory. Finally, the attack is converted to a preimage attack with a complexity of 2^{155}.

7   Concluding Remarks

We presented the first results on preimage resistance of RIPEMD-128 and -160. By using the initial-exchange technique, we discovered the (second) preimage attacks on the first 33, intermediate 35, and the last 32 steps of RIPEMD-128, and the first 30 and the last 31 steps of RIPEMD-160.

RIPEMD-128 and -160, have been believed to be more secure than RIPEMD. This may be true with respect to the collision resistance due to the differences between CF^L and CF^R. However, meet-in-the-middle attacks do not care most of the components except for the message order, and their security could be the same level as RIPEMD with respect to the preimage resistance.

References

1. U.S. Department of Commerce, National Institute of Standards and Technology: Federal Register/vol. 72, No. 212/Friday, November 2, 2007/Notices (2007)
2. Wang, X., Yu, H.: How to break MD5 and other hash functions. In: Cramer, R. (ed.) EUROCRYPT 2005. LNCS, vol. 3494, pp. 19–35. Springer, Heidelberg (2005)
3. Wang, X., Yin, Y.L., Yu, H.: Finding collisions in the full SHA-1. In: Shoup, V. (ed.) CRYPTO 2005. LNCS, vol. 3621, pp. 17–36. Springer, Heidelberg (2005)
4. Wang, X., Lai, X., Feng, D., Chen, H., Yu, X.: Cryptanalysis of the hash functions MD4 and RIPEMD. In: Cramer, R. (ed.) EUROCRYPT 2005. LNCS, vol. 3494, pp. 1–18. Springer, Heidelberg (2005)

5. Mendel, F., Rijmen, V.: Cryptanalysis of the tiger hash function. In: Kurosawa, K. (ed.) ASIACRYPT 2007. LNCS, vol. 4833, pp. 536–550. Springer, Heidelberg (2007)
6. Guo, J., Ling, S., Rechberger, C., Wang, H.: Advanced meet-in-the-middle preimage attacks: First results on full Tiger, and improved results on MD4 and SHA-2. Cryptology ePrint Archive, Report 2010/016 (2010)
7. Lamberger, M., Mendel, F., Rechberger, C., Rijmen, V., Schläffer, M.: Rebound distinguishers: Results on the full whirlpool compression function. In: Matsui, M. (ed.) ASIACRYPT 2009. LNCS, vol. 5912, pp. 126–143. Springer, Heidelberg (2009)
8. Saarinen, M.-J.O.: A meet-in-the-middle collision attack against the new FORK-256. In: Srinathan, K., Rangan, C.P., Yung, M. (eds.) INDOCRYPT 2007. LNCS, vol. 4859, pp. 10–17. Springer, Heidelberg (2007)
9. Dobbertin, H., Bosselaers, A., Preneel, B.: RIPEMD-160: A strengthened version of RIPEMD. In: Gollmann, D. (ed.) FSE 1996. LNCS, vol. 1039, pp. 71–82. Springer, Heidelberg (1996)
10. RIPE Integrity Primitives: Integrity Primitives for Secure Information Systems, Final RIPE Report of RACE Integrity Primitives Evaluation, RIPE-RACE 1040 (1995)
11. International Organization for Standardization: ISO/IEC 10118-3:2004, Information technology – Security techniques – Hash-functions – Part 3: Dedicated hash-functions (2004)
12. Mendel, F., Pramstaller, N., Rechberger, C., Rijmen, V.: On the collision resistance of RIPEMD-160. In: Katsikas, S.K., López, J., Backes, M., Gritzalis, S., Preneel, B. (eds.) ISC 2006. LNCS, vol. 4176, pp. 101–116. Springer, Heidelberg (2006)
13. Wang, G., Wang, S.: Preimage attack on hash function RIPEMD. In: Bao, F., Li, H., Wang, G. (eds.) ISPEC 2009. LNCS, vol. 5451, pp. 274–284. Springer, Heidelberg (2009)
14. Sasaki, Y., Aoki, K.: Meet-in-the-middle preimage attacks on double-branch hash functions: Application to RIPEMD and others. In: Boyd, C., González Nieto, J. (eds.) ACISP 2009. LNCS, vol. 5594, pp. 214–231. Springer, Heidelberg (2009)
15. Hong, D., Chang, D., Sung, J., Lee, S.-J., Hong, S.H., Lee, J.S., Moon, D., Chee, S.: A new dedicated 256-bit hash function: FORK-256. In: Robshaw, M.J.B. (ed.) FSE 2006. LNCS, vol. 4047, pp. 195–209. Springer, Heidelberg (2006)
16. Aoki, K., Sasaki, Y.: Preimage attacks on one-block MD4, 63-step MD5 and more. In: Avanzi, R.M., Keliher, L., Sica, F. (eds.) SAC 2008. LNCS, vol. 5381, pp. 103–119. Springer, Heidelberg (2009)
17. den Boer, B., Bosselaers, A.: An attack on the last two rounds of MD4. In: Feigenbaum, J. (ed.) CRYPTO 1991. LNCS, vol. 576, pp. 194–203. Springer, Heidelberg (1992)
18. Menezes, A.J., van Oorschot, P.C., Vanstone, S.A.: Handbook of applied cryptography. CRC Press, Boca Raton (1997)
19. Leurent, G.: MD4 is not one-way. In: Nyberg, K. (ed.) FSE 2008. LNCS, vol. 5086, pp. 412–428. Springer, Heidelberg (2008)
20. Sasaki, Y., Aoki, K.: Finding preimages in full MD5 faster than exhaustive search. In: Joux, A. (ed.) EUROCRYPT 2009. LNCS, vol. 5479, pp. 134–152. Springer, Heidelberg (2009)

Pseudo-Cryptanalysis of Luffa

Keting Jia[1,2], Yvo Desmedt[3], Lidong Han[1], and Xiaoyun Wang[1,2,⋆]

[1] Key Laboratory of Cryptologic Technology and Information Security, Ministry of Education,
Shandong University, China
{ktjia,hanlidong}@mail.sdu.edu.cn
[2] Institute for Advanced Study, Tsinghua University, China
xiaoyunwang@mail.tsinghua.edu.cn
[3] Department of Computer Science, University College London, UK
y.desmedt@cs.ucl.ac.uk

Abstract. In this paper, we present the pseudo-collision, pseudo-second-preimage and pseudo-preimage attacks on the SHA-3 candidate algorithm Luffa. The pseudo-collisions and pseudo-second-preimages can be found easily by computing the inverse of the message injection function at the beginning of Luffa. We explain in details the pseudo-preimage attacks. For Luffa-224/256, given the hash value, only 2 iteration computations are needed to get a pseudo-preimage. For Luffa-384, finding a pseudo-preimage needs about 2^{64} iteration computations with 2^{67} bytes memory by the extended generalized birthday attack. For Luffa-512, the complexity is 2^{128} iteration computations with 2^{132} bytes memory.

It is noted that, we can find the pseudo-collision pairs and the pseudo-second images only changing a few different bits of initial values. That is directly converted to the forgery attack on NMAC in related key cases.

Keywords: Luffa, pseudo-collision, pseudo-second-preimage, pseudo-preimage, generalized birthday attack.

1 Introduction

A cryptographic hash function is defined as a function that computes a fixed size message digest from arbitrary size messages. It has been widely used as a fundamental primitive in many cryptographic schemes and protocols, such as electronic signature, authentication of messages, electronic commerce and bit commitment, etc. In the past years, the cryptanalysis of hash functions has achieved tremendous progress with the construction of collisions. In particular, Wang et al. proposed new techniques to find efficiently collisions on the main hash functions from the MD4 family (e.g., MD4 [8], RIPEMD [8], MD5 [11], SHA-0 [9] and SHA-1 [10]). Moreover the techniques can be applied to explore the second-preimage of MD4 [12], forgery and partial key-recovery attacks on HMAC and NMAC [3,4]. Kelsey and Schneier [5] provided a second preimage attack on the iterated hash functions with Merkle-Damgård strengthening, which shows a vulnerability of the Merkle-Damgård construction. Responding to advances in the cryptanalysis of hash functions, NIST held two hash workshops to evaluate the

---

⋆ Corresponding author.

X. Lai, M. Yung, and D. Lin (Eds.): Inscrypt 2010, LNCS 6584, pp. 187–198, 2011.

security of its approved hash functions and to solicit public comments on its crypto-graphic hash function policy and standard. Finally, NIST opened a public competition to develop a new hash function called "SHA-3", similar to the development process of the Advanced Encryption Standard (AES). There are 64 new proposals for hash func-tions have been submitted to the SHA-3 project, of which 51 submissions have come into the first round. In July, 2009, NIST has selected 14 second round candidates of the SHA-3. Luffa [2] is one of them, proposed by De Cannière, Sato and Watanabe.

In this paper, we give some cryptanalytic results of Luffa with free initial values. The pseudo-collision and pseudo-second-preimage can be obtained easily by the message injection function of Luffa, which only changes a few bits of the initial values. This pa-per shows a pseudo-collision and pseudo-second-preimage example for Luffa-256 and gives the actual attacks. For Luffa-224/256, only 2 iteration computations are needed to get the pseudo-preimage. A pseudo preimage example for Luffa-256 is shown in this paper, which only changes 2 256-bit words of the initial values with 3 256-bit words. We use the extended generalized birthday attack [7] to compute the pseudo-preimage of Luffa-384 with 2^{64} iteration computations and 2^{64} table lookups. The time complexity and data complexity are both 2^{128} to get the pseudo-preimage for Luffa-512.

This paper is organized as follows. In Section 2, we list some notations and give a brief description of Luffa. Section 3 shows the pseudo-collision and pseudo-second-preimage attacks on Luffa. The pseudo-preimage attacks for Luffa is given in Section 4. The improved pseudo-preimage attacks for Luffa-384/512 are shown in Section 5. Finally, we summarize our results in Section 6.

2   Preliminaries and Notations

In this section, we first list some notations used in this paper, and then give a brief description of Luffa.

2.1   Notations

$X \| Y$: the concatenation of two messages X and Y.
$h_w(X)$: the w most significant bits of X.
$l_w(X)$: the w least significant bits of X.
$\lfloor a \rfloor$: the greatest integer less than or equal to a.
$(b_0, b_1, \ldots, b_m)^T$: the transposed matrix of $(b_0, b_1, \ldots, b_m)$, where $b_i(1 \leq i \leq m)$ are column vectors.
$a \lll j$: left rotation of a by j bits.

2.2   Description of Luffa

Luffa [2], a candidate algorithm for the second round of the SHA-3, was proposed by De Cannière et al. The chaining of Luffa is a variant of a sponge function. Fig.1 depicts the basic structure. For any message, Luffa can produce the hash values with 224, 256, 384 or 512 bits, which are denoted as Luffa-224/256/384/512 respectively. The message padding method consists of appending a single bit '1' followed by the minimum bits of '0' such that the length of the result is a multiple of 256. Let $M = M_0 \| \cdots \| M_{m-1}$ be a message after padding, where $M_i (0 \leq i < m)$ are 256-bit blocks. The *iteration function* of Luffa is a composition of a message injection function MI and a permutation P with w 256-bit inputs, where $w = 3, 4$ or 5 for Luffa-224/256, Luffa-384 and Luffa-512 respectively. The permutation P includes w permutations $Q_0, Q_1, \ldots, Q_{w-1}$, where Q_j is the permutation with 256-bit input, $j = 0, 1, \ldots, w - 1$. Let the input of the i−th iteration be $(H_0^{(i-1)}, \ldots, H_{w-1}^{(i-1)}, M_{i-1})$, the i−th iteration is computed as follows,

$$X_0 \| \cdots \| X_{w-1} = MI(H_0^{(i-1)}, \ldots, H_{w-1}^{(i-1)}, M_{i-1}),$$
$$H_j^{(i)} = Q_j(X_j), j = 0, 1, \ldots, w - 1,$$

where $(H_0^i, \ldots, H_{w-1}^i)$ is the i-th iteration output, and $(H_0^0, \ldots, H_{w-1}^0)$ is the initial value. Final operations, called a *finalization* are used to the chaining value $(H_0^{(m-1)}, \ldots, H_{w-1}^{(m-1)})$. For Luffa-224/256, the finalization consists of a blank iteration and a XOR operation OF, where the blank iteration means an iteration with a fixed message $M_m = \mathbb{0}$, where $\mathbb{0}$ denotes 256-bit zeros, the operation OF XORs w 256-bit values and outputs the result 256-bit value. For Luffa-384/512, the finalization includes two blank iterations and two XOR operations, see Fig. 1. The output of Luffa-256 is Z_0, the output of Luffa-512 is $Z_0 \| Z_1$. The outputs of Luffa-224 and Luffa-384 are the truncation of the Luffa-256 and Luffa-512 respectively. Here

$$Z_i = \bigoplus_{j=0}^{w-1} H_j^{(m+i)}, \quad i = 0, 1.$$

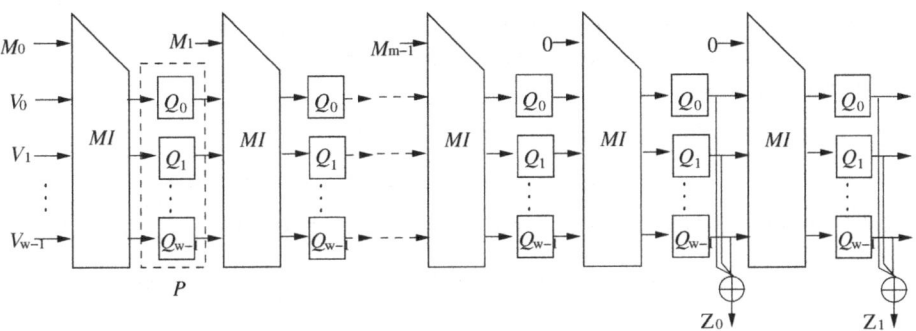

Fig. 1. The Structure of Luffa Hash Function

Message Injection Function MI. The message injection functions MI can be represented by the matrix over a field $GF(2^8)$. The multiplication over the field $GF(2^8)$ is modulo $\phi(x) = x^8 + x^4 + x^3 + x + 1$, corresponding to "0x11b". The map from 8 32-bit words $(h_0, \ldots, h_7)$ to 32 8-bit elements of the field is defined by $(\Sigma_{0 \leq k < 8} h_{k,l} x^k)_{0 \leq l < 32}$. Let $A_{w \times (w+1)} = (a_0, a_1, \ldots, a_{w-1}, a_w)$ represent the matrix of MI, where $a_i (0 \leq i \leq w)$ are column vectors. Then $(X_0, X_1, \ldots, X_{w-1})^T = A_{w \times (w+1)} \circ (H_0, H_1, \ldots, H_{w-1}, M)^T$. For Luffa-224/256, w=3,

$$A_{w \times (w+1)} = \begin{pmatrix} 0x3, 0x2, 0x2, 0x1 \\ 0x2, 0x3, 0x2, 0x2 \\ 0x2, 0x2, 0x3, 0x4 \end{pmatrix},$$

where the elements $0x1$, $0x2$, $0x3$, $0x4$ correspond to polynomials $1, x, x+1, x^2$ respectively.

For Luffa-384,

$$A_{w \times (w+1)} = \begin{pmatrix} 0x4, 0x6, 0x6, 0x7, 0x1 \\ 0x7, 0x4, 0x6, 0x6, 0x2 \\ 0x6, 0x7, 0x4, 0x6, 0x4 \\ 0x6, 0x6, 0x7, 0x4, 0x8 \end{pmatrix}.$$

For Luffa-512,

$$A_{w \times (w+1)} = \begin{pmatrix} 0x0F, 0x08, 0x0A, 0x0A, 0x08, 0x01 \\ 0x08, 0x0F, 0x08, 0x0A, 0x0A, 0x02 \\ 0x0A, 0x08, 0x0F, 0x08, 0x0A, 0x04 \\ 0x0A, 0x0A, 0x08, 0x0F, 0x08, 0x08 \\ 0x08, 0x0A, 0x0A, 0x08, 0x0F, 0x10 \end{pmatrix}.$$

The Permutation Q_j. The permutation Q_j is defined as a composition of an input tweak and 8 steps. Let $a_0, \ldots, a_7$ be the 256-bit input of the Q_j, $b_0, \ldots, b_7$ be the output of tweak. The tweak is defined as follows:

$$b_i = a_i, \text{for } 1 \leq i < 4;$$
$$b_i = a_i \lll j, \text{for } 4 \leq i < 8.$$

After tweak, there are 8 steps in the permutation, and each step consists of the following three functions: SubCrumb, MixWord and AddConstant.

SubCrumb is defined as:

$$x_{3,l} \| x_{2,l} \| x_{1,l} \| x_{0,l} = S(b_{3,l} \| b_{2,l} \| b_{1,l} \| b_{0,l}), 0 \leq l < 32,$$
$$x_{4,l} \| x_{7,l} \| x_{6,l} \| x_{5,l} = S(b_{4,l} \| b_{7,l} \| b_{6,l} \| b_{5,l}), 0 \leq l < 32,$$

where S denotes a S-box with 4-bit input and 4-bit output. MixWord is defined as:

$$\begin{aligned} y_{k+4} &= x_{k+4} \oplus x_k, & y_k &= x_k \lll 2, \\ y_k &= y_k \oplus y_{k+4}, & y_{k+4} &= y_{k+4} \lll 14, \\ y_{k+4} &= y_{k+4} \oplus y_k, & y_k &= y_k \lll 10, \\ y_k &= y_k \oplus y_{k+4}, & y_{k+4} &= y_{k+4} \lll 1. \end{aligned}$$

We do not give the description for AddConstant since it has no impact on our cryptanalysis. For more details about Luffa, consult [2].

3 Pseudo-Collision and Pseudo-Second-Preimage Attacks on Luffa

In this section, we give some cryptanalysis for Luffa when the initial value IV is free. Flipping 5 bits of IV for Luffa-256 is enough to get a pseudo-collision or pseudo-second-preimage. For Luffa-384, 7 bits of IV are needed to be changed to get a pseudo-collision or pseudo-second-preimage. There is a 12-bit difference in the IV to get a pseudo-collision or pseudo-second-preimage for Luffa-512. This can be used to construct the related key attack for the corresponding MACs using the secret key as initial value.

For the message injection function MI, the input is $(w+1)$ 256-bit words, and the output is w 256-bit words. So, it is a many-to-one function. It is easy to know that, any w columns of the MI matrix consists of an invertible matrix. So there are exactly 2^{256} inputs corresponding to any given output of MI. Given any MI output $(X_0, X_1, \ldots, X_{w-1})$, if one entry of $H_0, H_1, \ldots, H_{w-1}$ and M is fixed, we can easily compute the solution to other entries. Any pair of inputs with the same output of MI consists of a pseudo-collision of Luffa, that is the output difference of MI is zero.

For Luffa-224/256, the input difference is $(\Delta H_0, \Delta H_1, \Delta H_2, \Delta M)$, and the output difference of MI is $(0, 0, 0)$, here 0 denotes 256-bit zeros. They satisfy the following equations.

$$3 \circ \Delta H_0 \oplus 2 \circ \Delta H_1 \oplus 2 \circ \Delta H_2 \oplus \Delta M = 0,$$
$$2 \circ \Delta H_0 \oplus 3 \circ \Delta H_1 \oplus 2 \circ \Delta H_2 \oplus 2\Delta M = 0,$$
$$2 \circ \Delta H_0 \oplus 2 \circ \Delta H_1 \oplus 3 \circ \Delta H_2 \oplus 4\Delta M = 0.$$

From the equations, it is easy to get $\Delta H_0 = 0xf2 \circ \Delta M$, $\Delta H_1 = 0xf1 \circ \Delta M$ and $\Delta H_2 = 0xf7 \circ \Delta M$. Let IV be the standard initial value, given a message M, the message $M' = M \oplus \Delta M$, with another initial value $IV' = IV \oplus (\Delta H_0, \Delta H_1, \Delta H_2)$ is the pseudo-preimage of M, i.e. Luffa-256(IV, M)=Luffa-256(IV', M'). There are only 5 bits different between IV and IV', which is minimum, when the message difference $\Delta M = (2^i, 2^i, 0, 0, 0, 0, 0, 0)$, $(0, 2^i, 2^i, 0, 0, 0, 0, 0)$, $(0, 0, 2^i, 2^i, 0, 0, 0, 0)$, $(0, 0, 0, 2^i, 2^i, 0, 0, 0)$ or $(0, 0, 0, 0, 2^i, 2^i, 0, 0)$ for $(0 \le i < 32)$.

Let the input difference be $(\Delta H_0, \Delta H_1, \Delta H_2, \Delta H_3, \Delta M)$, and the output difference of MI be $(0, 0, 0, 0)$ for Luffa-384 such that

$$4 \circ \Delta H_0 \oplus 6 \circ \Delta H_1 \oplus 6 \circ \Delta H_2 \oplus 7 \circ \Delta H_3 \oplus \Delta M = 0,$$
$$7 \circ \Delta H_0 \oplus 4 \circ \Delta H_1 \oplus 6 \circ \Delta H_2 \oplus 6 \circ \Delta H_3 \oplus 2\Delta M = 0,$$
$$6 \circ \Delta H_0 \oplus 7 \circ \Delta H_1 \oplus 4 \circ \Delta H_2 \oplus 6 \circ \Delta H_3 \oplus 4\Delta M = 0,$$
$$6 \circ \Delta H_0 \oplus 6 \circ \Delta H_1 \oplus 7 \circ \Delta H_2 \oplus 4 \circ \Delta H_3 \oplus 8\Delta M = 0.$$

By the system of equations, we can deduce $\Delta H_0 = 8 \circ \Delta M$, $\Delta H_1 = 0xa \circ \Delta M$, $\Delta H_2 = 8 \circ \Delta M$ and $\Delta H_3 = 0xf \circ \Delta M$. There is a 7-bit difference in the initial values when $\Delta M = (2^i, 0, 2^i, 2^i, 0, 0, 0, 2^i)(0 \le i < 32)$. The message $M' = M \oplus \Delta M$ with $IV' = IV \oplus (\Delta H_0, \Delta H_1, \Delta H_2, \Delta H_3)$ is the pseudo-preimage of the given message M, that is to say Luffa-384(IV, M)=Luffa-384(IV', M').

Given the input difference of Luffa-512 $(\Delta H_0, \Delta H_1, \Delta H_2, \Delta H_3, \Delta H_4, \Delta M)$ and the output difference of MI $(0, 0, 0, 0, 0)$, we can compute that $\Delta H_0 = 0xbe \circ \Delta M$, $\Delta H_1 = 0x3c \circ \Delta M$, $\Delta H_2 = 0x25 \circ \Delta M$, $\Delta H_3 = 0x17 \circ \Delta M$ and $\Delta H_4 = 0x75 \circ \Delta M$ from the following equations.

$$0xf \circ \Delta H_0 \oplus 0x8 \circ \Delta H_1 \oplus 0xa \circ \Delta H_2 \oplus 0xa \circ \Delta H_3 \oplus 0x8 \circ \Delta H_4 \oplus \Delta M = 0,$$
$$0x8 \circ \Delta H_0 \oplus 0xf \circ \Delta H_1 \oplus 0x8 \circ \Delta H_2 \oplus 0xa \circ \Delta H_3 \oplus 0xa \circ \Delta H_4 \oplus 0x2\Delta M = 0,$$
$$0xa \circ \Delta H_0 \oplus 0x8 \circ \Delta H_1 \oplus 0xf \circ \Delta H_2 \oplus 0x8 \circ \Delta H_3 \oplus 0xa \circ \Delta H_4 \oplus 0x4\Delta M = 0,$$
$$0xa \circ \Delta H_0 \oplus 0xa \circ \Delta H_1 \oplus 0x8 \circ \Delta H_2 \oplus 0xf \circ \Delta H_3 \oplus 0x8 \circ \Delta H_4 \oplus 0x8\Delta M = 0,$$
$$0x8 \circ \Delta H_0 \oplus 0xa \circ \Delta H_1 \oplus 0xa \circ \Delta H_2 \oplus 0x8 \circ \Delta H_3 \oplus 0xf \circ \Delta H_4 \oplus 0x10\Delta M = 0.$$

When $\Delta M = (0, 2^i, 2^i, 2^i, 0, 2^i, 0, 0)$, $(2^i, 2^i, 0, 0, 2^i, 0, 0, 2^i)$ or $(0, 0, 2^i, 0, 0, 2^i, 2^i, 2^i)$ for $(0 \le i < 32)$, the number of bits with difference in the initial value is least, which is 12.

Table 1 shows a pseudo-second-preimage example for the message $M_0 = (0xaaaaaaaa,$ 0xaaaaaaaa, 0xaaaaaaaa, 0xaaaaaaaa, 0xaaaaaaaa, 0xaaaaaaaa, 0xaaaaaaaa, 0xaaaaaaaa).

From the above description, only a few bits are needed to be changed to get a collision pair or the second-preimage for a given message. It is obvious that we can directly construct the forgery attack on NMAC based on Luffa in the related key case, for the NMAC replaces the fixed IV in hash function with a secret key[1]. The NMAC function, on input message M and a pair of independent keys (K_1, K_2), is defined as:

$$\text{NMAC}_{(K_1, K_2)}(M) = H(K_1, H(K_2, M)).$$

When H is the Luffa hash function, a forgery message $M \oplus \Delta M$ with the same NMAC value as the message M in the related key case is given:

$$Luffa(K_1, Luffa(K_2, M)) = Luffa(K_1, Luffa(K_2 \oplus \Delta IV, M \oplus \Delta M)).$$

Where ΔM and ΔIV satisfy $MI(\Delta IV, \Delta M) = 0$.

4   The Pseudo-Preimage Attack on Luffa

For Luffa-256, given a hash value Z_0, the adversary can compute a pseudo-preimage with the following process. An example is shown in Table 2 with $Z_0 = 0$.

1. Select Y_0, Y_1 arbitrarily, and get $Y_3 = Z_0 \oplus Y_0 \oplus Y_1$.
2. Compute $X_0 = Q_0^{-1}(Y_0)$, $X_1 = Q_1^{-1}(Y_1)$, $X_2 = Q_2^{-1}(Y_2)$.
3. Because the message $M = 0$ for the blank iteration, the adversary can compute $MI^{-1}(X_0, X_1, X_2)$ as follows,

$$\begin{pmatrix} H_0 \\ H_1 \\ H_2 \end{pmatrix} = \begin{pmatrix} 0x3, 0x2, 0x2 \\ 0x2, 0x3, 0x2 \\ 0x2, 0x2, 0x3 \end{pmatrix}^{-1} \circ \begin{pmatrix} X_0 \\ X_1 \\ X_2 \end{pmatrix}.$$

4. For the chaining variables H_0, H_1, H_2, the adversary can obtain $X_0 = Q_0^{-1}(H_0)$, $X_1 = Q_1^{-1}(H_1)$, $X_2 = Q_2^{-1}(H_2)$.
5. For (X_0, X_1, X_2), the adversary computers (IV_1', IV_2', M) with the fixed IV_0 by the following equations,

$$\begin{pmatrix} IV_1' \\ IV_2' \\ M \end{pmatrix} = \begin{pmatrix} 0x2, 0x2, 0x1 \\ 0x3, 0x2, 0x2 \\ 0x2, 0x3, 0x4 \end{pmatrix}^{-1} \circ \begin{pmatrix} X_0 \oplus (3 \circ IV_0) \\ X_1 \oplus (2 \circ IV_0) \\ X_2 \oplus (2 \circ IV_0) \end{pmatrix}.$$

6. Output (IV_0, IV'_1, IV'_2, M) which is the pseudo-preimage of Z_0, i.e.,

$$\text{Luffa-256}(IV', M) = Z_0.$$

There are $w - 1$ 256-bit words changed of the initial value with w 256-bit words.

For Luffa-384, the hash value consists of Z_0 cascaded with the 128 most significant bits of Z_1, and

$$Z_1 = Z_{1,0} \| Z_{1,1} \| Z_{1,2} \| Z_{1,3} \| Z_{1,4} \| Z_{1,5} \| Z_{1,6} \| Z_{1,7},$$

where $Z_{1,i}$ for $0 \leq i < 8$ are 32-bit words. The adversary randomly chooses (H_0, H_1, H_2), and gets $H_3 = H_0 \oplus H_1 \oplus H_2 \oplus Z_0$, computes Z'_1 using the finalization function.

If the equation $Z'_{1,0} \| Z'_{1,1} \| Z'_{1,2} \| Z'_{1,3} = Z_{1,0} \| Z_{1,1} \| Z_{1,2} \| Z_{1,3}$ holds, let $Y_0 = H_0, Y_1 = H_1, Y_2 = H_2$. The adversary can now compute $(IV'_0, IV'_1, IV'_2, IV'_3)$ and message M_0 which has the same hash value $Z_0 \| Z_{1,0} \| Z_{1,1} \| Z_{1,2} \| Z_{1,3}$, using the similar method with Luffa-256. The total complexity is 2^{128} iteration computations.

For Luffa-512, the complexity is 2^{255} using a similar attack.

5   Improved Pseudo-Preimage Attacks on Luffa-384/512

In this section, we introduce an algorithm to improve the pseudo-preimage attack on Luffa-384/512 by the extended generalized birthday attack which is used to solve a system of equations, proposed by Schnorr [6]. The k-dimensional generalization of the birthday problem is, given k lists $L_0, L_1, \ldots, L_{k-1}$ independently at random from $\{0, 1\}^n$, to find k elements $x_i \in L_i$ for $0 \leq i \leq k - 1$ such that $x_0 \oplus x_1 \oplus \cdots \oplus x_{k-1} = 0$. Wagner's algorithm [7] builds a binary tree starting from the input lists $L_0, L_1, \ldots, L_{k-1}$. The time complexity and data complexity are both $t \cdot 2^{\frac{n}{1+t}}$, where $t = \lfloor \log_2 k \rfloor$.

5.1   The Extended Generalized Birthday Attack

We give a brief description of Wagner's generalized birthday attack in the following.

Wagner's Algorithm

1. The adversary constructs 2^t sets $S^0_0, S^0_1, \ldots, S^0_{2^t-1}$, where $t = \lfloor \log_2 k \rfloor$, $S^0_i = \{ x^j_i \mid x^j_i \in L_i, j = 0, 1, \ldots, 2^{\frac{n}{1+t}} - 1 \}$ for $1 \leq i < 2^t - 1$ and $S^0_{2^t-1} = \{ x^j_{2^t-1} \oplus x_{2^t} \oplus \cdots \oplus x_k \mid x^j_{2^t-1} \in L_{2^t-1}, j = 0, 1, \ldots, 2^{\frac{n}{1+t}} - 1 \}$, where $x_l \in L_l$ for $l = 2^t, \ldots, k - 1$.

2. The adversary searches $2^{\frac{n}{1+t}}$ element pairs $x^j_{2i} \in S^0_{2i}, x^k_{2i+1} \in S^0_{2i+1}$ with the same low $\frac{n}{1+t}$ bits by the birthday attack. Construct 2^{t-1} new sets $S^1_i, i = 0, 1, \ldots, 2^{t-1} - 1$, where $S^1_i = \{ x^j_{2i} \oplus x^k_{2i+1} \mid$ the low $\frac{n}{1+t}$ bits are zeros$\}$.

3. For $m = 2$ to $t - 1$, the adversary searches $2^{\frac{n}{1+t}}$ pairs $x^j_{2i} \in S^{m-1}_{2i}$ and $x^k_{2i+1} \in S^{m-1}_{2i+1}$ with the m-th low $\frac{n}{1+t}$ bits same. Construct 2^{t-m} new sets $S^m_i, i = 0, 1, \ldots, 2^{t-m} - 1$, where $S^m_i = \{ x^j_{2i} \oplus x^k_{2i+1} \mid$ the low $m \cdot \frac{n}{1+t}$ bits are zeros$\}$.

4. The adversary searches a pair $x^j_0 \in S^{t-1}_0, x^k_1 \in S^{t-1}_1$, s.t. $x^j_0 \oplus x^k_1 = 0$.

The above algorithm can find one solution $x_0, x_1, \ldots, x_{k-1}$ such that $x_0 \oplus x_1 \cdots \oplus x_{k-1} = 0$ with time complexity and data complexity being both $t \cdot 2^{\frac{n}{1+t}}$.

Now consider the solution to the following two equations instead of one equation.

$$f_1(x_1) \oplus f_2(x_2) \oplus \cdots \oplus f_k(x_k) = c_1, \tag{1}$$

$$g_1(x_1) \oplus g_2(x_2) \oplus \cdots \oplus g_k(x_k) = c_2, \tag{2}$$

where f_i and g_i $(1 \le i \le k)$ are random functions, $f_i : 2^m \to 2^{n_1}$, $g_i : 2^m \to 2^{n_2}$. The equations (1) and (2) can be solved together by the extended generalized birthday attack [6] described in the following.

It is easy to construct the following equation from equations (1) and (2):

$$(f_1(x_1) \| g_1(x_1)) \oplus (f_2(x_2) \| g_2(x_2)) \oplus \cdots \oplus (f_k(x_k) \| g_k(x_k)) = c_1 \| c_2. \tag{3}$$

For the new equation (3), the Wagner's algorithm can be applied to obtain $x_1, \ldots, x_k$. The data and time complexity is $t \cdot 2^{\frac{n_1+n_2}{1+t}}$, where $t = \lfloor \log_2 k \rfloor$ and $m \ge \frac{n_1+n_2}{1+t}$.

It is clear that, the algorithm can be extended to solve more equations.

$$f_1^{(1)}(x_1) \oplus f_2^{(1)}(x_2) \oplus \cdots \oplus f_k^{(1)}(x_k) = c_1,$$

$$f_1^{(2)}(x_1) \oplus f_2^{(2)}(x_2) \oplus \cdots \oplus f_k^{(2)}(x_k) = c_2,$$

$$\vdots$$

$$f_1^{(l)}(x_1) \oplus f_2^{(l)}(x_2) \oplus \cdots \oplus f_k^{(l)}(x_k) = c_l,$$

where $f_j^{(i)} : 2^m \to 2^{n_i}$ are random functions, $0 \le i \le l$, and $0 \le j \le k$. The data and time complexity is $t \cdot 2^{\frac{n_1+n_2+\cdots+n_t}{1+t}}$, where $t = \lfloor \log_2 k \rfloor$ and $m \ge \frac{n_1+n_2+\cdots+n_t}{1+t}$.

5.2   The Improved Pseudo-Preimage Attack on Luffa-384

Let $(H_0, H_1, H_2, H_3, \emptyset)$ be the input of the last blank iteration function, and (X_0, X_1, X_2, X_3) be the output of its MI. The hash value is $Z_0 \| \bar{Z}_1$, where $\bar{Z}_1 = Z_{1,0} \| Z_{1,1} \| Z_{1,2} \| Z_{1,3}$. Then

$$h_{128}(Q_0(X_0) \oplus Q_1(X_1) \oplus Q_2(X_2) \oplus Q_3(X_3)) = \bar{Z}_1. \tag{4}$$

From the message injection function MI, we know that $(H_0, H_1, H_2, H_3)^T = A_{4 \times 4}^{-1}(X_0, X_1, X_2, X_3)^T$, where $A_{4 \times 4}$ is the first 4 column vectors of the matrix $A_{4 \times 5}$, i.e.,

$$A_{4 \times 4} = \begin{pmatrix} 0x4, 0x6, 0x6, 0x7 \\ 0x7, 0x4, 0x6, 0x6 \\ 0x6, 0x7, 0x4, 0x6 \\ 0x6, 0x6, 0x7, 0x4 \end{pmatrix}.$$

It's inverse matrix is

$$A_{4 \times 4}^{-1} = \begin{pmatrix} 0x20, 0x43, 0x84, 0x11 \\ 0x11, 0x20, 0x43, 0x84 \\ 0x84, 0x11, 0x20, 0x43 \\ 0x43, 0x84, 0x11, 0x20 \end{pmatrix}.$$

From $H_0 \oplus H_1 \oplus H_2 \oplus H_3 = Z_0$, we can prove that,

$$X_0 \oplus X_1 \oplus X_2 \oplus X_3 = Z_0', \tag{5}$$

where $Z_0' = 0x3 \circ Z_0$.

Obviously, it is necessary for us to find the solution (X_0, X_1, X_2, X_3) to make equations (4) and (5) hold together. We search the solution by the extended generalized birthday attack and some specific properties of Luffa. The algorithm is as follows.

1. The adversary constructs four sets such that,

$$S_0 = \{X_0 \mid X_0 \in \{0,1\}^n, l_{192}(X_0) = c_0\},$$
$$S_1 = \{X_1 \mid X_1 \in \{0,1\}^n, l_{192}(X_1) = c_0 \oplus l_{192}(Z_0')\},$$
$$S_2 = \{X_2 \mid X_2 \in \{0,1\}^n, l_{192}(X_2) = c_1\},$$
$$S_3 = \{X_3 \mid X_3 \in \{0,1\}^n, l_{192}(X_3) = c_1\},$$

where c_0, c_1 are two 192-bit constants, and each set includes 2^{64} elements. It is clear that,

$$l_{192}(X_0 \oplus X_1 \oplus X_2 \oplus X_3) = l_{192}(Z_0'),$$

where $X_i \in S_i$ for $0 \le i \le 3$.

2. The adversary searches the solution (X_0, X_1, X_2, X_3) satisfying the following two equations by the extended generalized birthday attack.

$$h_{64}(X_0 \oplus X_1 \oplus X_2 \oplus X_3) = h_{64}(Z_0'),$$

$$h_{128}(Q_0(X_0) \oplus Q_1(X_1) \oplus Q_2(X_2) \oplus Q_3(X_3)) = \bar{Z}_1,$$

where $X_i \in S_i, i = 0,1,2,3$. It is clear that, The solution (X_0, X_1, X_2, X_3) guarantees the equations (4) and (5) hold together.

3. For (X_0, X_1, X_2, X_3), the adversary can calculate $(IV_0, IV_1', IV_2', IV_3')$ and the message M, and get the pseudo-preimage using the similar pseudo-preimage attack on Luffa-256.

There are 2^{64} Q_0, Q_1, Q_2, Q_3 computations and 2^{64} table lookups in the above algorithm. So the total complexity is about 2^{64} iteration computations and 2^{67} bytes memory.

5.3 The Improved Pseudo-Preimage Attack on Luffa-512

For Luffa-512, let $(H_0, H_1, H_2, H_3, H_4, \mathbb{0})$ be the input of the last blank iteration function, and $(X_0, X_1, X_2, X_3, X_4)$ be the output of MI. Then

$$Q_0(X_0) \oplus Q_1(X_1) \oplus Q_2(X_2) \oplus Q_3(X_3) \oplus Q_4(X_4) = Z_1. \tag{6}$$

For the message injection function MI, we know that, $(H_0, H_1, H_2, H_3, H_4)^T = A_{5\times5}^{-1}(X_0, X_1, X_2, X_3, X_4)^T$, where $A_{5\times5}$ is the first 5 column vectors of the matrix $A_{5\times6}$, i.e.,

$$A_{5\times5} = \begin{pmatrix} 0xf, 0x8, 0xa, 0xa, 0x8 \\ 0x8, 0xf, 0x8, 0xa, 0xa \\ 0xa, 0x8, 0xf, 0x8, 0xa \\ 0xa, 0xa, 0x8, 0xf, 0x8 \\ 0x8, 0xa, 0xa, 0x8, 0xf \end{pmatrix}.$$

Its inverse matrix is

$$A_{5\times5}^{-1} = \begin{pmatrix} 0xc7, 0x8b, 0xf4, 0xf4, 0x8b \\ 0x8b, 0xc7, 0x8b, 0xf4, 0xf4 \\ 0xf4, 0x8b, 0xc7, 0x8b, 0xf4 \\ 0xf4, 0xf4, 0x8b, 0xc7, 0x8b \\ 0x8b, 0xf4, 0xf4, 0x8b, 0xc7 \end{pmatrix}.$$

Since $H_0 \oplus H_1 \oplus H_2 \oplus H_3 \oplus H_4 = Z_0$, we obtain

$$X_0 \oplus X_1 \oplus X_2 \oplus X_3 \oplus X_4 = Z_0', \tag{7}$$

where $Z_0' = 0xf \circ Z_0$.

We can search a solution to equations (6) and (7) by the extended generalized birthday attack and some specific properties of Luffa.

1. The adversary constructs four sets such that,

$$S_0 = \{X_0 \mid X_0 \in \{0,1\}^n, l_{128}(X_0) = c_0\},$$
$$S_1 = \{X_1 \mid X_1 \in \{0,1\}^n, l_{128}(X_1) = c_0 \oplus l_{128}(Z_0')\},$$
$$S_2 = \{X_2 \mid X_2 \in \{0,1\}^n, l_{128}(X_2) = c_1\}$$
$$S_3 = \{(X_3, X_4) \mid X_3, X_4 \in \{0,1\}^n, l_{128}(X_3 \oplus X_4) = c_1\},$$

where c_0, c_1 are two 128-bit constants, and each set includes 2^{128} elements. It is clear that,

$$l_{128}(X_0 \oplus X_1 \oplus X_2 \oplus X_3 \oplus X_4) = l_{128}(Z_0').$$

2. The adversary searches a solution $(X_0, X_1, X_2, X_3, X_4)$ satisfying the following two equations by the extended generalized birthday attack.

$$h_{128}(X_0 \oplus X_1 \oplus X_2 \oplus X_3 \oplus X_4) = h_{128}(Z_0'),$$

$$Q_0(X_0) \oplus Q_1(X_1) \oplus Q_2(X_2) \oplus Q_3(X_3) \oplus Q_4(X_4) = \bar{Z}_1,$$

where $X_i \in S_i, i = 0, 1, 2$ and $(X_3, X_4) \in S_3$. It is clear that, The solution $(X_0, X_1, X_2, X_3, X_4)$ guarantees equations (6) and (7) hold.

3. For $(X_0, X_1, X_2, X_3, X_4)$, the adversary can calculate $(IV_0, IV_1', IV_2', IV_3', IV_4')$ and the message M, and get the pseudo-preimage using the similar pseudo-preimage attack on Luffa-256.

The total complexity is about 2^{128} iteration computations and 2^{132} bytes memory.

6   Conclusion

In this paper, we give pseudo-collision, pseudo-second-preimage and pseudo-preimage attacks on Luffa, one of the second round candidates of SHA-3. For any given output of the message injection function MI, it is easy to get the input to MI using the inverse operation of MI. So we can find pseduo-collisions and pseudo-second-preimages easily for Luffa by applying the MI property. It is noted that, the pseudo-collisions and pseudo-second-preimages only with a few different bits are easily searched. The attack can be directly converted to a forgery attack on NMAC with related keys.

Especially, we focus on the the pseudo-preimage attack on Luffa. For Luffa-224/256, the attack can find the the pseudo-preimage only with 2 iteration computations. It takes about 2^{64} iteration computations and 2^{67} bytes memory to search a pseudo-preimage for Luffa-384, and search a pseudo-preimage with 2^{128} iteration computations and 2^{132} bytes memory for Luffa-512 with the extended generalized birthday attack.

Acknowledgements. We would like to thank the anonymous reviewers for their valuable comments on this paper. This work is supported by the National "973" Program of China (Grant No.2007CB807902) and Tsinghua University Initiative Scientific Research Program (2009THZ01002). For the second author, a part of this work was done while funded by EPSRC EP/C538285/1, by BT(as BT Chair of Information Security) and while visiting Tsinghua University funded by 2007CB807902.

References

1. Bellare, M., Canetti, R., Krawczyk, H.: Keying Hash Functions for Message Authentication. In: Koblitz, N. (ed.) CRYPTO 1996. LNCS, vol. 1109, pp. 1–15. Springer, Heidelberg (1996)
2. Cannière, C.D., Sato, H., Watanabe, D.: Hash function Luffa Specification (2008), http://csrc.nist.gov/groups/ST/hash/sha-3/Round1/documents/Luffa.zip
3. Contini, S., Yin, Y.L.: Forgery and Partial Key-Recovery Attacks on HMAC and NMAC Using Hash Collisions. In: Lai, X., Chen, K. (eds.) ASIACRYPT 2006. LNCS, vol. 4284, pp. 37–53. Springer, Heidelberg (2006)
4. Fouque, P.-A., Leurent, G., Nguyen, P.Q.: Full Key-Recovery Attacks on HMAC/NMAC-MD4 and NMAC-MD5. In: Menezes, A. (ed.) CRYPTO 2007. LNCS, vol. 4622, pp. 13–30. Springer, Heidelberg (2007)
5. Kelsey, J., Schneier, B.: Second Preimages on n-Bit Hash Functions for Much Less than 2^n Work. In: Cramer, R. (ed.) EUROCRYPT 2005. LNCS, vol. 3494, pp. 474–490. Springer, Heidelberg (2005)
6. Schnorr, C.P.: Enhancing the Security of Perfect Blind DL-Signatures. Information Sciences 176(i10), 1305–1320 (2006)
7. Wagner, D.: A generalized birthday problem. In: Yung, M. (ed.) CRYPTO 2002. LNCS, vol. 2442, pp. 288–304. Springer, Heidelberg (2002)
8. Wang, X., Lai, X., Feng, D., Chen, H., Yu, X.: Cryptanalysis of the hash functions MD4 and RIPEMD. In: Cramer, R. (ed.) EUROCRYPT 2005. LNCS, vol. 3494, pp. 1–18. Springer, Heidelberg (2005)
9. Wang, X., Yu, H., Yin, Y.L.: Efficient collision search attacks on SHA-0. In: Shoup, V. (ed.) CRYPTO 2005. LNCS, vol. 3621, pp. 1–16. Springer, Heidelberg (2005)

10. Wang, X., Yin, Y.L., Yu, H.: Finding collisions in the full SHA-1. In: Shoup, V. (ed.) CRYPTO 2005. LNCS, vol. 3621, pp. 17–36. Springer, Heidelberg (2005)
11. Wang, X., Yu, H.: How to break MD5 and other hash functions. In: Cramer, R. (ed.) EURO-CRYPT 2005. LNCS, vol. 3494, pp. 19–35. Springer, Heidelberg (2005)
12. Yu, H., Wang, G., Zhang, G., Wang, X.: The second-preimage attack on MD4. In: Desmedt, Y.G., Wang, H., Mu, Y., Li, Y. (eds.) CANS 2005. LNCS, vol. 3810, pp. 1–12. Springer, Heidelberg (2005)

Appendix

In the appendix, we give two examples for the pseudo-second-preimage and pseudo-preimage.

Table 1. A Pseudo-second-preimage for Luffa-256

IV_0	0x6d251e69	0x44b051e0	0x4eaa6fb4	0xdbf78465	0x6e292011	0x90152df4	0xee058139	0xdef610bb
IV_1	0xc3b44b95	0xd9d2f256	0x70eee9a0	0xde099fa3	0x5d9b0557	0x8fc944b3	0xcf1ccf0e	0x746cd581
IV_2	0xf7efc89d	0x5dba5781	0x04016ce5	0xad659c05	0x0306194f	0x666d1836	0x24aa230a	0x8b264ae7
M_0	0xaaaaaaaa	0xaaaaaaaa	0xaaaaaaaa	0xaaaaaaaa	0xaaaaaaaa	0xaaaaaaaa	0xaaaaaaaa	0xaaaaaaaa
IV_0'	0x6d251e68	0x44b051e0	0x4eaa6fb5	0xdbf78464	0x6e292011	0x90152df4	0xee058139	0xdef610bb
IV_1'	0xc3b44b95	0xd9d2f256	0x70eee9a0	0xde099fa2	0x5d9b0557	0x8fc944b3	0xcf1ccf0e	0x746cd581
IV_2'	0xf7efc89d	0x5dba5780	0x4016ce5	0xad659c05	0x306194f	0x666d1836	0x24aa230a	0x8b264ae7
M_0'	0xaaaaaaab	0xaaaaaaab	0xaaaaaaaa	aaaaaaaa	0xaaaaaaaa	0xaaaaaaaa	0xaaaaaaaa	0xaaaaaaaa
X_0	0xe6333b1e	0x96d8e9f6	0x24d83129	0x6aa44be3	0x4da482a5	0x0a0bbb57	0x3d1e5ae2	0x71efd72c
X_1	0x48a26ee2	0xa110e0ea	0x1a9cb73d	0xc5f0fa8f	0xd4bc0d49	0x15d7d210	0x1c0714d5	0xdb751216
X_2	0x7cf9edea	0x2578453d	0xc4d998d2	0xb69cf929	0x208bbbfb	0x56d9243f	0xf7b1f8d1	0x243f8d70

Table 2. A Pseudo-preimage for Luffa-256

IV_0	0x6d251e69	0x44b051e0	0x4eaa6fb4	0xdbf78465	0x6e292011	0x90152df4	0xee058139	0xdef610bb
IV_1'	0x6a366118	0x3ee79df6	0x39643181	0x60793777	0x8ddc9066	0x1d50cebd	0xb1cfd39b	0x967da4e4
IV_2'	0x9622ac99	0xb752bbbb	0xd256db58	0x73db6cac	0x9ae49b27	0xeb1666b4	0x805027ed	0x8176bfc6
M	0x7c08aa09	0x52f9e2bf	0x27ce6bb9	0x11af8970	0x22c8478d	0x9eebde0e	0x78ae77ef	0xdafc7fa8
H_0	0xd42f102f	0x94316735	0xec5bb8a2	0xceb338ee	0x6d35036f	0x85d4ba8c	0xc9a85c96	0xed839a52
H_1	0x70238338	0x4461e9a7	0xa3012529	0xb6a10e0f	0xdfdf5bc0	0x2fd50d38	0xe98ddd20	0xf90f4fe9
H_2	0xe0d87b07	0x5704423f	0xb8ba00ed	0xeaa52759	0x8bc1b72b	0xc5720d53	0x41cde665	0x1288c8fc
Z_0	0	0	0	0	0	0	0	0

Distinguishing Attacks on LPMAC Based on the Full RIPEMD and Reduced-Step RIPEMD-{256, 320}*

Gaoli Wang[1,2]

[1] School of Computer Science and Technology, Donghua University,
Shanghai 201620, China
wanggaoli@dhu.edu.cn
[2] State Key Laboratory of Information Security Institute of Software,
Chinese Academy of Sciences, Beijing, China

Abstract. This paper presents the first distinguishing attack on the LPMAC based on RIPEMD, 58-step reduced RIPEMD-256 and 48-step reduced RIPEMD-320, and the LPMAC is the secret-prefix MAC with the message length prepended to the message before hashing. Wang et al. presented the first distinguishing attack on HMAC/NMAC-MD5 without the related-key setting in [27], then they extended this technique to give a distinguishing attack on the LPMAC based on 61-step SHA-1 in [24]. In this paper, we utilize the techniques in [24, 27] combined with our pseudo-near-collision differential path on the full RIPEMD, 58-step reduced RIPEMD-256 and 48-step reduced RIPEMD-320 to distinguish the LPMAC based on the full RIPEMD, 58-step reduced RIPEMD-256 and 48-step reduced RIPEMD-320 from the LPMAC based on a random function respectively. Because RIPEMD and RIPEMD-{256, 320} all contain two different and independent parallel lines of operations, the difficulty of our attack is to choose proper message differences and to find proper near-collision differential paths of the two parallel lines of operations. The complexity of distinguishing the LPMAC based on the full RIPEMD is about 2^{66} MAC queries. For the LPMAC based on 58-step reduced RIPEMD-256 and 48-step reduced RIPEMD-320, the complexities are about $2^{163.5}$ MAC queries and $2^{208.5}$ MAC queries respectively.

Keywords: Hash function, distinguishing attack, MAC, RIPEMD-family.

1 Introduction

Hash functions play an important role in modern cryptography, and many cryptographic schemes including the message authentication codes (MACs) use hash

* This work was supported by "Chen Guang" project (supported by Shanghai Municipal Education Commission and Shanghai Education Development Foundation); State Key Laboratory of Information Security (Institute of Software, Chinese Academy of Sciences); The Fundamental Research Funds for the Central Universities (2010D19).

X. Lai, M. Yung, and D. Lin (Eds.): Inscrypt 2010, LNCS 6584, pp. 199–217, 2011.

functions as primitives. A MAC algorithm based on hash function takes a message and a secret key as inputs and outputs a short digest. The MAC algorithm is used to ensure data integrity and authenticity, and it is widely used in security protocols, such as IPsec, SNMP, and SSL/TLS. A series attacks on hash functions [2–4, 7, 15, 16, 18, 21–23, 25, 26, 28, 30] etc. have shown that the prevailing hash functions such as MD4, HAVAL, MD5, SHA-0, SHA-1 etc. are not collision resistant. Therefore reevaluating the actual security of the MACs based on hash functions is a hot topic [5, 9, 11, 19, 20]. There are many methods to construct MACs based on hash functions such as the secret prefix method, secret suffix method, envelope method and HMAC/NMAC [1] etc.. The secret prefix method prepends a secret K to the message before hashing. In order to guarantee the security of the secret prefix MAC, one suggestion is appending the message length to the message before hashing [17], and this type of MAC is denoted as LPMAC in [24, 29].

There are mainly three kinds of attacks on MACs: distinguishing attack, forgery attack and key-recovery attack. The distinguishing attack can be divided into two kinds of attacks: $distinguishing-$R and $distinguishing-$H attacks[11]. The distinguishing-R attack means distinguishing a MAC from a random function, and distinguishing-H attack detects which kind of hash function is embedded in a MAC under the situation that the cryptanalyst somehow already knows that the output is produced by a MAC algorithm, but does not know the underlying hash function. Preneel and van Oorschot [12] proposed a general distinguishing-R attack on MAC by the birthday paradox. This attack requires about $2^{\frac{n}{2}}$ message queries, where n is the length of the initial value. For the distinguishing-H attack, there does not exist a general attack, and its ideal complexity is about 2^n message queries. In this paper, we only focus on the distinguishing-H attack on MACs based on hash functions, which is called distinguishing attack for simplicity.

Some attacks can be implemented successfully on the MACs based on MD4, HAVAL and SHA-0 [5, 9, 20] etc., because it's easy to find the differential paths with high probability for these hash functions. Generally, the pseudo-near-collision differential path holds with higher probability than the real differential path. Therefore, for the hash functions which are difficult to find the real differential path with high enough probability, the attacks on MACs use pseudo-near-collision differential paths, and most of these attacks are in the related-key setting. For example, for MD5, there is only one available dBB pseudo-collision path [6], and all the attacks [5, 9, 13, 20] on MACs based on MD5 are in the related-key setting. For SHA-1, [13] proposed attacks on 62-step HMAC-SHA-1 and 34-step NMAC-SHA-1, both attacks are in the related-key setting.

Wang et al. [27] presented a new distinguishing attack on HMAC/NMAC-MD5 and MD5-MAC without related-key setting. They use a distinguisher with a pair of two-block messages to detect a dBB collision from random collisions. The first iteration ensures the appearance of the dBB difference by the birthday attack, and the second iteration uses a dBB difference to make a collision. Wang et al. improved this work to give a distinguishing attack on the LPMAC based on

61-step SHA-1 [24]. The distinguisher also contains a pair of two-block messages, and it is used to detect an inner near-collision occurring in the second iteration. The first 960 bits of the messages (the first block in addition to 448 bits of the second block) ensure the presence of a specific difference in the 14-th step of the second block, and the last 64 bits messages distinguish the specific difference. By using the technique in [24], a distinguishing attack on LPMAC based on 39-step SHA-256 was proposed in [29] without related-key setting.

RIPEMD was developed in the European RIPE project [14]. RIPEMD−{128, 160, 256, 320} [8] were proposed in 1996. RIPEMD and RIPEMD−{128, 160, 256, 320} belong to RIPEMD-family, which uses two parallel lines of computations. In this paper, we apply the distinguishing techniques in [24, 27] to attack the LPMAC based on RIPEMD, 58-step RIPEMD-256 and 48-step RIPEMD-320 respectively. Firstly, we find a differential path of RIPEMD with probability $2^{-31} \times 2^{-31} = 2^{-62}$. Based on it, we give a distinguishing attack on the LP-MAC based on RIPEMD with complexity 2^{66}. Secondly, for RIPEMD-256, we find a 37-step differential path of Line1 operation with probability 2^{-12}, and a 42-step differential path of Line2 operation with probability 2^{-15}. By using the differential paths, we can give a distinguishing attack on the LPMAC based on 58-step RIPEMD-256 with complexity $2^{163.5}$. Thirdly, for RIPEMD-320, we find a 36-step differential path of Line1 operation with probability 2^{-16}, and a 33-step differential path of Line2 operation with probability 2^{-7}. Then we can give a distinguishing attack on the LPMAC based on 48-step RIPEMD-320 with complexity $2^{208.5}$. All of RIPEMD and RIPEMD−{256, 320} consist of two different and independent parallel operations called Line1 operation and Line2 operation. There are different constants, amounts of rotations and most importantly, different message schedules in Line1 and Line2 operations. Therefore, the difficulty of our attack is to choose proper message differences and to find proper differential paths of Line1 and Line2 operations.

The rest of the paper is organized as follows. In Section 2, we define some notations and give a brief description of RIPEMD and RIPEMD−{256, 320} and LPMAC. In Section 3, we describe our distinguishing attack on the LPMAC based on RIPEMD. In Section 4, we describe our distinguishing attack on 58-step RIPEMD-256. The distinguishing attack on 48-step RIPEMD-320 is described in Section 5. Finally, we summarize the paper in Section 6.

2   Background and Definitions

2.1   Notations

We introduce some notations in the follows, where $1 \leq j \leq 32$. $\neg, \wedge, \oplus, \vee$ denote bitwise complement, AND, XOR and OR respectively. $\lll s$ denotes circular shift s-bit positions to the left. $x\|y$ denotes concatenation of the two bitstrings x and y. $+, -$ denote addition and subtraction modulo 2^{32} respectively. Both x_i and m_i are 32-bit words. $x_{i,j}$ denotes the j-th bit of x_i, where the most significant bit is the 31-st bit. $\Delta m_i = m_i' - m_i$ denotes the modular subtraction difference of two words m_i and m_i', where $0 \leq i \leq 15$. $x_i' - x_i = [j]$ denotes $x_{i,j} = 0$, $x_{i,j}' = 1$, and the other bits of x_i and x'_i are all equal. $x'_i - x_i = [-j]$ denotes $x_{i,j} = 1$, $x'_{i,j} = 0$, and the other bits of x_i and x'_i are all equal. $M = (m_0, m_1, \ldots, m_{15})$ denotes 512-bit block, where m_i $(0 \leq i \leq 15)$ is a 32-bit word.

2.2 Description of RIPEMD

RIPEMD [14] was developed in the European RIPE project. Its compression function consists of two parallel copies of MD4's compression function, identical but for some internal constants. The results of both copies are combined to yield the output of RIPEMD's compression function. RIPEMD compresses any arbitrary length message into a message with the length of 128 bits. For each 512-bit padded message block, RIPEMD compresses it into a 128-bit hash value by a compression function.

The two copies of the compression function of RIPEMD are denoted by Line1 operation and Line2 operation respectively. Line1 and Line2 operations have the same initial value, and the initial value is: $(a, b, c, d) = (0x67452301, 0xefcdab89, 0x98badcfe, 0x10325476)$. The nonlinear functions in each round are as follows:
$F(X, Y, Z)$
$= (X \wedge Y) \vee (\neg X \wedge Z)$, $G(X, Y, Z) = (X \wedge Y) \vee (X \wedge Z) \vee (Y \wedge Z)$, $H(X, Y, Z) = X \oplus Y \oplus Z$. Here X, Y and Z are 32-bit words. The operations of the three functions are all bitwise. Each line has three rounds, and each round is composed of 16-step operations, and in each step, one of the four chaining variables is updated. $\phi_0(a, b, c, d, m_k, s) = (a + F(b, c, d) + m_k) \lll s, \phi_1(a, b, c, d, m_k, s) = (a + G(b, c, d) + m_k + 0x5a827999) \lll s, \phi_2(a, b, c, d, m_k, s) = (a + H(b, c, d) + m_k + 0x6ed9eba1) \lll s, \Phi_0(a, b, c, d, m_k, s) = (a + F(b, c, d) + m_k + 0x50a28be6) \lll s, \Phi_1(a, b, c, d, m_k, s) = (a + G(b, c, d) + m_k) \lll s, \Phi_2(a, b, c, d, m_k, s) = (a + H(b, c, d) + m_k + 0x5c4dd124) \lll s$.

For a 512-bit block $M = (m_0, m_1, \ldots, m_{15})$, let (aa, bb, cc, dd) and (aaa, bbb, ccc, ddd) be the inputs of Line1 and Line2 processes respectively. If M is the first block to be hashed, (aa, bb, cc, dd) and (aaa, bbb, ccc, ddd) are the initial values. Otherwise they are the outputs of the previous block of Line1 and Line2 processes respectively.

Line1 operation process. Perform the following 48 steps (three rounds):
For $j = 0, 1, 2$,   for $i = 0, 1, 2, 3$,
$aa = \phi_j(aa, bb, cc, dd, m_{j,4i}, s_{j,4i})$, $dd = \phi_j(dd, aa, bb, cc, m_{j,4i+1}, s_{j,4i+1})$, $cc = \phi_j(cc, dd, aa, bb, m_{j,4i+2}, s_{j,4i+2})$, $bb = \phi_j(bb, cc, dd, aa, m_{j,4i+3}, s_{j,4i+3})$.

Line2 operation process. Perform the following 48 steps (three rounds):
For $j = 0, 1, 2$,   For $i = 0, 1, 2, 3$,
$aaa = \Phi_j(aaa, bbb, ccc, ddd, m_{j,4i}, s_{j,4i})$, $ddd = \Phi_j(ddd, aaa, bbb, ccc, m_{j,4i+1}, s_{j,4i+1})$, $ccc = \Phi_j(ccc, ddd, aaa, bbb, m_{j,4i+2}, s_{j,4i+2})$, $bbb = \Phi_j(bbb, ccc, ddd, aaa, m_{j,4i+3}, s_{j,4i+3})$.

The ordering of message words and the details of the shift positions can be seen in Table 3. The compressing result for the message block M is $(H_1, H_2, H_3, H_4) = (b + cc + ddd, c + dd + aaa, d + aa + bbb, a + bb + ccc)$.

2.3   Description of RIPEMD-320

For each padded 512-bit message block, RIPEMD-320 compresses it into a 320-bit hash value by a compression function, which has two parallel lines denoted by Line1 operation and Line2 operation respectively. Each line has five rounds, and each round is composed of 16 steps. The nonlinear functions are: $f_1(X, Y, Z) = X \oplus Y \oplus Z, f_2(X, Y, Z) = (X \wedge Y) \vee (\neg X \wedge Z), f_3(X, Y, Z) = (X \vee \neg Y) \oplus Z, f_4(X, Y, Z) = (X \wedge Z) \vee (Y \wedge \neg Z), f_5(X, Y, Z) = X \oplus (Y \vee \neg Z)$. There is an interaction between Line1 operation and Line2 operation. After round 1, swap the contents of registers aa_{16} and aaa_{16}, after round 2, swap the contents of registers bb_{32} and bbb_{32}, etc. The details of RIPEMD-320 can refer to [8].

For a 512-bit block $M = (m_0, m_1, \ldots, m_{15})$, let $(aa_0, bb_0, cc_0, dd_0, ee_0)$ and $(aaa_0, bbb_0, ccc_0, ddd_0, eee_0)$ be the inputs of Line1 and Line2 processes respectively. If M is the first block to be hashed, $(aa_0, bb_0, cc_0, dd_0, ee_0)$ and $(aaa_0, bbb_0, ccc_0, ddd_0, eee_0)$ are the initial values. Otherwise they are the output of the previous block compressing of Line1 and Line2 processes respectively.

Line1 operation process.   Perform the following 80 steps (five rounds):
For $j = 1, 2, 3, 4, 5$, For $i = 16(j - 1) + 1, 16(j - 1) + 2, ..., 16(j - 1) + 16$,
$$TT_i = (aa_{i-1} + f_j(bb_{i-1}, cc_{i-1}, dd_{i-1}) + m_{ord_1(j,i)} + k_j^1) \lll s_{j,i}^1 + ee_{i-1},$$
$$aa_i = ee_{i-1}, \quad bb_i = TT_i, \quad cc_i = bb_{i-1}, \quad dd_i = cc_{i-1} \lll 10, \quad ee_i = dd_{i-1}.$$
$ord_1(j, i)$ denotes the value in the j-th row and $i - 16(j - 1)$-th column in Table 1. For example, $ord_1(2, 27)$ denotes the value 9. The ordering of message words can be seen in Table 1. The details of the shift positions can be seen in Table 9. The final chaining variables of Line1 operation is: $(hh_1, hh_2, hh_3, hh_4, hh_5)$ $= (aa_{80} + aa_0, bb_{80} + bb_0, cc_{80} + cc_0, dd_{80} + dd_0, ee_{80} + ee_0)$.

Line2 operation process.   Perform the following 80 steps (five rounds):
For $j = 1, 2, 3, 4, 5$,   For $i = 16(j - 1) + 1, 16(j - 1) + 2, ..., 16(j - 1) + 16$,
$$TTT_i = (aaa_{i-1} + f_{6-j}(bbb_{i-1}, ccc_{i-1}, ddd_{i-1}) + m_{ord_2(j,i)} + k_j^2) \lll s_{j,i}^2 + eee_{i-1},$$
$$aaa_i = eee_{i-1}, \quad bbb_i = TTT_i, \quad ccc_i = bbb_{i-1}, \quad ddd_i = ccc_{i-1} \lll 10, \quad eee_i = ddd_{i-1}.$$
$ord_2(j, i)$ denotes the value in the j-th row and $i - 16(j - 1)$-th column in Table 2. The ordering of message words can be seen in Table 2. The details of the shift positions can be seen in Table 11. The final chaining variables of Line2 operation is: $(hhh_1, hhh_2, hhh_3, hhh_4, hhh_5) = (aaa_{80} + aaa_0, bbb_{80} + bbb_0, ccc_{80} + ccc_0, ddd_{80} + ddd_0, eee_{80} + eee_0)$. Then $(hh_1, hh_2, hh_3, hh_4, hh_5, hhh_1, hhh_2, hhh_3, hhh_4, hhh_5)$ is the compressing result for the message block M.

Table 1. Ordering of the message words in Line1

0	1	2	3	4	5	6	7	8	9	10	11	12	13	14	15
7	4	13	1	10	6	15	3	12	0	9	5	2	14	11	8
3	10	14	4	9	15	8	1	2	7	0	6	13	11	5	12
1	9	11	10	0	8	12	4	13	3	7	15	14	5	6	2
4	0	5	9	7	12	2	10	14	1	3	8	11	6	15	13

Table 2. Ordering of the message words in Line2

5	14	7	0	9	2	11	4	13	6	15	8	1	10	3	12
6	11	3	7	0	13	5	10	14	15	8	12	4	9	1	2
15	5	1	3	7	14	6	9	11	8	12	2	10	0	4	13
8	6	4	1	3	11	15	0	5	12	2	13	9	7	10	14
12	15	10	4	1	5	8	7	6	2	13	14	0	3	9	11

2.4 Description of RIPEMD-256

For each padded 512-bit message block, RIPEMD-256 compresses it into a 256-bit hash value by a compression function, which has two parallel lines denoted by Line1 operation and Line2 operation respectively. Each line has four rounds, and each round is composed of 16-step operations. The nonlinear functions f_1, f_2, f_3, f_4 in each round are described above. There is an interaction between Line1 operation and Line2 operation. After round 1, swap the contents of registers aa_{16} and aaa_{16}, after round 2, swap the contents of registers bb_{32} and bbb_{32}, etc. The details of RIPEMD-256 can refer to [8].

For a 512-bit block $M = (m_0, m_1, \ldots, m_{15})$, let (aa_0, bb_0, cc_0, dd_0) and $(aaa_0, bbb_0, ccc_0, ddd_0)$ be the inputs of Line1 and Line2 processes respectively. If M is the first block to be hashed, (aa_0, bb_0, cc_0, dd_0) and $(aaa_0, bbb_0, ccc_0, ddd_0)$ are the initial values. Otherwise they are the outputs of the previous block compressing of Line1 and Line2 processes respectively.

Line1 operation process.   Perform the following 64 steps (four rounds): For $j = 1, 2, 3, 4$, For $i = 16(j - 1) + 1, 16(j - 1) + 2, ..., 16(j - 1) + 16$, $TT_i = (aa_{i-1} + f_j(bb_{i-1}, cc_{i-1}, dd_{i-1}) + m_{ord_1(j,i)} + k_j^1) \lll s_{j,i}^1$, $aa_i = dd_{i-1}$, $bb_i = TT_i$, $cc_i = bb_{i-1}$, $dd_i = cc_{i-1}$. The ordering of message words can be seen in Table 1. The details of the shift positions can be seen in Table 5. The final chaining variables of Line1 operation is: $(hh_1, hh_2, hh_3, hh_4) = (aa_{64} + aa_0, bb_{64} + bb_0, cc_{64} + cc_0, dd_{64} + dd_0)$.

Line2 operation process.   Perform the following 64 steps (four rounds): For $j = 1, 2, 3, 4$, For $i = 16(j - 1) + 1, 16(j - 1) + 2, ..., 16(j - 1) + 16$, $TTT_i = (aaa_{i-1} + f_{5-j}(bbb_{i-1}, ccc_{i-1}, ddd_{i-1}) + m_{ord_2(j,i)} + k_j^2) \lll s_{j,i}^2$, $aaa_i = ddd_{i-1}$, $bbb_i = TTT_i$, $ccc_i = bbb_{i-1}$, $ddd_i = ccc_{i-1}$. The ordering of message words can be seen in Table 2. The details of the shift positions can be seen in Table 7. The final chaining variables of Line1 operation is: $(hhh_1, hhh_2, hhh_3, hhh_4) = (aaa_{64} + aaa_0, bbb_{64} + bbb_0, ccc_{64} + ccc_0, ddd_{64} + ddd_0)$. Then $(hh_1, hh_2, hh_3, hh_4, hhh_1, hhh_2, hhh_3, hhh_4)$ is the compressing result for the message block M.

2.5 MAC Using Secret-Prefix Method and LPMAC

The secret prefix method is to append a message M to a secret key K before the hashing operation: $MAC(M) = h(k\|M)$. It was proposed in the 1980s, and suggested for MD4 independently in [10, 17]. The MAC using the secret prefix method is insecure: given a message-MAC, the given MAC value can be regarded as the initial chaining value for the appended message, an attacker can easily append any blocks to the message and update the MAC accordingly [12]. To avoid the above attack, a countermeasure is proposed in [17], and it prepends the length of the unpadded message before hashing, and this type of MAC is denoted as the LPMAC [24, 29]: $LPMAC_k(M) = h(k\|length\|\overline{M})$, where $\overline{M}$ is the padded message of M, and $k\|length$ is a complete block.

3 Distinguishing Attack against the LPMAC-RIPEMD

In this section and the following two sections, by using the techniques in [24, 27], we give distinguishing attacks on the LPMAC based on RIPEMD, 58-step RIPEMD-256 and 48-step RIPEMD-320. The difficulty in our attack is to find some differential paths with high enough probability because the compression function of RIPEMD-family contains two parallel and independent operations. Furthermore, there are different message schedules in two operations in RIPEMD$-\{256, 320\}$, so we must choose proper message difference to ensure the differential paths contain as many rounds as possible.

In the following, we will use the pseudo-near-collision of a compression function, so we present the definition of pseudo-near-collision first. The pseudo-near-collision of the compression function defined in [29] etc. is described as follows: for any compression function $f : \{0,1\}^n \times \{0,1\}^m \longmapsto \{0,1\}^n$, and $(h, x) \neq (h', x')$, if the Hamming distance between $f(h, x)$ and $f(h', x')$ is sufficiently small, then (h, x) and (h', x') is called a pseudo-near-collision of the compression function f. In this section, we apply the distinguisher in [27] to give an adaptive chosen message attack on the LPMAC-RIPEMD. The pseudo-near-collision differential path of RIPEMD is shown in Table 3.

3.1 The Pseudo-Near-Collision Differential Path for RIPEMD

We select $\Delta M = M' - M = (\Delta m_0, \Delta m_1, ..., \Delta m_{15})$ as follows: $\Delta M = (0, 0, 0, 0, 0, 2^{31}, 0, ..., 0)$. The input difference is $\Delta IV = (\Delta a_0, \Delta d_0, \Delta c_0, \Delta b_0) = (0, [17], 0, [23])$, and the pseudo-near-collision differential path is shown in Table 3. The output difference is $(\Delta H_1, \Delta H_2, \Delta H_3, \Delta H_4) = (\Delta b_0 + \Delta cc_{12} + \Delta ddd_{12}, \Delta c_0 + \Delta dd_{12} + \Delta aaa_{12}, \Delta d_0 + \Delta aa_{12} + \Delta bbb_{12}, \Delta a_0 + \Delta bb_{12} + \Delta ccc_{12}) = (2^{23} + 2^6, 0, 2^{17} \pm 2^{11}, \pm 2^{11} + 2^6)$. $\Delta IV = (0, [17], 0, [23])$ means $IV \oplus IV' = (a_0 \oplus a_0', d_0 \oplus d_0', c_0 \oplus c_0', b_0 \oplus b_0') = (0, 2^{17}, 0, 2^{23})$ and $d_{0,17} = 0, b_{0,23} = 0$. If $\Delta IV = (0, [17], 0, [23])$ is fulfilled, we say that the IV difference satisfies the R-condition.

According to the properties of the Boolean function F, G and H, it is easy to derive the sufficient conditions that ensure the differential path in Table 3 hold. There are 31 conditions in the differential path of Line1 or Line2 operation. The sufficient conditions are shown in Table 4. Therefore, if the input difference $\Delta IV = (0, [17], 0, [23])$ is fulfilled, the differential path of RIPEMD holds with probability $2^{-62} = 2^{-31} \times 2^{-31}$.

3.2 Adaptive Chosen Message Distinguishing Attack on LPMAC-RIPEMD

We apply the distinguishing attack technique presented in [27] to present a distinguishing attack on the LPMAC based on RIPEMD combined with the differential path in Table 3. The attack algorithm is as follows:

1. Randomly choose a structure $T = \{M^i | i = 1, ..., 2^{66}\}$ composed of 2^{66} different messages, and query their corresponding MAC values C^i.
2. Find two messages M^a and M^b such that C^a and C^b satisfies the R-condition by the birthday attack.
3. The paddings for M^a and M^b are denoted by pad^a and pad^b respectively. Randomly choose 2^{63} different messages M^j, and query the MACs of two sets of messages $\{M^a \| pad^a \| M^j | j = 1, ..., 2^{63}\}$ and $\{M^b \| pad^b \| M^j | j = 1, ..., 2^{63}\}$. Obviously, there are 2^{63} messages in each set.
4. Once a near-collision ($M^a \| pad^a \| M^c$ and $M^b \| pad^b \| M^c$) is found, we conclude that the LPMAC is based on RIPEMD. Otherwise, it is based on a random function.

Complexity Evaluation. The data complexity of the attack is $2^{66} + 2 \times 2^{63} \approx 2^{66}$ chosen messages. Step 1 takes 2^{66} MAC queries. We keep a table of 2^{66} entries in step 2, and there are 2^{66} table look-ups in step 2 by the birthday attack. There are 2^{64} MAC queries in step 3. So the time complexity is about 2^{66} MAC queries and 2^{66} table look-ups.

Success Rate. For two random messages M^a and M^b, the outputs C^a and C^b satisfy the R-condition with probability $\frac{1}{2^{128}} \times \frac{1}{2^2} = \frac{1}{2^{130}}$. From the birthday paradox, a near-collision pair (M^a, M^b) among the 2^{66} messages occurs with probability $1 - (1 - \frac{1}{2^{130}})^{C_{2^{66}}^2} \approx 1 - \frac{1}{e^2} \approx 0.86$. The following success rate analysis can be divided into two parts: If the LPMAC is based on RIPEMD, the attack succeeds when we can find a near-collision among 2^{63} messages. The success probability is $1 - (1 - \frac{1}{2^{62}})^{2^{63}} \approx 0.86$. If the LPMAC is based on a random function, the attack succeeds when no near-collision can be found. The success probability is $(1 - \frac{1}{2^{128}})^{2^{63}} \approx 1$. Therefore, the success rate of the whole attack is about $0.86 \times (\frac{1}{2} \times 0.86 + \frac{1}{2} \times 1) \approx 0.80$. The success probability can be improved by increasing the number of selected messages and repeating the attack several times.

4   Distinguishing Attack against the LPMAC Based on 58-Step RIPEMD-256

In this section, we apply the distinguisher in [24] to give an adaptive chosen message attack on the LPMAC based on 58-step RIPEMD-256. The Line1 and Line2 operations differential paths of RIPEMD-256 are shown in Tables 5 and 7 respectively. The pseudo-near-collision differential path in Table 5 can be divided into two parts. The first part is from step-7 to step-27, and the second part is from step-28 to step-64. For the first part, we only consider the output difference of step-27. It serves as the input of the second part, and the pseudo-near-collision differential path of the second part holds with probability 2^{-12}. Similarly, in Table 7, the pseudo-near-collision differential path can also be divided into two parts. The first part is from step-7 to step-22, and the second part is from step-23 to step-64. The pseudo-near-collision differential path of the second part holds with probability 2^{-15}. It is noted that the swap operation at the end of each round has no impact on the differential paths of Line1 and Line2 operations.

4.1 The Pseudo-Near-Collision Differential Path for 58-Step RIPEMD-256

Select the message difference $\Delta M = M' - M = (\Delta m_0, \Delta m_1, ..., \Delta m_{15}) = (0, ..., 0, 2^{31}, 0)$. RR_i and RRR_i denote the outputs of step i of Line1 and Line2 operations respectively.

The Pseudo-near-collision Differential Path of 58-Step Line1 Operation. For the pseudo-near-collision differential path from step-28 to step-64 of Table 5, the input difference $\Delta RR_{27} = (\Delta aa_{27}, \Delta bb_{27}, \Delta cc_{27}, \Delta dd_{27})$ is selected as $(0, [18], [24, 31], 0)$ (which means $RR_i' \oplus RR_i = (0, 2^{18}, 2^{24} + 2^{31}, 0)$, and $bb_{27,18} = 0$, $cc_{27,24} = 0$, $cc_{27,31} = 0$), and the output difference of ΔRR_{64} is $([7], 0, 0, 0)$. According to the properties of the Boolean function f_2, f_3 and f_4, it is easy to derive the sufficient conditions that ensure the differential path in Table 5 hold. There are 6 conditions in RR_{27} and 12 conditions in $RR_{28} \sim RR_{64}$. The sufficient conditions are shown in Table 6. Therefore, if the input difference $\Delta RR_{27} = (0, 2^{18}, 2^{24} + 2^{31}, 0)$ and 6 conditions in RR_{27} are fulfilled, the pseudo-near-collision differential path of Line1 operation holds with probability 2^{-12}.

The Pseudo-near-collision Differential Path of 58-Step Line2 Operation. For the pseudo-near-collision differential path from step-23 to step-64 of Table 7, the input difference $\Delta RRR_{22} = (\Delta aaa_{22}, \Delta bbb_{22}, \Delta ccc_{22}, \Delta ddd_{22})$ is selected as $(0, [2], [31], [31])$, and the output difference of ΔRRR_{64} is $(0, [7], 0, 0)$. According to the properties of the Boolean functions, it is easy to derive the sufficient conditions that ensure the differential path in Table 7 hold. There are 5 conditions in RRR_{22} and 15 conditions in $RRR_{23} \sim RRR_{64}$. The sufficient conditions are shown in Table 8. Therefore, if the input difference $\Delta RRR_{22} = (0, 2^2, 2^{31}, 2^{31})$ and 5 conditions in RRR_{22} are fulfilled, the pseudo-near-collision differential path of Line2 operation holds with probability 2^{-15}.

4.2 Distinguishing Algorithm on the LPMAC Based on 58-Step RIPEMD-256

We apply the technique in [24] to present a distinguishing attack on the LPMAC based on 58-step RIPEMD-256 combined with the differential path in Tables 5, 7. Firstly, we select a 448-bit messages $Y = (y_0, y_1, y_3, y_4, y_6, ..., y_{15})$ and two 64-bit messages $Z_1 = (z_{1,2}, z_{1,5})$, $Z_2 = (z_{2,2}, z_{2,5})$. Denote $W_1 = (y_0, y_1, z_{1,2}, y_3, y_4, z_{1,5}, y_6, ..., y_{13}, y_{14}, y_{15})$, $W_1' = (y_0, y_1, z_{1,2}, y_3, y_4, z_{1,5}, y_6, ..., y_{13}, y_{14}', y_{15})$, $W_2 = (y_0, y_1,$

$z_{2,2}, y_3, y_4, z_{2,5}, y_6, ..., y_{13}, y_{14}, y_{15})$, and $W_2' = (y_0, y_1, z_{2,2}, y_3, y_4, z_{2,5}, y_6, ..., y_{13},$ $y_{14}', y_{15})$, which are four fixed one-block messages. Both $\Delta W_1 = W_1' - W_1$ and $\Delta W_2 = W_2' - W_2$ satisfy the target message difference: $\Delta m_{14} = 2^{31}$, $\Delta m_i = 0$ $(i = 0, ..., 15, i \neq 14)$. Secondly, we find a 512-bit message pair (X, X') such that the message quadruple $(X\|W_1, X\|W_2, X'\|W_1', X'\|W_2')$ satisfy the following conditions:

1. (a) Let RR_{27} and RR_{27}' denote the 27-th step output of Line1 operation in the second block of $Line1(X\|W_1)$ and $Line1(X'\|W_1')$ respectively. ΔRR_{27} satisfies the target input difference of step 28 in Table 5 and RR_{27} satisfies the corresponding 6 conditions in Table 6.
   (b) The output of Line1 operation of the message quadruple satisfies the equation $Line1(X\|W_2) - Line1(X\|W_1) = Line1(X'\|W_2') - Line1(X'\|W_1')$.
2. (a) Let RRR_{22} and RRR_{22}' denote the 22-nd step output of Line2 operation in the second block of $Line2(X\|W_1)$ and $Line2(X'\|W_1')$ respectively. ΔRRR_{22} satisfies the target input difference of step 23 in Table 7 and RR_{22} satisfies the corresponding 5 conditions in Table 8.
   (b) The output of Line2 operation of the message quadruple satisfies the equation $Line2(X\|W_2) - Line2(X\|W_1) = Line2(X'\|W_2') - Line2(X'\|W_1')$.

If the above conditions 1 and 2 are satisfied, we call the message pair (X, X') as a *RIPEMD256-collision*. For a random 512-bit message pair (X, X'), the condition 1(a) above holds with probability $2^{-128} \times 2^{-6} = 2^{-134}$. The condition 2(a) holds with probability $2^{-128} \times 2^{-5} = 2^{-133}$. If the LPMAC is based on 58-step RIPEMD-256, the condition 1(b) can be satisfied when the two message pairs $(X\|W_1, X'\|W_1')$ and $(X\|W_2, X'\|W_2')$ both follow the differential path from step 28 to 64 of Line1 operation in Table 5, and the probability is $2^{-12} \times 2^{-12} = 2^{-24}$. Similarly, the condition 2(b) can be satisfied with probability $2^{-15} \times 2^{-15} = 2^{-30}$. Therefore, the message pair (X, X') is a RIPEMD256-collision with probability $2^{-134} \times 2^{-133} \times 2^{-24} \times 2^{-30} = 2^{-321}$. The distinguishing attack algorithm for the LPMAC based on 58-step RIPEMD-256 is as follows:

1. Randomly choose a set T which consists of $2^{161.5}$ one-block messages. For every $X \in T$, query the MACs with $X\|W_1$, $X\|W_1'$, $X\|W_2$ and $X\|W_2'$ respectively, and obtain the corresponding MACs.
2. Then perform the followings:
   (a) For Line1 operation, compute two sets of differences: $T_1^1 = \{Line1(X\|W_2) - Line1(X\|W_1)|X \in T\}$, $T_2^1 = \{Line1(X\|W_2') - Line1(X\|W_1')|X \in T\}$.
   (b) For Line2 operation, compute two sets of differences: $T_1^2 = \{Line2(X\|W_2) - Line2(X\|W_1)|X \in T\}$, $T_2^2 = \{Line2(X\|W_2') - Line2(X\|W_1')|X \in T\}$.
   (c) Find all the pairs (X, X') such that the following two conditions hold, and the set of all pairs is recorded as T_3. $Line1(X\|W_2) - Line1(X\|W_1) = Line1(X'\|W_2') - Line1(X'\|W_1')$, $Line2(X\|W_2) - Line2(X\|W_1) = Line2(X'\|W_2') - Line2(X'\|W_1')$.
3. For each pair $(X, X') \in T_3$: Compute $Line1(X'\|W_1') - Line1(X\|W_1)$ and denote it as δ_1. Compute $Line2(X'\|W_1') - Line2(X\|W_1)$ and denote it as δ_2. Denote $\overline{Z} = (\overline{z_{1,2}}, \overline{z_{1,5}})$, $\overline{W} = (y_0, y_1, \overline{z_{1,2}}, y_3, y_4, \overline{z_{1,5}}, y_6, ..., y_{13}, y_{14}, y_{15})$,

and $\overline{W'} = (y_0, y_1, \overline{z_{1,2}}, y_3, y_4, \overline{z_{1,5}}, y_6, ..., y_{13}, y'_{14}, y_{15})$. Randomly choose 2^{28} different 32-bit messages $\overline{Z}$ such that $(\overline{W}, \overline{W'})$ satisfy the target message difference: $\Delta m_{14} = 2^{31}$, $\Delta m_i = 0$ $(i = 0, ..., 15, i \neq 14)$. Query the MACs of all the 2^{28} message pairs $(X' \| \overline{W'}, X \| \overline{W})$. Compute $\overline{\delta_1} = Line1(X' \| \overline{W'}) - Line1(X \| \overline{W})$ and $\overline{\delta_2} = Line2(X' \| \overline{W'}) - Line2(X \| \overline{W})$. Check whether $\overline{\delta_1} = \delta_1$ and $\overline{\delta_2} = \delta_2$ hold simultaneously.

4. If a $\overline{Z}$ is found to match the differences δ_1 and δ_2, we claim the LPMAC is based on 58-step RIPEMD-256. Otherwise, it is based on a random function.

Complexity Evaluation. Step 1 takes $2^{161.5}$ messages and $4 \times 2^{161.5} = 2^{163.5}$ MAC queries. We keep a table of $2^{161.5}$ entries and need about $2^{161.5}$ table lookups in step 2. For the $2^{161.5}$ messages, it can produce about 2^{322} message pairs, so the expected number of pairs in T_3 is about $2^{322} \times 2^{-256} = 2^{66}$, in which about $2^{322} \times 2^{-321} = 2$ pairs are RIPEMD256-collisions. In step 3, for each pair, it needs 2^{28} message pairs to verify whether it is a RIPEMD256-collision, so the time complexity in step 3 is about $2^{28} \times 2^{66} = 2^{94}$. Therefore, the total data and time complexities are dominant by step 1 and they're about $2^{161.5}$ chosen messages and $2^{163.5}$ MAC queries respectively.

Success Rate. The success rate of the attack can be divided into two parts: If the LPMAC is based on 58-step RIPEMD-256, the attack succeeds when there is at least one RIPEMD256-collision in step 2, and a collision in step 3 is detected. The probability that there is at least one RIPEMD256-collision in step 2 is $1 - (1 - \frac{1}{2^{321}})^{2^{322}} = 1 - \frac{1}{e^2} \approx 0.86$. If the RIPEMD256-collision in step 2 is captured, a collision in step 3 can be detected with probability $1 - (1 - \frac{1}{2^{12} \times 2^{15}})^{2^{28}} = 1 - \frac{1}{e^2} \approx 0.86$. Therefore, if the LPMAC is based on 58-step RIPEMD-256, the distinguishing attack successes with probability $0.86 \times 0.86 \approx 0.72$. If the LPMAC is based on a random function, the attack succeeds when no RIPEMD256-collision can be found. The success probability is $((1 - \frac{1}{2^{256}})^{2^{28}})^{2^{67}} \approx 1$. Hence, the success rate of the whole attack is about $\frac{1}{2} \times 0.72 + \frac{1}{2} \times 1 = 0.87$. The success probability can be improved by increasing the number of selected messages and repeating the attack several times.

5   Distinguishing Attack against the LPMAC Based on 48-Step RIPEMD-320

In this section, we apply the distinguisher in [24] to give an adaptive chosen message attack on the LPMAC based on 48-step RIPEMD-320. The Line1 and Line2 operations differential paths of RIPEMD-256 are shown in Tables 9, 11 respectively. The pseudo-near-collision differential path in Table 9 can be divided into two parts. The first part is from step-1 to step-12, and the second part is from step-13 to step-48. We only consider the output difference of step-12 for the first part. The output of step-12 serves as the input of the the second part, and the pseudo-near-collision differential path of the second part holds with probability 2^{-16}. Similarly, in Table 11, the pseudo-near-collision differential path can also be divided into two parts. The first part is from step-1 to step-15, and the second part is from step-16 to step-48. The pseudo-near-collision differential path of the second part holds with probability 2^{-7}. We select the message difference $\Delta M = M' - M = (\Delta m_0, \Delta m_1, ..., \Delta m_{15})$ as follows: $\Delta M = (0, ..., 0, 2^{31}, 0, 0)$. Let RR_i and RRR_i denote the outputs after step i of Line1 operation and Line2 operation respectively.

It is noted that after round 1, the output differences are $\Delta RR_{16} = ([-7, 12], 0, 0, [31], [-25])$ in Line1 operation, and $\Delta RRR_{16} = ([18], [-9], [2], [-29], [16])$ in Line2 operation respectively. After swap aa_{16} with aaa_{16}, aa'_{16} with aaa'_{16} respectively, the input differences of step 17 are $([18], 0, 0, [31], [-25])$ in Line1 operation and $([-7, 12], [-9], [2], [-29], [16])$ in Line2 operation respectively.

The Pseudo-near-collision Differential Path of 48-Step Line1 Operation. For the pseudo-near-collision differential path from step-13 to step-48 of Table 9, the input chaining variable difference $\Delta RR_{12} = (\Delta aa_{12}, \Delta bb_{12}, \Delta cc_{12}, \Delta dd_{12}, \Delta ee_{12})$ is selected as $([-7, -9, 11, -14, -19, -23, 28, -30], [2, -29], [11, 15, 21, -26], [7, -15, -21, 27], [-0, 2, 4, 8, -14, 20, 25, 29])$, and the output difference of ΔRR_{48} is $(0, \pm 2^{19}, 0, 0, [14])$.

According to the properties of the Boolean function f_1, f_2 and f_3, it is easy to derive the sufficient conditions that ensure the differential path in Table 9 hold. There are 32 conditions in RR_{12} and 16 conditions in $RR_{13} \sim RR_{48}$. The sufficient conditions are shown in Table 10. Therefore, if the input difference $\Delta RR_{12} = (-2^7 - 2^9 + 2^{11} - 2^{14} - 2^{19} - 2^{23} + 2^{28} - 2^{30}, 2^2 - 2^{29}, 2^{11} + 2^{15} + 2^{21} - 2^{26}, 2^7 - 2^{15} - 2^{21} + 2^{27}, -1 + 2^2 + 2^4 + 2^8 - 2^{14} + 2^{20} + 2^{25} + 2^{29})$ and 32 conditions in RR_{12} are fulfilled, the pseudo-near-collision differential path of Line1 operation holds with probability 2^{-16}.

The Pseudo-near-collision Differential Path of 48-Step Line2 Operation. For the pseudo-near-collision differential path from step-16 to step-48 of Table 11, the input chaining variable difference $\Delta RRR_{15} = (\Delta aaa_{15}, \Delta bbb_{15}, \Delta ccc_{15}, \Delta ddd_{15}, \Delta eee_{15})$ is selected as $([-2, -12], [2], [-19], [16], [18])$, and the output difference of ΔRRR_{48} is $(0, 2^4, 0, 0, 0)$. According to the properties of the Boolean function f_3, f_4 and f_5, it is easy to derive the sufficient conditions that ensure the differential path in Table 11 hold. There are 13 conditions in RRR_{15} and 7 conditions in $RRR_{16} \sim RRR_{48}$. The sufficient conditions are shown in Table 12. Therefore, if the input difference $\Delta RRR_{15} = (-2^2 - 2^{12}, 2^2, -2^{19}, 2^{16}, 2^{18})$ and 13 conditions in RRR_{15} are fulfilled, the pseudo-near-collision differential path of Line2 operation holds with probability 2^{-7}.

We apply the technique presented in [24] to present a distinguishing attack on the LPMAC based on 48-step RIPEMD-320 combined with the differential path in Tables 9, 11. The distinguisher also contains a pair of two-block messages, and it is used to detect an inner near-collision occurring in the second iteration. The attack procedure is similarly to the descriptions in Section 4.2, we omit it because the page limit. The data complexity of the attack is about $2^{208.5}$ chosen messages, and the time complexity is about $2^{206.5}$ MAC queries. The success rate of the attack is about 0.87.

6   Conclusions

In this paper, we give the first distinguishing attack on the LPMAC based on the full RIPEMD, 58-step reduced RIPEMD-256 and 48-step reduced RIPEMD-320, and the attack is also applicable to the LPMAC based on extended MD4 which also belongs to the RIPEMD-family. The output difference of the differential path is non-zero, so it can't detect the target collision (R-collision, RIPEMD256-collision and RIPEMD320-collision respectively) by the outer function of HMAC/NMAC, and our distinguishing attack on the LPMAC is not applicable for the HMAC/NMAC.

Acknowledgments. The author would like to thank the anonymous reviewers for their very helpful comments on the paper.

References

1. Bellare, M., Canetti, R., Krawczyk, H.: Keying Hash Functions for Message Authentication. In: Koblitz, N. (ed.) CRYPTO 1996. LNCS, vol. 1109, pp. 1–15. Springer, Heidelberg (1996)
2. Biham, E., Chen, R.: Near-Collisions of SHA-0. In: Franklin, M. (ed.) CRYPTO 2004. LNCS, vol. 3152, pp. 290–305. Springer, Heidelberg (2004)
3. Biham, E., Chen, R., Joux, A., Carribault, P., Lemuet, C., Jalby, W.: Collisions of SHA-0 and Reduced SHA-1. In: Cramer, R. (ed.) EUROCRYPT 2005. LNCS, vol. 3494, pp. 36–57. Springer, Heidelberg (2005)
4. Chabaud, F., Joux, A.: Differential Collisions in SHA-0. In: Krawczyk, H. (ed.) CRYPTO 1998. LNCS, vol. 1462, pp. 56–71. Springer, Heidelberg (1998)
5. Contini, S., Yin, Y.L.: Forgery and Partial Key-recovery Attacks on HMAC and NMAC Using Hash Collisions. In: Lai, X., Chen, K. (eds.) ASIACRYPT 2006. LNCS, vol. 4284, pp. 37–53. Springer, Heidelberg (2006)
6. den Boer, B., Bosselaers, A.: Collisions for the Compression Function of MD5. In: Helleseth, T. (ed.) EUROCRYPT 1993. LNCS, vol. 765, pp. 293–304. Springer, Heidelberg (1994)
7. Dobbertin, H.: Cryptanalysis of MD4. In: Gollmann, D. (ed.) FSE 1996. LNCS, vol. 1039, pp. 53–69. Springer, Heidelberg (1996)
8. Dobbertin, H., Bosselaers, A., Preneel, B.: RIPEMD-160: A Strengthened Version of RIPEMD. In: Gollmann, D. (ed.) FSE 1996. LNCS, vol. 1039, pp. 71–82. Springer, Heidelberg (1996)
9. Fouque, P.-A., Leurent, G., Nguyen, P.Q.: Full Key-Recovery Attacks on HMAC/NMAC-MD4 and NMAC-MD5. In: Menezes, A. (ed.) CRYPTO 2007. LNCS, vol. 4622, pp. 13–30. Springer, Heidelberg (2007)
10. Galvin, J.M., McCloghrie, K., Davin, J.R.: Secure Management of SNMP Networks. Integrated Network Management II, 703–714 (1991)
11. Kim, J.-S., Biryukov, A., Preneel, B., Hong, S.H.: On the Security of HMAC and NMAC Based on HAVAL, MD4, MD5, SHA-0 and SHA-1 (Extended Abstract). In: De Prisco, R., Yung, M. (eds.) SCN 2006. LNCS, vol. 4116, pp. 242–256. Springer, Heidelberg (2006)
12. Preneel, B., van Oorschot, P.: MDx-MAC and building fast MACs from hash functions. In: Coppersmith, D. (ed.) CRYPTO 1995. LNCS, vol. 963, pp. 1–14. Springer, Heidelberg (1995)

13. Rechberger, C., Rijmen, V.: On Authentication with HMAC and Non-random Properties. In: Dietrich, S., Dhamija, R. (eds.) FC 2007 and USEC 2007. LNCS, vol. 4886, pp. 119–133. Springer, Heidelberg (2007)

14. RIPE, Integrity Primitives for Secure Information Systems, Final Report of RACE Integrity Primitives Evalution (RIPE-RACE 1040). LNCS, vol. 1007. Springer, Heidelberg (1995)

15. Van Rompay, B., Biryukov, A., Preneel, B., Vandewalle, J.: Cryptanalysis of 3-pass HAVAL. In: Laih, C.-S. (ed.) ASIACRYPT 2003. LNCS, vol. 2894, pp. 228–245. Springer, Heidelberg (2003)

16. Sasaki, Y., Aoki, K.: Meet-in-the-Middle Preimage Attacks on Double-Branch Hash Functions: Application to RIPEMD and Others. In: Boyd, C., González Nieto, J. (eds.) ACISP 2009. LNCS, vol. 5594, pp. 214–231. Springer, Heidelberg (2009)

17. Tsudik, G.: Message Authentication with One-Way Hash Functions. ACM Comput. Commun. Rev. 22(5), 29–38 (1992)

18. Wang, G.L., Wang, M.Q.: Cryptanalysis of reduced RIPEMD-128. Journal of Software 19(9), 2442–2448 (2008)

19. Wang, G.L., Wang, S.H.: Second Preimage Attack on 5-Pass HAVAL and Partial Key-Recovery Attack on HMAC/NMAC-5-Pass HAVAL. In: Preneel, B. (ed.) AFRICACRYPT 2009. LNCS, vol. 5580, pp. 1–13. Springer, Heidelberg (2009)

20. Wang, L., Ohta, K., Kunihiro, N.: New Key-Recovery Attacks on HMAC/NMAC-MD4 and NMAC-MD5. In: Smart, N.P. (ed.) EUROCRYPT 2008. LNCS, vol. 4965, pp. 237–253. Springer, Heidelberg (2008)

21. Wang, X.Y., Feng, D.G., Yu, X.Y.: An attack on HAVAL function HAVAL-128. Science in China Ser. F Information Sciences 48(5), 1–12 (2005)

22. Wang, X.Y., Lai, X.J., Feng, D.G., Chen, H., Yu, X.Y.: Cryptanalysis of the Hash Functions MD4 and RIPEMD. In: Cramer, R. (ed.) EUROCRYPT 2005. LNCS, vol. 3494, pp. 1–18. Springer, Heidelberg (2005)

23. Wang, X.Y., Lisa, Y., Yu, H.B.: Finding Collisions in the Full SHA-1. In: Shoup, V. (ed.) CRYPTO 2005. LNCS, vol. 3621, pp. 17–36. Springer, Heidelberg (2005)

24. Wang, X.Y., Wang, W., Jia, K.T., Wang, M.Q.: New Distinguishing Attack on MAC using Secret-Prefix Method. In: Dunkelman, O. (ed.) FSE 2009. LNCS, vol. 5665, pp. 363–374. Springer, Heidelberg (2009)

25. Wang, X.Y., Yu, H.B.: How to Break MD5 and Other Hash Functions. In: Cramer, R. (ed.) EUROCRYPT 2005. LNCS, vol. 3494, pp. 19–35. Springer, Heidelberg (2005)

26. Wang, X.Y., Yu, H.B., Lisa, Y.: Efficient Collision Search Attacks on SHA-0. In: Shoup, V. (ed.) CRYPTO 2005. LNCS, vol. 3621, pp. 1–16. Springer, Heidelberg (2005)

27. Wang, X.Y., Yu, H.B., Wang, W., Zhang, H.N., Zhan, T.: Cryptanalysis on HMAC/NMAC-MD5 and MD5-MAC. In: Joux, A. (ed.) EUROCRYPT 2009. LNCS, vol. 5479, pp. 121–133. Springer, Heidelberg (2009)

28. Yu, H.B., Wang, G.L., Zhang, G.Y., Wang, X.Y.: The Second-preimage Attack on MD4. In: Desmedt, Y.G., Wang, H., Mu, Y., Li, Y. (eds.) CANS 2005. LNCS, vol. 3810, pp. 1–12. Springer, Heidelberg (2005)

29. Yu, H.B., Wang, X.Y.: Distinguishing Attack on the Secret-Prefix MAC Based on the 39-Step SHA-256. In: Boyd, C., González Nieto, J. (eds.) ACISP 2009. LNCS, vol. 5594, pp. 185–201. Springer, Heidelberg (2009)

30. Yu, H.B., Wang, X.Y., Yun, A., Park, S.: Cryptanalysis of the Full HAVAL with 4 and 5 Passes. In: Robshaw, M.J.B. (ed.) FSE 2006. LNCS, vol. 4047, pp. 89–110. Springer, Heidelberg (2006)

Appendix

Table 3. Pseudo-near-collision differential path for RIPEMD

Step	m_i	Δm_i	Shift	Chaining value	The step difference
				a_0	0
				d_0	[17]
				c_0	0
				b_0	[23]
1	m_0		11	a_1	0
2	m_1		14	d_1	[31]
3	m_2		15	c_1	0
4	m_3		12	b_1	[3]
5	m_4		5	a_2	0
6	m_5	2^{31}	8	d_2	0
7	m_6		7	c_2	0
8	m_7		9	b_2	[12]
9	m_8		11	a_3	0
10	m_9		13	d_3	0
11	m_{10}		14	c_3	0
12	m_{11}		15	b_3	[27]
13	m_{12}		6	a_4	0
14	m_{13}		7	d_4	0
15	m_{14}		9	c_4	0
16	m_{15}		8	b_4	[3]
17	m_7		7	a_5	0
18	m_4		6	d_5	0
19	m_{13}		8	c_5	0
20	m_1		13	b_5	[16]
21	m_{10}		11	a_6	0
22	m_6		9	d_6	0
23	m_{15}		7	c_6	0
24	m_3		15	b_6	[31]
25	m_{12}		7	a_7	0
26	m_0		12	d_7	0
27	m_9		15	c_7	0
28	m_5	2^{31}	9	b_7	0
...	...	...	...	...	...
47	m_5	2^{31}	7	c_{12}	[6]
48	m_{12}		5	b_{12}	$\pm 2^{11}$

Table 4. Sufficient conditions for RIPEMD

Step	Conditions
	$d_{0,17} = 0$, $c_{0,23} = d_{0,23}$, $b_{0,17} = 1$, $b_{0,23} = 0$
1-3	$a_{1,23} = 0$, $a_{1,31} = b_{0,31}$, $d_{1,23} = 1$, $d_{1,31} = 0$, $c_{1,3} = d_{1,3}$, $c_{1,31} = 0$
4-8	$b_{1,3} = 0$, $b_{1,31} = 1$, $a_{2,3} = 0$, $d_{2,3} = 1$, $c_{2,12} = d_{2,12}$, $b_{2,12} = 0$
9-14	$a_{3,12} = 0$, $d_{3,12} = 1$, $c_{3,27} = d_{3,27}$, $b_{3,27} = 0$, $a_{4,27} = 0$, $d_{4,27} = 1$
15-20	$c_{4,3} = d_{4,3}$, $b_{4,3} = 0$, $a_{5,3} = c_{4,3}$, $d_{5,3} = a_{5,3}$, $c_{5,16} = d_{5,16}$, $b_{5,16} = 0$
21-26	$a_{6,16} = c_{5,16}$, $d_{6,16} = a_{6,16}$, $c_{6,31} = d_{6,31}$, $b_{6,31} = 0$, $a_{7,31} = c_{6,31}$, $d_{7,31} = a_{7,31}$
27-46	no conditions
47	$c_{12,6} = 0$

Table 5. Pseudo-near-collision differential path for Line1 in RIPEMD-256

Step	m_i	Δm_i	Shift	Δaa_i	Δbb_i	Δcc_i	Δdd_i
7	m_6		7	$-$	$-$	$-$	$-$
8	m_7		9	$-$	$-$	$-$	$-$
...	...	...	...	...	...	...	...
27	m_9		15	0	[18]	[24, 31]	0
28	m_5		9	0	0	[18]	[24, 31]
29	m_2		11	[24, 31]	0	0	[18]
30	m_{14}	2^{31}	7	[18]	[31]	0	0
31	m_{11}		13	0	[31]	[31]	0
32	m_8		12	0	0	[31]	[31]
33	m_3		11	[31]	0	0	[31]
34	m_{10}		13	[31]	0	0	0
35	m_{14}	2^{31}	6	0	0	0	0
...	...	...	...	...	...	...	...
61	m_{14}	2^{31}	8	0	[7]	0	0
62	m_5		6	0	0	[7]	0
63	m_6		5	0	0	0	[7]
64	m_2		12	[7]	0	0	0

Table 6. Sufficient conditions for Line1 in RIPEMD-256

Step	Conditions
27	$cc_{27,18} = dd_{27,18}(\Leftrightarrow bb_{26,18} = bb_{25,18})$, $cc_{27,24} = 0(\Leftrightarrow bb_{26,24} = 0)$, $cc_{27,31} = 0(\Leftrightarrow bb_{26,31} = 0)$, $bb_{27,18} = 0$, $bb_{27,24} = 0$, $bb_{27,31} = 0$
28	$bb_{28,18} = 0$, $bb_{28,24} = 1$, $bb_{28,31} = 1$
29-32	$bb_{29,18} = 1$, $bb_{29,31} = 1$, $bb_{30,31} = 0$, $bb_{31,31} = 0$, $bb_{32,31} = 0$
59-63	$bb_{59,7} = 0$, $bb_{60,7} = 1$, $bb_{61,7} = 0$, $bb_{63,7} = bb_{62,7}$

Table 7. Pseudo-near-collision differential path for Line2 in RIPEMD-256

Step	m_i	Δm_i	Shift	Δaa_i	Δbb_i	Δcc_i	Δdd_i
7	m_{11}		15	−	−	−	−
8	m_4		5	−	−	−	−
...	...	...	...	...	...	...	...
22	m_{13}		8	0	[2]	[31]	[31]
23	m_5		9	[31]	0	[2]	[31]
24	m_{10}		11	[31]	0	0	[2]
25	m_{14}	2^{31}	7	[2]	[9]	0	0
26	m_{15}		7	0	[9]	[9]	0
27	m_8		12	0	0	[9]	[9]
28	m_{12}		7	[9]	0	0	[9]
29	m_4		6	[9]	0	0	0
30	m_9		15	0	[24]	0	0
31	m_1		13	0	0	[24]	0
32	m_2		11	0	0	0	[24]
33	m_{15}		9	[24]	0	0	0
34	m_5		7	0	[31]	0	0
35	m_1		15	0	0	[31]	0
36	m_3		11	0	0	0	[31]
37	m_7		8	[31]	0	0	0
38	m_{14}	2^{31}	6	0	0	0	0
...	...	...	...	...	...	...	...
63	m_{10}		15	0	0	0	0
64	m_{14}	2^{31}	8	0	[7]	0	0

Table 8. Sufficient conditions for Line2 in RIPEMD-256

Step	Conditions
22	$ddd_{22,31} = 0 (\Leftrightarrow bbb_{20,31} = 0)$, $ccc_{22,2} = 0 (\Leftrightarrow bbb_{21,2} = 0)$, $ccc_{22,31} = 0 (\Leftrightarrow bbb_{21,31} = 0)$, $bbb_{22,2} = 0$, $bbb_{22,31} = 0$
23-26	$bbb_{23,2} = 1$, $bbb_{24,2} = 0$, $bbb_{24,9} = 0$, $bbb_{25,9} = 0$, $bbb_{26,9} = 0$
27-30	$bbb_{27,9} = 0$, $bbb_{29,24} = 0$, $bbb_{30,24} = 0$
31-34	$bbb_{31,24} = 1$, $bbb_{32,24} = 1$, $bbb_{33,31} = bbb_{32,31}$, $bbb_{34,31} = 0$
35-36	$bbb_{35,31} = 0$, $bbb_{36,31} = 1$
64	$bbb_{64,7} = 0$

Table 9. Pseudo-near-collision differential path for Line1 in RIPEMD-320

Step	m_i	Δm_i	Shift	Δaa_i	Δbb_i	Δcc_i	Δdd_i	Δee_i
1	m_0		11	−	−	−	−	−
2	m_1		14	−	−	−	−	−
...	...	...	...	...	...	...	...	...
12	m_{11}		15	$[-7,-9,11,-14,$ $-19,-23,28,-30]$	$[2,-29]$	$[11,15,$ $21,-26]$	$[7,-15,$ $-21,27]$	$[-0,2,4,8,-14,$ $20,25,29]$
13	m_{12}		6	$[-0,2,4,8,-14,$ $20,25,29]$	$[-15]$	$[2,-29]$	$[-4,21,$ $25,31]$	$[7,-15,$ $-21,27]$
14	m_{13}	2^{31}	7	$[7,-15,$ $-21,27]$	$[21]$	$[-15]$	$[-7,12]$	$[-4,21,$ $25,31]$
15	m_{14}		9	$[-4,21,$ $25,31]$	0	$[21]$	$[-25]$	$[-7,12]$
16	m_{15}		8	$[-7,12]$	0	0	$[31]$	$[-25]$
			swap	aa_{16} with aaa_{16}				
16	m_{15}		8	$[18]$	0	0	$[31]$	$[-25]$
17	m_7		7	$[-25]$	0	0	0	$[31]$
18	m_4		6	$[31]$	0	0	0	0
19	m_{13}	2^{31}	8	0	0	0	0	0
...	...	...	...	...	...	...	...	...
45	m_{13}	2^{31}	5	0	$[4]$	0	0	0
46	m_{11}		12	0	0	$[4]$	0	0
47	m_5		7	0	0	0	$[14]$	0
48	m_{12}		5	0	$\pm 2^{19}$	0	0	$[14]$

Table 10. Sufficient conditions for Line1 in RIPEMD-320

Step	Conditions
12	$aa_{12,i} = 0(i = 7, 11, 28)$, $aa_{12,i} = 1(i = 14, 19, 23, 30)$, $bb_{12,2} = 0$, $bb_{12,29} = 1$, $bb_{12,7} = cc_{12,7}$, $bb_{12,27} = cc_{12,27} + 1$, $bb_{12,11} = dd_{12,11} + 1$, $bb_{12,26} = dd_{12,26} + 1$, $bb_{12,15} = cc_{12,5} + 1 (\Longleftrightarrow cc_{13,15} = dd_{13,15} + 1)$, $cc_{12,i} = 0(i = 11, 15, 21)$, $cc_{12,26} = 1$, $cc_{12,2} = dd_{12,2} + 1$, $cc_{12,29} = dd_{12,29}$, $dd_{12,i} = 0(i = 7, 27)$, $dd_{12,i} = 1(i = 15, 21)$, $ee_{12,i} = 0(i = 2, 4, 8, 20, 25, 29)$, $ee_{12,i} = 1(i = 0, 14)$
13	$bb_{13,15} = 1$, $bb_{13,21} = cc_{13,21} + 1$, $bb_{13,25} = cc_{13,25} + 1$, $bb_{13,2} = dd_{13,2} + 1$, $bb_{13,29} = dd_{13,29}$
14	$cc_{14,21} = dd_{14,21} + 1$
14	$bb_{14,21} = 0$, $bb_{14,7} = cc_{14,7}$, $bb_{14,12} = cc_{14,12} + 1$, $bb_{14,15} = dd_{14,15}$
15	$bb_{15,25} = cc_{15,25}$, $bb_{15,21} = dd_{15,21} + 1$
16	$aa_{16,31} = 1$
45	$bb_{45,4} = 0$, $cc_{45,4} = 0$
46	$bb_{46,4} = 1$

Table 11. Pseudo-near-collision differential path for Line2 in RIPEMD-320

Step	m_i	Δm_i	Shift	Δaaa_i	Δbbb_i	Δccc_i	Δddd_i	Δeee_i
1	m_5		8	–	–	–	–	–
2	m_{14}		9	–	–	–	–	–
...	...	...	...	...	...	...	...	...
15	m_3		12	$[-2,-12]$	$[2]$	$[-19]$	$[16]$	$[18]$
16	m_{12}		6	$[18]$	$[-9]$	$[2]$	$[-29]$	$[16]$
			swap	aa_{16} with aaa_{16}				
16	m_{12}		6	$[-7,12]$	$[-9]$	$[2]$	$[-29]$	$[16]$
17	m_6		9	$[16]$	$[21]$	$[-9]$	$[12]$	$[-29]$
18	m_{11}		13	$[-29]$	0	$[21]$	$[-19]$	$[12]$
19	m_3		15	$[12]$	0	0	$[31]$	$[-19]$
20	m_7		7	$[-19]$	0	0	0	$[31]$
21	m_0		12	$[31]$	0	0	0	0
22	m_{13}	2^{31}	8	0	0	0	0	0
...	...	...	...	...	...	...	...	...
48	m_{13}	2^{31}	5	0	2^4	0	0	0

Table 12. Sufficient conditions for Line2 in RIPEMD-320

Step	Conditions
15	$aaa_{15,2} = 1$, $aaa_{15,12} = 1$, $bbb_{15,2} = 0$, $bbb_{15,11} = 0 (\Leftrightarrow ddd_{17,21} = 0)$, $bbb_{15,31} = 1 (\Leftrightarrow ddd_{17,9} = 1)$, $ccc_{15,24} = 1 (\Leftrightarrow ddd_{16,2} = 1)$, $ccc_{15,16} = 1$, $ccc_{15,19} = 1$, $ccc_{15,31} = 0 (\Leftrightarrow ddd_{16,9} = 0)$, $ddd_{15,2} = 0$, $ddd_{15,16} = 0$, $ddd_{15,19} = 0$, $eee_{15,18} = 0$
16	$bbb_{16,9} = 1$, $bbb_{16,29} = ccc_{16,29}$
17	$bbb_{17,21} = 0$, $bbb_{17,12} = ccc_{17,12}$
18	$ddd_{18,21} = 1$, $bbb_{18,19} = ccc_{18,19}$
19	$bbb_{19,31} = ccc_{19,31}$

How to Construct Secure and Efficient Three-Party Password-Based Authenticated Key Exchange Protocols

Weijia Wang[1,3], Lei Hu[2], and Yong Li[3]

[1] School of Science,
Beijing Jiaotong University, Beijing 100044, P.R. China
wangwj@bjtu.edu.cn
[2] State Key Laboratory of Information Security
(Graduate University of Chinese Academy of Sciences)
Beijing 100049, P.R. China
hu@is.ac.cn
[3] School of Electronic and Information Engineering,
Beijing Jiaotong University, Beijing 100044, P.R. China
liyong@bjtu.edu.cn

Abstract. Three-party password-based authenticated key exchange (3-party PAKE) protocols are attractive due to their convenience in many communication applications, and thus have been receiving much interest in the cryptographic research community. But, until now, how to build provably secure 4-round 3-party PAKE protocol in a formal way is still an open problem. In this paper, we introduce a target driven formal way to build a 4-round provably secure 3-Party PAKE protocol. Aiming at the security target and the efficiency one, we firstly present a new generic construction for 3PAKE protocols which enjoys perfect security. Furthermore, for obtaining a 4-round communication, we carefully simplify the above generic construction so as to get an improved version holding the target security. Finally, using the improved construction and some instantiation techniques, we present a provably secure 4-round 3-party PAKE protocol.

Keywords: password, authenticated key exchange, key distribution, multi-party protocol.

1 Introduction

The convenience of password-based authentication is obvious when two entities communicate on the Internet. Due to this advantage, password-based authenticated key exchange (PAKE) protocols play an important role in the field of secure communications. Recently, with the development of wireless communications for the Internet, the three-party password-based authenticated key exchange (3-party PAKE or 3PAKE) protocol has received growing attention in the research community. Using 3PAKE protocols, two communicating entities

X. Lai, M. Yung, and D. Lin (Eds.): Inscrypt 2010, LNCS 6584, pp. 218–235, 2011.
© Springer-Verlag Berlin Heidelberg 2011

in the Internet, who only share a weak (low entropy) password with a trusted server, respectively, is able to authenticate each other with the help of the trusted server and establish a strong session key for protecting their subsequent communications over the public channel. In the circumstance of 3PAKE, the server, who holds all the registered users' passwords, plays a role of the authentication agent. As a result, any communicating entity, who wants to build secure communications with another registered entity, does not need to remember all the other users' passwords, but holds a password shared with the server.

Compared with those public-key based schemes which rely on the Public Key Infrastructure (PKI), the password-based authenticated key exchange protocol is vulnerable to so-called *exhaustive dictionary attacks* as a password, with about 10-letter length, always distributes over a small set. According to the form of attacks, we can divide dictionary attacks into three classes [18]: *off-line dictionary attacks, undetectable on-line dictionary attacks* and *detectable on-line dictionary attacks*. In the first case, with the information captured in the channel, an attacker is able to guess a password and verify it off-linely. In the second one, an attacker is only able to guess and verify a password guess in an on-line way, and a failed guess is not detectable. In the last one, the actions of an attacker are still on-line, but any failed guess can be detected.

For a PAKE protocol, detectable on-line dictionary attacks are trivial and unavoidable. Undetectable on-line dictionary attacks are sometimes troublesome, but not serious, especially for the server, as it is able to be handled by additional precautions such as the logging limitation. In password-based settings, off-line dictionary attacks are fatal so that a secure password-based protocol must be resistant to this type of attacks. Certainly, it is more ideal for a PAKE protocol to resist both off-line attacks and the undetectable on-line ones.

Related work. Since Bellovin and Merrit [8] initiated research in the PAKE direction, a great number of research [6, 7, 5, 9–11, 14–16, 18–21, 24, 13, 12, 17, 1] has settled on the design or security analysis of the PAKE protocols, from heuristic arguments initially to formal treatments recently. So far, two-party password-based authenticated key exchange (2-party PAKE or 2PAKE) protocols have been fully studied in the random oracle/standard models. But much fewer formal work dealt with 3-party PAKE protocols.

In 2005, Abdalla et al. [2] presented the first provably secure 3-party PAKE protocol, which is actually a generic construction and built by using three cryptographic primitives as building blocks: Diffie-Hellman key exchange, Message Authentication code and 3-Party Key Distribution. Subsequently, to pursue higher efficiencies in computations and in communications, Abdalla et al. [3] built a 4-round 3-party PAKE protocol, based on the 2-party protocol in [11, 19], and proved its security by introducing a series of new non-standard variations of the standard Diffie-Hellman assumptions. However, unfortunately, these new assumptions were shortly broken by Michael Szydlo [22]. Although it is still possible that the 4-round 3PAKE protocol enjoys desirable security properties, but the search for a security proof becomes an open problem.

Additionally, for defending the undetectable dictionary attacks in a three party setting, Wang and Hu [23] also proposed a new generic construction for 3-party PAKE protocols and proved it secure under the model of Abdalla et al. [2]. But the protocol does not make contribution for improving the protocol efficiency.

Our contribution. In this paper, we focus on the design of 4-round provably secure 3-Party PAKE protocols. To this end, we introduce a target driven formal way in building the 4-round 3PAKE protocol as follows: Firstly, we make definite the security target and the efficiency one of the final protocol. Next, aiming at these targets, we present a new generic construction for 3PAKE protocols, called NWPAKE-1, which enjoys perfect securities. Furthermore, for obtaining a 4-round communication, we carefully simplify the above generic construction so as to get an improved version, called NWPAKE-2, which still holds the target security. Finally, using NWPAKE-2 and some instantiation techniques, we present a secure 4-round 3-party PAKE protocol.

Actually, to clarify the efficiency and security targets is equal to achieve an optimal tradeoff between them in the design of the protocol. In the 4 rounds communication setting, it is unimaginable for 3-party PAKE protocols to achieve the mutual authentication security between clients and the server. For instance, the 4-round 3-party PAKE protocol of Abdalla et al. [3] does not provide any unilateral authentication, not to mention the mutual one. The target security of the protocol is only the semantic security of the session key. As shown in [23], it is obvious that the above 4-round protocol suffers from the undetectable online attacks on both the server and the client.

The 4-round 3-party PAKE protocol presented in this paper enjoys both the semantic security and the unilateral authentication security from the server to clients except the unilateral authentication security from clients to the server. As a result, the protocol is resistant to the off-line attacks and undetectable on-line attacks on the client, but still vulnerable to undetectable on-line attacks on the server. The partiality for clients is reasonable since in general network circumstances the configurations of client are always lightweight, without any additional security precaution, on the contrary the servers are usually well equipped, capable of detecting and defending various on-line attacks.

Different from the building block design methods in Abdalla et al. [2] and Wang and Hu [23], with which the protocol designers mainly consider the security aspects of 3PAKE protocols and finish their work by providing a provably secure 3PAKE scheme without much concern for the efficiency of 3PAKE protocols, the target driven method requires that the designers always pay attention to both the efficiency target and the security one in the block building stage as well as in the instantiation stage. The reason we still resort to the block building technology in building the 4-round protocol is to make the process of the security proof simpler and more intuitive, and to avoid the dependency on some green security assumptions as in [2].

2   Security Model of 3-party PAKE Protocols

The model described in this section derives from the Real-Or-Random (ROR) one introduced in [2], which is an extension of the work of [7, 5]. In the ROR model the *Reveal* query is no longer accessible while the *Test* query can be asked as many as the adversary wants. As a result, under the model we can take a 2PAKE protocol as a black box to facilitate the proof of the 3PAKE scheme.

Furthermore, to address the security against on-line dictionary attacks, we give the authentication security definition, which follows closely the one provided in [11], as a supplement for the model of 3PAKE protocols.

2.1   Communication Model

Protocol participants. There are two sets of the participants: $\mathcal{U}$, the set of client users and $\mathcal{S}$, the one of trusted servers. For simplicity, we assume that $\mathcal{S}$ involves a single trusted server as in [2]. The set $\mathcal{U}$ can be divided into two disjoint subsets: $\mathcal{C}$, the set of honest clients and $\mathcal{E}$, the one of malicious client users, which correspond to the inside attackers in the 3-party setting.

Long-lived keys. Let pw_U denote the password held by the user $U \in \mathcal{U}$. The trusted server $S \in \mathcal{S}$ stores a vector $pw_S = \langle pw_S[U] \rangle_{U \in \mathcal{U}}$, where $pw_S[U]$ is identical to pw_U itself or its transformation as defined in [5].

Protocol execution. In the model the adversary $\mathcal{A}$ fully dominates the communication circumstance and interacts with the protocol via oracle queries, which model its capabilities in a real attack. The oracle queries are as follows, where U^i (S^j, respectively) denotes the i-th (j-th, respectively) instance of a participant U (S, respectively):

1. $Execute(U_1^{i_1}, S^j, U_2^{i_2})$: This query models passive eavesdropping attacks, in which the adversary obtains a transcript of all messages generated during the honest execution of the protocol among the client instances $U_1^{i_1}$ and $U_2^{i_2}$ and the trusted server instance S^j.

2. $SendClient(U^i, m)$: This query models an active attack against clients, in which the adversary sends a message m to the client instance U^i and gets the response from it.

3. $SendServer(S^j, m)$: This query models an active attack against a server, in which the adversary sends a message m to the server instance S^j and gets the response from it.

4. $Reveal(U^i)$: This query outputs the session key held by the instance U^i, which is used to model the misuse of session keys. If no session key is defined, then return $\perp$.

5. $Test(U^i)$: If the client instance U^i has not accepted, then return $\perp$. If its intended partner is dishonest, then return the real session key. Otherwise, the query replies the real session key held by U^i if $b = 1$ or a random number of the same size if $b = 0$, where b is the hidden bit selected randomly prior to the first call.

2.2   Security Definitions

Notation. We say an instance U^i is *opened* if the query $Reveal(U^i)$ has been asked by the adversary. An instance U^i is said to be *unopened* if it is not *opened*. Upon receiving its last expected message from the execution of the protocol, the client instance U^i is said to be *accepted*.

Partnering. Using the notion of session identifications (*sid*) introduced in [5], we define that two instances U_1^i and U_2^j are partners if the following conditions are satisfied: (1) Both U_1^i and U_2^j are *accepted*; (2) The *sid* of U_1^i is equal to the one of U_2^j; (3) U_1^i and U_2^j are partner identifications each other; and (4)No client instance except U_1^i and U_2^j accepts with a partner identification is U_1^i or U_2^j.

Freshness. A user instance U^i is said to be *fresh* if both it and its partner are unopened and honest, and it has been *accepted*.

Semantic security in the ROR model. During the execution of the protocol, the adversary $\mathcal{A}$ can ask multiple queries to the *Execute*, *SendClient* and *SendServer* oracles. The *Test* oracle is allowed to query only one time for each *fresh* instance of an honest client while the *Reveal* one is not available any more. Let b' be the output of the adversary, which is its guess for the bit b hidden in the Test oracle. Let $Pr[Succ]$ denote the probability of the event that the adversary $\mathcal{A}$ successfully guess the hidden bit, that is, $b' = b$. We define the advantage of $\mathcal{A}$ in breaking the semantic security of the protocol P and the advantage function of the protocol P, respectively, as follows:

$$Adv_{P,\mathcal{D}}^{ror-ake}(\mathcal{A}) = 2 \cdot Pr[Succ] - 1,$$
$$Adv_{P,\mathcal{D}}^{ror-ake}(t, R) = \max_{\mathcal{A}}\{Adv_{P,\mathcal{D}}^{ror-ake}(\mathcal{A})\},$$

where passwords are drawn from a dictionary $\mathcal{D}$, the *maximum* is taken over all $\mathcal{A}$ with time-complexity at most t and employing resources at most R (including the number of oracle queries).

A 3-party PAKE protocol P is said to be semantically secure if for every polynomial time adversary $\mathcal{A}$,

$$Adv_{P,\mathcal{D}}^{ror-ake}(t, R) < \frac{k \cdot n}{|\mathcal{D}|} + negl(),$$

where n is number of active sessions and k is a constant and ideally equal to 1.

Authentication security. To measure the capability of a 3PAKE protocol to resist undetectable on-line dictionary attacks, in this paper we consider the authentication securities between clients and the server. Let $Succ_{P,\mathcal{D}}^{auth(C \to S)}(\mathcal{A})$ (or $Succ_{P,\mathcal{D}}^{auth(S \to C)}(\mathcal{A})$) denote the probability that an adversary $\mathcal{A}$ successfully impersonates a client (or the server) instance during executing the protocol P without being detected. Also let $Succ_{P,\mathcal{D}}^{auth(C \to S)}(t, R) = \max_{\mathcal{A}}\{Succ_{P,\mathcal{D}}^{auth(C \to S)}(\mathcal{A})\}$ (or $Succ_{P,\mathcal{D}}^{auth(S \to C)}(t, R) = \max_{\mathcal{A}}\{Succ_{P,\mathcal{D}}^{auth(S \to C)}(\mathcal{A})\}$) denote the maximum over all $\mathcal{A}$ running in time at most t and using resources at most R. A 3-party PAKE protocol P is said to be client-to-server (or server-to-client) authentication secure if $Succ_{P,\mathcal{D}}^{auth(C \to S)}(t, R)$ (or $Succ_{P,\mathcal{D}}^{auth(S \to C)}(t, R)$) is at most $O(k/|\mathcal{D}|)$. Finally, we define

$$Succ_{P,\mathcal{D}}^{auth(mutual)}(t, R) = Succ_{P,\mathcal{D}}^{auth(C \to S)}(t, R) + Succ_{P,\mathcal{D}}^{auth(S \to C)}(t, R).$$

3   Security Primitives

In this section, we introduce serval cryptographic primitives which play the role of the security foundation in our scheme. Let $\mathbb{G}$ be a cyclic group of prime order q and let g be an arbitrary generator of $\mathbb{G}$.

Decisional Diffie-Hellman assumption (DDH): Let us consider the following two distributions:

$$\mathcal{D}_{\mathbb{G}}^{ddh-real} = \{g^x, g^y, g^{xy} | x, y \in_R \mathbb{Z}_q\},$$
$$\mathcal{D}_{\mathbb{G}}^{ddh-rand} = \{g^x, g^y, g^z | x, y, z \in_R \mathbb{Z}_q\}.$$

Let Γ be a probabilistic polynomial time (PPT) algorithm for these two cases: On input a triple of $\mathbb{G}$, outputting 0 or 1. And let the advantage function $Adv_{\mathbb{G}}^{ddh}(t)$ be the maximum value, over all probabilistic polynomial algorithms Γ running in time at most t, of:

$$|Pr[\Gamma(\mathcal{D}_{\mathbb{G}}^{ddh-real}) = 1] - Pr[\Gamma(\mathcal{D}_{\mathbb{G}}^{ddh-rand}) = 1)]|.$$

We say that the DDH assumption holds in $\mathbb{G}$ if $Adv_{\mathbb{G}}^{ddh}(t)$ is a negligible function of t.

Generalized Decisional Diffie-Hellman assumption (GDDH) [4]: Generalized Decisional Diffie-Hellman assumption can be taken regard as an extension of the DDH assumption. Similarly, let us consider two distributions:

$$\mathcal{D}_{\mathbb{G}}^{gddh-real} = \{g_1, g_2..., g_k, g_1{}^r, g_2{}^r..., g_k{}^r | g_1, ..., g_k \in_R \mathbb{G}, r \in_R \mathbb{Z}_q\},$$
$$\mathcal{D}_{\mathbb{G}}^{gddh-rand} = \{g_1, g_2..., g_k, u_1, u_2..., u_k, | g_1, ..., g_k, u_1, ..., u_k \in_R \mathbb{G}\}.$$

Γ is assumed to be a probabilistic polynomial distinguisher for these two cases: On input a k-tuple of $\mathbb{G}$, outputting 0 or 1, so that the advantage function $Adv_{\mathbb{G}}^{gddh}(t)$ is defined as the maximum value, over all probabilistic polynomial algorithms Γ running in time at most t, of:

$$|Pr[\Gamma(\mathcal{D}_{\mathbb{G}}^{gddh-real}) = 1] - Pr[\Gamma(\mathcal{D}_{\mathbb{G}}^{gddh-rand}) = 1)]|.$$

We say that the GDDH assumption holds in $\mathbb{G}$ if $Adv_{\mathbb{G}}^{gddh}(t)$ is a negligible function of t.

In the following, we consider the relationship between the DDH assumption and the GDDH one with $k = 3$. For simplicity, we define $GDDH_2$ and $GDDH_3$ problems as the $GDDH$ ones with $k = 2$ and $k = 3$, respectively. Let Γ be a probabilistic polynomial distinguisher for the $GDDH_k$. And let the advantage function $Adv_{\mathbb{G}}^{gddh_k}(t)$ be the maximum value, over all probabilistic polynomial algorithms Γ running in time at most t.

Lemma 1. *The $GDDH_2$ problem is equivalent to the $GDDH_3$ one for any prime order group $\mathbb{G}$ and any time complexity t, where*

Proof. The main idea of proving this lemma is to show that the existence of a PPT algorithm breaking $GDDH_2$ will lead the generation of another PPT algorithm to break $GDDH_3$, and visa versa. For more details, one can refer to [4]. □

Lemma 2. *The $GDDH_2$ assumption is equivalent to or weaker than the DDH assumption, that is,*

$$Adv_{\mathbb{G}}^{gddh_2}(t) \leq Adv_{\mathbb{G}}^{ddh}(t)$$

Proof. Let us assume that Γ_{gddh_2} is a distinguisher of the $GDHH_2$. We show that a distinguisher Γ_{ddh} against the DDH is able to be built by calling Γ_{gddh_2} as a subroutine. We denote the output of Γ_{gddh_2} as follows: If the input comes from $\mathcal{D}_{\mathbb{G}}^{gddh-real}$, it outputs 1 and 0 if the input tuple comes from $\mathcal{D}_{\mathbb{G}}^{gddh-rand}$. Therefore, we have

$$Pr[\Gamma_{ddh}(g^x, g^y, g^z) = 1|x, y \in_R \mathbb{G}, z = xy]$$
$$= Pr[\Gamma_{gddh_2}(g, g^x, g^y, g^z) = 1|x, y, \in_R \mathbb{G}, z = xy]$$
$$= Pr[\Gamma_{gddh_2}(g_1, g_2, u_1, u_2) = 1|g_1, g_2, u_1, u_2 \in_R \mathbb{G}]$$

And

$$Pr[\Gamma_{ddh}(g^x, g^y, g^z) = 0|x, y, z \in_R \mathbb{G}]$$
$$= Pr[\Gamma_{gddh_2}(g, g^x, g^y, g^z) = 0|x, y, z \in_R \mathbb{G}]$$
$$= Pr[\Gamma_{gddh_2}(g_1, g_2, g_1^r, g_2^r) = 0|g_1, g_2 \in_R \mathbb{G}, r \in R].$$

□

As for the further discussion on the GDDH assumption, one can refer to [4] for more details.

Message authentication codes (MAC). A message authentication code MAC = (Tag; Ver) can be addressed by the following algorithms:

- A MAC generation algorithm Tag, possibly probabilistic, which outputs a tag μ upon receiving a message m and a secret key sk.
- A MAC verification algorithm Ver, which takes a tag μ, a message m, and a secret key sk as the parameters, and outputs 1 if μ is a valid tag for m under sk or 0 otherwise.

We say that a MAC scheme is existential unforgeability under chosen-message attacks (euf-cma) [2] if the adversary is not able to produce a new valid message-tag pair from existing valid message-tag pairs. More specifically, let l be a security parameter and sk be a secret key selected uniformly at random from $\{0,1\}^l$. Assume an adversary $\mathcal{A}$ is allowed to access the MAC generation oracle $\text{Tag}(sk; \cdot)$ and the MAC verification oracle $\text{Ver}(sk; \cdot, \cdot)$ and outputs a message-tag pair $(m; \mu)$. Let $Adv^{euf-cma}(\mathcal{A})$ denote the probability of the event that $\mathcal{A}$ generates a legal message-tag pair which was not outputted by the $\text{Tag}(sk; \cdot)$ oracle on input m. We define $Adv_{MAC}^{euf-cma}(t, q_g, q_v)$ as the maximal value of $Adv^{euf-cma}(\mathcal{A})$ over all $\mathcal{A}$ with at most t in time and q_g and q_v queries to its MAC generation and verification oracles, respectively.

4 General Construction of 3-party PAKE Protocols

In this section, we present a new generic construction (referred to as NWPAKE-1) for 3-party PAKE protocols, which is a form of compiler transforming any secure 2-party PAKE protocol into a secure 3-party PAKE protocol. NWPAKE-1 consists of two components: a 2-party password-based key exchange and a 3-party MAC-based key exchange protocol. As a generic construction, using the secure building blocks aforementioned, it is able to enjoy the perfect securities: the semantic security and the mutual authentication security. Compared with the one provided by Abdalla et al. [2], the new construction does not have advantages in the communication round and the computation. Moreover, it is essentially an extension of the general construction proposed by Wang and Hu [23]. However, the price of its existence is to benefit the latter simplification and the design of a secure 4-round 3PAKE protocol.

4.1 Scheme Description

Let us assume that the participators are users A and B who in advance shares a passwords pw_A and pw_B with a trusted server S, respectively, and attempt to establish a secure session key with the help of the server. Roughly, NWPAKE-1 can be divided into two phases: the 2PAKE phase and the authenticated key exchange phase. In the former phase, the users A and B build two secure high-entropy session key sk_A and sk_B with the trusted server S, respectively, by using any semantic secure 2-party PAKE protocol. In the latter phase, with the session keys as the MAC key, A and B can concurrently authenticate and send their respective temporary Diffie-Hellman public keys (i.e., session key seeds) to the server S. Upon receiving and confirming the temporary public keys from the clients A and B, the server S applies modular exponentiations on the temporary public keys of A and B by using its own nonce s, respectively. Next, still using the secure MAC scheme, the server authenticates and transfers the results to B and A, respectively. In this manner, A and B finally finish establishing a session key (its value is equal to $g^{r_1 r_2 s}$) in an authenticated way. The protocol is also shown in Fig. 1 .

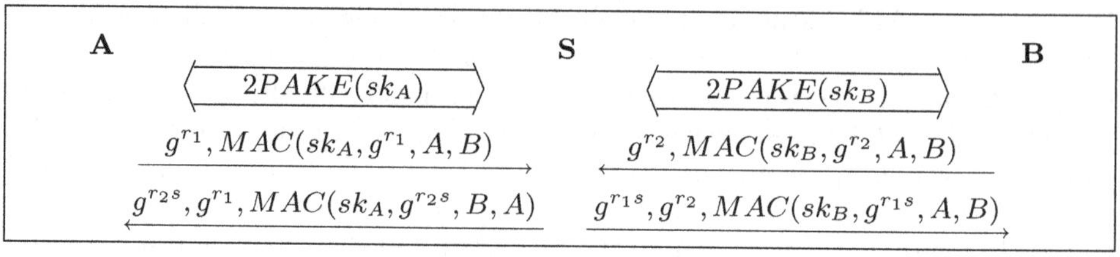

$$
\begin{array}{ccc}
\mathbf{A} & \mathbf{S} & \mathbf{B} \\
\end{array}
$$

Fig. 1. NWPAKE-1: A New generic construction for 3PAKE protocols

4.2   Security of Our Construction

We prove that NWPAKE-1 satisfies the semantic security and the mutual authentication security as long as the Decisional Diffie-Hellman assumption holds in $\mathbb{G}$ and the secure MAC tag exists.

Theorem 1. *Let 2PAKE be a semantic secure 2-party PAKE protocol and MAC be a secure MAC algorithm. Let q_{exe} and q_{test} denote the numbers of queries to Execute and Test oracles, and q_{send}^A, q_{send}^B, and q_{ake} be the numbers of queries to the SendClient and SendServer oracles with respect to each of the two 2PAKE protocols and the final two authenticated key exchange protocols. Then,*

$$
\begin{aligned}
Adv_{NWPAKE-1,\mathcal{D}}^{ror-ake}&(t, q_{exe}, q_{test}, q_{send}^A, q_{send}^B, q_{ake}) \leq \\
& 4 \cdot Adv_{2PAKE,\mathcal{D}}^{ror-ake}(t, q_{exe}, q_{exe} + q_{send}^A, q_{send}^A) \\
& + 4 \cdot Adv_{2PAKE,\mathcal{D}}^{ror-ake}(t, q_{exe}, q_{exe} + q_{send}^B, q_{send}^B) \\
& + 2 \cdot q_{ake} \cdot Adv_{MAC}^{euf-cma}(t, 2, 1) \\
& + 4 \cdot Adv_{\mathbb{G}}^{ddh}(t + 10(q_{exe} + q_{ake})\tau_{\mathbb{G}})
\end{aligned}
$$

and

$$
\begin{aligned}
Succ_{NWPAKE-1,\mathcal{D}}^{auth(mutual)}&(t, q_{exe}, q_{test}, q_{send}^A, q_{send}^B, q_{ake}) \leq \\
& 2Adv_{2PAKE,\mathcal{D}}^{ror-ake}(t, q_{exe}, q_{exe} + q_{send}^A, q_{send}^A) \\
& + 2Adv_{2PAKE,\mathcal{D}}^{ror-ake}(t, q_{exe}, q_{exe} + q_{send}^B, q_{send}^B) \\
& + q_{ake} \cdot Adv_{MAC}^{euf-cma}(t, 2, 1),
\end{aligned}
$$

where $\tau_{\mathbb{G}}$ denotes the exponentiation computational time in $\mathbb{G}$.

Proof. In the following, we partly inherit the proof technique of the reference [2]. For example, we still assume that the set of honest users involves only users A and B, which can be easily extended to the multiple-party case. Also assume that the adversary $\mathcal{A}$ attacks the protocol under the Real-Or-Random model. Let t be the upper bound of the $\mathcal{A}$'s running time-complexity, q_{exe} be the upper bound of the times of *Execute* queries, q_{test} be the one of *Test* query, q_{send}^A

be the one of queries to *SendClient* and *SendServer* oracles corresponding to the 2PAKE protocol between A and the trusted server S, q_{send}^B be the one of queries to the oracles corresponding to the protocol between B and S, q_{ake}^{AS} be the one of queries to *SendClient* and *SendServer* oracles corresponding to the authenticated key exchange (AKE) protocol between A and S, and q_{ake}^{BS} be the one of queries to the oracles corresponding to the protocol between B and S. We incrementally define a sequence of games starting at the real game G_0 and ending up at the game G_7 in which the advantage of the adversary is zero. Let $Succ_i$ denote the event that $\mathcal{A}$ succeeds in guessing the hidden bit b in game G_i.

Furthermore, we assume that when the game below aborts or stops with no answer for b hidden in the *Test* oracles from $\mathcal{A}$, we guess a random bit for b, in which the success probability of the adversary is straightforwardly $1/2$.

Game G_0: This game corresponds to the real attack environment, in which all communications are performed by oracle queries. By definition, we have

$$Adv_{NGPAKE,\mathcal{D}}^{ror-ake}(\mathcal{A}) = 2 \cdot Pr[Succ_0] - 1. \tag{1}$$

Game G_1: In this game, we use a random string sk_A', instead of the real session key sk_A, as the MAC key in the simulation of queries to the SendServer oracles. As the following lemma shows, the difference between the current and previous game is at most twice advantage of breaking the underlying 2PAKE protocol between A and S.

Lemma 3. $|Pr[Succ_1] - Pr[Succ_0]| < 2 \cdot Adv_{2PAKE,\mathcal{D}}^{ror-ake}(t, q_{exe}, q_{exe} + q_{send}^A, q_{send}^A)$.

Proof. Below, we show the existence of a distinguisher $\mathcal{A}_1$ for the event $Succ$ in G_0 and G_1 will grant an adversary $\mathcal{A}_{2PAKE}$ the power to break a provably secure 2PAKE protocol.

- Initializing. $\mathcal{A}_{2PAKE}$ initializes the simulation environment by choosing a bit b randomly, generating passwords uniformly from $\mathcal{D}$ for all clients in the system except the user A and providing $\mathcal{A}_1$ with passwords of all the malicious users. And then, it starts $\mathcal{A}_1$, in reply to its oracle quries.
- Answering Queries. For the queries *SendServer* or *SendClient* not involving the user A, $\mathcal{A}_{2PAKE}$ does respondence by using its holding passwords. For those queries corresponding to an instance of 2PAKE protocol between A and S, $\mathcal{A}_{2PAKE}$ can answer it by querying its own *Send* oracles. Once a *Send* query triggers the acceptance of a fresh instance of client A or S, $\mathcal{A}_{2PAKE}$ sends a *Test* query to the corresponding instance and returns the result as the session key shared between A and S. For the *Test* query by $\mathcal{A}_1$, $\mathcal{A}_{2PAKE}$ returns the real session key if b=1 or a random string, otherwise. As for the *Execute* query, since it can be simulated by *SendClient* and *SendServer*, we can easily deal with it as above.
- Output. Let b' be the output of $\mathcal{A}_1$. $\mathcal{A}_{2PAKE}$ outputs 1 if $b' = b$, otherwise 0.

The above simulation indicates that the probability that $\mathcal{A}_1$ succeeds in G_0 is exactly the probability that $\mathcal{A}_{2PAKE}$ outputs 1 when its *Test* oracles returns the real session key. Similarly, the probability of $\mathcal{A}_1$'s succeeding in G_1 is exactly the one that $\mathcal{A}_{2PAKE}$ outputs 1 when the corresponding answer is a random string. Hence, we have

$$Pr(Output(\mathcal{A}_{2PAKE}) = 1 | Its\ Test\ oracle\ returns\ real\ session\ key)$$
$$= Pr(\mathcal{A}_1 succeeds | sk_A\ works\ as\ MAC\ key)$$
$$= Pr(\mathcal{A}_1 succeeds | in\ Game\ G_0)$$
$$= Pr(Succ_0)$$

and

$$Pr(Output(\mathcal{A}_{2PAKE}) = 1 | Its\ Test\ oracle\ returns\ random\ string)$$
$$= Pr(\mathcal{A}_1 succeeds | sk'_A\ works\ as\ MAC\ key)$$
$$= Pr(\mathcal{A}_1 succeeds | in\ Game\ G_1)$$
$$= Pr(Succ_1).$$

As a result, the lemma follows easily with the following inequation

$$Adv_{2PAKE,\mathcal{D}}^{ror-ake}(t, q_{exe}, q_{exe} + q_{send}^A, q_{send}^A)$$
$$\geq |\frac{1}{2} \cdot Pr(Output(\mathcal{A}_{2PAKE}) = 1 | Its\ Test\ oracle\ returns\ real\ session\ key) -$$
$$\frac{1}{2} \cdot Pr(Output(\mathcal{A}_{2PAKE}) = 1 | Its\ Test\ oracle\ returns\ random\ string)|,$$

where $\mathcal{A}_{2PAKE}$ runs at most time-complexity t and sends at most $q_{exe} + q_{send}^A$ queries to its $Test$ oracle, at most q_{exe} queries to its Execute oracle, and at most q_{send}^A queries to its $Send$ oracle.   □

Game G_2: Similarly, we modify this game by using a random string sk'_B as the MAC key in all of the sessions between B and S, instead of the real session key sk_B between B and S. By the same arguments, we can prove the following lemma.

Lemma 4. $|Pr[Succ_2] - Pr[Succ_1]| < 2 \cdot Adv_{2PAKE,\mathcal{D}}^{ror-ake}(t, q_{exe}, q_{exe} + q_{send}^B, q_{send}^B).$
                                                                              □

Game G_3: In this game, once a query includes a legal message-tag occurs in the authentication between A and S, which is not previously generated by the simulated oracle, we set it be invalid and abort the game. Since the MAC scheme adopted in the construction is secure, the following lemma shows that the difference of the success probabilities between in the current game and in the previous is negligible.

Lemma 5. $|Pr[Succ_3] - Pr[Succ_2]| \leq q_{ake}^{AS} \cdot Adv_{MAC}^{euf-cma}(t, 2, 1).$

Proof. To prove the lemma, we employ the so-called "hybrid arguments" technique, in which the total number of hybrids is q_{ake}^{AS}. In each hybrid E_i ($0 \leq i \leq q_{ake}^{AS}$), the $Send$ queries in the first i authentications between A and S are answered as in game G_3 and the remaining ones are treated as in game G_2.

Let $\mathcal{A}_3^i$ be a distinguisher for hybrids E_i and E_{i-1}. By using it, we can build an adversary $\mathcal{A}_{mac}^i$ against the security of the MAC scheme. Let F_i be the event that in the ith authentication process between A and S a legal message-tag pair is not generated by the oracle, which leads the game termination in hybrid E_{i-1} but does not in hybrid E_i. With the time upper bound t, at most two queries to the MAC generation and one queries to the verification oracle, the probability that $\mathcal{A}_{mac}^i$ forges a message-tag pair is at most $Adv_{MAC}^{euf-cma}(t, 2, 1)$. Since the success probabilities of $\mathcal{A}_3^i$ in hybrids E_i and in E_{i-1} are same if F does not occur (i.e. $Pr[Succ_{E_i} \wedge \neg F] = Pr[Succ_{E_{i-1}} \wedge \neg F]$), we can easily obtain $|Pr[Succ_{E_i}] - Pr[Succ_{E_{i-1}}]| \leq Adv_{MAC}^{euf-cma}(t, 2, 1)$. The lemma follows with at most q_{ake}^{AS} hybrids. $\square$

Game G_4: The modification of the *SendClient* or *SendServer* queries in the authentications between B and S are similar as in the previous game. Hence, we can get the following lemma.

Lemma 6. $|Pr[Succ_4] - Pr[Succ_3]| \leq q_{ake}^{BS} \cdot Adv_{MAC}^{euf-cma}(t, 2, 1).$ $\square$

Notice that the proof on the authentication security in Theorem 1 is finished by combining the previous lemmas.

Game G_5: To simplify the following reduction from the protocol to DDH assumption, we change the *Send* oracles by using a random DDH triple $(X; Y; Z)$, where $X = g^x$, $Y = g^y$, and $Z = g^{xy}$.

For the *SendClient*$(A^i, *)$ query during the authentication phase, our simulator computes $X_0 = X^{a_0} g^{x_0}$ by choosing two random values x_0 and a_0 in Z_p, returns X_0 and stores the quintuple $(a_0, x_0, X_0, \Delta, id)$ in a list Λ_A, where Δ, a placeholder, says that the item is empty, and id is identifer used for distinguishing each protocol instance, which is generated according to the MAC key. For the corresponding *SendClient*$(B^j, *)$, it selects b_0 and y_0, computes Y_0 and stores them in a list Λ_B in the same measure. When the following *SendServer*$(S^K, X_0, *)$ query from A^i arrives, the simulator validates its legitimacy and then seeks for X_0 in the list Λ_A. If successful, our simulator checks the fourth item of the quintuple whether assigned or not. If not, it randomly generates a value s in Z_p, and answers the query by returning $(X_0)^s$. As for the corresponding *SendServer*$(S^K, Y_0, *)$ query from B^j, our simulator similarly seeks Y_0 in Λ_A, obtains the value s from the corresponding quintuple in Λ_A and then returns $(Y_0)^s$. Once the acceptation of a protocol instance was triggered by a *Send* query, the simulator locates X_0 and Y_0 in the lists, Λ_A and Λ_B, respectively. If both of them exist, it computes $Z_0 = (Z^{a_0 b_0} \times Y^{x_0 b_0} \times X^{a_0 y_0} \times g^{x_0 y_0})^s$ for answering the *Test* query. Otherwise, the instance halts without accepting. The remaining simulations are same as the previous game.

Since MAC forgeries have been excluded in the previous game, the simulator is always able to answer the *Test* query to a fresh instance by using the precomputed Z_0. The difference between G_4 and G_5 exists in the choice way of random variables. But the distributions of the random variables in the two games are identical. As a result, this game is equivalent to the previous one and we have $Pr[Succ_4] = Pr[Succ_5]$.

Game G_6: We modify the game by replacing the DDH triple with a random triple $(g^x; g^y; g^z)$ in the simulation of the authentication phase. As the following lemma shows, the two games, G_5 and G_6, are indistinguishable if the DDH assumption holds in $\mathbb{G}$.

Lemma 7. $|Pr[Succ_6] - Pr[Succ_5] \leq Adv_{\mathbb{G}}^{ddh}(t + 10(q_{exe} + q_{ake})\tau_{\mathbb{G}}).$

Proof. This is a classic reduction from the DDH assumption to the gap between before and after the two games. Let us assume $\mathcal{A}_6$ is a distinguisher for G_5 and G_6. Using it, we are able to build an adversary $\mathcal{A}^{ddh}$ against the DDH problem in $\mathbb{G}$.

Firstly, with a triple $(X; Y; Z)$ as the input, $\mathcal{A}^{ddh}$ randomly selects a bit b and generates the passwords for all users in the system according to the distribution of $\mathcal{D}$, and then starts running $\mathcal{A}_6$. Next, by using the secrets generated randomly and the input triple, $\mathcal{A}^{ddh}$ simulates the oracles of $\mathcal{A}_6$ to answer its *SendClient*, *SendServer*, and *Test* queries. Finally, $\mathcal{A}_6$ outputs its guess bit b' after a certain number of the *Test* queries. If its guess is correct (i.e. $b' = b$), then $\mathcal{A}^{ddh}$ returns 1 or 0, otherwise. Therefore, one can easily see that $\mathcal{A}$ just runs in game G_5 if the triple $(X; Y; Z)$ is a DDH triple, but in game G_6 if it is a random one. As a result, $Pr[Succ_5]$ is the probability that $\mathcal{A}^{ddh}$ outputs 1 in G_5, but $Pr[Succ_6]$ is the one that $\mathcal{A}^{ddh}$ does in G_6. The lemma follows from the fact that $\mathcal{A}^{ddh}$ has time-complexity at most $t + 10(q_{exe} + q_{ake})\tau_{\mathbb{G}}$, where $10(q_{exe} + q_{ake})\tau_{\mathbb{G}}$ is the additional time for the reducibility. □

Game G_7: In this game, we use three random numbers s_1, s_2 and s_3, instead of one value s, as the nonce of the server to accomplish the key exchange. In other words, a set of random variables $(X_0, Y_0, Z_0, X_0^s, Y_0^s, Z_0^s)$ are substituted by $(X_0, Y_0, Z_0, X_0^{s_1}, Y_0^{s_2}, Z_0^{s_3})$ to answer the oracle queries in G_7. As the following lemma shows, the game is indistinguishable from the previous game if the GDDH assumption holds in $\mathbb{G}$.

Lemma 8. $|Pr[Succ_7] - pr[Succ_6] \leq Adv_{\mathbb{G}}^{ddh}(t + 10(q_{exe} + q_{ake})\tau_{\mathbb{G}}).$

Proof. Similar as the proof in the game G_6, let $\mathcal{A}_7$ be a distinguisher for G_5 and G_6. By running it, the adversary $\mathcal{A}^{gddh_3}$ breaks the $GDDH_3$ problem in $\mathbb{G}$.

On the input $(g_1, g_2, g_3, u_1, u_2, u_3)$, the adversary $\mathcal{A}^{gddh_3}$ selects a bit b at random and initializes the simulation environment by producing the passwords for all users. Next, it runs $\mathcal{A}_7$, answering *Execute, SendClient*, *SendServer*, and *Test* queries from the distinguisher. Concretely, in the simulation of the authentication phase of each protocol instance, g_1, g_2, u_1, u_2 and u_3 are used as X_0, Y_0, X_0^s, Y_0^s and the session key, respectively. Finally, $\mathcal{A}_7$ outputs the guess bit b' after finishing the attacks. If its guess is correct (i.e. $b' = b$), then $\mathcal{A}^{gddh_3}$ returns 1, or 0 otherwise. Therefore, one can easily see that $\mathcal{A}$ just runs in game G_6 if the $(g_1, g_2, g_3, u_1, u_2, u_3)$ is a $GDDH_3$ tuple, but in game G_7 if it is a random one. As a result, $Pr[Succ_6]$ is the probability that $\mathcal{A}^{gddh_3}$ outputs 1 in G_6, but $Pr[Succ_7]$ is the one that $\mathcal{A}^{gddh_3}$ does in G_7. Combining with the result of the lemma 1 and 2 on the relation between DDH and $GDDH_3$, we prove the lemma by the fact that $\mathcal{A}^{ddh}$ has time-complexity at most $t + 10(q_{exe} + q_{ake})\tau_{\mathbb{G}}$, where $10(q_{exe} + q_{ake})\tau_{\mathbb{G}}$ is the additional time for the reducibility.   □

So far, all knowledge captured by the adversary in the active manner or the passive one have nothing with the final session key. This means that no information on the hidden bit b is leaked to the adversary, i.e. $Pr[Succ_7] = 1/2$. Consequently, the result on the semantic security in Theorem 1 is proved by joining with all the previous lemmas.   □

5   Simplification and Instantiation

The advantage of building protocols by using a generic construction method is to simplify both the forming process and the security proof of the protocol. According to the construction law, step by step, using specific 2-party PAKE protocols and MAC schemes, one can easily get a provably secure 3-party PAKE protocol. But the number of the communication rounds of the resulting protocol is at least 8. Therefore, for building a 4-round provably secure 3-party PAKE protocol, we simplify the generic construction NWPAKE-1 and utilize some instantiation techniques to achieve a optimal trade-off between the efficiency and the security.

Let us consider the message from clients to the server in the authentication key exchange phase of NWPAKE-1. It consists of a session key seed (g^{r_1} or g^{r_2}) of the key exchange and a MAC tag which is used to authenticate the maker of the seed. This structure of the message results in that the whole authentication key exchange phase must begin after the two party session keys have been generated by the 2PAKE protocol between each client and the server. To eliminate the above limitation, we adopt an alternative way that in the authenticated key exchange phase the session key seed is sent first and is authenticated later. The modified generic construction, named NWPAKE-2, is shown in Fig. 2.

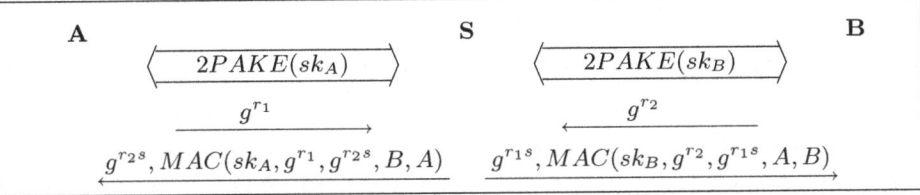

Fig. 2. NWPAKE-2: The modified generic construction for 3PAKE protocols

Using the improved generic construction NWPAKE-2, one is able to reduce the communication rounds of the result protocol. It is since without the MAC tag, the session key seeds provided by clients are random and independent of the message produced in the 2PAKE phase so that they can be delivered together with the message of 2PAKE, which causes that the communication rounds for transmitting session key seeds in the authenticated key exchange phase can be removed. Certainly, there is no free lunch in this world. The result protocol will lose the authentication security from clients to the server since the MAC tags from clients to the server are omitted in the simplification. But the protocol still holds the crucial securities of the 3-party setting: the semantic security and the authentication security from the server to clients, which is presented in Theorem 2. Actually, if a server is able to operate stably in an open network circumstance, additional security precautions are absolutely necessary, which protects it from various on-line attacks, such as illegal access and excessive links. In this case, the loss of the authentication from clients to server security is no big deal.

Theorem 2. *Let 2PAKE be a semantic secure 2-party PAKE protocol and MAC be a secure MAC algorithm. Let q_{exe} and q_{test} denote the numbers of queries to Execute and Test oracles, and q_{send}^A, q_{send}^B, and q_{ake} be the numbers of queries to the SendClient and SendServer oracles with respect to each of the two 2PAKE protocols and the final two authenticated key exchange protocols. Then,*

$$Adv_{NWPAKE-2,\mathcal{D}}^{ror-ake}(t, q_{exe}, q_{test}, q_{send}^A, q_{send}^B, q_{ake}) \leq$$
$$4 \cdot Adv_{2PAKE,\mathcal{D}}^{ror-ake}(t, q_{exe}, q_{exe} + q_{send}^A, q_{send}^A)$$
$$+ 4 \cdot Adv_{2PAKE,\mathcal{D}}^{ror-ake}(t, q_{exe}, q_{exe} + q_{send}^B, q_{send}^B)$$
$$+ 2 \cdot q_{ake} \cdot Adv_{MAC}^{euf-cma}(t, 1, 1)$$
$$+ 4 \cdot Adv_{\mathbb{G}}^{ddh}(t + 10(q_{exe} + q_{ake})\tau_{\mathbb{G}}),$$

and

$$Succ_{NWPAKE-2,\mathcal{D}}^{auth(S\rightarrow C)}(t, q_{exe}, q_{test}, q_{send}^A, q_{send}^B, q_{ake}) \leq$$
$$2Adv_{2PAKE,\mathcal{D}}^{ror-ake}(t, q_{exe}, q_{exe} + q_{send}^A, q_{send}^A)$$
$$+ 2Adv_{2PAKE,\mathcal{D}}^{ror-ake}(t, q_{exe}, q_{exe} + q_{send}^B, q_{send}^B)$$
$$+ q_{ake} \cdot Adv_{MAC}^{euf-cma}(t, 1, 1),$$

where $\tau_{\mathbb{G}}$ denotes the exponentiation computational time in $\mathbb{G}$.

Proof. The proof of this theorem is very similar as the one of Theorem 1. The only difference exists in the game G_3 and G_4, where simulator identify the session key seeds from the clients by using the MAC tag answered by the server. As the length limits, we do not repeatedly present the homologous specifications.   □

Additionally, the securities of both our generic constructions have no requirement on the random oracle model. Both of them can be easily instantiated in the standard model. For instance, by using a semantically secure 2-party PAKE protocol such as KOY protocol [16], it is easy to build a secure 3-party PAKE protocol in the standard model. Also, one is able to use any 2-party PAKE scheme with the semantic security in the random oracle model to get a secure 3PAKE protocol in the random oracle model. In the following, we present a secure 4-round

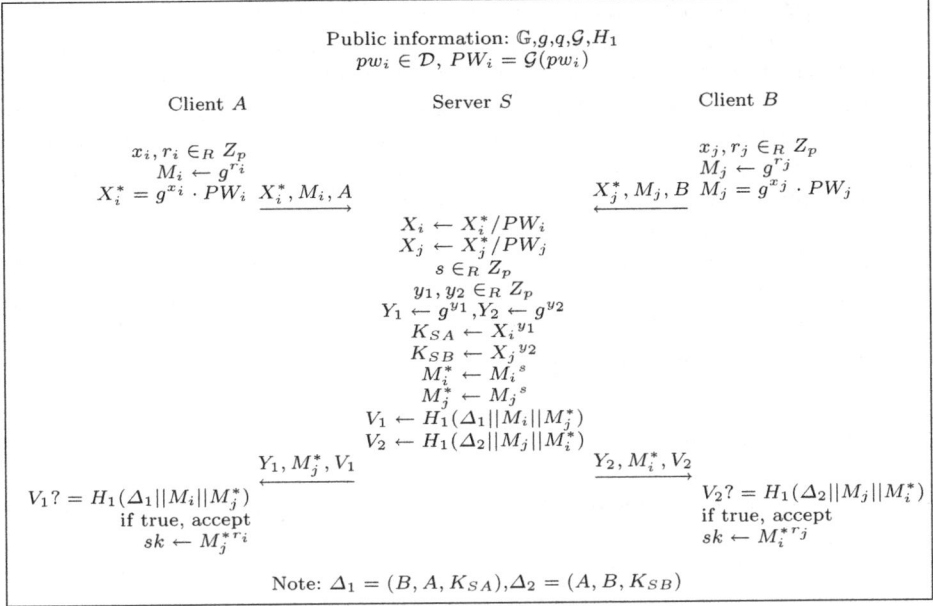

Fig. 3. A provably secure 4-round 3PAKE protocol instantiated from the NWPAKE-2

3PAKE protocol, which is essentially an instantiation of NWPAKE-2 by using the OMDHKE protocol [11] as the 2PAKE components.

According to the NWPAKE-2 structure, one puts the OMDHKE protocol on each 2PAKE position and then put forward some measures to further simplify the result 3PAKE scheme. As we all known, the random oracle assumption is stronger than the existential unforgeability MAC one. Therefore, in the instantiating process one substitutes the Hash functions (i.e, random oracles) for all the MAC schemes, which keeps the result protocol as the same security as the original scheme NWPAKE-2 in the random oracle model. Furthermore, to refine the result protocol during the instantiation, one combines two hash functions in the message from the server to each client into a single one (i.e., combine two authenticators into a single one). Since the inputs of the two hash functions are independent, this change do no harm to the security of the result protocol. Finally, as shown in Fig. 3, one obtains a 4-round 3-party PAKE protocol which is provably secure in the random oracle model as the security of the OMDHKE protocol is proved in the same model.

6 Conclusion

In this paper, we present two generic constructions for the 3PAKE protocol, and prove their securities in the standard model. By using the second construction NWPAKE-2, we instantiate a provably secure 3-party PAKE protocol which only has 4 rounds in communications. If we apply other generic construction such as GPAKE [2] or NGPAKE [23] to build a 3PAKE protocol, the result protocol has at least 8 rounds in communication[1]. On the other hand, compared with the efficient 3PAKE protocol presented by Abdalla *et.al.* [3], our result protocol has the same number of rounds in communication, but has 6 more times modular exponentiations, where 2 times modular exponentiations in clients can be pre-computed. It is obvious that the above scheme of Abdalla *et.al.* enjoys higher computation efficiency, but it is not provably secure since its security assumption has been broken. In contrast, the securities of our 4-round 3PAKE protocol directly inherits the ones of NWPAKE-2, and only relies on the standard security primitives. To the best of our knowledge, our scheme is the only 4-round 3PAKE protocol holding the provable security.

Acknowledgement

We would like to thank the anonymous referees for their invaluable suggestions. The work of the first and third authors is partially supported by the 863 Program of China under grant No. 2009AA01Z423 and the Fundamental Research Fund for the Central Universities under Grant 2009JBM101, 2009JBM004. The second author is supported by the NSFC under grant No. 60773134,10990011 and the 973 Program of China under grant No. 2007CB311201.

References

1. Abdalla, M., Bohli, J.-M., González Vasco, M.I., Steinwandt, R. (Password) authenticated key establishment: From 2-party to group. In: Vadhan, S.P. (ed.) TCC 2007. LNCS, vol. 4392, pp. 499–514. Springer, Heidelberg (2007)
2. Abdalla, M., Fouque, P.-A., Pointcheval, D.: Password-based authenticated key exchange in the three-party setting. In: Vaudenay, S. (ed.) PKC 2005. LNCS, vol. 3386, pp. 65–84. Springer, Heidelberg (2005)
3. Abdalla, M., Pointcheval, D.: Interactive diffie-hellman assumptions with applications to password-based authentication. In: Patrick, A.S., Yung, M. (eds.) FC 2005. LNCS, vol. 3570, pp. 341–356. Springer, Heidelberg (2005)
4. Bao, F., Deng, H.R., Zhu, H.F.: Efficient and provably secure generic construction of three-party password-based authenticated key exchange protocols. In: Qing, S., Gollmann, D., Zhou, J. (eds.) ICICS 2003. LNCS, vol. 2836, pp. 301–312. Springer, Heidelberg (2003)
5. Bellare, M., Pointcheval, D., Rogaway, P.: Authenticated key exchange secure against dictionary attacks. In: Preneel, B. (ed.) EUROCRYPT 2000. LNCS, vol. 1807, pp. 139–155. Springer, Heidelberg (2000)
6. Bellare, M., Rogaway, P.: Entity authentication and key distribution. In: Stinson, D.R. (ed.) CRYPTO 1993. LNCS, vol. 773, pp. 232–249. Springer, Heidelberg (1994)

---

[1] Each of the known provably secure 2-party PAKE protocol has at least 2 rounds in communications and the total number of rounds for key distribution and the authentication key exchange is at least 4.

7. Bellare, M., Rogaway, P.: Provably secure session key distribution: the three party case. In: STOC 1995, pp. 57–66. ACM, New York (1995)
8. Bellovin, S.M., Merritt, M.: Encrypted key exchange: Password-based protocols secure against dictionary attacks. In: Proceedings of the 1992 IEEE Symposium on Security and Privacy, pp. 72–84. IEEE Computer Society Press, Los Alamitos (1992)
9. Boyko, V., MacKenzie, P.D., Patel, S.: Provably secure password-authenticated key exchange using diffie-hellman. In: Preneel, B. (ed.) EUROCRYPT 2000. LNCS, vol. 1807, pp. 156–171. Springer, Heidelberg (2000)
10. Bresson, E., Chevassut, O., Pointcheval, D.: Security proofs for an efficient password-based key exchange. In: Jajodia, S., Atluri, V., Jaeger, T. (eds.) CCS 2003, pp. 241–250. ACM, New York (2003)
11. Bresson, E., Chevassut, O., Pointcheval, D.: New security results on encrypted key exchange. In: Bao, F., Deng, R.H., Zhou, J. (eds.) PKC 2004. LNCS, vol. 2947, pp. 145–158. Springer, Heidelberg (2004)
12. Gennaro, R.: Faster and shorter password-authenticated key exchange. In: Canetti, R. (ed.) TCC 2008. LNCS, vol. 4948, pp. 589–606. Springer, Heidelberg (2008)
13. Gennaro, R., Lindell, Y.: A framework for password-based authenticated key exchange. ACM Trans. Information and System Security 9(2), 181–234
14. Goldreich, O., Lindell, Y.: Session-key generation using human passwords only. In: Kilian, J. (ed.) CRYPTO 2001. LNCS, vol. 2139, pp. 408–432. Springer, Heidelberg (2001)
15. Jablon, D.P.: Strong password-only authenticated key exchange. ACM Computer Communication Review 26, 5–26 (1996)
16. Katz, J., Ostrovsky, R., Yung, M.: Efficient password-authenticated key exchange using human-memorable passwords. In: Pfitzmann, B. (ed.) EUROCRYPT 2001. LNCS, vol. 2045, pp. 475–494. Springer, Heidelberg (2001)
17. Katz, J., Vaikuntanathan, V.: Smooth projective hashing and password-based authenticated key exchange from lattices. In: Matsui, M. (ed.) ASIACRYPT 2009. LNCS, vol. 5912, pp. 636–652. Springer, Heidelberg (2009)
18. Lin, C.-L., Sun, H.-M., Steiner, M., Hwang, T.: Three-party encrypted key exchange without server public-keys. IEEE Commun. Lett. 5(12), 497–499 (2001)
19. MacKenzie, P.D.: The pak suite: Protocols for password-authenticated key exchange. Submission to IEEE P1363.2 (2002)
20. MacKenzie, P.D., Patel, S., Swaminathan, R.: Password-authenticated key exchange based on RSA. In: Okamoto, T. (ed.) ASIACRYPT 2000. LNCS, vol. 1976, pp. 599–613. Springer, Heidelberg (2000)
21. Steiner, M., Tsudik, G., Waidner, M.: Refinement and extension of encrypted key exchange. Operating Systems Review 29(3), 22–30 (1995)
22. Szydlo, M.: A note on chosen-basis decisional diffie-hellman assumptions. In: Di Crescenzo, G., Rubin, A. (eds.) FC 2006. LNCS, vol. 4107, pp. 166–170. Springer, Heidelberg (2006)
23. Wang, W., Hu, L.: Efficient and provably secure generic construction of three-party password-based authenticated key exchange protocols. In: Barua, R., Lange, T. (eds.) INDOCRYPT 2006. LNCS, vol. 4329, pp. 118–132. Springer, Heidelberg (2006)
24. Yeh, H.-T., Sun, H.-M., Hwang, T.: Efficient three-party authentication and key agreement protocols resistant to password guessing attacks. J. Inf. Sci. Eng. 19(6), 1059–1070 (2003)

Redesigning Group Key Exchange Protocol Based on Bilinear Pairing Suitable for Various Environments

Yvo Desmedt[1,*] and Atsuko Miyaji[2,**]

[1] University College London and RCIS (AIST)
y.desmedt@cs.ucl.ac.uk
[2] Japan Advanced Institute of Science and Technology
miyaji@jaist.ac.jp

Abstract. Group key exchange (GKE) allows a group of n parties to share a common secret key over insecure channels. Since key management is important, NIST is now looking for a standard. The goal of this paper is to redesign GKE using bilinear pairings, proposed by Desmedt and Lange, from the point of view of arrangement of parties. The arrangement of parties is called a party tree in this paper. Actually, we are able to *redesign* the party tree, to reduce the computational and communicational complexity compared with the previous scheme, when GKE is executed among a small group of parties. We also redesign the general party tree for a large number of parties, in which each party is in a different environment such as having large or limited computational resources, electrical power, etc.

Keywords: group key exchange, pairing, party tree, graph theory.

1 Introduction

A group key exchange protocol (GKE) allows a group of n parties to share a common secret key over an insecure channel and, thus, parties in the group can encrypt and decrypt messages among group members. Secure communication among many parties has become an integral part of many applications. For example, ad hoc wireless networks are deployed in many areas such as homes, schools, disaster areas, etc., where a network is susceptible to attacks ranging from passive eavesdropping to active interference. Besides ad hoc networks, another environment where ad hoc groups are popular is in the context of new emerging social networks. The most well-known examples are Facebook and the professional network LinkedIn. Note that, as pointed out by Katz-Yung [15] some dynamic GKE protocols are slower than restarting from scratch with an efficient GKE. So, we do not consider making our protocols dynamic.

---

[*] A part of this work was done while funded by EPSRC EP/C538285/1 and by BT, (as BT Chair of Information Security).
[**] This study is partly supported by Grant-in-Aid for Scientific Research (A), 21240001.

X. Lai, M. Yung, and D. Lin (Eds.): Inscrypt 2010, LNCS 6584, pp. 236–254, 2011.

Some previous GKEs are based on the DH-key exchange protocol [7,8]. These GKEs were defined over a finite field, however, it can also be naturally defined over an elliptic curve for efficiency, denoted by GKE-ECDH. Some GKEs [10,12], based on Joux's tripartite key exchange protocols [14] using a bilinear pairing, follow constructions by [7,8], which are denoted by GKE-BP. Other GKEs [1,2,3] are not based on [7,8], which combine DH-key over an elliptic curve and Joux's tripartite key exchange. In this paper, we focus on GKE-BP proposed by Desmedt and Lange [12].

Let us discuss the differences between GKE-ECDH and GKE-BP from the point of view of arrangement of parties. A party-arrangement tree is called a *party tree* in this paper. GKE-ECDH is based on a two-party GKE and, thus, the generalization to an n-party GKE uses a binary tree. On the other hand, GKE-BP is based on Joux's [14] three-party GKE. In order to generalize the three-party GKE-BP to an n-party GKE-BP, n parties are simply arranged in a triplet tree. As a result, GKE-BP has the merit of reducing the height of the tree which arranges parties. In addition to this fact, GKE-BP is fit for combination with the short signature [6], since both GKE-BP and the short signature are based on a bilinear pairing over elliptic curve, using similar technology. However, there might be room for improvement in the arrangement of multiple triangles from the point of view of communicational or computational complexity; and the most efficient party tree might be different according to the number of parties. Previous protocols [12] based on GKE-BP, denoted by BDI-BP and BDII-BP[1] in this paper, do not focus on the party tree, and use a triplet tree to arrange parties by connecting the triangles at the nodes. In fact, few generalizations were developed to achieve an n-party version, although Joux's 3-party GKE-BP is a heavily cited paper.

In this paper, we explore the improvement of n-party versions of GKE-BP by redesigning the party tree, and investigate what type of party tree is suitable for given each condition: for example, the number of parties is decided according to application, or in the case of a large number of parties, each party may be under a different environment, such as having limited computational resources, electrical power, etc. As a result, we succeed in constructing a new GKE based on bilinear pairings which uses a new party tree and arranges parties by connecting the triangles at the edges, which we call an *edge-based GKE*. Compared with our edge-based GKE, BDII-BP is called a node-based GKE. We also analyze the performance of our edge-based GKE, and, the node-based GKE carefully, and show that the most efficient party arrangement is different, according to the number of parties, n. In addition, each tree has various strengths and weaknesses. Edge-based scheme has an advantage over node-based GKE in sent message complexity for parties with low computational resources. On the other hand, node-based GKE has an advantage over Edge-based scheme in received message complexity. Edge-based scheme is suitable in the case of a small number of parties. From the point of view of computational complexity, our edge-based GKE can work more efficiently than node-based GKE for $4 \leq n \leq 9$ and $16 \leq n \leq 21$.

---

[1] We focus on BDII-BP in this paper since BDII-BP is more efficient than BDI-BP.

We also investigate GKE in the case of a large number of parties. In such a case, each party may be in a different environment. For example, some parties may have large computational resources, but others may have few resources; and some parties may have almost unlimited electrical power, but others may run on small batteries. In [12], a GKE among a group with two types of parties is discussed. n_1 parties have large computational resources and n_2 parties have few resources. In this paper, we give the general and systematic construction of a GKE among a group by redesigning the party tree, in which $n_1, n_2, \cdots,$ n_m parties have computational resources in descending order, which we call an $(n_1, n_2, \cdots, n_m)$-GKE. From a practical point of view, the necessary features for GKE depend on the application. By using our results, we can choose the optimal party tree according to each application.

This paper is organized as follows. Section 2 summarizes computational assumptions, security assumptions, and security definitions of GKE, together with notations. Section 3 reviews the previous GKEs based on bilinear pairings. Section 4 presents our new edge-based GKE using bilinear pairings, after making clear the differences between edge-based and node-based GKE. Section 5 shows how to construct $(n_1, n_2, \cdots, n_m)$-GKE, in which $n_1, n_2, \cdots, n_m$ parties have computational resources in descending order.

2   Preliminary

This section summarizes notations, assumptions, and the basic security notions used in this paper.

2.1   The Bilinear Map, Its Related Assumptions, and Security Model of GKE

Let $\mathbb{G}_1$ and $\mathbb{G}_2$ be two cyclic groups of prime order q. $\mathbb{G}_1$ (resp. $\mathbb{G}_2$) is represented additively (resp. multiplicatively), where $\mathcal{O}$ (resp. 1) represents the zero element (identity element) for addition (multiplication) in $\mathbb{G}_1$ (resp. $\mathbb{G}_2$). The following bilinear map $\hat{e} : \mathbb{G}_1 \times \mathbb{G}_1 \to \mathbb{G}_2$ is defined over $\mathbb{G}_1$.

1. Bilinearity: $\hat{e}(G_0 + G_1, G_2) = \hat{e}(G_0, G_2) * \hat{e}(G_1, G_2)$, $\hat{e}(G_0, G_1 + G_2) = \hat{e}(G_0, G_1) * \hat{e}(G_0, G_2) \; \forall G_0, G_1, G_2 \in \mathbb{G}_1$.
2. Non-degeneracy: $\hat{e}(G, G) \neq 1$ for any $G \in \mathbb{G}_1 \setminus \{\mathcal{O}\}$.
3. Computability: There is an efficient algorithm to compute $\hat{e}(G_0, G_1)$ for any $G_0, G_1 \in \mathbb{G}_1$.

Let k be a security parameter. A DBDH (Decision Bilinear Diffie Hellman) parameter generator $\mathcal{IG}$ is a probabilistic polynomial time (PPT) algorithm that on input 1^k, outputs a description of the above $(\mathbb{G}_1, \mathbb{G}_2, \hat{e})$. The *DBDH problem* with respect to $\mathcal{IG}$ is: given random $G, Y_1, Y_2, Y_3 \in \mathbb{G}_1$ and $z \in \mathbb{G}_2$ where $Y_i = \alpha_i G$ $(i = 1, \cdots, 3)$ to decide whether $z = \hat{e}(G, G)^{\alpha_1 \alpha_2 \alpha_3}$ or not. More precisely, we say that $\mathcal{IG}$ satisfies the *DBDH assumption* if $|p_1 - p_2|$ is negligible (in k) for all PPT algorithms A, where $p_1 = \Pr[(\mathbb{G}_1, \mathbb{G}_2, \hat{e}) \leftarrow \mathcal{IG}(1^k); G, Y_1 = \alpha_1 G, Y_2 = \alpha_2 G, Y_3 = \alpha_3 G \leftarrow \mathbb{G}_1 : A(\mathbb{G}_1, \mathbb{G}_2, \hat{e}, G, Y_1, Y_2, Y_3, \hat{e}(G, G)^{\alpha_1 \alpha_2 \alpha_3}) = 0]$ and $p_2 = \Pr[(\mathbb{G}_1, \mathbb{G}_2, \hat{e}) \leftarrow \mathcal{IG}(1^k); G, Y_1 = \alpha_1 G, Y_2 = \alpha_2 G, Y_3 = \alpha_3 G \leftarrow \mathbb{G}_1, z \leftarrow \mathbb{G}_2 : A(\mathbb{G}_1, \mathbb{G}_2, \hat{e}, G, Y_1, Y_2, Y_3, z) = 0]$. This assumption is believed to hold if $\hat{e}$ is a Weil/Tate pairing on either a supersingular elliptic curve or an ordinary elliptic curve [18].

Let Π be a GKE protocol with n parties, let k be a security parameter, and let $\mathcal{P} = \{P_1, \cdots, P_n\}$ be a set of n parties, where n is bounded above by a polynomial in k. We follow the security model described in [15]. Here we review their definitions while focusing on models used in this paper.

We assume that parties do not deviate from the protocol and an adversary $\mathcal{A}$ is an outsider, that is, never participates as a party in the protocol. The interaction between $\mathcal{A}$ and parties occurs only via the following oracle queries, where Π_P^i denotes the i-th instance of party P; sk_P^i denotes the session key after execution of the protocol by Π_P^i; sid_P^i denotes the session identity for instance Π_P^i; and pid_P^i denotes the partner identity for instance Π_P^i.

Send(P, i, m): This sends message m to instance Π_P^i, and outputs the reply generated by this instance. This query models an active attack.

Execute$(P_1, i_1, \cdots, P_n, i_n)$: This executes the protocol between the unused instances $\{\Pi_{P_j}^{i_j}\}_{1 \leq j \leq n}$ and outputs the transcript of the execution;

Reveal(P, i): This outputs a session key sk_P^i for a terminated instance Π_P^i.

Corrupt(P): This outputs the long-term secret key of a party P.

Test(P, i): This query is asked only once, at any time during the adversary's execution. A bit $b \in \{0, 1\}$ is chosen uniformly at random. The adversary is given sk_P^i if $b = 1$, and a random session key if $b = 0$.

A passive adversary is given access to the Execute, Reveal, Corrupt, and Test oracles, while an active adversary is additionally given access to the Send oracle. The adversary can query Send, Execute, Reveal, and Corrupt oracles several times, but Test oracle is asked only once and on a fresh instance[2].

Finally, the adversary outputs a guess bit b'. Then, Succ, the event in which $\mathcal{A}$ wins the game for a protocol Π, occurs if $b = b'$ where b is the hidden bit used by the Test oracle. The advantage of $\mathcal{A}$ is defined as $\mathrm{Adv}_\Pi(k) = |\mathrm{Prob}[\mathrm{Succ}] - 1/2|$. We say Π is a secure group key exchange protocol if, for any PPT passive adversary $\mathcal{A}$, $\mathrm{Adv}_\Pi^{\mathrm{KE}}$ is negligible (in k). We say Π is a secure group authenticated key exchange protocol if, for any PPT active adversary $\mathcal{A}$, $\mathrm{Adv}_\Pi^{\mathrm{AKE}}$ is negligible (in k). The requirement of forward secrecy is already included in the above definition, since $\mathcal{A}$ is allowed to access the Corrupt oracle in each case.

The Katz-Yung compiler [15], or a variant of [13], transforms any GKE which is secure against a passive adversary with or without forward secrecy into one that is secure against active adversaries with or without forward secrecy, respectively. Let us briefly describe how the compiler transforms any passive-adversary-secure GKE into active-adversary-secure GKE: to avoid replay

---

[2] Π_P^i is a fresh instance unless one of the following is true: (1) $\mathcal{A}$, at some point, queried Reveal (P, i) or Reveal (P', j) with $P' \in \mathsf{pid}_P^i$; or (2) $\mathcal{A}$ queried Corrupt(P'') with $(P'' \in \mathsf{pid}_P^i)$ before a query of Send$(P, i, *)$ or Send$(P', j, *)$ with $(P' \in \mathsf{pid}_P^i)$.

attacks, the compiler introduces a fresh random nonce for each party for each execution of the protocol, adds a message number for each party, and makes a signature on message, the message number, and the nonce by using a strongly unforgeable signature under adaptive chosen message attack. As for the detailed construction, refer to [15,13]. This paper focuses on redesigning BDII-BP from the graph-theory point of view, and investigates the optimal party tree for a given condition, where BDII-BP is secure against a passive attack and does not have a long-term secret key. Therefore, we focus solely on the passive case without long-term secret key. Note that, our scheme will be shown to be secure against passive adversaries, and, thus, both our scheme and BDII-BP are transformed to become secure against active adversaries.

2.2   Assumptions Regarding Computational Complexity

We make some assumptions necessary to compute the computational complexity. The GKE we will build consists of scalar multiplications on $\mathbb{G}_i$ ($i = 1, 2$), multiplications on $\mathbb{G}_i$, and pairings $\hat{e}$. We denote the computational complexity of a single scalar multiplication on $\mathbb{G}_i$, a single multiplication on $\mathbb{G}_i$, and a single pairing, by SM_i, M_i, and e, respectively, where $i = 1$ or 2. Based on the current security parameters, the size of $\mathbb{G}_2$ is 6 or more times larger than $\mathbb{G}_1$. Using the conventional algorithm [16], the ratio of computational complexity of M_2 versus M_1 can be set to $M_1 = \left(\frac{|\mathbb{G}_1|}{|\mathbb{G}_2|}\right)^2 M_2$. Similarly, the ratio of the computational complexity of SM_i versus M_i can be set to $SM_i = \frac{3|\mathbb{G}_i|}{2} M_i$ for each $\mathbb{G}_i$. The computational complexity of these operations, in descending order, is $e > SM_2 > SM_1 > M_2 > M_1$. In our evaluation, we focus primarily on the computational complexity of e, SM_1, and M_2. Note that we do not use a scalar multiplication on $\mathbb{G}_2$ in any GKE presented in this paper.

2.3   Notation and Assumptions Regarding GKE

This paper deals with each computational resources or electrical power slightly precisely. For this purpose, we introduce notation, (n_1, n_2)-GKE, which means GKE among n_1 parties that have large computational resources and enough electrical power, and n_2 parties that have low computational resources or are running on batteries. More generally, we explore $(n_1, n_2, \cdots, n_m)$-GKE among n_1, n_2, $\cdots$, n_m parties, each with computational resources or electrical power levels in descending order.

   Let us first make some observations regarding GKE. In this paper, when we evaluate the communicational complexity per party, it is from the point of view of the party with the maximum *sent* and *received* data. We distinguish between point-to-point and broadcast communication, while we do not distinguish between multicast and broadcast communication. We use $\mathbf{p}_i$ (resp. $\mathbf{b}_i$) to denote a message in $\mathbb{G}_i$ ($i = 1, 2$) sent/received through point-to-point (resp. broadcast) communication.

Another measure for comparing protocols is the computational complexity per party. Keeping the discussion in Section 2.2 in mind, we focus on the computational complexity of e, SM_1, and M_2.

We also introduce a concept, *"auxiliary elements"*. In some GKEs, some parties can compute a shared key by themselves, that is, they can compute a shared key using their own secret key and public data. Some parties, however, cannot compute a shared key by themselves, that is, they need some additional data computed and sent by others. Moreover, this data has to be received and stored by the recipient. The maximum number of auxiliary elements a party receives is denoted by MAE. MAE is also a good characteristic for evaluating each GKE.

To express these evaluations in detail we use the notation $(n_1\text{-}[\#e, \#SM_1, \#M_2], n_2\text{-}[\#e, \#SM_1, \#M_2], \cdots, n_m\text{-}[\#e, \#SM_1, \#M_2]; \#MAE)\text{-GKE}$. For example, $(n_1\text{-}[3, 4, 5], n_2\text{-}[1, 1, 0]; 2)\text{-GKE}$ indicates that n_1 parties compute $3e + 4SM_1 + 5M_2$; n_2 parties compute $1e + 1SM_1$; some parties need to receive 2 auxiliary elements for the shared key.

For the sake of completeness, we define a triplet tree. A triplet tree is a hypergraph [4] (V, E) in which each hyperedge is a 3-set, and the intersection of two edges is a single vertex or empty. Note that some of our constructions are not triplet trees (see Section 4). Our constructions can also be regarded as a hypergraph (V, E) in which each hyperedge is a 3-set, and which is vertex-connected. When such a hyperedge involves the vertices a, b, c we often denote it as Δ_{abc}. We also denote an edge which involves the vertices a, b as E_{ab}. Although we use a normal graph to represent this hypergraph, the hyperedge will be obvious.

3   Background

This section summarizes previous GKEs based on bilinear maps. The original GKE, called BDI [7] and BDII [8], are constructed over a finite field or an elliptic curve. They were adapted to work using pairings in [10,12]. BDI using pairings was proposed by [10], but it is neither more efficient than [12] nor adapted to the situation of parties with different computational resources since it is fully contributory. We are interested in dealing with parties having different computational resources each other and, thus, redesigning the asymmetric party tree. This is why we focus on BDII based on pairings [12], which we call BDII-BP.

In BDII-BP, parties are arranged in a tree based on a triangle, in which each node is connected to two other triangles (See Fig 1). We denote the parent, the two left children, or the two right children of i by $\mathtt{par}(i)$, $\mathtt{l.child.1}(i)$ and $\mathtt{l.child.2}(i)$, or $\mathtt{r.child.1}(i)$ and $\mathtt{r.child.2}(i)$, respectively, and the sibling of i, who is in the same triangle, by $\mathtt{sib}(i)$ (See Fig 2). The concepts of child and parent of i are defined by using the distance from a shaded triangle Δ_{123}. In these figures, one party is set to each node; black nodes correspond to parties with large computational resources; white nodes correspond to parties with low computational resources; and a shaded triangle corresponds to the exact triangle of a shared key.

Protocol 1 (BDII-BP[12])

1. *Each P_i computes $Z_i = r_i G$ for a secretly chosen $r_i \in \mathbb{Z}_q^*$ and sends it to 6 parties such as its 2 left children, 2 right children, the sibling, and the parent.*

2. *Each P_i computes both $X_{\text{left},i}$ and $X_{\text{right},i}$ and multicasts these respectively to its left and right descendants, where*

$$X_{\text{left},i} = \frac{\hat{e}(Z_{\text{par}(i)}, Z_{\text{sib}(i)})^{r_i}}{\hat{e}(Z_{\text{l.child.1}(i)}, Z_{\text{l.child.2}(i)})^{r_i}} = \frac{\hat{e}(Z_{\text{par}(i)}, r_i Z_{\text{sib}(i)})}{\hat{e}(Z_{\text{l.child.1}(i)}, r_i Z_{\text{l.child.2}(i)})}$$
$$= \hat{e}(r_i Z_{\text{par}(i)}, Z_{\text{sib}(i)}) \cdot \hat{e}(Z_{\text{l.child.1}(i)}, -r_i Z_{\text{l.child.2}(i)}),$$
$$X_{\text{right},i} = \frac{\hat{e}(Z_{\text{par}(i)}, Z_{\text{sib}(i)})^{r_i}}{\hat{e}(Z_{\text{r.child.1}(i)}, Z_{\text{r.child.2}(i)})^{r_i}} = \frac{\hat{e}(Z_{\text{par}(i)}, r_i Z_{\text{sib}(i)})}{\hat{e}(Z_{\text{r.child.1}(i)}, r_i Z_{\text{r.child.2}(i)})}$$
$$= \hat{e}(r_i Z_{\text{par}(i)}, Z_{\text{sib}(i)})\hat{e}(Z_{\text{r.child.1}(i)}, -r_i Z_{\text{r.child.2}(i)}).$$

3. *Each P_i computes a shared key $K = \hat{e}(r_i Z_{\text{par}(i)}, Z_{\text{sib}(i)}) \prod_{j \in \text{ ancestor}(i)} X_j = \hat{e}(G, G)^{r_1 r_2 r_3}$.*

BDII-BP works[3] in $(\frac{n}{4} - \frac{3}{4}, \frac{3n}{4} + \frac{3}{4})$-GKE, where $\frac{n}{4} - \frac{3}{4}$ parties execute $3e + 4SM_1 + (\log_4(n+1))M_2$ at most by keeping and reusing $\hat{e}(r_i Z_{\text{par}(i)}, Z_{\text{sib}(i)})$, and $\frac{3n}{4} + \frac{3}{4}$ parties execute $e + 2SM_1 + (\log_4(n+1) - 1)M_2$ at most.

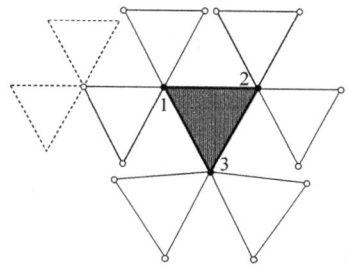

Fig. 1. BDII-BP using a bilinear map

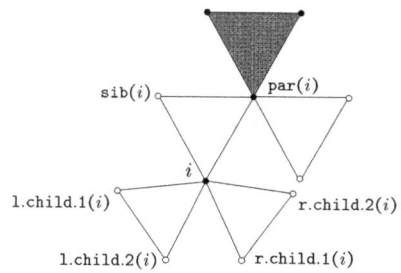

Fig. 2. Neighbors of P_i

4 Redesigning GKE Based on Bilinear Pairing

In this section, we present our basic new GKEs, which use a new arrangement of parties by using triangles that overlap at edges. When viewing the triangles as hyperedges, this formally corresponds with hyperedges at which an intersection corresponds to two vertices. Any previous GKE based on bilinear pairings uses a triplet tree, and so triangles were connected to each other at single nodes. Before showing our new edge-based GKE, let us investigate the differences between edge-based and node-based GKEs when using bilinear pairings.

---

[3] From now on we will drop the notations (both $\lfloor \ \rfloor$ and $\lceil \ \rceil$) when there is no confusion.

4.1   Differences between Edge-Based and Node-Based GKE

We present three GKEs (Protocols 2, 3, and 4) between 7 parties, and investigate
the differences among them, where Figures 3, 4, and 5 show each arrangement of
parties, respectively. In these figures, arrows correspond to the flow to compute
the shared key and other descriptions such as nodes and a shaded triangles are
the same as in Section 3. Protocol 2 is a node-based GKE using bilinear pairings;
this protocol is easily derived from the previous GKE [12]. Protocols 3 and 4 are
edge-based GKEs, which are new arrangements introduced in this paper. Let us
compare Protocols 3 and 4 and, then, Protocols 2 and 4 after we describe these
protocols.

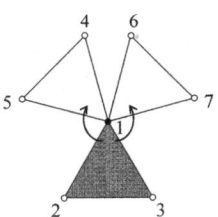

Fig. 3. Protocol 2   **Fig. 4.** Protocol 3   **Fig. 5.** Protocol 4

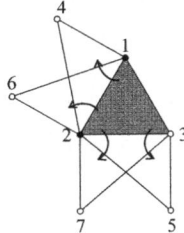

Protocol 2 $((1 - [3, 4, 2], 4 - [1, 2, 1], 2 - [1, 2, 0]; 1)$-GKE$)$.

1. *Each party P_i computes $Z_i = r_i G$ for a (private) randomly chosen $r_i \in \mathbb{Z}_q^*$*
   and sends it to its neighbors.
2. *P_1 computes two auxiliary elements $X_{4,5}$ and $X_{6,7}$ and sends them to (P_4, P_5)*
   and (P_6, P_7), respectively, where

$$X_{4,5} = \frac{\hat{e}(Z_2, Z_3)^{r_1}}{\hat{e}(Z_4, Z_5)^{r_1}} = \hat{e}(r_1 Z_2, Z_3)\hat{e}(Z_4, -r_1 Z_5) \ (reusing \ \hat{e}(r_1 Z_2, Z_3));$$

$$X_{6,7} = \frac{\hat{e}(Z_2, Z_3)^{r_1}}{\hat{e}(Z_6, Z_7)^{r_1}} = \hat{e}(r_1 Z_2, Z_3)\hat{e}(Z_6, -r_1 Z_7)$$

3. *A shared key is given as $K = \hat{e}(G, G)^{r_1 r_2 r_3}$. P_1 computes this as $K = \hat{e}(r_1 Z_2, Z_3)$; P_2 as $K = \hat{e}(r_2 Z_1, Z_3)$; P_3 as $K = \hat{e}(r_3 Z_1, Z_2)$; P_4 as $K = X_{4,5}\hat{e}(r_4 Z_1, Z_5)$; P_5 as $K = X_{4,5}\hat{e}(r_5 Z_1, Z_4)$; P_6 as $K = X_{6,7}\hat{e}(r_6 Z_1, Z_7)$; and P_7 as $K = X_{6,7}\hat{e}(r_7 Z_1, Z_6)$ and this shared key is depicted in Figure 3 as computed from the shaded area.*

Protocol 3 $((2 - [3, 3, 0], 1 - [1, 2, 2], 3 - [1, 2, 1], 1 - [1, 2, 0]; 2)$-GKE$)$.

1. *Each party P_i computes $Z_i = r_i G$ for a (private) randomly chosen $r_i \in \mathbb{Z}_q^*$*
   and sends it to its neighbors.

2. P_1 and P_2 compute 2 auxiliary elements (X_4, X_6) and (X_5, X_7) and send them to (P_4, P_6) and (P_5, P_7), respectively, where

$$P_1 : X_4 = \frac{\hat{e}(Z_2, Z_3)^{r_1}}{\hat{e}(Z_2, Z_4)^{r_1}} = \hat{e}(r_1 Z_2, (Z_3 - Z_4)) \ (\text{reusing } r_1 Z_2);$$

$$X_6 = \frac{\hat{e}(Z_3, Z_2)^{r_1}}{\hat{e}(Z_3, Z_6)^{r_1}} = \hat{e}(Z_3, r_1(Z_2 - Z_6));$$

$$P_2 : X_5 = \frac{\hat{e}(Z_3, Z_1)^{r_2}}{\hat{e}(Z_3, Z_5)^{r_2}} = \hat{e}(r_2 Z_3, (Z_1 - Z_5)) \ (\text{reusing } r_2 Z_3);$$

$$X_7 = \frac{\hat{e}(Z_5, Z_3)^{r_2}}{\hat{e}(Z_5, Z_7)^{r_2}} = \hat{e}(Z_5, r_2(Z_3 - Z_7)).$$

3. A shared key is given as $K = \hat{e}(G, G)^{r_1 r_2 r_3}$. P_1 computes this as $K = \hat{e}(r_1 Z_2, Z_3)$; P_2 as $K = \hat{e}(Z_1, r_2 Z_3)$; P_3 as $K = \hat{e}(r_3 Z_1, Z_2)$; P_4 as $K = X_4 \hat{e}(r_4 Z_1, Z_2)$; P_5 as $K = X_5 \hat{e}(r_5 Z_2, Z_3)$; P_6 as $K = X_6 \hat{e}(r_6 Z_1, Z_3)$; and P_7 as $K = X_5 X_7 \hat{e}(r_7 Z_5, Z_2)$.

Protocol 4 $((2\text{-}[3, 2, 0], 4\text{-}[1, 2, 1], 1\text{-}[1, 2, 0]; 1)\text{-GKE})$.

1. Each party P_i computes $Z_i = r_i G$ for a (private) randomly chosen $r_i \in \mathbb{Z}_q^*$ and sends it to its neighbors.
2. P_1 and P_2 compute two auxiliary elements (X_4, X_6) and (X_5, X_7) and send them to (P_4, P_6) and (P_5, P_7), respectively, where

$$P_1 : X_4 = \frac{\hat{e}(Z_2, Z_3)^{r_1}}{\hat{e}(Z_2, Z_4)^{r_1}} = \hat{e}(r_1 Z_2, Z_3 - Z_4) \ (\text{reusing } r_1 Z_2);$$

$$X_6 = \frac{\hat{e}(Z_3, Z_2)^{r_1}}{\hat{e}(Z_3, Z_6)^{r_1}} = \hat{e}(r_1 Z_3, Z_2 - Z_6);$$

$$P_2 : X_5 = \frac{\hat{e}(Z_3, Z_1)^{r_2}}{\hat{e}(Z_3, Z_5)^{r_2}} = \hat{e}(r_2 Z_3, Z_1 - Z_5) \ (\text{reusing } r_2 Z_3);$$

$$X_7 = \frac{\hat{e}(Z_3, Z_1)^{r_2}}{\hat{e}(Z_3, Z_7)^{r_2}} = \hat{e}(r_2 Z_3, Z_1 - Z_7).$$

3. A shared key is given as $K = \hat{e}(G, G)^{r_1 r_2 r_3}$. P_1 computes this as $K = \hat{e}(r_1 Z_2, Z_3)$; P_2 as $K = \hat{e}(Z_1, r_2 Z_3)$; P_3 as $K = \hat{e}(r_3 Z_1, Z_2)$; P_4 as $K = X_4 \hat{e}(r_4 Z_1, Z_2)$; P_5 as $K = X_5 \hat{e}(r_5 Z_2, Z_3)$; P_6 as $K = X_6 \hat{e}(r_6 Z_1, Z_3)$; and P_7 as $K = X_7 \hat{e}(r_7 Z_2, Z_3)$.

We now compare these protocols by focusing on how to compute auxiliary elements. The computational complexity of each of these 3 GKEs are summarized in Table 1. Here we assume that parties with large computational resources compute at least three pairings, and these with low computational resources compute at most one.

In Protocol 2, Δ_{123}, Δ_{154} and Δ_{167} share a node (not edge) with party P_1 and, thus, the computational complexity of one auxiliary element is $2e + 2SM_1 + M_2$. To compute another auxiliary element, $e + SM_1$ can be *reused*, and, thus the

Table 1. Computational complexity of GKE among 7 parties

Party Type	large computational resources			low computational resources					
	$\#e$	$\#SM_1$	$\#M_2$	$\#e$	$\#SM_1$	$\#M_2$	$\#e$	$\#SM_1$	$\#M_2$
(node-based GKE) Protocol 2	3	4	2	1	2	1	1	2	0
(edge-based GKE) Protocol 3	3	3	0	1	2	2(1)	1	2	0
(edge-based GKE) Protocol 4	3	2	0	1	2	1	1	2	0

additional computational complexity is $e + SM_1 + M_2$. One auxiliary element enables 2 parties to compute the shared key. P_1 also can compute the shared key itself during computation of the auxiliary element. Remark that MAE, the maximum number of auxiliary elements, is 1. In Protocol 3, Δ_{123} shares one edge E_{12} with Δ_{124} and another edge E_{13} with Δ_{136}. Thus, the computational complexity of one auxiliary element such as X_4 or X_6 is $e+SM_1$. In this protocol, computation of each auxiliary element is independent, and, thus, that of another auxiliary element is $e+SM_1$. However, SM_1 can be *reused* to compute the shared key, and, thus only additional computation of e is required for the computation of the shared key. One auxiliary element enables 1 party to compute the shared key. Remark that MAE is 2, and, thus, there exists a party which needs two auxiliary elements. In Protocol 4, Δ_{123} shares one edge E_{12} with Δ_{124} and the same edge E_{12} with Δ_{126}. Thus, the computational complexity of one auxiliary element is $e + SM_1$. To compute another auxiliary element, SM_1 can be *reused*, and, thus the additional computational complexity is e. Furthermore, SM_1 can be *reused* to compute the shared key, and, thus only additional computation of e is required for the computation of the shared key. One auxiliary element enables 1 party to compute the shared key. Remark that MAE is 1.

Let us compare the two edge-based GKEs, Protocols 3 and 4. The differences are:

1. In Protocol 4, no party needs to use two auxiliary elements to compute the shared key. This is due to the "parallel" locations of P_5 and P_7, while in Protocol 3 these two parties are arranged "serially". So, in Protocol 3, P_7 needs 2 auxiliary elements to compute the shared key. (When using a graph (E, E') as used to explain the triplet tree in Section 2.3, then Δ_{257} is at distance 2 from the shaded Δ_{123}, while no triangle is at such a distance in Figure 5.)

2. In Protocol 4, computations of auxiliary elements are not independent. In Protocol 3, computation of auxiliary elements is independent. This is due to the "edge-sharing" of Δ_{124} and Δ_{126} in Protocol 4, while in Protocol 3 these two triangles Δ_{124} and Δ_{136} do not share any edge. So, the computations of auxiliary elements X_4 and X_6 in Protocol 3 are done independently.

Comparing the node-based GKE (Protocol 2) with the better edge-based GKE (Protocol 4), the edge-based GKE can reduce the computational complexity of parties with large computational resources by $2SM_2$. As for parties with low computational resources, both the node-based GKE and the edge-based GKE need $e+2SM_1$. The concepts developed in Protocol 4 are applied to construct the edge-based GKE among any group in order to reduce MAE and reuse computations.

4.2 New Edge-Based GKE

We show the generalization of Protocol 4 as Protocol 5. All parties are arranged in a graph which consists of triangles, seen in Figure 6. Figure 7 shows the party tree which describes the relation between a parent and two children, where all nodes except leaves have two children, and a parent node generates two auxiliary elements for its two children to compute a shared key. The parties P_1, P_2, and P_3 are parents to each other, that is, P_1(resp. P_2, resp. P_3) is the parent of P_3(rep. P_1, resp. P_2). In detail, P_i is arranged in a tree that starts with P_1, P_2, or P_3, where the tree is decided by the residue class of i in $\mathbb{Z}_3$, and nodes in leaves correspond to parties with low computational resources or small batteries. Figure 8 shows neighbors of a party P_i, which is a close-up of the structure of Figure 6. Let a party P_i be an inner node in Figure 7. Then, neighbors of P_i are described in Figure 8: $P_{\mathrm{par}(i)}$ (resp. $P_{\mathrm{par}(\mathrm{par}(i))}$) corresponds to the parent of P_i (resp. $P_{\mathrm{par}(i)}$) and $P_{\mathrm{l.child}(i)}$ and $P_{\mathrm{r.child}(i)}$ correspond to left and right children of P_i in Figure 7. P_i computes auxiliary elements for parties $P_{\mathrm{l.child}(i)}$ and $P_{\mathrm{r.child}(i)}$. By using the residue class of i in $\mathbb{Z}_3$, i can be represented by $i = 3 \cdot j_i + a_i$ for $a_i = 1, 2, 3$ and $j_i \geq 0$. So, two children $P_{\mathrm{l.child}(i)}$ and $P_{\mathrm{r.child}(i)}$ of P_i $(i \geq 1)$ are denoted by $P_{3(2j_i+1)+a_i}$ and $P_{3(2j_i+2)+a_i}$, respectively.

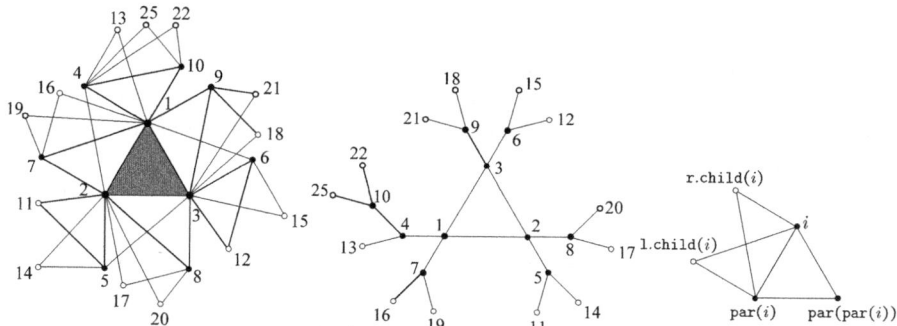

Fig. 6. Protocol 5   **Fig. 7.** Party tree of Proto-   **Fig. 8.** Neighbors of P_i
col 5

Protocol 5 $((\frac{n-3}{2}$ -$[3, 2, \log_2(\frac{n}{3}+1)-1], \frac{n+3}{2}$ -$[1, 2, \log_2(\frac{n}{3}+1)];$
$\log_2(\frac{n}{3}+1))$-GKE).

1. *Each party P_i computes $Z_i = r_i G$ using a (private) uniformly random chosen $r_i \in \mathbb{Z}_q^*$ and sends Z_i to its parent, children, and grandchildren.*
2. *Let P_i be an inner-node party, where $i = 3j_i + a_i$ ($a_i = 1, 2, 3$). Then, P_i computes two auxiliary elements, $X_{3(2j_i+b)+a_i}$ ($b \in \{1, 2\}$), and multicasts each to its left and right descendants, where*

$$X_{3(2j_i+b)+a_i} = \frac{\hat{e}(Z_{\text{par}(i)}, Z_{\text{par}(\text{par}(i))})^{r_i}}{\hat{e}(Z_{\text{par}(i)}, Z_{3(2j_i+b)+a_i})^{r_i}} = \hat{e}(r_i Z_{\text{par}(i)}, Z_{\text{par}(\text{par}(i))} -$$
$$Z_{3(2j_i+b)+a_i})\ (reusing\ r_i Z_{\text{par}(i)}).$$

3. *Let P_i ($i = 1, \cdots, n$) be a party, represented by $i = 3j_i + a_i$ ($a_i = 1, 2, 3$); and the sequence of ancestors of i be $\mathcal{A}_i = v_{i,1} \cdots v_{i,\ell}$, where $v_{i,1} = a_i$ and $v_{i,\ell} = i$. Then, P_i computes a shared key*

$$K = \hat{e}(r_i Z_{\text{par}(i)}, Z_{\text{par}(\text{par}(i))}) \cdot \prod_{t \in \mathcal{A}_i, t=v_{i,\ell}}^{v_{i,1}} X_t.$$

Remarks 1
1. Note that the numbering of the nodes may seem strange. A quick check of Figure 7, however, will show that the computational (and communication) load is balanced among the inner nodes. For this reason we call our protocol balanced.
2. Let us call n_l the number of leaves in the tree of Figure 7 and n_c the number of non-leaves. A quick check shows that $n_l \leq n_c + 3$. For this reason it is an $(\frac{n-3}{2}, \frac{n+3}{2})$-GKE.
3. Computing one auxiliary element costs $e + SM_1$ and another auxiliary element costs e by reusing SM_1.

4.3   Comparison and Discussion

Table 2 summarizes the communicational complexity of Protocols 5 and BDII-BP [12] for $n \geq 4$ and Table 3 summarizes their computational complexity[4]. We see that the sent message complexity of Protocol 5 is less than that of BDII-BP for parties with low computational resources. On the other hand, that of BDII-BP is less than that of Protocol 5 for parties with large computational resources. The received message complexity of BDII-BP is less than that of Protocol 5.

Let us compare both Protocol 5 and BDII-BP from the point of view of computational complexity. Both protocols execute the same number of times of $\hat{e}$ for parties with large and low computational complexity. To simplify the comparison, we focus on M_2 and SM_1 and remove e for formulae, where $\text{Comp}_{\text{BDII-Large}}$ and $\text{Comp}_{\text{Our-Large}}$ are the computational complexity of BDII-BP and Protocol 5 for parties with large computational complexity; and $\text{Comp}_{\text{BDII-Low}}$ and $\text{Comp}_{\text{Our-Low}}$ are for parties with low computational complexity,

$$\text{Comp}_{\text{BDII-Large}} = 2SM_1 + \lceil \log_4 (n+1) \rceil M_2, \ \text{Comp}_{\text{Our-Large}} = (\lceil \log_2 (\frac{n}{3} + 1) \rceil - 2)M_2,$$

$$\text{Comp}_{\text{BDII-Low}} = (\lceil \log_4 (n+1) \rceil - 1)M_2, \ \text{Comp}_{\text{Our-Low}} = (\lceil \log_2 (\frac{n}{3} + 1) \rceil - 1)M_2.$$

The differences between $\text{Comp}_{\text{BDII-Large}}$ and $\text{Comp}_{\text{Our-Large}}$ ($\text{Comp}_{\text{BDII-Low}}$ and $\text{Comp}_{\text{Our-Low}}$) depend on the number of parties, and choice of $\mathbb{G}_1$ and $\mathbb{G}_2$. We

---

[4] Protocols 5 and BDII-BP are coincident with Joux's three-party GKE for $n = 3$.

Table 2. Sent/received message complexity of several GKEs among n parties

	sent message complexity		received message complexity	
Party Type	large comp.	low comp.	large comp.	low comp.
BDII-BP				
$(\frac{n}{4} - \frac{3}{4}, \frac{3n}{4} + \frac{3}{4})$-GKE	$2\mathbf{b}_2 + 6\mathbf{p}_1$	$2\mathbf{p}_1$	$\log_4(n+1)\mathbf{b}_2 + 6\mathbf{p}_1$	$\log_4(n+1)\mathbf{b}_2 + 2\mathbf{p}_1$
Protocol 5				
$(\frac{n-3}{2}, \frac{n+3}{2})$-GKE	$2\mathbf{b}_2 + 7\mathbf{p}_1$	$\mathbf{p}_1$	$\log_2(\frac{n}{3} + 1)\mathbf{b}_2 + 4\mathbf{p}_1$	$\log_2(\frac{n}{3} + 1)\mathbf{b}_2 + 2\mathbf{p}_1$

Table 3. Computational complexity of several GKEs among n parties

Party Type	large computational resources			low computational resources		
	$\#e$	$\#SM_1$	$\#M_2$	$\#e$	$\#SM_1$	$\#M_2$
BDII-BP						
$(\frac{n}{4} - \frac{3}{4}, \frac{3n}{4} + \frac{3}{4})$-GKE	3	4	$\lceil \log_4(n+1) \rceil$	1	2	$\lceil \log_4(n+1) \rceil - 1$
Protocol 5						
$(\frac{n-3}{2}, \frac{n+3}{2})$-GKE	3	2	$\lceil \log_2(\frac{n}{3} + 1) \rceil - 2$	1	2	$\lceil \log_2(\frac{n}{3} + 1) \rceil - 1$

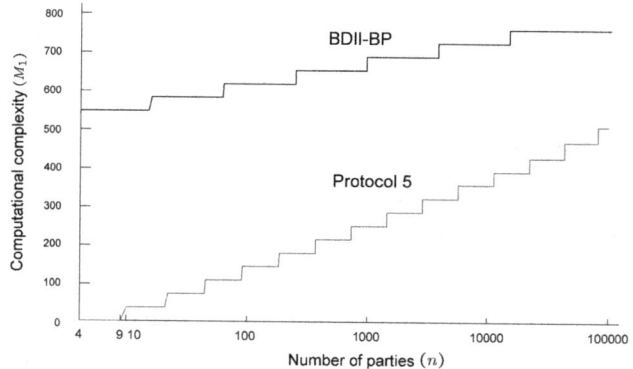

Fig. 9. Comparison of $\mathrm{Comp}_{\mathtt{BDII-Large}}$ and $\mathrm{Comp}_{\mathtt{Our-Large}}$ (Estimated by M_1. $|\mathbb{G}_1| = 160$, $|\mathbb{G}_2|/|\mathbb{G}_1| = 6$.)

investigate computational complexity when $|\mathbb{G}_1| = 160$ and $|\mathbb{G}_2|/|\mathbb{G}_1| = 6$. Figure 9 shows each computational complexity of $\mathrm{Comp}_{\mathtt{BDII-Large}}$ and $\mathrm{Comp}_{\mathtt{Our-Large}}$ with the number of parties $n \leq 10^5$, and Figure 10 shows each complexity of $\mathrm{Comp}_{\mathtt{BDII-Low}}$ and $\mathrm{Comp}_{\mathtt{Our-Low}}$ with $n \leq 10^5$. Formulae are measured by M_1 and conversion of both SM_1 and M_2 to M_1 were shown in Section 2.2. We see that Protocol 5 can always reduce computational complexity for parties with large computational resources in BDII-BP under the above conditions. However, the computational complexity for parties with low computational resources in Protocol 5 is equal to that for those in BDII-BP for $4 \leq n \leq 9$ and $16 \leq n \leq 21$,

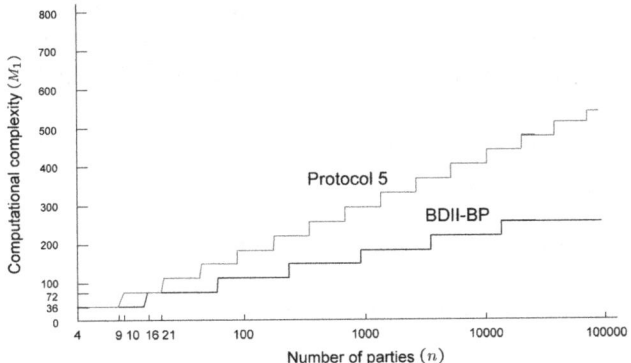

Fig. 10. Comparison of $\text{Comp}_{\text{BDII}-\text{Low}}$ and $\text{Comp}_{\text{Our}-\text{Low}}$ (Estimated by M_1. $|\mathbb{G}_1| = 160$, $|\mathbb{G}_2|/|\mathbb{G}_1| = 6$.)

as we have seen in the case of $n = 7$ in Section 4.1. Protocol 5 is slightly worse than BDII-BP for other n.

In summary, we have seen that the optimal party tree is different according to the number of parties. In addition, each tree has various strengths and weaknesses. Protocol 5 has an advantage over BDII-BP in sent message complexity for parties with low computational resources. On the other hand, BDII-BP has an advantage over Protocol 5 in received message complexity. Protocol 5 has an advantage over BDII-BP in computational complexity among a small number of parties. On the other hand, BDII-BP has an advantage over Protocol 5 in computational complexity among a large number of parties. From a practical point of view, the necessary features for GKE depend on the application. By using our results, we can choose the optimal party tree according to each application.

4.4   Security of Protocol 5

We show that a passive adversary that can break Protocol 5 can be used to solve the DBDH Problem. The detailed proof will be shown in the final paper due to the lack of space.

Theorem 1. *Assuming the DBDH problem over $\mathbb{G}$ is hard, Protocol 5, denoted simply by Π, is a secure group GKE protocol. Namely,*

$$\text{Adv}_{\Pi}^{\text{KE}}(t, q_{ex}) \leq \text{Adv}_{\mathbb{G}}^{\text{DBDH}}(t'),$$

where $\text{Adv}_{\Pi}^{\text{KE}}(t, q_{ex})$ is an adversary to Π with q_{ex} Execute queries and in t time, and $\text{Adv}_{\mathbb{G}}^{\text{DBDH}}(t')$ is an adversary to DBDH in $t' = t + (n-3)q_{ex}(e + 2SM_1)$ time for the number of parties n.

The Katz-Yung compiler [15] and a variant [13] turn Protocol 5 into an authenticated GKE protocol which is secure against active attack, as we have reviewed in Section 2.

Corollary 1. *The authenticated GKE Π' obtained from Protocol 5, denoted simply by Π, by applying the compiler is secure against active adversary. Namely, for the number of* Send *queries, q_s, and the number of* Execute *queries, q_{ex}, we obtain*

$$\mathsf{Adv}_{\Pi'}^{\mathsf{AKE-fs}}(t, q_{ex}, q_s) \leq \mathsf{Adv}_{\Pi}^{\mathsf{KE}}(t', q_{ex}) + \frac{q_s}{2}\mathsf{Adv}_{\Pi}^{\mathsf{KE}}(t', 1) + n\mathsf{Succ}_{\Sigma}(t') + \frac{q_s^2 + q_{ex}q_s}{2^k},$$

where $\mathsf{Adv}_{\Pi'}^{\mathsf{AKE-fs}}(t, q_{ex}, q_s)$ is an adversary to Π', $t' = t + (nq_{ex} + q_s)t_{\Pi'}$, $t_{\Pi'}$ is the time required for an execution of Π' by any party, and Succ_{σ} is the success probability against the signature scheme used, Σ.

5   Construction of GKE among a Large Group

In this section, we will deal with a large group. In such a group, some parties may have large computational resources and electrical power, while others do not, that is, the resources may be different for each party. As we have seen in Section 4, node-based GKEs are suitable for a large group. We will further redesign a party tree of node-based GKEs from the point of view of different *weight*, to construct GKEs suitable for a large group among parties with different resources.

5.1   Variants of Node-Based GKEs

In order to apply node-based GKEs to parties with different resources, we re-design variants of Protocol 2, in such a way that one party has large computational resources and electrical power to compute all auxiliary elements.

Protocol 6 ($(1 - [\frac{n-3}{2} + 1, \frac{n-3}{2} + 2, \frac{n-3}{2}], (n-3) - [1, 2, 1], 2 - [1, 2, 0]; 1)$-GKE)
Figure 11 shows an arrangement of parties, which is a variant of $(1, 6)$-GKE (Protocol 2) for the case in which 1 party constructs all auxiliary elements.

1. $n - 3$ *parties are set under U_1, which are denoted by $U_{1,i}$ ($i = 1, \cdots, n-3$).*
2. *Each party U_i ($i = 1, 2, 3$) computes $Z_i = r_i G$ for a (private) randomly chosen $r_i \in \mathbb{Z}_q^*$ and sends it to its neighbors. Only U_1 broadcasts Z_1 to all parties. Each party $U_{1,i}$ ($i = 1, \cdots, n-3$) computes $Z_{1,i} = r_{1,i} G$ and sends it to its neighbors (including U_1).*
3. U_1 *computes $\lceil \frac{n-3}{2} \rceil$ auxiliary elements and sends them to the corresponding parties $\{U_{1,2j-1}, U_{1,2j}\}$ ($j = 1, \cdots, \lceil \frac{n-3}{2} \rceil$),*

$$X_j = \frac{\hat{e}(Z_2, Z_3)^{r_1}}{\hat{e}(Z_{1,2j-1}, Z_{1,2j})^{r_1}} = \hat{e}(r_1 Z_2, Z_3)\hat{e}(-r_1 Z_{1,2j-1}, Z_{1,2j}) \text{ (reusing } \hat{e}(r_1 Z_2, Z_3)).$$

(1)

4. *A shared key is given as $K = \hat{e}(G, G)^{r_1 r_2 r_3}$, where U_1 computes $K = \hat{e}(r_1 Z_2, Z_3)$; U_2 computes $K = \hat{e}(r_2 Z_1, Z_3)$; U_3 computes $K = \hat{e}(r_3 Z_1, Z_2)$; and $U_{1,2j-1}$ and $U_{1,2j}$ ($j = 1, \cdots, \lceil \frac{n-3}{2} \rceil$) compute $K = X_j \hat{e}(r_{1,2j-1} Z_1, Z_{1,2j})$ and $K = X_j \hat{e}(r_{1,2j} Z_1, Z_{1,2j-1})$, respectively.*

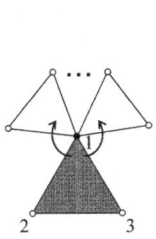 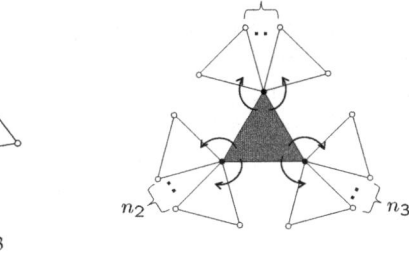 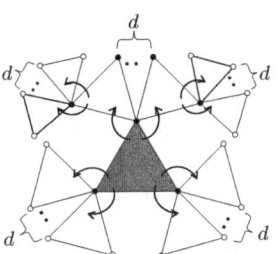

Fig. 11. Protocol 6   **Fig. 12.** Variants of Protocol 6   **Fig. 13.** Protocol 7

Remarks 2

1. As we have discussed in Protocol 2, computing $(n-3)$-party auxiliary elements costs $(\frac{n-3}{2}+1)e+(\frac{n-3}{2}+2)SM_1+\frac{n-3}{2}M_2$ by reusing $e+SM_1$ for every auxiliary element. Note that the shared key itself is computed during this computation.

2. Protocol 6 can be executed as a $(2, n-2)$ or a $(3, n-3)$-GKE by using the computational resources and electrical power of 2 or 3 parties instead of 1 party. It can also be generalized to $(1, 1, 1, 2n_1 + 2n_2 + 2n_3)$-GKE for $n_1 \geq n_2 \geq n_3$ as seen in Figure 12.

3. Protocol 6 can be modified in such a way that n parties $\{U_i\}_{i=1}^n$ have already shared a key K; $2t$ parties $\{U_{i,j}\}_{j=1}^{2t}$ are set under each U_i; each U_i computes t auxiliary elements and sends each auxiliary element to the appropriate party, $\{U_{i,j}\}_{j=1}^{2t}$, and, thus, $n + 2tn$ parties share the key K by changing Equation (1) to $X_{i,j} = K\hat{e}(-r_i Z_{i,2j}, Z_{i,2j+1})$. This achieves $(n$ -$[1, 2, 1], 2tn$ -$[1, 2, 1]; 1)$-GKE.

We show that a passive adversary that can break Protocol 6 can be used to solve the DBDH Problem. The detailed proof will be shown in the final paper due to the lack of space.

Theorem 2. *Assuming the DBDH problem over $\mathbb{G}$ is hard, Protocol 6, denoted simply by Π, is a secure group GKE protocol. Namely,*

$$\mathsf{Adv}_\Pi^{\mathrm{KE}}(t, q_{ex}) \leq \mathsf{Adv}_\mathbb{G}^{\mathrm{DBDH}}(t'),$$

where $\mathsf{Adv}_\Pi^{\mathrm{KE}}(t, q_{ex})$ is an adversary to Π with q_{ex} Execute queries and in t time, and $\mathsf{Adv}_\mathbb{G}^{\mathrm{DBDH}}(t')$ is an adversary to DBDH in $t' = t + \frac{n-3}{2} q_{ex}(e + 5SM_1)$ time for the number of parties n.

In the same way as Protocol 5, Protocol 6 can be turned into an authenticated GKE protocol, as we have seen in Section 4.4. We avoid the repetition of the same corollary here.

5.2 Construction of GKE in Different Environments

We investigate $(n_1, \cdots, n_k, m)$-GKE from the following point of view: the computational resources or electrical power required by $n_1, \cdots, n_k$ parties are arranged according to the allowable number of computations of pairings[5] with $d_1 > \cdots > d_k \geq 3$; and m parties with the lowest computational resources or electrical power can share the key by computing 1 pairing.

For the sake of simplicity, we will show the case of $k = 1$, i.e. (n, m)-GKE, where n parties with large computational resources and electrical power compute d pairings with $d \geq 3$; and m parties with low computational resources or which are using small batteries compute 1 pairing.

Protocol 7 $((n, m)$-GKE)
STEP 1. CHECK THE CONDITIONS
  If $m > (d-1)^h$ *for the height* $h = \lceil \log_{2(d-1)} (\frac{n(2d-3)}{3} + 1) \rceil - 1$, *then stop and output "Computational resources are not sufficient".*
STEP 2. ARRANGE PARTIES ACCORDING TO THE GIVEN ENVIRONMENT OF (n, m)
  Arrange a party tree in such a way that each node has $(d - 1)$ *triangles, that is,* $2(d - 1)$ *children; then set* n *parties to inner nodes on the party tree; finally set* m *parties to leaves on the party tree.*
STEP 3. KEY EXCHANGE AMONG $n + m$ PARTIES BASED ON A VARIANT OF PROTOCOL 6
  See Figures 12 and 13. First, Step 1 in Protocol 6 is executed; then, n *parties compute* $(d - 1)$ *auxiliary elements and send them to their descendants; and finally,* $K = \hat{e}(G, G)^{r_1 r_2 r_3}$ *is shared.*

Protocol 7 realizes $(n\text{-}[d, d + 1, h - 1],\ m\text{-}[1, 2, h];\ h)$-GKE for $h = \lceil \log_{2(d-1)} (\frac{n(2d-3)}{3} + 1) \rceil - 1$.

6   Concluding Remarks

Earlier schemes [10,12] developed to achieve an n-party GKE based on Joux's tripartite scheme, were based on combining several 3-party Joux based GKEs, in which the 3 parties involved were represented by a triangle. Earlier schemes did not focus on arrangement of parties, and, thus, simply, these triangles only had at most one node in common.

We discovered that by just redesigning the arrangement in such a way that these triangles overlap in two parties, we can reduce the communicational or computational complexity according to the number of parties. To obtain this advantage, we used an ingenuous trick by exploiting the mathematics of bilinear pairings (i.e., a new method to compute auxiliary elements) and proposed Protocol 5. By redesigning this arrangement, we can point out that the most efficient party arrangement is different, according to the number of parties. In fact, Protocol 5 can work more efficiently than BDII-BP for $4 \leq n \leq 9$ and $16 \leq n \leq 21$, from the point of view of computational complexity.

---

[5] n_i parties with large computational resources should be able to compute $d_i \geq 3$ pairings. If $d_i \leq 2$, those parties are assumed to be those with the least computational resources.

Although earlier schemes already discussed asymmetric computational resources, they characterized all machines into two classes based on their resources. Moreover, roughly half the nodes had large computational resources, while the other half had few resources. We also simply generalized this by redesigning the arrangement of parties, so that we can use more than two classes, and for some of our schemes we do not require a 50-50 division into two classes.

This paper enables us to give the optimal party tree for given either communication or computation complexity. The following open problem still remains: For given each upper bound on P_i's available computation and communication complexity, what is the optimal hyper-graph by using a bilinear-based group key exchange?

References

1. Dutta, R., Barua, R.: Dynamic Group Key Agreement in Tree-Based Setting. In: Boyd, C., González Nieto, J.M. (eds.) ACISP 2005. LNCS, vol. 3574, pp. 101–112. Springer, Heidelberg (2005)
2. Barua, R., Dutta, R., Sarkar, P.: Extending Joux's Protocol to Multi Party Key Agreement. In: Johansson, T., Maitra, S. (eds.) INDOCRYPT 2003. LNCS, vol. 2904, pp. 205–217. Springer, Heidelberg (2003)
3. Dutta, R., Barua, R., Sarkar, P.: Provably Secure Authenticated Tree Based Group Key Agreement. In: López, J., Qing, S., Okamoto, E. (eds.) ICICS 2004. LNCS, vol. 3269, pp. 92–104. Springer, Heidelberg (2004)
4. Berge, C.: Graphs and Hypergraphs. Elsevier Science (1985)
5. Abdel-Hafez, A., Miri, A., Orozco-Barbosa, L.: Authenticated group key agreement protocols for ad hoc wireless networks. Journal of Network Security (2007)
6. Boneh, D., Boyen, X.: Short signatures without random oracles and the SDH assumption in bilinear groups. J. Cryptology 21(2), 149–177 (2008)
7. Burmester, M., Desmedt, Y.G.: A secure and efficient conference key distribution system. In: De Santis, A. (ed.) EUROCRYPT 1994. LNCS, vol. 950, pp. 275–286. Springer, Heidelberg (1995)
8. Burmester, M., Desmedt, Y.: Efficient and secure conference key distribution. In: Lomas, M. (ed.) Security Protocols 1996. LNCS, vol. 1189, pp. 119–130. Springer, Heidelberg (1997)
9. Boneh, D., Franklin, M.: Identity-Based Encryption from the Weil Pairing. In: Kilian, J. (ed.) CRYPTO 2001. LNCS, vol. 2139, pp. 213–229. Springer, Heidelberg (2001)
10. Choi, K.Y., Hwang, J.Y., Lee, D.-H.: Efficient ID-based group key agreement with bilinear maps. In: Bao, F., Deng, R., Zhou, J. (eds.) PKC 2004. LNCS, vol. 2947, pp. 130–144. Springer, Heidelberg (2004)
11. Ciet, M., Joye, M., Lauter, K., Montgomey, P.L.: Trading inversions for multiplications in elliptic curve cryptography. In: Designs, Codes and Cryptography, vol. 39(2), pp. 189–206. Springer, Netherlands (2006)
12. Desmedt, Y., Lange, T.: Revisiting pairing based group key exchange. In: Tsudik, G. (ed.) FC 2008. LNCS, vol. 5143, pp. 53–68. Springer, Heidelberg (2008)
13. Desmedt, Y., Lange, T., Burmester, M.: Scalable authenticated tree based group key exchange for ad-hoc groups. In: Dietrich, S., Dhamija, R. (eds.) FC 2007 and USEC 2007. LNCS, vol. 4886, pp. 104–118. Springer, Heidelberg (2007)

14. Joux, A.: A One Round Protocol for Tripartite Diffie-Hellman. J. Cryptology 17(4), 263–276 (2004)
15. Katz, J., Yung, M.: Scalable Protocols for Authenticated Group Key Exchange. In: Boneh, D. (ed.) CRYPTO 2003. LNCS, vol. 2729, pp. 110–125. Springer, Heidelberg (2003)
16. Knuth, D.E.: The Art of Computer Programming. In: Seminumerical Algorithms, 2nd edn., vol. 2. Addison-Wesley, Reading (1981)
17. Konstantinou, E.: Cluster-based group key agreement for wireless ad hoc networks. in: ARES 2008 (2008)
18. Miyaji, A., Nakabayashi, M., Takano, S.: New explicit conditions of Elliptic Curve Traces under FR-reduction. IEICE Trans. Fundamentals E84-A(5), 1234–1243 (2001)

Multi-Factor Authenticated Key Exchange Protocol in the Three-Party Setting

Ying Liu, Fushan Wei, and Chuangui Ma

Zhengzhou Information Science and Technology Institute, Zhengzhou, Henan
Province, 450002, China
hellen1984129@163.com

Abstract. A great deal of authenticated key exchange (AKE) protocols
have been proposed in recent years. Most of them were based on 1-factor
authentication. In order to increase the security for AKE protocols, various authentication means can be used together. In fact, the existing
multi-factor AKE protocols provide an authenticated key exchange only
between a client and a server. This paper presents a new multi-factor
AKE protocol in the three-party settings (3MFAKE), in which the authentication means combine a password, a secure device, and biometric
authentications. We also prove the security of the protocol in the random
oracle model.

Keywords: Multi-factor, Three-party, Authenticated key exchange, Random oracle model.

1 Introduction

Motivation. Multi-factor authentication key exchange (MFAKE) protocol uses
various authentication means. A MFAKE protocol is designed to remain secure
even if all but one of the factors has been compromised, so it can provide an
enhanced level of assurance in higher security scenarios such as online banking,
virtual private network access, and physical access. For example, there are security attacks of phishing and spyware on the Internet nowadays. They aim to
get a user's username and password, then the adversary can use the personal
information to impersonate the user. The MFAKE protocol can resist to such attacks, since the security doesn't only rely on the password. In our security model,
the authentication is based on "something you know" (a password), "something
you have" (an unclonable secure device with a secret key), and "something you
are" (a biometric). Although two-party MFAKE protocols are quite useful for
client-server architectures, they are not suitable for large scale communication
environment. In two-party MFAKE protocols, if a client want to communicate
with other clients, he needs to know a large number of authentication means. Apparently, it is very inconvenient for client-to-client communications. The three-party MFAKE protocols can avoid this inconvenience. In a three-party MFAKE
protocol two clients A, B and a server S participate. A, B can authenticate
each other and establish a session key which is known to nobody but both of

X. Lai, M. Yung, and D. Lin (Eds.): Inscrypt 2010, LNCS 6584, pp. 255–267, 2011.

them with the help of the trusted server S. Each client only needs to share the authentication means with the trusted server.

Contributions. In this paper, we design a three-party multi-factor authenticated key exchange protocol based on MFAKE protocol [1] that was proposed by David Pointcheval et al. in 2008. Pontcheval's protocol is applied only in two party settings, and our new protocol works in the three-party settings, called 3MFAKE protocol. We provide the formal security proof of 3MFAKE protocol in the random oracle model. Even if two authentication means are corrupted, the new session key still remain semantically secure. In other words, the protocol is provably as secure as the strongest remaining factor: when the password is the last factor not to be corrupted, dictionary attacks are the most efficient attacks; when the biometric is the last one, the adversary's probability to be accepted is nearly equal to the false-acceptance probability; when the secret is the last one, the adversary make the protocol insecure that means the adversary break the Diffie-Hellman problem. Like many previous three-party protocols, we also assume that the server is honest but curious. Under this assumption our protocol can guarantee that the session key is private to the server.

Related Work. The literatures about 1-factor AKE protocol are rich of many results [2][3][4][5], but the literatures don't tell much on multi-factor authentication protocols. In 2006, an encoding for fingerprints is presented by Bhargav-Spantzel et al. [6], which is thereafter included in the design of a two-factor authentication protocol. In 2008, Pointcheval and Zimmer [1] proposed a multi-factor authenticated key exchange protocol, which is quite secure, since it allows a lot of information leakage for the adversary.

Due to the practical aspects, password authentication key exchange (PAKE) protocols in the three-party model have become the subject of extensive work in recent years. In 1978, Needhan and Schroeder [7] proposed the first three-party PAKE protocol which inspired the Kerberos distributed system. In 2005, a generic construction of three-party PAKE protocol was presented by Abdalla, Fouque, and Pointcheval [8], and it is the first provably-secure PAKE protocol in the three-party setting. Since then, there have been some published works aimed to improve the model in the three-party setting [9][10][11][12]. To the best of our knowledge, there is not multi-factor AKE protocol in three-party setting.

Outline. The rest of the paper is organized as follows. In section 2, we present the formal secure model for three-party MFAKE protocols. In section 3, we review some building blocks. In section 4, we propose the 3MFAKE protocol and prove it's security under the CDH assumption in the random oracle model. We conclude in section 5.

2 The Formal Model

In this section, we describe the security model for three-party multi-factor authenticated key exchange protocols, which in turn builds upon those of Bellare and Rogaway [13][14] and that of Bellare, Pointcheval and Rogaway [15].

2.1   Communication Model

Protocol participants. Each participant in a three-party MFAKE is either a client $U \in \mathcal{U}$ or a trusted server $S \in \mathcal{S}$. The set $\mathcal{S}$ is assumed to involve only a single trusted server for the simplicity of the proof, which can be easily extended to the case considering multiple servers. The set of clients $\mathcal{U}$ is made up of two disjoint sets: $\mathcal{C}$, the set of honest clients, and $\mathcal{E}$, the set of malicious clients. The malicious set $\mathcal{E}$ corresponds to the set of inside attackers, who exist only in the 3-party setting.

Long-Lived Keys. Each client $U \in \mathcal{U}$ owns a tuple $t_U = (\mathcal{D}_U, sk_U, pwd_U)$, where $\mathcal{D}_U$ is a probability distribution for his biometric, while sk_U and pwd_U are a high-entropy private key and a low-entropy password respectively. The server holds a list of tuples $t_S =< t_S[U] >$, where $t_S[U]$ is a transformed-tuple of t_U.

Biometric Templates. For each client U, $\mathcal{D}_U$ defines the probability distribution of his biometric. We use the encoding and the Hamming distance to deal with the matching process. There are two kinds of the matching decision:

- the distance between two templates W_U and W'_U of the same biometric is low with great probability. More concretely, there is a threshold m, such that for any U, $\Pr[W_U \leftarrow \mathcal{D}_U, W'_U \leftarrow \mathcal{D}_U : d_H(W_U, W'_U) \leq m] \geq 1 - \varepsilon_{fr}$, where the subscript fr stands for "false rejection".
- for any pair of distinct clients $U \neq U'$, the distance between W_U and W'_U is high with great probability. More precisely, there exist a threshold $\mathcal{M} \geq m$, such that for any $U \neq U'$, $\Pr[W_U \leftarrow \mathcal{D}_U, W_{U'} \leftarrow \mathcal{D}_{U'} : d_H(W_U, W_{U'}) > \mathcal{M}] \geq 1 - \varepsilon_{fa}$, where the subscript fa stands for "false acceptance".

Liveness Assumption. Because recovering a fingerprint from the object someone has just touched is an easy task, we assume the biometric to possibly be public. How do we prevent an adversary from impersonating an honest user? We use the liveness assumption to guarantee the biometrics really from the living human being under control. The liveness assumption means that the biometric is fresh, comes from a real living person, and that the computations are made from this biometric honestly.

We define a computation oracle $Compute(U^i, W', sk, pwd)$ to model this assumption: according to the state of the client instance U^i, from the secrets sk, pwd and a random value of W', it computes honestly the message which would have been generated by U with these inputs, following the protocol.

With the liveness assumption for the client U, we consider that all the messages involving the biometric, claimed to be sent by U, have been previously generated by the computation oracle.

Execution of the protocol. The interaction between an adversary $\mathcal{A}$ and the participants occurs only by making various queries, which model adversary capabilities in a real attack. During the execution, the adversary may create several concurrent instances of a participant.

- $Execute(U_1^{i_1}, S^j, U_2^{i_2})$: This query models passive attacks, where the attacker eavesdrops on honest executions among client instances $U_1^{i_1}$ and $U_2^{i_2}$ and the server instance S^j. The output of this query consists of the messages that were exchanged during the honest execution of the protocol.
- $SendClient(U^i, m)$: This query models an active attack against clients. This query allows the adversary to play with the client instance U^i, by intercepting, forwarding, modifying or creating messages. The output of this query is the message that the client instance U^i would generate upon receipt of message m. As stated above, if the liveness assumption still holds for the client U, and if the computation of m involves the biometric, then m has to have been previously generated through a $Compute(U^j, W', sk, pwd)$ query.
- $SendServer(S^j, m)$: This query models an active attack against the server, in which the adversary sends a message to server instance S^j. It outputs the message that server instance S^j would generate upon receipt of message m.
- $Reveal(U^i)$: This query models the misuse of session keys by instance U^i. It returns to the adversary the session key of client instance U^i, if the latter is defined.
- $Corrupt(U, a)$: This query models corruption capabilities of the adversary. The adversary can get one or several authentication factors of clients.
  - If a=1, the query outputs the password pwd_U of U.
  - If a=2, the query outputs the secret key sk_U of U.
  - If a=3, the query outputs the message involving the biometry. It models the adversary against the liveness assumption.

  We don't allow the corruption be performed during a session, but before a new session starts.
- $Test(U^i)$: This query is used to measure the semantic security of the session key of instance U^i, if the latter is defined. If the key isn't defined, it returns $\perp$. Otherwise, it returns either the session key held by instance U^i if $b = 0$ or a random key of the same size if $b = 1$. The query can be asked at most once by the adversary.

2.2   Security Notions

Partnering. The definition of partnering uses session identifications and partner identifications. More specifically, the session identification of a client instance is a function of the partial transcript of the conversation between the clients and the server before the acceptance. Let the partner identification of a client instance be the instance with which a common secret key is to be established. Two instances U_1^i and U_2^j are said to be partners if the following conditions are satisfied:

1. Both U_1^i and U_2^j accepted.
2. Both U_1^i and U_2^j share the same session identification.
3. The partner identification for U_1^i is U_2^j and vice-versa.
4. No instance other than U_1^i and U_2^j accepts with a partner identification equal to U_1^i and U_2^j.

Freshness. We say an instance U^i is fresh if all of the following hold: it has been accepted; no Reveal query has been made to it or its partner and less than 3 Corruptkey queries has been asked since the beginning of the game.

AKE semantic security. The security notions take place in the context of executing P in the presence of the adversary $\mathcal{A}$. When playing the game $Game^{ake}(\mathcal{A}, P)$, the goal of the adversary is to guess the bit b involved in the Test-query by outputting this guess b'.

We denote the AKE advantage as the probability that $\mathcal{A}$ correctly guesses the value of b. More precisely, we define $Adv_P^{ake} = 2\Pr[b = b'] - 1$. Furthermore, $Adv_p^{ake}(t, Q) = \max\{Adv_p^{ake}(\mathcal{A})\}$ is defined as the maximum over all $\mathcal{A}$ running in time at most t and using resources at most R. The protocol P is said to be AKE-secure if $\mathcal{A}$'s advantage is negligible in the security parameter.

3   Buliding Blocks

3.1   Message Authentication Codes (MAC)

A message authentication code $MAC = (Tag, Ver)$ is defined by the following two algorithms: (1) A MAC generation algorithm Tag, possibly probabilistic, which given a message m and a secret key $sk \in \{0,1\}^l$, produces a tag $\mu = MAC_{sk}(m)$; (2) A MAC verification algorithm Ver, which given a tag μ, a message m, and a secret key sk, outputs 1 if μ is a valid tag and 0, otherwise. The security notion that we need for the MAC scheme is strong existential unforgeability under chosen-message attacks. In this notion, the adversary should be unable to create a new valid message-tag pair, even after seeing many such valid pairs. The security of MAC is modeled by the security game $Game_{\mathcal{A}_{mac}}^{euf-cma}(k)$ between a challenger and an adversary $\mathcal{A}_{mac}$. It runs as follows: First, the adversary $\mathcal{A}_{mac}$ outputs a message-tag pair (m, μ). Second, the challenger verify whether $V(\mu, m, sk) = 1$ or not. If $V(\mu, m, sk) = 1$ the output of $Game_{\mathcal{A}_{mac}}^{euf-cma}(k)$ is set to 1 and otherwise set to 0.

We denote the advantage of such an adversary $\mathcal{A}_{mac}$:

$$Adv_{MAC}^{euf-cma}(\mathcal{A}) = \Pr[Game_{\mathcal{A}_{mac}}^{euf-cma}(k) = 1]$$

$$Adv_{MAC}^{euf-cma}(T_{mac}, q_t, q_v, k) = Max_{\mathcal{A}_{mac}}\{Adv_{\mathcal{A}_{mac}}^{euf-cma}(k)\}$$

where maximum is over all $\mathcal{A}_{mac}$ with time-complexity at most T_{mac} and asking at most q_t and q_v queries to its MAC generation and verification oracles.

A MAC scheme is said to be existential unforgeability if the advantage of any polynomial time adversary is a negligible function in time T_{mac}.

3.2   Computational Diffie-Hellman Assumption

Let $\mathbb{G} = \langle g \rangle$ be a finite cyclic group of order an l-bit prime number q, where the operation is denoted multiplicatively. A $(t, \varepsilon) - CDH$ attacker in $\mathbb{G}$ is a probabilistic machine Δ running in time t such that its success probability $Succ_{g,\mathbb{G}}^{cdh}(\Delta)$, given random elements g^x and g^y to output g^{xy}, is greater than ε.

$$Succ_{g,\mathbb{G}}^{cdh}(\Delta) = \Pr_{x,y}[\Delta(g^x, g^y) = g^{xy}] \geq \varepsilon$$

We denote by $Succ_{g,\mathbb{G}}^{cdh}(t)$ the maximal success probability over all adversaries running within time t.

4   Three-Party MFAKE Protocol

In this section, we describe our 3MFAKE protocol, and prove its security in the random oracle model.

4.1   Description of the Scheme

The arithmetic is in a finite $\mathbb{G} = \langle g \rangle$ of order q, where g is an element in $\mathbb{Z}_p^*$. Then, u and v are random elements in $\mathbb{G}$. Define hash functions $H, H_1 : \{0,1\}^* \rightarrow \{0,1\}^k$. Let A, B be the identifications of the clients and S be the identification of the server. The client A and the server S share the password pwd_A. A has the secret key $sk_A = x_A$, and S stores the public key $h_A = g^{x_A}$. A owns the biometric template $W_A = (W_{A_i})_{i \leq M}$, where W_{A_i} is the i-th bit of W_A and M is the length of the public key h_A, and S stores a tuple of pairs $(g^{r_{A_i}}, h^{r_{A_i}} g^{W_{A_i}})_i$ which is an ELGamal encryption of the reference biometric template W_A. The status between B and S is same with the status between A and S as above.

The protocol proceeds as follows (see Fig.1).

1. Client A randomly chooses a private number $x_1 \in_R \mathbb{Z}_q$, computes $X_1 = g^{x_1}$ and $X_1^* = X_1 \cdot v^{pwd_A}$. Finally A sends (A, S, B, X_1^*).
2. Client B randomly chooses a private number $y_1 \in_R \mathbb{Z}_q$, computes $Y_1 = g^{y_1}$ and $Y_1^* = Y_1 \cdot v^{pwd_B}$. Finally B sends (B, S, A, Y_1^*).
3. For $1 \leq i \leq M$, the server randomly chooses r'_{A_i} and r'_{B_i}, computes $g^{S_{A_i}}$, $g^{S_{B_i}}$, $h^{S_{A_i}}$ and $h^{S_{B_i}}$. Then the server randomly chooses private number $x_2 \in_R \mathbb{Z}_q$ and $y_2 \in_R \mathbb{Z}_q$, computes X_2^* and Y_2^* respectively. Following the protocol S computes $Z_{SA} = (\frac{X_1^*}{v^{pwd_A}})^{x_2}$, $Z_{SB} = (\frac{Y_1^*}{v^{pwd_B}})^{y_2}$, $Z_{SA}^i = h^{S_{A_i}} \cdot g^{W_{A_i}}$ and $Z_{SB}^i = h^{S_{B_i}} \cdot g^{W_{B_i}}$, then S computes $H(A||S||(g^{S_{A_i}})_i||X_1^*||X_2^*||Y_1^*||Y_2^*||Z_{SA}||Z_{SA}^i||pwd_A||i) = \alpha_{A_i}||\beta_{A_i}||k_{A_i}$ and $H(B||S||(g^{S_{B_i}})_i||Y_1^*||Y_2^*||X_1^*||X_2^*||Z_{SB}||Z_{SB}^i||pwd_B||i) = \alpha_{B_i}||\beta_{B_i}||k_{B_i}$. Then, S sends $(S, A, B, (g^{S_{A_i}})_i, (\alpha_{A_i})_i, X_2^*, Y_1^*, Y_2^*)$ to A and $(S, B, A, (g^{S_{B_i}})_i, (\alpha_{B_i})_i, Y_2^*, X_1^*, X_2^*)$ to B respectively.
4. For $1 \leq i \leq M$, A computers Z_A and Z_A^i using the messages from S. Then, A computes $H(A||S||(g^{S_{A_i}})_i||X_1^*||X_2^*||Y_1^*||Y_2^*||Z_A||Z_A^i||pwd_A||i) = \alpha'_{A_i}||\beta'_{A_i}||k'_{A_i}$. A checks α_{A_i} and α'_{A_i}, if the number of the incorrect authenticators is less than m, A computes K'_A. Then, the client randomly chooses a private number $x \in_R \mathbb{Z}_q$, and computes $E_{A1} = g^x || MAC_{K'_A}(g^x)$. Finally, A sends $(A, S, B, (\beta'_{A_i})_i, E_{A1})$.

$ClientA$ $\qquad\qquad$ $ServerS$ $\qquad\qquad$ $ClientB$

$ClientA$:
$$x_1 \in_R \mathbb{Z}_q,\; X_1 = g^{x_1}$$
$$X_1^* = X_1 \cdot v^{pwd_A}$$
$$\xrightarrow{\;A, S, B, X_1^*\;}$$

$ClientB$:
$$y_1 \in_R \mathbb{Z}_q,\; Y_1 = g^{y_1}$$
$$Y_1^* = Y_1 \cdot v^{pwd_B}$$
$$\xleftarrow{\;B, S, A, Y_1^*\;}$$

$ServerS$ — For $1 \le i \le M$:
$$r'_{A_i} \in_R \mathbb{Z}_q,\; r'_{B_i} \in_R \mathbb{Z}_q$$
$$g^{S_{A_i}} = g^{r'_{A_i}} \cdot g^{r_{A_i}}$$
$$h^{S_{A_i}} \cdot g^{W_{A_i}} = h^{r'_{A_i}} \cdot h^{r_{A_i}} \cdot g^{W_{A_i}}$$
$$g^{S_{B_i}} = g^{r'_{B_i}} \cdot g^{r_{B_i}}$$
$$h^{S_{B_i}} \cdot g^{W_{B_i}} = h^{r'_{B_i}} \cdot h^{r_{B_i}} \cdot g^{W_{B_i}}$$
$$\text{choose } x_2 \in_R \mathbb{Z}_q$$
$$X_2 = g^{x_2},\; X_2^* = X_2 \cdot u^{pwd_A}$$
$$\text{choose } y_2 \in_R \mathbb{Z}_q$$
$$Y_2 = g^{y_2},\; Y_2^* = Y_2 \cdot u^{pwd_B}$$
$$Z_{SA} = \left(\frac{X_1^*}{v^{pwd_A}}\right)^{x_2},\; Z_{SA}^i = h^{S_{A_i}} \cdot g^{W_{A_i}}$$
$$H(A||S||(g^{S_{A_i}})_i||X_1^*||X_2^*||Y_1^*||Y_2^*||Z_{SA}||Z_{SA}^i||pwd_A||i)$$
$$= \alpha_{A_i}||\beta_{A_i}||k_{A_i}$$
$$Z_{SB} = \left(\frac{Y_1^*}{v^{pwd_B}}\right)^{y_2},\; Z_{SB}^i = h^{S_{B_i}} \cdot g^{W_{B_i}}$$
$$H(B||S||(g^{S_{B_i}})_i||Y_1^*||Y_2^*||X_1^*||X_2^*||Z_{SB}||Z_{SB}^i||pwd_B||i)$$
$$= \alpha_{B_i}||\beta_{B_i}||k_{B_i}$$

$$\xleftarrow{\; S, A, B, (g^{S_{A_i}})_i, (\alpha_{A_i})_i, X_2^*, Y_1^*, Y_2^* \;}$$
$$\xrightarrow{\; S, B, A, (g^{S_{B_i}})_i, (\alpha_{B_i})_i, Y_2^*, X_1^*, X_2^* \;}$$

$ClientA$ — For $1 \le i \le M$:
$$Z_A = \left(\frac{X_2^*}{u^{pwd_A}}\right)^{x_1}$$
$$Z_A^i = (g^{S_{A_i}})^{x_A} \cdot g^{W'_{A_i}}$$
$$H(A||S||(g^{S_{A_i}})_i||X_1^*||X_2^*||Y_1^*||Y_2^*||Z_A||Z_A^i||pwd_A||i)$$
$$= \alpha'_{A_i}||\beta'_{A_i}||k'_{A_i}$$
$$\text{If } \#\{i: \alpha_{A_i} \ne \alpha'_{A_i}\} \le m$$
$$K'_A = lsb_k\Big(\big\|_{i:\alpha_{A_i}=\alpha'_{A_i}} k'_{A_i}\Big)$$
$$x \in_R \mathbb{Z}_q$$
$$E_{A1} = g^x || MAC_{K'_A}(g^x)$$

$ClientB$ — For $1 \le i \le M$:
$$Z_B = \left(\frac{Y_2^*}{u^{pwd_B}}\right)^{y_1}$$
$$Z_B^i = (g^{S_{B_i}})^{x_B} \cdot g^{W'_{B_i}}$$
$$H(B||S||(g^{S_{B_i}})_i||Y_1^*||Y_2^*||X_1^*||X_2^*||Z_B||Z_B^i||pwd_B||i)$$
$$= \alpha'_{B_i}||\beta'_{B_i}||k'_{B_i}$$
$$\text{If } \#\{i: \alpha_{B_i} \ne \alpha'_{B_i}\} \le m$$
$$K'_B = lsb_k\Big(\big\|_{i:\alpha_{B_i}=\alpha'_{B_i}} k'_{B_i}\Big)$$
$$y \in_R \mathbb{Z}_q$$
$$E_{B1} = g^y || MAC_{K'_B}(g^y)$$

$$\xrightarrow{\; A, S, B, (\beta'_{A_i})_i, E_{A1} \;}$$
$$\xleftarrow{\; B, S, A, (\beta'_{B_i})_i, E_{B1} \;}$$

$ServerS$ — For $1 \le i \le M$:
$$\text{If } \#\{i: \beta_{A_i} \ne \beta'_{A_i}\} \le m$$
$$K_A = lsb_k\Big(\big\|_{i:\beta_{A_i}=\beta'_{A_i}} k_{A_i}\Big)$$
$$\text{If } \#\{i: \beta_{B_i} \ne \beta'_{B_i}\} \le m$$
$$K_B = lsb_k\Big(\big\|_{i:\beta_{B_i}=\beta'_{B_i}} k_{B_i}\Big)$$
$$\text{Check } E_{A1} \text{ and } E_{B1}$$
$$E_{A2} = g^y || MAC_{K_A}(g^y)$$
$$E_{B2} = g^x || MAC_{K_B}(g^x)$$

$$\xleftarrow{\; S, A, B, E_{A2} \;}$$
$$\xrightarrow{\; S, B, A, E_{B2} \;}$$

$ClientA$:
Check the value of E_{A2}
if failed then reject, else
$$sk = H_1(g^{xy}, A, B, S, X_1^*, X_2^*, Y_1^*, Y_2^*)$$

$ClientB$:
Check the value of E_{B2}
if failed then reject, else
$$sk = H_1(g^{xy}, A, B, S, X_1^*, X_2^*, Y_1^*, Y_2^*)$$

Fig. 1. Our 3MFAKE protocol

5. For $1 \leq i \leq M$, B computes Z_B and Z_B^i using the messages from S. Then, B computes $H(B||S||(g^{S_{B_i}})_i||Y_1^*||Y_2^*||X_1^*||X_2^*||Z_B||Z_B^i||pwd_B||i) = \alpha'_{B_i}||\beta'_{B_i}||k'_{B_i}$. B checks α_{B_i} and α'_{B_i}, if the numbers of the incorrect authenticators is less than m, B computes K'_B. Then, the client randomly chooses a private number $y \in_R \mathbb{Z}_q$, and computes $E_{B1} = g^y||MAC_{K'_B}(g^y)$. Finally, B sends $(B, S, A, (\beta'_{B_i})_i, E_{B1})$.

6. For $1 \leq i \leq M$, the server S checks $\beta_{A_i}, \beta'_{A_i}$ and $\beta_{B_i}, \beta'_{B_i}$, if the numbers of the incorrect authenticators are more than m, S rejects. Otherwise, S check E_{A1} and E_{B1}, if both are correct, computes E_{A2} and E_{B2}. Finally, S sends (S, A, B, E_{A2}) to A and (S, B, A, E_{B2}) to B, respectively.

7. Upon receiving the messages from the server, A and B check E_{A2} and E_{B2} respectively, if failed then abort, else each client computers Diffie-Hellman key $sk = H_1(g^{xy}, A, B, S, X_1^*, X_2^*, Y_1^*, Y_2^*)$.

4.2   Security of the Protocol

Theorem 1. *Let us consider the protocol, where passwords is a finite dictionary of size N equipped with the uniform distribution. For any adversary $\mathcal{A}$ within a time bound t, with less than q_S (i.e. $q_{sendclient} + q_{sendserver}$) active interaction with the parties and q_P passive eavesdroppings, and asking q_h queries to the random oracle. Then we have*

$$Adv^{AKE}(\mathcal{A}) \leq \frac{(q_S + q_P)^2}{(q-1)} + \frac{q_h^2}{2^l} + 2\frac{q_S}{N} + 4\frac{q_h}{q} + 2q_S\frac{M^m(2^l-1)^m}{2^{lM}(m-1)!} + 2(2q_h^2 + q_p) \cdot$$

$$Succ_g^{cdh}(T + 4T_e) + 2(q_S + q_P)Adv_{A_{mac}}^{cma}(T_{mac}) + 2q_{sendserver}\left(\varepsilon_{fa} + \frac{\binom{M}{M-m}}{2^{l(M-m)}}\right)$$

where T_e denotes the computational time for one exponentiation.

Proof. The security proof for the protocol defines a sequence of games, starting with the real attack and ending in a game in which the adversary has no advantage.

For each game *Game* G_n, we define the event S_n.

– S_n (for semantic security), which occurs if the adversary $\mathcal{A}$ correctly guesses the bit b chosen at the beginning of the game.

Game G_0. This is the real protocol. By definition, we have

$$Adv^{ake}(\mathcal{A}) = 2\Pr[\mathbf{S}_0] - 1$$

Game G_1. In this game, we simulate the hash oracles H and H_1, but also an additional function H', which will be using later. We also simulate all the instances, as the real players would do, for the Send-queries and for the Execute, Reveal and Test-queries. From this simulation, we easily see that the experiment is perfectly indistinguishable from the real attack. So we have, $\Pr[S_1] = \Pr[S_0]$

Game G_2. For an easier analysis in the following, we cancel games in which some collisions appear: collisions on the transcripts and collisions on the outputs of hash oracles.

The probability is bounded by the birthday paradox:

$$|\Pr[S_2] - \Pr[S_1]| \leq \frac{(q_S + q_P)^2}{2(q-1)} + \frac{q_h^2}{2^{l+1}}$$

Game G_3. In this game, we modify the Execute oracle so that the session key sk of the instance is selected uniformly at random. Concretely, the session key sk is set equal to a random number selected from $\{0,1\}^k$, rather than the output of the random oracle H_1.

In game G_2, the session key sk is the output of the random oracle H_1 on the input $(g^{xy}, A, B, S, X_1^*, X_2^*, Y_1^*, Y_2^*)$. If the adversary doesn't know g^{xy}, he can't distinguish the output of H_1 from a random number uniformly selected from $\{0,1\}^k$. Hence, the games G_3 and G_2 are indistinguishable unless the adversary can solve the CDH-problem. It shows that modifying the Execute oracle in this way affects the advantage of the adversary by a negligible value.

$$|\Pr[S_3] - \Pr[S_2]| \leq q_p \times Succ_g^{cdh}(T)$$

Game G_4. Now, we consider the MAC message via the Execute query. We replace the $MAC_{K_B/K_{A'}}(g^x)$ and $MAC_{K_A/K_{B'}}(g^y)$ instead of random numbers selected from $\{0,1\}^k$.

Because the secret keys of MAC scheme aren't known by the adversary, the games G_4 and G_3 are indistinguishable unless the adversary can break the MAC scheme. So we have

$$|\Pr[S_4] - \Pr[S_3]| \leq q_p \times Adv_{A_{mac}}^{cma}(T_{mac})$$

Game G_5. In this game, we continue considering attacks generated via Execute query. In such a case, we replace the generation of the authenticators with a private oracle H' instead of H: $H'(A||S||(g^{S_{A_i}})_i||X_1^*||X_2^*||Y_1^*||Y_2^*||g^{W_{A_i}}||i)$, $H'(B||S||(g^{S_{B_i}})_i||Y_1^*||Y_2^*||X_1^*||X_2^*||g^{W_{B_i}}||i)$.

We note that we don't use X_1, X_2, Y_1 and Y_2 anymore, therefore we can change the computations of X_1^*, X_2^*, Y_1^* and Y_2^* : $x_1^*, x_2^*, y_1^*, y_2^* \in_R Z_q$, $X_1^* = g^{x_1^*}$, $X_2^* = g^{x_2^*}$, $Y_1^* = g^{y_1^*}$ and $Y_2^* = g^{y_2^*}$. Since we don't use neither the password nor the secret key, we can choose them at the last moment.

The games G_5 and G_4 are indistinguishable unless the following event occurs: the adversary $\mathcal{A}$ queries the hash functions H on $A||S||(g^{S_{A_i}})_i||X_1^*||X_2^*||Y_1^*||Y_2^*||Z_{A/SA}||Z_{A/SA}^i||pwd_A||i$ or $B||S||(g^{S_{B_i}})_i||Y_1^*||Y_2^*||X_1^*||X_2^*||Z_{B/SB}||Z_{B/SB}^i||pwd_B||i$. We denote the event by $AskH_5$.

Then we have $|\Pr[S_5] - \Pr[S_4]| \leq \Pr[AskH_5]$.

If event $AskH_5$ occurs, this means that $\mathcal{A}$ can distinguish whether the simulator has used the private oracle or the public one. In other words, the Diffie-Hellman key lie in the hash list Λ_H, which means that $\mathcal{A}$ can break the CDH-problem.

To show that, we introduce a random CDH instance (X, Y) to the executions of the protocol. We set $u = X$ and $v = Y$. Assume that there is a tuple

$(X_1^*, X_2^*, D = CDH(X_1^*/u^{pwd_A}, X_2^*/v^{pwd_A}))$ such that $A||S||(g^{S_{A_i}})_i||X_1^*||X_2^*||$
$Y_1^*||Y_2^*||Z_{A/SA}||Z_{A/SA}^i||pwd_A||i$ or $(Y_1^*, Y_2^*, D = CDH(Y_1^*/v^{pwd_A}, Y_2^*/u^{pwd_B}))$
such that $B||S||(g^{S_{B_i}})_i||Y_1^*||Y_2^*||X_1^*||X_2^*||Z_{B/SB}||Z_{B/SB}^i||pwd_B||i$ is in Λ_H. Now
we assume the former happens.

Because the corresponding transcript $((A, S, B, X_1^*), (S, A, B, (g^{S_{A_i}})_i, X_2^*, Y_1^*$
$, Y_2^*))$ comes from an execution, we know both X_1^* and X_2^* have been simulated.
In other words, we know the discrete logarithms x_1^* and x_2^*, and $CDH_g(X_1^*/u^{pwd_A}$
$, X_2^*/v^{pwd_A}) = \frac{g^{x_1^* x_2^*}(v^{x_1^*}u^{x_2^*})^{pwd_A}}{CDH_g(v,u)^{pwd^2}}$.

Since pwd_A is non-zero in $\mathbb{Z}_q$, it can be inverted modulo q, then we obtain
$CDH_g(X, Y) = (\frac{g^{x_1^* x_2^*}(v^{x_1^*}u^{x_2^*})^{pwd_A}}{CDH_g(X_1^*/u^{pwd_A}, X_2^*/v^{pwd_A})})^{1/pwd_A^2}$:

$$\Pr[AskH_5] \leq q_h \times Succ_g^{cdh}(T + 4T_e)$$

Finally, we have $|\Pr[S_5] - \Pr[S_4]| \leq q_h \times Succ_g^{cdh}(T + 4T_e)$.

We know that the Execute oracle queries are not of too much help to the adversary. Now we go no showing that that send oracle calls only provide negligible advantage to the adversary.

Game G_6. In this game, we abort the game if the MAC message $E_{A1/A2}$ or $E_{B1/B2}$ is not generated by the simulator.

The games G_6 and G_5 are indistinguishable unless the adversary break the MAC scheme since the adversary don't get the secret key of the MAC scheme.

$$|\Pr[S_6] - \Pr[S_5]| \leq q_S \times Adv_{A_{mac}}^{cma}(T_{mac})$$

Game G_7. In this game, we consider a client instance $A^{i_1}(or B^{i_2})$ that receives an adversarially-generated message $(S, A, B, (g^{S_{A_i}})_i, (\alpha_{A_i})_i, X_2^*, Y_1^*, Y_2^*)$
$(or(S, (g^{S_{B_i}})_i, (\alpha_{B_i})_i, Y_2^*, X_1^*, X_2^*)$. In this case, if $A^{i_1}(B^{i_2})$ accepts, then the game is halted and we say the adversary have succeeded. If this happens, we split the event in two sub-cases:

1. CBad1: The hash query hasn't been asked, but the authenticator α_{A_i/B_i} is valid.
2. CBad2: the adversary manages to build a valid authenticator by asking the hash oracle.

We have $|\Pr[S_7] - \Pr[S_6]| \leq \Pr[CBad1] + \Pr[CBad2]$.

In the first case, the adversary tries to guess the α_{A_i/B_i} at random, since $|\alpha_{A_i/B_i}| = l$, then we can easily see that the probability is upper-bounded by:

$$q_{sendclient} \frac{1}{2^{Ml}} \sum_{k=0}^{m} (2^l - 1)^k \leq q_{sendclient} \frac{M^m (2^l - 1)^m}{2^{lM}(m-1)!}$$

Then we have

$$\Pr[CBad1] \leq q_{sendclient} \frac{1}{2^{Ml}} \sum_{k=0}^{m} (2^l - 1)^k$$

$$\leq q_{sendclient} \frac{M^m (2^l - 1)^m}{2^{lM} (m-1)!}$$

Now we deal with the second case. Note that if the adversary correctly guesses the secret key x_c and the password of the user, then it is trivial for him to generate a valid authenticator. Otherwise, we can solve the CDH-problem with the help of the adversary.

Then we can get:

$$\Pr[CBad2] \leq \frac{q_h}{q} + \frac{q_{sendclient}}{N} + q_h^2 \cdot Succ_g^{cdh}(T + 3T_e)$$

So we have: $|\Pr[S_7] - \Pr[S_6]| \leq q_{sendclient} \frac{M^m (2^l - 1)^m}{2^{lM} (m-1)!} + \frac{q_h}{q} + \frac{q_{sendclient}}{N}$

$$+ q_h^2 \cdot Succ_g^{cdh}(T + 3T_e)$$

Game G_8. In this game, we change the simulation of the oracle so that the authenticator $(\beta'_{A_i/B_i})_i$ which is generated by the adversary will be rejected.

The games G_8 and G_7 are indistinguishable unless a valid authenticator has been rejected. We split the event in three sub-cases:

1. SBad1: the hash query hasn't been asked, but the authenticator $(\beta'_{A_i/B_i})_i$ is valid.
2. SBad2: the adversary manages to build a valid authenticator by asking the hash oracle.
3. SBad3: the adversary uses the compute-oracle, the authenticator is generated through a trusted computation oracle.

We have $|\Pr[S_8] - \Pr[S_7]| \leq \Pr[SBad1] + \Pr[SBad2] + \Pr[SBad3]$.

In this game, the $(\alpha_i)_i$, the $(\beta_i)_i$ and the key are computed from a private random oracle. Therefore, whatever the bit b involved in the Test-query, the answer is random, and independent for all the sessions.

So we have $\Pr[S_8] = \frac{1}{2}$.

In the first case, the analysis is similar with the case CBad1, so we can easily see that:

$$\Pr[SBad1] \leq q_{sendserver} \frac{1}{2^{Ml}} \sum_{k=0}^{m} (2^l - 1)^k$$

$$\leq q_{sendserver} \frac{M^m (2^l - 1)^m}{2^{lM} (m-1)!}$$

As to the second case, because the server accepted a non-Compute-oracle-generated, it means that the biometric corrupt query has been made for the corresponding client A/B. Thereafter, the same analysis, according to the secret key and the password, as the case CBad2 can be done.

With a similar argument to *Game G_7*, we can get:

$$\Pr[SBad2] \leq \frac{q_h}{q} + \frac{q_{sendserver}}{N} + q_h^2 \cdot Succ_g^{cdh}(T + 3T_e)$$

In the third case, sice the adversary uses the computer-oracle by her own biometric W', which is, with high probability, quite different from the client biometric, her probability to succeed is equal to the false-acceptance probability.

It is easy to see that our protocol increase the false-acceptance probability but it doesn't increase the false-rejection probability. The increasing is upper-bounded by

$$\Pr[\#\{i : \alpha'_{A_i} \neq \alpha_{A_i}\} \leq m | d_H(W'_A, W_A) > \mathcal{M}] \leq \frac{\binom{\mathcal{M}}{\mathcal{M}-m}}{2^{l(\mathcal{M}-m)}}$$

$$\Pr[\#\{i : \alpha'_{B_i} \neq \alpha_{B_i}\} \leq m | d_H(W'_B, W_B) > \mathcal{M}] \leq \frac{\binom{\mathcal{M}}{\mathcal{M}-m}}{2^{l(\mathcal{M}-m)}}$$

So we have

$$\Pr[SBad3] \leq q_{sendserver} \left(\varepsilon_{fa} + \frac{\binom{\mathcal{M}}{\mathcal{M}-m}}{2^{l(\mathcal{M}-m)}} \right)$$

Finally, we have $| \Pr[S_8] - \Pr[S_7]| \leq q_{sendserver} \frac{M^m(2^l-1)^m}{2^{lM}(m-1)!} + \frac{q_h}{q} + \frac{q_{sendserver}}{N} +$ $q_h^2 \cdot Succ_g^{cdh}(T + 3\mathcal{T}_e) + q_{sendserver} \left(\varepsilon_{fa} + \frac{\binom{\mathcal{M}}{\mathcal{M}-m}}{2^{l(\mathcal{M}-m)}} \right).$

Combining all the above equations one get the announced result.

Key Privacy with Respect to the Server. We consider the key privacy for the server, the idea that the session key shared between two instances should only be known to these two instances and nobody else, including the trusted server. The goal is to limit the amount of trust put into the server. That is, although we rely on the server to help clients establish session keys between themselves, we still want to guarantee the server can't compute these session keys. In fact, this is the main difference between a key distribution protocol (in which the session key is known to the server) and a three-party key exchange protocol (for which the session key remains unknown to the server). In our protocol, the server knows g^x and g^y but he doesn't compute g^{xy}. In other words, the server can't compute the session key unless he can break the CDH assumption.

5   Conclusion

In this paper, we present a new three-party MFAKE protocol with the assistance of the trusted server, called 3MFAKE protocol, which combines a password, a secure device, and biometric authentications. To the best of our knowledge, it is the first try to give a MFAKE protocol in the three-party settings. Our 3MFAKE protocol is more secure and efficient because the adversary would have to break the three protections in order to win. We also provide a formal security proof of 3MFAKE protocol under the CDH assumption and the random oracle model.

Acknowledgment

This work was in part supported by the National High Technology Research and Development Program of China (No.2009AA01Z417) and Key Scientific and Technological Project of Henan Province (No.092101210502).

References

1. Pointcheval, D., Zimmer, S.: Multi-Factor Authenticated Key Exchange. In: Bellovin, S.M., Gennaro, R., Keromytis, A.D., Yung, M. (eds.) ACNS 2008. LNCS, vol. 5037, pp. 277–295. Springer, Heidelberg (2008)
2. Bresson, E., Chevassut, O., Pointcheval, D.: Security proofs for an efficient password-based key exchange. In: Proc. of the 10th ACM Conference on Computer and Communicate Security, pp. 241–250 (2003)
3. Canetti, R., Halevi, S., Katz, J., Lindell, Y., MacKenzie, P.: Universally composable password-based key exchange. In: Cramer, R. (ed.) EUROCRYPT 2005. LNCS, vol. 3494, pp. 404–421. Springer, Heidelberg (2005)
4. Abdalla, M., Bresson, E., Chevassut, O., Moller, B., Pointcheval, D.: Provably secure password-based authentication in TLS. In: Proc. 2006 ACM Symposium on Information, Computer and Communications Security, pp. 35–45. ACM Press, New York (2006)
5. Abdalla, M., Chevassut, O., Pointcheval, D.: One-time verifier-based encrypted key exchange. In: Vaudenay, S. (ed.) PKC 2005. LNCS, vol. 3386, pp. 47–64. Springer, Heidelberg (2005)
6. Bhargav-Spantzel, A., Squicciarini, A.C., Modi, S., Young, M., Bertino, E., Elliot, S.J.: Privacy preserving multi-factor authentication with biometrics. In: Juels, A. (ed.) Proceedings of ACM DIM 2006 Workshop, pp. 63–72. ACM Press, New York (2006)
7. Needham, R.M., Schroeder, M.D.: Using encryption for authentication in large networks of computers. Communications of the Association for Computing Machinery 21(12), 993–999 (1978)
8. Abdalla, M., Fouque, P., Pointcheval, D.: Password-based authenticated key exchange in the three-party setting. In: Vaudenay, S. (ed.) PKC 2005. LNCS, vol. 3386, pp. 65–84. Springer, Heidelberg (2005)
9. Sun, H.M., Chen, B.C., Hwang, T.: Secure key agreement protocols for three-party against guessing attacks. The Journal of Systems and Software 75, 63–68 (2005)
10. Choo, K.K.R., Boyd, C., Hitchcock, Y.: The importance of proofs of security for key establishment protocols: formal analysis of Jan-Chen, Yang-Shen-Shieh, Kim-Huh-Hwang-Lee, Lin-Sun-Hwang, and Yeh-Sun protocols. Computer Communications 29(15), 2788–2797 (2006)
11. Lu, R., Cao, Z.: Simple three-party key exchange protocol. Computers and Security 26, 94–97 (2007)
12. Nam, J., Lee, Y., Kim, S., Won, D.: Security weakness in a three-party pairing-based protocol for password authenticated key exchange. Information Sciences 177(6), 1364–1375 (2007)
13. Bellare, M., Rogaway, P.: Entity authentication and key distribution. In: Stinson, D.R. (ed.) CRYPTO 1993. LNCS, vol. 773, pp. 232–249. Springer, Heidelberg (1994)
14. Bellare, M., Rogaway, P.: Provably secure session key distribution-the three party case. In: Proc. of the 28th Annual ACM Symposium on Theory of Computing, pp. 57–66 (1996)
15. Bellare, M., Pointcheval, D., Rogaway, P.: Authenticated key exchange secure against dictionary attacks. In: Preneel, B. (ed.) EUROCRYPT 2000. LNCS, vol. 1807, pp. 139–155. Springer, Heidelberg (2000)

KALwEN+: Practical Key Management Schemes for Gossip-Based Wireless Medical Sensor Networks

Zheng Gong[1], Qiang Tang[1], Yee Wei Law[2], and Hongyang Chen[3]

[1] Faculty of EWI, University of Twente, The Netherlands
{z.gong, q.tang}@utwente.nl
[2] Department of EEE, The University of Melbourne, Australia
yee.wei.law@gmail.com
[3] Institute of Industrial Science, The University of Tokyo, Japan
hongyang@mcl.iis.u-tokyo.ac.jp

Abstract. The constrained resources of sensors restrict the design of a key management scheme for wireless sensor networks (WSNs). In this work, we first formalize the security model of ALwEN, which is a gossip-based wireless medical sensor network (WMSN) for ambient assisted living. Our security model considers the node capture, the gossip-based network and the revocation problems, which should be valuable for ALwEN-like applications. Based on Shamir's secret sharing technique, we then propose two key management schemes for ALwEN, namely the KALwEN+ schemes, which are proven with the security properties defined in the security model. The KALwEN+ schemes not only fit ALwEN, but also can be tailored to other scalable wireless sensor networks based on gossiping.

Keywords: Wireless medical sensor network, Gossiping, Key management.

1 Introduction

Following the improvement of wireless technologies and embedded systems, the potential of wireless sensor networks (WSNs) for various applications has been drawing a great deal of attention from the academia and the industry. For WSNs, one of the promising applications is healthcare. A wireless medical sensor network (WMSN, sometimes also called body sensor network) [19], which can be developed from a WSN, is a developing technology for long term monitoring of biological events or any abnormal condition of patients for realizing Ambient Assisted Living (AAL) [1]. In general, a WMSN is a moderate-scale wireless network of low-cost sensors. The purpose of WMSN is to monitor the user's physiological parameters and the related information in environment, e.g., ECG, EMG, EEG, SpO_2 and blood pressure. The collected data will be sent to doctors or nurses for daily diagnosis. A typical scenario of WMSN is illustrated in Figure 1.

X. Lai, M. Yung, and D. Lin (Eds.): Inscrypt 2010, LNCS 6584, pp. 268–283, 2011.

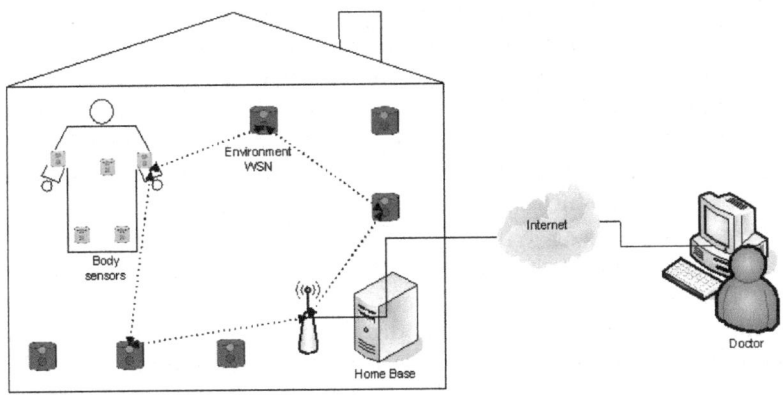

Fig. 1. A Scenario of Wireless Medical Sensor Network

In practice, sensors used in WMSNs also have limited computational abilities and small memories, typically with a low-end CPU and RAM in KBytes level. These factors are important not only in the implantable but also in the external sensor settings because they determine how "hidden" and "pervasive" the sensors are. A gossip protocol is a style of computer-to-computer communication protocol inspired by the form of gossip seen in social networks. Since gossip-based network protocol is proven to be energy-efficient, it would be a low-cost candidate for realizing a WMSN via gossiping [10]. Recently, the ALwEN project [2] built a gossip-based wireless sensor network with 1000 nodes. The estimated lifetime of the network can be 1-2 years, which is a promising property in practice.

Although gossip-based WSN is energy-efficient, designing a appropriate key management scheme for WMSN is a challenging task. In the gossip mode, each node will send out messages to 1-hop neighbor nodes with a well-chosen probability. Thus the security model should consider the situations that all nodes can receive the message, and the message might be dropped during multi-hops. Moreover, the security and privacy problems related to healthcare systems are critical [3]. As a recent study has demonstrated, medical devices that do not support any confidentiality and authentication function are prone to eavesdropping and attacks [11]. Basically, solving these problems requires a key management scheme, which handles the cryptographic keys in a right manner, to provide data confidentiality and authenticity. In the literature, many key management schemes have been proposed for broadcast/gossip WSNs [8,13,16]. However, a WMSN-oriented key management must consider the following differences. Firstly, in WMSN applications, nodes might be added or removed frequently. For the ease of a user, the initialization or revocation of such nodes should be designed as agile as possible. Since we suppose the added/removed nodes might be tampered, the resilience of compromise becomes serious in WMSN key management. Secondly, a typical WMSN is a moderate-scale WSN, so probabilistic key sharing schemes that are designed for large-scale WSNs are not suitable [6,7,12]. For practical applications, a good WMSN key management scheme must consider the above differences carefully, whilst balancing the applicability and the security.

Recently, Law et al. propose a novel WMSN key management scheme, which is called KALwEN [14]. But KALwEN relies on a smart Faraday cage and unicast communication channels, which might be impractical in some cases. In this work, our main contribution are two new key management schemes, namely the KALwEN+ schemes, which are secure against active and aggressive adversaries respectively. Compared to KALwEN, KALwEN+ does not require a Faraday cage, and the communication can be fully broadcast for satisfying gossip-based networks. Based on Shamir's secret sharing technique, KALwEN+ schemes support an efficient way to add/remove nodes. Using formal analysis, we prove that the KALwEN+ schemes are secure in our formalized security model. Based on their theoretical performances, the KALwEN+ schemes not only fit ALwEN, but also can be tailored to other scalable wireless sensor networks based on gossiping.

The rest of this paper is organized as follows. In Section 2, we first describe the system environment, then define the security model for KALwEN+. In Section 3, we describe the KALwEN+ scheme secure against active adversaries and prove its security in our security model. In Section 4, we describe the KALwEN+ scheme secure against aggressive adversaries and prove its security in our security model. In Section 5, we present the performance analysis for KALwEN+ schemes. In Section 6, we conclude the paper.

2   Key Distribution Schemes for Gossip-Based WMSN

In this section we first describe the system environment, then formulate the security properties of key distribution schemes which are specifically tailored to gossip-based WMSN. The security formulations follow that of Bellare and Rogaway [4].

2.1   Environment of Gossip-Based WMSN

Due to the special setting of gossip-based WMSN as shown in Figure 2, at the beginning of the key distribution, a node denoted as the *sink node* is connected to trusted device Dev (e.g., a home-based computer) and key distribution messages will be broadcast by the sink node as an initiator. Then, the sink node and other nodes will engage in a key management scheme. The resultant session keys will be used to protect the data collection and the gossip communications.

2.2   Description of Key Distribution Schemes

We consider an environment which can consist of maximal N sensor nodes, say $node_i$ ($1 \leq i \leq N$), and a trusted device Dev, such as a PC or a programmer or any other trusted infrastructure, which serves as a fully trusted third party (TTP). All nodes are honest and follow the pre-configured instructions, unless they are compromised by an adversary. In addition, we note that the trusted device Dev typically does not have the ability to connect to any node through

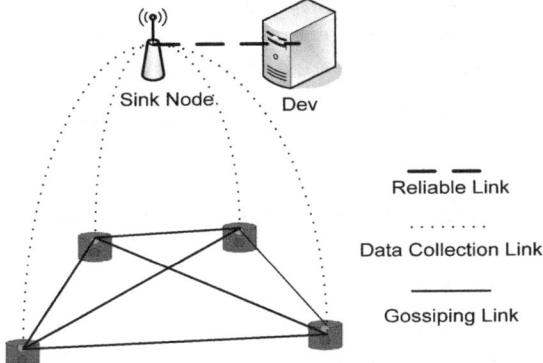

Fig. 2. Environment of Gossip-based WMSN

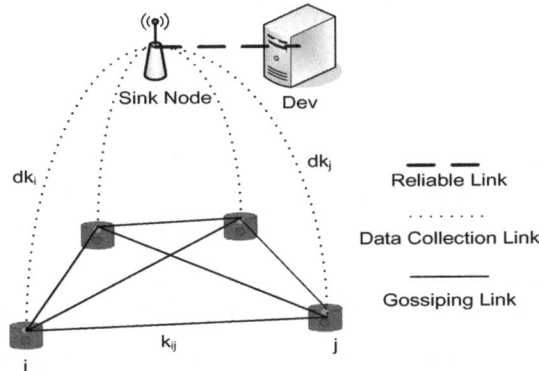

Fig. 3. Key Distribution of WMSN

wireless communication. To facilitate the establishment of our security model, we assume that a key distribution scheme for gossip-based WMSN consists of the following three phases.

1. *System setup*. In this phase, the trusted device Dev generates the long-term credentials. In the symmetric-key setting, a global key k_G is generated, while in the public-key setting a public/private key pair (PK_G, SK_G) is generated. In addition, the trusted device Dev generates some public system parameters *params*.

2. *Node setup*. In this phase, every node $node_i$ is initialized by the trusted device Dev. In the symmetric-key setting, the global key k_G is stored in the node. In the public-key setting, the trusted device Dev generates a public/private key pair (PK_i, SK_i) and stores $(PK_G, Cert_i, PK_i, SK_i, params)$ in $node_i$, where $Cert_i$ is a certificate of PK_i generated with PK_G.

Note that the above two steps can be executed outside the key distribution scheme. The manufacturer can generate the certificates and the global key, and then distribute them to the trusted device and the nodes beforehand.

3. *Key distribution.* In this phase, the following two types of session keys will be distributed to a group of nodes, say $node_i$ $(1 \leq i \leq N')$ and $N' \leq N$.

   - The first type is *data collection keys* used for data collection. For node $node_i$, the data collection key is denoted as dk_i. This key is used for end-to-end communication between $node_i$ and the data collection gateway (namely, the sink node).

   - The second type is *pairwise keys* used for nodes to securely communicate with each other. For a pair of nodes $node_i$ and $node_j$, the the pairwise key is denoted as $k_{i,j}$.

In addition, we assume that the trusted device Dev keeps a counter *ctr* to count all the key distribution sessions. Identified by the counter *ctr*, we denote an invocation of the key distribution protocol as a *session*.

2.3   Security Properties and Their Formulations

In our security model, we only consider attacks from adversaries, whose main focus is to obtain information about the session keys, including cluster keys and pairwise keys, in a certain session. We make the following assumptions:

1. No adversary is present in the *system setup* and *node setup* phases, so that no information about the long-term credentials will be leaked in both phases.

2. An adversary may mount a denial of service (DoS) attack against the key distribution process. How to make a key distribution scheme secure in this case is beyond the scope of our model.

With respect to the secrecy of the data collection keys and pairwise keys, we consider the following types of adversaries.

- *Passive Adversary* ($\mathcal{A}^-$). This type of adversary can only passively eavesdrop on the wireless communications in the network.

- *Active Adversary* ($\mathcal{A}$). This type of adversary can not only eavesdrop on, but also manipulate the wireless communications in the network. The possible manipulation of communication includes delaying, deleting, inserting, and replacing messages.

It is worth noting that both types of adversaries are outsiders since we assume all nodes are honest. In addition, since active adversaries are more powerful than the passive ones, a scheme secure against the former will also be secure against the latter.

Following the work by Bellare and Rogaway [4], the security of a key distribution scheme for gossip-based WMSN is evaluated by the attack game between a

1. Setup: the challenger generates the parameters for the trusted device Dev and publishes the public parameters.

2. Phase 1: Besides delivering messages for all sessions, the adversary is allowed to issue the following types of queries.

   (a) Invoke($set, node_i$): The trusted device Dev initiates a new session to distribute cluster keys and pairwise keys to the nodes in the set set which is a subset of $\{node_j | 1 \leq j \leq N\}$. The node $node_i$ belongs to the set set and acts as the sink node.

   (b) Corrupt$_k$($ctr, node_j$): If the session identified by ctr has successfully ended and $node_j$ has been involved in the session, the challenger sends the data collection key and pairwise keys of $node_j$ to the adversary. Otherwise, the challenger returns nothing.

   At some point, the adversary chooses a counter value ctr^* and a user index j, such that, in the session identified by ctr^*, $node_j$ has successfully ended with $dk_j^*, pk_{j,t}^*$ for all t such that $node_t$ is also involved in the session. This is subject to the restriction that there has been no Corrupt$_k$($ctr^*, node_t$) query for any t.

3. Challenge: Select $b \in_R \{0, 1\}$. If $b = 0$, send $dk_j^*, pk_{j,t}^*$ for all t such that $node_t$ is also involved in the session, otherwise send a replacement to the adversary, where the keys are replaced by a set of random values.

4. Phase 2: The adversary is allowed to issue the same types of queries as in Phase 1, and is subject to the same restriction. At some point, the adversary terminates by outputting a guess bit b'.

Fig. 4. The Attack Game

challenger and an adversary, as shown in Fig. 4, where the adversary's advantage is defined to be $| \Pr[b = b'] - \frac{1}{2} |$. It is worth noting that the challenger faithfully simulates all these activities of the trusted device Dev and all the nodes.

Definition 1. *A key distribution scheme for gossip-based WMSN is secure against (passive and) active adversaries, if any polynomial-time adversary has only negligible advantage in the attack game defined in Fig. 4.*

It is worth stressing that in the attack game defined in Fig. 4, the adversary is allowed to obtain all data collection keys and pairwise keys in all sessions except ctr^*. As a result, a secure scheme under this definition achieves known-key security [15].

Compared with other settings, in gossip-based WMSN, it is reasonable to assume that it is very difficult for an adversary to physically capture the nodes since they will be locked indoor or worn by patients. In other words, key distribution schemes secure against passive and active adversaries provide adequate security guarantees in most application scenarios. However, in some scenarios, higher security level may be required in the presence of an *aggressive adversary* $\mathcal{A}^+$. Besides eavesdropping on and manipulating wireless communications, this type of adversary is also capable of physically compromising some wireless nodes in the network even before the key management.

1. Setup: the challenger generates the parameters for the trusted device Dev and publishes the public parameters.

2. Phase 1: Besides delivering messages for all sessions, the adversary is allowed to issue the following types of queries.

   (a) Invoke($set, node_i$): The trusted device Dev initiates a new session to distribute cluster keys and pairwise keys to the nodes in the set set which is a subset of $\{node_j | 1 \leq j \leq N\}$. The node $node_i$ belongs to the set set and acts as the sink node.

   (b) Corrupt$_k$($ctr, node_j$): If the session identified by ctr has successfully ended and $node_j$ has been involved in the session, the challenger sends the data collection key and pairwise keys of $node_j$ to the adversary. Otherwise, the challenger returns nothing.

   (c) Corrupt$_l$($index$): The challenger returns the long-term public/private keys of $node_{index}$ to the adversary.

   At some point, the adversary chooses a counter value ctr^* and a user index j, such that, in the session identified by ctr^*, $node_j$ has successfully ended with $dk_j^*, pk_{j,t}^*$ for all t which satisfies that $node_t$ is also involved in the session. This is subjected to the following restrictions.

   (a) Suppose the node $node_i$ is the sink node in the session identified by ctr^*. There has been no Corrupt$_l$(i) and Corrupt$_k$($ctr^*, node_i$) queries. The requirement also applies to $node_j$. Note that the adversary may choose $j = i$ in the challenge.

   (b) Suppose set^* is the set of nodes in the session identified by ctr^* satisfying that if $node_j \in set^*$ then there has been no Corrupt$_k$($ctr^*, node_j$) query and no Corrupt$_l$(j) query. The size of set^* is at least 2.

   (c) In the session identified by ctr^*, at most $t-1$ nodes have been issued a Corrupt$_k$ query.

3. Challenge: Select $b \in_R \{0, 1\}$. If $b = 0$, send $dk_j^*, pk_{j,t}^*$ for all t which satisfies that $node_t$ is also involved in the session and there has been no Corrupt$_k$($ctr^*, node_t$) query and and no Corrupt$_l$(t) query, otherwise send a replacement to the adversary, where the keys are replaced by a set of random values.

4. Phase 2: The adversary is allowed to issue the same types of queries as in Phase 1, with the following restriction.

   (a) There has been no Corrupt$_k$($ctr^*, node_h$) query for any h satisfying that there has been no Corrupt$_k$($ctr^*, node_h$) query in Phase 1.

   At some point, the adversary terminates by outputting a guess bit b'.

Fig. 5. The Enhanced Attack Game

The security against an aggressive adversary is evaluated by the attack game between a challenger and an adversary, as shown in Fig. 5, where the adversary's advantage is defined to be $| \Pr[b = b'] - \frac{1}{2}|$.

Definition 2. *A key distribution scheme for WMSN is secure against an aggressive adversary, if any polynomial-time adversary has only negligible advantage in the attack game defined in Fig. 5.*

It is worth stressing that in the attack game defined in Fig. 5, the adversary is allowed to obtain all data collection keys and pairwise keys in all sessions except ctr^*, and it is also allowed to obtain all long-term private keys of all nodes in Phase 2. As a result, a secure scheme under this definition achieves known-key security and perfect forward security [15].

3 Scheme Secure against Active Adversaries

In this section, we propose a key distribution scheme which is secure against active adversaries. In this scheme we use symmetric key cryptographic primitives, including message authentication code (MAC) algorithms [15] and symmetric key encryption schemes. We make use of Shamir's secret sharing scheme [17] to deal with the issues such as adding nodes and key recovery in emergency situations.

3.1 Preliminaries

A MAC algorithm is a family of functions $\{\mathsf{MAC}_k\}$, parameterised by a secret key k, with the following properties:

1. Ease of computation: for a known function MAC_k, given a value k and an input x, $\mathsf{MAC}_k(x)$ is easy to compute. This result is called the MAC-value or MAC.
2. Compression: MAC_k maps an input x of arbitrary finite bit-length to an output $\mathsf{MAC}_k(x)$ of fixed bit-length.

Definition 3. *A MAC algorithm is said to be secure against existential forgery if, for any fixed key k (not known to the attacker), and given any number of MAC queries $\mathsf{MAC}_k(x)$, where the values of x may be chosen by the adversary after observing the results of previous queries, a adversary can only succeed with a negligible probability in finding a pair $(x^*, \mathsf{MAC}_k(x^*))$ where x^* (which could be chosen by the attacker) was not in the set of MAC queries.*

Shamir's secret sharing scheme [17] is based on the polynomial interpolation: given k points $(x_1, y_1), (x_2, y_2), \cdots, (x_k, y_k)$, where all elements are from a finite field $\mathbb{F}$ and x_i ($1 \le i \le k$) are distinct, there is one and only one polynomial $f(x)$ of degree $k-1$ such that $f(x) = y_i$ for all is. To hide a secret d, first pick a random $k-1$ degree polynomial $f(x) = d + a_1 x + \cdots + a_{k-1} x^{k-1}$ and sets $d_j = f(j)$ for $1 \le j \le n$ where $n \ge k$. It is straightforward to verify that, given any subset of k tuples of the set $\{(i, d_i)|1 \le i \le n\}$, we can find the coefficients of $f(x)$ by interpolation and then obtain $d = f(0)$. Given just $k-1$ of these values, d is indistinguishable from a random element from $\mathbb{F}$.

Let $\mathsf{F} : K \times D \to R$ be a function family, where $K = \{0,1\}^x, D = \{0,1\}^y, R = \{0,1\}^z$ for some integers x, y, z. F is said to be a pseudorandom function family if, given the input-output behaviors, an adversary can only distinguish $\mathsf{F}(k, \cdot)$ from Ran with a negligible probability, where k is randomly chosen from $\{0,1\}^x$ and $\mathsf{Ran} : D \to R$ is a random function [9].

3.2 Description of the Scheme

In the *system setup* phase, the trusted device Dev selects a symmetric encryption algorithm (ENC, DEC), an MAC algorithm MAC, and a symmetric key $k_G = (k_1, k_2)$. It also choose a finite field $\mathbb{F}$ for Shamir's secret sharing.

In the *node setup* phase, $(k_G, \mathbb{F})$ is stored in the node. For simplicity, we assume all nodes have been programmed to perform all the operations in the key distribution scheme. The key distribution scheme is as follows.

1. A node $node_i$, which is connected to the trusted device Dev, becomes a sink node, broadcasts a bootstrap message to the network. The bootstrap message is defined as follows

$$node_i + \mathsf{Dev} \to * : ctr, \ \mathsf{ENC}_{k_1}(k_s), \ \mathsf{MAC}_{k_2}(1||ctr||\mathsf{ENC}_{k_1}(k_s)), \quad (1)$$

   where k_s is a randomly-chosen ephemeral key for MAC.
2. After receiving the message, if the value of ctr is smaller than the local counter value, $node_j$ terminates by broadcasting a failure message. Otherwise, it sets the local counter value to be ctr, decrypts $\mathsf{ENC}_{k_1}(k_s)$, and checks

$$\mathsf{MAC}_{k_2}(1||ctr||\mathsf{ENC}_{k_1}(k_s)).$$

   If the MAC code is correct, it sends $(n_j, \mathsf{MAC}_{H(1||k_s)}(2||ctr||ID_j||n_j)$ to the sink node, where n_j is a nonce.

$$node_j \to node_i : n_j, \mathsf{MAC}_{H(1||k_s)}(2||ctr||ID_j||n_j). \quad (2)$$

3. After receiving the message from $node_j$, the sink node first checks the MAC code $\mathsf{MAC}_{H(1||k_s)}(2||ctr||ID_j||n_j)$. If the check fails, it terminates by broadcasting a failure message. Otherwise, it continues. *At a certain point, the sink node learns that session keys need to be distributed to a group of nodes, say $node_j$ ($1 \le j \le N'$) and $N' \le N$.* The sink node computes an ephemeral key pool $\Gamma = \{ek_1, ek_2, \cdots, ek_{N'}, ek'_1, ek'_2, \cdots, ek'_{N'}\}$, where $1 \le j \le N', j \ne i$

   (a) Using Shamir's (t, N)-threshold secret sharing technique, generate N shares $\{(j, sh_j)|1 \le i \le N\}$ to hide a secret $r \in_R \mathbb{F}$.

   (b) Send the following message to the node $node_j$

$$node_i \to node_j : \mathsf{ENC}_{H(2||ID_j||k_s)}(j||sh_j||sk_j||T_j),$$
$$\mathsf{MAC}_{k_2}(ID_j||n_j||ctr||\mathsf{ENC}_{H(2||ID_j||k_s)}(j||sh_j||sk_j||T_j)), \quad (3)$$

   where $sk_j = \mathsf{H}(3||ctr||ID_j||r)$ and T_j is a concatenation of $pk_{t,j}$ for all t such that $ek_t \in \Gamma$ and $t \ne j$. $pk_{t,j}$ is set to be $\mathsf{H}(4||ctr||ID_t||ID_j||r)$ if $t < j$, and $\mathsf{H}(4||ctr||ID_j||ID_t||r)$ otherwise. Consequently, $pk_{t,j} = pk_{j,t}$ holds.

   (c) The sink nodes stores r and the shares $\{(j, sh_j)|N'+1 \le i \le N\}$ at the trusted device Dev.

4. After receiving the message, $node_j$ first checks the MAC code. If the check fails, it terminates by broadcasting a failure message. Otherwise, it decrypts $\text{ENC}_{\text{H}(2||ID_j||k_s)}(j||sh_j||sk_j||T_j)$ to obtain the data collection key sk_j, pairwise keys T_j, and the share (j, sh_j). It also updates ctr to be $ctr + 1$.

Lemma 1. *The proposed scheme is secure under Definition 1 given that the MAC algorithm is secure against existential forgery, the encryption algorithm is a pseudorandom function, and* H *is a random oracle.*

Proof sketch. Suppose that an adversary has the advantage ϵ the attack game shown in Fig. 4. We first have the following observation, which implies the integrity of messages received by all nodes (the adversary is not able to manipulate the messages without being detected by some users).

Observation. *During the attack game, in the session identified by ctr^* (and in any other sessions), $node_j$, for any j such that $node_j$ is involved in the session, is supposed to receive the following values:*

$$ctr^*, \text{ENC}_{k_1}(k_s), \text{MAC}_{k_2}(1||ctr^*||\text{ENC}_{k_1}(k_s)),$$

$$\text{ENC}_{\text{H}(2||k_s)}(j||sh_j||sk_j||T_j),$$

$$\text{MAC}_{k_2}(ID_j||n_j||ctr^*||\text{ENC}_{\text{H}(2||k_s)}(j||sh_j||sk_j||T_j)),$$

If $node_j$ accepts the values, the probability that these values are not generated (or, simulated) by the challenger is negligible. Intuitively, the reason is that, in the proposed scheme, only sink nodes will generate messages in these format, and based on the existential forgeability of the MAC algorithm an adversary can only forge such messages with a negligible probability. The proof is straightforward so that we skip it here.

The rest of the security proof is done through a sequence of games [18].

Game$_0$: In this game, the challenger faithfully simulates the protocol execution and answers the oracle queries from $\mathcal{A}$. Let $\delta_0 = \Pr[b' = b]$, as we assumed at the beginning, $|\delta_0 - \frac{1}{2}| = \epsilon$.

Game$_1$: The challenger performs faithfully as in Game$_0$, except that the challenger stops if the values described in the above observation are not generated by the challenger (referred to as the event Ent_1). Let $\delta_1 = \Pr[b' = b]$ at the end of this game. From the Difference Lemma in [18], we have $|\delta_1 - \delta_0| \leq \Pr[Ent_1]$ which is negligible.

Game$_2$: The challenger performs faithfully as in Game$_1$, except that, in the session identified by ctr^*, in step 3 of the scheme the messages sent to $node_j$, for any j such that $node_j$ is involved in the session, are replaced with the following, where Ran$_j$ is random function.

$$\text{Ran}_j(j||sh_j||sk_j||T_j),$$

$$\text{MAC}_{k_2}(ID_j||n_j||ctr||\text{Ran}_j(j||sh_j||sk_j||T_j)),$$

Since H is a random oracle and the encryption algorithm is a pseudorandom function, Game_2 is identical to Game_1 unless the adversary queries H with $*\|k_s\|*$ (referred to as the event Ent_2), where $*$ can be any string. Furthermore, since the encryption algorithm is a pseudorandom function, $\Pr[Ent_2]$ is negligible. Let $\delta_2 = \Pr[b' = b]$ at the end of this game. From the Difference Lemma in [18], we have $|\delta_2 - \delta_1| \leq \Pr[Ent_2]$ which is negligible.

In Game_2, since the encryption of the session keys and shares is provided by random functions, the probability $\delta_2 = \frac{1}{2}$. As a result, we have

$$\epsilon = |\delta_0 - \frac{1}{2}|$$
$$\leq |\delta_1 - \delta_0| + |\delta_2 - \delta_1| + |\delta_2 - \frac{1}{2}|$$
$$\leq \Pr[Ent_1] + \Pr[Ent_2]$$

Since $\Pr[Ent_1]$ and $\Pr[Ent_2]$ are negligible, the lemma now follows.   □

3.3   Further Remarks

If a key distribution execution has been carried out for $node_j$ ($1 \leq j \leq N'$), later on $node_v$ for any $N' + 1 \geq v \geq N$ may need to join the communications. With respect to the key distribution scheme, there are two possibilities to add a new node into a group. Note the fact that $node_v$ should have been initialized and share the key K_G with the trusted device Dev.

In the first case, if Dev is available, then it can just generate the corresponding data collection key and pairwise keys for $node_v$ based on the secret value r and sends these keys and a share (v, sh_v) to $node_v$ through a secure channel provided by the shared long-term key K_G.

In the second case, if Dev is unavailable, then the secret r can be recovered by $node_j$ ($1 \leq j \leq N'$) using their shares (j, sh_j) ($1 \leq j \leq N'$). Then the corresponding data collection key and pairwise keys for $node_v$ can be generated and transmitted to $node_v$ in the same way as the above case.

4   Scheme Secure against Aggressive Adversaries

In this section, we propose a key distribution scheme which is secure against aggressive adversaries. Compared with the previous scheme, we use public key cryptographic techniques, including digital signature schemes and Diffie-Hellman key exchange, in order to deter the effect of compromised nodes by aggressive adversaries. Nonetheless, both key distribution schemes make use of the secret sharing technique, therefore, the remarks in Section 3.3 apply to this scheme and we skip it here [1].

---

[1] The only difference is that a secure channel between Dev and a new node can be provided using a symmetric key resulted from a standard Diffie-hellman key exchange.

4.1 Preliminaries

Digital signature schemes provide a means by which an entity can bind its identity (or public key) to a piece of information (usually referred to as a message). A digital signature scheme is made up of the following algorithms [15]:

1. KeyGen: which takes a security parameter ℓ as input, and outputs a public (verification) key pk and a private (signing) key sk.
2. Sign: which takes as input a message m and a private key sk and produces a signature σ for the message m.
3. Verify: which takes as input a message m, a public key pk and a signature σ, and outputs either accept (denoted by 1) or reject (denoted by 0).

The existential unforgeability of a digital signature scheme is defined as follows:

Definition 4. *A digital signature scheme is existentially unforgeable under an adaptive chosen message attack if the probability of success of any polynomially bounded attacker in the following game is negligible. The attack game is carried out between an attacker $\mathcal{A}$ and the hypothetical challenger $\mathcal{C}$.*

1. *Initialisation: $\mathcal{C}$ runs KeyGen(ℓ) to generate a public key pk and a private key sk.*
2. *Challenge: The attacker runs $\mathcal{A}$ on the input pk and terminates by outputting a pair m^*, σ^*. During its execution, $\mathcal{A}$ can query the Sign oracle with any input m $(m \neq m^*)$.*

The attacker wins the game if Verify(m^*, pk, σ^*) = 1, and, the attacker's advantage is defined to be $\Pr[\text{Verify}(m^*, pk, \sigma^*) = 1]$.

Given a group $\mathbb{G}$ of order p, the computational Diffie-Hellman assumption holds if, given g^x and g^y where x, y are randomly chosen from $\mathbb{Z}_p$, an adversary can compute g^{xy} only with a negligible probability.

4.2 Description of the Proposed Scheme

In the *system setup* phase, the trusted device Dev selects a digital signature algorithm (KeyGen, Sign, Verify) and a public/private key pair (PK_G, SK_G). It also chooses a group $\mathbb{G}$ for Diffie-Hellman key exchange [5] and a finite field $\mathbb{F}$ for Shamir's secret sharing.

In the *node setup* phase, every node $node_i$ is initialized by the trusted device Dev: a public/private key pair (PK_i, SK_i) is generated and the parameters $(PK_G, Cert_i, PK_i, SK_i, \mathbb{G}, \mathbb{F})$ are stored in the node, where $Cert_i$ is a signature of $PK_i \| ID_i$ signed with SK_G. For simplicity, we assume all nodes have been programmed to perform all the operations in the key distribution scheme. The key distribution scheme is as follows.

1. A node $node_i$, which is connected to the trusted device Dev, becomes a sink node, broadcasts a bootstrap message to the network. The bootstrap message is defined as follows.

$$node_i + \text{Dev} \rightarrow * : ctr, \ g^{r_i}, \ \text{Sign}_{SK_G}(ctr\|g^{r_i}). \tag{4}$$

2. After receiving the bootstrap message, every node $node_j$ verifies the signature. If the signature is not valid or the value of ctr is smaller than the local counter value, $node_j$ terminates by broadcasting a failure message. Otherwise, it sets its local counter value to be ctr, and sends the following message to the sink node.

$$node_j \rightarrow node_i : g^{r_j}, \; \mathsf{Sign}_{SK_j}(ctr||g^{r_i}||g^{r_j}). \tag{5}$$

The node $node_j$ computes two ephemeral keys ek_j and ek'_j, where

$$ek_j = \mathsf{H}(1||g^{r_i r_j}||ctr||ID_i||ID_j), \; ek'_j = \mathsf{H}(2||g^{r_i r_j}||ctr||ID_i||ID_j).$$

3. After receiving the message from $node_j$, the sink node first checks the counter value and the signature. If the check fails, it terminates by broadcasting a failure message. Otherwise, it continues. *At a certain point, the sink node learns that session keys need to be distributed to a group of nodes, say $node_j$* $(1 \leq j \leq N')$ *and $N' \leq N$.* The sink node computes an ephemeral key pool $\Gamma = \{ek_1, ek_2, \cdots, ek_{N'}, ek'_1, ek'_2, \cdots, ek'_{N'}\}$, where for $1 \leq j \leq N', j \neq i$

$$ek_j = \mathsf{H}(1||g^{r_i r_j}||ctr||ID_i||ID_j), \; ek'_j = \mathsf{H}(2||g^{r_i r_j}||ctr||ID_i||ID_j).$$

The sink node then does the following.

(a) Using Shamir's (t, N)-threshold secret sharing technique, generate N shares $\{(j, sh_j)|1 \leq j \leq N\}$ to hide a secret $r \in_R \mathbb{F}$.

(b) Send the following message to the node $node_j$

$$node_i \rightarrow node_j : \mathsf{ENC}_{ek_j}(ctr||j||sh_j||sk_j||T_j),$$
$$\mathsf{MAC}_{ek'_j}(ctr||\mathsf{ENC}_{ek_j}(ctr||sk_j||T_j)), \tag{6}$$

where $sk_j = \mathsf{H}(3||ctr||ID_j||r)$ and T_j is a concatenation of $pk_{t,j}$ for all $ek_t \in \Gamma$ and $t \neq i$. The value $pk_{t,j}$ is set to be $\mathsf{H}(4||ctr||ID_t||ID_j||r)$ if $t < j$, and $\mathsf{H}(4||ctr||ID_j||ID_t||r)$ otherwise. Consequently, $pk_{t,j} = pk_{j,t}$ holds.

4. After receiving the message, $node_j$ first checks the MAC code. If the check fails, it terminates by broadcasting a failure message. Otherwise, it decrypts $\mathsf{ENC}_{ek_j}(j||sh_j||sk_j||T_j)$ to obtain the data collection key sk_j, pairwise keys T_j, and the share (j, sh_j). It also update ctr to be $ctr + 1$.

Lemma 2. *The proposed scheme is secure under Definition 2 based on the computational Diffie-Hellman (CDH) assumption, given that the digital signature scheme is existentially unforgeable, the encryption algorithm is a pseudorandom function, and H is a random oracle.*

Proof sketch. Suppose that an adversary has the advantage ϵ the attack game shown in Fig. 5. We first have the following observation.

Observation. *During the attack game, in the session identified by ctr^*, $node_j$, for any j such that $node_j$ is involved in the session, is supposed to receive the following value:*

$$ctr^*, \; g^{r_i}, \; \mathsf{Sign}_{SK_G}(ctr^*\|g^{r_i}),$$

$$\mathsf{ENC}_{ek_j}(ctr^*\|j\|sh_j\|sk_j\|T_j), \; \mathsf{MAC}_{ek'_j}(ctr^*\|\mathsf{ENC}_{ek_j}(ctr^*\|sk_j\|T_j)).$$

Based on the existential unforgeability of the signature scheme, the probability that the first message is not generated (or, simulated) by the challenger is negligible. Based on the CDH assumption and the existential unforgeability of the MAC algorithm, the probability that an adversary can forge the second message is negligible given that H is a random oracle. Therefore, these values are generated by the challenger, and the proof is straightforward so that we skip it here.

The rest of the security proof is done through a sequence of games [18].

Game_0: In this game, the challenger faithfully simulates the protocol execution and answers the oracle queries from $\mathcal{A}$. Let $\delta_0 = \Pr[b' = b]$, as we assumed at the beginning, $|\delta_0 - \frac{1}{2}| = \epsilon$.

Game_1: The challenger performs faithfully as in Game_0, except that the challenger stops if the values described in the above observation are not generated by the challenger (referred to as the event Ent_1). Let $\delta_1 = \Pr[b' = b]$ at the end of this game. From the Difference Lemma in [18], we have $|\delta_1 - \delta_0| \leq \Pr[Ent_1]$ which is negligible.

Game_2: The challenger performs faithfully as in Game_1, except that, in the session identified by ctr^*, in step 3 of the scheme the messages sent to $node_j$, for any j such that $node_j$ is involved in the session and $node_j$ has not been issued any $\mathsf{Corrupt}_l$ query, are replaced with the following, where Ran_j is a random function.

$$\mathsf{Ran}_j(j\|sh_j\|sk_j\|T_j),$$

$$\mathsf{MAC}_{ek'_j}(ID_j\|ctr^*\|\mathsf{Ran}_j(j\|sh_j\|sk_j\|T_j)),$$

Since H is a random oracle and the encryption algorithm is a pseudorandom function, Game_2 is identical to Game_1 unless the event Ent_2 occurs: the adversary has queried H with $*\|r\|*$ or $*\|g^{r_i r_j}\|*$ for any j such that $node_j$ has not been issued any $\mathsf{Corrupt}_l$ query. Based on the CDH assumption and the security of the Shamir secret sharing scheme, $\Pr[Ent_2]$ is negligible. Let $\delta_2 = \Pr[b' = b]$ at the end of this game. From the Difference Lemma in [18], we have $|\delta_2 - \delta_1| \leq \Pr[Ent_2]$ which is negligible.

In Game_2, since the encryption is provided by random functions, the probability $\delta_2 = \frac{1}{2}$. As a result, we have

$$\epsilon = \left|\delta_0 - \frac{1}{2}\right|$$

$$\leq |\delta_1 - \delta_0| + |\delta_2 - \delta_1| + \left|\delta_2 - \frac{1}{2}\right|$$

$$\leq \Pr[Ent_1] + \Pr[Ent_2]$$

Since $\Pr[Ent_1]$ and $\Pr[Ent_2]$ are negligible, the lemma now follows.   □

5   Performance Analysis

Based on the theoretical results, here we give a performance analysis of KALwEN+. Let T_e be the time for a symmetric key encryption, and T_m be the time for computing a MAC value. Let T_p be time for one exponentiation computation. T_s denotes the time for the (t, N)-threshold secret sharing algorithm which is used in KALwEN+. Let T_{sig} and T_{ver} be the time costs for generating and verifying a signature, respectively. For a gossip sensor network with n nodes, the performance of KALwEN+ is estimated as follows.

Table 1. The Performance Estimation of KALwEN+

KALwEN+	Against Active Adversary	Against Aggressive Adversary
Sink node costs	$(n+1)T_e+(n+1)T_m+1T_s$	$1T_{sig}+(n+1)T_p+nT_e+nT_m+1T_s$
Member node costs	$2T_m+2T_e$	$1T_{ver}+1T_{sig}+1T_p+1T_e+1T_m$
Communication rounds	3-Rounds	3-Rounds
Storage costs	O(n)	O(n)

For the estimated performance, the potential bottleneck of the scheme will be the sink node. Especially in a large network, a typical sensor node can hardly afford the computational costs of (t, N)-threshold secret sharing by itself. Since the sink node can be connected to a trusted device, the computational costs would possibly be shared by the device while the scalability of network is large.

6   Conclusion

By simply using the Shamir's secret sharing techniques and the Diffie-Hellman algorithm, a family of novel key management schemes that named KALwEN+ has been proposed for wireless medical sensor network. The KALwEN+ schemes can be fully based on broadcast communication, and does not require special equipment like some existing schemes do. The secret sharing technique used in KALwEN+ not only supports efficient node addition/removal, but also elegantly ensures security against key-exposure. For applications with highly-constrained resources, the KALwEN+ scheme that fully based on symmetric cryptographic primitives is a reasonable choice. For future work, we will investigate the practical performance and the interoperability of KALwEN+ in a multi-user scenario.

Acknowledgement. We would like to thank Frits van der Wateren and Teun Hendriks for their helpful advice during ALwEN workshops. And also thank many anonymous reviewers for their valuable comments. Zheng Gong acknowledges the support of SenterNovem for the ALwEN project, grant PNE07007. Yee Wei Law is supported by the Australian Research Council Research Network on Intelligent Sensors, Sensor Networks and Information Processing (ISSNIP), and the ARC DP1095452.

References

1. AAL. European union. the ambient assisted living (aal) joint programme (January 2008), http://www.aal-europe.eu/about-aal
2. ALwEN. Ambient living with embedded networks (January 2010), http://www.alwen.nl
3. Anderson, R.: A security policy model for clinical information systems. In: IEEE Symposium on Security and Privacy, pp. 30–43 (1996)
4. Bellare, M., Rogaway, P.: Entity authentication and key distribution. In: Stinson, D.R. (ed.) CRYPTO 1993. LNCS, vol. 773, pp. 232–249. Springer, Heidelberg (1994)
5. Diffie, W., Hellman, M.: New directions in cryptography. IEEE Transactions on Information Theory IT-22(6), 644–654 (1976)
6. Dutta, R., Chang, E.-C., Mukhopadhyay, S.: Efficient self-healing key distribution with revocation for wireless sensor networks using one way key chains. In: Katz, J., Yung, M. (eds.) ACNS 2007. LNCS, vol. 4521, pp. 385–400. Springer, Heidelberg (2007)
7. Dutta, R., Mukhopadhyay, S., Dowling, T.: Generalized self-healing key distribution in wireless adhoc networks with trade-offs in user's pre-arranged life cycle and collusion resistance. In: Q2SWinet 2009: Proceedings of the 5th ACM Symposium on QoS and Security for Wireless and Mobile Networks, pp. 80–87. ACM Press, New York (2009)
8. Eschenauer, L., Gligor, V.D.: A key-management scheme for distributed sensor networks. In: CCS 2002: Proceedings of the 9th ACM Conference on Computer and Communications Security, pp. 41–47. ACM, New York (2002)
9. Goldreich, O., Goldwasser, S., Micali, S.: How to construct random functions. J. ACM 33(4), 792–807 (1986)
10. Haas, Z.J., Halpern, J.Y., Li, L.: Gossip-based ad hoc routing. IEEE/ACM Transactions on Networking (TON) 14(3), 479–491 (2006)
11. Halperin, D., Heydt-Benjamin, T.S., Ransford, B., Clark, S.S., Defend, B., Morgan, W., Fu, K., Kohno, T., Maisel, W.H.: Pacemakers and implantable cardiac defibrillators: Software radio attacks and Zero-Power defenses. In: 29th IEEE Symposium on Security and Privacy, Oakland, California, pp. 129–142. IEEE Computer Society, Los Alamitos (2008)
12. Kausar, F., Hussain, S., Park, J.H., Masood, A.: Secure group communication with self-healing and rekeying in wireless sensor networks. In: Zhang, H., Olariu, S., Cao, J., Johnson, D.B. (eds.) MSN 2007. LNCS, vol. 4864, pp. 737–748. Springer, Heidelberg (2007)
13. Khalili, A., Katz, J., Arbaugh, W.A.: Toward secure key distribution in truly ad-hoc networks. In: IEEE/IPSJ International Symposium on Applications and the Internet Workshops, p. 342 (2003)
14. Law, Y., Moniava, G., Gong, Z., Hartel, P., Palaniswami, M.: KALwEN: A New Practical and Interoperable Key Management Scheme for Body Sensor Networks. In: Security and Communication Networks (2010) (in press)
15. Menezes, A.J., van Oorschot, P.C., Vanstone, S.A.: Handbook of Applied Cryptography. CRC Press, Boca Raton (1997)
16. Oliveira, L.B., Wong, H.C., Bern, M., Dahab, R., Loureiro, A.A.F.: Secleach - a random key distribution solution for securing clustered sensor networks. In: IEEE International Symposium on Network Computing and Applications, pp. 145–154 (2006)
17. Shamir, A.: How to share a secret. Commun. ACM 22(11), 612–613 (1979)
18. Shoup, V.: Sequences of games: a tool for taming complexity in security proofs (2006), http://shoup.net/papers/
19. Yang, G.Z.: Body Sensor Network. Springer, London (2003)

Determining Parameters of Key Predistribution Schemes via Linear Codes in Wireless Sensor Networks

Qi Chen, Dingyi Pei, and Junwu Dong

College of Mathematics and Information Science, Guangzhou University,
Guangzhou 510006, China
chenqi.math@gmail.com, gztcdpei@scut.edu.cn,
djunwu1971@yahoo.com.cn

Abstract. In INSCRYPT 2008, Ruj and Roy proposed deterministic key predistribution schemes using codes. Particularly, they used Reed Solomon codes to present key predistribution schemes. They calculate the connectiviey and resiliency of the network when the schemes are based on Reed Solomon codes. However, the connectivity and resiliency of the network for the schemes using other codes haven't been calculated so far. In the present paper, we will determine the key parameters of predistribution schemes via linear codes in wireless sensor networks. We calculate the connective probability, the probability $fail(1)$ and the upper bound of the fraction of links broken when s nodes are compromised. We use the theory of matroid. We find that it is very surprising that these parameters can be calculated by making use of the chromatic polynomial of the matroid associated to the codes used in the resulting schemes.

Keywords: Key predistribution scheme, Combinatorial design, Linear code, Matroid, Sensor network.

1 Introduction

Sensor nodes are typically low-cost, battery powered, and highly resource constrained. In a distributed sensor network (DSN), the sensor nodes are distributed in a random way, hence the network topology is unknown before the deployment. A sensor node can communicate with other nodes within its neighborhood, which is the radio coverage area formed as a circle of fixed radius centering that node. Once the nodes are deployed, they scan their neighborhoods in order to find out their neighbors.

In this paper, secure communication of DSN is studied. To establish pairwise keys between sensor nodes is essential in enabling them to communicate securely with each other using cryptographic techniques. One method is to use the public-key infrastructure. However, the asymmetric cryptographic primitives are associated with expensive computational cost and demanding huge storage

X. Lai, M. Yung, and D. Lin (Eds.): Inscrypt 2010, LNCS 6584, pp. 284–299, 2011.

consumption. Therefore, a key predistribution scheme (KPS) is preferred, where a set of secret keys is installed in each node before the sensor nodes are deployed.

A KPS consists of three phases: key predistribution, shared-key discovery, and path-key establishment. A sensor node is initially loaded with a fixed number of keys. Each key is assigned a unique identifier. After the deployment of the DSN, the shared-key discovery phase takes place, where any two nodes in wireless communication range exchange their list of key identifiers to each other, and look for their common keys. If they share one or more common keys, they can pick one of them as their secret key for cryptographic communication. The path-key establishment phase takes place if there is no common key between a pair of nodes. A sequence of nodes is called a path. To establish a secure path with node j, a node i needs to find a path between itself and the node j such that any two adjacent nodes (in the radio coverage range) in the path have a common key. Thus messages from the node i can reach the node j securely.

Probabilistic key predistribution is proposed by Eschenauer and Gliger [11]. The main idea is to let each sensor node pick randomly a set of keys from a key pool before deployment so any two sensor nodes have a certain probability of sharing at least one common key. Extensions and variations of this approach can be found in [11,7,10,16].

To construct deterministic KPS for DSN using combinatorial design is another strategy, proposed by Çamtepe and Yener [5]. Further study in this context can be found in [2,6,8,9,15,14,17,21,22,23]. A combinatorial design is a pair of sets $(X, \mathscr{B})$, where X is a finite set of points, $\mathscr{B}$ is a finite set of subsets of X, called blocks. Let $X = \{x_i | 1 \leq i \leq v\}$ and $\mathscr{B} = \{B_j | 1 \leq j \leq b\}$ where each block B_j has n points of X. Any combinatorial design can be used to establish a KPS for a DSN. Assume the DSN has b sensor nodes denoted by $N_1, \ldots, N_b$. In such a scheme, the points in X are mapped to a set of v keys, where each key K_i, for $1 \leq i \leq v$, is chosen randomly from some special key space. Each B_j is assigned to a sensor node N_j and is used to specify which keys are given to the node, i.e. the sensor node N_j receives the set of n keys corresponding to the points in B_j. Deterministic designs have the advantage of efficient shared key discovery and path key establishment, which was pointed out by Lee and Stinson [13] and Ruj and Roy [20].

Recently, Ruj and Roy [19] proposed a class of deterministic KPSs using codes. According to their technique, codewords are mapped to the sensor nodes and (x, i) is mapped to the keys, where x is the i-th symbol of a codeword. In particular they construct deterministic KPSs by making use of the Reed Solomon codes of length $n = q - 1$ over a finite field $\mathbb{F}_q$. They consider the problem of node compromise and calculate the resiliency of the network as the fraction of links broken and nodes disconnected, and present experimental results for these parameters and support them by calculating the upper bounds when the schemes are based on the Reed Solomon codes of length $n = q - 1$ over a finite field $\mathbb{F}_q$. The most important advantage of their scheme is that the network can be made scalable. This means more nodes can be introduced if need arises. However the keys in the already existing nodes need not be changed or redistributed. Moreover their scheme resist the selective node capture attack and some measures of resiliency to random node capture attack are presented in [19].

However, they didn't calculate the connectivity and resiliency of the network for the KPSs using other codes. In this paper, we will determine these parameters for the KPSs based on general linear codes. We first construct the combinatorial designs based on general linear codes, and then construct KPSs based on the resulting combinatorial designs. The main contributions of this paper are summarized as follows.

1) We construct the combinatorial designs based on general linear codes, and propose a technique that can be used to calculate the number of blocks in $\mathscr{B}$ which exactly contain some given u-subset of X for $1 \leq u \leq n$ by making use of matroid theory.

2) We determining the key parameters of KPS via general linear codes. We extend the Ruj and Roy's approaches [19] to calculate the connective probability and the upper bound of the fraction of links broken when s nodes are compromised, combining with matroid theory. Moreover, we calculate the probability $fail(1)$ by using the technique presented in [9].

The rest of this paper is arranged as follows. In Section 2, as the preliminaries, we introduce some knowledge about matroids and some connections between codes and matroids. In Section 3, we construct the combinatorial designs based on general linear codes, and propose a technique that can be used to calculate the number of blocks in $\mathscr{B}$ which exactly contain some given u-subset of X for $1 \leq u \leq n$. In Section 4, we determine the key parameters of KPS via general linear codes. We calculate the connective probability and the upper bound of the fraction of links broken when s nodes are compromised of the resulting schemes. Moreover, we compute the probability $fail(1)$ of the resulting schemes by means of the properties of the corresponding combinatorial designs. In Section 5, we give some examples of KPSs based on codes. We construct KPSs using MDS codes and the codes of $d^{\perp} \geq \lfloor n/2 \rfloor$, and analyze their parameters.

2   Preliminaries

In this section we review some background on matroids, and discuss some connections between codes and matroids. A matroid is an axiomatic abstraction of linear independence. There are several equivalent axiomatic systems to describe matroids: by independent sets, by bases, by the rank function, or, as done here, by circuits. For more background on matroid theory the reader is referred to [24,18].

Definition 1. *A matroid M is an ordered pare $(S, \mathscr{F})$ consisting of a finite set S and a collection $\mathscr{F}$ of subset of S (called independent sets) such that (1)-(3) are satisfied.*

(1) $\emptyset \in \mathscr{F}$;

(2) If $X \in \mathscr{F}$ and $Y \subseteq X$ then $Y \in \mathscr{F}$;

(3) If U, V are members of $\mathscr{F}$ with $|U| = |V| + 1$ there exists $x \in U \backslash V$ such that $V \cup \{x\} \in \mathscr{F}$.

If M is the matroid $(S, \mathscr{F})$ then M is called a matroid on S. A subset of S not belonging to $\mathscr{F}$ is called *dependent*.

Example 1. Let V be a finite vectors space and let $\mathscr{F}$ be the collection of linearly independent subsets of vectors of V. then $(V, \mathscr{F})$ is a matroid.

Following the analogy with vector spaces we make the following definitions.

A *base* of M is a maximal independent subset of S, the collection of bases is denoted by $\mathcal{B}$ or $\mathcal{B}(M)$.

Definition 2. *The* rank function *of a matroid is a function* $\rho : 2^S \to \mathbb{Z}$ *defined by*

$$\rho(A) = max\{|X| \, | \, X \subseteq A \subseteq S, \ X \in \mathscr{F}\}.$$

The *rank of the matroid* M sometimes denoted by $\rho(M)$, is the rank of the set S.

Definition 3. *A matroid M on S is representable over a field $\mathbb{F}$ if there is a vector space V over $\mathbb{F}$ and a map $\phi : S \to V$ which preserves rank.*

As usual, a code C of length n, dimension k, and minimum distance d (resp., at least d) is called an $[n, k, d]$-code (resp., $[n, k, \geq d]$-code) which is a k-dimensional subspace of $\mathbb{F}_q^n$. We sometimes write $d(C)$ to mean the minimum distance of the code C. Moreover, let $d^\perp$ denotes the minimum distance of the dual code $C^\perp$ for a code C.

In general, the matrix G is a generator matrix of a $[n, k, d]$-linear code C over $\mathbb{F}_q$. The columns of G define a $\mathbb{F}_q$-representable matroid $M_C = (S, \mathscr{F})$, where S denotes the set of columns of the matrix G and $\mathscr{F}$ denotes the collection of the linearly independent sets of columns of G. This matroid depends only on the code C, that is, it does not depend on the choice of the generator matrix G. In this situation, we say that M_C is the matroid associated to the code C and also that the code C is a $\mathbb{F}_q$-representation of the matroid M_C. Observe that different codes can represent the same matroid. Important properties about the weight distribution of a linear code can be studied from its associated matroid. Several results on this relation between matroids and codes are given in [1,3,4,12] and other works.

Definition 4. *If $\{B_i : i \in I\}$ is the set of bases of a matroid M on S then $\{S \setminus B_i : i \in I\}$ is the set of bases of a matroid M^* on S. We call M^* the* dual matroid *of M.*

Obviously the relation between M and M^* is symmetrical, that is $(M^*)^* = M$. The different notions of duality that are defined for codes and for matroids are closely related. The matroid M associated to the dual code $C^\perp$ is the dual matroid of the matroid M_G corresponding to C.

Definition 5. *For any matroid M on a set S we define the* chromatic polynomial *of M, $P(M; z)$ by*

$$P(M; z) = \sum_{A \subseteq S} (-1)^{|A|} z^{\rho(S) - \rho(A)},$$

the (Whitney) rank generating function of M, $R(M; x, y)$ by

$$R(M; x, y) = \sum_{A \subseteq S} x^{\rho(S) - \rho(A)} y^{\rho^*(S) - \rho^*(S \backslash A)},$$

and the Tutte polynomial of M, $T(M; x, y)$ by

$$T(M; x, y) = R(M; x - 1, y - 1),$$

where ρ, ρ^* as usual are the rank function of M, M^* respectively.

Note that

$$P(M; z) = (-1)^{\rho(S)} R(M; -z, -1) = (-1)^{\rho(S)} T(M; 1 - z, 0).$$

Example 2. An $[n, k, d]$-code is said to be *maximum distance separable (MDS)* if $d = n - k + 1$.

If C is an $[n, k, d]$ MDS code, then for the matroid M_C, the collection $\mathscr{F}$ of independent sets is

$$\mathscr{F} = \{I \subseteq \{1, \ldots, n\} : |I| \leq k\}.$$

Such a matroid is called a *uniform matroid*, denoted by $U_{k,n}$. Its chromatic polynomial is that

$$P(U_{k,n}; z) = \sum_{i=0}^{k-1} \binom{n}{i} (-1)^i (z^{k-i} - 1).$$

3   Combinatorial Design from Linear Codes

In this section, we will construct the combinatorial designs based on general linear codes, and propose a technique that can be used to calculate the number of blocks in $\mathscr{B}$ which exactly contain some given u-subset of X for $1 \leq u \leq n$ by making use of matroid theory.

Let C be an $[n, k, d]$-code over $\mathbb{F}_q$. Set $\bar{G}$ be the $q^k \times n$ matrix, whose rows are the codewords of the code C.

The matrix $\bar{G}$ can be used to construct combinatorial designs. Regard symbols in different columns as different points in X, hence X has $v = nq$ elements; and take each row of $\bar{G}$ as block, so that each block has n elements. Therefore, we get a combinatorial design $C(X, \mathscr{B})$, where $b = |\mathscr{B}| = q^k$.

Hereinafter, suppose the first k rows of $\bar{G}$ is the generator matrix G of the code C. Then the columns of G define a $\mathbb{F}_q$-representable matroid M_G.

Let S' denote the set consist of the whole columns of $\bar{G}$. For any $A' \in S'$, $\bar{G}_{A'}$ denotes the $q^k \times |A'|$ matrix consist of all columns of the set A'. In the combinatorial design $C(X, \mathscr{B})$, any u-subset P appearing in some block B of $\mathscr{B}$ must be corresponding a row vector of $\bar{G}_{A'}$, where $|A'| = u$, $u = 1, \ldots, n$. Hence if we can determine the number of occurrences of any row vector in $\bar{G}_{A'}$ for any $A' \in S'$, then we can determine the number of occurrences of any u-subset P in all blocks of $\mathscr{B}$.

From now on, let S denote the set consist of the whole columns of G. we can prove the following Lemma (we provide the proof in Appendix):

Lemma 1. *For any $A' \in S'$, all columns of $\bar{G}_{A'}$ are linearly dependent over $\mathbb{F}_q$ if and only if all columns of G_A are linearly dependent over $\mathbb{F}_q$, where $A \in S$ and every column of A is consist of the first k elements in the correspond column of A'.*

Of course, from this Lemma, we can conclude that for any $A' \in S'$, all columns of $\bar{G}_{A'}$ are linearly independent over $\mathbb{F}_q$ if and only if all columns of G_A are linearly independent over $\mathbb{F}_q$, where $A \in S$ and every column of A is consist of the first k elements in the correspond column of A'.

Lemma 2. *Let S denote the set consist of the columns of G. For any $A' \in S'$, any row of $\bar{G}_{A'}$ is corresponding to some $|A'|$-subset of X, which appears in $q^{k-\rho(A)}$ blocks in the combinatorial design $C(X, \mathcal{B})$, where $A \in S$ and every column of A consist of the first k elements in the correspond column of A'.*

The proof of Lemma 2 is provided in Appendix.

In the design $C(X, \mathcal{B})$, given a block $B \in \mathcal{B}$, there are $\binom{n}{u}$ u-subsets in B for $u = 1, \ldots, n$. Let P_{u_v} denote the u-subset in B where $v = 1, \ldots, \binom{n}{u}$. Let $\lambda_{P_{u_v}}$ denote the number of occurrences of the set P_{u_v} in all blocks of $\mathcal{B}$. Then there exists a subset A'_{u_v} of S', which is corresponding to the set P_{u_v} and whose i-th column is corresponding to the i-th element of P_{u_v}. Let $A_{u_v} \in S$ where every column vector of A_{u_v} is consist of the first k elements in the correspond column of A'_{u_v}. From Lemma 2, we can conclude that the following corollary.

Corollary 1. $\lambda_{P_{u_v}} = q^{k-\rho(A_{u_v})}$.

4   KPS from Linear Codes

The KPS from linear codes in wireless sensor networks can be constructed by making use of the design $C(X, \mathcal{B})$. Each B_j of $\mathcal{B}$ is assigned to a sensor node N_j and is used to specify which keys are given to the node, i.e. the sensor node N_j receives the set of n keys corresponding to the points in B_j where $j = 1, \ldots, q^k$. We will determine some key parameters such as connective probability and resiliency, which have not been calculated so far.

4.1   Connective Probability

The number of common keys between any two nodes equals the number of common points between the corresponding two codewords. The number of common keys between any two nodes may be any one from $[0, 1, \ldots, n]$. If two nodes share one or more common keys, they can pick one of them as their secret key for cryptographic communication.

The connective probability p is defined by the probability that any pair of sensor nodes shares a link, i.e., the nodes of a pair have at least one common key. Suppose $B \in \mathcal{B}$ is a block, it is easy to see that the connective probability p, which is independent of the specified block B by the symmetry of combinatorial designs. Each sensor node can communicate with nodes only within its neighborhood. Suppose that two nodes N_i and N_j are in each other's neighborhood. The connective probability that N_i and N_j share at least one key is

$$p = \frac{\#\{B' \in \mathscr{B} | B' \cap B \neq \emptyset\}}{b-1}.$$

This probability is expected to be as large as possible, since it measures the effectiveness of the sensor network.

Now let $\mu_B = \#\{B' \in \mathscr{B} | B' \cap B \neq \emptyset\}$.

Lemma 3. $\mu_B = \sum\limits_{\substack{A \subseteq S \\ 0 \neq \rho(A) < k}} (-1)^{(|A|-1)}(q^{k-\rho(A)} - 1).$

Proof. Given the node B, let $\lambda_{P_{u_v}}$ denote the number of occurrences of the set P_{u_v} in B. Then there exists a subset A'_{u_v} of S' which is corresponding to the set P_{u_v}. Let $A_{u_v} \in S$ where every column vector of A_{u_v} is consist of the first k elements in the correspond column of A'_{u_v}.

Since the number of blocks in $\mathscr{B}$ which intersects with B at all u-set is that

$$\sum\nolimits_{v=1}^{\binom{n}{u}} \left(\lambda_{P_{u_v}} - 1\right) = \sum\nolimits_{v=1}^{\binom{n}{u}} \left(q^{k-\rho(A_{u_v})} - 1\right),$$

it follows that

$$\begin{aligned}
\mu_B &= \sum_{u=1}^{n} (-1)^{u+1} \left(\sum\nolimits_{v=1}^{\binom{n}{u}} \left(\lambda_{P_{u_v}} - 1\right) \right) \\
&= \sum_{u=1}^{n} (-1)^{u+1} \left(\sum\nolimits_{v=1}^{\binom{n}{u}} \left(q^{k-\rho(A_{u_v})} - 1\right) \right) \\
&= \sum_{\substack{A \subseteq S \\ 0 \neq \rho(A) < k}} (-1)^{(|A|-1)}(q^{k-\rho(A)} - 1).
\end{aligned}$$

$\square$

Lemma 4. $P(M; z) = \sum\limits_{\substack{A \subseteq S \\ \rho(A) \neq k}} (-1)^{|A|}(z^{k-\rho(A)} - 1).$

Proof. $\begin{aligned}
P(M; z) &= \sum_{A \subseteq S} (-1)^{|A|} z^{\rho(S)-\rho(A)} \\
&= \sum_{\substack{A \subseteq S \\ \rho(A) \neq k}} (-1)^{|A|} z^{k-\rho(A)} + \sum_{\substack{A \subseteq S \\ \rho(A) = k}} (-1)^{|A|} \\
&= \sum_{\substack{A \subseteq S \\ \rho(A) \neq k}} (-1)^{|A|} z^{k-\rho(A)} - \sum_{\substack{A \subseteq S \\ \rho(A) \neq k}} (-1)^{|A|} + \sum_{A \subseteq S} (-1)^{|A|}.
\end{aligned}$

Since $\sum_{A \subseteq S}(-1)^{|A|} = 0$, it follows that

$$P(M; z) = \sum_{\substack{A \subseteq S \\ \rho(A) \neq k}} (-1)^{|A|}(z^{k-\rho(A)} - 1).$$

$\square$

Theorem 1. $p = 1 - \frac{P(M;q)}{q^k - 1}.$

Proof. Since

$$P(M; q) = \sum_{\substack{A \subseteq S \\ \rho(A) \neq k}} (-1)^{|A|}(q^{k-\rho(A)} - 1)$$

$$= q^k - 1 + \sum_{\substack{A \subseteq S \\ 0 \neq \rho(A) < k}} (-1)^{|A|}(q^{k-\rho(A)} - 1)$$

$$= q^k - 1 - \sum_{\substack{A \subseteq S \\ 0 \neq \rho(A) < k}} (-1)^{(|A|-1)}(q^{k-\rho(A)} - 1)$$

$$= q^k - 1 - \mu_B,$$

it follows that

$$\mu_B = q^k - 1 - P(M; q).$$

Hence

$$p = 1 - \frac{P(M;q)}{q^k - 1}.$$

$\square$

4.2 Resiliency

4.2.1 Analysis of $fail(1)$

If a sensor node is detected as being compromised, then all the keys it possesses should no longer be used by any node in the sensor network. Suppose the sensor nodes N_i and N_j have at least one common key (which means that there is a link between the pair of N_i and N_j). If all the common keys of the pair of N_i and N_j are contained in the compromised sensor node, then N_i and N_j no longer communicate directly, i.e., the link between N_i and N_j is lost. And the probability of links being affected is defined as

$$fail(1) = \frac{the\ lost\ connectivities\ when\ one\ nodes\ are\ compromised}{the\ original\ connectivities}.$$

Generally, we expect $fail(1)$ to be as small as possible, since it measures the resilience of the sensor network, when a random sensor node is compromised.

Suppose that $C(X; \mathscr{B})$ is a combinatorial design constructed by a linear code. Suppose $B \in \mathscr{B}$ is a block, and $P_{u_v} \in B$ denote some u-set in B where $u = 1, \ldots, n$ and $v = 1, \ldots, \binom{n}{u}$. Let $u' = u, u+1, \ldots, n$, $P_{u'_{v'}} = P_{u_v} \cup P$ where $P \subseteq B \setminus P_{u_v}$ and $|P| = u' - u$. There are $\binom{n-u}{v'-u}$ $P_{u'_{v'}}$ in B. Now let $v' = 1, \ldots, \binom{n-u}{v'-u}$. Let $\mu_B(P_{u_v}) = \#\{B' \in \mathscr{B} | B' \cap B = P_{u_v}\}$.

It is easy to see that the following recursion relation holds for $u = 1, \ldots, n$ and $v = 1, \ldots, \binom{n}{u}$:

$$\mu_B(P_{u_v}) = \sum_{u'=u}^{n} \left((-1)^{u'-u} \left(\sum_{v'=1}^{\binom{n-u}{u'-u}} (\lambda_{P_{u'_{v'}}} - 1) \right) \right),$$

from which we can calculate the number $\mu_B(P_{u_v})$ for all $u = 1, \ldots, n$ and $v = 1, \ldots, \binom{n}{u}$. Then we can calculate the probability $fail(1)$ as the following:

$$fail(1) = \frac{\sum\limits_{u=1}^{n} \sum\limits_{v=1}^{\binom{n}{u}} \lambda_{P_{u_v}} \mu_B(P_{u_v})}{b \mu_B} = \frac{\sum\limits_{u=1}^{n} \sum\limits_{v=1}^{\binom{n}{u}} q^{k-\rho(A_{u_v})} \mu_B(P_{u_v})}{q^k(q^k - 1 - P(M;q))}.$$

(We follow the notation used in [14]).

4.2.2 Analysis of $E(s)$

$E(s)$ is defined to be the fraction of links broken when s nodes are compromised. Mathematically, $E(s)$ is given by

$$E(s) = \frac{Number\ of\ links\ disconnected\ when\ s\ nodes\ are\ compromised}{Number\ of\ links\ before\ compromise}.$$

Ruj and Roy [19] calculated the upper bound for $E(s)$ when the KPS is based on the Reed Solomon code of length $n = q - 1$. We will calculate the upper bound for $E(s)$ when the KPSs is based on general linear codes in this section.

Upper bound for $E(s)$. The value of $E(s)$ depends on which s nodes are compromised. Accordingly some keys are exposed. When nodes are compromised randomly it is difficult to predict which set of s nodes are compromised. But it is clear that the maximum number of links will be broken when keys exposed are all distinct.

Theorem 2. $E(s) \leq 1 - \frac{q^k - 1 - (\frac{q-s}{q})^k P(M; \frac{q^2}{q-s}) + (\frac{q-s}{q})^k P(M; \frac{q}{q-s})}{q^k - 1 - P(M; q)}.$

Proof. Suppose s nodes are compromised. Let the compromised nodes be denoted by $N_1, N_2, \ldots, N_s$. Let the exposed keys be denoted by $x_{11}, x_{12}, \ldots, x_{1n}, x_{21}, x_{22}, \ldots, x_{2n}, \ldots, x_{s1}, x_{s2}, \ldots, x_{sn}$. It is clear that maximum nodes will be broken when all the exposed keys are distinct. So while calculating the upper bound of $E(s)$, we consider the number of links disconnected when all the exposed keys are distinct.

the total number of links before compromise is given by

$$\sum_{u=1}^{n}(-1)^{u-1}\left(\sum_{v=1}^{\binom{n}{u}} q^{\rho(A_{uv})}\binom{q^{k-\rho(A_{uv})}}{2}\right).$$

The number of links connected after s nodes are compromised is

$$\sum_{u=1}^{n}(-1)^{u-1}\left(\sum_{v=1}^{\binom{n}{u}} (q-s)^{\rho(A_{uv})}\binom{q^{k-\rho(A_{uv})}}{2}\right).$$

Hence

$$E(s) \leq 1 - \frac{\sum_{u=1}^{n}(-1)^{u-1}\left(\sum_{v=1}^{\binom{n}{u}} (q-s)^{\rho(A_{uv})}\binom{q^{k-\rho(A_{uv})}}{2}\right)}{\sum_{u=1}^{n}(-1)^{u-1}\left(\sum_{v=1}^{\binom{n}{u}} q^{\rho(A_{uv})}\binom{q^{k-\rho(A_{uv})}}{2}\right)}.$$

We know that

$$\sum_{u=1}^{n}(-1)^{u-1}\left(\sum_{v=1}^{\binom{n}{u}} q^{\rho(A_{uv})}\binom{q^{k-\rho(A_{uv})}}{2}\right)$$
$$= \frac{1}{2}\sum_{u=1}^{n}(-1)^{u-1}\left(\sum_{v=1}^{\binom{n}{u}} q^{\rho(A_{uv})} q^{k-\rho(A_{uv})}(q^{k-\rho(A_{uv})} - 1)\right)$$
$$= \frac{1}{2} q^k \sum_{u=1}^{n}(-1)^{u-1}\left(\sum_{v=1}^{\binom{n}{u}} (q^{k-\rho(A_{uv})} - 1)\right)$$
$$= \frac{1}{2} q^k \sum_{\substack{A \subseteq S \\ 0 \neq \rho(A) < k}} (-1)^{(|A|-1)}(q^{k-\rho(A)} - 1)$$
$$= \frac{1}{2} q^k \mu_B$$

$$= \tfrac{1}{2} q^k \big(q^k - 1 - P(M; q) \big),$$

and

$$\sum_{u=1}^{n} (-1)^{u-1} \Big(\sum_{v=1}^{\binom{n}{u}} (q-s)^{\rho(A_{uv})} \binom{q^{k-\rho(A_{uv})}}{2} \Big)$$

$$= \tfrac{1}{2} \sum_{u=1}^{n} (-1)^{u-1} \Big(\sum_{v=1}^{\binom{n}{u}} (q-s)^{\rho(A_{uv})} q^{k-\rho(A_{uv})} (q^{k-\rho(A_{uv})} - 1) \Big)$$

$$= \tfrac{1}{2} q^k \sum_{u=1}^{n} (-1)^{u-1} \Big(\sum_{v=1}^{\binom{n}{u}} \frac{(q-s)^{\rho(A_{uv})}}{q^{\rho(A_{uv})}} (q^{k-\rho(A_{uv})} - 1) \Big)$$

$$= \tfrac{1}{2} q^k \sum_{u=1}^{n} (-1)^{u-1} \Big(\sum_{v=1}^{\binom{n}{u}} (1 - \tfrac{s}{q})^{\rho(A_{uv})} (q^{k-\rho(A_{uv})} - 1) \Big)$$

$$= \tfrac{1}{2} q^k \sum_{\substack{A \subseteq S \\ 0 \neq \rho(A) < k}} (-1)^{(|A|-1)} (1 - \tfrac{s}{q})^{\rho(A)} (q^{k-\rho(A)} - 1).$$

Hence

$$E(s) \leq 1 - \frac{\sum\limits_{\substack{A \subseteq S \\ 0 \neq \rho(A) < k}} (-1)^{(|A|-1)} (1 - \tfrac{s}{q})^{\rho(A)} (q^{k-\rho(A)} - 1)}{q^k - 1 - P(M; q)}.$$

Now let $P(M; z_1, z_2) = \sum_{A \subseteq S} (-1)^{|A|} z_1^{k-\rho(A)} z_2^{\rho(A)}$. Then

$$P(M; z_1, z_2) = \sum_{\substack{A \subseteq S \\ \rho(A) < k}} (-1)^{|A|} z_1^{k-\rho(A)} z_2^{\rho(A)} + \sum_{\substack{A \subseteq S \\ \rho(A) = k}} (-1)^{|A|} z_2^k$$

$$= \sum_{\substack{A \subseteq S \\ \rho(A) < k}} (-1)^{|A|} (z_1^{k-\rho(A)} - 1) z_2^{\rho(A)} + \sum_{\substack{A \subseteq S \\ \rho(A) < k}} (-1)^{|A|} z_2^{\rho(A)} + \sum_{\substack{A \subseteq S \\ \rho(A) = k}} (-1)^{|A|} z_2^k$$

$$= \sum_{\substack{A \subseteq S \\ \rho(A) < k}} (-1)^{|A|} (z_1^{k-\rho(A)} - 1) z_2^{\rho(A)} + \sum_{A \subseteq S} (-1)^{|A|} z_2^{\rho(A)}.$$

In addition, if $z_2 \neq 0$, then

$$\sum_{A \subseteq S} (-1)^{|A|} z_2^{\rho(A)} = z_2^k \sum_{A \subseteq S} (-1)^{|A|} z_2^{\rho(A)-k} = z_2^k P(M; \tfrac{1}{z_2}).$$

Hence if $z_2 \neq 0$, then

$$P(M; z_1, z_2) = \sum_{\substack{A \subseteq S \\ \rho(A) < k}} (-1)^{|A|} (z_1^{k-\rho(A)} - 1) z_2^{\rho(A)} + z_2^k P(M; \tfrac{1}{z_2}).$$

Additionally, when $z_2 \neq 0$,

$$P(M; z_1, z_2) = z_2^k \sum_{A \subseteq S} (-1)^{|A|} z_1^{k-\rho(A)} z_2^{\rho(A)-k}$$

$$= z_2^k \sum_{A \subseteq S} (-1)^{|A|} (\tfrac{z_1}{z_2})^{k-\rho(A)}$$

$$= z_2^k P(M; \tfrac{z_1}{z_2}).$$

Hence

$$\sum_{\substack{A \subseteq S \\ \rho(A) < k}} (-1)^{|A|} (z_1^{k-\rho(A)} - 1) z_2^{\rho(A)}$$

$$= P(M; z_1, z_2) - z_2^k P(M; \tfrac{1}{z_2})$$

$$= z_2^k P(M; \tfrac{z_1}{z_2}) - z_2^k P(M; \tfrac{1}{z_2}).$$

Since

$$\sum_{\substack{A \subseteq S \\ \rho(A) < k}} (-1)^{|A|} (z_1^{k-\rho(A)} - 1) z_2^{\rho(A)}$$

$$= z_1^k - 1 + \sum_{\substack{A \subseteq S \\ 0 \neq \rho(A) < k}} (-1)^{|A|} (z_1^{k-\rho(A)} - 1) z_2^{\rho(A)}$$

$$= z_1^k - 1 - \sum_{\substack{A \subseteq S \\ 0 \neq \rho(A) < k}} (-1)^{(|A|-1)} (z_1^{k-\rho(A)} - 1) z_2^{\rho(A)},$$

it follows that

$$\sum_{\substack{A \subseteq S \\ 0 \neq \rho(A) < k}} (-1)^{(|A|-1)} (z_1^{k-\rho(A)} - 1) z_2^{\rho(A)} = z_1^k - 1 - z_2^k P(M; \tfrac{z_1}{z_2}) + z_2^k P(M; \tfrac{1}{z_2}).$$

Hence

$$\sum_{\substack{A \subseteq S \\ 0 \neq \rho(A) < k}} (-1)^{(|A|-1)} (1 - \tfrac{s}{q})^{\rho(A)} (q^{k-\rho(A)} - 1)$$

$$= q^k - 1 - (\tfrac{q-s}{q})^k P(M; \tfrac{q^2}{q-s}) + (\tfrac{q-s}{q})^k P(M; \tfrac{q}{q-s}).$$

From this the result follows. $\qquad\square$

5 Examples of KPS from Codes

5.1 KPS from MDS Codes

Suppose a KPS based on an $[n, k, d]$ MDS code, then since the matroid M_C is uniform matroid $U_{k,n}$. Its chromatic polynomial is that

$$P(U_{k,n}; z) = \sum_{i=0}^{k-1} \binom{n}{i} (-1)^i (z^{k-i} - 1),$$

it follows that

$$p = 1 - \tfrac{1}{q^k - 1} \sum_{i=0}^{k-1} \binom{n}{i} (-1)^i (q^{k-i} - 1)$$

$$= \tfrac{1}{q^k - 1} \sum_{i=1}^{k-1} \binom{n}{i} (-1)^{i-1} (q^{k-i} - 1)$$

and

$$E(s) \leq 1 - \frac{q^k - 1 - (\tfrac{q-s}{q})^k P(U_{k,n}; \tfrac{q^2}{q-s}) + (\tfrac{q-s}{q})^k P(U_{k,n}; \tfrac{q}{q-s})}{q^k - 1 - P(U_{k,n}; q)}.$$

Additionally, for any u-set P in B, $\lambda(P) = q^{k-u}$ for $u < k$ and $\lambda(P) = 1$ for $k \leq u < n$. Hence

$$\mu_B(P_{u_v}) = \sum_{u'=u}^{n} \left((-1)^{u'-u} \left(\sum_{v'=1}^{\binom{n-u}{u'-u}} (\lambda_{P_{u'_{v'}}} - 1) \right) \right)$$

$$= \sum_{u'=u}^{k-1} \left((-1)^{u'-u} \binom{n-u}{u'-u} (q^{k-u'} - 1) \right)$$

for any $v = 1, \ldots, \binom{n}{u}$. Then

$$fail(1) = \frac{\sum_{u=1}^{k-1} \binom{n}{u} q^{k-u} \left(\sum_{u'=u}^{k-1} \left((-1)^{u'-u} \binom{n-u}{u'-u} (q^{k-u'}-1) \right) \right)}{q^k (q^k - 1 - P(M;q))}$$

$$= \frac{\sum_{u=1}^{k-1} \sum_{u'=u}^{k-1} (-1)^{u'-u} \binom{n}{u} \binom{n-u}{u'-u} q^{k-u} (q^{k-u'}-1)}{q^k \sum_{i=1}^{k-1} \binom{n}{i} (-1)^{i-1} (q^{k-i}-1)}.$$

A class of transversal design $TD(n; N)$, where N is a prime and $n < N$, was constructed in [14]. In the resulting scheme, every two sensor nodes share at most one common key, the number of nodes $b = N^2$, the connective probability $p = n/(N+1)$ and $Fail(1) = (N-2)/(N^2 - 2)$. It was pointed out that the KPS using Reed Solomon code in [19] and the KPS based on orthogonal Arrays in [9] are better than Lee and Stinson's [14] using Transversal Designs.

By using the Reed Solomon codes of length $n = q - 1$ over $\mathbb{F}_q$, we can get the KPS constructed by Ruj and Roy [19]. Dong, et al. [9] constructed KPSs based on orthogonal Arrays. The orthogonal Arrays used by Dong, et al. are corresponding to a class MDS codes of length $n = q+1$ over $\mathbb{F}_q$, so their constructions are special cases of our constructions based on MDS codes. Moreover, suppose q is a prime, by using the $[n, 2, d]$ MDS codes over $\mathbb{F}_q$, we can get the KPSs of connective probability $p = n/(q+1)$, which have the same parameters with the KPSs sing Transversal Designs.

Suppose per node has the same number n of keys, then in the schemes of Dong, et al., $b = (n-1)^k$ and in Ruj and Roy's [19] schemes, $b = (n+1)^k$. Since there exist MDS codes of length n over $\mathbb{F}_q$ where $q > n+1$ and $1 \le k \le n$, we can construct KPSs for larger size of DSN based on MDS codes.

5.2   KPS from Codes of $d^\perp \ge \lfloor n/2 \rfloor$

Generally, it is difficult to calculate the the chromatic polynomial $P(M; z)$. Let $d^\perp$ denotes the minimum distance of the dual code $C^\perp$ for an $[n, k, d]$-code C. The following Corollary give the bounds of $P(M; z)$ for $z \ge 1$.

Corollary 2. *If $d^\perp \ge \lfloor n/2 \rfloor$, then for $z \ge 1$, the following holds*

$(1) \displaystyle\sum_{i=0}^{d^\perp - 1} \binom{n}{i} (-1)^i (z^{k-i} - 1) \le P(M; z) \le \sum_{i=0}^{d^\perp - 2} \binom{n}{i} (-1)^i (z^{k-i} - 1)$, *if $d^\perp$ is even,*

$(2) \displaystyle\sum_{i=0}^{d^\perp - 2} \binom{n}{i} (-1)^i (z^{k-i} - 1) \le P(M; z) \le \sum_{i=0}^{d^\perp - 1} \binom{n}{i} (-1)^i (z^{k-i} - 1)$, *if $d^\perp$ is odd.*

Proof. There are $\binom{n}{u}$ u-subsets in B for $u = 1, \ldots, n$. If $d^\perp \ge \lfloor n/2 \rfloor$, then $\binom{n}{i} \ge \binom{n}{i+1}$ for $d^\perp \le i \le n$. Hence

$$\sum_{\substack{A \subseteq S, |A|=i \\ \rho(A) \ne k}} (z^{k-\rho(A)} - 1) \ge \sum_{\substack{A \subseteq S, |A|=i+1 \\ \rho(A) \ne k}} (z^{k-\rho(A)} - 1)$$

for $d^\perp \leq i \leq n$. Since

$$
\begin{aligned}
P(M; z) &= \sum_{\substack{A \subseteq S \\ \rho(A) \neq k}} (-1)^{|A|} (z^{k-\rho(A)} - 1) \\
&= \sum_{\substack{A \subseteq S \\ |A| \leq d^\perp - 1}} (-1)^{|A|} (z^{k-\rho(A)} - 1) + \sum_{\substack{A \subseteq S, |A| \geq d^\perp \\ \rho(A) \neq k}} (-1)^{|A|} (z^{k-\rho(A)} - 1) \\
&= \sum_{i=0}^{d^\perp - 1} \binom{n}{i} (-1)^i (z^{k-i} - 1) + \sum_{\substack{A \subseteq S, |A| \geq d^\perp \\ \rho(A) \neq k}} (-1)^{|A|} (z^{k-\rho(A)} - 1),
\end{aligned}
$$

the result follow.   □

This Corollary can be applied to give the bounds of the connective probability p and $E(s)$ for KPSs using codes of $d^\perp \geq \lfloor n/2 \rfloor$.

6   Conclusions

In this paper, we calculated the connective probability p, the probability $fail(1)$, and the upper bound of $E(s)$ for KPSs via general linear codes. We found there exist some connections between these parameters and the chromatic polynomial of the matroid associated the linear code used in the construction of the resulting KPS. These parameters can be calculated as long as the chromatic polynomial of the matroid associated the linear code can be determined. We think that other codes can be used to construct better KPS, and it is interesting to find which codes are best to construct KPSs for WSN.

Acknowledgments

We would like to thank the anonymous referees for their valuable comments. This work was supported by the National Natural Science Foundation of China (Grant No. 10971246).

References

1. Barg, A.: On some polynomials related to weight enumerators of linear codes. SIAM J. Discrete Math. 15, 155–164 (2002)
2. Blackburn, S.R., Etzion, T., Martin, K.M., Paterson, M.B.: Efficient key predistribution for grid-based wireless sensor networks. In: Safavi-Naini, R. (ed.) ICITS 2008. LNCS, vol. 5155, pp. 54–69. Springer, Heidelberg (2008)
3. Britz, T.: MacWilliams identities and matroid polynomials. Electron. J. Combin. 19, Research Paper 19, 16 (2002)
4. Cameron, P.J.: Cycle index, weight enumerator, and Tutte polynomial. Electron. J. Combin. 9, Note 2, 10 (2002)
5. Çamtepe, S.A., Yener, B.: Combinatorial design of key distribution mechanisms for wireless sensor networks. In: Samarati, P., Ryan, P.Y.A., Gollmann, D., Molva, R. (eds.) ESORICS 2004. LNCS, vol. 3193, pp. 293–308. Springer, Heidelberg (2004)

6. Chakrabarti, D., Maitra, S., Roy, B.: A key pre-distribution scheme for wireless sensor networks: merging blocks in combinatorial design. Int. J. Inf. Security 5, 105–114 (2006)
7. Chan, H., Perrig, A., Song, D.: Random key predistribution schemes for sensor networks. In: IEEE Symposium on Research in Security and Privacy, Washington DC, pp. 197–213 (2003)
8. Dong, J., Pei, D., Wang, X.: A key predistribution scheme based on 3-designs. In: Pei, D., Yung, M., Lin, D., Wu, C. (eds.) Inscrypt 2007. LNCS, vol. 4990, pp. 81–92. Springer, Heidelberg (2008)
9. Dong, J., Pei, D., Wang, X.: A class of key predistribution schemes based on orthogonal arrays. JCST 23(5), 825–831 (2008)
10. Du, W., Deng, J., Han, Y.S., et al.: A pairwise key predistribution scheme for wireless sensors. In: Proceeding of the 10th ACM Conference on Computer and Communications Security (CCS), Washington DC, pp. 42–51 (2003)
11. Eschenauer, L., Gligor, V.B.: A key-management scheme for distributed sensor networks. In: Proceedings of the 9th ACM Conference on Computer and Communications Security, Washington, DC, USA, pp. 41–47 (2002)
12. Greene, C.: Weight enumeration and the geometry of linear codes. Studies in Appl. Math. 55, 119–128 (1976)
13. Lee, J., Stinson, D.R.: On the construction of practical key predistribution schemes for distributed sensor networks using combinatorial designs. ACM Trans. Inf. Syst. Secur. 11(2) (2008)
14. Lee, J., Stinson, D.R.: A combinatorial approach to key predistribution for distributed sensor networks. In: IEEE Wireless Communications and Networking Conference, WCNC 2005, New Orleans, LA, USA, pp. 1200–1205 (2005)
15. Lee, J., Stinson, D.R.: Deterministic key predistribution schemes for distributed sensor networks. In: Handschuh, H., Hasan, M.A. (eds.) SAC 2004. LNCS, vol. 3357, pp. 294–307. Springer, Heidelberg (2004)
16. Liu, D., Ning, P.: Establishing pairwise keys in distributed sensor networks. In: Jajodia, S., Atluri, V., Jaeger, T. (eds.) ACM Conference on Computer and Communications Security, pp. 52–61. ACM, New York (2003)
17. Martin, K.M.: On the Applicability of Combinatorial Designs to key predistribution for wireless sensor networks. In: Chee, Y.M., Li, C., Ling, S., Wang, H., Xing, C. (eds.) IWCC 2009. LNCS, vol. 5557, pp. 124–145. Springer, Heidelberg (2009)
18. Oxley, J.G.: Matroid Theory. Oxford University Press, Oxford (1992)
19. Ruj, S., Roy, B.: Key predistribution schemes using codes in wireless sensor networks. In: Yung, M., Liu, P., Lin, D. (eds.) Inscrypt 2008. LNCS, vol. 5487, pp. 275–288. Springer, Heidelberg (2009)
20. Ruj, S., Roy, B.: Key establishment algorithms for some deterministic key predistribution schemes. In: Rodrguez, A., Yage, M., Fernndez-Medina, E. (eds.) Workshop on Security In Information Systems, INSTICC (2008)
21. Ruj, S., Roy, B.: Key predistribution using partially balanced designs in wireless sensor networks. In: Stojmenovic, I., Thulasiram, R.K., Yang, L.T., Jia, W., Guo, M., de Mello, R.F. (eds.) ISPA 2007. LNCS, vol. 4742, pp. 431–445. Springer, Heidelberg (2007)
22. Pei, D.Y., Dong, J.W., Rong, C.M.: A novel key pre-distribution scheme for wireless distributed sensor networks. Sci. China Inf. Sci. 53, 288–298 (2010)
23. Wei, R., Wu, J.: Product construction of key distribution schemes for sensor networks. In: Handschuh, H., Hasan, M.A. (eds.) SAC 2004. LNCS, vol. 3357, pp. 280–293. Springer, Heidelberg (2004)
24. Welsh, D.J.A.: Matroid Theory. Academic Press, London (1976)

A   Proofs of Lemma 1 and 2

A.1   Proofs of Lemma 1

Proof. Let

$$
\bar{G}_{A'} = \begin{pmatrix}
a_{1i_1} & a_{1i_2} & \cdots & a_{1i_{|a'|}} \\
\vdots & \vdots & \vdots & \vdots \\
a_{ki_1} & a_{ki_2} & \cdots & a_{ki_{|a'|}} \\
\vdots & \vdots & \vdots & \vdots \\
a_{q^k i_1} & a_{q^k i_2} & \cdots & a_{q^k i_{|a'|}}
\end{pmatrix}.
$$

Suppose all columns of $\bar{G}_{A'}$ are linearly dependent over $\mathbb{F}_q$, then there exist $|A'|$ elements, which are not all zero, $b_1, b_2, \ldots, b_{|A'|} \in \mathbb{F}_q$ such that

$$
b_1 \begin{pmatrix} a_{1i_1} \\ \vdots \\ a_{ki_1} \\ \vdots \\ a_{q^k i_1} \end{pmatrix} + b_2 \begin{pmatrix} a_{1i_2} \\ \vdots \\ a_{ki_2} \\ \vdots \\ a_{q^k i_2} \end{pmatrix} + \cdots + b_{|A'|} \begin{pmatrix} a_{1i_{|a'|}} \\ \vdots \\ a_{ki_{|a'|}} \\ \vdots \\ a_{q^k i_{|a'|}} \end{pmatrix} = 0.
$$

Hence for all $j = 1, 2, \ldots, q^k$, we have

$$
b_1 a_{ji_1} + b_2 a_{ji_2} + \cdots + b_{|A'|} a_{ji_{|A'|}} = 0.
$$

Therefore

$$
b_1 \begin{pmatrix} a_{1i_1} \\ \vdots \\ a_{ki_1} \end{pmatrix} + b_2 \begin{pmatrix} a_{1i_2} \\ \vdots \\ a_{ki_2} \end{pmatrix} + \cdots + b_{|A'|} \begin{pmatrix} a_{1i_{|a'|}} \\ \vdots \\ a_{ki_{|a'|}} \end{pmatrix} = 0.
$$

Hence all columns of G_A are linearly dependent over $\mathbb{F}_q$.

Suppose all columns of G_A are linearly dependent over $\mathbb{F}_q$. Since any row of G' can be denoted by $\boldsymbol{\xi} G$ where

$$
\boldsymbol{\xi} = (\xi_1, \xi_2, \ldots, \xi_k) \in \mathbb{F}_q^k,
$$

any row of $\bar{G}_{A'}$ can also be denoted by $\boldsymbol{\xi} G_A$. Since

$$
\begin{aligned}
\boldsymbol{\xi} G_A &= (\xi_1, \xi_2, \ldots, \xi_k) G_A \\
&= \xi_1 (a_{1i_1}, a_{1i_2}, \ldots, a_{1i_{|A'|}}) + \xi_2 (a_{2i_1}, a_{2i_2}, \ldots, a_{2i_{|A'|}}) + \cdots \\
&\quad + \xi_k (a_{ki_1}, a_{ki_2}, \ldots, a_{ki_{|A'|}}) \\
&= \Big(\sum_{j=1}^{k} \xi_j a_{ji_1}, \sum_{j=1}^{k} \xi_j a_{ji_2}, \ldots, \sum_{j=1}^{k} \xi_j a_{ji_{|A'|}} \Big),
\end{aligned}
$$

and

$$b_1 \sum_{j=1}^{k} \xi_j a_{ji_1} + b_2 \sum_{j=1}^{k} \xi_j a_{ji_2} + \cdots + b_{|A'|} \sum_{j=1}^{k} \xi_j a_{ji_{|A'|}}$$
$$= \xi_1 \sum_{j=1}^{|A'|} b_j a_{1i_j} + \xi_2 \sum_{j=1}^{|A'|} b_j a_{2i_j} + \cdots + \xi_k \sum_{j=1}^{|A'|} b_j a_{ki_j}$$
$$= 0,$$

it follows that all columns of $\bar{G}_{A'}$ are also linearly dependent over $\mathbb{F}_q$.   □

A.2 Proofs of Lemma 2

Proof. At first, we give the technique that computing the number of occurrences of any row vector of $\bar{G}_{A'}$ in $\bar{G}_{A'}$ for any $A' \in S'$.

Let z denote any row of A'. The number of times that a $|A'|$-tuple z appears as a row in $\bar{G}_{A'}$ is equal to the number of $\boldsymbol{\xi}$ such that

$$\boldsymbol{\xi} G_A = z$$

where $\boldsymbol{\xi} \in \mathbb{F}_q^k$. Since G_A has rank $\rho(A)$, this number is $q^{k-\rho(A)}$ for all z. There, according to the constructing method of $C(X, \mathscr{B})$, we can get the conclusion. □

Fully-Secure and Practical Sanitizable Signatures

Junqing Gong[1], Haifeng Qian[1,*], and Yuan Zhou[2]

[1] Department of Computer Science and Technology,
East China Normal University, China
hfqian.ecnu@gmail.com

[2] Network Emergency Response Technical Team/Coordination Center, China

Abstract. Sanitizable signatures have been introduced recently to provide a means for the signer to authorize a censor to modify some parts of the signed message without the help of the original signer. This paper presents the following three contributions. (1) We point out the weaknesses of Brzuska et al.'s (PKC 2009) and Canard et al.'s (CT-RSA 2010) constructions respectively. Namely we show that their constructions are not signer-accountable. (2) We point out the weakness of Brzuska et al.'s security model (PKC 2009) for sanitizable signatures by showing some potential attacks neglected in their original model. (3) We present a stronger security model based on Brzuska et al.'s model and a fully-secure construction based on both Brzuska et al.'s and Canard et al.'s constructions. We must note that our proposed construction is much more practical than prior ones. In detail, the computation costs of signing, sanitizing and verification algorithm are *constant* and the signature size is *constant* as well.

Keywords: sanitizable signatures, chameleon hashes, provable security.

1 Introduction

BACKGROUND. Digital signatures are designed to guarantee the integrity of the released messages. Unforgeability of digital signatures prevents the released messages from being tampered with. After being introduced, digital signatures have been studied widely and play an important role in many fields.

However, in certain scenarios, one may wish to legitimately modify a message signed in advance by another entity without disturbing the original signer for various purposes. Ateniese et al. [2] have shown us a number of examples in the real world. For instance, the database administrator may wish to personalize the commercials signed beforehand by the sponsors in order to guard against annoying spam at a relatively low cost; a set of signed medical records may be released for research purposes after some necessary modifications so as to safeguard the sensitive personal information. For more examples in practice and more detailed explanations, refer to Ateniese et al.'s original paper [2].

Obviously, plain digital signatures do not work well in such a type of scenarios since any modification of a signed message (such as personalizing the commercial

---

* Corresponding author.

X. Lai, M. Yung, and D. Lin (Eds.): Inscrypt 2010, LNCS 6584, pp. 300–317, 2011.

and de-identifying the medical records) is regarded as a malicious behavior. Therefore, sanitizable signatures are introduced and designed to provide integrity as well as flexibility, where the signer is capable of authorizing a censor to sanitize some admissible parts of the signed message without the knowledge of the private signing key. Then, after producing the signature by using sanitizable signature schemes, the signer does not need to engage in any further modification of this released message. Moreover such a modification is controllable, that is both the censor and its sanitizing rights are pre-determined by the original signer at the signing stage. Due to these attractive characteristics, sanitizable signatures are applicable to those aforementioned scenarios.

PRIOR WORK. At ESORICS 2005, Ateniese et al. [2] are the first to give the notion of sanitizable signatures with such desirable property. They defined the elementary algorithms of a sanitizable signature scheme and listed five elementary security requirements, i.e., unforgeability, immutability, privacy, transparency and accountability. In this paper, a sanitizable signature scheme is said to be *fully secure* if it satisfies all these five requirements simultaneously. As a matter of fact, they only formalized unforgeability in a game-based style. Besides that, they also proposed the first construction for sanitizable signatures by using chameleon hashes [24]. However their construction has been shown insecure definitely by Canard et al. [9] recently.

Nevertheless, so far we know, most subsequent constructions (including ours) still follow their paradigm. For instance, Klonowski et al. [23] suggested several extensions of plain sanitizable signatures in [2] to provide a number of additional desirable features, such as limiting the range of some block, achieving strong transparency, etc. Afterwards Canard et al. [10] introduced the notion of trapdoor sanitizable signatures and formalized the security requirements at ACNS 2008. In addition, they also proposed a generic construction for trapdoor sanitizable signatures by using identity-based chameleon hashes [3]. Note that the signer can delegate the rights of sanitizing some message to more than one entity at any time in their model.

At PKC 2009, Brzuska et al. [6] first introduced another two algorithms, i.e., proof and judge algorithm, to give a complete definition of sanitizable signatures, then formalized all the security requirements proposed by Ateniese et al. [2] and also revealed the relationship between them, that is, transparency implies privacy, accountability implies unforgeability. Also, a generic construction derived from Ateniese et al.'s [2] was given, which was claimed to be secure in their proposed formal security model. Especially, they introduced tags that is either produced by the signer using pseudorandom functions and pseudorandom generators or chosen randomly by the censor in order to provide accountability.

Recently, at CT-RSA 2010, Canard et al. [9] first analyzed the weakness of Ateniese et al.'s construction [2] and put forward another construction by introducing an additional sanitizable block as [10] to reach higher efficiency. They principally extended Brzuska et al.'s security model for plain sanitizable signatures [6] to capture several additional features (most of which were suggested by Klonowski et al. [23]), pointed out the weaknesses of two constructions of

Klonowski *et al.* [23] and proposed three extended sanitizable signature schemes that are claimed to be secure in their extended security model.

Very recently, at PKC 2010, Brzuska *et al.* [8] introduced a new security requirement, i.e., unlinkability, and presented a new generic construction based on group signatures [4,5,12,13,14,15,22], which satisfies this new requirement as well as five aforementioned elementary requirements. Though their novel construction reveals a new paradigm for sanitizable signatures, their construction is less efficient due to the relatively lower efficiency of the underlying group signature schemes.

OTHER RELATED WORK. In fact, there are many other definitions, security models and constructions for sanitizable signatures so far, such as those shown in [11,17,19,20,21,25,26,27,28,29,31]. In 2008, Yuen *et al.* [31] summarized and classified these definitions, models and constructions carefully by state controllability, sanitized message, designated sanitizer and transparency respectively. For more details, refer to Yuen *et al.*'s original paper (see Section 3.4 and Section 5.2 in [31]). During the last two years, a few new definitions, security models and constructions have been put forward continuously after Yuen *et al.*'s work [31], such as [18,1,7]. However these sanitizable signature schemes do not follow the definition or security requirements of Ateniese *et al.* [2] and are out of the scope of our discussion. Hence, in the rest of paper, terminology *sanitizable signature* only indicates the sanitizable signature scheme that follows Ateniese *et al.*'s definition and security requirements [2] for simplicity.

OUR CONTRIBUTIONS. To the best of our knowledge, Brzuska *et al.*'s security model [6] is the only formal model for sanitizable signatures so far. [1] And the constructions of Brzuska *et al.* [6] and Canard *et al.* [9] are the only two schemes that are based on chameleon hashes and claimed to be secure in Brzuska *et al.*'s formal model. We revisit both this formal security model and these constructions, and present the following three contributions:

1. **Point out the weaknesses of the existing constructions.** Compared with Ateniese *et al.*'s construction [2], both Brzuska *et al.*'s [6] and Canard *et al.*'s [9] constructions provide more effective accountability. However, we must point out that, in fact, these two constructions have not reached the signer-accountability formalized by Brzuska *et al.* [6] yet. We show an attack on Brzuska *et al.*'s construction [6] and another similar attack on Canard *et al.*'s [9]. Through these two attacks, we can see that both these two constructions allow the adversary to re-use the witnesses generated for other messages or by other signers to mislead the judge about the origin of the current controversial message. Hence we name such a type of attacks *witness re-use attack* here.

---

[1] As mentioned earlier, Brzuska *et al.* [8] reinforced the security model in [6] by introducing a new requirement but the definitions of other five elementary requirements remain unchanged. Hence we consider that the security model in [6] is the only formal model for elementary requirements.

2. **Point out the weakness of the existing security model.** Brzuska *et al.*'s security model [6] offers the designers a powerful formal tool to analyze the security of sanitizable signature schemes and provides a means to comprehend the relationship of these security requirements. Unfortunately, we realize that their security model is not complete yet. In particular, they do not take the description ADM (see Section 2) into account and thus their security model fails to capture the corresponding potential attacks, i.e., *rights forge attack*.

3. **Provide a stronger model and a provably secure construction.** Having shown the flaws in the existing constructions and the weakness of the existing security model, we first expand Brzuska *et al.*'s security model [6] to overcome its weakness. Second, we draw lessons from Brzuska *et al.*'s [6] and Canard *et al.*'s [9] constructions and combine them together to conclude our secure construction. Besides higher security level, our construction also achieves higher efficiency (including both space and time efficiency). In detail, the computational costs of involved algorithms (signing, sanitizing and verification algorithm) are *constant* and the signature size is also *constant*. The constant computational costs of algorithms provide not only high response speed but also low response jitter, meanwhile the constant signature size helps to save bandwidth and storage resources and simplifies the implementation of the scheme as well. Hence our proposed construction is much more practical than prior ones.

ORGANIZATION. In the rest of this paper, we first review the definition of sanitizable signatures as well as some necessary building blocks in Section 2. In Section 3, we review the security model due to Brzuska *et al.* [6] and analyze the constructions of Brzuska *et al.* [6] and Canard *et al.* [9] respectively. In Section 4, we present the weakness of Brzuska *et al.*'s security model. In Section 5, we provide our stronger security model and an efficient and secure construction with formal proof. Finally, we conclude the entire paper in Section 6.

2   Preliminaries

We first recall the definition of sanitizable signatures given by Brzuska *et al.* [6] and then review the definitions and security notions of digital signatures, chameleon hashes with tags, pseudorandom functions and pseudorandom generators respectively.

2.1   Definition of Sanitizable Signatures

Brzuska *et al.*'s definition [6] involves two important descriptions, i.e., sanitizing rights ADM and sanitizing instruction MOD. The description ADM consists of the block length followed by a series of indexes of sanitizable blocks, namely ADM $\in$ $\mathbb{N} \times 2^{\mathbb{N}}$. For simplicity, we abuse the notation $i \in$ ADM to denote the fact that message block m_i is sanitizable. Thus the sanitizing instruction is defined as follows: MOD $= \{(i, m'[i]) : \forall i \in \text{ADM}\}$ where $m'[i]$ is the new content of the i-th message block. For brevity, let MOD(m) denote the updated message derived from the original one m according to sanitizing instruction MOD, which is used to denote the general message modification in [6].

Definition 1 (Sanitizable Signature Scheme). *A sanitizable signature scheme* SS *is composed of the following seven p.p.t. algorithms:*

- **Key generation algorithm for signer** SigKeyGen *takes as input the security parameter* λ *and outputs the key pair* (ssk, spk) *for the signer, that is* $(ssk, spk) \leftarrow \text{SS.SigKeyGen}(1^\lambda)$.
- **Key generation algorithm for censor** SanKeyGen *takes as input the security parameter* λ *and outputs the key pair* (csk, cpk) *for the censor, that is* $(csk, cpk) \leftarrow \text{SS.SanKeyGen}(1^\lambda)$.
- **Signing algorithm** Sign *takes as input the message* m, *the public key* cpk *of the censor, the description* ADM *and the private key* ssk *of the signer and outputs a signature* σ *on this message, that is* $\sigma \leftarrow \text{SS.Sign}(ssk, m, cpk, \text{ADM})$.
- **Sanitizing algorithm** Sanitize *takes as input the message-signature pair* (m, σ), *the public key* spk *of the original signer, the sanitizing instruction* MOD *and the private key* csk *of the censor and outputs an updated message-signature pair* (m', σ'), *that is* $(m', \sigma') \leftarrow \text{SS.Sanitize}(csk, m, \sigma, spk, \text{MOD})$.
- **Verification algorithm** Verify *takes as input the message-signature pair* (m, σ), *the public key* spk *of the original signer and the public key* cpk *of the censor and outputs a binary bit* $d \in \{\text{Valid}, \text{Invalid}\}$ *to indicate whether* (m, σ) *is valid or not, that is* $d \leftarrow \text{SS.Verify}(m, \sigma, spk, cpk)$.
- **Proof algorithm** Prove *takes as input the message-signature pair* (m, σ), *the public key* cpk *of the censor, the private key* ssk *of the original signer and an internal database* $\mathfrak{DB}$ *and outputs a witness* π *for* (m, σ), *that is* $\pi \leftarrow \text{SS.Prove}(ssk, m, \sigma, cpk, \mathfrak{DB})$.
- **Judge algorithm** Judge *takes as input the message-signature pair* (m, σ), *the public key* spk *of the original signer, the public key* cpk *of the censor and the witness* π *and outputs a binary bit* $d \in \{\text{Sig}, \text{San}\}$ *to indicate the actual originator of the given message-signature pair, that is* $d \leftarrow \text{SS.Judge}(m, \sigma, \pi, spk, cpk)$. *Note that if* $\pi = \bot$, *then the judge outputs* $d = \text{Sig}$.

A meaningful sanitizable signature scheme should meet three correctness requirements: *signing correctness* means that any well-established message-signature pair output by SS.Sign should be accepted by SS.Verify; *sanitizing correctness* means that any well-established message-signature pair output by SS.Sanitize should also be accepted by SS.Verify; and *proof correctness* means that any well-established witness for any sanitized message should let the judge accuse the sanitizer. For more precise definitions, refer to [6].

2.2   Building Blocks

DIGITAL SIGNATURES. We recall the definition of digital signatures in Definition 2. Here we follow the security notion of Goldwasser, Micali and Rivest [16], i.e., existentially unforgeability against adaptively chosen message attacks (EU-CMA) and review its notion in Definition 3.

Definition 2 (Digital Signature). *A digital signature scheme* DS *consists of three p.p.t. algorithms:*

- *Key generation algorithm* KeyGen *takes as input the security parameter λ and outputs the signing key and verification key (sk, vk), which is denoted by $(sk, vk) \leftarrow$ DS.KeyGen(1^λ).*
- *Signing algorithm* Sign *takes as input the message m and the signing key sk of the signer and outputs a signature σ on this message, which is denoted by $\sigma \leftarrow$ DS.Sign(sk, m).*
- *Verification algorithm* Verify *takes as input the message-signature pair (m, σ), the verification key vk of the signer and outputs a binary bit $d \in \{$Valid, Invalid$\}$ to indicate whether (m, σ) is valid or not, which is denoted by $d \leftarrow$ DS.Verify(vk, m, σ).*

Definition 3 (EU-CMA). *A digital signature scheme* DS *is said to be (q_s, t, ϵ)-existentially unforgeable against adaptively chosen message attacks (EU-CMA) if* $\Pr[\text{Exp}_{\text{EU-CMA}}(\mathcal{A}) = \text{True}] \leq \epsilon$ *for any adversary $\mathcal{A}$ after at most q_s signing queries and at most t steps, where* $\text{Exp}_{\text{EU-CMA}}$ *is defined as follows.*

EXPERIMENT $\text{Exp}_{\text{EU-CMA}}(\mathcal{A})$:

$(sk^*, vk^*) \leftarrow$ DS.KeyGen(1^λ).

$(m^*, \sigma^*) \leftarrow \mathcal{A}^{\mathcal{O}_{Sig}}(1^\lambda, vk^*)$ where $\forall\, i \in [1, q_s]$, $\sigma_i \leftarrow \mathcal{O}_{Sig}(m_i)$.

$\text{Exp}_{\text{EU-CMA}}(\mathcal{A}) = \text{True iff}$ DS.Verify$(vk^*, m^*, \sigma^*) = \text{Valid and } \forall\, i \in [1, q_s],\ m^* \neq m_i$.

CHAMELEON HASHES WITH TAGS. We recall the concept of chameleon hashes with tags in Definition 4. Here we follow the security notion proposed by Brzuska *et al.* [6], that is collision-resistance under random tagging attacks (CR-RTA) and recall this security notion in Definition 5.

Definition 4 (Chameleon Hashes with Tags). *A chameleon hash scheme* CH *consists of three p.p.t. algorithms:*

- *Key generation algorithm* KeyGen *takes as input the security parameter λ and outputs the adaptation key and hashing key (ak, hk), which is denoted by $(ak, hk) \leftarrow$ CH.KeyGen(1^λ).*
- *Hashing algorithm* Hash *takes as input the message m, tag t, randomness r and the hashing key hk and outputs a hash value h on this message, which is denoted by $h \leftarrow$ CH.Hash$(hk, m, t; r)$.*
- *Adaptation algorithm* Adapt *takes as input the old message m, the old tag t, the old randomness r, the new message m, the new tag t and the adaptation key ak and outputs a new randomness r' such that* CH.Hash$(hk, m, t; r) =$ CH.Hash$(hk, m', t'; r')$, *which is denoted by $r' \leftarrow$ CH.Adapt(ak, m, t, r, m', t'). Furthermore, it is required that the distribution of r' is identical to that of r.*

Definition 5 (CR-RTA). *A chameleon hash scheme* CH *is said to be (q_a, t, ϵ)-collision-resistant under random tagging attacks (CR-RTA) if* $\Pr[\text{Exp}_{\text{CR-RTA}}(\mathcal{A}) = \text{True}] \leq \epsilon$ *for any adversary $\mathcal{A}$ after at most q_a adaptation queries and at most t steps, where* $\text{Exp}_{\text{CR-RTA}}$ *is defined as follows.*

EXPERIMENT $\mathrm{Exp}_{\mathrm{CR-RTA}}(\mathcal{A})$:
$(ak^*, hk^*) \leftarrow \mathrm{CH.KeyGen}(1^\lambda)$.
$(m, t, r, m', t', r') \leftarrow \mathcal{A}^{\mathcal{O}_{Adapt}}(1^\lambda, hk^*)$ where
$\forall\, i \in [1, q_a]$, $(t'_i, r'_i) \leftarrow \mathcal{O}_{Adapt}(m_i, t_i, r_i, m'_i)$ where
$t'_i \overset{R}{\leftarrow} \{0,1\}^{2\lambda}$ and $r'_i \leftarrow \mathrm{CH.Adapt}(ak^*, m_i, t_i, r_i, m'_i, t'_i)$.
$\mathrm{Exp}_{\mathrm{CR-RTA}}(\mathcal{A}) = \mathrm{True}$ iff $\mathrm{CH.Hash}(hk^*, m, t; r) = \mathrm{CH.Hash}(hk^*, m', t'; r')$ and
$(t, m) \neq (t', m')$ and $\forall\, i \in [1, q_a]$, $\{(t, m), (t', m')\} \neq \{(t_i, m_i), (t'_i, m'_i)\}$ and
$\forall\, i, j \in [1, q_a]$, $\{(t, m), (t', m')\} \neq \{(t'_i, m'_i), (t'_j, m'_j)\}$.

PSEUDORANDOM FUNCTIONS AND PSEUDORANDOM GENERATORS. In our construction, we also employ a pseudorandom function $\mathrm{PRF} : \{0,1\}^\lambda \times \{0,1\}^\lambda \rightarrow \{0,1\}^\lambda$ and a pseudorandom generator $\mathrm{PRG} : \{0,1\}^\lambda \rightarrow \{0,1\}^{2\lambda}$ as in [6]. We require that both PRF and PRG are pseudorandom.

Definition 6. *Assume that function* $\mathrm{TRF} : \{0,1\}^\lambda \times \{0,1\}^\lambda \rightarrow \{0,1\}^\lambda$ *is a truly random function. A function* PRF *is said to be* (t, ϵ)-*pseudorandom if*

$$\left| \Pr[\mathcal{A}^{\mathrm{TRF}} = 1] - \Pr[\mathcal{A}^{\mathrm{PRF}} = 1] \right| \leq \epsilon$$

for any p.p.t. adversary $\mathcal{A}$ *after at most* t *steps.*

Definition 7. *Let* U_1 *be a uniform distribution over* $\{0,1\}^\lambda$ *and* U_2 *be a uniform distribution over* $\{0,1\}^{2\lambda}$. *A function* PRG *is said to be* (t, ϵ)-*pseudorandom if*

$$\left| \Pr[\mathcal{A}(\mathrm{PRG}(U_1)) = 1] - \Pr[\mathcal{A}(U_2) = 1] \right| \leq \epsilon$$

for any p.p.t. adversary $\mathcal{A}$ *after at most* t *steps.*

3   Cryptanalysis on Previous Constructions

Though both Brzuska *et al.* [6] and Canard *et al.* [9] claimed that their constructions are secure in Brzuska *et al.*'s model [6]. However, we show that it is not the case. In this section, we first review the security model due to Brzuska *et al.* [6]. Then we recall these two constructions and present the attacks on them respectively.

3.1   Review of Brzuska *et al.*'s Security Model

When introducing the notion of sanitizable signatures, Ateniese et al. [2] listed the following five elementary requirements:

- *Unforgeability*: Any outsider is not able to forge any signature in the name of either the signer or the censor.
- *Immutability*: An authorized censor is allowed to sanitize *only* admissible blocks pre-determined by the original signer.
- *Privacy*: No one except the signer and the censor is able to recover the sanitized message blocks.
- *Transparency*: No one except the signer and the censor is able to tell whether the message has been sanitized.

– *Accountability*: Any judge is able to reveal the actual originator of the controversial message correctly.

Brzuska *et al.* [6] formalized these five security requirements in a game-based style and revealed the relationship of them. Note that they consider two flavors of accountability. Hence their security model for sanitizable signatures consists of six definitions corresponding to unforgeability, immutability, privacy, transparency, *signer-accountability* as well as *sanitizer-accountability* respectively. In this paper, a sanitizable signature scheme is said to be *fully secure* if it meets all the above requirements. Since transparency implies privacy and the following discussion about this security model does not involve this requirement, we omit the corresponding experiment and definition here. The experiments and definitions corresponding to other requirements are shown as follows.

EXPERIMENT $\text{Exp}_{\text{Unf}}(\mathcal{A})$:
$(ssk^*, spk^*) \leftarrow \text{SS.SigKeyGen}(1^\lambda), (csk^*, cpk^*) \leftarrow \text{SS.SanKeyGen}(1^\lambda)$.
$(m^*, \sigma^*) \leftarrow \mathcal{A}^{\mathcal{O}_{Sig}, \mathcal{O}_{San}, \mathcal{O}_{Prf}}(1^\lambda, spk^*, cpk^*)$ where
$\forall\, i \in [1, q_s], \sigma_i \leftarrow \mathcal{O}_{Sig}(m_i, cpk_i, \text{ADM}_i), \forall\, j \in [1, q_c], (m'_j, \sigma'_j) \leftarrow \mathcal{O}_{San}(m_j, \sigma_j, spk_j, \text{MOD}_j)$.
$\text{Exp}_{\text{Unf}}(\mathcal{A}) = \text{True iff SS.Verify}(m^*, \sigma^*, spk^*, cpk^*) = \text{Valid and}$
$\forall\, i \in [1, q_s], (cpk^*, m^*) \neq (cpk_i, m_i)$ and $\forall\, j \in [1, q_c], (spk^*, m^*) \neq (spk_j, m'_j)$.

EXPERIMENT $\text{Exp}_{\text{Imm}}(\mathcal{A})$:
$(ssk^*, spk^*) \leftarrow \text{SS.SigKeyGen}(1^\lambda)$.
$(cpk^*, m^*, \sigma^*) \leftarrow \mathcal{A}^{\mathcal{O}_{Sig}, \mathcal{O}_{Prf}}(1^\lambda, spk^*)$ where $\forall\, i \in [1, q_s], \sigma_i \leftarrow \mathcal{O}_{Sig}(m_i, cpk_i, \text{ADM}_i)$.
$\text{Exp}_{\text{Imm}}(\mathcal{A}) = \text{True iff SS.Verify}(m^*, \sigma^*, spk^*, cpk^*) = \text{Valid and}$
$\forall\, i \in [1, q_s], cpk^* \neq cpk_i$ or $m^*[j_i] \neq m_i[j_i]$ for some $j_i \notin \text{ADM}_i$.

EXPERIMENT $\text{Exp}_{\text{Trans}}(\mathcal{A})$:
$(ssk^*, spk^*) \leftarrow \text{SS.SigKeyGen}(1^\lambda), (csk^*, cpk^*) \leftarrow \text{SS.SanKeyGen}(1^\lambda), b \leftarrow \{\text{Sig}, \text{San}\}$.
$b' \leftarrow \mathcal{A}^{\mathcal{O}_{Sig}, \mathcal{O}_{San}, \mathcal{O}_{Prf}, \mathcal{O}_{SoS}}(1^\lambda, spk^*, cpk^*)$ where
$\forall\, i \in [1, q_o], (m'_i, \sigma'_i) \leftarrow \mathcal{O}_{SoS}(m_i, \text{ADM}_i, \text{MOD}_i)$ where
$m'_i = \text{MOD}(m_i)$ and $\sigma'_i = \text{SS.Sign}(ssk^*, m'_i, cpk^*, \text{ADM}_i)$ if $b = \text{Sig}$, or
$\sigma'_i = \text{SS.Sanitize}(csk^*, m_i, \text{SS.Sign}(ssk^*, m_i, cpk^*, \text{ADM}_i), spk^*, \text{MOD}_i)$.
$\text{Exp}_{\text{Trans}}(\mathcal{A}) = \text{True iff } b = b'$.

EXPERIMENT $\text{Exp}_{\text{SanAcc}}(\mathcal{A})$:
$(ssk^*, spk^*) \leftarrow \text{SS.SigKeyGen}(1^\lambda)$.
$(cpk^*, m^*, \sigma^*) \leftarrow \mathcal{A}^{\mathcal{O}_{Sig}, \mathcal{O}_{Prf}}(1^\lambda, spk^*)$ where $\forall\, i \in [1, q_s], \sigma_i \leftarrow \mathcal{O}_{Sig}(m_i, cpk_i, \text{ADM}_i)$.
$\pi^* \leftarrow \text{SS.Prove}(ssk^*, m^*, \sigma^*, cpk^*, \{(m_i, \sigma_i)\}_{i \in [1, q_s]})$.
$\text{Exp}_{\text{SanAcc}}(\mathcal{A}) = \text{True iff SS.Verify}(m^*, \sigma^*, spk^*, cpk^*) = \text{Valid and}$
$\text{SS.Judge}(m^*, \sigma^*, \pi^*, spk^*, cpk^*) = \text{Sig and } \forall\, i \in [1, q_s], (m^*, cpk^*) \neq (m_i, cpk_i)$.

EXPERIMENT $\text{Exp}_{\text{SigAcc}}(\mathcal{A})$:
$(csk^*, cpk^*) \leftarrow \text{SS.SanKeyGen}(1^\lambda)$.
$(spk^*, m^*, \sigma^*, \pi^*) \leftarrow \mathcal{A}^{\mathcal{O}_{San}}(1^\lambda, cpk^*)$ where $\forall\, i \in [1, q_c], (m'_i, \sigma'_i) \leftarrow \mathcal{O}_{San}(m_i, \sigma_i, spk_i, \text{MOD}_i)$.
$\text{Exp}_{\text{SigAcc}}(\mathcal{A}) = \text{True iff SS.Verify}(m^*, \sigma^*, spk^*, cpk^*) = \text{Valid and}$
$\text{SS.Judge}(m^*, \sigma^*, \pi^*, spk^*, cpk^*) = \text{San and } \forall\, i \in [1, q_c], (m^*, spk^*) \neq (m'_i, spk_i)$.

Definition 8 (Unforgeability). *A sanitizable signature scheme* SS *is said to be* $(q_s, q_c, q_p, t, \epsilon)$-*unforgeable if* $\Pr[\text{Exp}_{\text{Unf}}(\mathcal{A}) = \text{True}] \leq \epsilon$ *for any adversary* $\mathcal{A}$ *after at most* q_s *signing queries,* q_c *sanitizing queries and* q_p *proof queries and* t *steps.*

Definition 9 (Immutability). *A sanitizable signature scheme* SS *is said to be* (q_s, q_p, t, ϵ)*-immutable if* $\Pr[\text{Exp}_{\text{Imm}}(\mathcal{A}) = \text{True}] \leq \epsilon$ *for any adversary* $\mathcal{A}$ *after at most* q_s *signing queries and* q_p *proof queries and* t *steps.*

Definition 10 (Transparency). *A sanitizable signature scheme* SS *is said to be* $(q_s, q_c, q_p, q_o, t, \epsilon)$*-transparent if* $|\Pr[\text{Exp}_{\text{Trans}}(\mathcal{A}) = \text{True}] - 1/2| \leq \epsilon$ *for any adversary* $\mathcal{A}$ *after at most* q_s *signing queries,* q_c *sanitizing queries,* q_p *proof queries and* q_o *sig-or-san queries and* t *steps.*

Definition 11 (Sanitizer-Accountability). *A sanitizable signature scheme* SS *is said to be* (q_s, q_p, t, ϵ)*-sanitizer-accountable if* $\Pr[\text{Exp}_{\text{SanAcc}}(\mathcal{A}) = \text{True}] \leq \epsilon$ *for any adversary* $\mathcal{A}$ *after at most* q_s *signing queries and* q_p *proof queries and* t *steps.*

Definition 12 (Signer-Accountability). *A sanitizable signature scheme* SS *is said to be* (q_c, t, ϵ)*-signer-accountable if* $\Pr[\text{Exp}_{\text{SigAcc}}(\mathcal{A}) = \text{True}] \leq \epsilon$ *for any adversary* $\mathcal{A}$ *after at most* q_c *sanitizing queries and* t *steps.*

3.2   Flaw in Brzuska *et al.*'s Construction

BRIEF REVIEW OF BRZUSKA *et al.*'S CONSTRUCTION [6]. We call their construction BFFL from now on and briefly review its as follow:

- BFFL.SigKeyGen acquires a key pair (sk, vk) by running DS.KeyGen and chooses a random key $\kappa \leftarrow \{0,1\}^\lambda$ for pseudorandom function. It outputs key pair $(ssk, spk) = ((sk, \kappa), vk)$.
- BFFL.SanKeyGen acquires a key pair (ak, hk) by running CH.KeyGen and outputs $(csk, cpk) = (ak, hk)$.
- BFFL.Sign first selects nonce $n \leftarrow \{0,1\}^\lambda$ and computes tag $t = \text{PRG}(x)$ where $x = \text{PRF}(\kappa, n)$. For each $i \in$ ADM, it sets $h[i] \leftarrow \text{CH.Hash}(hk, (i, m[i], spk), t; r[i])$ where $r[i] \leftarrow \{0,1\}^\lambda$. For each $i \notin$ ADM, it sets $h[i] \leftarrow m[i]$. Then it constructs h by concatenating all $h[i]$ and sets $\sigma = (\hat{\sigma}, t, n, \text{ADM}, \{r[i]\})$ where $\hat{\sigma} \leftarrow \text{DS}(sk, (h, cpk, \text{ADM}))$.
- BFFL.Sanitize first selects new nonce $n' \leftarrow \{0,1\}^\lambda$ and new tag $t' \leftarrow \{0,1\}^{2\lambda}$. Then it replaces each $r[i]$ with

$$r'[i] \leftarrow \text{CH.Adapt}(ak, (i, m[i], spk), t, r[i], (i, m'[i], spk), t')$$

and outputs the updated message and signature.
- BFFL.Verify recovers h and outputs $d = \text{DS.Verify}(vk, (h, cpk, \text{ADM}), \hat{\sigma})$.
- BFFL.Prove searches for tuple $(t_j, (i, m_j[i], spk), r_j[i])$ in the internal database $\mathfrak{DB}$ such that

$$\text{CH.Hash}(hk, t, (i, m[i], spk); r[i]) = \text{CH.Hash}(hk, t_j, (i, m_j[i], spk); r_j[i]).$$

  The witness π consists of this tuple and $x_j \leftarrow \text{PRF}(\kappa, n_j)$.
- BFFL.Judge checks whether the witness indicates a non-trivial collision and $t_j = \text{PRG}(x_j)$. If not, it outputs $d \leftarrow$ Sig; otherwise it outputs $d \leftarrow$ San.

WITNESS RE-USE ATTACK ON BRZUSKA *et al.*'S CONSTRUCTION. Here we show that the adversary can always win the experiment $\mathsf{Exp}_{\mathsf{SigAcc}}$ (see Definition 12) by re-using the witness. In this attack, the adversary $\mathcal{A}$ acts as a signer holding a key pair (ssk^*, spk^*) chosen by itself and does as follows:

1. construct a message-signature pair (m, σ) under spk^* such that only the i-th block is sanitizable,
2. make a sanitizing query $(m, \sigma, spk^*, \mathtt{MOD})$ where $\mathtt{MOD} = \{(i, m'[i])\}$ and get an updated message-signature pair (m', σ'),
3. produce a valid witness $\pi = (t, (i, m[i], spk^*), r[i], x)$ for this updated pair (m', σ') using ssk^* and keep track of t' and $r'[i]$ in σ',
4. create a new message $m^* \neq m'$ but $m^*[i] = m'[i]$ and $i \in \mathtt{ADM}^*$, and sign this message using t' and $r'[i]$ to obtain new signature σ^*,
5. output $(spk^*, m^*, \sigma^*, \pi)$ to the challenger.

First, it is obvious that the message-signature pair (m^*, σ^*) is valid since the signature is produced by using correct signing key ssk^*. Then we can see that the simulator who acts as a censor has never created the signature on message m^* due to the fourth step. Thirdly, the witness is acceptable since the tuples $(t, (i, m[i], spk^*), r[i])$ and $(t', (i, m'[i], spk^*), r'[i])$ still form a valid collision in the current setting and x remains unchanged. Hence the adversary always wins the experiment $\mathsf{Exp}_{\mathsf{SigAcc}}$. This witness re-use attack means that the signer can release any message containing block $m'[i]$ without being responsible for it once the censor has replaced $m[i]$ with $m'[i]$ using its private key.

3.3 Flaw in Canard *et al.*'s Construction

REVIEW OF CANARD *et al.*'S CONSTRUCTION [9]. We call their construction CJ from now on and briefly review it as follow. Note that they use chameleon hashing without tags here.

- CJ.SigKeyGen and CJ.SanKeyGen work as BFFL.SigKeyGen and BFFL.SanKeyGen respectively.
- CJ.Sign first selects nonce $n \leftarrow \{0,1\}^\lambda$ and computes tag $t = \mathsf{PRG}(x)$ where $x = \mathsf{PRF}(\kappa, n)$. For each $i \in \mathtt{ADM}$, it sets $h[i] \leftarrow \mathsf{CH.Hash}(hk, i||m[i]; r[i])$ where $r[i] \leftarrow \{0,1\}^\lambda$. For each $i \notin \mathtt{ADM}$, it sets $h[i] \leftarrow i||m[i]$. Then it sets $h_c \leftarrow \mathsf{CH.Hash}(hk, m||t; r_c)$ where $r_c \leftarrow \{0,1\}^\lambda$. Next it constructs h by concatenating all $h[i]$ as well as h_c, and sets $\sigma = (\hat{\sigma}, t, n, \mathtt{ADM}, \{r[i]\}, r_c)$ where $\hat{\sigma} \leftarrow \mathsf{DS}(sk, h||cpk)$.
- CJ.Sanitize first selects new nonce $n' \leftarrow \{0,1\}^\lambda$ and new tag $t' \leftarrow \{0,1\}^{2\lambda}$. Then replace $r[i]$ with $r'[i] \leftarrow \mathsf{CH.Adapt}(ak, i||m[i], r[i], i||m'[i])$ for all $i \in \mathtt{ADM}$ and $m[i] \neq m'[i]$, and substitute r_c for $r'_c \leftarrow \mathsf{CH.Adapt}(ak, m||t, m'||t', r_c)$. It outputs the updated message and signature.
- CJ.Verify recovers h and outputs $d = \mathsf{DS.Verify}(vk, h||cpk)$.
- CJ.Prove searches for $(t_i||m_i, r_{c,i})$ in the internal database $\mathfrak{DB}$ such that $\mathsf{CH.Hash}(hk, t||m; r_c) = \mathsf{CH.Hash}(hk, t_i||m_i; r_{c,i})$. The witness π consists of $(spk, t_i, m_i, r_{c,i})$ and $x_i \leftarrow \mathsf{PRF}(\kappa, n_i)$.
- CJ.Judge checks whether the witness indicates a legal collision and $t_i \leftarrow \mathsf{PRG}(x_i)$. If not, it outputs $d \leftarrow \mathsf{Sig}$; otherwise it outputs $d \leftarrow \mathsf{San}$.

WITNESS RE-USE ATTACK ON CANARD *et al.*'S CONSTRUCTION. Similarly, we show that the adversary can always win the experiment $\mathrm{Exp_{SigAcc}}$ (see Definition 12) by re-using the witness. On this occasion, adversary $\mathcal{A}$ acts as a signer holding two distinct key pairs (ssk, spk) and (ssk^*, spk^*) chosen by itself. Then it does as follows:

1. construct a message-signature pair (m, σ) under the public key spk,
2. make a sanitizing query $(m, \sigma, spk, \mathrm{MOD})$ and get an updated message-signature pair (m', σ'),
3. produce a valid witness π for this updated pair (m', σ') using ssk,
4. replace $\hat{\sigma}'$ in σ' with the signature on $h||cpk^*$ under another public key spk^* to obtain a new signature σ^*,
5. replace spk in π with spk^* to produce π^* and output $(spk^*, m', \sigma^*, \pi^*)$ to the challenger.

First, it is obvious that the message-signature pair (m^*, σ^*) is valid since the signature is produced by using correct signing key ssk^*. Then we can see that the simulator who acts as a censor has never sanitized the the message signed under spk^*. Thirdly, the witness is acceptable since the tuples $(t||m, r_c)$ and $(t'||m', r'_c)$ still form a valid collision in the current setting and x remains unchanged. Hence the adversary always wins the experiment $\mathrm{Exp_{SigAcc}}$. This witness re-use attack means that the signer can release message m' without being responsible for it once the censor has released the same message signed by another signer and corresponding witness is available.

3.4   Lesson and Countermeasure

We have shown the attacks on BFFL and CJ respectively. In both attacks, the re-use of the witness results from the re-use of the collision found by the censor in the sanitizing stage. It is because that the collision is actually independent of the entire message (in the attack on BFFL) or the identity of the signer (in the attack on CJ). It is easy to overcome this flaw by hashing both the entire message and also the signer's identity (e.g., signer's public key) when producing each h_i for $i \in \mathrm{ADM}$ in BFFL or computing h_c in CJ. Note that this modification can also be applied to the extensions of CJ in [9] directly.

4   Weakness of Brzuska *et al.*'s Security Model

Brzuska *et al.* [6] proposed the first and sole formal security model for sanitizable signatures. However their security model neglects the importance of the description ADM that indicates the sanitizing rights of the authorized censor. In this section, we present a type of potential attacks and explain its harmfulness.

4.1   Potential Attacks: Rights Forge Attacks

We first consider as an example the experiment $\mathrm{Exp_{Unf}}$ (see Definition 8). The adversary wins the experiment if it produces a correct pair (m^*, σ^*) and it holds that $(cpk^*, m^*) \neq (cpk_i, m_i)$ for all i and $(spk^*, m^*) \neq (spk_j, m'_j)$ for all j. Assume there exists an adversary who outputs another valid pair such that $(cpk^*, m^*) = (cpk_i, m_i)$ for some i but $\text{ADM}^* \neq \text{AMD}_i$ or $(spk^*, m^*) = (spk_j, m'_j)$ for some j but $\text{ADM}^* \neq \text{AMD}_j$. Obviously, this adversary fails in this experiment according to the definition, but it may actually have benefited from this attack. Similar attacks also exist in the formal model for immutability as well as two flavors of accountability. In a word, this model does not consider the attack that the description of sanitizing rights is modified maliciously by the adversary. Here we call this type of attacks *rights forge attack in terms of unforgeability (immutability, signer-accountability or sanitizer-accountability)*.

4.2 Rights Forge Attacks Are Harmful

In Ateniese *et al.*'s work [2], they actually mentioned two flavors of transparency, i.e., weak and strong transparency. To be precise, these are two different levels of transparency.

A sanitizable signature scheme with strong transparency does not reveal the sanitizing rights of the censor (i.e., the description ADM) to the verifier. For instance, one of Klonowski *et al.*'s extensions [23] achieves strong transparency. In addition, Agrawal *et al.* [1] gave two constructions with strong transparency based on Waters signature scheme [30] recently. Generally speaking, transparency always means weak one, which allows the sanitizing rights of the censor to be revealed to the verifiers. Ateniese *et al.*'s [2], Brzuska *et al.*'s [6] and Canard *et al.*'s [9] constructions are all weak transparent. Of course, Brzuska *et al.*'s security model is also for weak transparency.

Due to its visibility, the description ADM should also be considered as an indispensable element of the information released by the signer in such a case. In [6], Brzuska *et al.* said that a sanitized message block may be less valuable if the outsider knows the fact that this block has been sanitized, which is one of the reasons why transparency is necessary. Similarly, the fact that some block is sanitizable may also make this message block less valuable. It is clear that ADM that has been tampered with can color the outsider's judgement on the use value of certain message block. Hence any modification of ADM should also be regarded as a malicious behavior and captured by the security model.

In terms of signer-accountability, both Brzuska *et al.*'s [6] and Canard *et al.*'s [9] constructions actually suffer from rights forge attacks. The attacks are similar with witness re-use attacks shown before except that the adversary will not change the message itself and signer's public key in this case. On the other hand, they can resist rights forge attacks in terms of other experiments, since they always signs ADM. However we must note that the conceptual weakness of formal model may lead to a provably secure construction that is actually not.

5   Expanded Security Model and Improved Construction

Having shown the flaws in the existing constructions [6,9] and the weakness of the existing security model [6], we first expand Brzuska *et al.*'s security model to overcome the weakness of the original model and then present an efficient construction based on Brzuska et al.'s [6] and Canard et al.'s [9], which is provably secure in our expanded security model.

5.1   Expanded Security Model for Sanitizable Signatures

To expand Brzuska et al.'s model, we still follow the style of the original security model and only refine the criteria of adversary's success in experiment Exp_{Unf}, Exp_{Imm}, $\text{Exp}_{\text{SanAcc}}$ and $\text{Exp}_{\text{SigAcc}}$ respectively as follows.

$\text{Exp}_{\text{Unf}}(\mathcal{A}) = \text{True iff SS.Verify}(m^*, \sigma^*, spk^*, cpk^*) = \text{Valid and}$ $\forall\, i \in [1, q_s],\ (cpk^*, m^*, \boxed{\text{ADM}^*}) \neq (cpk_i, m_i, \boxed{\text{ADM}_i})$ and $\forall\, j \in [1, q_c],\ (spk^*, m^*, \boxed{\text{ADM}^*}) \neq (spk_j, m'_j, \boxed{\text{ADM}_j}).$
$\text{Exp}_{\text{Imm}}(\mathcal{A}) = \text{True iff SS.Verify}(m^*, \sigma^*, spk^*, cpk^*) = \text{Valid and}$ $\forall\, i \in [1, q_s],\ (cpk^*, m^*[j_i], \boxed{\text{ADM}^*}) \neq (cpk_i, m_i[j_i], \boxed{\text{ADM}_i})$ for some $j_i \notin \text{ADM}_i.$
$\text{Exp}_{\text{SanAcc}}(\mathcal{A}) = \text{True iff SS.Verify}(m^*, \sigma^*, spk^*, cpk^*) = \text{Valid and}$ $\text{SS.Judge}(m^*, \sigma^*, \pi^*, spk^*, cpk^*) = \text{Sig and } \forall\, i \in [1, q_s],\ (m^*, cpk^*, \boxed{\text{ADM}^*}) \neq (m_i, cpk_i, \boxed{\text{ADM}_i}).$
$\text{Exp}_{\text{SigAcc}}(\mathcal{A}) = \text{True iff SS.Verify}(m^*, \sigma^*, spk^*, cpk^*) = \text{Valid and}$ $\text{SS.Judge}(m^*, \sigma^*, \pi^*, spk^*, cpk^*) = \text{San and } \forall\, i \in [1, q_c],\ (m^*, spk^*, \boxed{\text{ADM}^*}) \neq (m'_i, spk_i, \boxed{\text{ADM}_i}).$

Here we use box to indicate the new criteria added to Brzuska et al.'s original model [6]. Obviously, our expanded security model captures rights forge attacks successfully, since any illegal ADM^* will also lead to the success of $\mathcal{A}$.

According to this expanded model, the relationship of these five elementary security requirements still follow the results of Brzuska et al. [6], that is transparency implies privacy, and signer- and sanitizer-accountability implies unforgeability. The formal proofs of these results are much the same as those for the original model. In addition, it is also easy to see that our expanded model implies the original one [6].

5.2   Our Improved Construction: SS$^+$

Our construction SS$^+$ is a modification of BFFL [6] and CJ [9]. Besides the improvement shown in Section 3.4, we now no longer hash each message block separately so as to provide higher efficiency. In this regard, our strategy is similar with those in [7,8]. However the former employs plain digital signature scheme and the latter adopts group signature scheme, while our construction uses chameleon hashes.

Let "$||$" denote the concatenation of two bit strings. Here we require that any string formed by concatenating two or more sub-strings is recoverable, that is one can recover all the original sub-strings exactly. In addition, for each message $m = m[1]||m[2]||\cdots||m[l]$, we define $\bar{m} \leftarrow i_1||m[i_1]||\cdots||i_\mu||m[i_\mu]$ for all $i_k \in$ ADM, where $1 \leq k \leq \mu$, and $\tilde{m} \leftarrow j_1||m[j_1]||\cdots||j_\nu||m[j_\nu]$ for all $j_k \notin$ ADM, where $1 \leq k \leq \nu$. Note that $\mu + \nu = l$. We describe our construction SS$^+$ as follows.

- $SS^+.SigKeyGen$ takes as input the security parameter λ and does as follows:
    1. $(sk, vk) \leftarrow DS.KeyGen(1^\lambda)$;
    2. choose $\kappa \leftarrow_R \{0,1\}^\lambda$;
    and outputs the key pair $(ssk, spk) = ((sk, \kappa), vk)$.
- $SS^+.SanKeyGen$ takes as input the security parameter λ and does as follows:
    $(ak, hk) \leftarrow CH.KeyGen(1^\lambda)$ and outputs the key pair $(csk, cpk) = (ak, hk)$.
- $SS^+.Sign$ takes as input the message m, the public key $cpk = hk$, description
    ADM and the private key $ssk = (sk, \kappa)$ and does as follows:
    1. choose $n \leftarrow_R \{0,1\}^\lambda$ and $r \leftarrow_R \{0,1\}^\lambda$, and compute $x \leftarrow PRF(\kappa, n)$ and
       $t \leftarrow PRG(x)$;
    2. set $h \leftarrow CH.Hash(hk, spk||\tilde{m}||\bar{m}, t; r)$;
    3. $\hat{\sigma} \leftarrow DS.Sign(sk, cpk||\tilde{m}||h)$;
    and outputs signature $\sigma = (\hat{\sigma}, ADM, n, t, r)$. Finally, it inserts this pair (m, σ)
    into the internal database $\mathfrak{DB}$.
- $SS^+.Sanitize$ takes as input the message-signature pair (m, σ) where $\sigma =$
    $(\hat{\sigma}, ADM, n, t, r)$, the public key spk, the sanitizing instruction MOD and the
    private key $csk = ak$ and does as follows:
    1. check whether $SS^+.Verify(m, \sigma, spk, cpk) = Valid$, if not abort;
    2. choose $n' \leftarrow_R \{0,1\}^\lambda$ and $t' \leftarrow_R \{0,1\}^{2\lambda}$;
    3. let $m' = MOD(m)$ and construct $\bar{m}' = i_1||m'[i_1]||\cdots||i_\mu||m'[i_\mu]$;
    4. $r' \leftarrow CH.Adapt(ak, spk||\tilde{m}||\bar{m}, t, r, spk||\tilde{m}||\bar{m}', t')$;
    and outputs the new pair $(m', \sigma') = (MOD(m), (\hat{\sigma}, ADM, n', t', r'))$.
- $SS^+.Verify$ takes as input the pair (m, σ) where $\sigma = (\hat{\sigma}, ADM, n, t, r)$, the
    public key $spk = vk$ and the public key $cpk = hk$, and reconstruct $\bar{m}$, $\tilde{m}$ and
    h as $SS^+.Sign$ does and outputs $d = DS.Verify(cpk||\tilde{m}||h, \hat{\sigma}, vk)$.
- $SS^+.Prove$ takes as input the pair (m, σ), the public key $cpk = hk$, the
    private key $ssk = (sk, \kappa)$ and the internal database $\mathfrak{DB} = \{(m_i, \sigma_i)\}$ and
    does as follows:
    1. for (m, σ) where $\sigma = (\hat{\sigma}, ADM, n, t, r)$, reconstruct $\bar{m}$ and $\tilde{m}$;
    2. for $(m_i, \sigma_i) \in \mathfrak{DB}$ where $\sigma_i = (\hat{\sigma}_i, ADM_i, n_i, t_i, r_i)$, reconstruct $\bar{m}_i$ and
       $\tilde{m}_i$;
    3. search for a message-signature pair (m_π, σ_π) with t_π, r_π, n_π, $\bar{m}_\pi$ and $\tilde{m}_\pi$
       such that $t_\pi = PRG(x_\pi)$ where $x_\pi = PRF(\kappa, n_\pi)$ and

$$CH.Hash(hk, spk||\tilde{m}||\bar{m}, t; r) = CH.Hash(hk, spk||\tilde{m}_\pi||\bar{m}_\pi, t_\pi; r_\pi); \quad (1)$$

    and outputs witness $\pi = (spk||\tilde{m}_\pi||\bar{m}_\pi, t_\pi, r_\pi, x_\pi)$ or $\bot$ if the search fails.
- $SS^+.Jdg$ takes as input the pair (m, σ), the public key spk, the public key
    $cpk = hk$ and the witness $\pi = (spk||\tilde{m}_\pi||\bar{m}_\pi, t_\pi, r_\pi, x_\pi)$ and does as follows:
    1. if $\pi = \bot$, output $d \leftarrow Sig$;
    2. reconstruct $\bar{m}$ and $\tilde{m}$ for m, and check whether Eq. (1) holds and $t_\pi =$
       $PRG(x_\pi)$. If so, output $d \leftarrow San$, if not, still return $d \leftarrow Sig$.

It is trivial to demonstrate that the following construction meets all the correctness requirements recalled in Section 2.1. We must note that both $\tilde{m}$ and $\bar{m}$ actually include ADM since they contain the indexes of all admissible or all inadmissible blocks and operation "$||$" is recoverable.

5.3 Security Analysis

Now we show that our construction SS^+ is immutable (Theorem 1), transparent (Theorem 2), sanitizer-accountable (Theorem 3) and signer-accountable (Theorem 4) and thus unforgeable and private according to the relationship of elementary requirements [6]. Hence our proposed construction is *fully secure* in our expanded security model. Due to the lack of space, we omit the formal proofs of these theorems. Indeed, the core idea is the same as [6].

Theorem 1. *Assume that* DS *is* (q_s, t, ϵ)-*existentially unforgeable against chosen message attacks,* SS^+ *is* $(q_s', q_p, t', \epsilon')$-*immutable where* $q_s = q_s'$, $t = t' + \mathcal{O}(q_s' + q_p)$ *and* $\epsilon = \epsilon'$.

Theorem 2. *Assume that* PRF *is* (t_1, ϵ_1)-*pseudorandom and* PRG *is* (t_2, ϵ_2)-*pseudorandom,* SS^+ *is* $(q_s, q_c, q_p, q_o, t, \epsilon)$-*transparent where* $t_1 = t + \mathcal{O}(q_s + q_c + q_p + q_o)$, $t_2 = t + \mathcal{O}(q_s + q_c + q_p + q_o)$ *and* $\epsilon \le \epsilon_1 + \epsilon_2$.

Theorem 3. *Assume that* DS *is* (q_s, t, ϵ)-*existentially unforgeable against chosen message attacks,* SS^+ *is* $(q_s', q_p, t', \epsilon')$-*sanitizer-accountable where* $q_s = q_s'$, $t = t' + \mathcal{O}(q_s' + q_p)$ *and* $\epsilon = \epsilon'$.

Theorem 4. *Assume that* CH *is* (q_a, t, ϵ)-*collision-resistant under random tagging attacks,* SS^+ *is* (q_c, t', ϵ')-*signer-accountable where* $q_a = q_c$, $t = t' + \mathcal{O}(q_c)$ *and* $\epsilon = \epsilon' - q_c 2^{-\lambda}$.

5.4 Efficiency Analysis

Now we compare our improved construction SS^+ with BFFL [6] and CJ [9] in terms of both space and time efficiency, all of which follow the paradigm of Ateniese *et al.* [2] and are based on chameleon hashes. Brzuska et al.'s group signature-based construction in [8] achieves additional security property (i.e., unlinkability), but sacrifices its efficiency (due to relatively low efficiency of the underlying group signatures [4,13,14,15,22]). Hence we do not consider this group signature-based construction in the following discussion on efficiency.

We assume that the message to be signed consists of l blocks, $l_s = |ADM|$ blocks are sanitizable and l_m blocks are actually sanitized (i.e. all block i such that $m[i] \ne m'[i]$). When it comes to the space efficiency, we focus on the number of random values in the resulting signatures since other portions of the signatures are identical. When we talk about the time efficiency, we only consider the number of hashing operations involved in algorithm Sign and Verify and the number of adaptation operations involved in algorithm Sanitize because other corresponding computational costs of these three constructions are identical. The comparison is shown in Table 1.

SPACE EFFICIENCY. It is obvious that the signature size of SS^+ is much shorter. The most important point is that the signature sizes of both BFFL and CJ depend on l_s, while that of SS^+ is *constant*. As mentioned above, the decisive factor is

Table 1. Comparison between our proposal and the related schemes

Schemes	Number of Random Values	Number of Hashing or Adaptation		
		Sig(Hashing)	San(Adaptation)	Vfy(Hashing)
BFFL [6]	l_s	l_s	l_s	l_s
CJ [9]	$l_s + 1$	$l_s + 1$	$l_m + 1$	$l_s + 1$
SS$^+$	1	1	1	1

the number of random values. Especially, each signature of BFFL has l_s random values, that of CJ has $l_s + 1$ random values and SS$^+$ produces signatures with only one random value. Short and constant signature size not only saves bandwidth and storage resources but also simplifies the implementation of our construction. Hence our construction is applicable to some bandwidth-restricted or storage-restricted scenarios such as wireless network.

TIME EFFICIENCY. It is also clear that the algorithms of SS$^+$ are much faster either. Namely the costs of the signing, sanitizing and verification algorithms of SS$^+$ are *constant*. By contrast, the costs of these algorithms of BFFL and CJ are dependent on l_s or l_m respectively. To our best knowledge, both the hashing and the adaptation algorithm of chameleon hashes (with tags) schemes are still expensive, which is non-negligible in general. Hence our construction provides very high response speed. On the other hand, constant computational cost also provides low response jitter. Therefore our construction is applicable to batch processing such as de-identifying thousands of medical records or other real-time system such as personalizing commercials in a multimedia database.

6   Conclusion

In this paper, we have pointed out the flaws in Brzuska *et al.*'s and Canard *et al.*'s construction as well as the weakness of Brzuska *et al.*'s security model. Furthermore, we expand Brzuska *et al.*'s security model to capture potential attacks and thus overcome the weakness of the original model. Meanwhile, we also provide an improved construction for sanitizable signatures based on previous techniques, which not only fulfills all the security requirements defined in our expanded model but also achieves higher space and time efficiency.

Acknowledgments. We want to thank the anonymous reviewers for their constructive comments. This work has been partially supported by the National Natural Science General Foundation of China Grant No. 60703004, 60873217 and 60703031, the Research Fund for the Doctoral Program of Higher Education of China Grant No. 20070269005.

References

1. Agrawal, S., Kumar, S., Shareef, A., Rangan, C.P.: Sanitizable signatures with strong transparency in the standard model. In: Bao, F., Yung, M., Lin, D., Jing, J. (eds.) Inscrypt 2009. LNCS, vol. 6151, pp. 93–107. Springer, Heidelberg (2010)

2. Ateniese, G., Chou, D.H., de Medeiros, B., Tsudik, G.: Sanitizable signatures. In: de Capitani di Vimercati, S., Syverson, P.F., Gollmann, D. (eds.) ESORICS 2005. LNCS, vol. 3679, pp. 159–177. Springer, Heidelberg (2005)

3. Ateniese, G., de Medeiros, B.: Identity-Based Chameleon Hash and Applications. In: Juels, A. (ed.) FC 2004. LNCS, vol. 3110, pp. 164–180. Springer, Heidelberg (2004)

4. Bellare, M., Micciancio, D., Warinschi, B.: Foundations of Group Signatures: Formal Definitions, Simplified Requirements, and a Construction Based on General Assumptions. In: Biham, E. (ed.) EUROCRYPT 2003. LNCS, vol. 2656, pp. 614–629. Springer, Heidelberg (2003)

5. Boneh, D., Boyen, X.: Short signatures without random oracles. In: Cachin, C., Camenisch, J.L. (eds.) EUROCRYPT 2004. LNCS, vol. 3027, pp. 56–73. Springer, Heidelberg (2004)

6. Brzuska, C., Fischlin, M., Freudenreich, T., Lehmann, A., Page, M., Schelbert, J., Schröder, D., Volk, F.: Security of Sanitizable Signatures Revisited. In: Jarecki, S., Tsudik, G. (eds.) PKC 2009. LNCS, vol. 5443, pp. 317–336. Springer, Heidelberg (2009)

7. Brzuska, C., Fischlin, M., Lehmann, A., Schröder, D.: Sanitizable Signatures: How to Partially Delegate Control for Authenticated Data. In: Brömme, A., Busch, C., Hühnlein, D. (eds.) BIOSIG 2009: Biometrics and Electronic Signatures. LNI, vol. P-155, pp. 117–128. Gesellschaft für Informatik, Bonn (2009)

8. Brzuska, C., Fischlin, M., Lehmann, A., Schröder, D.: Unlinkability of Sanitizable Signatures. In: Nguyen, P.Q., Pointcheval, D. (eds.) PKC 2010. LNCS, vol. 6056, pp. 444–461. Springer, Heidelberg (2010)

9. Canard, S., Jambert, A.: On Extended Sanitizable Signature Schemes. In: Pieprzyk, J. (ed.) CT-RSA 2010. LNCS, vol. 5985, pp. 179–194. Springer, Heidelberg (2010)

10. Canard, S., Laguillaumie, F., Milhau, M.: *Trapdoor* Sanitizable Signatures and Their Application to Content Protection. In: Bellovin, S.M., Gennaro, R., Keromytis, A.D., Yung, M. (eds.) ACNS 2008. LNCS, vol. 5037, pp. 258–276. Springer, Heidelberg (2008)

11. Chang, E., Lim, C., Xu, J.: Short Redactable Signatures Using Random Trees. In: Fischlin, M. (ed.) CT-RSA 2009. LNCS, vol. 5473, pp. 133–147. Springer, Heidelberg (2009)

12. Chaum, D., van Heyst, E.: Group signatures. In: Davies, D.W. (ed.) EUROCRYPT 1991. LNCS, vol. 547, pp. 257–265. Springer, Heidelberg (1991)

13. Delerablée, C., Pointcheval, D.: Dynamic Fully Anonymous Short Group Signatures. In: Nguyên, P.Q. (ed.) VIETCRYPT 2006. LNCS, vol. 4341, pp. 193–210. Springer, Heidelberg (2006)

14. Groth, J.: Simulation-Sound NIZK Proofs for a Practical Language and Constant Size Group Signatures. In: Lai, X., Chen, K. (eds.) ASIACRYPT 2006. LNCS, vol. 4284, pp. 444–459. Springer, Heidelberg (2006)

15. Groth, J.: Fully Anonymous Group Signatures Without Random Oracles. In: Kurosawa, K. (ed.) ASIACRYPT 2007. LNCS, vol. 4833, pp. 164–180. Springer, Heidelberg (2007)

16. Goldwasser, S., Micali, S., Rivest, R.: A Digital Signature Scheme Secure Against Adaptive Chosen-Message Attacks. SIAM Journal of Computing 17(2), 281–308 (1988)

17. Haber, S., Hatano, Y., Honda, Y., Horne, W., Miyazaki, K., Sander, T., Tezoku, S., Yao, D.: Efficient signature schemes supporting redaction, pseudonymization, and data deidentification. In: ASIACCS 2008, pp. 353–362. ACM, New York (2008)

18. Izu, T., Kunihiro, N., Ohta, K., Sano, M., Takenaka, M.: Sanitizable and Deletable Signature. In: Chung, K.-I., Sohn, K., Yung, M. (eds.) WISA 2008. LNCS, vol. 5379, pp. 130–144. Springer, Heidelberg (2009)
19. Izu, T., Kunihiro, N., Ohta, K., Takenaka, M., Yoshioka, T.: A sanitizable signature scheme with aggregation. In: Dawson, E., Wong, D.S. (eds.) ISPEC 2007. LNCS, vol. 4464, pp. 51–64. Springer, Heidelberg (2007)
20. Izu, T., Kanaya, N., Takenaka, M., Yoshioka, T.: PIATS: A partially sanitizable signature scheme. In: Qing, S., Mao, W., López, J., Wang, G. (eds.) ICICS 2005. LNCS, vol. 3783, pp. 72–83. Springer, Heidelberg (2005)
21. Johnson, R., Molnar, D., Song, D., Wagner, D.: Homomorphic signature schemes. In: Preneel, B. (ed.) CT-RSA 2002. LNCS, vol. 2271, pp. 244–262. Springer, Heidelberg (2002)
22. Kiayias, A., Yung, M.: Group Signatures with Efficient Concurrent Join. In: Cramer, R. (ed.) EUROCRYPT 2005. LNCS, vol. 3494, pp. 198–214. Springer, Heidelberg (2005)
23. Klonowski, M., Lauks, A.: Extended Sanitizable Signatures. In: Rhee, M.S., Lee, B. (eds.) ICISC 2006. LNCS, vol. 4296, pp. 343–355. Springer, Heidelberg (2006)
24. Krawczyk, H., Rabin, T.: Chameleon signatures. In: Proceedings of the Network and Distributed Systems Security Symposium (NDSS 2000), pp. 143–154 (2000)
25. Miyazaki, K., Hanaoka, G., Imai, H.: Digitally signed document sanitizing scheme based on bilinear maps. In: ASIACCS 2006, pp. 343–354. ACM, New York (2006)
26. Miyazaki, K., Iwamura, M., Matsumoto, T., Sasaki, R., Yoshiura, H., Tezuka, S., Imai, H.: Digitally Signed Document Sanitizing Scheme with Disclosure Condition Control. The Institute of Electronics, Information and Communication Engineers (IEICE) Trans. on Fundamentals E88-A(1), 239–246 (2005)
27. Miyazaki, K., Susaki, S., Iwamura, M., Matsumoto, T., Sasaki, R., Yoshiura, H.: Digital Documents Sanitizing Problem. The Institute of Electronics, Information and Communication Engineers (IEICE) technical report, ISEC 2003-20 (May 2003)
28. Steinfeld, R., Bull, L., Zheng, Y.: Content extraction signatures. In: Kim, K.-c. (ed.) ICISC 2001. LNCS, vol. 2288, pp. 285–304. Springer, Heidelberg (2002)
29. Suzuki, M., Isshiki, T., Tanaka, K.: Sanitizable signature with secret information. In: Symposium on Cryptography and Information Security, vol. 4A1-2 (2006)
30. Waters, B.: Efficient identity-based encryption without random oracles. In: Cramer, R. (ed.) EUROCRYPT 2005. LNCS, vol. 3494, pp. 114–127. Springer, Heidelberg (2005)
31. Yuen, T., Susilo, W., Liu, J., Mu, Y.: Sanitizable Signatures Revisited. In: Franklin, M.K., Hui, L.C.K., Wong, D.S. (eds.) CANS 2008. LNCS, vol. 5339, pp. 80–97. Springer, Heidelberg (2008)

Rigorous Security Requirements for Designated Verifier Signatures

Kazuki Yoneyama[1], Mebae Ushida[2,*], and Kazuo Ohta[2]

[1] NTT Information Sharing Platform Laboratories
[2] The University of Electro-Communications
yoneyama.kazuki@lab.ntt.co.jp

Abstract. In this paper, we point out that previous security models for the Designated Verifier Signature (DVS) are not sufficient because some serious problems may be caused such that the verifier cannot confirm the validity of the signature even if a scheme satisfies previous security models. Hence, our aim is to clarify rigorous security requirements for the DVS. We use the universal composability (UC) framework. First, we define an ideal DVS functionality within the UC framework. Next, we propose a new security model for the DVS and show that it is necessary and sufficient by proving the equivalence between the DVS functionality and the proposed model. By our reconsideration, it emerges that the DVS requires stronger unforgeability than previous definitions but privacy of signer's identity considered in previous definitions is unnecessary. Finally, we revisit the security of previous DVS schemes according to our rigorous security model. Then, we justify the DVS functionality in feasibility by showing some DVS schemes can satisfy the proposed model.

Keywords: designated verifier signature, strong unforgeability, universally composable security.

1 Introduction

Background. Digital signature schemes provide the authentication of a signer by the *public* verification of the signature and are widely used in many kinds of cryptographic protocols. On the other hand, in some application, it may be preferable that the signature cannot be verified publicly. According to this motivation, the Designated Verifier Signature (DVS) was introduced in 1996 by Jakobsson, Sako and Impagliazzo [1]. In DVS schemes, a signer designates a verifier and only the designated verifier is able to verify the validity of signatures. The DVS is useful for fair e-businesses where a signer expects that the validity of the signature is confirmed by only a specific person but cannot be confirmed by others. Specifically, we consider the situation that a company A offers a service to a client X for a price with the signature of the content of the offer. A does not hope that the validity of the signature is confirmed by a person except A, much less is confirmed by a competitor B. If B can verify the signature, X may

---

* Presently with FUJITSU LABORATORIES LTD.

X. Lai, M. Yung, and D. Lin (Eds.): Inscrypt 2010, LNCS 6584, pp. 318–335, 2011.
© Springer-Verlag Berlin Heidelberg 2011

leak A's offer in order to obtain better price of an offer from B. By using the DVS, A is able to prevent the leak of A's offer because B cannot confirm the validity of the signature.

The DVS is classified into two types. One is called the *ordinary* DVS [1, 2, 3, 4, 5, 6, 7, 8, 9, 10]. In the ordinary DVS, a person except the designated verifier cannot confirm that a signature is exactly generated by the signer, but third parties can know that either the signer or the designated verifier generates the signature (i.e., the signature is related to secret keys of either the signer or the designated verifier). This property is defined as non-transferability or deniability. By allowing the designated verifier to generate a *dummy signature* which is indistinguishable with an *original* signature generated by the signer for the same message, any third party cannot distinguish whether a signature is generated by the signer or the designated verifier even if the designated verifier reveals his secret key. The other is called the *strong* DVS [11, 12, 13, 14, 15, 16, 17]. In the strong DVS, anyone except the designated verifier cannot know any information about the signer from the signature. That is, third parties cannot even narrow the candidate of the signer to two entities. Thus, the strong DVS can guarantee stronger privacy of the validity of the signature than the ordinary DVS. The formal difference between the ordinary DVS and the strong DVS will be described in Section 2.

Motivating Problem. In previous works, various security models of the DVS were proposed and it seems that there is no exact consensus. Since the DVS is a kind of digital signature schemes, *unforgeability* is indispensable property and all of known DVS schemes are proved (or claimed) to satisfy unforgeability. Most of previous works defined unforgeability based on *existential unforgeability against chosen message attacks* (EUF-CMA) studied in the context of digital signature. In EUF-CMA, the forger is allowed to pose signing queries for chosen messages, but the forger is prohibited to output a valid signature as the forged signature for a message previously posed by any signing query. For the context of digital signature, this definition has no problem practically. However, is this definition also appropriate for the context of the DVS?

Unfortunately, our answer is negative. We can show that only EUF-CMA for the DVS cannot prevent some serious problems as follows:

Case of the ordinary DVS. EUF-CMA cannot guarantee *strong* existential unforgeability (i.e., the forger cannot forge a valid signature of a message (m^*, σ^*) even when the forger obtains the other valid signature of this message (m^*, σ)) [18]. Thus, the forger may play strong forgery attack, that is, generating (m^*, σ^*) from (m^*, σ). On the other hand, in order to guarantee non-transferability, a designated verifier needs to be able to output a dummy signature which is indistinguishable from an original signature for the same message. We consider a situation that the designated verifier outputs a dummy signature of a message (m, σ_D) and the forger outputs forged signatures of this message (m, σ^*) by strong forgery attack using the dummy signature. After that, even if the signer generates an original signature of this message, the designated verifier cannot confirm that the signer exactly generates a signature for m because the designated verifier cannot decide whether the original signature is contained in the valid signatures or not. Thus, completeness of the DVS may be lost.[1]

Case of the strong DVS. The strong DVS does not necessarily allow the designated verifier to generate dummy signatures because anonymity of the signer has to be guaranteed without dummy signatures. Thus, the problem in the above case of the ordinary DVS may not occur as long as the designated verifier does not generate dummy signatures. But, we can show that EUF-CMA is also insufficient for the strong DVS because of another problem of *non-repudiation*. Non-repudiation is essential property of signature schemes, that is, the verifier of a correctly generated signature of a message can hold the signer responsible to the contents of the message. In the strong DVS, the signer should be responsible to the contents of a message for a specific designated verifier, but the signer does not need to have responsibility to the contents of this message for other people. However, since EUF-CMA does not guarantee unforgeability for *multiple* verifiers (i.e., the forger cannot forge a valid signature of a message (m, σ^*) for a designated verifier V^* even where the forger obtains the other valid signature of this message (m, σ) for *another* designated verifier V), the forger may generate valid signatures of the same message m for multiple verifiers (V^* and V). Then, though the signer hopes that he is responsible to m for only V, the signer is plunged into responsible to m for also V^* because there is a valid signature of m for V^*. Thus, non-repudiation of the DVS may be lost.

Therefore, EUF-CMA is insufficient for both the ordinary DVS and the strong DVS, and at least strong existential unforgeability for multiple verifiers is required for the DVS.

Our Contribution. Our first contribution is to show the defect of (most of) previous security models clearly as in the above motivating problem. By this result, we can see that DVS schemes have to satisfy strong existential unforgeability. Then, our next question is what are *necessary and sufficient* security requirements for the DVS. Thus, in this paper, we will clarify such rigorous security requirements for the DVS as follows:

1. We define an ideal DVS functionality within the universal composability (UC) framework [19]. The UC framework enables to guarantee that the composed protocol is secure in the sense of the framework if each building block is modularized and all modules satisfy UC security respectively. We say a scheme is UC secure if the scheme is indistinguishable from the ideal world

---

[1] One may think that the designated verifier should ignore any other signature on a message which he has created a dummy signature on the same message. However, in this case, the designated verifier cannot generate dummy signatures on messages which the signer may generate an original signature. For such an important message, non-transferability is not guaranteed. Thus, the problem cannot be solved by this counter.

containing the ideal functionality. Since the ideal functionality is defined to represent essential function and security of the protocol, we can capture the essence of security requirements of the DVS naturally. We define DVS functionalities for both the ordinary DVS and the strong DVS respectively because of the difference between functions of them. As far as we know, our functionalities are first ideal DVS functionalities.

2. Based on the proposed DVS functionalities, we propose a new security model for the DVS. The proposed model is designed to be equivalent with the DVS functionalities. Thus, we also have to consider different models for both the ordinary DVS and the strong DVS respectively. We prove the equivalence between the proposed model and the DVS functionality. As a result, we clarify that the ordinary DVS has to satisfy strong unforgeability, non-transferability and non-coincidental property, and the strong DVS has to satisfy strong unforgeability, non-transferability and private decidability. That is, previous models are lacking in unforgeability but are surplus to privacy of signer's identity because private decidability is exactly weaker than privacy of signer's identity.

3. Regardless of the equivalence, if there was no scheme realizing the proposed functionalities, the functionalities would be meaningless. Hence, we show that there are some previous schemes realizing the proposed functionalities in order to justify the formulation of them. Specifically, we show that the ordinary DVS scheme by Lipmaa et al. [3] satisfies the proposed model for the ordinary DVS and the strong DVS scheme by Laguillaumie and Vergnaud [12] satisfies the proposed model for the strong DVS. By the equivalence, these schemes can realize the proposed functionalities and so our functionalities are reasonable.

Related Works. Security requirements of the DVS have been studied in many literatures.

Laguillaumie and Vergnaud [12] firstly defined the notion of privacy of signer's identity for the strong DVS. Privacy of signer's identity requires that for any distinguisher and a chosen message m a signature σ_0 signed by a signing key SK_0 of m to a designated verifier Ver cannot be distinguishable from a signature σ_1 signed by another signing key SK_1 of m to Ver. Thus, the anonymity property of the strong DVS can be guaranteed by privacy of signer's identity. In this paper, we will show that private decidability which is weaker than privacy of signer's identity is enough to guarantee the anonymity property of the strong DVS.

Lipmaa et al. [3] introduced the notion of non-delegatability. Non-delegatability requires that the signer cannot delegate his signing ability with respect to a designated verifier to a third party, without revealing his secret key or making it possible for the third party to sign with respect to other designated verifiers. This property is useful for many applications of the DVS. However, it is not crucial for the DVS because there is a case that delegatability is useful, e.g., using the DVS with a proxy. The aim of this paper is to clarify (crucially) necessary and sufficient requirements for the DVS. Thus, we deal with non-delegatability as outside the scope of this work.

2 Preliminaries

In this section, we recall the model of the DVS. Due to space limitations, we cannot explain the UC framework. Please see [19].

In the DVS, a signature has to be regarded as to be valid if the designated verifier convinces that the signature is correctly generated by the signer. Unlike basic digital signatures, the verification procedure may not complete only if the signature is accepted by the verification algorithm, especially in the ordinary DVS. Thus, we can generally model the verification of a signature by dividing two procedures: Decision and Distinction. By Decision, the signature is checked whether it is *accepted* by a decision procedure[2]. By Distinction, the accepted signature is checked whether it is exactly generated by the signer. In this paper, we call a signature which is accepted by Decision *an acceptable signature*, and a signature which is acceptable and generated by the signer *a valid signature*. The verification of a signature completes if the signature is valid by performing Decision and Distinction.

In the ordinary DVS, to guarantee non-transferability the verifier can also generate an acceptable signature for any message. We call such an acceptable signature *a dummy signature*, while we call an acceptable signature generated by a signer *an original signature*. Only the original signature must be confirmed as the valid signature. Any third party should be unable to distinguish the original signature from dummy signatures. Even if a third party knows that a signature is acceptable by Decision, he is unable to confirm whether the signature is the original signature or a dummy signature. Thus, the third party is unable to verify the validity of the signature, while the verifier can decide whether the signature is the original signature by using his own list of dummy signatures generated by himself. Also, the verifier cannot convince a third party the validity of any signature because the signature may be generated by the verifier even if the verifier leaks his secret key. Hence, non-transferability is guaranteed.

In several DVS schemes [1, 2, 3, 5, 10], anyone can perform the decision procedure. Thus, anyone can know that an acceptable signature is generated by the signer or the designated verifier. But, any third party cannot confirm the validity of a signature because he cannot perform Distinction. We call such DVS schemes the *ordinary* DVS. On the other hand, the *strong* DVS [11, 12, 14] allows only the verifier to perform the decision procedure. In the strong DVS, any third party cannot know even that a signature is generated by the signer or the designated verifier. In this paper, we call this property *private decidability*. Owing to private decidability, the verifier need not be able to generate dummy signatures, that is, Distinction finishes when Decision finishes.

Definition 1 (Model of Ordinary DVS). *An ordinary DVS scheme consists of following seven algorithms.*

Common parameter generation (SetUp) : *A probabilistic algorithm, on input k, which outputs the public parameters params.*

---

[2] This procedure corresponds to the verification process whether the signature is generated with correct secret key of the signer in the basic digital signature.

Signer's key generation (SKeyGen) : *A probabilistic algorithm, on input params, which outputs the signer's public and secret key PK_s and SK_s.*

Verifier's key generation (VKeyGen) : *A probabilistic algorithm, on input params, which outputs the verifier's public and secret key PK_v and SK_v.*

Designated signing (DSign) : *An algorithm, on input params, a message m, the signer's secret key SK_s and the verifier's public key PK_v, which outputs an original signature σ.*

Transcript simulation (TSim) : *An algorithm, on input params, a message m, the signer's public key PK_s and the verifier's secret key SK_v, which outputs a dummy signature σ'.*

Decision (Decision) : *A deterministic algorithm, on input params, a message m, a signature σ, and public keys PK_s and PK_v, which outputs accept or reject.*

Distinction (Dist) : *A deterministic algorithm, on input a pair of the message and the acceptable signature (m, σ), which outputs valid or invalid.*

Definition 2 (Model of Strong DVS). *A strong DVS scheme consists of following seven algorithms.* SetUp, SKeyGen, VKeyGen, DSign, TSim, Dist *are the same as the ordinary DVS.*

Decision (Decision) : *A deterministic algorithm, on input params, a message m, a signature σ, public keys PK_s and PK_v, and the verifier's secret key SK_v, which outputs accept or reject.*

3   Designated Verifier Signature Functionality

In this section, we define an ideal DVS functionality within the UC framework.

3.1   Basic Idea

First, we show the basic idea of defining the DVS functionality.

KeyGen. When the functionality receives a Signer's Key Generation request from some party P_i, it issues a signer's public key pk_i for P_i and records the fact that P_i is a signer and P_i's public key is pk_i. For a Verifier's Key Generation, the DVS functionality proceeds as above except that it records that the party is a verifier.

Signing. Upon receiving a signing request on a message m, the functionality issues a signature σ. The functionality receives signing request from not only the signer but also the verifier. Then, the functionality records the fact that σ is surely issued on m in the "Signature List" with which the signer or the verifier the functionality outputs (m, σ) to.

Verification. Upon receiving a verification request, the functionality outputs the results of the verification by using the Signature List. In the DVS, there are two kinds of verification requests: Decision and Dist. For a Decision request, the functionality outputs *accept* if (m, σ) is recorded in the Signature

List, otherwise outputs *reject*. For a Dist request, the functionality outputs *valid* for only (m, σ) which is recorded in the Signature List and is issued to the signer. In order to designate the verifier, the functionality outputs such a verification result to only the verifier.

There are two kinds of the DVS: the ordinary DVS and the strong DVS. In the ordinary DVS, for Dist requests the functionality outputs the verification result to only the verifier, but for Decision requests the functionality outputs the verification result for any party. Else, in the strong DVS, for both Decision and Dist requests, the functionality outputs the verification result to only the verifier.

Corrupt and Reveal. The DVS functionality allows two types of corruption of parties to the simulator. The simulator $\mathcal{S}$ (adversary in the ideal model) can corrupt any party, and request to the signer and the verifier to reveal the secret key through the environment $\mathcal{Z}$. We say that "a party is corrupted" if the party reports all current states and the value of his secret key (if he has a secret key). We say that "a party reveals" if the party reveals only the value of his secret key.

3.2   Fault of Basic Idea and Remedy

Unfortunately, the functionality in the basic idea is too weak, that is, there exists an insecure DVS scheme which realizes the functionality. There exists an environment $\mathcal{Z}'$ which can distinguish whether it is interacting with the real life model or with the ideal process for the DVS functionality as follows.

$\mathcal{Z}'$ poses Signing requests to both the signer and the verifier for a fixed message m. Though, in the real model, contents of outputted signatures depend on each DVS scheme, in the ideal model, the functionality may output the same signature σ for the signer and the verifier. If $\mathcal{Z}'$ receives the same signature σ, $\mathcal{Z}'$ poses the Verification request for (m, σ) to the verifier.

The verifier ought to think that σ is generated by himself because he remembers that he previously generated σ for m. Thus, the verifier should output *invalid* in the secure DVS. However, in the ideal model, the functionality returns *valid* because (m, σ) is listed on the signer's Signature List. Hence, even if the DVS scheme is insecure (i.e., the verifier outputs *valid* for such a situation), the scheme can realize the functionality.

In order to avoid such a fault, we can add a following function (1) or (2) to the DVS functionality.

(1). restrict the signer and the verifier to issue coincidental signatures for same messages.

(2). restrict the verifier to issue dummy signatures.

In the ordinary DVS, in order to guarantee non-transferability, the verifier needs to be able to issue a dummy signature. Hence, we define the ordinary DVS functionality by combining basic idea and the function (1) as $\mathcal{F}_{DVS}^{ord}$. Also, we define the strong DVS functionality by combining basic idea and the function (2) as $\mathcal{F}_{DVS}^{str}$.

3.3   Ideal Functionality of DVS

First, we present the ideal functionality $\mathcal{F}_{\mathsf{DVS}}^{ord}$ for the ordinary DVS.

Functionality $\mathcal{F}_{\mathsf{DVS}}^{ord}$

Signer's Key Generation: On input (**SKeyGen**, sid) from some party Sig, hand (**SKeyGen**, sid) to the simulator. Upon receiving (**SKeys**, sid, sk_i, pk_i) from the simulator, output (**SVerKey**, sid, pk_i) to Sig and record the tuple (Sig, sk_i, pk_i, sid) in the Signer List.

Verifier's Key Generation: On input (**VKeyGen**, sid) from some party Ver, hand (**VKeyGen**, sid) to the simulator. Upon receiving (**VKeys**, sid, sk_j, pk_j) from the simulator, output (**VVerKey**, sid, pk_j) to Ver and record the tuple (Ver, sk_j, pk_j, sid) in the Verifier List.

Designated signing: On input (**DSign**, sid, m, pk_i', pk_j') from Sig, verify that there exists (Sig, sk_i, pk_i, sid) in the Signer List and $pk_i' = pk_i$. If not, then ignore the request. Else, send (**DSign**, sid, m, pk_i', pk_j') to the simulator. Upon receiving (**Signature**, sid, m, σ, pk_i', pk_j') from the simulator, verify that there exists the entry $(m, \sigma, pk_i', pk_j', *, 0)$. If it does, then output an error message to Sig and halt. Else, search $(Ver', sk_j', pk_j', sid)$ in the Verifier List and check that $(m, \sigma, pk_i', pk_j', Ver', 1)$ is recorded. If it does, then output an error message to Sig and halt. Else, output (**OriginalSignature**, sid, m, σ) to Sig and record the entry $(m, \sigma, pk_i', pk_j', Sig, 1)$.

Transcript simulation: On input (**TSim**, sid, m, pk_i', pk_j') from Ver, verify that there exists (Ver, sk_j, pk_j, sid) in the Verifier List and $pk_j' = pk_j$. If not, then ignore the request. Else, send (**TSim**, sid, m, pk_i', pk_j') to the simulator. Upon receiving (**Signature**, sid, m, σ, pk_i', pk_j') from the simulator, verify that there exists the entry $(m, \sigma, pk_i', pk_j', *, 0)$. If it does, then output an error message to Ver and halt. Else, search $(Sig', sk_i', pk_i', sid)$ in the Signer List and check $(m, \sigma, pk_i', pk_j', Sig', 1)$ is recorded. If it does, then output an error message to Ver and halt. Else, output (**DummySignature**, sid, m, σ) to Ver, and record the entry $(m, \sigma, pk_i', pk_j', Ver, 1)$.

Decision: On input (**Decide**, sid, m, σ, pk_i', pk_j') from some party P, hand (**Decide**, sid, m, σ, pk_i', pk_j') to the simulator. Upon receiving (**Decided**, sid, m, ϕ, ϕ') from the simulator, do:

1. If the entry $(m, \sigma, pk_i', pk_j', *, b)$ is recorded, then set $f = b$.
2. Else, if $(*, *, pk_i', sid)$ is recorded in the Signer List, $(*, *, pk_j', sid)$ is recorded in the Verifier List, no entry $(m, \sigma, pk_i', pk_j', *, b)$ is recorded, and
   - the signer and the verifier are uncorrupted and do not reveal, then set $f = 0$ and record the entry $(m, \sigma, pk_i', pk_j', Ver, 0)$.
   - only the signer is corrupted or reveals, then set $f = \phi$ and record the entry $(m, \sigma, pk_i', pk_j', Sig, \phi)$.
   - only the verifier is corrupted or reveals, then set $f = \phi$ and record the entry $(m, \sigma, pk_i', pk_j', Ver, \phi)$.

- the signer and the verifier are corrupted or reveal, then set $f = \phi$ and record the entry $(m, \sigma, pk'_i, pk'_j, \phi', \phi)$.

3. Otherwise, let $f = \phi$ and record the entry $(m, \sigma, pk'_i, pk'_j, \phi', \phi)$.

Output (**Decided**, sid, m, f) to P.

Distinction: On input (**Distinct**, sid, m, σ, pk'_i, pk'_j) from some party P, if there does not exist (P, sk'_j, pk'_j, sid) in the Verifier List, then output the error message and halt. Else, hand (**Distinct**, sid, m, σ, pk'_i, pk'_j) to the simulator. Upon receiving (**Distincted**, sid, m, ϕ') from the simulator, do:

1. If $(*, *, pk'_i, sid)$ is not recorded in the Signer List or $(P, *, pk'_j, sid)$ is not recorded in the Verifier List, then output the error message and halt.
2. Else, if there is no entry $(m, \sigma, pk'_i, pk'_j, *, 1)$, then set $f' = \phi'$.
3. Else, if the entry $(m, \sigma, pk'_i, pk'_j, Sig, 1)$ is recorded, then set $f' = 1$.
4. Else, if the entry $(m, \sigma, pk'_i, pk'_j, Ver, 1)$ is recorded, then set $f' = 0$.

Output (**Distincted**, sid, m, f') to P.

Next, we present the ideal functionality $\mathcal{F}_{\mathsf{DVS}}^{str}$ for the strong DVS.

Functionality $\mathcal{F}_{\mathsf{DVS}}^{str}$

Signer's Key Generation, Verifier's Key Generation, Distinction: the same as $\mathcal{F}_{\mathsf{DVS}}^{ord}$.

Designated signing: On input (**DSign**, sid, m, pk'_i, pk'_j) from Sig, verify that there exists (Sig, sk_i, pk_i, sid) in the Signer List and $pk'_i = pk_i$. If not, then ignore the request. Else, send (**DSign**, sid, m, pk'_i, pk'_j) to the simulator. Upon receiving (**Signature**, $sid, m, \sigma, pk'_i, pk'_j$) from the simulator, verify that the entry $(m, \sigma, pk'_i, pk'_j, *, 0)$. If it does, then output an error message to Sig and halt. Else, output (**OriginalSignature**, sid, m, σ) to Sig, and record the entry $(m, \sigma, pk'_i, pk'_j, Sig, 1)$.

Transcript simulation: On input (**TSim**, sid, m, pk'_i, pk'_j) from Ver, verify that there exists (Ver, sk_j, pk_j, sid) in the Verifier List and $pk'_j = pk_j$. If not, then ignore the request. Else, if the Ver does not only reveals, then ignore the request. Else, send (**TSim**, sid, m, pk'_i, pk'_j) to the simulator. Upon receiving (**Signature**, $sid, m, \sigma, pk'_i, pk'_j$) from the simulator, verify that the entry $(m, \sigma, pk'_i, pk'_j, Ver, 0)$ is recorded. If it does, then output an error message to Ver and halt. Else, output (**DummySignature**, sid, m, σ) to Ver, and record the entry $(m, \sigma, pk'_i, pk'_j, Ver, 1)$.

Decision: On input (**Decide**, $sid, m, \sigma, pk'_i, pk'_j$) from P, if there does not exist (P, sk'_j, pk'_j, sid) in the Verifier List, then output the error message and halt. Else, hand (**Decide**, $sid, m, \sigma, pk'_i, pk'_j$) to the simulator. Upon receiving (**Decided**, sid, m, ϕ, ϕ') from the simulator, perform the procedure which is the same as Decision of $\mathcal{F}_{\mathsf{DVS}}^{ord}$.

---

4   Rigorous Security Definition

In this section, we clarify the rigorous security definition for the secure DVS which realizes the proposed DVS functionality in Section 3.

4.1   Security Requirements for Secure DVS

In this section, we define the security requirements for the DVS.

Correctness. We say that the DVS satisfies correctness if an original signature and a dummy signature are surely judged "accepted" by the decision procedure.

Definition 3 (Correctness). [3] *A DVS scheme is said to satisfy correctness, if for any m,*

$$\Pr[accept \leftarrow \mathsf{Decision}(params, m, \sigma, PK_s, PK_v)|$$
$$params \leftarrow \mathsf{SetUp}(k);$$
$$(SK_s, PK_s) \leftarrow \mathsf{SKeyGen}(params);$$
$$(SK_v, PK_v) \leftarrow \mathsf{VKeyGen}(params);$$
$$(\sigma \leftarrow \mathsf{DSign}(m, SK_s, PK_v)) \vee (\sigma \leftarrow \mathsf{TSim}(m, PK_s, SK_v))]$$
$$\geq 1 - \epsilon$$

Consistency. We say that DVS satisfies consistency if for any message and signature pair (m, σ), outputs of Decision for (m, σ) are always the same.

Definition 4 (Consistency). [3] *A DVS scheme is said to satisfy consistency, if for any m,*

$$\Pr[b_1 \neq b_2|$$
$$b_1 \leftarrow \mathsf{Decision}(params, m, \sigma, PK_s, PK_v)$$
$$b_2 \leftarrow \mathsf{Decision}(params, m, \sigma, PK_s, PK_v)$$
$$\leq \epsilon$$

Strong Unforgeability. In basic digital signatures, the security notion of strong unforgeability is proposed by [18]. We define strong unforgeability for multiple signers and verifiers.

Definition 5 (Strong Unforgeability). [3] *Let $\mathcal{A}$ be a strong-forgery for multiple signers and verifiers under chosen message attack (sEUF-CMA)-adversary, $\Sigma_{S(SK_s, \cdot)}(\cdot)$ be the original signing oracle, $\Sigma_{T(\cdot, SK_v)}(\cdot)$ be the dummy signing oracle and $\Upsilon_{(\cdot, SK_v)}(\cdot)$ be the verification oracle[4]. Let $\{(m_1, \sigma_1), \cdots, (m_{qs}, \sigma_{qs})\}$*

---

[3] This definition is for the ordinary DVS. In the strong DVS case, $\mathsf{Decision}(params, m, \sigma, PK_s, PK_v)$ changes to $\mathsf{Decision}(params, m, \sigma, PK_s, SK_v)$.

[4] For the ordinary DVS, the verification oracle need not be considered.

be a set of message and signature pair which is given to $\mathcal{A}$ by oracle $\Sigma_{S(\mathsf{SK}_s,\cdot)}(\cdot)$, and $\{(m'_1, \sigma'_1), \cdots, (m'_{q_T}, \sigma'_{q_T})\}$ be a set of message and signature pair which is given to $\mathcal{A}$ by oracle $\Sigma_{T(\cdot,\mathsf{SK}_v)}(\cdot)$. Let k be a security parameter. We consider the following random experiment:

Experiment $\mathsf{Exp}_{DVS,\mathcal{A}}^{seuf-cma}(k)$

$params \overset{R}{\leftarrow} \mathsf{Setup}(k)$

$(PK_s, SK_s) \overset{R}{\leftarrow} \mathsf{SKeyGen}(params)$

$(PK_v, SK_v) \overset{R}{\leftarrow} \mathsf{VKeyGen}(params)$

$(m^*, \sigma^*) \leftarrow \mathcal{A}^{\Sigma_{S(\mathsf{SK}_s,\cdot)}(\cdot),\Sigma_{T(\cdot,\mathsf{SK}_v)}(\cdot),\Upsilon_{(\cdot,\mathsf{SK}_v)}(\cdot)}(params, PK_s, PK_v)$

s.t. $(m^*, \sigma^*) \notin \{(m_1, \sigma_1), \cdots, (m_{q_S}, \sigma_{q_S})\} \cup \{(m'_1, \sigma'_1), \cdots, (m'_{q_T}, \sigma'_{q_T})\}$

Return 1 iff $\mathsf{Decision}(params, m^*, \sigma^*, PK_s, PK_v) = accept$

We define the success probability of the adversary $\mathcal{A}$ by

$$\mathsf{Succ}_{DVS,\mathcal{A}}^{seuf-cma}(k) = \Pr[\mathsf{Exp}_{DVS,\mathcal{A}}^{seuf-cma}(k) = 1].$$

A DVS scheme is said to be (k, τ, ϵ)-sEUF-CMA secure, if no adversary $\mathcal{A}$ running in time τ has $\mathsf{Succ}_{DVS,\mathcal{A}}^{seuf-cma}(k) \geq \epsilon$.

Non-transferability. A property of non-transferability guarantees that even if a third party who has signer's and verifier's secret keys cannot distinguish the original signature from the dummy signature, and that only the verifier (and the signer) can perform Distinction procedure.

Definition 6 (Non-transferability). *Let $\mathcal{A}$ be an arbitrary non-transferability adversary against the DVS. Let k be a security parameter. We consider the following random experiment:*

Experiment $\mathsf{Exp}_{DVS,\mathcal{A}}^{nt}(k)$

$params \overset{R}{\leftarrow} \mathsf{Setup}(k)$

$(PK_s, SK_s) \overset{R}{\leftarrow} \mathsf{SKeyGen}(params)$

$(PK_v, SK_v) \overset{R}{\leftarrow} \mathsf{VKeyGen}(params)$

$m^* \leftarrow \mathcal{A}(params, PK_s, PK_v, SK_s, SK_v)$

$r \leftarrow_R \{0, 1\}$

if $r = 1 : \sigma^* \leftarrow \mathsf{DSign}(params, m^*, SK_s, PK_v)$

otherwise : $\sigma^* \leftarrow \mathsf{TSim}(params, m^*, PK_s, SK_v)$

$r' \leftarrow \mathcal{A}(params, m^*, \sigma^*, PK_s, PK_v, SK_s, SK_v)$

Return 1 iff $r' = r$

We define the advantage of the adversary $\mathcal{A}$ by

$$\mathsf{Adv}^{nt}_{DVS,\mathcal{A}}(k) = |\mathsf{Pr}[\mathsf{Exp}^{nt}_{DVS,\mathcal{A}}(k) = 1] - \tfrac{1}{2}|.$$

A DVS scheme is said to satisfy (k, τ, ϵ)-non-transferability, if no adversary $\mathcal{A}$ running time τ has $\mathsf{Adv}^{nt}_{DVS,\mathcal{A}}(k) \geq \epsilon$.

Private Decidability. Private decidability guarantees that a third party who has only public information cannot decide that any message and signature pair is acceptable or not. This property is considered in only the strong DVS, and ordinary DVS schemes never satisfy private decidability due to the definition.

Definition 7 (Private Decidability). *Let $\mathcal{A}$ be a private decidability adversary against the DVS, $\Sigma_{S(\mathsf{SK_s}, \cdot)}(\cdot)$ be the original signing oracle, $\Sigma_{T(\cdot, \mathsf{SK_v})}(\cdot)$ be the dummy signing oracle and $\Upsilon_{(\cdot, \mathsf{SK_v})}(\cdot)$ be the verification oracle. Let k be a security parameter. We consider the following experiment.*

$$\boxed{\text{Experiment } \mathsf{Exp}^{pd-i}_{DVS,A}(k)}$$

$params \xleftarrow{R} \mathsf{Setup}(k)$

$(PK_s, SK_s) \xleftarrow{R} \mathsf{SKeyGen}(params)$

$(PK_v, SK_v) \xleftarrow{R} \mathsf{VKeyGen}(params)$

$m^* \leftarrow \mathcal{A}^{\Sigma_{S(\mathsf{SK_s}, \cdot)}(\cdot), \Sigma_{T(\cdot, \mathsf{SK_v})}(\cdot), \Upsilon_{(\cdot, \mathsf{SK_v})}(\cdot)}(params, PK_s, PK_v)$

$\sigma_i \leftarrow \mathsf{DSign}(params, m^*, SK_s, PK_v)$

$\sigma_{\bar{i}} \leftarrow_R \Sigma = \{\sigma; \mathsf{Decision}(m, \sigma) = 0\}$

$\text{Return } i' \leftarrow \mathcal{A}^{\Sigma_{S(\mathsf{SK_s}, \cdot)}(\cdot), \Sigma_{T(\cdot, \mathsf{SK_v})}(\cdot), \Upsilon_{(\cdot, \mathsf{SK_v})}(\cdot)}(params, m^*, \sigma_i, \sigma_{\bar{i}}, PK_s, PK_v)$

We define the advantage of the adversary $\mathcal{A}$ by

$$\mathsf{Adv}^{pd}_{DVS,\mathcal{A}}(k) = |\mathsf{Pr}[\mathsf{Exp}^{pd-1}_{DVS,\mathcal{A}}(k) = 1] - \mathsf{Pr}[\mathsf{Exp}^{pd-0}_{DVS,\mathcal{A}}(k) = 1]|.$$

A DVS scheme is said to satisfy (k, τ, ϵ)-private decidability, if no adversary $\mathcal{A}$ running in time τ has $\mathsf{Adv}^{pd}_{DVS,\mathcal{A}}(k) \geq \epsilon$.

Non-Coincidental Property. For a message m, if the probability that $\sigma_{DSign} = \sigma_{TSim}$ such that σ_{DSign} from DSign and σ_{TSim} from TSim is non-negligible, the verifier cannot confirm the validity of the signature because he cannot distinguish (m, σ_{DSign}) from the dummy signature (m, σ_{TSim}) he issued before. Hence, the DVS must satisfy the property that the probability that the original signature for a message is identical with the dummy signature for the message is negligible. In this paper, we call this property *non-coincidental property*.

Definition 8 (Non-coincidental Property). *A DVS scheme is said to have (k, ϵ)-non-coincidental property, if for any m,*

$$\Pr[\sigma_{DSign} = \sigma_{TSim} | params \leftarrow \mathsf{SetUp}(k);$$
$$(SK_s, PK_s) \leftarrow \mathsf{SKeyGen}(params);$$
$$(SK_v, PK_v) \leftarrow \mathsf{VKeyGen}(params);$$
$$\sigma_{DSign} \leftarrow \mathsf{DSign}(m, SK_s, PK_v);$$
$$\sigma_{TSim} \leftarrow \mathsf{TSim}(m, PK_s, SK_v)]$$
$$\leq \epsilon.$$

4.2 Security Definition

We define the rigorous definition for secure DVS schemes.

Notations. We use following notations in order to describe our main theorem. Σ is a DVS scheme. $\mathsf{Cor} : \{\Sigma\} \rightarrow \{0, 1\}$ is a Boolean function which outputs 1 if Σ satisfies correctness, otherwise outputs 0. In the same way, Con, sEUF, NT, PD and NCP are Boolean functions which output 1 if Σ satisfies consistency, strong unforgeability, non-transferability, private decidability and non-coincidental property, respectively. Let $\mathsf{NTSim} : \{DVS \; player\} \rightarrow \{0, 1\}$ is a Boolean function which outputs 1 if the verifier does not generate any dummy signature, otherwise outputs 0.

Intuition of Definition. If a DVS scheme does not satisfy sEUF-CMA (i.e., sEUF=0), there is an acceptable signature which is not either an original signature or a dummy signature. In this case, the verifier cannot decide the validity of signature by Dist because it is impossible for the verifier to decide that a signature which is not in the list of dummy signatures is the original signature. Thus, the DVS must satisfy sEUF=1.

If a DVS scheme does not satisfy non-transferability (i.e., NT=0), a third party who is given signer's and verifier's secret keys is able to distinguish the original signature from the dummy signature. In this case, a third party can confirm the validity of the signature using these keys. Thus, the DVS scheme must satisfy NT=1.

If a DVS scheme does not satisfy non-coincidental property (i.e., NCP=0), the following situation occurs: The verifier issues a dummy signature (m, σ_{TSim}). After that, the signer generates an original signature (m, σ_{DSign}). If Coll=0, $\sigma_{DSing} = \sigma_{TSim}$ holds with non-negligible probability. Then, the verifier misunderstands that (m, σ_{DSign}) is the dummy signature and so invalid. Thus, the DVS scheme must satisfy NCP=1.

Even if NCP=0, the verifier is able to confirm the validity of the signature when he never issues dummy signatures for any message (i.e., NTSim=1). However, in the DVS, the verifier's ability to generate a dummy signature prevents a third party from confirming the validity of the signature. If a third party could know that the verifier never issues dummy signatures and confirm the validity of the signature, it would be impossible to satisfy non-transferability. Hence, if NTSim=1, the DVS must satisfy private decidability (i.e., PD=1). If the DVS scheme satisfies private decidability, any third party cannot know any signer of the signature even if the verifier never generates dummy signatures. Thus, if NTSim=1, the DVS must also satisfy the PD=1. This case corresponds to the strong DVS.

Definition 9 (Secure DVS). *We say a DVS scheme is secure if the following condition holds:* $\mathsf{Cor} \wedge \mathsf{Con} \wedge \mathsf{sEUF} \wedge \mathsf{NT} \wedge (\mathsf{NCP} \vee (\mathsf{PD} \wedge \mathsf{NTSim})) = 1$. *The condition* $\mathsf{Cor} \wedge \mathsf{Con} \wedge \mathsf{sEUF} \wedge \mathsf{NT} \wedge \mathsf{NCP} = 1$ *is for the ordinary DVS and* $\mathsf{Cor} \wedge \mathsf{Con} \wedge \mathsf{sEUF} \wedge \mathsf{NT} \wedge \mathsf{PD} \wedge \mathsf{NTSim} = 1$ *is for the strong DVS.*

5 Equivalence

We show that the proposed DVS functionalities $\mathcal{F}_{\mathsf{DVS}}^{ord}$ and $\mathcal{F}_{\mathsf{DVS}}^{str}$ are equivalent with the proposed security definition in Section 4.

5.1 Translation to Protocol

First, we describe how to translate an ordinary DVS scheme and a strong DVS scheme into protocols respectively.

Translation for the Ordinary DVS. We describe how to translate a ordinary DVS scheme $\Sigma_{ordDVS} = (\mathsf{SetUp}, \mathsf{SKeyGen}, \mathsf{VKeyGen}, \mathsf{DSign}, \mathsf{TSim}, \mathsf{Decision}, \mathsf{Dist})$ into a protocol $\pi_{\Sigma_{ordDVS}}$.

- First, the public parameter is generated as $params \leftarrow \mathsf{SetUp}(1^k)$.
- When a party Sig receives an input (**SKeyGen**, sid), it runs $(SK_s, PK_s) \leftarrow \mathsf{SKeyGen}(params)$, keeps the secret key SK_s and outputs (**SVerKey**, sid, PK_s).
- When a party Ver receives an input (**VKeyGen**, sid), it runs $(SK_v, PK_v) \leftarrow \mathsf{VKeyGen}(params)$, keeps the secret key SK_v and outputs (**VVerKey**, sid, PK_v).
- When Sig receives an input (**DSign**, sid, m, pk'_i, pk'_j) for Sig who has a secret key SK_s and $pk'_i = PK_s$, Sig sets $\sigma \leftarrow \mathsf{DSign}(params, m, SK_s, pk'_j)$, and outputs (**OriginalSignature**, sid, m, σ).
- When Ver receives an input (**TSim**, sid, m, pk'_i, pk'_j) for Ver who has a secret key SK_v and $pk'_j = Pk_v$, Ver sets $\sigma \leftarrow \mathsf{TSim}(params, m, pk'_i, SK_v)$, and outputs (**DummySignature**, sid, m, σ).
- When P receives an input (**Decide**, $sid, m, \sigma, pk'_i, pk'_j$), P runs $f \leftarrow \mathsf{Decision}(params, m, \sigma, pk'_i, pk'_j)$, and outputs (**Decided**, sid, m, f).
- When Ver receives an input (**Distnct**, $sid, m, \sigma, pk'_i, pk'_j$) for Ver. If $pk'_j = PKv$, Ver runs $f \leftarrow \mathsf{Decision}(params, m, \sigma, pk'_i, PK_v)$. If $f = 1$ and (m, σ) is not issued as (**DummySignature**, sid, m, σ) for pk'_i before, let $f' = 1$. Else $f' = 0$. It outputs (**Distincted**, sid, m, f'). Else ignore the request.

Translation for the Strong DVS. We describe how to translate a strong DVS scheme $\Sigma_{strDVS} = (\mathsf{SetUp}, \mathsf{SKeyGen}, \mathsf{VKeyGen}, \mathsf{DSign}, \mathsf{TSim}, \mathsf{Decision}, \mathsf{Dist})$ into a protocol $\pi_{\Sigma_{strDVS}}$.

- First, the public parameter is generated as $params \leftarrow \mathsf{SetUp}(1^k)$.
- When a party Sig receives an input (**SKeyGen**, sid), it runs $(SK_s, PK_s) \leftarrow$ SKeyGen($params$), keeps the secret key SK_s and outputs (**SVerKey**, sid, PK_s).
- When a party Ver receives an input (**VKeyGen**, sid), it runs $(SK_v, PK_v) \leftarrow$ VKeyGen($params$), keeps the secret key SK_v and outputs (**VVerKey**, sid, PK_v).
- When Sig receives an input (**DSign**, sid, m, pk'_i, pk'_j) for Sig who has the secret key SK_s and $pk'_i = PK_s$, Sig sets $\sigma \leftarrow$ DSign($params, m, SK_s, pk'_j$), and outputs (**OriginalSignature**, sid, m, σ).
- When Ver receives an input (**TSim**, sid, m, pk'_i, pk'_j) for Ver who has $pk'_j = PK_v$, if Ver does not only reveals then ignores the request. Else, it sets $\sigma \leftarrow$ TSim($params, m, pk'_i, SK_v$), and outputs (**DummySignature**, sid, m, σ).
- When Ver receives an input (**Decide**, $sid, m, \sigma, pk'_i, pk'_j$), if $pk'_j = PK_v$, Ver runs $f \leftarrow$ Decision($params, m, \sigma, pk'_i, SK_v$) and outputs (**Decided**, ID, m, f). Otherwise Ver ignores the request.
- When Ver receives an input (**Dist**, $sid, m, \sigma, pk'_i, pk'_j$) for Ver who has a secret key SK_v. If $pk'_j = PK_v$, it runs $f \leftarrow$ Decision($params, m, \sigma, pk'_i, SK_v$). If $f = 1$ and (m, σ) is not issued as (**DummySignature**, sid, m, σ) for pk'_i, let $f' = 1$. Else $f' = 0$. Ver outputs (**Distinction**, sid, m, f'). Else ignore the request.

5.2   Main Theorems

Theorem 1 (Equivalence between Secure Ordinary DVS and $\mathcal{F}_{\mathsf{DVS}}^{ord}$). *Let* Σ_{ordDVS} = (SKeyGen, VKeyGen, DSign, TSim, Decision, Dist) *be an ordinary DVS. Then* $\pi_{\Sigma_{ordDVS}}$ *securely realize* $\mathcal{F}_{\mathsf{DVS}}^{ord}$ *if and only if* Σ_{ordDVS} *is a secure ordinary DVS which satisfies* Cor $\wedge$ Con $\wedge$ sEUF $\wedge$ NT $\wedge$ NCP $= 1$.

Theorem 2 (Equivalence between Secure Strong DVS and $\mathcal{F}_{\mathsf{DVS}}^{str}$). *Let* Σ_{strDVS} = (SKeyGen, VKeyGen, DSign, TSim, Decision, Dist) *be a strong DVS. Then* $\pi_{\Sigma_{strDVS}}$ *securely realize* $\mathcal{F}_{\mathsf{DVS}}^{str}$ *if and only if* Σ_{strDVS} *is a secure strong DVS which satisfies* Cor $\wedge$ Con $\wedge$ sEUF $\wedge$ NT $\wedge$ NTSim $\wedge$ PD $= 1$.

Due to space limitations, we will show the proof of Theorem 1 and 2 in the full version of this paper.

5.3   Difference from Previous Requirements

Unforgeability.   In the previous unforgeability definitions for the DVS, the adversary is not prevented to output a forged signature of a message for a verifier where the adversary posed the message to the signing oracle for another verifier. Thus, the serious problems described in Section 1 may occur. In the proposed sEUF-CMA, the adversary cannot forge any signature of messages for the target verifier even where the adversary posed the messages to the signing oracle for another verifier. Hence, such problems do not occur if the DVS scheme satisfies our sEUF-CMA. That is, the previous unforgeability definitions are not sufficient.

Privacy of Signer's Identity and Private Decidability. The proposed private decidability is exactly weaker than the notion of privacy of signer's identity which is considered as necessary requirement in previous works.

Theorem 3. *If a DVS scheme satisfies privacy of signer's identity, then the scheme satisfies private decidability.*

Proof. We construct the adversary $\mathcal{A}_{PSI}$ who breaks privacy of signer's identity by assuming the successful adversary $\mathcal{A}_{PD}$ against private decidability. First, $\mathcal{A}_{PSI}$ receives (PK_{s0}, PK_{s1}, PK_v), chooses $b' \leftarrow \{0,1\}$ randomly, set $PK_s = PK_{sb'}$, and inputs (PK_s, PK_v) to $\mathcal{A}_{PD}$. When $\mathcal{A}_{PD}$ outputs m^*, $\mathcal{A}_{PSI}$ outputs m^* as his challenge. The challenger chooses $b \leftarrow \{0,1\}$ randomly, computes $\sigma^* \leftarrow \mathsf{DSign}(SK_{sb}, PK_v, m^*)$ and returns σ_* to $\mathcal{A}_{PSI}$. $\mathcal{A}_{PSI}$ sets $\sigma_{b''} = \sigma^*$. Also, $\mathcal{A}_{PSI}$ poses m^* to the original signing oracle for $s\bar{b'}$, obtains the signature and sets it as $\sigma_{\bar{b''}}$. $\mathcal{A}_{PSI}$ returns $\sigma_{b''}, \sigma_{\bar{b''}}$ to $\mathcal{A}_{PD}$. When $\mathcal{A}_{PD}$ outputs b''^*, $\mathcal{A}_{PSI}$ outputs b''^*. If $b = b'$, $\mathcal{A}_{PD}$ outputs $b''^* = b''$ with probability non-negligibly larger than $1/2$. Thus, $\mathcal{A}_{PSI}$ also succeeds with probability non-negligibly larger than $1/2$. □

However, we show that private decidability is sufficient for secure DVSs. That is, privacy of signer's identity is unnecessarily strong.

6   Security of Previous Schemes

In this section, we show some previous DVS schemes satisfy our proposed security model. From a point of view, this fact justifies the proposed DVS functionality because there exist DVS schemes realize it. Specifically, we show that the Lipmaa et al.'s ordinary DVS [3] (LWB DVS) and the Laguillaumie-Vergnaud strong DVS [12] (LV DVS) are secure in the sense of Definition 9. From Theorem 1 and 2, these schemes realize the proposed DVS functionality.

LWB DVS. First, we show the security of the LWB DVS. The protocol of the LWB DVS is described below.

SetUp. For input a security parameter k, set the public parameter $params = (p, q, g, H)$ shared between the users: p is a large prime s.t. $2^k < p < 2^{k+1}$, q is a prime factor of $p - 1$, $(g_1, g_2) \in \mathbb{Z}_q^{*2}$ are two elements such that nobody knows the mutual discrete logarithm of g_1 and g_2. $H : \{0,1\}^* \to \mathbb{Z}_q$ is a one-way hash function.
SKeyGen. For input $params$, pick $x_s \in \mathbb{Z}_q$, let x_s be the signer's secret key SK_s and compute $y_{s1} = g_1^{x_s}$ and $y_{s2} = g_2^{x_s}$. Let the signer's public key $PK_s = (y_{s1}, y_{s2})$.
VKeyGen. For input $params$, pick $x_v \in \mathbb{Z}_q$, let x_v be the verifier's secret key SK_v and compute $y_{v1} = g_1^{x_v}$ and $y_{v2} = g_2^{x_v}$. Let the verifier's public key $PK_v = (y_{v1}, y_{v2})$.

DSign. For input $params$, a message m, SK_s and PK_v, select three random values $r, \omega, t \in \mathbb{Z}_q$, set $a_1 = g_1^r \mod p$, $a_2 = g_2^r \mod p$, $c = g_1^\omega y_{v1}^t \mod p$ and $h = H(PK_s, PK_v, a_1, a_2, c, m)$, and compute $z = r + (h + \omega)x_s \mod q$. Let (ω, t, h, z) be the signature σ of the message m.

Decision. For input $params$, a message m, signature $\sigma = (\omega, t, h, z)$, PK_s and PK_v, check whether $h = H(PK_s, PK_v, g_1^z y_{s1}^{-(h+\omega)} \mod p, g_2^z y_{s2}^{-(h+\omega)} \mod p, g_1^\omega y_{v1}^t \mod p, m)$.

TSim. For input $params$, a message m, SK_v and PK_s, select three random values $z, \alpha, \beta \in \mathbb{Z}_q$, set $a_1 = g_1^z y_{s1}^{-\beta} \mod p$, $a_2 = g_2^z y_{s2}^{-\beta} \mod p$ and $h = H(PK_s, PK_v, a_1, a_2, g_1^\alpha \mod p, m)$, and compute $\omega = \beta - h \mod q$ and $t = (\alpha - \omega)x_v^{-1} \mod q$. Let (ω, t, h, z) be the signature σ of the message m.

Theorem 4. *The LWB DVS is secure in the sense of Definition 9 in the random oracle model if the Decisional Diffie-Hellman (DDH) problem is hard.*

Due to space limitations, we will show the proof of Theorem 4 in the full version of this paper.

LV DVS. Next, we show the security of the LV DVS. The protocol of the LV DVS is described below.

SetUp. For input a security parameter k, set the public parameter $params = (q, G, G_T, g, H, H')$ shared between the users: q is a large prime, G is a pairing group and $e : G \times G \to G_T$ is an admissible bilinear map. Let $H : \{0,1\}^* \to \{0,1\}^k$ and $H' : \{0,1\}^* \to G$ be hash functions.

SKeyGen. Let $x_s \in \mathbb{Z}_q$ be the signer's secret key SK_s and $y_s = g^{x_s}$ be the signer's public key PK_s.

VKeyGen. Let $x_v \in \mathbb{Z}_q$ be the verifier's secret key SK_v and $y_v = g^{x_v}$ be the verifier's public key PK_v.

DSign. For input a message m, SK_s and PK_v, select a random string r of length k, and compute $s = H(e(y_v, H'(m, r)^{x_s}))$. Let (s, r) be the signature σ of the message m.

Decision. For input a message m, a signature $\sigma = (s, r)$, PK_s and SK_v, check whether $s = H(e(y_s, H'(m, r)^{x_v}))$.

Theorem 5. *The LV DVS is secure in the sense of Definition 9 in the random oracle model if the Gap-Bilinear Diffie-Hellman (GBDH) problem is hard.*

Due to space limitations, we will show the proof of Theorem 5 in the full version of this paper.

References

1. Jakobsson, M., Sako, K., Impagliazzo, R.: Designated Verifier Proofs and Their Applications. In: Maurer, U.M. (ed.) EUROCRYPT 1996. LNCS, vol. 1070, pp. 143–154. Springer, Heidelberg (1996)
2. Rivest, R.L., Shamir, A., Tauman, Y.: How to Leak a Secret. In: Boyd, C. (ed.) ASIACRYPT 2001. LNCS, vol. 2248, pp. 552–565. Springer, Heidelberg (2001)

3. Lipmaa, H., Wang, G., Bao, F.: Designated Verifier Signature Schemes: Attacks, New Security Notions and a New Construction. In: Caires, L., Italiano, G.F., Monteiro, L., Palamidessi, C., Yung, M. (eds.) ICALP 2005. LNCS, vol. 3580, pp. 459–471. Springer, Heidelberg (2005)
4. Steinfeld, R., Bull, L., Wang, H., Pieprzyk, J.: Universal Designated-Verifier Signatures. In: Laih, C.-S. (ed.) ASIACRYPT 2003. LNCS, vol. 2894, pp. 523–542. Springer, Heidelberg (2003)
5. Steinfeld, R., Wang, H., Pieprzyk, J.: Efficient Extension of Standard Schnorr/RSA Signatures into Universal Designated-Verifier Signatures. In: Bao, F., Deng, R., Zhou, J. (eds.) PKC 2004. LNCS, vol. 2947, pp. 86–100. Springer, Heidelberg (2004)
6. Zhang, F., Susilo, W., Mu, Y., Chen, X.: Identity-Based Universal Designated Verifier Signatures. In: EUC Workshops 2005, pp. 825–834 (2005)
7. Zhang, R., Furukawa, J., Imai, H.: Short Signature and Universal Designated Verifier Signature Without Random Oracles. In: Ioannidis, J., Keromytis, A.D., Yung, M. (eds.) ACNS 2005. LNCS, vol. 3531, pp. 483–498. Springer, Heidelberg (2005)
8. Vergnaud, D.: New extensions of pairing-based signatures into universal designated verifier signatures. In: Bugliesi, M., Preneel, B., Sassone, V., Wegener, I. (eds.) ICALP 2006. LNCS, vol. 4052, pp. 58–69. Springer, Heidelberg (2006)
9. Huang, X., Susilo, W., Mu, Y., Wu, W.: Universal Designated Verifier Signature Without Delegatability. In: Ning, P., Qing, S., Li, N. (eds.) ICICS 2006. LNCS, vol. 4307, pp. 479–498. Springer, Heidelberg (2006)
10. Shahandashti, S.F., Safavi-Naini, R.: Construction of Universal Designated-Verifier Signatures and Identity-Based Signatures from Standard Signatures. In: Cramer, R. (ed.) PKC 2008. LNCS, vol. 4939, pp. 121–140. Springer, Heidelberg (2008)
11. Saeednia, S., Kremer, S., Markowitch, O.: An Efficient Strong Designated Verifier Signature Scheme. In: Lim, J.-I., Lee, D.-H. (eds.) ICISC 2003. LNCS, vol. 2971, pp. 40–54. Springer, Heidelberg (2004)
12. Laguillaumie, F., Vergnaud, D.: Designated Verifier Signatures: Anonymity and Efficient Construction from Any Bilinear Map. In: Blundo, C., Cimato, S. (eds.) SCN 2004. LNCS, vol. 3352, pp. 105–119. Springer, Heidelberg (2005)
13. Laguillaumie, F., Vergnaud, D.: Multi-designated Verifiers Signatures. In: López, J., Qing, S., Okamoto, E. (eds.) ICICS 2004. LNCS, vol. 3269, pp. 495–507. Springer, Heidelberg (2004)
14. Susilo, W., Zhang, F., Mu, Y.: Identity-Based Strong Designated Verifier Signature Schemes. In: Wang, H., Pieprzyk, J., Varadharajan, V. (eds.) ACISP 2004. LNCS, vol. 3108, pp. 313–324. Springer, Heidelberg (2004)
15. Laguillaumie, F., Libert, B., Quisquater, J.-J.: Universal Designated Verifier Signatures Without Random Oracles or Non-black Box Assumptions. In: De Prisco, R., Yung, M. (eds.) SCN 2006. LNCS, vol. 4116, pp. 63–77. Springer, Heidelberg (2006)
16. Chow, S.S.M.: Identity-Based Strong Multi-Designated Verifiers Signatures. In: Atzeni, A.S., Lioy, A. (eds.) EuroPKI 2006. LNCS, vol. 4043, pp. 257–259. Springer, Heidelberg (2006)
17. Huang, Q., Yang, G., Wong, D.S., Susilo, W.: Efficient Strong Designated Verifier Signature Schemes without Random Oracles or Delegatability. In: Cryptology ePrint Archive: 2009/518 (2009)
18. An, J.H., Dodis, Y., Rabin, T.: On the Security of Joint Signature and Encryption. In: Knudsen, L.R. (ed.) EUROCRYPT 2002. LNCS, vol. 2332, pp. 83–107. Springer, Heidelberg (2002)
19. Canetti, R.: Universally Composable Security: A New Paradigm for Cryptographic Protocols. In: FOCS 2001, pp. 136–145 (2001)

Quasi-Dyadic CFS Signatures

Paulo S.L.M. Barreto[1,*], Pierre-Louis Cayrel[2],
Rafael Misoczki[1], and Robert Niebuhr[3]

[1] Departamento de Engenharia de Computação e Sistemas Digitais (PCS),
Escola Politécnica, Universidade de São Paulo, Brazil
{pbarreto,rmisoczki}@larc.usp.br
[2] CASED – Center for Advanced Security Research Darmstadt,
Mornewegstrasse, 32
64293 Darmstadt
Germany
pierre-louis.cayrel@cased.de
[3] Technische Universität Darmstadt
Fachbereich Informatik
Kryptographie und Computeralgebra,
Hochschulstraße 10
64289 Darmstadt
Germany
rniebuhr@cdc.informatik.tu-darmstadt.de

Abstract. Courtois-Finiasz-Sendrier (CFS) digital signatures critically depend on the ability to efficiently find a decodable syndrome by random sampling the syndrome space, previously restricting the class of codes upon which they could be instantiated to generic binary Goppa codes. In this paper we show how to construct t-error correcting quasi-dyadic codes where the density of decodable syndromes is high, while also allowing for a reduction by a factor up to t in the key size.

Keywords: post-quantum cryptography, coding-based cryptography, digital signatures, efficient parameters and algorithms.

1 Introduction

Digital signatures are among the most useful and pervasive cryptographic primitives, either *per se* or as part of more elaborate, derived protocols. Yet the overwhelming majority of actually deployed signature schemes seem to rely on the hardness of certain computational problems that are efficiently solvable by quantum computers [19]. Should quantum computers become a technological reality, the task of ensuring that suitable quantum-resistant signatures are available for deployment becomes critical.

The signature algorithm proposed by Courtois, Finiasz and Sendrier, or CFS for short [4], is one of the few and most promising schemes known based on the

* Supported by the Brazilian National Council for Scientific and Technological Development (CNPq) under research productivity grant 303163/2009-7.

X. Lai, M. Yung, and D. Lin (Eds.): Inscrypt 2010, LNCS 6584, pp. 336–349, 2011.

difficulty of decoding linear error-correcting codes. However, it has the drawback that public keys tend to be exceedingly large [9], all the more so due to an attack due to Bleichenbacher (unpublished, but described in [9]).

Part of the difficulty resides in obtaining codes with high density of decodable syndromes, since the CFS signing mechanism involves sampling random syndromes until a decodable one is found. Essentially the only family of suitable codes for this purpose is that of binary Goppa codes, for which one can actually correct all t design errors, leading to a signing complexity of $O(t!)$. In comparison, for other classes of codes, no decoding method is known that is capable of efficiently correcting more than about half as many errors; since one has then to design the error correcting capacity twice as high, the CFS signing complexity becomes $O((2t)!) \approx O((t!)^2 \cdot 4^t/\sqrt{t})$, far too much for any secure parameter set.

Quasi-dyadic (QD) codes [14], which constitute a proper subfamily of Goppa codes, have been proposed to address the problem of key reduction in the related McEliece and Niederreiter cryptosystems [13,15]. However, the original QD construction only yields codes with a fairly low density of decodable syndromes, comparable to generic alternant codes rather than to other Goppa codes.

Our contribution: In this paper we modify the construction algorithm for t-error correcting quasi-dyadic codes [14], where the density of decodable syndromes is high, while also allowing for a reduction by a factor up to t in the key size. This yields dense binary Goppa codes as needed for practical instantiation of CFS signatures.

Recently, in an independent unpublished work Kobara [12] proposed another construction (dubbed flexible quasi-dyadic, or FQD for short) for the same problem, based on selecting distinct linear combinations from the rows of a certain nonsingular matrix, with the associated computational effort of this kind of operation[1]. In contrast, our proposed algorithm is more accurately seen as a natural extension of the original quasi-dyadic construction, whereby a stringent condition on the length of private codes is dropped and replaced by a straightforward consistency validation for the resulting parity-check matrix. It is also computationally simpler, since no linear combinations of rows from the parity-check matrix have to be generated and compared. Besides, contrary to [12] we provide a security assessment of binary QD codes against certain recent structural attacks [7,20] against this and other families of error-correcting codes. In particular, we argue that, in spite of those attacks being successful against non-binary QD codes (and quasi-cyclic codes as well), binary QD codes remain unscathed and are hence suitable for cryptographic applications.

The remainder of this paper is organized as follows. Section 2 introduces some basic concepts of coding theory. We proceed by describing the CFS signature scheme and its security in Section 3. In Section 4 we review the class of quasi-dyadic codes and propose a modification of the generation algorithm, enlarging that class with codes where the density of decodable syndromes increases by

---

[1] We note *en passant* that, although [12] claims that the FQD construction further reduces key sizes, this does not hold since that method does not produce any code that is not defined by [14, Theorem 2].

an exponential factor in the number of errors. We discuss security issues of the resulting quasi-dyadic CFS scheme in Section 5. We conclude in Section 6.

2   Preliminaries

In what follows all vector and matrix indices are numbered from zero onwards.

Definition 1. *Given a ring $\mathcal{R}$ and a vector $h = (h_0, \ldots, h_{n-1}) \in \mathcal{R}^n$, the dyadic matrix $\Delta(h) \in \mathcal{R}^{n \times n}$ is the symmetric matrix with components $\Delta_{ij} = h_{i \oplus j}$, where $\oplus$ stands for bitwise exclusive-or on the binary representations of the indices. The sequence h is called its* signature. *The set of dyadic $n \times n$ matrices over $\mathcal{R}$ is denoted $\Delta(\mathcal{R}^n)$. Given $t > 0$, $\Delta(t, h)$ denotes $\Delta(h)$ truncated to its first t rows.*

One can recursively characterize a dyadic matrix when n is a power of 2: any 1×1 matrix is dyadic, and for $k > 0$ any $2^k \times 2^k$ dyadic matrix M has the form

$$M = \begin{bmatrix} A & B \\ B & A \end{bmatrix},$$

where A and B are $2^{k-1} \times 2^{k-1}$ dyadic matrices. It is not hard to see that the signature of a dyadic matrix coincides with its first row. Dyadic matrices form a commutative subring of $\mathcal{R}^{n \times n}$ as long as $\mathcal{R}$ is commutative [11]. We will consider here only the case where $\mathcal{R} = \mathbb{F}_q$, the finite field with q (a power of 2) elements.

Definition 2. *A dyadic permutation is a dyadic matrix $\Pi^i \in \Delta(\{0,1\}^n)$ whose signature is the i-th row of the identity matrix.*

Definition 3. *A quasi-dyadic matrix is a (possibly non-dyadic) block matrix whose component blocks are dyadic submatrices. A quasi-dyadic (QD) code is a linear error-correcting code that admits a quasi-dyadic parity-check matrix.*

Definition 4. *Given two disjoint sequences $z = (z_0, \ldots, z_{t-1}) \in \mathbb{F}_q^t$ and $L = (L_0, \ldots, L_{n-1}) \in \mathbb{F}_q^n$ of distinct elements, the Cauchy matrix $C(z, L)$ is the $t \times n$ matrix with elements $C_{ij} = 1/(z_i - L_j)$, i.e.*

$$C(z, L) = \begin{bmatrix} \dfrac{1}{z_0 - L_0} & \cdots & \dfrac{1}{z_0 - L_{n-1}} \\ \vdots & \ddots & \vdots \\ \dfrac{1}{z_{t-1} - L_0} & \cdots & \dfrac{1}{z_{t-1} - L_{n-1}} \end{bmatrix}.$$

Cauchy matrices have the property that all of their submatrices are nonsingular [18]. Notice that, in general, Cauchy matrices are not dyadic and vice-versa, although the intersection of these two classes is non-empty in characteristic 2.

Definition 5. *Given $t > 0$ and a sequence $L = (L_0, \ldots, L_{n-1}) \in \mathbb{F}_q^n$, the Vandermonde matrix $\mathrm{vdm}(t, L)$ is the $t \times n$ matrix with elements $V_{ij} = L_j^i$.*

Definition 6. *Given a sequence $L = (L_0, \ldots, L_{n-1}) \in \mathbb{F}_q^n$ of distinct elements and a sequence $D = (D_0, \ldots, D_{n-1}) \in \mathbb{F}_q^n$ of nonzero elements, the* General-ized Reed-Solomon code $GRS_t(L, D)$ *is the* $[n, k, t]$ *linear error-correcting code defined by the parity-check matrix*

$$H = \text{vdm}(t - 1, L) \cdot \text{diag}(D).$$

An alternant code *is a subfield subcode of a Generalized Reed-Solomon code.*

Let p be a prime power, let $q = p^d$ for some d, and let $\mathbb{F}_q = \mathbb{F}_p[x]/b(x)$ for some irreducible polynomial $b(x) \in \mathbb{F}_p[x]$ of degree d. Given a code specified by a parity-check matrix $H \in \mathbb{F}_q^{t \times n}$, the *trace construction* derives from it an $\mathbb{F}_p$-subfield subcode by fixing a basis of $\mathbb{F}_q$ over $\mathbb{F}_p$, writing the $\mathbb{F}_p$-coefficients of each $\mathbb{F}_q$-component of H onto d successive rows of a parity-check matrix $T_d(H) \in \mathbb{F}_p^{dt \times n}$ for the subcode. The related *co-trace* parity-check matrix $T'_d(H) \in \mathbb{F}_p^{dt \times n}$, equivalent to $T_d(H)$ by a left permutation, is obtained from H by writing the $\mathbb{F}_p$-coefficients of terms of equal degree from all components from a column of H onto successive rows of $T'_d(H)$.

Thus, given $\mathbb{F}_q$ elements $u_i(x) = u_{i,0} + \cdots + u_{i,d-1}x^{d-1}$, the (co-)trace construction maps a column $(u_0, \ldots, u_{t-1})^\mathsf{T}$ from H to the column $(u_{0,0}, \ldots, u_{0,d-1}; \ldots; u_{t-1,0}, \ldots, u_{t-1,d-1})^\mathsf{T}$ on the trace matrix $T_d(H)$, and to the column $(u_{0,0}, \ldots, u_{t-1,0}; \ldots; u_{0,d-1}, \ldots, u_{t-1,d-1})^\mathsf{T}$ on the co-trace matrix $T'_d(H)$.

Definition 7. *Given a prime power p, $q = p^d$ for some d, a sequence $L = (L_0, \ldots, L_{n-1}) \in \mathbb{F}_q^n$ of distinct elements, and a polynomial $g(x) \in \mathbb{F}_q[x]$ of degree t such that $g(L_i) \neq 0$ for $0 \leqslant i < n$, the* Goppa code $\Gamma(L, g)$ *over $\mathbb{F}_p$ is the alternant code over $\mathbb{F}_p$ corresponding to $GRS_t(L, D)$, where $D = (g(L_0)^{-1}, \ldots, g(L_{n-1})^{-1})$.*

A binary Goppa code can correct up to t errors, sometimes slightly more [17,2], regardless of whether the generator $g(x)$ is irreducible or not. For all other cases, no method is generally known to correct more than about $t/2$ errors.

Consider a t-error correcting $\mathbb{F}_p$-alternant code of length n derived from a code over $\mathbb{F}_{p^m}$. The syndrome space has size p^{mt}. However, the decodable syndromes are only those that correspond to error vectors of weight not exceeding t. In other words, only $\sum_{w=1}^t \binom{n}{w}(p-1)^w$ nonzero syndromes are decodable, and hence their density is

$$\delta = \frac{1}{p^{mt}} \sum_{w=1}^t \binom{n}{w}(p-1)^w.$$

If the code length is a fraction $1/p^c$ for some $c \geqslant 0$ of the full length, i.e. $n = p^{m-c}$, the density can be approximated as

$$\delta \approx (n^t/t!)(p-1)^t/p^{mt} = (p^{m-c})^t(p-1)^t/(p^{mt}t!) = (p-1)^t/(p^{ct}t!).$$

A particularly good case is therefore $\delta \leqslant 1/t!$, which occurs when $(p^c/(p-1))^t \leqslant 1$, i.e. $c \leqslant \log_p(p-1)$, or $n \geqslant p^m/(p-1)$. Unfortunately this also means that for binary codes the highest densities are attained only by full or nearly full length codes, otherwise the density is reduced by a factor 2^{ct}. For full length binary codes ($p = 2$, $n = 2^m$) the density simplifies to

$$\delta \approx \frac{1}{2^{mt}} \frac{n^t}{t!} = \frac{1}{t!}.$$

3   CFS Signature Scheme

Courtois, Finiasz and Sendrier proposed in [4] the first practical signature scheme based on coding theory. The Full Domain Hash (FDH) approach assumes that all the hash values can be inverted by decryption.

3.1   Description

The CFS signature scheme is based on the Niederreiter cryptosystem: signing a document requires hashing it to a syndrome and then decoding it to an error vector of a certain weight t. Since not all syndromes are decodable, a counter is hashed with the message, and the signer tries successive counter values until a decodable syndrome is found. The signature consists of both the error pattern of weight t corresponding to the syndrome, and the counter value yielding this syndrome.

Let $\mathcal{H} : \{0,1\}^* \times \mathbb{N} \to \mathbb{F}_q^k$ be a random oracle for a given vector space $\mathbb{F}_q^k$ over a finite field $\mathbb{F}_q$. Formally, the CFS signature scheme consists of the following algorithms:

- Keygen: For the desired security level expressed by suitable integers q, n, k, t, choose a linear t-error correcting $[n, k]$-code over $\mathbb{F}_q$ defined by a public parity-check matrix H with a private decoding trapdoor $\mathcal{T}$. The private-public key pair is $(\mathcal{T}, H)$.
- Sign: Let $m \in \{0,1\}^*$ be the message to sign. Find $c \in \mathbb{N}$ (either sequentially or by random sampling) such that $s \leftarrow \mathcal{H}(m, c)$ is a decodable syndrome. Using the decoding trapdoor $\mathcal{T}$, find $e \in \mathbb{F}_q^n$ of weight $\mathsf{wt}(e) \leqslant t$ such that $He^{\mathrm{T}} = s^{\mathrm{T}}$. The signature is the pair (e, c).
- Verify: Let (e, c) be a purported signature for message m. Compute $s \leftarrow \mathcal{H}(m, c)$, and accept iff $\mathsf{wt}(e) \leqslant t$ and $He^{\mathrm{T}} = s^{\mathrm{T}}$.

The original description of the CFS scheme [4] suggests using a binary Goppa code and scanning over the c values sequentially. Random counter sampling (limited to r bits, i.e. from the set $\{0 \ldots 2^r - 1\}$) was proposed in [5] to obtain a security proof in the random oracle model, assuming the intractability of the following problems:

Definition 8 (Goppa Parametrized Bounded Decoding (GPBD)).
Given a matrix $H \in \mathbb{F}_2^{r \times n}$ and a syndrome $s \in \mathbb{F}_2^r$, is there a word $e \in \mathbb{F}_2^n$ of weight $\mathsf{wt}(e) \leqslant r/\lg n$ such that $He^T = s^T$?

Definition 9 (Goppa Code Distinguishing (GD)). *Given* $m, t, n \in \mathbb{N}$ *and a matrix* $H \in \mathbb{F}_2^{mt \times n}$, *is* H *the parity-check matrix of a binary t-error correcting* $[n, n - mt]$ *Goppa code?*

The main drawback of the CFS scheme is the key size. For the 80-bit security level, the authors of [4] suggest taking $m = 16$ and $t = 9$, leading to 1152 KiB keys. In the next section, we propose a construction that allows for smaller keys (and faster arithmetic), by using quasi-dyadic Goppa codes.

4   Quasi-Dyadic Codes

We recap the original construction of binary QD Goppa codes [14]. These are characterized by Theorem 1, which in turn suggests Algorithm 1, taken from the same reference.

Theorem 1 ([14]). *Let* $H \in \mathbb{F}_q^{n \times n}$ *with* $n > 1$ *be simultaneously a dyadic matrix* $H = \Delta(h)$ *for some* $h \in \mathbb{F}_q^n$ *and a Cauchy matrix* $H = C(z, L)$ *for two disjoint sequences* $z \in \mathbb{F}_q^n$ *and* $L \in \mathbb{F}_q^n$ *of distinct elements. Then* $\mathbb{F}_q$ *is a binary field, h satisfies*

$$\frac{1}{h_{i \oplus j}} = \frac{1}{h_i} + \frac{1}{h_j} + \frac{1}{h_0}, \tag{1}$$

and $z_i = 1/h_i + \omega$, $L_j = 1/h_j + 1/h_0 + \omega$ *for some* $\omega \in \mathbb{F}_q$.

4.1   Quasi-Dyadic Codes for CFS Signatures

Because the sequences z and L must be disjoint and consist of distinct elements, the length of the codes Algorithm 1 produces are upper bounded by $n \leqslant 2^{m-1}$, and hence the syndrome density is bound by $1/(2^t t!)$. Clearly, if z and L were not disjoint at least one element $H_{ij} = 1/(z_i - L_j)$ of matrix H would be undefined due to division by zero.

However, the CFS signature scheme only needs a very small t (say, $t \lesssim m$), meaning that most elements of the sequence z, and hence the corresponding rows of the largest possible matrix $\Delta(h)$, are left unused anyway when defining the actual code. It is therefore possible to allow matrix $\Delta(h)$ to contain undefined entries, as long as the rows and columns containing those entries are removed afterwards, and that $\Delta(t, h)$ itself contains only well-defined entries. This means the code length can be naturally extended all the way up to $2^m - t$, corresponding to an exact partition of the field elements from $\mathbb{F}_{2^m}$ into two disjoint sequences z and L.

In principle, this strategy can fail, i.e. the first t rows could contain an undefined element. This can be handled by either choosing a different code, or else by carefully rearranging the dyadic signature h into some h' in order to permute the rows of $\Delta(h)$ and eliminate undefined elements from $\Delta(t, h')$. As it turns out, the probability that an improper element will appear on the first t rows of $\Delta(h)$ is extremely low. As a consequence, the simpler strategy of just trying another code, if this is ever necessary in practice, is much simpler to implement without any measurable impact on either security or efficiency.

Algorithm 1. Constructing a purely dyadic binary Goppa code

INPUT: q (a power of 2), $n \leqslant q/2$, t.

OUTPUT: Support L, generator polynomial g, dyadic parity-check matrix H for a Goppa code $\Gamma(L, g)$ of length n and design distance $2t + 1$ over $\mathbb{F}_q$.

1: $U \leftarrow \mathbb{F}_q \setminus \{0\}$

 ▷ Choose the dyadic signature $(h_0, \ldots, h_{n-1})$. N.B. Whenever h_j with $j > 0$ is taken from U, so is $1/(1/h_j + 1/h_0)$ to prevent a potential spurious intersection between z and L.

2: $h_0 \xleftarrow{\$} U$, $U \leftarrow U \setminus \{h_0\}$

3: **for** $s \leftarrow 0$ **to** $\lceil \lg n \rceil - 1$ **do**

4:      $i \leftarrow 2^s$

5:      $h_i \xleftarrow{\$} U$, $U \leftarrow U \setminus \{h_i, 1/(1/h_i + 1/h_0)\}$

6:      **for** $j \leftarrow 1$ **to** $i - 1$ **do**

7:           $h_{i+j} \leftarrow 1/(1/h_i + 1/h_j + 1/h_0)$

8:           $U \leftarrow U \setminus \{h_{i+j}, 1/(1/h_{i+j} + 1/h_0)\}$

9:      **end for**

10: **end for**

11: $\omega \xleftarrow{\$} \mathbb{F}_q$

 ▷ Assemble the Goppa generator polynomial:

12: **for** $i \leftarrow 0$ **to** $t - 1$ **do**

13:      $z_i \leftarrow 1/h_i + \omega$

14: **end for**

15: $g(x) \leftarrow \prod_{i=0}^{t-1} (x - z_i)$

 ▷ Compute the support:

16: **for** $j \leftarrow 0$ **to** $n - 1$ **do**

17:      $L_j \leftarrow 1/h_j + 1/h_0 + \omega$

18: **end for**

19: $h \leftarrow (h_0, \ldots, h_{n-1})$

20: $H \leftarrow \Delta(t, h)$

21: **return** L, g, H

This idea is captured in Algorithm 2, which in practice is as simple to implement and as efficient as Algorithm 1. In a sense it is actually somewhat simpler, since less field elements have to be computed and discarded from the remaining allowed set U. Notice that improper array elements, whose evaluation would cause division by zero, are represented by a zero value, since this cannot ever occur on a proper array entry.

Algorithm 2 produces a code that is amenable to the same treatment as a generic Goppa code when instantiating the CFS signature scheme, namely, apply the trace construction of a binary alternant code from the code over $\mathbb{F}_{2^m}$, permute the columns of the corresponding parity-check matrix, and put the result in systematic form to get a CFS public key. However, this simple technique does not benefit from a possible reduction in key size since it destroys the quasi-dyadic structure. Algorithm 2 is designed to preserve that structure by removing the entire $t \times t$ block where one (or more) improper column lies.

Algorithm 2. Constructing a purely dyadic, CFS-friendly code

INPUT: m, n, t.

OUTPUT: A dyadic signature h from which a CFS-friendly t-error correcting binary Goppa code of length n can be constructed from a code over $\mathbb{F}_{2^m}$, and the sequence b of all consistent blocks of columns (i.e. those that can be used to define the code support).

1: $q \leftarrow 2^m$
2: **repeat**
3:     $U \leftarrow \mathbb{F}_q \setminus \{0\}$
4:     $h_0 \xleftarrow{\$} U, U \leftarrow U \setminus \{h_0\}$
5:     **for** $s \leftarrow 0$ **to** $m - 1$ **do**
6:         $i \leftarrow 2^s$
7:         $h_i \xleftarrow{\$} U, U \leftarrow U \setminus \{h_i\}$
8:         **for** $j \leftarrow 1$ **to** $i - 1$ **do**
9:             **if** $h_i \neq 0$ **and** $h_j \neq 0$ **and** $1/h_i + 1/h_j + 1/h_0 \neq 0$ **then**
10:                 $h_{i+j} \leftarrow 1/(1/h_i + 1/h_j + 1/h_0)$
11:             **else**
12:                 $h_{i+j} \leftarrow 0 \triangleright$ undefined entry
13:             **end if**
14:             $U \leftarrow U \setminus \{h_{i+j}\}$
15:         **end for**
16:     **end for**
17:     $c \leftarrow 0 \triangleright$ also: $U \leftarrow \mathbb{F}_q$
18:     **if** $0 \notin \{h_0, \ldots, h_{t-1}\}$ **then** $\triangleright$ consistent root set
19:         $b_0 \leftarrow 0, c \leftarrow 1 \triangleright$ also: $U \leftarrow U \setminus \{1/h_i, 1/h_i + 1/h_0 \mid i = 0, \ldots, t-1\}$
20:         **for** $j \leftarrow 1$ **to** $\lfloor q/t \rfloor - 1$ **do**
21:             **if** $0 \notin \{h_{jt}, \ldots, h_{(j+1)t-1}\}$ **then** $\triangleright$ consistent support block
22:                 $b_c \leftarrow j, c \leftarrow c+1 \triangleright$ also: $U \leftarrow U \setminus \{1/h_i + 1/h_0 \mid i = jt, \ldots, (j+1)t-1\}$
23:             **end if**
24:         **end for**
25:     **end if**
26: **until** $ct \geqslant n \triangleright$ consistent roots and support
27: $h \leftarrow (h_0, \ldots, h_{q-1}), b \leftarrow (b_0, \ldots, b_{c-1}) \triangleright$ also: $\omega \xleftarrow{\$} U$
28: **return** $h, b \triangleright$ also: ω

The strategy to get shorter keys is then to permute the blocks (or a large subset thereof) among themselves, dyadic-permute each block individually, and apply the co-trace construction to get a binary quasi-dyadic alternant code. This has to be done carefully so as to fully hide the code structure. The obvious approach is to delete more blocks and/or to replace them (and also the blocks that contain improper columns) by random dyadic blocks (the latter case corresponds to Wieschebrink's technique). One has to be careful here as well, since if only a fraction $1/2^c$ of the columns remain, the syndrome density effectively decreases by a factor 2^{ct} as seen above. A sensible choice, which we will usually adopt, is to take a fraction $2^{-1/t}$ of full code length (i.e. $c = 1/t$), since this only increases the average signing time by a factor of 2.

Table 1. Suggested parameters for practical security levels

level	m	t	$n = \lfloor 2^{m-1/t} \rfloor$	$k = n - mt$	key size (KiB)
80	15	12	30924	30744	169
100	20	12	989724	989484	7248
120	25	12	31671168	31670868	289956

Typical parameter combinations are put forward on Table 1. We will later examine some possible parameter choices in the context of, and as a result of, the security discussion in Section 5.

5   Security

Most of the time, the most threatening attacks are based on decoding algorithms for generic linear codes. There are two main families of generic algorithms, (Generalized) Birthday Algorithm (GBA) and Information Set Decoding (ISD). However, due to the peculiar nature of QD codes one has to take care of structural attacks as well. We provide an overview of these attacks and their impact on the choice of parameters for a quasi-dyadic CFS instantiation.

5.1   (Generalized) Birthday Attacks

An attack due to Daniel Bleichenbacher against the CFS scheme is described in [9]. We can shortly describe this attack as follows:

- build 3 lists L_0, L_1, and L_2 of XORs of respectively t_0, t_1 and t_2 columns of H (with $t = t_0 + t_1 + t_2$).
- merge the two lists L_0 and L_1 into a list L_0' of XORs of $t_0 + t_1$ columns of H, keeping only those starting with λ zeros.
- repeat the following steps:
  - choose a counter and compute the corresponding document hash,
  - XOR this hash with all elements of L_2 matching on the first λ bits,
  - look up each of these XORs in L_0': any complete match gives a valid signature.

Due to this attack, the values of m and t proposed in the original CFS scheme are not enough to ensure a proper security level. Therefore, instead of $m = 16$ and $t = 9$, the authors of [9] propose $m = 21$ and $t = 10$, or $m = 19$ and $t = 11$, or $m = 15$ and $t = 12$, as new parameters for a security of more than 2^{80} binary operations.

5.2   Decoding Attacks

The authors of [9] derive lower bounds on the work factor of idealized versions of the ISD and of the GBA. Table 2 shows the cost of these two attacks against various parameter sets, calculated according to [9]. Table 3 lists for each t the

Table 2. Time complexity (given as lg) for the ISD / GBA attack against the CFS scheme using binary codes with various parameter sets

n \ t	2^{15}	2^{16}	2^{17}	2^{18}	2^{19}	2^{20}	2^{21}
9	66.4/60.3	72.2/63.3	78.1/66.4	83.9/69.5	89.8/72.5	95.6/75.6	101.5/78.7
10	72.8/63.1	79.5/66.2	86.2/69.3	93.0/72.4	99.8/75.4	106.5/78.5	113.3/81.5
11	79.0/67.2	86.6/71.3	94.3/75.4	102.0/79.5	109.6/83.6	117.4/87.6	125.1/91.7
12	85.2/81.5	93.7/85.6	102.2/89.7	110.8/93.7	119.4/97.8	128.1/101.9	136.7/105.9

Table 3. Minimum m to yield time complexity of at least 2^{80}, expected number of signing attempts, and key sizes

(t,m)	$(8,25)$	$(9,22)$	$(10,21)$	$(11,19)$	$(12,15)$	$(13,14)$	$(14,14)$	$(15,13)$	$(16,13)$
sec level	$2^{81.7}$	$2^{81.7}$	$2^{81.5}$	$2^{83.6}$	$2^{81.5}$	$2^{80.7}$	$2^{84.1}$	$2^{80.7}$	$2^{84.6}$
avg sign atts	$2^{16.3}$	$2^{19.5}$	$2^{22.8}$	$2^{26.3}$	$2^{29.8}$	$2^{33.5}$	$2^{37.3}$	$2^{41.3}$	$2^{45.3}$
key size (KiB)	93902	93862	25080	12560	169	346	187	187	13

minimum m such that the security level is about 2^{80} or larger, taking both ISD and GBA into account, and the resulting key sizes.

For simplicity, on Table 2 we assume full-length codes with $n = 2^m$. In practice we would adopt slightly shorter punctured codes, taking e.g. $n = 2^{m-1}/t$ since this keeps the signing time within a factor of 2 from the corresponding time for full-length codes; this choice is adopted in Table 3. While the key size may be too large for smaller t, and conversely the signing complexity may be too large for larger t, intermediate combinations like $m = 15$, $t = 12$ may be just right in practice for this security level.

5.3 Structural Attacks

Structural attacks attempt to benefit from the symmetries existent in the public and private information. As an example of the potential of such attacks, the technique described in [16] successfully extracts the private key from the quasi-cyclic codes proposed in [10]. That scheme takes a binary quasi-cyclic subcode of a BCH code of length n as the secret code. The structure is hidden by a heavily constrained permutation in order to produce a quasi-cyclic public code. This implies that the permutation transformation is completely described with n_0^2 binary entries where $n_0 \ll n$ is the quasi-cyclic index. The attack takes advantage of the fact that the secret is a subcode of completely known BCH code. The idea is to construct a system of linear equations by exploiting the public generator matrix and a known parity-check matrix of the BCH code, so as to get an overdefined (and easily solvable) system satisfied by the unknown permutation matrix.

We show how to adapt this attack to our variant. Let H_0 be a private parity-check matrix of the underlying $[n, k, 2t+1]$ Goppa code, for which a decoding trapdoor is known to exist (or at least revealing that trapdoor, as is the case for the purely dyadic parity-check matrix $\Delta(t, h)$ constructed in Section 4.1). Consider matrix $G = [G_P \mid O]$ where G_P is a generator matrix of the code defined by the public parity-check matrix H, and O is the zero matrix with $N - n$ columns. Clearly, there exists an $N \times N$ matrix X such that:

$$H_0 X G^{\mathrm{T}} = O. \tag{2}$$

Writing $N = N_0 t$, X is an $N_0 \times N_0$ block matrix whose blocks are either the $t \times t$ zero matrix or a $t \times t$ dyadic permutation (the actual permutation varying from block to block). Let $n_0 < N_0$ be the number of nonzero blocks in X (all of them on the n_0 leftmost columns of X, , without loss of generality because of the structure of G). There are therefore $\binom{N_0}{n_0} n_0! t^{n_0}$ possibilities for X. The situation is almost the same as for quasi-cyclic alternant codes [1]. The main difference is that, rather than having small powers of a fixed value whose successive powers are on the diagonal, here we have one single element whose position assumes one out of t possibilities (and this is not fixed). Therefore solving the system given by Equation (2) reveals all the private information.

The first obstacle, however, is obtaining H_0. The attack against quasi-cyclic codes simply guesses the private parity-check matrix since there are only $O(2^m)$ possibilities. In the QD case, on the other hand, guessing H_0 would already incur a superpolynomial cost $O(2^{m^2})$. To makes things worse, for each guess of H_0, the attacker would have to mount and solve a linear system over the ring of dyadic $t \times t$ matrices, containing $n_0 \times N_0$ unknowns, or alternatively a system over $\mathbb{F}_2$ directly, increasing the number of unknowns by a factor t^2. In either case the total amount of work is prohibitively high. The attacker might try to guess X instead, or at least the positions of its nonzero dyadic blocks, but this incurs an extra cost factor $\binom{N_0}{n_0} n_0!$, which is too high for practical parameters. A further difficulty is that the systems are highly underdefined (typically containing hundreds of thousands of equations in tens of millions of unknowns).

None of the above ideas seems to lead to any promising strategy for a structural attack based on systems of linear equations. We next examine the possibility of using systems of quadratic equations to reduce the overall attack complexity.

5.4   Attacks Based on Multivariate Quadratic Equations

The structural attacks outlined above are based on solving certain systems of linear equations after guessing part of the unknown information, a task that, the attacker hopes, is made easier by the structure of the underlying codes, but as we saw the chances of these ideas ever succeeding are meagre at best. Recently, Faugère et al. [7] proposed to reduce the decoding problem for quasi-dyadic codes (and others) to the problem of solving systems of multivariate quadratic equations (MQE) instead. The overall idea is to find an alternant decoder for the public code directly, i.e. to write the public parity-check matrix as $H = VD$ for an unknown Vandermonde matrix V and an unknown diagonal matrix D defined over the public field $\mathbb{F}_{2^d}$, where $d \mid m$. The unknown components of V and D in the defining equation $H = VD$ give rise to an instance of the MQE problem. By making careful use of the structure of H, the authors of [7] are able to reduce the complexity of such instances, since many component equations become linear, and the truly quadratic part involves a reduced number of variables. This way they are able to break all parameters proposed in [1] and [14] over extension fields.

Apart from the fact that the attack complexity increases steeply as the codes are defined over ever smaller extension fields, to the effect that no actual attack was described against any of the published *binary* parameters, we argue that this strategy, at least as it is presented, cannot yield an attack against binary QD codes, even if it succeeds (at an impractically high cost but still faster than other methods) against e.g. quasi-cyclic codes. The reason is that the attack principle is to construct an *alternant* trapdoor directly from the public code defined by H, which is *not* a Goppa code except with overwhelmingly low probability. This trapdoor can be used to correct about $t/2$ errors at most, where t is the design number of errors. For all alternant codes except binary Goppa codes this is exactly the same as the number of errors that can be introduced and then successfully corrected using the *private* trapdoor, which explains why the attack is successful as long as the associated MQE instance can be solved in practice.

This is the case for codes over extension fields, as demonstrated in [7] (see also [20]). Whether or not this is also the case for non-Goppa binary codes is at best unclear for the time being as we pointed out. However, for the specific case of binary Goppa codes, including binary QD codes, this attack can only correct *half* as many errors as can be introduced and then corrected using the private Goppa trapdoor.

If the underlying QD code were used for encryption, the attacker would have to guess the remaining $t/2$ errors before using the obtained alternant trapdoor. This would mean repeating the attempted decoding $\binom{n}{t/2} / \binom{t}{t/2}$ times, which is clearly infeasible for properly chosen practical parameters. For CFS signatures no guessing is possible, since the messages to be signed are hashed directly onto syndromes, not onto words with errors. Thus the attacker faces the difficulty of finding a syndrome that decodes into a $t/2$-error vector. Such syndromes only occur with exceedingly low density.

We conclude that existing attacks based on solving instances of the MQE problem fail against properly chosen, yet still practical, binary QD codes.

Remark 1. A recent paper by Faugère et al. [8] analyzes the problem of distinguishing binary Goppa codes from random codes. The authors show that, under certain conditions (essentially for the parameters used for signatures), this problem is no longer hard (for binary Goppa codes and binary quasi-dyadic Goppa codes).

6 Conclusion

In this paper, we have presented a new way to instantiate CFS-like signature schemes. The adoption of binary quasi-dyadic (QD) codes allows for a reduction of key sizes by a factor of 4 in practice. Although the number of signing attempts increases by a factor of 2, a proper implementation of the more efficient arithmetic enabled by QD codes is likely to make the actual signing time comparable to plain CFS, possibly faster.

The resulting QD-CFS scheme can be adapted to schemes derived from CFS signatures like [3], [21], or [6]. Binary QD codes can also be applied to other code-based primitives like FSB (hash function), Stern (identification and signature scheme) or SYND (stream cipher). We leave these possibilities for further research.

References

1. Berger, T.P., Cayrel, P.-L., Gaborit, P., Otmani, A.: Reducing key length of the mcEliece cryptosystem. In: Preneel, B. (ed.) AFRICACRYPT 2009. LNCS, vol. 5580, pp. 77–97. Springer, Heidelberg (2009)
2. Bernstein, D.J.: List decoding for binary Goppa codes. Preprint (2008), http://cr.yp.to/papers.html#goppalist
3. Cayrel, P.-L., Gaborit, P., Galindo, D., Girault, M.: Improved identity-based identification using correcting codes. CoRR, abs/0903.0069 (2009)
4. Courtois, N.T., Finiasz, M., Sendrier, N.: How to achieve a mcEliece-based digital signature scheme. In: Boyd, C. (ed.) ASIACRYPT 2001. LNCS, vol. 2248, pp. 157–174. Springer, Heidelberg (2001)
5. Dallot, L.: Towards a concrete security proof of courtois, finiasz and sendrier signature scheme. In: Lucks, S., Sadeghi, A.-R., Wolf, C. (eds.) WEWoRC 2007. LNCS, vol. 4945, pp. 65–77. Springer, Heidelberg (2008), http://users.info.unicaen.fr/~ldallot/download/articles/CFSProof-dallot.pdf
6. Dallot, L., Vergnaud, D.: Provably secure code-based threshold ring signatures. In: Parker, M.G. (ed.) CC 2009. LNCS, vol. 5921, pp. 222–235. Springer, Heidelberg (2009)
7. Faugère, J.-C., Otmani, A., Perret, L., Tillich, J.-P.: Algebraic cryptanalysis of mcEliece variants with compact keys. In: Gilbert, H. (ed.) EUROCRYPT 2010. LNCS, vol. 6110, pp. 279–298. Springer, Heidelberg (2010)
8. Faugère, J.-C., Otmani, A., Perret, L., Tillich, J.-P.: A distinguisher for high rate mceliece cryptosystems. Cryptology ePrint Archive, Report 2010/331 (2010), http://eprint.iacr.org/
9. Finiasz, M., Sendrier, N.: Security bounds for the design of code-based cryptosystems. In: Matsui, M. (ed.) ASIACRYPT 2009. LNCS, vol. 5912, pp. 88–105. Springer, Heidelberg (2009)
10. Gaborit, P.: Shorter keys for code based cryptography. In: International Workshop on Coding and Cryptography – WCC 2005, Bergen, Norway, pp. 81–91. ACM Press, New York (2005)
11. Gulamhusein, M.N.: Simple matrix-theory proof of the discrete dyadic convolution theorem. Electronics Letters 9(10), 238–239 (1973)
12. Kobara, K.: Flexible quasi-dyadic code-based public-key encryption and signature. Cryptology ePrint Archive, Report 2009/635 (2009)
13. McEliece, R.: A public-key cryptosystem based on algebraic coding theory. The Deep Space Network Progress Report, DSN PR 42–44 (1978), http://ipnpr.jpl.nasa.gov/progressreport2/42-44/44N.PDF

14. Misoczki, R., Barreto, P.S.L.M.: Compact mcEliece keys from goppa codes. In: Jacobson Jr., M.J., Rijmen, V., Safavi-Naini, R. (eds.) SAC 2009. LNCS, vol. 5867, pp. 376–392. Springer, Heidelberg (2009)
15. Niederreiter, H.: Knapsack-type cryptosystems and algebraic coding theory. Problems of Control and Information Theory 15(2), 159–166 (1986)
16. Otmani, A., Tillich, J.-P., Dallot, L.: Cryptanalysis of two McEliece cryptosystems based on quasi-cyclic codes. Mathematics in Computer Science 3(2), 129–140 (2010)
17. Patterson, N.J.: The algebraic decoding of Goppa codes. IEEE Transactions on Information Theory 21(2), 203–207 (1975)
18. Schechter, S.: On the inversion of certain matrices. Mathematical Tables and Other Aids to Computation 13(66), 73–77 (1959), http://www.jstor.org/stable/2001955
19. Shor, P.W.: Polynomial-time algorithms for prime factorization and discrete logarithms on a quantum computer. SIAM Journal on Computing 26, 1484–1509 (1995)
20. Umana, V.G., Leander, G.: Practical key recovery attacks on two McEliece variants. In: International Conference on Symbolic Computation and Cryptography – SCC 2010 (2010) (to appear)
21. Zheng, D., Li, X., Chen, K.: Code-based ring signature scheme. I. J. Network Security 5(2), 154–157 (2007)

Online/Offline Verification of Short Signatures

Yilian Zhang[1], Zhide Chen[1], and Fuchun Guo[2]

[1] Key Lab of Network Security and Cryptology
School of Mathematics and Computer Science
Fujian Normal University, Fuzhou, China
fjyilian@gmail.com,
zhidechen@fjnu.edu.cn
[2] Centre for Computer and Information Security Research
School of Computer Science and Software Engineering
University of Wollongong, Wollongong NSW2522, Australia
fg278@uow.edu.au

Abstract. Fast signature verification is desirable in many applications, especially when signature recipients need to make response quickly. In this paper, we present an efficient *online/offline verification of short signature (OVS)* scheme without random oracles. Besides message signing, signature verification can be also separated into offline phase and online phase. Only one multi-exponentiation is required for the verifier in the online phase. In addition, our signature is short which gives about 480 bits for 80-bit security. Our scheme indeed improves the efficiency of signature verification since no pairing operation is required in the online phase. We also give a generic construction of OVS schemes using the idea of double trapdoor chameleon hash.

Keywords: Online/Offline Verification, Chameleon Hash, Short Signatures.

1 Introduction

Online/offline signatures were first introduced by Even, Goldreich and Micali [15]. The idea is to split signing algorithm into two phases. The first phase is performed in the *offline* phase before the message to be signed is presented, and the second phase is performed in the *online* phase after the message is given. Most of costly computations are accomplished in the offline phase, and the signer can generate a signature quickly in the online phase with the aid of offline tokens. In 2001, Shamir and Tauman [14] improved online/offline signature schemes utilizing the idea of chameleon hash. The online phase is very fast with modular multiplications only. Since the seminal work due to Shamir and Tauman, many subsequent works are proposed [12,7,17,18,4,9,8]. Recently, in CT-RSA 2009, Gao et al. [8] introduced the notion of divisible online/offline signature, where the signer can send partial signatures to the verifier in the offline phase. We note that online/offline signatures are proposed to speed up message signing. Signature verification is still slow for these online/offline signature schemes.

X. Lai, M. Yung, and D. Lin (Eds.): Inscrypt 2010, LNCS 6584, pp. 350–358, 2011.
© Springer-Verlag Berlin Heidelberg 2011

Many devices such as smart cards are low powerful devices and cannot perform heavy computations quickly. The well-known pairing-based signature schemes (e.g., [3,2,6,16,10]) capture some good properties but at the cost of heavy verification which requires expensive pairing operations. It is therefore very inefficient for these devices to perform signature verification for pairing-based signatures. Note that batch verification [1,5] can speed up signature verification, but it cannot be applied to verify one signature.

Our Contributions. In this paper, we borrow the notion of "online/offline" and propose an efficient *online/offline verification of short signature* (OVS) scheme without random oracles. This signature scheme can be seemed as an extension of divisible online/offline signatures [8], and the construction is a modification of Boneh-Boyen short signature scheme [2]. In our signature scheme, not only the signer can send partial signatures to the verifier but also the verifier can verify them in the offline phase. In the online phase, the computation cost for signer and verifier are modular multiplications and one multi-exponentiation respectively. In particular, no pairing computation is required for the verifier in the online phase. Our signature is short with 480 bits for 80-bit security and the security is based on the q-SDH assumption. We also give a generic construction of OVS scheme that can be constructed from traditional signatures using double trapdoor chameleon hash [4].

The organization of the paper is as follows. In Section 2, we provide related definitions, including the definition of our OVS scheme, bilinear pairing and the q-SDH assumption. We present our concrete OVS scheme in Section 3 and a generic construction in Section 4. Section 5 is our conclusion.

2   Definitions

2.1   Definition of OVS

Our OVS scheme is composed of the following five algorithms.

KeyGen: On input a security parameter 1^λ, the key generation algorithm returns a random verification (public) key VK and a private (signing) key SK.

OffSign: On input SK, the offline signing algorithm returns an offline signature token Σ^{off} and the state information St.

OffVer: On input VK and the offline signature Σ^{off}, the verification algorithms returns *accept* if Σ^{off} is valid; otherwise outputs *reject*.

OnSign: On input SK, the state information St and a message m, the online signing algorithm returns an online signature token Σ^{on}.

OnVer: On input VK, a message m, the online signature Σ^{on} and the offline signature token Σ^{off}, the verification algorithms returns *accept* if Σ^{on} is valid; otherwise output *reject*. The signature of m is defined as $\sigma = (\Sigma^{off}, \Sigma^{on})$.

2.2 Security Model

The security of an OVS scheme should be existential unforgeable under chosen-message attacks (EU-CMA), where a game between a challenger $\mathcal{C}$ and an adversary $\mathcal{A}$ are described as follows:

Setup: The challenger $\mathcal{C}$ runs algorithm KeyGen to obtain a pair of a verification key and a private key (VK, SK). VK is given to the adversary $\mathcal{A}$.

OffSign Queries: $\mathcal{A}$ makes a query for the ith offline signature token. $\mathcal{C}$ responds to the query by computing (Σ_i^{off}, St_i). Σ_i^{off} is sent to $\mathcal{A}$ while St_i is stored by $\mathcal{C}$. Let $\mathcal{A}$ make q_1 queries at most in this phase.

OnSign Queries: $\mathcal{A}$ makes a query for the ith online signature token on message m_i. We assume that the adversary must make queries for offline signature tokens before making queries for online signature tokens. $\mathcal{C}$ computes the online token Σ_i^{on} using St_i, and Σ_i^{on} is returned to $\mathcal{A}$. Let $\mathcal{A}$ make q_2 queries at most in this phase.

Forgery: $\mathcal{A}$ outputs a signature pair (m^*, σ^*) and wins the game if

(1) $\mathcal{A}$ did not make a query for the online signature token on m^*;

(2) σ^* is a valid signature on m^* signed with SK.

Definition 1. *An OVS scheme is (t, q_1, q_2, ϵ)-secure against EU-CMA attack if no adversary $\mathcal{A}$ who runs in time t, makes at most q_1 queries for offline signature token and q_2 queries for online signature tokens can win the above game with probability ϵ at least.*

2.3 Bilinear Pairing

Let $\mathbb{G}$ and $\mathbb{G}_T$ be two cyclic groups of prime order p. A map $e : \mathbb{G} \times \mathbb{G} \to \mathbb{G}_T$ is called a bilinear map if this map satisfies the following properties:

- Bilinear: for all $u, v \in \mathbb{G}$ and $a, b \in \mathbb{Z}_p$, we have $e(u^a, v^b) = e(u, v)^{ab}$;
- Non-degeneracy: $e(g, g) \neq 1$. In other words, if g be a generator of $\mathbb{G}$, then $e(g, g)$ is a generator of $\mathbb{G}_T$;
- Computability: It is efficient to compute $e(u, v)$ for all $u, v \in \mathbb{G}$.

2.4 Complexity Assumption

Let $\mathbb{G}$ be a cyclic group of prime order p, and g be a generator of $\mathbb{G}$. The q-SDH problem [2] in $\mathbb{G}$ is to compute any pair $(c, g^{1/(a+c)})$ for some $c \in \mathbb{Z}_p$ given $g, g^a, g^{(a^2)}, \cdots, g^{(a^q)}$ as input. We say that the q-SDH problem is (t, ϵ)-hard if for any t-time adversary $\mathcal{A}$, we have

$$Pr\left[\mathcal{A}(g, g^a, g^{(a^2)}, \cdots, g^{(a^q)}) = (c, g^{\frac{1}{a+c}}), c \in \mathbb{Z}_p\right] < \epsilon$$

where ϵ is negligible.

Definition 2. *We say that the q-SDH assumption holds with (t, ϵ) in $\mathbb{G}$ if no t-time algorithm has advantage at least ϵ in solving the q-SDH problem in $\mathbb{G}$.*

2.5 Double Trapdoor Chameleon Hash

Let $\mathbb{G}$ be the group of prime order p, $g \in \mathbb{G}$ be a generator and y, z be two random values from $\mathbb{Z}_p^*$. Set the element $g_2 = g^y, g_3 = g^x$. The verification key is (g, g_2, g_3) and the private key is (y, z). The input elements of chameleon hash is a triple (m, r, w) from $\mathbb{Z}_p$ and the output is an element of $\mathbb{G}$, where the chameleon hash is defined as

$$H(m, r, w) = g^m \cdot g_2^r \cdot g_3^w.$$

Given a new $m' \neq m$ and (y, z), firstly choose a random r'(or w'), and compute $w' = ((m - m') + (r - r')y + wz)z^{-1}$ (or $r' = ((m - m') + (w - w')z + ry)y^{-1}$) such that $H(m', r', w') = H(m, r, w)$. However, when the triple (m, r, w) is given and the private key is unknown, no adversary can find a new triple (m', r', w') in polynomial time such that both $m' \neq m$ and $H(m', r', w') = H(m, r, w)$ hold. The security proof of double chameleon hash functions was given in [4].

3 Online/Offline Verification of Short Signatures

3.1 Construction

Let $e : \mathbb{G} \times \mathbb{G} \to \mathbb{G}_T$ be the bilinear map, where $\mathbb{G}$ and $\mathbb{G}_T$ be two cyclic groups of prime order p, and g be the corresponding generator in $\mathbb{G}$. The proposed OVS scheme consists of five algorithms (**KeyGen, OffSign, OffVer, OnSign, OnVer**), and they are described as follows.

KeyGen: Randomly choose three integers $x, y, z \in \mathbb{Z}_p^*$ and two generators $g, u \in \mathbb{G}$. Set $g_1 = g^x$, $g_2 = g^y$, $g_3 = g^z$, and $v = e(u, g) \in \mathbb{G}_T$. The verification key and private key are respectively as follows:

$$VK = (u, g, g_1, g_2, g_3, v, \mathbb{G}, \mathbb{G}_T), \quad SK = (x, y, z).$$

OffSign: Given the private key $SK = (x, y, z)$, the signer randomly chooses an integer $\rho \in \mathbb{Z}_p \backslash \{-x\}$, and computes $\sigma = u^{\frac{1}{x+\rho}}$, where $\frac{1}{x+\rho}$ is the inverse of $(x + \rho)$ in $\mathbb{Z}_p^*$. Then, computes $\eta = g_1 g^\rho$, and output (Σ^{off}, St) defined as

$$(\Sigma^{off}, St) = \Big((\sigma, \eta), \rho\Big).$$

OffVer: Given the verification key $VK = (u, g, g_1, g_2, g_3, v, \mathbb{G}, \mathbb{G}_T)$ and an offline signature token $\Sigma^{off} = (\sigma, \eta)$, verify that

$$e(\sigma, \eta) = v.$$

Correctness:

$$\begin{aligned}
e(\sigma, \eta) &= e(u^{1/x+\rho}, g_1 g^\rho) \\
&= e(u^{1/x+\rho}, g^{x+\rho}) \\
&= e(u, g) \\
&= v.
\end{aligned}$$

OnSign: Given the message m to be signed, retrieving the state information $St = \rho$ from the memory, the signer randomly picks $r \in \mathbb{Z}_p$, and computes $s \in \mathbb{Z}_p$, such that

$$m + ry + sz = \rho \mod p.$$

Output the online signature token $\Sigma^{on} = (r, s)$.

OnVer: Given the verification key VK, Σ^{off} and a signed message (r, s), verify that

$$\eta = g_1 \cdot g^m \cdot g_2^r \cdot g_3^s.$$

If the equality holds, store (σ, η, r, s) as the signature on m; otherwise invalid.

Correctness:

$$\eta = g_1 \cdot g^\rho$$
$$= g_1 \cdot g^{m+ry+sz}$$
$$= g_1 \cdot g^m \cdot g_2^r \cdot g_3^s.$$

3.2   Efficiency

We give a concrete computation cost of our OVS scheme. Let E denote one exponentiation, P denote one pairing computation, M denote one modular multiplication, and E_M denote one multi-exponentiation of three exponentiations. We have the result of our OVS scheme in the following table.

Table 1. Computation Cost of Our OVS Scheme

	Offline Computation	Online Computation
Signer	2E	1 M
Verifier	1P	1 E_M

Note that the pairing-based signature scheme [2] requires one pairing and one multi-exponentiation (two exponentiations) for the verifier. Since the offline phase can be carried out and pre-done before knowing messages, we have successfully reduced the pairing computation for the verifier in the online phase.

Our signature is composed of the four elements (σ, η, r, s). It is easy to verify that it can be reduced to (σ, r, s) if the signature is valid. Given the signature (σ, r, s), any other parties can verify it by checking

$$e\left(\sigma, g_1 \cdot g^m \cdot g_2^r \cdot g_3^s\right) = v.$$

We can also use the asymmetric pairing described in [3,2] for shorter signature length. For 80-bit security, we have that each element represents 160 bits and therefore our signature is 480 bits in length.

3.3   Security

We now show the security of our scheme without random oracles with the aid of proofs in [8,2].

Theorem 1. *Let $q = q_1 + 1$. Then our OVS scheme is (t, q_1, q_2, ϵ)-secure against EU-CMA assuming the q-SDH assumption holds with complexity (t', ϵ').*

$$\epsilon' \geq \frac{\epsilon}{3} - \frac{q_s}{p}, \quad t' = t + O(q_s^2 t_e)$$

Where t_e is the maximum time for an exponentiation in $\mathbb{G}$.

Proof. Suppose $\mathcal{A}$ is the adversary that (t, q_1, q_s, ϵ)-breaks our signature scheme, we construct an algorithm $\mathcal{B}$ that solves the q-SDH problem in time t' with advantage ϵ'. Algorithm $\mathcal{B}$ is given an instance $g, g^a, g^{(a^2)}, \cdots, g^{(a^q)}$ of the q-SDH problem for some unknown $a \in \mathbb{Z}_p$, and its goal is to produce a pair $(\rho, g^{1/(a+\rho)})$ for some $\rho \in \mathbb{Z}_p$. Let $f(x) = \prod_{i=1}^{q_s}(x+c_i)$ be a q_s-degree polynomial function, where $c_1, \cdots, c_{q_s} \in \mathbb{Z}_p$ are randomly chosen. Set $u = g^{f(a)}$, $\delta = g^a$ and $v = e(u, g)$. The attack from $\mathcal{A}$ falls into the following three types:

Type-1: $g^{m^*} g_2^{r^*} g_3^{s^*} \neq g^{m_i} g_2^{r_i} g_3^{s_i}$ for all $i = 1, \ldots, q_s$.
Type-2: $g^{m^*} g_2^{r^*} g_3^{s^*} = g^{m_i} g_2^{r_i} g_3^{s_i}$ for some $i = 1, \ldots, q_s$, but $r^* \neq r_i$.
Type-3: $g^{m^*} g_2^{r^*} g_3^{s^*} = g^{m_i} g_2^{r_i} g_3^{s_i}$ for some $i = 1, \ldots, q_s$, but $r^* = r_i$ and $s^* \neq s_i$.

[Type–1.]

KeyGen: Algorithm $\mathcal{B}$ randomly chooses two values $y, z \in \mathbb{Z}_p^*$ and sets $SK = (a, y, z)$. $\mathcal{B}$ gives the verification key $VK = (u, g, g_1, g_2, g_3, v, \mathbb{G}, \mathbb{G}_T)$ to $\mathcal{A}$, where g_1 is set to δ, g_2 is set to g^y, and g_3 is set to g^z.

Offline Queries: $\mathcal{A}$ makes a query for the ith offline token, where $1 \leq i \leq q_1$. $\mathcal{B}$ responds to the query by computing $\Sigma_i^{off} = (\sigma_i, \eta_i) = (u^{1/a+c_i}, \delta g^{c_i})$. Σ_i^{off} is sent to $\mathcal{A}$ while c_i is stored by $\mathcal{B}$. (σ_i, η_i) is a valid offline signature token for VK since

$$e(\sigma_i, \eta_i) = e(u^{1/a+c_i}, g^a g^{c_i}) = e(u, g) = v.$$

Online Queries: $\mathcal{A}$ makes a query for the ith online token on message m_i, where $1 \leq i \leq q_s$. $\mathcal{B}$ randomly chooses $r_i \in \mathbb{Z}_p^*$, and sets $s_i = (c_i - m_i - yr_i)z^{-1}$ mod p. The online signature token (r_i, s_i) is returned to $\mathcal{A}$. $(, r_i, s_i)$ is a valid online signature token on the message m_i for VK since

$$\eta_i = g^a \cdot g^{c_i} = g_1 \cdot g^{m_i + r_i y + s_i z} = g_1 \cdot g^{m_i} \cdot g_2^{r_i} \cdot g_3^{s_i}.$$

Forgery: Finally, $\mathcal{A}$ returns a valid forgery $(m^*, \sigma^*, \eta^*, r^*, s^*)$ satisfying the condition in *Type 1*. We have $c^* = m^* + yr^* + zs^* \neq c_i$. $\mathcal{B}$ outputs $(c_*, g^{1/(a+c_*)})$ as the solution to the q-SDH assumption. Therefore *Type 1* occurs with probability $\epsilon/3$, and $\mathcal{B}$ can successfully solve the q-SDH problem with probability at least $\epsilon/3$.

[Type–2.]

KeyGen: Algorithm $\mathcal{B}$ randomly chooses two values $x, z \in \mathbb{Z}_p^*$ and sets $SK = (x, a, z)$. $\mathcal{B}$ gives the verification key $VK = (u, g, g_1, g_2, g_3, v, \mathbb{G}, \mathbb{G}_T)$ to $\mathcal{A}$, where g_1 is set to g^x, g_2 is set to δ, and g_3 is set to g^z.

Offline Queries: $\mathcal{A}$ makes a query for the ith offline token, where $1 \leq i \leq q_1$. $\mathcal{B}$ randomly chooses $r_i \in \mathbb{Z}_p^*$, and returns $\Sigma_i^{off} = (\sigma_i, \eta_i) = (u^{1/(a+c_i)})^{\frac{1}{r_i}}$ as the i-th offline signature token while (r_i, c_i) is stored by $\mathcal{B}$. This (σ_i, η_i) is a valid offline signature token for VK since

$$e(\sigma_i, \eta_i) = e((u^{1/(a+c_i)})^{\frac{1}{r_i}}, g^{r_i a} g^{r_i c_i}) = e(u^{1/a+c_i}, g^a g^{c_i}) = e(u, g) = v.$$

Online Queries: $\mathcal{A}$ makes a query for the ith online token on message m_i, where $1 \leq i \leq q_s$. $\mathcal{B}$ sets $s_i = (c_i r_i - x - m_i)z^{-1} \bmod p$. The online signature token (r_i, s_i) is returned to $\mathcal{A}$. $(\sigma_i, \eta_i, r_i, s_i)$ is a valid online signature token on the message m_i for VK since

$$\eta_i = \delta^{r_i} \cdot g^{r_i c_i} = g_2^{r_i} \cdot g^{m_i + x + s_i z} = g_2^{r_i} \cdot g^{m_i} \cdot g_1 \cdot g_3^{s_i}.$$

Forgery: From above description, we know that *Type 2* occurs with probability at least $\epsilon/3$, and $r^* = r_i$ occurs with probability at most q_s/p. If $\mathcal{A}$ returns a value forgery $(m^*, \sigma^*, \eta^*, r^*, w^*)$ satisfying the condition in *Type 2*, which for some i, $g^{m^*} g_2^{r^*} g_3^{s^*} = g^{m_i} g_2^{r_i} g_3^{s_i}$ and $r_* \neq r_i$ hold, then $\mathcal{B}$ will not abort. $\mathcal{B}$ can compute $a = y = \big((s_i - s_*)z + (m_i - m_*)\big)(r_* - r_i)^{-1} \bmod p$. Therefore $\mathcal{B}$ can succeed with probability at least $\epsilon/3 - q_s/p$ to solve the q-SDH problem.

[Type–3.]

KeyGen: Algorithm $\mathcal{B}$ randomly chooses two values $x, y \in \mathbb{Z}_p^*$ and sets $SK = (x, y, a)$. $\mathcal{B}$ gives the verification key $VK = (u, g, g_1, g_2, g_3, v, \mathbb{G}, \mathbb{G}_T)$ to $\mathcal{A}$, where g_1 is set to g^x, g_2 is set to g^y, and g_3 is set to δ.

Offline Queries: $\mathcal{A}$ makes a query for the ith offline token, where $1 \leq i \leq q_1$. $\mathcal{B}$ chooses a random $s_i \in \mathbb{Z}_p^*$, and returns $(\sigma_i, \eta_i) = ((u^{1/(a+c_i)})^{\frac{1}{s_i}}$ as the i-th offline signature token, while (r_i, c_i) is stored by $\mathcal{B}$. This (σ_i, η_i) is a valid offline signature token for VK since

$$e(\sigma_i, \eta_i) = e((u^{1/(a+c_i)})^{\frac{1}{s_i}}, g^{s_i a} g^{s_i c_i}) = e(u^{1/a+c_i}, g^a g^{c_i}) = e(u, g) = v.$$

Online Queries: $\mathcal{A}$ makes a query for the ith online token on message m_i, where $1 \leq i \leq q_s$. $\mathcal{B}$ sets $r_i = (c_i s_i - x - m_i)y^{-1} \bmod p$. The online signature token (r_i, s_i) is returned to $\mathcal{A}$. $(\sigma_i, \eta_i, r_i, s_i)$ is a valid signature on the message m_i for VK since

$$\eta_i = \delta^{s_i} g^{s_i c_i} = g_3^{s_i} \cdot g^{m_i + x + r_i y} = g_3^{s_i} \cdot g^{m_i} \cdot g_1 \cdot g_2^{r_i}.$$

Forgery: The proof of *Type 3* is similar to that of *Type 2*. Likewise, $\mathcal{B}$ can compute $a = z = (m_i - m_*)(s_* - s_i)^{-1} \bmod p$ for some i with probability at least $\epsilon/3 - q_s/p$ to solve the q-SDH problem, where $(m_*, \sigma_*, \eta_*, r_*, s_*)$ is a valid signature forged by $\mathcal{A}$ satisfying Type 3.

Since three Types are independent with uniform distribution, there exists an algorithm $\mathcal{B}$, which can solve the q-SDH problem with probability at least $\epsilon/3 - q_s/p$ in polynomial time. This completes the full proof.

4   Generic Construction

Using the double trapdoor chameleon hash, we show how to achieve the generic construction of OVS scheme from any secure signature scheme. Let $(\mathcal{G}, \mathcal{S}, \mathcal{V})$ be a provably secure signature scheme, which denotes key generation, signing and verification, respectively. The generic OVS signature can be described as the following five algorithms (**KeyGen, OffSign, OffVer, OnSign, OnVer**).

KeyGen: Let (vk, sk) be a pair of verification/private key from $\mathcal{G}$, randomly choose two values $y, z \in \mathbb{Z}_p$ and set $g_2 = g^y$, $g_3 = g^z$. The final verification/private key of (VK, SK) is $VK = (vk, g_2, g_3)$, $SK = (sk, y, z)$.

OffSign: Randomly choose three integers $m, r, w \in \mathbb{Z}_p$, and compute $H_{ch} = g^m g_2^r g_3^w$. Store the state information $St = (m, r, w)$. Let σ_{sk} be a signature on H_{ch}. The offline signature tokens is $\Sigma^{off} = (\sigma_{sk}, H_{ch})$

OffVer: On input the verification key VK and $\Sigma^{off} = (\sigma_{sk}, H_{ch})$, the verification algorithms outputs *accept* if σ_{sk} is a valid signature on H_{ch} signed with sk; otherwise outputs *reject*.

OnSign: Given the message $m' \in \mathbb{Z}_p$ to be signed, firstly choose a random $r' \in \mathbb{Z}_p$, and compute $w' = ((m - m') + (r - r')y + w)z^{-1}$. The online signature token on m' is $\Sigma^{on} = (r', w')$.

OnVer: Given the online signature token (r', w'), verification key VK and a message $m' \in \mathbb{Z}_p$, check that $H_{ch} = g^{m'} g_2^{r'} g_3^{w'}$. The verifier outputs *accept* if it is correct, otherwise output *reject*. The final signature on m' is (σ_{sk}, r', w').

The security proof of our generic construction is similar to the Theorem 1, and we omit it here.

5   Conclusion

In this paper, we proposed an efficient online/offline verification of short signatures without random oracles. In our scheme, both signer and verifier can separate their computations into offline phase and online phase. In particular, only one multi-exponentiation is required for the verifier in the online phase and no pairing computation is required. Our signature is short with 480 bits for 80-bit security. We also gave a generic construction of OVS scheme from double trapdoor chameleon hash.

Acknowledgement

The authors would like to thank the anonymous reviewers of *Inscrypt 2010* for their helpful comments on this work.

References

1. Bellare, M., Garay, J., Rabin, T.: Fast batch verification for modular exponentiation and digital signatures. In: Nyberg, K. (ed.) EUROCRYPT 1998. LNCS, vol. 1403, pp. 236–250. Springer, Heidelberg (1998)
2. Boneh, D., Boyen, X.: Short signatures without random oracles. In: Cachin, C., Camenisch, J.L. (eds.) EUROCRYPT 2004. LNCS, vol. 3027, pp. 56–73. Springer, Heidelberg (2004)
3. Boneh, D., Lynn, B., Shacham, H.: Short signatures from the weil pairing. In: Boyd, C. (ed.) ASIACRYPT 2001. LNCS, vol. 2248, pp. 514–532. Springer, Heidelberg (2001)
4. Bresson, E., Catalano, D., Gennaro, R.: Improved on-line/Off-line threshold signatures. In: Okamoto, T., Wang, X. (eds.) PKC 2007. LNCS, vol. 4450, pp. 217–232. Springer, Heidelberg (2007)
5. Camenisch, J.L., Hohenberger, S., Pedersen, M.Ø.: Batch verification of short signatures. In: Naor, M. (ed.) EUROCRYPT 2007. LNCS, vol. 4515, pp. 246–263. Springer, Heidelberg (2007)
6. Camenisch, J., Lysyanskaya, A.: Signature schemes and anonymous credentials from bilinear maps. In: Franklin, M. (ed.) CRYPTO 2004. LNCS, vol. 3152, pp. 56–72. Springer, Heidelberg (2004)
7. Catalano, D., Di Raimondo, M., Fiore, D., Gennaro, R.: Off-line/on-line signatures: theoretical aspects and experimental results. In: Cramer, R. (ed.) PKC 2008. LNCS, vol. 4939, pp. 101–120. Springer, Heidelberg (2008)
8. Gao, C., Wei, B., Xie, D., Tang, C.: Divisible on-Line/off-Line signatures. In: Fischlin, M. (ed.) CT-RSA 2009. LNCS, vol. 5473, pp. 148–163. Springer, Heidelberg (2009)
9. Guo, F., Mu, Y.: Optimal online/Offline signature: How to sign a message without online computation. In: Baek, J., Bao, F., Chen, K., Lai, X. (eds.) ProvSec 2008. LNCS, vol. 5324, pp. 98–111. Springer, Heidelberg (2008)
10. Hohenberger, S., Waters, B.: Realizing hash-and-sign signatures under standard assumptions. In: Joux, A. (ed.) EUROCRYPT 2009. LNCS, vol. 5479, pp. 333–350. Springer, Heidelberg (2009)
11. Krawczyk, H., Rabin, T.: Chameleon signatures. In: NDSS 2000, pp. 143–154. Internet Society, San Diego (2000)
12. Kurosawa, K., Schmidt-Samoa, K.: New online/Offline signature schemes without random oracles. In: Yung, M., Dodis, Y., Kiayias, A., Malkin, T. (eds.) PKC 2006. LNCS, vol. 3958, pp. 330–346. Springer, Heidelberg (2006)
13. Au, M.H., Susilo, W., Mu, Y.: Is the Notion of Divisible On-Line/Off-Line Signatures Stronger than On-Line/Off-Line Signatures? In: Pieprzyk, J., Zhang, F. (eds.) ProvSec 2009. LNCS, vol. 5848, pp. 129–139. Springer, Heidelberg (2009)
14. Shamir, A., Tauman, Y.: Improved online/offline signature schemes. In: Kilian, J. (ed.) CRYPTO 2001. LNCS, vol. 2139, pp. 355–367. Springer, Heidelberg (2001)
15. Even, S., Goldreich, O., Micali, S.: On-line/Off-line digital signatures. In: Brassard, G. (ed.) CRYPTO 1989. LNCS, vol. 435, pp. 263–275. Springer, Heidelberg (1990)
16. Waters, B.: Efficient identity-based encryption without random oracles. In: Cramer, R. (ed.) EUROCRYPT 2005. LNCS, vol. 3494, pp. 114–127. Springer, Heidelberg (2005)
17. Xu, S., Mu, Y., Susilo, W.: Online/Offline Signatures and Multisignatures for AODV and DSR Routing Security. In: Batten, L.M., Safavi-Naini, R. (eds.) ACISP 2006. LNCS, vol. 4058, pp. 99–110. Springer, Heidelberg (2006)
18. Yu, P., Tate, S.R.: Online/Offline signature schemes for devices with limited computing capabilities. In: Malkin, T. (ed.) CT-RSA 2008. LNCS, vol. 4964, pp. 301–317. Springer, Heidelberg (2008)

Acquiring Key Privacy from Data Privacy

Rui Zhang[1,2]

[1] State Key Laboratory of Information Security,
Institute of Software, Chinese Academy of Sciences, Beijing, China
`r-zhang@is.iscas.ac.cn`
[2] Research Center for Information Security (RCIS),
National Institute of Advanced Industrial Science and Technology (AIST), Japan
`r-zhang@aist.go.jp`

Abstract. A primary functionality of public key encryption schemes is data privacy, while in many cases key privacy (aka. anonymity of public keys) may also be important. Traditionally, one has to separately design/prove them, because data privacy and key privacy were shown to be independent from each other [5,40]. Existing constructions of anonymous public key encryption usually take either of the following two approaches:

1. Directly construct it from certain number theoretic assumptions.
2. Find a suitable anonymous encryption scheme with key privacy yet without chosen ciphertext security, then use some dedicated transforms to upgrade it to one with key privacy and chosen ciphertext security.

While the first approach is intricate and a bit mysterious, the second approach is unnecessarily a real solution to the problem, namely, how to acquire key privacy. In this paper, we show how to build anonymous encryption schemes from a class of key encapsulation mechanisms with only weak data privacy, in the random oracle model. Instantiating our generic construction, we obtain many interesting anonymous public key encryption schemes. We note that some underlying schemes are based on gap assumptions or with bilinear pairings, which were previously well-known not anonymous.

Keywords: public key encryption, key privacy, data privacy, anonymity.

1 Introduction

Key privacy, also called anonymity, is an interesting property for public key encryption, which was first formulated in [5]. Key privacy concerns the anonymity of the receiver, namely, the identity of the receiver should not be easily inferred from a ciphertext to him, even with some non-trivial interactions between the adversary and the receiver. Informally speaking, anonymity of public keys is related to the so-called public verifiability in the multi-user setting, where anyone without the decryption key, can verify the validity of a ciphertext under a certain user's public key. Anonymous encryption has many applications, e.g., anonymous BCC email, anonymous credential system, e-auction, etc.. We refer to [5] and the references therein for further descriptions for the applications.

On the other hand, unlike data privacy [23,31,35,19,7], key privacy is comparatively not well-understood. Some research has investigated relations between

X. Lai, M. Yung, and D. Lin (Eds.): Inscrypt 2010, LNCS 6584, pp. 359–372, 2011.

anonymity and data privacy for public key encryption schemes [5,27,40], showing that key privacy and data privacy are independent, namely, a very secure data private encryption scheme may be not anonymous at all, and vice versa. This result forces that the anonymity of each encryption scheme should be studied independently. Known constructions for key privacy start either from certain number theoretic assumptions [5,26], or from some schemes with weak anonymity [27,40,33], namely, anonymity without chosen ciphertext security (CCA).

The former method is intricate, since everything has to be designed from scratch, while the latter seems a bit tricky: the difficult problem of constructing an anonymous encryption scheme has actually been changed to how to upgrade an encryption scheme with key privacy without CCA security to one with CCA security. This somehow seems easier, thanks to the rich literature: [31,20,36,18,15,34] in the standard model and [9,7,22,32] in the random oracle model. But it actually does not solve the problem how to acquire anonymity.

It becomes natural to ask the following questions: First, *can one have a more intelligent way to build key privacy?* Second, since data privacy is the essential functionality of a public key encryption scheme, *can we build key privacy based on data privacy?* In this paper, we give an affirmative answer to both questions. We propose a generic construction for anonymity from very weak data privacy. Contrary to previous constructions [27,40,33], we don't pose any requirement on the anonymity of the underlying schemes. Alternatively, we assume the underlying encryption admits weak data privacy security as well as a special property called reproducibility which is explained below. To remark, a reproducible KEM can be not anonymous at all. In Section 5.2, we give a few concrete examples.

Our main tool is key encapsulation mechanism (KEM) [39] with reproducibility [6,4]. In such a system, a ciphertext $c = (\psi, \tau)$ is produced by two sub-algorithms KEM.enc1 and KEM.enc2. Here KEM.enc1 takes a system parameter sp that is shared by all the users, produce a partial ciphertext ψ and an internal state ω. KEM.enc2 takes a public key pk and ω, and produces the other part of the ciphertext τ and the session key dk. Informally, the reproducibility property is that with input (sp, ψ), a receiver, with knowledge of the secret key sk, can reconstruct τ using an additional algorithm KEM.rp, denoted as $\tau \leftarrow$ KEM.rp(sp, sk, ψ).

With the above description, it is easy to see that if a sender erases τ from the ciphertext encapsulating the same dk, because of reproducibility, a receiver can still recover τ, thus decrypt. We then claim this new key encapsulation mechanism scheme with shortened ciphertext ψ is actually anonymous. The intuition is that ψ only depends on sp, which is shared system-wide, thus will not leak information of the receiver's public key. But a problem arises that we don't know how to demonstrate a meaningful security reduction, if we only assume the underlying KEM is secure.

To solve this problem, we modify the key derivation algorithm, such that the final session key is forced to depend on both (ψ, τ) and encapsulated key dk of the underlying KEM scheme. A simple idea is to let the session key be $H(pk, c, dk)$, where H is a key derivation function, which is regarded as a random oracle in security analysis. In this way, we only require weak data privacy for the underlying reproducible KEM scheme, namely one-wayness against session key checking attack [3]. We remark that the resulting PKE scheme achieves not only key privacy, but strong data privacy as well, which we will briefly discuss in Section 4.

We remark that the above construction relies on random oracles, while a proof in the random oracle model says nothing about its security if the random oracles are instantiated with practical hash functions [14]. However, a proof in the random oracle at least shows the scheme has no inherent defect in its design, and is definitely better than no proof at all. We hope this will help to motivate more ideas in constructing efficient anonymous encryption in the standard model.

1.1 Related Work

A classical security notion for encryption schemes is data privacy, which is defined in terms of indistinguishability against chosen ciphertext attack (IND-CCA) [23,35,19,7]. An independent security notion, key privacy or anonymity, was formalized by Bellare, Boldyreva, Desai and Pointcheval [5], and was further studied in [5,26,24,27,40,21].

Recently, Naccache, Steinwandt and Yung formulate the notion reverse public key encryption (RPKE) [30], which is a weaker form of key privacy. In such a model, an adversary is not allowed to choose which message to encrypt in its target ciphertext. But this was shown to be already enough for secure message transmission (though of bad bandwidth usually): The the real message is encoded by possible choices of public keys.

Key encapsulation mechanism (KEM) was first formulated by Shoup [39]. While the initial motivation of KEM was to construct efficient hybrid encryption schemes, it turned out that this has many other applications. E.g., Baek, Zhou and Bao introduced KEM with reproducibility [4], which can be used to build stateful encryption schemes [8].[1] We note that reproducibility was first introduced in [6], whose intension was to build multi-recipient encryption. We note that known multi-recipient encryption and stateful encryption may not be anonymous, even they satisfy reproducibility.

2   Preliminary

In this section, we review some useful notations and definitions.

NOTATIONS. If x is a string, let $|x|$ denotes its length, while if S is a set then $|S|$ denotes its size. If S is a set then $s \leftarrow S$ denotes the operation of picking an element s of S uniformly at random. We write $z \leftarrow \mathcal{A}(x, y, \ldots)$ to indicate that $\mathcal{A}$ is an algorithm with inputs $(x, y, \ldots)$ and an output z. If $k \in \mathbb{N}$, a function $f(k)$ is negligible if $\exists\, k_0 \in \mathbb{N},\ \forall\, k > k_0,\ f(k) < 1/k^c$, where $c > 0$ is a constant.

---

[1] In particular, reproducibility was crucial for the proof of their scheme in the known secret key model [8,4].

2.1   Public Key Encryption

SYNTAX. A public key encryption scheme PKE = (PKE.setup, PKE.kg, PKE.enc, PKE.dec) consists of 4 algorithms.

- PKE.setup: taking a security parameter k as input, the randomized algorithm generates the system parameter sp (including k), denoted as $sp \leftarrow$ PKE.setup(k).
- PKE.kg: taking a system parameter sp as input, the randomized algorithm generates a public/secret key pair (pk, sk), denoted as $(pk, sk) \leftarrow$ PKE.kg(sp).
- PKE.enc: taking a system parameter sp, a public key pk, a plaintext m as input, the possibly randomized algorithm computes a ciphertext c, denoted as $c \leftarrow$ PKE.enc(sp, pk, m).
- PKE.dec: taking a system parameter sp, a secret key sk, a ciphertext c as input, the deterministic algorithm outputs a plaintext m, or a specially symbol "$\perp$" (indicating "invalid ciphertext"), denoted as $m/\perp \leftarrow$ PKE.dec(sp, sk, c).

We require the correctness condition, namely, $\forall \ sp \leftarrow$ PKE.setup(k) and (pk, sk) $\leftarrow$ PKE.kg(sp), we have $m =$ PKE.dec$(sp, sk,$ PKE.enc$(sp, pk, m))$.

Definition 1 (ANON-CCA security for PKE). *We say an encryption scheme is (ϵ, t)-ANON-CCA secure, if for any adversary $\mathcal{A}$ with running time at most t, has advantage ϵ in the following experiment. The interaction between $\mathcal{A}$ and a decryption oracle $\mathcal{DO}$ is shown in Fig. 1. In particular, $\mathcal{A}$ is not allowed to query (c^*, j) $(j \neq 0, 1)$ to the decryption oracle. We say the encryption scheme is ANON-CCA secure, if for any probabilistic polynomial Turing-machine (PPT) $\mathcal{A}$, ϵ is negligible.*

$$\text{Adv}_{\mathcal{A}}^{\text{anon-cca}}(k) = |\Pr[sp \leftarrow \text{PKE.setup}(k); (pk_0, sk_0) \leftarrow \text{PKE.kg}(sp);$$
$$(pk_1, sk_1) \leftarrow \text{PKE.kg}(sp); (m, st) \leftarrow \mathcal{A}^{\mathcal{DO}}(pk_0, pk_1, sp); b \leftarrow \{0, 1\};$$
$$c^* \leftarrow \text{PKE.enc}(sp, pk_b, m); b' \leftarrow \mathcal{A}^{\mathcal{DO}}(c^*, st) : b = b'] - 1/2|$$

The above experiment considers only the 2-user case, but we note it is possible to extend the definition to the n-user case, as long as n is polynomially bounded.

2.2   Key Encapsulation Mechanism (KEM)

We review an important tool, reproducible key encapsulation mechanism [4]. A reproducible key encapsulation mechanism KEM = (KEM.setup, KEM.kg, KEM.enc1, KEM.enc2, KEM.dec, KEM.rp) consists of 6 algorithms.

Oracle Query	Action Taken	Response
$\mathcal{DO}(c, j)$, $j \in \{0, 1\}$	$m \leftarrow$ PKE.dec(sp, sk_j, c)	m

Fig. 1. Decryption Oracle in ANON-CCA Game for PKE.

- KEM.setup: taking a security parameter k as input, the randomized algorithm generates the system parameter sp (including k), denoted as $sp \leftarrow$ KEM.setup(k).
- KEM.kg: taking a system parameter sp as input, the randomized algorithm generates a public/secret key pair (pk, sk), denoted as $(pk, sk) \leftarrow$ KEM.kg(sp).
- KEM.enc1: taking a system parameter sp as input, with internal coin-flipping, output a partial ciphertext ψ and internal state ω, denoted as $(\psi, \omega) \leftarrow$ KEM.enc1(sp).
- KEM.enc2: taking sp, a public key pk and ω as input, outputs a partial ciphertext τ and the encapsulated key dk, denoted as $(\tau, dk) \leftarrow$ KEM.enc2(sp, pk, ω).
- KEM.dec: taking a system parameter sp, a secret key sk, a ciphertext c as input, the deterministic algorithm outputs a session key dk, or a special symbol "$\perp$" (indicating "invalid ciphertext"), denoted as $dk/\perp \leftarrow$ KEM.dec(sp, sk, c).
- KEM.rp: Denote $(pk, sk) \leftarrow$ KEM.kg(sp) as a pair of public/secret keys. Let $(\psi, \omega) \leftarrow$ KEM.enc1(sp) as defined above. KEM.rp takes sk and ψ as input, outputs (τ, dk), denoted as $(\tau, dk) \leftarrow$ KEM.rp(sp, sk, ψ). We say a KEM scheme is reproducible, if KEM.rp always outputs the valid remaining partial ciphertext τ_1 and the valid session key dk, namely $\Pr[(\tau, dk) =$ KEM.enc2(sp, pk, ω)] $= 1$.

We require the standard correctness, namely, $\forall \ sp \leftarrow$ KEM.setup(k) and $\forall$ $(pk, sk) \leftarrow$ KEM.kg(sp), we have $dk =$ KEM.dec(sp, sk, c), where $c = (\psi, \tau)$ is produced by $(\psi, \omega) \leftarrow$ KEM.enc1(sp) and $(\tau, dk) \leftarrow$ KEM.enc2(sp, pk, ω).

Remark 1. Our definition of the reproducibility is weaker (thus more general) than that given in [4]. In particular, we don't insist the input for KEM.rp involves multiple key pairs, since this is already enough for our purpose. Most of the known DH-based KEM schemes, in the random oracle [2,12,37,17], or in the standard model [18,29,16,25], meet these two properties.

We consider a very weak security notion for data privacy, namely one-wayness against key checking attack (OW-KCA) [3], which is formally defined below.

Definition 2 (OW-KCA security for KEM). *We say a KEM scheme is (ϵ, t)-OW-KCA secure, if for any adversary $\mathcal{A}$ with running time at most t, has advantage ϵ in the following experiment. The interaction between $\mathcal{A}$ and a key checking oracle $\mathcal{KCO}$ is shown in Fig. 2. In particular, we say a reproducible KEM is OW-KCA secure if for any PPT $\mathcal{A}$, ϵ is negligible.*

$$\mathrm{Adv}_{\mathcal{A}}^{\mathrm{ow\text{-}kca}}(k) = \Pr[sp \leftarrow \mathsf{KEM.setup}(k); (pk, sk) \leftarrow \mathsf{KEM.kg}(sp);$$
$$(\psi, w) \leftarrow \mathsf{KEM.enc1}(sp, pk); (\tau, dk) \leftarrow \mathsf{KEM.enc2}(sp, pk, w);$$
$$c^* \leftarrow (\psi, \tau); dk' \leftarrow \mathcal{A}^{\mathcal{KCO}}(pk, c^*) : dk = dk']$$

Oracle Query	Action Taken	Response
$\mathcal{KCO}(pk_j, c, dk)$, $j \in \{0, 1\}$	If $dk = \mathsf{KEM.dec}(sp, sk_j, c)$	1
	If $dk \neq \mathsf{KEM.dec}(sp, sk_j, c)$	0

Fig. 2. Plaintext Checking Oracle in the OW-KCA Game for KEM

Oracle Query	Action Taken	Response
$\mathcal{EO}(m)$	$e \leftarrow \mathsf{SE.enc}(dk_b, m)$	e
$\mathcal{DO}(c)$	$m \leftarrow \mathsf{SE.dec}(dk_b, c)$	m

Fig. 3. Oracles in the IND-CCA Game for SE

2.3 Symmetric Encryption

A symmetric key encryption scheme $\mathsf{SE} = (\mathsf{SE.enc}, \mathsf{SE.dec})$ consists of 2 algorithms associated with a key space $\mathcal{K}$:

- $\mathsf{SE.enc}$: taking a key $dk \in \mathcal{K}$ and a plaintext m as input, the encryption algorithm outputs a ciphertext e, denoted as $e \leftarrow \mathsf{SE.enc}(dk, m)$.
- $\mathsf{SE.dec}$: taking a key $dk \in \mathcal{K}$, and a ciphertext e as input, the decryption algorithm outputs a plaintext m, or a specially symbol "$\perp$" (indicating "invalid ciphertext"), denoted as $m/\perp \leftarrow \mathsf{SE.dec}(dk, e)$.

Unlike public key encryption, the anonymity of symmetric key schemes are quite related to its data privacy. We note if all the users share the same system parameters thus the same key space, the symmetric key scheme is already anonymous. We review the definition of data privacy (indistinghushability) and anonymity of symmetric key encryption.

Definition 3 (IND-ANON-CCA security for SE). *Consider the advantage of an adversary $\mathcal{A}$ in the following experiment, where $\mathcal{A}$ can either query $\mathsf{SE.enc}$ with (m_0, m_1) or query $\mathsf{SE.dec}$ with (e_0, e_1). The limitation of $\mathcal{A}$ when querying the oracles are: it cannot query an oracle with an output it obtained previously from the other oracle. The interactions between $\mathcal{A}$ and the oracles are shown Fig. 3. We say SE is IND-ANON-CCA secure, if for any probabilistic polynomial time (PPT) $\mathcal{A}$, ϵ is negligible.*

$$\mathrm{Adv}_{\mathcal{A}}^{\mathsf{ind\text{-}anon\text{-}cca}}(k) = |[dk_0 \leftarrow \mathcal{K}; dk_1 \leftarrow \mathcal{K}; b \leftarrow \{0, 1\};$$
$$b' \leftarrow \mathcal{A}^{\mathcal{EO}, \mathcal{DO}}(k, \mathcal{K}) : b' = b] - 1/2|$$

3 A Generic Construction for Key Privacy

In this section, we present a generic transform that turns any reproducible KEM with one-wayness against key checking attack (OW-PCA) into a PKE scheme with anonymous against chosen ciphertext attack (ANON-CCA). To remark, this transform also enhances data privacy of the underlying KEM, namely, the resulting

KEM is IND-CCA secure. For completeness, a brief discussion is given in Section 4. Here we focus on the detailed description of our scheme and prove its anonymity.

3.1 Our Construction

Denote KEM = (KEM.setup, KEM.kg, KEM.enc1, KEM.enc2, KEM.dec, KEM.rp) as a reproducible KEM scheme. Denote H as a hash function (modeled as a random oracle in security analysis) with compatible range and domain. Our generic construction is shown in Fig 4. Here $H : \{0,1\}^* \to \mathcal{K}$ is a secure key derivation function (KDF), and $\mathcal{K}$ is the key space of a secure symmetric encryption SE = (SE.enc, SE.dec).

PKE.setup(k)	PKE.kg(sp)
$sp \leftarrow$ KEM.setup(k);	$(pk_1, sk_1) \leftarrow$ KEM.kg(sp);
Return sp;	Pick a key derivation function H;
	$pk \leftarrow (pk_1, H)$;
	$sk \leftarrow sk_1$
	Return (pk, sk);
PKE.enc(sp, pk, m)	PKE.dec(sp, sk, c)
Parse $pk = (pk, H)$;	Parse $c = (\psi, e)$;
$(\psi, \omega) \leftarrow$ KEM.enc1(sp);	$\tau \leftarrow$ KEM.rp(sp, sk, ψ);
$(\tau, dk) \leftarrow$ KEM.enc2(sp, pk, ω);	$dk \leftarrow$ KEM.dec($sp, sk, (\psi, \tau)$);
$dk' \leftarrow H(pk, \tau, dk)$;	abort if $dk = \perp$;
$e \leftarrow$ SE.enc(dk', m);	$dk' \leftarrow H(pk, \tau, dk)$;
$c \leftarrow (\psi, e)$;	Return SE.dec(dk', c);
Return c;	

Fig. 4. Generic Construction of ANON-CCA PKE from Reproducible KEM

The correctness of the construction can be verified from the description of algorithms. We focus on the ANON-CCA security. The following theorem guarantees its anonymity.

Theorem 1. *The PKE scheme (Fig. 4) is $(\epsilon_1 + \epsilon_2, t_1 + t_2 + O(kq))$-ANON-CCA secure, assuming the KEM is (ϵ_1, t_1)-OW-KCA secure, and the SE is (ϵ_2, t_2)-ANON-CCA secure, where k is the security parameter, q is the total number of queries $\mathcal{A}$ makes in the game.*

Proof Idea. We introduce the proof strategy before give the details. Since τ doesn't appear explicitly in the challenge ciphertext, the simulator can fake the session key for the challenge by a randomly chosen one. Later, to have the knowledge of b, the real τ and dk must appear in the adversary's the random oracle query, thus the simulator can extract dk. The only thing left is how to answer the decryption queries. For decryption queries on valid ciphertexts, if it has appeared in the previous hash queries, then the simulator can extract the correct session key for the hash list, then decrypt. For invalid queries, note that the simulator knows every session key, it will reject. More exactly, even if it encounters a new ciphertext whose session key it does not know, it can randomly sample a new one. Later when τ and dk are queried by the adversary, it can fill up the early unfinished record. Thus for every type of query, the simulator makes perfect simulation. We elaborate the details below.

Proof. We build a simulator $\mathcal{B}$ that utilizes an ANON-CCA adversary $\mathcal{A}$ to break the underlying reproducible KEM. $\mathcal{B}$ controls the random oracle H, and simulates the challenger in the ANON-CCA game as follows.

Hash Query: $\mathcal{B}$ maintains a hash list with 6-entry $(pk, \psi, \tau, dk, dk', \beta)$ ($\beta \in \{0, 1\}$ is a boolean value), initially empty. When there is a hash query of the form (pk_j, ψ, τ, dk), where ($j \in \{0, 1\}$ is the index of the public key), $\mathcal{B}$ searches the hash list for an entry of the form $(pk_j, \psi, \tau, dk, dk', ?)$, where "?" means "don't care". If there is such a record, it returns corresponding dk' as reply.

If there is not such a record, $\mathcal{B}$ queries its own session key checking oracle $\mathcal{KCO}$ with (pk_j, ψ, τ, dk). If $\mathcal{KCO}$'s answer is "valid", $\mathcal{B}$ further searches for a record of the form $(pk_j, \psi, \cdot, \cdot, dk', 1)$, where "·" means "empty". If there is such a record, $\mathcal{B}$ fills τ and dk in and completes the record, otherwise $\mathcal{B}$ chooses randomly $dk' \leftarrow \mathcal{K}$ and adds a new record $(pk_i, \psi, \tau, dk, dk', 1)$ to the list. If $\mathcal{KCO}$'s answer is "invalid", $\mathcal{B}$ then chooses randomly $dk' \leftarrow \mathcal{K}$, returns dk' as the output and adds a new record $(pk_i, \psi, \tau, dk, dk', 0)$ to the hash list.

Decryption Query: On a decryption query (pk_j, ψ, e), $\mathcal{B}$ first searches the hash list for a record of the form $(pk_j, \psi, ?, ?, dk', 1)$. If there is such an record, $\mathcal{B}$ returns $m \leftarrow \mathsf{SE.dec}(dk', c)$ as the answer. If there is not such an record, $\mathcal{B}$ chooses $dk' \leftarrow \mathcal{K}$, adds $(pk_j, \psi, \cdot, \cdot, dk', 1)$ to the hash list, and returns $m \leftarrow \mathsf{SE.dec}(dk', c)$ as the answer.

Encryption Query: On query m^* submitted by $\mathcal{A}$, $\mathcal{B}$ flips a fair coin b to produce the challenge (ψ^*, τ^*) under public key pk_b. Moreover, $\mathcal{B}$ sets $e \leftarrow \mathsf{SE.enc}(dk'^*, m^*)$, where $dk'^* \leftarrow \mathcal{K}$. $\mathcal{B}$ then gives $c^* = (\psi^*, e)$ to $\mathcal{A}$. Especially, $\mathcal{B}$ adds $(pk_b, \psi^*, \tau^*, \cdot, dk'^*, 1)$ to the hash list.

When $\mathcal{A}$ terminates and outputs its guess a bit b', $\mathcal{B}$ searches the hash list for $(pk_{b'}, \psi^*, \tau^*, dk^*, dk'^*, 1)$. If there is such an entry, $\mathcal{B}$ recovers dk^*, i.e., $\mathcal{B}$ has broken the OW-KCA security of the underlying KEM. If there is no such an entry, $\mathcal{B}$ aborts. This completes the description of $\mathcal{B}$.

Now we calculate $\mathcal{B}$'s success probability. Notice the decryption query is answered perfectly, since $\mathcal{B}$ always is able to tell all invalid ciphertexts. Because of the random oracle, $\mathcal{B}$ is always able to compute the correct dk' for valid ciphertexts. The encryption query is also perfectly answered.

Note that if dk^* was not queried during the game, due to the assumption on the symmetric key encryption, $\mathcal{A}$'s advantage is bounded by ϵ_2. Otherwise, $\mathcal{B}$ can find dk^* with probability 1. We have

$$\mathrm{Adv}_{\mathcal{B}}(k) = \epsilon_1 = \Pr[\mathrm{Adv}_{\mathcal{A}} \wedge dk^* \in H\text{-list}] - \Pr[\mathrm{Adv}_{\mathcal{A}} \wedge dk^* \notin H\text{-list}]$$
$$\geq \epsilon - \epsilon_2$$

We have $\epsilon \leq \epsilon_1 + \epsilon_2$, which proves our statement. The claimed time bound can be verified from the description of $\mathcal{B}$.

Relation to a scheme from [4] In the context of building efficient stateful encryption schemes [8], Baek, Zhou and Bao proposed a transform in the random oracle model [4], which is somehow similar to our transform. We remark that instead of hiding τ in the key derivation function as we did, they require τ to be transmitted as a part of the ciphertext. Thus the bandwidth of their scheme is worse than ours. Instead, a receiver doesn't need to compute τ himself. On the other hand, because τ depends on the receiver's public key, their scheme cannot be anonymous in general. Note that their original goal was not key privacy.

4   Data Privacy of the Proposed Scheme

The proposed construction actually provides IND-CCA security assuming the reproducible KEM is OW-KCA secure. Here we only give the definition of IND-CCA and sketch the proof, since majority of the proof overlaps the one given in Section 3.

Definition 4 (IND-CCA security for PKE). *We say an encryption scheme is (ϵ, t)-IND-CCA secure, if for any adversary $\mathcal{A}$ with running time at most t, has advantage ϵ in the following experiment. The interaction between $\mathcal{A}$ and a decryption oracle $\mathcal{DO}$ is shown in Fig. 5. In particular, $\mathcal{A}$ is not allowed to query c^* to the decryption oracle. We say the encryption scheme is IND-CCA secure, if for any polynomially bounded t, ϵ is negligible.*

$$\mathrm{Adv}_{\mathcal{A}}^{\mathsf{ind\text{-}cca}}(k) = |\Pr[sp \leftarrow \mathsf{PKE.setup}(k); (pk, sk) \leftarrow \mathsf{PKE.kg}(sp);$$
$$(m_0, m_1, st) \leftarrow \mathcal{A}^{\mathcal{DO}}(pk, sp); b \leftarrow \{0, 1\}; c^* \leftarrow \mathsf{PKE.enc}(sp, pk, m_b);$$
$$b' \leftarrow \mathcal{A}^{\mathcal{DO}}(c^*, st) : b = b'] - 1/2|$$

Oracle Query	Action Taken	Response
$\mathcal{DO}(c)$	$m \leftarrow \mathsf{PKE.dec}(sp, sk, c)$	m or $\bot$

Fig. 5. Decryption Oracle in the IND-CCA Game for PKE

We have the following statements on data privacy of the scheme:

Theorem 2. *The PKE scheme (Fig. 4) is $(\epsilon_1 + \epsilon_2, t_1 + t_2 + O(kq))$-ANON-CCA secure, assuming the KEM is (ϵ_1, t_1)-OW-KCA secure, and the SE is (ϵ_2, t_2)-IND-CCA secure, where k is the security parameter, q is the total number of queries $\mathcal{A}$ makes in the game.*

The proof is almost the same as the one shown in Sect. 3. We only sketch the difference. For key generation, a simulator $\mathcal{B}$ will only generates one key pair $\mathcal{B}$. Hash query and decryption query will be answered exactly as before. For encryption query, $\mathcal{B}$ flips a fair coin b and chooses a random session key $dk'^* \leftarrow \mathcal{K}$, sets $e \leftarrow \mathsf{SE.enc}(dk'^*, m_b)$ and gives (ψ^*, e^*) as the challenge ciphertext for $\mathcal{A}$. Recall that (ψ^*, τ^*) is $\mathcal{B}$'s own challenge. $\mathcal{B}$ also adds $(pk, \psi^*, \tau, \cdot, dk', 1)$ to the hash list. When $\mathcal{A}$ successfully guesses b, $\mathcal{B}$ can then extract dk^* from the hash list.

It is not hard to verify that $\mathcal{B}$'s simulation is perfect. With a similar discussion on $\mathcal{B}$'s success probability, we obtain the bounds in Thm. 2. The claimed time bounds can be easily verified also.

5   Extensions and Instantiations

We discuss some further extensions of our results.

5.1   Extensions

Anonymous Key Encapsulation Mechanism. Our construction is designed for anonymous public key encryption, however, it is easy to derive the corresponding key encapsulation mechanism (KEM) scheme. E.g., in Fig. 4, instead of letting the encryption algorithm calling SE.enc, we output dk' as the encapsulated key as the session key. The decapsulation algorithm then outputs dk' without calling SE.dec. We can prove the anonymity of this resulting KEM scheme similarly as Thm. 1.

Anonymous Identity Based Encryption. The discussion here is mainly for public key encryption, and it is easy to generate all the above discussions to the identity based encryption (IBE) [38,12,1]. An anonymous IBE has applications such as public key encryption with keyword search (PEKS) [11]. We omit the details here and only claim it is not so much different: plug anonymous ID-based KEMs into our generic construction, one will get anonymous IBE/IBKEM schemes.

A Benchmark for Our Transform. Since OW-KCA security is implied by chosen ciphertext security (IND-CCA) in most interesting cases, we have the following useful corollary.

Corollary 1. *If the generic construction given in Fig. 4 is applied to an* IND-CCA *secure reproducible KEM, the resulting scheme is also* ANON-CCA *secure.*

This corollary is very useful, since it gives a "benchmark" of the usability of our generic construction. There are many schemes known to have IND-CCA security. We can then quickly judge whether a scheme can be used for our purpose or not, by just "looking" at the encryption algorithms. On the other hand, IND-CCA is redundant for our purpose, and most of the occasions, we can make weaker assumptions, since we are already in the random oracle world. However, we note that the transformed schemes always achieves tight security reduction, thanks to the key checking oracle!

5.2   Practical Instantiations

We give some instantiations for our generic construction, which result in some new anonymous public key encryption schemes. For the sake of space, we only focus on the schemes built on gap groups, or pairings. In such schemes, the validity of ciphertexts can be publicly verified, thus there is no anonymity. Using our transform, we can build anonymous public key encryption schemes with anonymity and improved bandwidth efficiency. We remark some of them can be further optimized, and here we focus on the effectiveness of our transform.

DH KEM [2,39]. A classical reproducible KEM is DH KEM, which is based on Diffie-Hellman key exchange. The algorithms of DH KEM is reviewed below:

- DH.setup(k): Choose a cyclic group $\mathbb{G} = <g>$ of prime order q. Return $sp = (\mathbb{G}, q, g)$.
- DH.kg(sp): Choose $x \leftarrow \mathbb{Z}_q$, and compute $y \leftarrow g^x$. Choose a key derivation function $H : \mathbb{G} \rightarrow \mathcal{K}$, where $\mathcal{K}$ is the key space for the associated symmetric key encryption. Return $pk = (y, H)$ and $sk = (x, H)$.
- DH.enc1(sp): Pick $r \leftarrow \mathbb{Z}_q$, compute $\psi = g^r$. return (ψ, r)
- DH.enc2($sp, pk, \psi \| r$): Compute $dk \leftarrow H(y^r)$. Note that τ is equal to an empty string. Output (τ, dk).
- DH.dec(sp, sk, ψ): Output $dk \leftarrow H(\psi^x)$, if ψ is an element of $\mathbb{G}$.
- DH.rp(sp, sk, ψ): Always output an empty string.

Sine τ is simply an empty string, it is trivially reproducible. Previous results [5,40] have shown that the PKE version of DH KEM is ANON-CPA secure without random oracles under the decisional Diffie-Hellman assumption (DDH) is hard. From our result, we know it is actually ANON-CCA secure under the gap Diffie-Hellman assumption (GDH). Interestingly, this coincides with data privacy of DH KEM [39].

BMW KEM [13]. Boyen, Mei and Waters proposed an efficient KEM based on bilinear pairings from the BB1 IBE [10]. The algorithms are reviewed below.

- BMW.setup(k): Generate bilinear map $e : \mathbb{G}_1 \times \mathbb{G}_2 \rightarrow \mathbb{G}_T$. $\mathbb{G}_1$, $\mathbb{G}_2$ and $\mathbb{G}_T|$ are of prime order q. g and h are generators for $\mathbb{G}_1$ and $\mathbb{G}_2$, respectively. Picks a collision resistant hash function $H : \mathbb{G}_1 \rightarrow \mathbb{Z}_q$. sp is set as $(k, q, e, \mathbb{G}_1, \mathbb{G}_T, g, h, H)$.
- BMW.kg(sp): Choose $\alpha \leftarrow \mathbb{Z}_q$ and $\ell \leftarrow h^\alpha$. Compute $Z \leftarrow e(g, \ell)$, $u \leftarrow g^x$ and $v \leftarrow g^y$, where $x, y \leftarrow \mathbb{Z}_q$. Return $pk = (Z, u, v)$ and $sk = (pk, \ell, x, y)$.
- BMW.enc1(sp): $r \leftarrow \mathbb{Z}_q$, $\psi \leftarrow g^r$. Return (r, ψ).
- BMW.enc2(sp, pk, st): Parse $st = (r, \psi)$. $w \leftarrow H(\psi)$, $\tau \leftarrow u^r v^{rw}$, and $dk \leftarrow Z^r$. Return (τ, dk).
- BMW.dec(sp, sk, c): Parse $c = (\psi, \tau)$. $w \leftarrow H(\psi)$, $w' \leftarrow x + yw$. If $\psi^{w'} = \tau$, return $dk \leftarrow e(\psi, \ell)$. Otherwise, return $\perp$.
- BMW.rp(sp, sk, ψ):

It has been shown in [4] that the BMW KEM has separability and reproducibility. It was also shown in [13] that it has IND-CCA security. Then it also has OW-KCA security according to Corollary 1.

It is easily verifiable that the original BMW KEM is not anonymous. Using our transform we can build a variant of the BMW KEM which is anonymous under the computational bilinear Diffie-Hellman assumption (CBDH) in the random oracle model. We next show some concrete examples.

Kiltz KEM [28]. Kiltz proposed another efficient KEM based on the so-called gap hashed Diffie-Hellman assumption, which is an interactive assumption. The algorithms are reviewed below.

- K.setup(k): Pick a cyclic group $\mathbb{G}$ prime order q. g is a generator for $\mathbb{G}$. Picks a target collision resistant hash function $H : \mathbb{G} \to \mathbb{Z}_q$ and a key derivation function $G : \mathbb{G} \to \mathcal{K}$, where $\mathcal{K}$ is the key space for symmetric key encryption. sp is set as $(k, q, \mathbb{G}, g, H, G)$.
- K.kg(sp): Choose $x, y \leftarrow \mathbb{Z}_q$ and set $u \leftarrow g^x$ and $v \leftarrow g^y$. Return $pk = (u, v)$ and $sk = (x, y)$.
- K.enc1(sp): $r \leftarrow \mathbb{Z}_q$, $\psi \leftarrow g^\omega$. Let $\omega \leftarrow c_1||r$. Return (ψ, ω).
- K.enc2(sp, pk, ω): Parse $\omega = \psi||r$. $\tau \leftarrow (u^{H(\psi)}v)^r$, and $dk \leftarrow G(u^r)$. Return (τ, dk).
- K.dec(sp, sk, c): Parse $c = (\psi, \tau)$. $t \leftarrow H(\psi)$. If $\tau = \psi^{xt+y}$, let $dk \leftarrow G(\psi^x)$. Otherwise, return $\perp$.
- K.rp(sp, sk, ψ): Parse $sk = (x, y)$. For $t \leftarrow H(\psi)$, output ψ^{xt+y}.

Under gap hashed Diffie-Hellman assumption (HGDH), the above scheme is IND-CCA secure. Furthermore, it is briefly mentioned in [28] that under gap Diffie-Hellman assumption (GDH) the scheme is OW-CCA [28]. Then it is easily verified that the scheme also satisfies OW-KCA under the same assumption, namely, gap Diffie-Hellman assumption (GDH). Instantiating this scheme, we havd an anonymous variant of it whose ANON-CCA security can be proved either under the HGDH assumption or the GDH assumption, both with random oracles. We remark that the resulting scheme is not as efficient as the DH-KEM, however, it may help to provide a different way in understanding the key privacy of Kiltz KEM.

6   Conclusion

In this paper, we propose a simple and efficient method to obtain strong key privacy from weak data privacy, as well as upgrading data privacy of the underlying KEM scheme for a class of public key encryption schemes in the random oracle model. We also provide some interesting instantiations where the underlying KEMs may be not anonymous. It is worth mentioning that it is still open whether efficient transforms achieving the same goal can exist without random oracles.

References

1. Abdalla, M., Bellare, M., Catalano, D., Kiltz, E., Kohno, T., Lange, T., Malone-Lee, J., Neven, G., Paillier, P., Shi, H.: Searchable Encryption Revisited: Consistency Properties, Relation to Anonymous IBE, and Extensions. In: Shoup, V. (ed.) CRYPTO 2005. LNCS, vol. 3621, pp. 205–222. Springer, Heidelberg (2005)
2. Abdalla, M., Bellare, M., Rogaway, P.: The Oracle Diffie-Hellman Assumptions and an Analysis of DHIES. In: Naccache, D. (ed.) CT-RSA 2001. LNCS, vol. 2020, pp. 143–158. Springer, Heidelberg (2001)
3. Abe, M.: Combining Encryption and Proof of Knowledge in the Random Oracle Model. The Computer Journal 47(1), 58–70 (2004)
4. Baek, J., Zhou, J., Bao, F.: Generic Constructions of Stateful Public Key Encryption and Their Applications. In: Bellovin, S.M., Gennaro, R., Keromytis, A.D., Yung, M. (eds.) ACNS 2008. LNCS, vol. 5037, pp. 75–93. Springer, Heidelberg (2008)

5. Bellare, M., Boldyreva, A., Desai, A., Pointcheval, D.: Key-Privacy in Public-Key Encryption. In: Boyd, C. (ed.) ASIACRYPT 2001. LNCS, vol. 2248, pp. 566–582. Springer, Heidelberg (2001)
6. Bellare, M., Boldyreva, A., Staddon, J.: Randomness Re-use in Multi-recipient Encryption Schemes. In: Desmedt, Y.G. (ed.) PKC 2003. LNCS, vol. 2567, pp. 85–99. Springer, Heidelberg (2002)
7. Bellare, M., Desai, A., Pointcheval, D., Rogaway, P.: Relations among Notions of Security for Public-Key Encryption Schemes. In: Krawczyk, H. (ed.) CRYPTO 1998. LNCS, vol. 1462, pp. 26–45. Springer, Heidelberg (1998)
8. Bellare, M., Kohno, T., Shoup, V.: Stateful Public-Key Cryptosystems: How to Encrypt with One 160-bit Exponentiation. In: ACM CCS 2006, pp. 380–389. ACM, New York (2006)
9. Bellare, M., Rogaway, P.: Random Oracles Are Practical: A Paradigm for Designing Efficient Protocols. In: ACM CCS 1993, pp. 62–73. ACM Press, New York (1993)
10. Boneh, D., Boyen, X.: Efficient Selective-ID Secure Identity-Based Encryption Without Random Oracles. In: Cachin, C., Camenisch, J.L. (eds.) EUROCRYPT 2004. LNCS, vol. 3027, pp. 223–238. Springer, Heidelberg (2004)
11. Boneh, D., Di Crescenzo, G., Ostrovsky, R., Persiano, G.: Public Key Encryption with Keyword Search. In: Cachin, C., Camenisch, J.L. (eds.) EUROCRYPT 2004. LNCS, vol. 3027, pp. 506–522. Springer, Heidelberg (2004)
12. Boneh, D., Franklin, M.: Identity-Based Encryption from the Weil Pairing. In: Kilian, J. (ed.) CRYPTO 2001. LNCS, vol. 2139, pp. 213–229. Springer, Heidelberg (2001)
13. Boyen, X., Mei, Q., Waters, B.: Direct Chosen Ciphertext Security from Identity-Based Techniques. In: ACM CCS 2005, pp. 320–329. ACM Press, New York (2005)
14. Canetti, R., Goldreich, O., Halevi, S.: The Random Oracle Methodology, Revisited. In: STOC 1998, pp. 557–594. ACM, New York (1998), http://eprint.iacr.org/1998/011.pdf
15. Canetti, R., Halevi, S., Katz, J.: Chosen-Ciphertext Security from Identity-Based Encryption. In: Cachin, C., Camenisch, J.L. (eds.) EUROCRYPT 2004. LNCS, vol. 3027, pp. 207–222. Springer, Heidelberg (2004)
16. Cash, D.M., Kiltz, E., Shoup, V.: The Twin Diffie-Hellman Problem and Applications. In: Smart, N.P. (ed.) EUROCRYPT 2008. LNCS, vol. 4965, pp. 127–145. Springer, Heidelberg (2008)
17. Chen, L., Cheng, Z.: Security proof of sakai-kasahara's identity-based encryption scheme. In: Smart, N.P. (ed.) CC 2005. LNCS, vol. 3796, pp. 442–459. Springer, Heidelberg (2005)
18. Cramer, R., Shoup, V.: Universal Hash Proofs and a Paradigm for Adaptive Chosen Ciphertext Secure Public-Key Encryption. In: Knudsen, L.R. (ed.) EUROCRYPT 2002. LNCS, vol. 2332, pp. 45–64. Springer, Heidelberg (2002)
19. Dolev, D., Dwork, C., Naor, M.: Non-Malleable Cryptography. In: STOC 1991, pp. 542–552. ACM, New York (1991)
20. Dolev, D., Dwork, C., Naor, M.: Nonmalleable Cryptography. SIAM Journal on Computing 30(2), 391–437 (2000)
21. El Aimani, L.: Anonymity from public key encryption to undeniable signatures. In: Preneel, B. (ed.) AFRICACRYPT 2009. LNCS, vol. 5580, pp. 217–234. Springer, Heidelberg (2009)
22. Fujisaki, E., Okamoto, T.: Secure Integration of Asymmetric and Symmetric Encryption Schemes. In: Wiener, M. (ed.) CRYPTO 1999. LNCS, vol. 1666, pp. 537–544. Springer, Heidelberg (1999)

23. Goldwasser, S., Micali, S.: Probabilistic Encryption. Journal of Computer and System Sciences 28(2), 270–299 (1984)
24. Halevi, S.: A sufficient condition for key-privacy. Cryptology ePrint Archive, Report 2005/005 (2005)
25. Hanaoka, G., Kurosawa, K.: Efficient Chosen Ciphertext Secure Public Key Encryption under the Computational Diffie-Hellman Assumption. In: Pieprzyk, J. (ed.) ASIACRYPT 2008. LNCS, vol. 5350, pp. 308–325. Springer, Heidelberg (2008)
26. Hayashi, R., Okamoto, T., Tanaka, K.: An RSA Family of Trap-Door Permutations with a Common Domain and Its Applications. In: Bao, F., Deng, R., Zhou, J. (eds.) PKC 2004. LNCS, vol. 2947, pp. 291–304. Springer, Heidelberg (2004)
27. Hayashi, R., Tanaka, K.: PA in the Two-Key Setting and a Generic Conversion for Encryption with Anonymity. In: Batten, L.M., Safavi-Naini, R. (eds.) ACISP 2006. LNCS, vol. 4058, pp. 271–282. Springer, Heidelberg (2006)
28. Kiltz, E.: Chosen-Ciphertext Secure Key-Encapsulation Based on Gap Hashed Diffie-Hellman. In: Okamoto, T., Wang, X. (eds.) PKC 2007. LNCS, vol. 4450, pp. 282–297. Springer, Heidelberg (2007)
29. Kurosawa, K., Desmedt, Y.G.: A New Paradigm of Hybrid Encryption Scheme. In: Franklin, M. (ed.) CRYPTO 2004. LNCS, vol. 3152, pp. 426–442. Springer, Heidelberg (2004)
30. Naccache, D., Steinwandt, R., Yung, M.: Reverse public key encryption. In: BIOSIG. LNI, vol. 155, pp. 155–169. GI (2009)
31. Naor, M., Yung, M.: Public-key Cryptosystems Provably Secure against Chosen Ciphertext Attacks. In: STOC 1990, pp. 427–437. ACM, New York (1990)
32. Okamoto, T., Pointcheval, D.: REACT: Rapid Enhanced-Security Asymmetric Cryptosystem Transform. In: Naccache, D. (ed.) CT-RSA 2001. LNCS, vol. 2020, pp. 159–175. Springer, Heidelberg (2001)
33. Paterson, K.G., Srinivasan, S.: Building Key-Private Public-Key Encryption Schemes. In: Boyd, C., González Nieto, J. (eds.) ACISP 2009. LNCS, vol. 5594, pp. 276–292. Springer, Heidelberg (2009)
34. Peikert, C., Waters, B.: Lossy Trapdoor Functions and Their Applications. In: STOC 2008, pp. 187–196. ACM, New York (2008); Available as Eprint Archive Report 2007/279
35. Rackoff, C., Simon, D.R.: Non-interactive Zero-Knowledge Proof of Knowledge and Chosen Ciphertext Attack. In: Feigenbaum, J. (ed.) CRYPTO 1991. LNCS, vol. 576, pp. 433–444. Springer, Heidelberg (1992)
36. Sahai, A.: Non-Malleable Non-Interactive Zero Knowledge and Adaptive Chosen-Ciphertext Security. In: FOCS 1999, pp. 543–553. IEEE Computer Society, Los Alamitos (1999)
37. Sakai, R., Kasahara, M.: ID based Cryptosystems with Pairing on Elliptic Curve. Eprint Archive Report 2003/054 (2003)
38. Shamir, A.: Identity-Based Cryptosystems and Signature Schemes. In: Blakely, G.R., Chaum, D. (eds.) CRYPTO 1984. LNCS, vol. 196, pp. 47–53. Springer, Heidelberg (1985)
39. Shoup, V.: ISO 18033-2: An Emerging Standard for Public-Key Encryption (committee draft) (June 2001), http://shoup.net/iso/
40. Zhang, R., Hanaoka, G., Imai, H.: Orthogonality between Key Privacy and Data Privacy, Revisited. In: Pei, D., Yung, M., Lin, D., Wu, C. (eds.) Inscrypt 2007. LNCS, vol. 4990, pp. 313–327. Springer, Heidelberg (2008)

Private Information Retrieval with a Trusted Hardware Unit – Revisited[*]

Łukasz Krzywiecki, Mirosław Kutyłowski[**], Hubert Misztela,
and Tomasz Strumiński

Institute of Mathematics and Computer Science,
Wrocław University of Technology, Wybrzeże Wyspiańskiego 27,
50-370 Wrocław, Poland
{firstname.secondname}@pwr.wroc.pl

Abstract. During ISC'2008 Yanjiang Yang, Xuhua Ding, Robert H. Deng, and Feng Bao presented a construction for holding an encrypted database in a cloud so that the access pattern remains hidden. The scheme is designed for the case when a user holds a trusted hardware unit, which serves as an interface between the owner of the database and the untrusted environment where the encrypted database is stored. The scheme is relatively efficient and has some provable privacy properties.

In this paper we analyze an idealized version of the above protocol and prove rigorously strong privacy conditions in a model with a powerful adversary observing all operations occurring in the cloud. On the other hand, we show that the full version of the protocol (with some implementation details), as proposed at ISC'2008, leaks some information about the access pattern of the user. This shows that the protocol does not fulfil the property of ideally private information retrieval. While this is not a general full scale attack, at some specific situations information leakage presented might have practical value for an adversary.

Keywords: private information retrieval, cloud computing, database, probability distribution.

1 Introduction

1.1 Problem Statement

Nowadays, quite often databases are kept in environments that are not under sole control of the data owners. Such a situation is a standard one in business applications: information is stored and processed in service centers on servers that guarantee high reliability (protection against hardware crushes, round the clock availability, access control, guaranteed response time and so on). It is also

---

[*] This research has been partially supported by Polish Ministry of Science and Higher Education, grant N N206 1842 33. Later, it has been also supported by Foundation for Polish Science within the MISTRZ Programme. Some results from this paper are also contained in the Master Dissertation [7] of the third author.

[**] Contact author.

X. Lai, M. Yung, and D. Lin (Eds.): Inscrypt 2010, LNCS 6584, pp. 373–386, 2011.

increasingly popular to keep databases in a cloud, without any control who and how actually keeps it. In such a case it might be critical to protect information stored in the database as well as information about database usage. In fact, it seems to be one of central problems for cloud computing paradigm. Without a satisfactory solution keeping a database in a cloud may remain limited to a very small range of applications.

Obviously, one can keep the entries of the database in an encrypted form. In this case the party holding the database has no access to information stored in the records of the database. The encryption scheme used should guarantee that the observer cannot detect repetitions of the same value stored in the database at different positions. One of possible solutions is to use a probabilistic encryption scheme.

However, even the best encryption does not hide all information concerning the database. For instance, in the database there might be more and less popular entries. If the positions of the entries stored are not changed, then frequency of access requests to particular positions of the encrypted database reveal some information about their contents. This is especially important, if an observer has some prior knowledge about the database. Access pattern characteristics can also be treated as a fingerprint of the database contents enabling the adversary to categorize encrypted databases. Potential privacy violations of this kind might prohibit migration of the database to an external environment. Keeping the database in a sole physical control of the user would remain the only reasonable solution, increasing substantially the running costs and decreasing ease of keeping the database.

The problem mentioned has been in focus of *private information retrieval (PIR)* research in the recent years, initiated by [1]. There is a rich literature on this topic (for some starting points see a survey [8]). There are many clever solutions that are concentrated on reduction of communication complexity: the trivial solution is to fetch the whole database, but to decrypt only the entry the user is interested in. In case of large databases this solution is useless, despite the fact that no information is leaked which entry is read by the user.

In practice, the owner of the database is not only formulating the queries to the database. We may assume that she or he uses a terminal that is under his sole control, and the terminal has certain computational and storage capacity. This terminal can be regarded as kind of a protected cache memory of the database. Moreover, the interface between the local system and the database can be implemented in a trusted hardware unit [4,5,9].

The main issue for solutions based on trusted hardware unit is to reduce the communication cost. For instance, [9] assumes frequent rewriting of the whole database, which is quite impractical. The paper [10] reduces significantly the amount of this work without loosing privacy properties (to some extent, as we shall see).

Our contribution. The main goal of this paper is to inspect the privacy guarantees given by the scheme from paper [10]. We prove that the ideal version of the protocol guarantees substantially higher privacy level than previously claimed.

We prove that knowledge about the access pattern (location of read and write operations) does not bring *any knowledge* in information-theoretic sense about the ordering of touched records in the memory.

On the other hand, we show that there are some information leakages in the full scheme that takes into account all implementation details. They do not seem to lead directly to large scale practical attacks at the moment, but also show that we cannot claim that the scheme provides full privacy guarantees. At least, further investigations are required to exclude possibility of practical attacks.

Following paper [10], we concern the following model. The user runs all database operations through a trusted hardware unit. The unit performs all crypto operations as well as governs the locations of individual records, keeping track of all information that need to be stored locally. The hardware unit is assumed to be secure – no information is leaked to an outside observer. On the other hand, it is assumed pessimistically that the adversary may observe which encrypted database entries are fetched by the hardware unit and which are overwritten.

1.2   The Solution of Yang et al.

In this subsection we sketch the idea of the solution presented in [10]. An overview seems to be necessary, since the original description and pseudo-code is rather hard to follow for the reader and there are a few bugs in the pseudo-code. In fact, we present a simplified version that in our opinion is equivalent to the original one from the point of view of the adversary.

We assume that a database D consists of records $d_1, \dots, d_n$ of the same size. The trusted hardware unit T is capable of storing k records; we assume that $k \ll n$. So T can be regarded as a kind of cache memory.

At database initialization, all entries are stored in an encrypted form, but the trusted hardware unit T knows a function σ translating the keys into locations in the encrypted database D_0, i.e. an entry with key i is stored at location $\sigma(i)$ in D_0.

Running the database accesses is divided into epochs. During an epoch data are loaded into the cache of T, no write operation are performed into the database. The epoch terminates, when the cache memory is full. Then all records from the memory are written into the database. Additionally, the database becomes reorganized in the way described below.

The central idea of the construction is the notion of white and black records. A record is *white*, if it has never been read since the system initialization (from time to time the system is re-initialized – so we count the time from the last initialization). A record that has been fetched at least once becomes *black*.

When a user wants to fetch a record from the database and the record is not in the cache, then there are two cases:

the record requested is black: in this case T fetches the requested black record and a white record chosen at random,

the record requested is white: in this case T fetches the requested white record and one black record – namely a record chosen at random from the set of the black records that have not been read yet in the current epoch.

In both cases the observer sees that T fetches

- one white record,
- one black record from those that have not been touched yet in the current epoch.

Let us remark that the white record fetched becomes automatically black. So within an epoch, the protocol execution is in some sense oblivious: there is no obvious behavior feature that depends on the number of requests for black records. The epoch lasts $k/2$ steps, as the cache has place for k entries in total.

The key part of the protocol is the procedure executed at the end of an epoch. The contents of the cache is flushed and at the same time the black records are permuted at random. Consequently, the adversary should not be aware of the new positions of the records read during the current epoch.

Permuting black records – security challenges. Mixing the old black records and the records from the cache is necessary, since otherwise the adversary could see that, for instance, in the next epoch the user is not asking for the records that he has fetched during the last epoch. Or vice versa: that the same records are fetched. Leaking such data – even if this is not exactly the access pattern of the user – is unacceptable and would mean failure of very basic privacy requirements.

Permuting the black records at random is not as trivial as one can think at first. We must be aware that, in the assumed model, the adversary can trace all operations executed in the database. The adversary cannot say which data are written at a given place, but he is aware of time and location of any write and read operation in the database. Of course, T can perform any operation in the cache and this remains hidden from the adversary. However, the size of the cache is small compared to the number of black records and T cannot fetch all of them at once. The assumption that makes this problem hard are efficiency requirements: the number of read/write operations should be linear in the number of black records. The ultimate goal would be to touch each black position exactly once during permutation procedure (going below that is impossible, since the adversary would know that some blacks are not used). As we shall see in Proposition 1, if we have a small cache and each database position is read and overwritten exactly once, then the adversary gets a lot of knowledge about permutation performed. Namely, most permutations are impossible for a given pattern of read/write operations. At this point the reader may doubt, if the sketched scheme is plausible at all, as it is impossible to permute the black elements at random without revealing some information to the adversary.

According to paper [10] a partial shuffle procedure at the end of the epoch s is performed according to a random permutation π_{s+1} which will lead the database to the epoch $s+1$. The hardware unit T updates the black positions sequentially via quite perplexed algorithm that uses composition of π_{s+1}^{-1}, and π_s from the previous epoch. As a result the previous black positions and new white positions from the cache are randomly mixed. However, these records are not mixed at random from the adversary's point of view, as he may observe the operations performed in the database. That is because the cache size is limited and the shuffling algorithm at each iteration reads and writes exactly one elements for re-encryption. To illustrate how this can improve adversary's knowledge about the permutation consider the following example. Consider the ith element read in by T. One of the main features of the algorithm from [10] is that at the moment of reading already $i - 1$ elements have been written to destination places. So the permutation of black records is not purely random from the adversary's point of view: the ith element is not stored in the first $i - 1$ places. In particular, the last element read can be placed at $k + 1$ places only. The fraction of permutations that fulfill these properties is very small.

Simplified scheme. To set up attention, and to make the analysis more readable we provide below a concise variant of original shuffling procedure from [10]. Since some properties of permutation over all black elements are revealed to the adversary we should not rely on it. Instead, in our simplified approach we suggest that the one thing the adversary cannot deduce are the destination places of elements read in to the cache during the retrieval phase. In this variant the trusted hardware does not have to hold a random permutation over the whole set of black records in the cache. Instead, it uses a random injective function with the domain of the cache cardinality to define new position for cache items in the next epoch database. Thus it is easier to narrow the analysis to the cases where, from adversary's point of view, items from the cache are put somewhere among the untouched black records of the currently finished epoch. Now, despite this modification that potentially advantages adversary's reasoning, the shuffling achieves the same level of security as the original scheme.

Assume that there are together m plus k black records – m black records that have not been fetched to the cache during the current epoch and k black records in the cache. k records residing in the cache at the beginning of this procedure will be called *cache records*, the other black records will be called *untouched*. T uses some canonical ordering of the locations of these records, but for ease of presentation we assume that the locations of the untouched black records come first.

The procedure is the following:

1. T chooses at random destinations for all cache records. That is, T chooses an injective function $\phi : \{1, \ldots, k\} \to \{1, \ldots, m + k\}$ at random.
2. m steps are executed. At step j (for $j \leq m$):
   - the untouched black record from position j is read,
   - if there is no i such that $\phi(i) = j$, then the untouched black record read from the database at this step is re-encrypted and written back to position j,
   - if $\phi(i) = j$, then the ith cached record is re-encrypted and written into position j; the untouched black record read into the cache is retained in the cache.
3. After reading all m positions, the contents of the cache is flushed into the k remaining places of black records. k steps are executed, numbered $m + 1$ through $m + k$. At step j:

- if $\phi(i) = j$, then the ith cache record is re-encrypted and stored in position j,
- if there is no i such that $\phi(i) = j$, then one of the untouched black records left in the cache is written to position j. Namely, this is the untouched black record that is in the cache for the longest time.

Essentially, the procedure could be slightly different. Really important features for the proof are that:

- the positions for cache black records are chosen at random (by the choice of ϕ),
- and that the remaining black records are written in the way that is uniquely determined by ϕ (even if ϕ does not explicitly define the positions for records other than cache records).

This determinism requirement is counterintuitive, but it is really necessary to prove privacy properties.

1.3   Basic Scheme and Privacy Issues

For the so called *Basic Scheme*, the authors of [10] assume that T can keep information concerning black records, so that it knows all positions of black records in the database (and so all positions of white elements), and the position of each single black element.

Of course, in certain situations this assumption is unrealistic – in order to keep a database in a cloud T has to store a database of about the same number of records internally! On the other hand, if the number of records is relatively low but the records are long, this might be feasible. The mechanism used to work in the general case will be described in Sect. 3.

In [10], it has been proved that an observer looses control over location of a single black record. Namely, they show:

Lemma 1 (Uniform Shuffle), page 70 : probability that a given black position contains a given black record is $1/b$, where b is the current number of the black records.

Lemma 2 (Uniform Access), page 70: given the past access pattern, and two positions: x of a black record and y of the white record, then the probability that x and y are chosen at the current step conditioned on the current query, is the same for each query.

Privacy challenges. At a first look it may seem that Lemma 1 from [10] shows that the black records are permuted uniformly at random. However, this is not the case: the difference is in fact dramatic. To see it assume that the shuffling scheme has the property that at each step a circular shift is performed, with the new item appended immediately after the last item appended so far. For such a procedure, if the circular shifts are chosen uniformly at random, the position of a given item is uniformly distributed. On the other hand, if two items are next to each other they remain to be neighbors. Hence in particular, if an adversary learns a position of a single item, he will learn positions of all items. On the other hand, the adversary can always provoke the user to fetch some known black record. Therefore, the whole allocation of the black records would be revealed. This is true despite that Lemma 1 holds for such permuting method.

Fortunately, the procedure of handling the black records does not even remotely resemble the example with circular shifts. However, there might be serious doubts about quality of shuffling due to the following fact:

Proposition 1. *Consider a shuffling procedure that starts with k elements and m black records in the database, and such that:*

- *each black position is read exactly once,*
- *the black positions are read in some fixed predefined order,*
- *after reading a black record, some black record (may be the same) is immediately written into the same position.*

The number of permutations on the set of $m+k$ positions that can be generated by this procedure is not higher than $k^m \cdot k!$. Hence, the ratio of these permutations to the number of all permutations on $m + k$ positions is at most

$$\frac{k^m \cdot k!}{(m+k)!} \leq \frac{k^m \cdot k^{k+0.5} \cdot e^{-k+1/12k}}{(m+k)^{m+k+0.5} \cdot e^{-m-k+1/(12(m+k)+1)}} \approx (\frac{k}{m+k})^{m+k+0.5} \cdot e^m \ .$$

In particular, if $5k < m$, then the above fraction is lower than 2^{-m}.

Proposition 1 shows how difficult it is to permute at random a set of elements if the permutation must be performed in place, apart from a small cache memory. In particular, if the procedure must work in a single pass through data, then only an exponentially small fraction of permutations can be obtained.

Due to Proposition 1, one cannot claim that rewriting of black records at the end of epoch is a random permutation of the black records. It is not even remotely related to a uniform one. Therefore, it is fully justified to ask the the following question:

Problem 1. *What is the probability distribution of the allocation of black records conditioned by the information available for the external observer seeing all read and write operations performed by T.*

Our main result in the next section will be that this probability distribution is uniform in a model with a powerful adversary, despite all problems observed.

2   Privacy for the Basic Scheme

When we consider the probability distribution of the black records we condition it on the following information that we call *access pattern*. For each step, the access pattern specifies

- the positions from which the black records has been fetched to the cache,
- the values of these black records.

Access pattern contains all information that potentially can be available for an attacker in the most pessimistic situation. In particular, an adversary can somehow know all queries asked by the database owner until the current moment. However, we assume that an observer can neither corrupt the device T nor break ciphertexts produced by T.

Below we use the following notation:

- let the black records read up to the end of epoch t be denoted by $d_{r(t,1)}, \ldots,$ $d_{r(t,z)}$ for $z = k + (t-1) \cdot \frac{k}{2}$, where $r(t,j) < r(t,j+1)$ for each $j < z$,
- let at the end of epoch t the (black) positions of the black records in the database will be denoted by $p_1, \ldots, p_z$, where $p_j < p_{j+1}$ for each $j < z$ according to some fixed ordering of positions in the database.
- let π_t indicate the allocation of the black records to the black positions, that is, immediately after epoch t let $d_{r(t,i)}$ be stored in $p_{\pi_t(i)}$.

For an observer aware of an access pattern A up to the end of epoch t, the permutation π_t is a random variable. We are interested in probability distribution of this random variable in the set of all permutations over $\{1, 2, \ldots, k + (t-1) \cdot \frac{k}{2}\}$. We prove the following theorem that says that we achieve perfect shuffling of all black records:

Theorem 1. *Probability distribution of π_t conditioned on the access pattern A observed up to the end of epoch t is uniform in the set of all permutations over $\{1, 2, \ldots, k + (t-1) \cdot \frac{k}{2}\}$.*

Before we start the proof, let us emphasize that Theorem 1 does not say that there are no correlations between the permutations π_{t-1} and π_t. In fact, there are very strong correlations due to the fact that shuffling at the end of epoch t is quite restricted by the small size of the cache memory used. So in fact Theorem 1 shows that the initial randomness of allocation of the records is maintained despite all information revealed and seemingly imperfect shuffling at the end of each epoch.

Proof. The proof is by induction on t. For $t = 1$, the claim of the theorem is obvious, since T permutes at random all black records (as they are stored in the cache).

Now let us consider the essential case of $t > 1$. Let σ denote the injection chosen by T for execution at the end of epoch t. Note that σ determines some of the values of π_t. Namely, if $d_{r,i_1}, \ldots, d_{r,i_k}$ are all cache records at epoch t, then $\pi_t(i_j) = \sigma(j)$ for $j \leq k$. Let $\pi_t \setminus \sigma$ denote π_t restricted to the arguments, for which the value is not defined by σ.

Since σ is chosen uniformly at random, it suffices to show that given a realization of the random variable σ, each realization of $\pi_t \setminus \sigma$ is equally probable. So let us consider a fixed mapping ζ that can be a value of $\pi_t \setminus \sigma$. We have to show that $\Pr(\pi_t \setminus \sigma = \zeta)$ does not depend on ζ.

Let us recall the procedure of flushing the cache and rewriting the black records in the database at the end of an epoch. The following claim follows directly from the construction:

Claim. Given σ, ζ and the positions of the elements from which the cache records have been read during epoch t, there is *exactly one* allocation of black records to black positions at the end of epoch $t - 1$.

Indeed, the procedure is deterministic in the sense that once we have σ, for each black record at the end of epoch t we can indicate its position at the end of epoch $t - 1$. If we have also ζ, then we can explicitly show the contents of each black position at the end of epoch $t - 1$.

Now we have to use the inductive hypothesis for epoch $t - 1$. It says that the allocation of black records is done according to uniform distribution over the set of permutations on $\{1, 2, \ldots, k + (t - 2) \cdot \frac{k}{2}\}$, conditioned on the access pattern restricted to epochs 1 through $t - 1$. In epoch t the observer learns positions some of the black records – namely those $k/2$ black records that are read into the cache. But still, the probability distribution of the remaining untouched black records is according to uniform distribution over the set of mappings to the remaining positions. So each such a mapping is achieved with some fixed probability q.

As we have seen above, each realization ζ of the random variable $\pi_t \setminus \sigma$ corresponds in a 1-1 fashion to a configuration of untouched black elements (from epoch t) at the beginning of the epoch t. Therefore each ζ has the same probability q. This terminates the proof of the claim that $\Pr(\pi_t \setminus \sigma = \zeta)$ does not depend on ζ. This terminates also the proof of the inductive step.   □

Let us finally remark that that there is a fine issue related to our model. If we consider π_t and the access pattern for more than t epochs, then it is no longer true that π_t is uniformly distributed. Indeed, an observer may learn some positions of black records by persuading the user to fetch some concrete black records. Nevertheless, this does not change the knowledge of the observer concerning the remaining black records. In this sense the algorithm of Yang et al. with our modification is very clever: if the observer forces the user to fetch some records, he does not learn anything about the other records, while on the other hand all information about the position of the records fetched is lost at the end of the epoch, when the cache is flushed.

3   General Scheme

The main problem with implementing Basic Scheme is that T needs to know, for each incoming query from the user, if it concerns a black or a white record. The problem is that the number of black records grows and quickly becomes much higher than the size of the cache. Of course, in some cases it is possible to keep this information – e.g. in form of Bloom filters. However, the authors of [10] make an effort to provide an efficient implementation that would work for any size of the database and of the records. In the solution proposed the information about black records is kept in a tree outside T, in the same area as the encrypted database.

Let us recall some details of the construction. Let D_s be the database after executing epoch s, let $b = k + (s - 1) \cdot \frac{k}{2}$ be the number of black records at this moment. The black records are represented by b pairs of tuples $\langle x, y \rangle$, where x is a position in D_0 and y is the corresponding position in D_s. T generates a sorted array L of half-encrypted pairs, i.e.

$$L = [(f_u(x_1), y_1), (f_u(x_2), y_2), \ldots, (f_u(x_b), y_b)] \, ,$$

where $y_1 < \ldots < y_b$, $f_u(x) = \mathcal{H}(e_u(x))$, $\mathcal{H}$ is a hash function and e_u is deterministic symmetric encryption with a secret key u.

T also builds a labeled binary search tree Γ, where the tuples in L are the leaves in Γ, each leaf labeled by its value $f_u(x)$. From the left to the right, the leaves are sorted in order of $f_u(x)$ values. The label of an inner node is an integer randomly chosen in the interval determined by the labels of its children.

At the beginning of each session, T chooses key u at random and generates L and Γ. Then they are stored by the system H responsible for holding database records in the cloud. Each time T needs to check if a record is black or white it communicates with H, asking for a leaf from tree Γ. Of course, T wants to hide the need for retrieving a black element, therefore this communication always takes place, but sometimes it involves picking a leaf from Γ at random. The search in tree Γ is performed via asking for the labels of the intermediate nodes. After receiving the label of a current node T says to H whether to go to the left son or to the right son of the current node.

Assuming that a record with index x is to be retrieved, the following situation needs to be considered:

the record is already in cache – T is aware of this fact and he chooses a leaf from Γ uniformly at random by coin toss at each of inner nodes of Γ.

the record is black but not in the cache – in this case the searched record is represented by some leaf in tree Γ (but T might be unaware of this). T runs a binary search for $f_u(\sigma(x))$ in Γ, the search terminates at a leaf $\langle f_u(\sigma(x)), y \rangle$, where y is the position in D_s of the requested item. T recognizes that the leaf corresponds to the item with index x by finding the value $f_u(x)$ in the leaf.

the record is white – this means that there is no representation of the record with index x in tree Γ. As in the previous case T runs a binary search for $f_u(\sigma(x))$ in Γ, the search terminates at a leaf $\langle f_u(x'), y \rangle$, where $x' \neq \sigma(x)$. As the searched item is not in Γ, the element with index y is chosen as the random black element to be fetched. Then the search continues in the set of white elements.

After determining a black element to be fetched to T, a white element is chosen. This is facilitated by the fact that the white elements are not relocated since the initial placement. However, it is necessary to keep track which positions are already occupied by black records. This is done by an appropriate data structure.

From the H's perspective determining a black record to be fetched is performed by a walk on tree Γ from the root to one of its leafs, according to the instructions obtained from T.

3.1   Information Leakage

The construction adapted for the general case is quite clever, but still causes some problems. We start with relatively simple issues and end up with the most complicated problem of non-uniformity of the interval lengths.

Number of collisions. The first source of information leakage is occurrence of collisions when searching black records. By a collision we mean here choosing the same leaf in Γ as before in the same epoch. To understand what is the mechanism of collisions consider two situations:

case 1: the user makes no repetitions – always asks about the records he has not seen since initialization,
case 2: the user is repeatedly asking for the same $k/2$ records.

In the first case the elements sought are never represented in Γ – so the search in Γ always fails and each time a random black record is fetched. The procedure can therefore be described by a process of throwing balls into bins. Of course, as long as the number of bins is not high compared to the number of balls it may happen with a fairly high probability that one bin obtains more than one ball. Such collisions become rare, if the number of bins is at least quadratic in the number of balls. If the number of balls and bins are not far from each other, then there are not only collisions, but also some bins with relatively many balls.

In the second case, when search is performed in the tree of black records, it is always successful and never a hit occurs at the same leaf of the tree as before in the same epoch. The point is that such an access pattern to the leaves of the tree of black records has quite low probability, if the first case occurs. So we see that an observer can derive some information about the behavior of the user.

Of course, one can apply diverse countermeasures, like starting with some dummy operations so that the number of black records reaches some minimal value. Still this is a heuristic approach without firm analytic guarantees.

Repeated hit. Now consider again a situation when during an epoch the same leaf of the tree of black elements is reached. Let x be the black record corresponding to this leaf. This situation shows that the user is either asking for a white element (and the repetition is due to the process of random search of a leaf in the tree), or the user is asking for a black element already in the cache (again, the procedure will choose a random leaf in the tree of black records). However, it is impossible that the user is asking for a black record not seen during this epoch.

3.2   Uniformity of leafs in Γ

Since the hash function $\mathcal{H}$ should behave like a random function, the black records are represented in leaf of Γ in an order that seem to be chosen uniformly at random. So searching for a black record looks like choosing a leaf at random. As we shall see below, this is not true when the searched record with index x is white.

Let us simplify consideration and treat $\mathcal{H}$ as a random assignment with a range $[0, 1]$, where each value is determined by choosing a point in $[0, 1]$ uniformly at random. A similar simplification was used for investigation of Chord P2P network [6,2].

Let $X_1, \ldots X_n$ be random variables representing independent uniformly distributed (over the interval $[0, 1]$) values $f_u(x_j) = \mathcal{H}(e_u(x))$. Leafs of Γ are ordered according to the order statistics

$$X_{(1)} < X_{(2)} < \ldots < X_{(|B|)} \; .$$

The set $\{X_{(1)}, \ldots, X_{(n)}\}$ induces a partition of $[0, 1]$ into $n + 1$ subintervals, whose lengths will be denoted by $x_1, \ldots, x_{n+1}$.

It is obvious that the expected value of the length of uniformly chosen interval equals to $\frac{1}{n+1}$. This is why, the authors of [10] suggest that the probability of stopping at particular leaf of Γ tree while searching for a white record is $\frac{1}{n+1}$. However, this may not be true in particular situations. In fact, with a high probability significant differences may appear between the interval of the minimal length $m_{n+1} = \min\{x_1, \ldots, x_{n+1}\}$, the interval with the maximal length $M_{n+1} = \max\{x_1, \ldots, x_{n+1}\}$, and the average length of the random interval. To be more precise, it has been shown that

$$E[m_{n+1}] = \frac{1}{(n+1)^2} \; ,$$

while

$$E[M_{n+1}] = \frac{\ln n + 1 + \gamma}{n+1} + o(\frac{1}{n+1}) \; .$$

As noticed in [11] for every $\delta_1 \geq 0, \ldots, \delta_{n+1} \geq 0$ the following formula holds

$$\Pr[x_1 > \delta_1, \ldots, x_{n+1} > \delta_{n+1}] = (1 - (\delta_1 + \ldots + \delta_{n+1}))^n.$$

From this formula, we get

$$\Pr[m_{n+1} > \delta] = (1 - (n+1)\delta)^n.$$

When we set $\delta = E[m_{n+1}] = \frac{1}{(n+1)^2}$ we immediately deduce that

$$\Pr\left[m_{n+1} > \frac{1}{(n+1)^2}\right] = \left(1 - \frac{1}{n+1}\right)^n.$$

This means, that the probability that there is a interval of length smaller or equal to $\frac{1}{(n+1)^2}$ is, already for relatively small n, close to $1 - \frac{1}{e} \approx 0.632121$. Since the number of epochs can be quite high, the probability that such an event (a significantly shorter interval corresponding to a leaf of Γ) occurs at all is even higher.

Notice that if the search procedure in Γ terminates in a leaf corresponding to a small interval, then the observer may tend to assume that the search was for a black element and not for a white one.

Of course, the analysis presented so far does not exactly concern the situation of the intervals in the tree Γ – there are subtle mathematical issues related to the choice of labels of internal nodes. However, the problem still exists: the fake search of a black element chooses the leaves of Γ uniformly at random, while behavior of the search performed for white records depends very much on the size of intervals corresponding to the leaves of Γ. This difference is hard to hide, even if the number of black records is already high.

One method of alleviating the problems mentioned above is to modify the search in Γ: instead of terminating the search in a leaf of Γ, one can stop the search one level above the leaves and return both leaves below the current node. The idea is that the lengths of the intervals corresponding to nodes at level 1 are much more uniform than the lengths of the intervals corresponding to the leaves. To understand this phenomenon consider again the random variables $X_1, \ldots X_n$ representing independent uniformly distributed (over the interval $[0, 1]$) values $f_u(x_j) = \mathcal{H}(e_u(x))$. The length of intervals corresponding to the nodes at level 1 are related to the values $x_i + x_{i+1}$, in the sense that if none of these sums is small, then also none of the intervals corresponding to the nodes at level 1 should be small. Let us recall a result from [3, Theorem 3] which says that the expected number of i's such that

$$x_i + x_{i+1} \leq \frac{\sqrt{2}}{n^{1.5}}$$

converges to 1 with $n \to \infty$ and converges to zero for

$$x_i + x_{i+1} \leq \frac{\sqrt{2}}{n^{1.5+c}}$$

and $c > 0$. So we see that the shortest interval has the length of order $1/n^{1.5}$ instead of $1/n^2$.

The downside of stopping at level 1 is that we retrieve 2 black elements instead of 1. This makes flushing the cache more frequent.

4   Open Problems and Conclusions

As proved before, the smart way of retrieving elements and mixing them up preserves the user's privacy defined in [10]. However, when considering the suggested implementation of those ideas one have to be careful. Namely, we know the situations in which the adversary with probability significantly higher than $1/2$ can distinguish whether the user is interested in black or white element. This of course violates the twin retrieval policy, and therefore leads to a violation of PIR security definition from [10].

Even if we have seen that the general scheme proposed in [10] leaks some information, it does not mean that it has been broken. We only show that further investigations are necessary for estimating difference between probability distributions for the access patterns in the basic case and the probability distribution for access patterns conditioned by the information seen by an observer for the full implementation. This difference should be stated in terms of such privacy measures as variation distance between probability distributions.

The main problem is determining whether a record asked by the user is black or not. So the problem would be solved, if we could find a data structure to be used in the cloud that would enable testing if a given record is black without revealing any information to the observer. As we have seen in Sect. 3.2, some countermeasures providing partial solutions are possible; their effectiveness in the practical setting should be investigated.

References

1. Chor, B., Kushilevitz, E., Goldreich, O., Sudan, M.: Private information retrieval. In: Proceedings of IEEE FOCS 1995, pp. 41–50 (1995)
2. Cichoń, J., Klonowski, M., Krzywiecki, Ł., Różański, B., Zieliński, P.: Random Subsets of the Interval and P2P Protocols. In: Charikar, M., Jansen, K., Reingold, O., Rolim, J.D.P. (eds.) RANDOM 2007 and APPROX 2007. LNCS, vol. 4627, pp. 409–421. Springer, Heidelberg (2007)
3. Cichoń, J., Kapelko, R., Marchwicki, K.: Uniformity of improved versions of Chord. In: Zhu, R., Zhang, Y., Liu, B., Liu, C. (eds.) ICICA 2010. LNCS, vol. 6377, pp. 431–438. Springer, Heidelberg (2010)
4. Iliev, A., Smith, S.: Private information storage with logarithm-space secure hardware. In: Proceedings of International Information Security Workshops, pp. 199–214 (2004)
5. Iliev, A., Smith, S.: Protecting client privacy with trusted computing at the server. IEEE Security & Privacy 3(2), 20–28 (2005)
6. King, V., Saia, J.: Choosing a Random Peer. In: POD 2004. ACM, New York, 1581138024/04/0007 (2004)
7. Misztela, H.: Anonimization of access to data resources. Master Dissertation, Wrocław University of Technology, Institute of Mathematics and Computer Science (2010)
8. Ostrovsky, R., Skeith III, W.E.: A Survey of Single-Database Private Information Retrieval: Techniques and Applications. In: Okamoto, T., Wang, X. (eds.) PKC 2007. LNCS, vol. 4450, pp. 393–411. Springer, Heidelberg (2007)
9. Wang, S., Ding, X., Deng, R.H., Bao, F.: Private Information Retrieval Using Trusted Hardware. In: Gollmann, D., Meier, J., Sabelfeld, A. (eds.) ESORICS 2006. LNCS, vol. 4189, pp. 49–64. Springer, Heidelberg (2006)
10. Yang, Y., Ding, X., Deng, R.H., Bao, F.: An Efficient PIR Construction Using Trusted Hardware. In: Wu, T.-C., Lei, C.-L., Rijmen, V., Lee, D.-T. (eds.) ISC 2008. LNCS, vol. 5222, pp. 64–79. Springer, Heidelberg (2008)
11. Feller, W.: An Introduction to Probability Theory and Its Applications, vol. II. John Wiley and Sons Inc., New York (1992)

Algebraic Precomputations in Differential and Integral Cryptanalysis

Martin Albrecht[1], Carlos Cid[1], Thomas Dullien[2],
Jean-Charles Faugère[3], and Ludovic Perret[3]

[1] Information Security Group, Royal Holloway, University of London
Egham, Surrey TW20 0EX, United Kingdom
{M.R.Albrecht,carlos.cid}@rhul.ac.uk
[2] Lehrstuhl für Kryptologie und IT-Sicherheit, Ruhr-Universität Bochum
44780 Bochum, Germany
Thomas.Dullien@ruhr-uni-bochum.de
[3] SALSA Project - INRIA (Centre Paris-Rocquencourt)
UPMC, Univ Paris 06 - CNRS, UMR 7606, LIP6
104, avenue du Président Kennedy 75016 Paris, France
jean-charles.faugere@inria.fr, ludovic.perret@lip6.fr

Abstract. Algebraic cryptanalysis is a general tool which permits one to assess the security of a wide range of cryptographic schemes. Algebraic techniques have been successfully applied against a number of multivariate schemes and stream ciphers. Yet, their feasibility against block ciphers remains the source of much speculation. In this context, algebraic techniques have mainly been deployed in order to solve a system of equations arising from the cipher, so far with limited success. In this work we propose a different approach: to use Gröbner basis techniques to compute *structural* features of block ciphers, which may then be used to improve "classical" differential and integral attacks. We illustrate our techniques against the block ciphers PRESENT and KTANTAN32.

1 Introduction

Algebraic cryptanalysis is a general tool which permits one to assess the security of a wide range of cryptographic schemes [21,20,19,17,18,23,24,22]. As pointed out in the report [13], *"the recent proposal and development of algebraic cryptanalysis is now widely considered an important breakthrough in the analysis of cryptographic primitives"*. The basic principle of algebraic cryptanalysis is to model a cryptographic primitive by a set of algebraic equations. The system of equations is constructed in such a way as to have a correspondence between its solutions and some secret information of the cryptographic primitive (for instance, the secret key of a block cipher). The secret can thus be derived by solving the equation system.

Such algebraic techniques have been successfully applied against a number of multivariate schemes and in stream cipher cryptanalysis. On the other hand,

X. Lai, M. Yung, and D. Lin (Eds.): Inscrypt 2010, LNCS 6584, pp. 387–403, 2011.

their feasibility against block ciphers remains the source of much speculation [15,14,19]. One of the reasons is that the sizes of the resulting equation systems are usually beyond the capabilities of current solving algorithms. Furthermore, the complexity estimates are complicated as the algebraic systems are highly structured; a situation where known complexity bounds are no longer valid [4,2,3].

While it is currently infeasible to *cryptanalyse* a block cipher by algebraic means alone, these techniques nonetheless have practical applications for block cipher cryptanalysis. For instance, Albrecht and Cid proposed in [1] to combine differential cryptanalysis with algebraic attacks and demonstrated the feasibility of their techniques against reduced-round versions of the block cipher PRESENT [7]. In this approach, the key recovery was approached by solving (or showing lack of solutions in) equation systems that were much simpler than the one arising from the full cipher.

In this paper, we further shift the focus away from attempting to solve the full system of equations. Instead, we use Gröbner basis techniques to compute *structural features* of block ciphers. It turns out that significant information can be gained without solving the equation system in the classical sense. This information, computed via algebraic means, can in turn be potentially used to improve other, "non-algebraic" cryptanalytic methods. We illustrate our techniques by considering the differential cryptanalysis of reduced-round variants of PRESENT and KTANTAN32 [11], as well bit-pattern based integral attacks against PRESENT [31].

The paper is organised as follows. In Section 2 we briefly recall some of the cryptanalytic concepts of relevance to this paper. In Section 3 we provide a high-level description of the main idea behind this work, and briefly describe the ciphers that we use to demonstrate our ideas. These ideas are then applied to improve differential cryptanalysis (Section 4) and integral cryptanalysis (Section 5); experimental results are also presented in both sections.

2   Block Cipher Cryptanalysis

Differential cryptanalysis was formally introduced by Biham and Shamir in [6], and has since been successfully used to attack a wide range of block ciphers. By considering the distribution of output *differences* for the non-linear components of the cipher (e.g. the S-Box), the attacker may be able to construct *differential characteristics* $P' \oplus P'' = \Delta P \to \Delta C = C' \oplus C''$ for a number of rounds N that are valid with non-negligible probability p. A plaintext pair (P', P'') for which the characteristic holds is called a *right pair*, and this behaviour may be used to distinguish the cipher from a random permutation. By modifying the attack, one may use it to potentially recover key information: instead of characteristics for the full N-round cipher, the attacker considers characteristics valid for r rounds only ($r = N - R$, with $R > 0$). The attacker can partially decrypt the known ciphertexts and verify if the result matches the one predicted by the characteristic. Candidate (last round) keys are counted, and as random noise is expected for wrong key guesses, eventually a peak may be observed in the candidate key counters, pointing to the correct round key.

The chances of success and data requirements of differential attacks are typically estimated based on the idea of *signal to noise ratio*. Assume such a differential attack, making use of m plaintext pairs. If the attacker is attempting to recover k subkey bits, it can count the number of occurrences of the possible key values in 2^k counters. If β is the ratio of discarded pairs, based on some criteria to *filter* wrong pairs (e.g. ciphertext difference), and α is the average number of k-bit subkeys suggested by each pair, we expect the counters to contain on average $(m \cdot \alpha \cdot \beta)/2^k$ counts. The right subkey value is counted $m \cdot p$ times due to right pairs, plus the random counts for all the possible subkeys. The signal to noise ratio is therefore:

$$S/N = \frac{m \cdot p}{m \cdot \alpha \cdot \beta / 2^k} = \frac{2^k \cdot p}{\alpha \cdot \beta}.$$

Albrecht and Cid considered in [1] several ideas on how to use algebraic techniques to improve "classical" differential cryptanalysis. In the most promising method, named in [1] *Attack-C*, Gröbner basis computations (applied to the algebraic system arising from the outer rounds in differential cryptanalysis) are used to distinguish right pairs. These Gröbner basis computations could however only be performed during the online phase of the attack. This limitation prevented them from applying their techniques to PRESENT-80 with more than 16 rounds, since computation time would exceed exhaustive key search. In this work, we extend the idea but take a different approach: we only perform Gröbner basis computations in a precomputation (or offline) phase. We show that these computations can also be used to improve the success of differential attacks (for instance, one can increase the signal to noise ratio S/N by using algebraic techniques).

Integral attacks were originally proposed for byte-oriented ciphers such as the AES, and can be viewed as a special form of higher-order differential attacks [27]. In such an attack, one uses sets of plaintexts that satisfy a particular structure (e.g. take on all possible values in one byte and a fixed arbitrary value in all other plaintext bytes). For some ciphers this leads to a predictable feature relating the ciphertexts after a few rounds, which in turn may be used to attack the cipher. In [31] Reza Z'Aba et al. extend the notion of integral attacks to bit-oriented ciphers, considering the block ciphers PRESENT, NOEKEON and SERPENT.

The first work combining algebraic and higher-order differential attacks is [25] by Faugère and Perret. The authors used higher-order differentials to explain the improved runtime of their Gröbner basis algorithms against the Curry and Flurry families of block ciphers [10]. In this work, we also use algebraic techniques to improve integral cryptanalysis: we focus on recovering symbolic representations for relations that must hold on the output after a few rounds, illustrated on an attack against reduced-round variants of PRESENT.

3   Symbolic Precomputation in Block Ciphers

The main idea explored in this paper involves shifting the emphasis of previous algebraic attacks away from attempting to solve an equation system towards using *ideal membership as implication*. In others words, instead of trying to solve an equation system arising from the cipher to recover secret key information, we use Gröbner basis methods to compute what a particular input pattern *implies*.

We use a small example to illustrate the main idea. Consider the block cipher PRESENT [7]. Its 4-bit S-Box can be completely described by a set of polynomials that express each output bit in terms of the input bits. Let $X_{i,j}$ and $Y_{i,j}$ denote the jth input and output bits of the ith S-Box, respectively. In differential cryptanalysis, one considers a *pair* of inputs $X'_{i,0}, \ldots, X'_{i,3}$ and $X''_{i,0}, \ldots, X''_{i,3}$ and the corresponding output bits $Y'_{i,0}, \ldots, Y'_{i,3}$ and $Y''_{i,0}, \ldots, Y''_{i,3}$. Since the output bits are described as polynomials in the input bits, it is easy to build a set of polynomials describing the parallel application of the S-Box to the pair of input bits. For example, assume the fixed input difference of $(0, 0, 0, 1)$ holds for this S-Box. This can be described algebraically by adding the equations $X'_{i,3} + X''_{i,3} = 1$, $X'_{i,j} + X''_{i,j} = 0$ for $0 \leq j < 3$ to the set. As usual, we add to this system (as well as in all calculations performed in this work) the field equations $X_{i,j}^2 + X_{i,j} = 0$ and $Y_{i,j}^2 + Y_{i,j} = 0$.

The set of equations now forms a description of the parallel application of the S-Box to two inputs with a fixed input difference. The ideal I spanned by these polynomials contains *all* polynomials that are *implied* by the set. If all polynomials in the generating set of the ideal evaluate to zero, it is clear that any element of I will also evaluate to zero. In particular *any polynomial in the ideal will vanish* if it is assigned values corresponding to the application of the S-Box with a pair of inputs with the above-mentioned input difference.

From a cryptographic point of view, it may be desirable to understand what relations between output bits will hold for a particular input difference. This can be done by considering the polynomials in *the output bits only* that are contained in I. Algebraically, we are trying to find elements in the ideal $I_Y = I \bigcap \mathbb{F}_2[Y'_{i,0}, \ldots, Y'_{i,3}, Y''_{i,0}, \ldots, Y''_{i,3}]$, where I is the ideal spanned by our original equations.

A *deglex* Gröbner basis G_Y of this ideal can be computed using standard elimination techniques.[1] For this, we can for example set up a block or product ordering where all output variables are lexicographically smaller than any other variable in the system. In addition, we fix the *deglex* ordering among the output variables. Computing the Gröbner basis with respect to such an ordering gives us the Gröbner basis G_Y of I_Y. We note that G_Y will contain the relations of lowest degree of I_Y due to the choice of term ordering. In our example we have:

---

[1] We refer the reader unfamiliar with Gröbner bases theory and techniques to [5] for the algebraic geometry concepts relevant to the remaining of this section.

$$G_Y = [Y'_{i,3} + Y''_{i,3} + 1,$$
$$Y'_{i,0} + Y'_{i,2} + Y''_{i,0} + Y''_{i,2} + 1,$$
$$Y''_{i,0}Y''_{i,2} + Y'_{i,2} + Y''_{i,0} + Y''_{i,1} + Y''_{i,3},$$
$$Y''_{i,0}Y''_{i,1} + Y''_{i,0}Y''_{i,3} + Y''_{i,1}Y''_{i,2} + Y''_{i,2}Y''_{i,3} + Y'_{i,1} + Y''_{i,0} + Y''_{i,1},$$
$$Y'_{i,2}Y''_{i,2} + Y''_{i,1}Y''_{i,2} + Y''_{i,2}Y''_{i,3},$$
$$Y'_{i,2}Y''_{i,0} + Y''_{i,1}Y''_{i,2} + Y''_{i,2}Y''_{i,3} + Y'_{i,1} + Y'_{i,2} + Y''_{i,0} + Y''_{i,3},$$
$$Y'_{i,1}Y''_{i,2} + Y'_{i,2}Y''_{i,1} + Y'_{i,2}Y''_{i,3} + Y''_{i,1}Y''_{i,2} + Y'_{i,1} + Y'_{i,2} + Y''_{i,1},$$
$$Y'_{i,1}Y''_{i,1} + Y''_{i,1}Y''_{i,3} + Y''_{i,1}Y''_{i,2} + Y''_{i,1}Y''_{i,3} + Y''_{i,2}Y''_{i,3} + Y''_{i,1},$$
$$Y'_{i,1}Y''_{i,0} + Y'_{i,2}Y''_{i,1} + Y'_{i,2}Y''_{i,3} + Y''_{i,0}Y''_{i,3} + Y''_{i,1}Y''_{i,2} + Y''_{i,2}Y''_{i,3} + Y'_{i,1} + Y''_{i,3},$$
$$Y'_{i,1}Y'_{i,2} + Y'_{i,2}Y''_{i,3} + Y''_{i,1}Y''_{i,2} + Y''_{i,2}Y''_{i,3} + Y'_{i,2}].$$

There is no other linear or quadratic polynomial $p \in I_Y$ which is not a simple algebraic combination of the polynomials in G_Y. In other words, all *simple* relations involving only the output bits can be derived in a straightforward way from the set G_Y.

In order to formalise this idea, consider a function $\mathcal{E}$ (for example a block cipher), and assume $\mathcal{E}$ can be expressed as a set of algebraic equations F over a finite field $\mathbb{F}$. We can consider d parallel applications of $\mathcal{E}$, with inputs and outputs $P_0, \ldots, P_{d-1}$ and $C_0, \ldots, C_{d-1}$, respectively, and denote the corresponding polynomial systems by F_i. Now assume some property Λ holds on $P_0, \ldots, P_{d-1}$, and can be expressed by a set of algebraic equations F_Λ. A natural question to ask is: how do properties on the input set $P_0, \ldots, P_{d-1}$ affect properties on the output set $C_0, \ldots, C_{d-1}$?

We can simply combine the equation systems into the set $\overline{F} = F_\Lambda \cup (\bigcup_{i=0}^{d-1} F_i)$ and consider the ideal $I = \langle \overline{F} \rangle$. As discussed above, the unique reduced Gröbner basis G_C of the ideal $I_C = I \cap \mathbb{F}[C_0, \ldots, C_{d-1}]$ contains all "relevant" polynomials in $C_0, \ldots, C_{d-1}$, where "relevant" is determined by the term ordering. As soon as we compute the Gröbner basis G_C for the d parallel applications of the function $\mathcal{E}$, we only need to collect the right polynomials from G_C to obtain the properties on the output set $C_0, \ldots, C_{d-1}$ which are implied by Λ.

We note however that for many functions $\mathcal{E}$, computing G_C may be infeasible using current Gröbner basis techniques, implementations and computing power. Thus in practice, we may need to relax some conditions hoping that we still can recover useful information using a similar technique. We provide below a few heuristics and techniques that may still allow recovering *some* relevant equations.

Early Abort. To recover some properties we might not need to compute the complete Gröbner basis; instead we may opt to stop the computation at some degree D.

Replacing Symbols by Constants. It is possible to replace the symbols P_0, $\ldots, P_{d-1}$ by some constants (values) satisfying the constraint Λ which further simplifies the computation. Of course any polynomial recovered from such a computation would have to be checked against other values to verify whether it actually holds in general or with high probability.

Choosing a Different Term Ordering. Instead of computing with respect to an elimination ordering, which is usually more expensive than a degree compatible ordering, we may choose to perform our computations with respect to a more efficient ordering such as *degrevlex*. Used together with **Early Abort**, we have no assurances about the completeness of the recovered system; yet we might still be able to recover some useful information.

3.1 Block Ciphers

We briefly introduce the block ciphers used to demonstrate our techniques.

PRESENT [7] was proposed at CHES 2007 as an ultra-lightweight block cipher, enabling a very compact implementation in hardware, and therefore particularly suitable for RFIDs and similar devices. There are two variants of PRESENT: one for 80-bit keys and one for 128-bit keys, denoted as PRESENT-80 and PRESENT-128 respectively.

PRESENT is an SP-network with a blocksize of 64 bits and both versions have 31 rounds. Each round of the cipher has three layers of operations: keyAddLayer, sBoxLayer and pLayer. The operation keyAddLayer is a simple subkey addition to the current state, while the sBoxLayer operation consists of 16 parallel applications of a 4-bit S-Box. The operation pLayer is a permutation of wires. In this work we consider round-reduced variants of PRESENT denoted PRESENT-Ks-Nr where $Ks \in \{80, 128\}$ and the number of rounds is $0 < Nr \leq 31$.

The designers of PRESENT give a security analysis of their cipher by showing resistance against well-known attacks such as differential and linear cryptanalysis [7]. The best published differential attacks are for 16 rounds of PRESENT-80 [30] and 17 (and possibly up to 19) rounds [1] for PRESENT-128. Results on linear cryptanalysis for up to 26 rounds are available in [12,26]. Bit-pattern based integral attacks [31] are successful up to seven rounds of PRESENT. A new type of attack, called statistical saturation attack, was proposed in [16] and expected to be applicable to up to 24 rounds of PRESENT.

KTANTAN32 was proposed at CHES 2009 and is the smallest cipher in a family of block ciphers proposed in [11]. It allows a very compact implementation in hardware. It has a blocksize of 32 bits and accepts an 80-bit key. The input is loaded into two registers L_2 and L_1 of 19 and 13 bit length respectively. A round transformation is then applied to these registers 254 times. This round function updates two bits using a quadratic function and performs rotations on the registers. After 254 rounds the content of L_2 and L_1 is output as the ciphertext.

The designers of KTANTAN consider a wide range of attacks in their security argument and show evidence that the cipher is secure against differential, linear, impossible differential, algebraic attacks, as well as some combined attacks. However strong cryptanalytic results against the cipher have recently been proposed in [8].

4   Algebraic Precomputation in Differential Cryptanalysis

In this section we show how to use the techniques discussed previously to improve the differential cryptanalysis of some block ciphers. More specifically, we attempt to increase the chances of success of such an attack by increasing the signal to noise ratio S/N; we illustrate the method against reduce-round versions of PRESENT and KTANTAN32.

4.1   Reducing the Noise

We briefly recall the basic principles of the main attack proposed in [1]. The proposed technique (referred to as *Attack-C*) was used to discard wrong pairs during a differential attack. The attacker would consider the equation systems modelling only the rounds $> r$ (the R outer rounds in the differential attack based on a characteristic valid for r rounds) for each plaintext–ciphertext pair. We denote these equation systems arising from the encryption of P' to C' and P'' to C'', by F'_R and F''_R respectively. The algebraic part of *Attack-C* of [1] consists of a Gröbner basis computation on the polynomial system

$$F = F'_R \cup F''_R \cup \{X'_{r+1,i} + X''_{r+1,i} + \delta X_{r+1,i}\},$$

where the last set refers to the (linear) polynomials arising from the output difference $\delta X_{r+1,i}$ predicted by the characteristic. Whenever the Gröbner basis of the ideal $\langle F \rangle$ is equivalent to $\{1\}$, we know that the system has no solution, and the pair (P', P'') cannot be a right pair (it can thus be discarded). We note however that no strong assurances are given in [1] as to how many pairs are actually discarded by this technique (we refer the reader to [1] for a more detailed description of the proposed algebraic techniques in differential cryptanalysis).

In the present work, we consider the same system of equations as in *Attack-C* but replace the values of C' and C'' by symbols (i.e. variables). By computing a Gröbner basis for the right elimination ordering (cf. Section 3), we can recover relations in the variables C' and C'' that must evaluate to zero whenever the input difference for round $r+1$ holds. We note that this computation can be done *offline*, as the actual values for the plaintexts and ciphertexts are not required. These equations may be used to improve the quality of the algebraic *filter* used to discard wrong pairs (in other words, to decrease the value of β in the expression of S/N). An estimate about the quality of this filter can calculated by computing the probability that the polynomials obtained evaluate to zero for random values of C' and C''.

4.2   Case Study: PRESENT

We consider the differential from [30] and construct filters for PRESENT reduced to $14 + R$ rounds. The same filter also applies to $10 + R$, $6 + R$ and $2 + R$ rounds since the characteristic is iterative with a period of four rounds. The explicit polynomials in this section do not differ for PRESENT-80 and PRESENT-128.

PRESENT 2R. We consider the polynomial ring

$$P = \mathbb{F}_2[\, K_{0,0}, \ldots, K_{0,79}, \; K_{1,0}, \ldots, K_{1,63},$$
$$Y'_{1,0}, \ldots, Y'_{1,63}, \quad Y''_{1,0}, \ldots, Y''_{1,63}, \quad X'_{1,0}, \ldots, X'_{1,63}, \quad X''_{1,0}, \ldots, X''_{1,63},$$
$$\ldots, \qquad K_{15,0}, \ldots, K_{15,3},$$
$$Y'_{15,0}, \ldots, Y'_{15,63}, Y''_{15,0}, \ldots, Y''_{15,63}, X'_{15,0}, \ldots, X'_{15,63}, X''_{15,0}, \ldots, X''_{15,63},$$
$$Y'_{16,0}, \ldots, Y'_{16,63}, Y''_{16,0}, \ldots, Y''_{16,63}, X'_{16,0}, \ldots, X'_{16,63}, X''_{16,0}, \ldots, X''_{16,63},$$
$$C'_0, \ldots, C'_{63}, \qquad C''_0, \ldots, C''_{63}]$$

and use the following block ordering:

$$\underbrace{K_{0,0}, \ldots, X''_{16,63}}_{\text{degrevlex}}, \underbrace{C'_0, \ldots, C'_{63}, C''_0, \ldots, C''_{63}}_{\text{degrevlex}}.$$

We set up an equation system as in [1], except that the ciphertext bits are symbols (C'_i and C''_i). Then, we compute the Gröbner basis up to degree $D = 3$) using POLYBORI 0.6.3 [9,29] with the option deg_bound=3 and filter out any polynomial that contains non-ciphertext variables.

This computation returns 64 polynomials, 46 of which are linear. Forty linear polynomials are of the form $C'_i + C''_i$ and encode the information that the last round output difference of 10 S-Boxes must be zero (cf. [30]). The remaining 24 polynomials are split into two sets F_0, F_2 of 12 polynomials in 24 variables each; furthermore the sets F_j do not share any variables with each other or the first 40 linear polynomials. The systems F_j are listed in Figure 2 in the Appendix. The probability that all polynomials evaluate to zero for a random point is $\approx 2^{-50.669}$. We recall that Wang's filter from [30] passes with probability $2^{-40} \cdot (5/16)^6 \approx 2^{-50.07}$. Thus, our filter improves upon Wang's by a factor of $2^{0.59} \approx 1.51$.

In order to estimate how close to optimal our filter is, we construct random pairs C', C'' which pass our polynomial filter and notice that for *Attack-C* from [1] mounted using a SAT-solver, roughly every second such pair for PRESENT-80 and 317 out of 512 for PRESENT-128 will pass. Thus, the most precise filter that can be constructed only using the ciphertext bits and the output difference of round r will accept a pair with probability $\approx 2^{-51.669}$ for PRESENT-80 and with probability $\approx 2^{-51.361}$ for PRESENT-128.

PRESENT 3R. We extend the ring and the block ordering in the obvious way and compute a Gröbner basis with degree bound 3. The computation returns 28 polynomials, 16 of which are linear. The linear polynomials have the form $C'_i + C''_i$ for

$$i \in \{3, 7, 11, 15, 19, 23, 27, 31, 35, 39, 43, 47, 51, 55, 59, 63\}.$$

The remaining 12 polynomials are quadratic and cubic (cf. Figure 3 in the Appendix). The probability that all polynomials evaluate to zero on a random point is $\approx 2^{-18.296}$. In order to estimate how close to optimal this filter is, we construct random pairs C', C'' which pass this polynomial filter. *Attack-C* using a SAT-solver will accept roughly 6 in 1024 pairs for PRESENT-80 and 9 out of 1024 pairs for PRESENT-128. Thus, we expect an optimal filter – based on the output difference of round r and the ciphertext bits – to pass with probability $\approx 2^{-25.711}$ for PRESENT-80 and $2^{-25.126}$ for PRESENT-128. That is, there is a factor of $2^{7.4} \approx 168$ between our filter and this optimal filter.

PRESENT 4R. We again extend the ring and the block ordering in the obvious way and compute a Gröbner basis with degree bound 3, to we recover

$$(C'_{32+j} + C''_{32+j} + 1)(C'_j + C''_j + 1)(C'_{16+j} + C'_{48+j} + C''_{16+j} + C''_{48+j})$$

for $0 \leq j < 16$. The probability that all polynomials evaluate to zero on a random point is $\approx 2^{-3.082}$.

We verified experimentally that this bound is optimal by using the SAT solver CRYPTOMINISAT [28] on *Attack-C* systems in a 4R attack against PRESENT-80-14. The solver returned an assignment which satisfies the equation system with probability $\approx 2^{-3}$. Thus, we conclude that our filter is optimal among the filters which only consider only the output difference of round r and the ciphertext bits.

4.3   Case Study: KTANTAN

In Table 1 we give our results against KTANTAN32. We used the best characteristic for 42 rounds as provided by the designers and extended it to 71 rounds. The characteristic is valid with probability 2^{-31}. We present results for computation with degree bound $D = 4$ and 5. For each D we give the number of polynomials of degree 1 to 5 found (denoted as $d = *$). In the last column of each experiment we give the approximate probability that all the equations we found evaluate to zero for random values (denoted $\log_2 p$).

4.4   Increasing the Signal

In this section, we consider the problem of increasing the amount of correct data that has to agree with and is always suggested by a right pair. Increasing this value usually has considerable costs attached to it. First, more data needs to be managed and thus usually the counter tables become larger. On average, we can expect each additional bit considered to double the size of these tables. Second, in order to generate more data, more partial decryptions must be performed which in turn increases the computation time. Additionally, the number of key bits that can be trial decrypted may be limited by the number of rounds R we can consider because of the quality of the filter.

In this work we use (non-linear) relations available from the first few rounds instead of the last R rounds. Assume that we have an SP-network, a differential characteristic $\Delta = (\Delta P, \Delta Y_1, \dots, \Delta Y_r)$ valid for r rounds with probability p, and (P', P'') a right pair for Δ (so that $\Delta P = P' \oplus P''$ and ΔY_r holds for the output of round r). For simplicity, let us assume that only one S-Box is active in round 1, and by abuse of notation, that X'_1, X''_1 and K_0 denote the S-Box

Table 1. Decreasing the noise for KTANTAN32

N	degree bound = 4						degree bound = 5					
	$d=1$	$d=2$	$d=3$	$d=4$	$d=5$	$\log_2 p$	$d=1$	$d=2$	$d=3$	$d=4$	$d=5$	$\log_2 p$
72	32	0	0	0	0	-32.0	32	0	0	0	0	-32.0
74	32	0	0	0	0	-32.0	32	0	0	0	0	-32.0
76	32	0	0	0	0	-32.0	32	0	0	0	0	-32.0
78	31	3	0	0	0	-32.0	31	3	0	0	0	-32.0
80	28	11	0	0	0	-31.4	28	11	0	0	0	-31.4
82	25	23	0	0	0	-31.0	25	23	0	0	0	-31.0
84	20	32	4	8	0	-29.0	20	32	4	32	0	-29.0
86	16	44	19	8	0	-25.7	16	46	23	75	106	< -24
88	12	39	54	96	0	-24.0	12	51	103	371	745	< -23
90	8	41	129	287	0	-23.0	8	42	133	612	1762	< -22
92	4	28	113	285	0	-20.0	4	33	133	743	2646	-20.4
94	1	20	94	244	0	-16.3	1	25	124	662	2345	-18.5
96	0	8	38	96	0	-12.8	0	8	52	287	1264	-14.3
98	0	3	8	29	0	-7.0	0	3	10	46	156	-9.1
100	0	1	3	13	0	-3.7	0	1	3	18	47	-4.6
102	0	0	0	2	0	-0.8	0	0	0	4	9	-0.9
103	0	0	0	1	0	-0.4	0	0	0	2	4	-0.4
104	0	0	0	0	0	0.0	N/A	N/A	N/A	N/A	N/A	N/A

input *vectors* corresponding to the plaintext *vectors* P_1', P_1'' (also restricted to the S-Box) and initial key whitening, respectively. Thus we have the relations

$$S(P_1' \oplus K_0) = S(X_1') = Y_1' \text{ and } S(P_1'' \oplus K_0) = S(X_1'') = Y_1''.$$

The S-Box operation S can be described by a (vectorial) Boolean function, expressing each bit of the output Y_1' as a polynomial function (over $\mathbb{F}_2$) on the input bits of X_1' and K_0. If (P', P'') is a right pair, then the polynomial equations arising from the relation $\Delta Y_1 = Y_1' \oplus Y_1'' = S(P_1' \oplus K_0) \oplus S(P_1'' \oplus K_0)$ give us a very simple equation system to solve, with only the key variables $K_{0,j}$ as unknowns (and which do not vanish identically because we are considering nonzero differences). Consequently, right pairs suggest additional information about the key from the first round difference. In particular, if ΔY_1 holds with probability 2^{-b} then we can recover b bits of information about the key, as soon as we have a right pair.

There is no *a priori* reason to restrict this argument (which was considered in [1]) to the first round only. Let Δ, r, P', P'' be as before. We set up two equation systems F' and F'' involving P', C' and P'', C'' respectively and discard any polynomials from the rounds $> s$, where s is small (the discussion above refers to the case $s = 1$). We can then add linear equations as suggested by the characteristic up to s rounds and use this system to potentially recover information about the key from the first s rounds.

In order to avoid the potentially costly Gröbner basis computation for every candidate pair, we replace the vectors of constants P' and P'' by vectors of symbols. Using the idea from Section 3 we can compute polynomials involving only key variables and the newly introduced plaintext variables P' and P''. Assume that we can indeed compute the Gröbner basis, with P' and P'' as symbols, for the first s rounds combined with the linear equations arising from the characteristic. Assume further that the characteristic restricted to s rounds holds with a probability 2^{-b} and that we computed m_s polynomials in the variables K_0, P' and P''. This means that we can recover b bits of information when we evaluate all m_s polynomials, by replacing the variables in P' and P'' by their actual values.

This means that we have b bits of extra information and thus can write $S/N = \frac{2^{k+b} \cdot p}{\alpha \cdot \beta}$ without the overhead of performing any partial decryptions. However, we have to perform m_s polynomial evaluations (where we replace P' and P'' by their actual values) of relatively small low degree polynomials.

Case Study: PRESENT. We consider the first two encryption rounds and the characteristic from [30]. We set up a polynomial ring with two blocks such that the variables P_i and K_i are lexicographically smaller than any other variable. Within the blocks we chose a degree lexicographical term ordering. We set up an equation system covering the first two encryption rounds and added the linear equations suggested by the characteristic. Then, we eliminated all linear leading terms which are not in the variables P_i and K_i and computed a Gröbner basis up to degree five. This computation returned 22 linear and quadratic polynomials (we give the Gröbner basis for these polynomials in Figure 4). This system gives 8 bits of information about the key. Note that the first two rounds of the characteristic is valid with probability 2^{-8}.

Case Study: KTANTAN32. We consider the first 24 rounds of KTANTAN32 and compute the full Gröbner basis. This computation recovers 39 polynomials. We list an excerpt in Figure 1 in the Appendix. As expected we observe that the characteristic also imposes restrictions on the plaintext. These eight equations allow us to recover up to four bits (depending on the value of P'_{19}) of information about the key.

5   Algebraic Precomputation in Integral Cryptanalysis

In [31] *bit-pattern based integral attacks* against up to 7 rounds of PRESENT were proposed. These attacks are based on a 3.5 round distinguisher. The attacker prepares 16 chosen plaintexts which agree in all bit values except the bits at the positions 51, 55, 59, 63. These four bits take all possible values $(0, 0, 0, 0), (0, 0, 0, 1), \ldots, (1, 1, 1, 1)$. The authors of [31] show that the input bits to the 4th round are then balanced. That is, the sum of all bits at the same bit position across all 16 encryptions is zero. If $X_{i,j,k}$ denotes the k-th input bit of the j-th round of the i-th encryption, we have that $0 = \sum_{i=0}^{15} X_{i,4,k}$ for $0 \le k < 64$.

We show below that more algebraic structure can be found. For this purpose we set up an equation system for PRESENT-80-4 for 16 plaintexts of the form given above. We also added all information about relations between encryptions from [31] to the system in algebraic form. These relations are of the form $\sum_{i \in I} X_{i,j,k}$ for $I \subset \{0 \ldots, 15\}$. These relations would be found by the Gröbner basis algorithm eventually, but adding them directly can speed up the computation. Then we computed a Gröbner basis up to degree 2 only using POLYBORI. This computation takes about 5 minutes and returns more than 500 linear polynomials in the input variables to the fourth round. All these polynomials relate bits from different encryptions, that is they contain $X_{i,j,k}$ and $X_{i',j',k'}$ with $i \neq i'$. In Figure 5 of the Appendix we provide a selection in order to illustrate the form of these polynomials.

The exact number of subkey bits we can recover using these polynomials varies with the values of the ciphertext bits. On average we can recover 50 subkey bits from the last round key of PRESENT-80-4 using 2^4 chosen plaintexts by performing trial decryptions and comparing the relations between the inputs of the 4th round with the expected relations[2].

The same strategy for finding algebraic relations can be applied to PRESENT-80-5 where we look for polynomials which relate the input variables for the 5th round. Using POLYBORI with the same options as above, we found 26 linear polynomials. We can represent 12 of them as

$$X_{i,5,k} + X_{i+1,5,k} + X_{6,5,k} + X_{7,5,k} + X_{8,5,k} + X_{9,5,k} + X_{14,5,k} + X_{15,5,k},$$

with $i \in \{0, 2, 4\}$ and $k \in \{51, 55, 59, 63\}$.

Another 12 polynomials are of the form

$$X_{i,5,k} + X_{i,5,k+32} + X_{i+1,5,k} + X_{i+1,5,k+32} + X_{i+8,5,k} + X_{i+8,5,k+32} +$$
$$X_{i+9,5,k} + X_{i+9,5,k+32} + X_{6,5,k} + X_{6,5,k+32} + X_{7,5,k} + X_{7,5,k+32} +$$
$$X_{14,5,k} + X_{14,5,k+32} + X_{15,5,k} + X_{15,5,k+32}.$$

for $i \in \{0, 2, 4\}$ and $k \in \{3, 7, 11, 15\}$.

The remaining two polynomials can be represented by

$$X_{4,5,k} + X_{4,5,k+32} + X_{4,5,k+48} + X_{5,5,k} + X_{5,5,k+32} + X_{5,5,k+48} +$$
$$X_{6,5,k} + X_{6,5,k+32} + X_{6,5,k+48} + X_{7,5,k} + X_{7,5,k+32} + X_{7,5,k+48} +$$
$$X_{12,5,k} + X_{12,5,k+32} + X_{12,5,k+48} + X_{13,5,k} + X_{13,5,k+32} + X_{13,5,k+48} +$$
$$X_{14,5,k} + X_{14,5,k+32} + X_{14,5,k+48} + X_{15,5,k} + X_{15,5,k+32} + X_{15,5,k+48}$$

for $k \in \{3, 7\}$.

Using the 26 polynomials listed above we expect to recover the round-key for the last round of PRESENT-80-5 using $3 \cdot 2^4$ chosen plaintexts. For each S-box we have to guess the four subkey bits which separate the S-box output

---

[2] We note that considering the full equation system for all rounds instead of only the equations of the 4th round we can recover the full encryption key using 2^4 chosen plaintext by performing a classical algebraic attack. The overall Gröbner basis computation for this task takes only a few minutes but the running time varies between instances.

from the ciphertext. For each of the S-Boxes $12, 13, 14$ and 15, we have 3 linear equations to filter out wrong guesses on four bits. For each pair of S-boxes $(0, 8)$, $(1, 9)$, $(2, 10)$ and $(3, 11)$ we have again three linear equations to filter out wrong guesses, however this time we are filtering on eight bits. Thus, we need $2 \cdot 2^4$ chosen plaintexts to recover 16 bits and $3 \cdot 2^4$ chosen plaintext to recover 64 subkey bits. In [31], one required $5 \cdot 2^4$ chosen plaintexts. We mention that we can reduce the number of required texts further to 2^4 if we consider the polynomials from PRESENT-80-4 and PRESENT-80-5 together.

We were unable to obtain any polynomials for the input variables of the sixth round. However, just as in [31] we can extend our attack on PRESENT-80-5 to an attack on PRESENT-80-6 by guessing bits in the first round. Our improvements for PRESENT-80-5 translate directly into an improvement for PRESENT-80-6, dropping the data complexity from $2^{22.4}$ to 2^{21} chosen plaintexts (or 2^{20} if we consider the relations arising for the 4th round as well). Similarly, this additional information can be exploited for the PRESENT-128-7 attack from [31].

6   Conclusion

In this work, we have introduced a novel application for algebraic cryptanalysis of block ciphers. We propose a method which can improve "classical" differential and integral cryptanalysis, by applying algebraic tools in a pre-computation phase. As such, we shift the focus from attempting to solve large systems of polynomial equations to recovering symbolic information about the underlying cipher. We note that the use of algebraic techniques in general, and Gröbner basis methods in particular, in block cipher cryptanalysis has received some criticism within the cryptographic community, as it has been often the case that "simpler" techniques can perform favourably in many situations. However in this paper we showed that the rich algebraic structure of Gröbner basis can offer many advantages and may give one a more subtle insight of the cipher structure. This can in turn be used in the cryptanalysis of the cipher. We note that *in principle* our techniques can recover an optimal amount of information and that in most cases considered in this work we were (almost) able to accomplish this. We expect that this approach is applicable to other cryptanalytical techniques and consider applying it as an area of future work.

Acknowledgements

The work described in this paper has been supported in part by the Royal Society grant JP090728 and by the European Commission through the ICT programme under contract ICT-2007-216676 ECRYPT II. The first author was supported by the Royal Holloway Valerie Myerscough Scholarship. The two last authors were also supported in part by the french ANR under the Computer Algebra and Cryptography (CAC) project ANR-09-JCJCJ-0064-01. We would like to thank Stanislav Bulygin for helpful comments. We would also like to thank William Stein for access to his computers (purchased under National Science Foundation Grant No. DMS-0821725).

References

1. Albrecht, M., Cid, C.: Algebraic techniques in differential cryptanalysis. In: Dunkelman, O. (ed.) FSE 2009. LNCS, vol. 5665, pp. 193–208. Springer, Heidelberg (2009)
2. Bardet, M., Faugère, J.-C., Salvy, B.: Complexity of Gröbner basis computation for semi-regular overdetermined sequences over F_2 with solutions in F_2. Technical Report 5049, INRIA (December 2003), http://www.inria.fr/rrrt/rr-5049.html
3. Bardet, M., Faugère, J.-C., Salvy, B.: On the complexity of Gröbner basis computation of semi-regular overdetermined algebraic equations. In: Proc. International Conference on Polynomial System Solving (ICPSS), pp. 71–75 (2004)
4. Bardet, M., Faugère, J.-C., Salvy, B., Yang, B.-Y.: Asymptotic behaviour of the degree of regularity of semi-regular polynomial systems. In: Proc. of MEGA 2005, Eighth International Symposium on Effective Methods in Algebraic Geometry (2005)
5. Becker, T., Weispfenning, V.: Gröbner Bases - A Computational Approach to Commutative Algebra. Springer, Heidelberg (1991)
6. Biham, E., Shamir, A.: Differential cryptanalysis of DES-like cryptosystems. In: Menezes, A., Vanstone, S.A. (eds.) CRYPTO 1990. LNCS, vol. 537, pp. 2–21. Springer, Heidelberg (1991)
7. Bogdanov, A.A., Knudsen, L.R., Leander, G., Paar, C., Poschmann, A., Robshaw, M.J.B., Seurin, Y., Vikkelsoe, C.: PRESENT: An ultra-lightweight block cipher. In: Paillier, P., Verbauwhede, I. (eds.) CHES 2007. LNCS, vol. 4727, pp. 450–466. Springer, Heidelberg (2007), http://www.crypto.rub.de/imperia/md/content/texte/publications/conferences/present_ches2007.pdf
8. Bogdanov, A., Rechberger, C.: Generalizing meet-in-the-middle attacks: Cryptanalysis of the lightweight block cipher ktantan. In: Proceedings of Selected Areas in Cryptography 2010 (2010)
9. Brickenstein, M., Dreyer, A.: PolyBoRi: A framework for Gröbner basis computations with Boolean polynomials. In: Electronic Proceedings of MEGA 2007 (2007), http://www.ricam.oeaw.ac.at/mega2007/electronic/26.pdf
10. Buchmann, J., Pyshkin, A., Weinmann, R.-P.: Block ciphers sensitive to gröbner basis attacks. In: Pointcheval, D. (ed.) CT-RSA 2006. LNCS, vol. 3860, pp. 313–331. Springer, Heidelberg (2006)
11. De Cannière, C., Dunkelman, O., Knežević, M.: KATAN and KTANTAN — A family of small and efficient hardware-oriented block ciphers. In: Clavier, C., Gaj, K. (eds.) CHES 2009. LNCS, vol. 5747, pp. 272–288. Springer, Heidelberg (2009)
12. Cho, J.Y.: Linear cryptanalysis of reduced-round PRESENT. Cryptology ePrint Archive, Report 2009/397 (2009), http://eprint.iacr.org/2009/397
13. Cid, C.: D.STVL.7 algebraic cryptanalysis of symmetric primitives (2008), http://www.ecrypt.eu.org/ecrypt1/documents/D.STVL.7.pdf
14. Cid, C., Leurent, G.: An analysis of the XSL algorithm. In: Roy, B. (ed.) ASIACRYPT 2005. LNCS, vol. 3788, pp. 333–352. Springer, Heidelberg (2005)
15. Cid, C., Murphy, S., Robshaw, M.J.B.: Small scale variants of the AES. In: Gilbert, H., Handschuh, H. (eds.) FSE 2005. LNCS, vol. 3557, pp. 145–162. Springer, Heidelberg (2005), http://www.isg.rhul.ac.uk/~sean/smallAES-fse05.pdf
16. Collard, B., Standaert, F.-X.: A statistical saturation attack against the block cipher PRESENT. In: Fischlin, M. (ed.) CT-RSA 2009. LNCS, vol. 5473, pp. 195–210. Springer, Heidelberg (2009)
17. Courtois, N.T.: Fast algebraic attacks on stream ciphers with linear feedback. In: Boneh, D. (ed.) CRYPTO 2003. LNCS, vol. 2729, pp. 176–194. Springer, Heidelberg (2003)

18. Courtois, N.T.: Higher order correlation attacks,XL algorithm and cryptanalysis of toyocrypt. In: Lee, P.J., Lim, C.H. (eds.) ICISC 2002. LNCS, vol. 2587, pp. 182–199. Springer, Heidelberg (2003)
19. Courtois, N.T., Bard, G.V.: Algebraic cryptanalysis of the data encryption standard. In: Galbraith, S.D. (ed.) CC 2007. LNCS, vol. 4887, pp. 152–169. Springer, Heidelberg (2007), pre-print available at http://eprint.iacr.org/2006/402
20. Courtois, N.T., Meier, W.: Algebraic attacks on stream ciphers with linear feedback. In: Biham, E. (ed.) EUROCRYPT 2003. LNCS, vol. 2656, pp. 345–359. Springer, Heidelberg (2003)
21. Courtois, N.T., Pieprzyk, J.: Cryptanalysis of block ciphers with overdefined systems of equations. In: Zheng, Y. (ed.) ASIACRYPT 2002. LNCS, vol. 2501, pp. 267–287. Springer, Heidelberg (2002)
22. Faugère, J.-C., Levy-dit-Vehel, F., Perret, L.: Cryptanalysis of minRank. In: Wagner, D. (ed.) CRYPTO 2008. LNCS, vol. 5157, pp. 280–296. Springer, Heidelberg (2008)
23. Faugère, J.-C., Joux, A.: Algebraic cryptanalysis of hidden field equation (HFE) cryptosystems using gröbner bases. In: Boneh, D. (ed.) CRYPTO 2003. LNCS, vol. 2729, pp. 44–60. Springer, Heidelberg (2003)
24. Faugère, J.-C., Perret, L.: Cryptanalysis of 2R$^-$ schemes. In: Dwork, C. (ed.) CRYPTO 2006. LNCS, vol. 4117, pp. 357–372. Springer, Heidelberg (2006)
25. Faugère, J.-C., Perret, L.: Algebraic cryptanalysis of Curry and Flurry using correlated messages. Cryptology ePrint Archive, Report 2008/402 (2008), http://eprint.iacr.org/2008/402.pdf
26. Nakahara Jr., J., Sepehrdad, P., Zhang, B., Wang, M.: Linear (Hull) and algebraic cryptanalysis of the block cipher PRESENT. In: Garay, J.A., Miyaji, A., Otsuka, A. (eds.) CANS 2009. LNCS, vol. 5888, pp. 58–75. Springer, Heidelberg (2009)
27. Knudsen, L.R.: Truncated and higher order differentials. In: Preneel, B. (ed.) FSE 1994. LNCS, vol. 1008, pp. 196–211. Springer, Heidelberg (1995)
28. Soos, M., Nohl, K., Castelluccia, C.: Extending SAT solvers to cryptographic problems. In: Kullmann, O. (ed.) SAT 2009. LNCS, vol. 5584, pp. 244–257. Springer, Heidelberg (2009)
29. Stein, W., et al.: SAGE Mathematics Software. The Sage Development Team (2008), http://www.sagemath.org
30. Wang, M.: Differential cryptanalysis of reduced-round PRESENT. In: Vaudenay, S. (ed.) AFRICACRYPT 2008. LNCS, vol. 5023, pp. 40–49. Springer, Heidelberg (2008)
31. Z'aba, M.R., Raddum, H., Henricksen, M., Dawson, E.: Bit-pattern based integral attack. In: Nyberg, K. (ed.) FSE 2008. LNCS, vol. 5086, pp. 363–381. Springer, Heidelberg (2008)

A   Explicit Polynomials

$$(P'_{19} + 1)(P'_3 P'_8 + P'_{10} P'_{12} + K_3 + K_{53} + P'_7 + P'_{18} + P'_{23}),$$
$$P'_8 P'_{10} P'_{19} + K_8 P'_{19} + P'_3 P'_8 + P'_6 P'_{19} + P'_{10} P'_{12} +$$
$$P'_{16} P'_{19} + K_3 + K_{53} + P'_7 + P'_{18} + P'_{19} + P'_{23},$$
$$P'_{19} P'_{22} + K_1 + K_{11} + P'_6 + P'_{11} + P'_{17} + P'_{21} + P'_{26},$$
$$P'_{23} P'_{26} + K_{65} + P'_{21} + P'_{25} + P'_{30},$$
$$P'_1 + 1, P'_2, P'_5 + 1, P'_9 + 1$$

Fig. 1. Polynomials for the first two rounds of KTANTAN32

$$(C'_{57+j} + C''_{57+j})(C'_{53+j} + C''_{53+j} + 1)(C'_{17+j} + C''_{17+j}),$$
$$(C'_{57+j} + C''_{57+j})(C'_{53+j} + C''_{53+j} + 1)(C'_{33+j} + C''_{33+j}),$$
$$(C'_{57+j} + C''_{57+j} + 1)(C'_{25+j} + C''_{25+j}),$$
$$(C'_{57+j} + C''_{57+j} + 1)(C'_{41+j} + C''_{41+j}),$$
$$(C'_{53+j} + C''_{53+j} + 1)(C'_{21+j} + C''_{21+j}),$$
$$(C'_{53+j} + C''_{53+j} + 1)(C'_{37+j} + C''_{37+j}),$$
$$(C'_{53+j} + C''_{53+j} + 1)(C'_{49+j} + C'_{57+j} + C''_{49+j} + C''_{57+j} + 1),$$
$$(C'_{49+j} + C''_{49+j} + 1)(C'_{17+j} + C''_{17+j}),$$
$$(C'_{49+j} + C''_{49+j} + 1)(C'_{33+j} + C''_{33+j}),$$
$$C'_{1+j} + C'_{33+j} + C'_{49+j} + C''_{1+j} + C''_{33+j} + C''_{49+j},$$
$$C'_{5+j} + C'_{37+j} + C'_{53+j} + C''_{5+j} + C''_{37+j} + C''_{53+j},$$
$$C'_{9+j} + C'_{41+j} + C'_{57+j} + C''_{9+j} + C''_{41+j} + C''_{57+j},$$

Fig. 2. 2R polynomials for PRESENT with $j \in \{0, 2\}$

$$(C'_{36} + C''_{36})((C'_4 + C''_4)(C'_{20} + C'_{52} + C''_{20} + C''_{52} + 1) + (C'_{20} + C''_{20} + 1)(C'_{52} + C''_{52} + 1)),$$
$$(C'_{37} + C''_{37})((C'_5 + C''_5)(C'_{21} + C'_{53} + C''_{21} + C''_{53} + 1) + (C'_{21} + C''_{21} + 1)(C'_{53} + C''_{53} + 1)),$$
$$(C'_{40} + C''_{40})((C'_8 + C''_8)(C'_{24} + C'_{56} + C''_{24} + C''_{56} + 1) + (C'_{24} + C''_{24} + 1)(C'_{56} + C''_{56} + 1)),$$
$$(C'_{41} + C''_{41})((C'_9 + C''_9)(C'_{25} + C'_{57} + C''_{25} + C''_{57} + 1) + (C'_{25} + C''_{25} + 1)(C'_{57} + C''_{57} + 1)),$$
$$(C'_{45} + C''_{45})((C'_{13} + C''_{13})(C'_{29} + C'_{61} + C''_{29} + C''_{61} + 1) + (C'_{29} + C''_{29} + 1)(C'_{61} + C''_{61} + 1)),$$
$$(C'_{46} + C''_{46})((C'_{14} + C''_{14})(C'_{30} + C'_{62} + C''_{30} + C''_{62} + 1) + (C'_{30} + C''_{30} + 1)(C'_{62} + C''_{62} + 1)),$$
$$(C'_{06} + C''_{06})((C'_{22} + C''_{22})(C'_{38} + C'_{54} + C''_{38} + C''_{54} + 1) + (C'_{38} + C''_{38} + 1)(C'_{54} + C''_{54} + 1)),$$
$$(C'_{10} + C''_{10})((C'_{26} + C''_{26})(C'_{42} + C'_{58} + C''_{42} + C''_{58} + 1) + (C'_{42} + C''_{42} + 1)(C'_{58} + C''_{58} + 1)),$$
$$(C'_{12} + C''_{12})((C'_{28} + C''_{28})(C'_{44} + C'_{60} + C''_{44} + C''_{60} + 1) + (C'_{44} + C''_{44} + 1)(C'_{60} + C''_{60} + 1)),$$
$$(C'_{52} + C''_{52} + 1)(C'_{20} + C''_{20} + 1)(C'_4 + C'_{36} + C''_4 + C''_{36}),$$
$$(C'_{60} + C''_{60} + 1)(C'_{28} + C''_{28} + 1)(C'_{12} + C'_{44} + C''_{12} + C''_{44}),$$
$$(C'_{10} + C'_{42} + C'_{58} + C''_{10} + C''_{42} + C''_{58})(C'_2 + C'_{34} + C'_{50} + C''_2 + C''_{34} + C''_{50}).$$

Fig. 3. 3R polynomials for PRESENT

$(K_1 + P_1' + 1)(K_0 + K_3 + K_{29} + P_0' + P_3'),$

$(K_2 + P_2')(K_0 + K_3 + K_{29} + P_0' + P_3'),$

$K_1 K_2 + K_1 P_2' + K_2 P_1' + P_1' P_2' + K_0 + K_1 + K_3 + K_{29} + P_0' + P_1' + P_3',$

$(K_9 + P_9' + 1)(K_8 + K_{11} + K_{31} + P_8' + P_{11}'),$

$(K_{10} + P_{10}')(K_8 + K_{11} + K_{31} + P_8' + P_{11}'),$

$K_9 K_{10} + K_9 P_{10}' + K_{10} P_9' + P_9' P_{10}' + K_8 + K_9 + K_{11} + K_{31} + P_8' + P_9' + P_{11}',$

$(K_{49} + P_{49}' + 1)(K_{41} + K_{48} + K_{51} + P_{48}' + P_{51}'),$

$(K_{50} + P_{50}')(K_{41} + K_{48} + K_{51} + P_{48}' + P_{51}'),$

$K_{49} K_{50} + K_{49} P_{50}' + K_{50} P_{49}' + P_{49}' P_{50}' + K_{41} + K_{48} + K_{49} + K_{51} + P_{48}' + P_{49}' + P_{51}',$

$(K_{57} + P_{57}' + 1)(K_{43} + K_{56} + K_{59} + P_{56}' + P_{59}'),$

$(K_{58} + P_{58}')(K_{43} + K_{56} + K_{59} + P_{56}' + P_{59}'),$

$K_{57} K_{58} + K_{57} P_{58}' + K_{58} P_{57}' + P_{57}' P_{58}' + K_{43} + K_{56} + K_{57} + K_{59} + P_{56}' + P_{57}' + P_{59}',$

$K_5 + K_7 + P_5' + P_7',$

$K_6 + K_7 + P_6' + P_7',$

$K_{53} + K_{55} + P_{53}' + P_{55}',$

$K_{54} + K_{55} + P_{54}' + P_{55}'$

Fig. 4. Polynomials for the first two rounds of PRESENT

$X_{14,4,0} + X_{14,4,32} + X_{14,4,56} + X_{14,4,62} + X_{15,4,0} + X_{15,4,32} + X_{15,4,56} + X_{15,4,62} + 1,$

$X_{14,4,1} + X_{14,4,33} + X_{14,4,49} + X_{15,4,1} + X_{15,4,33} + X_{15,4,49},$

$X_{14,4,2} + X_{14,4,34} + X_{14,4,58} + X_{14,4,62} + X_{15,4,2} + X_{15,4,34} + X_{15,4,58} + X_{15,4,62},$

$X_{14,4,3} + X_{14,4,35} + X_{14,4,51} + X_{15,4,3} + X_{15,4,35} + X_{15,4,51},$

$X_{14,4,4} + X_{14,4,36} + X_{14,4,52} + X_{15,4,4} + X_{15,4,36} + X_{15,4,52},$

$X_{14,4,5} + X_{14,4,37} + X_{14,4,53} + X_{15,4,5} + X_{15,4,37} + X_{15,4,53},$

$X_{14,4,6} + X_{14,4,38} + X_{14,4,54} + X_{15,4,6} + X_{15,4,38} + X_{15,4,54},$

$X_{14,4,7} + X_{14,4,39} + X_{14,4,55} + X_{15,4,7} + X_{15,4,39} + X_{15,4,55},$

$X_{14,4,8} + X_{14,4,40} + X_{14,4,56} + X_{15,4,8} + X_{15,4,40} + X_{15,4,56},$

$X_{14,4,9} + X_{14,4,41} + X_{14,4,57} + X_{15,4,9} + X_{15,4,41} + X_{15,4,57},$

$X_{14,4,10} + X_{14,4,42} + X_{14,4,58} + X_{15,4,10} + X_{15,4,42} + X_{15,4,58},$

$X_{14,4,11} + X_{14,4,43} + X_{14,4,59} + X_{15,4,11} + X_{15,4,43} + X_{15,4,59},$

$X_{14,4,12} + X_{14,4,44} + X_{14,4,62} + X_{15,4,12} + X_{15,4,44} + X_{15,4,62} + 1,$

$X_{14,4,13} + X_{14,4,45} + X_{14,4,61} + X_{15,4,13} + X_{15,4,45} + X_{15,4,61},$

$X_{14,4,14} + X_{14,4,46} + X_{14,4,62} + X_{15,4,14} + X_{15,4,46} + X_{15,4,62},$

$X_{14,4,15} + X_{14,4,47} + X_{14,4,63} + X_{15,4,15} + X_{15,4,47} + X_{15,4,63},$

$X_{14,4,48} + X_{14,4,56} + X_{14,4,62} + X_{15,4,48} + X_{15,4,56} + X_{15,4,62} + 1,$

$X_{14,4,49} + X_{14,4,57} + X_{14,4,61} + X_{15,4,49} + X_{15,4,57} + X_{15,4,61},$

$X_{14,4,50} + X_{14,4,58} + X_{14,4,62} + X_{15,4,50} + X_{15,4,58} + X_{15,4,62},$

$X_{14,4,51} + X_{14,4,59} + X_{15,4,51} + X_{15,4,59} + 1,$

$X_{14,4,60} + X_{14,4,62} + X_{15,4,60} + X_{15,4,62} + 1,$

$X_{14,4,63} + X_{15,4,63} + 1.$

Fig. 5. Polynomials for four round integral attack against PRESENT

A Note on Fast Algebraic Attacks and Higher Order Nonlinearities

Qichun Wang[1,2,*] and Thomas Johansson[2]

[1] The Shanghai Key Lab of Intelligent Information Processing, School of Computer Science, Fudan University, Shanghai 200433, P.R. China
032018023@fudan.edu.cn
[2] Dept. of Electrical and Information Technology, Lund University,
P.O. Box 118, 221 00 Lund, Sweden
Thomas.Johansson@eit.lth.se

Abstract. In this note, we deduce a bound between fast algebraic immunity and higher order nonlinearity (it is the first time that a bound between these two cryptographic criteria is given), and find that a Boolean function should have high r-order nonlinearity to resist fast algebraic attacks. As a corollary, we find that no matter how much effort we make, the Tu-Deng functions cannot be repaired in a standard way to behave well against fast algebraic attacks. Therefore, we should give up repairing this class of Boolean functions and try to find other classes of functions with good cryptographic properties or to prove that the Carlet-Feng function behaves well.

Keywords: Boolean functions, stream ciphers, fast algebraic attacks, higher order nonlinearities.

1 Introduction

To resist many kinds of attacks, Boolean functions used in stream ciphers should have good cryptographic properties: balancedness, high algebraic immunity, high algebraic degree, high nonlinearity and good immunity to fast algebraic attacks. Up to now, many classes of Boolean functions achieving optimum algebraic immunity have been introduced [1, 2, 3, 4, 5, 6, 7, 8, 32]. In [7], Carlet and Feng proposed an infinite class of balanced functions with optimum algebraic degree, optimum algebraic immunity and a much better nonlinearity than all the previously known infinite classes of functions. However, the lower bound they deduced is not enough to assert resistance to fast correlation attacks [21, 22]. In [8], Tu and Deng introduced another class of balanced functions with optimum algebraic degree, optimum algebraic immunity and a provable good nonlinearity provided that a certain conjecture is true. Some researchers have done work on this conjecture [28, 29]. However, the Tu-Deng functions are also weak against

* Research supported by 973 Program with No. 2010CB327906, NSFC with No. 60873178, 60772131 and 60832001, and Grant No.09DZ2271800 of Shanghai Committee of Science and Technology.

X. Lai, M. Yung, and D. Lin (Eds.): Inscrypt 2010, LNCS 6584, pp. 404–414, 2011.

fast algebraic attacks. Carlet found this weakness and also tried to repair it [9]. The repair of this weakness should give an infinite class of balanced functions having optimum algebraic degree, optimum algebraic immunity, good nonlinearity and a good behavior against fast algebraic attacks. Then it will be the best construction of an infinite class of Boolean functions in cryptographic literature.

The higher order nonlinearity is an important cryptographic criterion [10,11, 12,13], and many bounds on it have been deduced [14,15,16,17,18,19]. However, no bound between fast algebraic immunity and higher order nonlinearity was previously given. In fact, given a class of Boolean functions, it may be hard to compute the fast algebraic immunity of them. Therefore, it may be a good choice if we can assess it by its higher order nonlinearities, and in fact, it is sometimes easy to prove bad higher order nonlinearity.

In this note, we deduce a bound between fast algebraic immunity and higher order nonlinearity, and find that a Boolean function should have high r-order nonlinearity to resist fast algebraic attacks. As a corollary, we find that no matter how much effort we make, the Tu-Deng functions cannot be repaired in a standard way to behave well against fast algebraic attacks. Therefore, we should give up repairing this classes of Boolean functions and try to find other class of functions with good cryptographic properties or to prove that the Carlet-Feng function behaves well.

The note is organized as follows. In Section 2, the necessary background is established. We then deduce a bound between fast algebraic immunity and higher order nonlinearity in Section 3. In Section 4, we then show that the Tu-Deng functions cannot be repaired in a standard way such that they behave well against fast algebraic attacks. We end in Section 5 with a few conclusions.

2   Preliminaries

Let $\mathbb{F}_2^n$ be the n-dimensional vector space over the finite field $\mathbb{F}_2$. A Boolean function of n variables is a function from $\mathbb{F}_2^n$ into $\mathbb{F}_2$. We denote by B_n the set of all n-variable Boolean functions.

Any $f \in B_n$ can be uniquely represented as a multivariate polynomial in $\mathbb{F}_2[x_1, \cdots, x_n]$,

$$f(x_1, ..., x_n) = \sum_{K \subseteq \{1,2,...,n\}} a_K \prod_{k \in K} x_k,$$

which is called its algebraic normal form (ANF). The algebraic degree of f, denoted by $\deg(f)$, is the number of variables in the highest order term with nonzero coefficient.

A Boolean function is affine if there exists no term of degree strictly greater than 1 in the ANF and the set of all affine functions is denoted by A_n.

Let

$$1_f = \{x \in \mathbb{F}_2^n | f(x) = 1\}, \ 0_f = \{x \in \mathbb{F}_2^n | f(x) = 0\}.$$

The cardinality of 1_f, denoted by $wt(f)$, is called the Hamming weight of f. The Hamming distance between two functions f and g, denoted by $d(f, g)$, is the Hamming weight of $f + g$. We say that an n-variable Boolean function f is balanced if $wt(f) = 2^{n-1}$.

Let $f \in B_n$. The nonlinearity of f is its distance from the set of all n-variable affine functions, i.e.,

$$nl(f) = \min_{g \in A_n} d(f, g).$$

The r-order nonlinearity, denoted by $nl_r(f)$, is its distance from the set of all n-variable functions of degree at most r.

The nonlinearity of an n-variable Boolean function is upper bounded by $2^{n-1} - 2^{n/2-1}$, and a function is said to be bent if it can achieve this bound. Clearly, bent functions exist only for even n and it is known that the algebraic degree of a bent function is upper bounded by $\frac{n}{2}$ [24].

For any $f \in B_n$, a nonzero function $g \in B_n$ is called an annihilator of f if $fg = 0$, and the algebraic immunity of f, denoted by $\mathcal{AI}(f)$, is the minimum value of d such that f or $f + 1$ admits an annihilator of degree d. It is known that the algebraic immunity of an n-variable Boolean function is upper bounded by $\lceil \frac{n}{2} \rceil$ [25].

To resist algebraic attacks, a Boolean function f used in stream ciphers should have a high algebraic immunity, which implies that the nonlinearity of f is also not very low since [30]

$$nl(f) \geq 2 \sum_{i=0}^{AI(f)-2} \binom{n-1}{i}.$$

A typical filter generator uses an m-sequence $\mathbf{s} = s_0, s_1, s_2, \ldots$ and a filter function $f \in B_n$. Denote the output of the filter generator by $c_0, c_1, c_2, \ldots$. Any term s_t of the m-sequence $\mathbf{s}$ is uniquely determined by a linear function of the initial state $(s_0, s_1, \ldots, s_{N-1})$, where N is the length of the register. Let

$$f(L'(s_t, s_{t+1}, \ldots, s_{t+N-1})) = c_t, t = 0, 1, 2, \ldots,$$

where L' is linear from F_2^N to F_2^n. Then we have

$$f(L'(L^t(s_0, s_1, \ldots, s_{N-1}))) = c_t, t = 0, 1, 2, \ldots,$$

where L^t are vectorial Boolean functions from $\mathbb{F}_2^N$ into $\mathbb{F}_2^N$ and all components are linear functions. An algebraic attack is an approach to solve this system of equations efficiently. To resist algebraic attacks, f should have high algebraic immunity. Otherwise, there exists a $g \in B_n$ of low degree such that $fg = 0$. Then

$$f(L'(L^t(s_0, s_1, \ldots, s_{N-1})))g(L'(L^t(s_0, s_1, \ldots, s_{N-1})))$$
$$= c_t g(L'(L^t(s_0, s_1, \ldots, s_{N-1}))) = 0.$$

Therefore, each time $c_t = 1$, we have $g(L'(L^t(s_0, s_1, \ldots, s_{N-1}))) = 0$, and many equations of low degree are derived. They can be solved more efficiently than the initial system. The complexity of the standard algebraic attack is roughly $O(D^3)$ in time and $O(D)$ in data, where $D = \sum_{i=0}^{\mathcal{AI}(f)} \binom{N}{i}$.

To resist fast algebraic attacks, a high algebraic immunity is not sufficient. Assume that we can find g of low degree and h of reasonable degree such that $fg = h$. Then

$$h(L'(L^t(s_0, s_1, \ldots, s_{N-1}))) = c_t g(L'(L^t(s_0, s_1, \ldots, s_{N-1}))), t = 0, 1, 2, \ldots.$$

Then there exists a linear combination of the first $\sum_{i=0}^{\deg(h)} \binom{N}{i}$ equations that sum the left hand side to 0. We find this by using the Berlekamp-Massey algorithm or through an explicit algebraic calculation [23]. After summing up we arrive at one equation of degree at most $\deg(g)$. The fast algebraic attack has a pre-computation step of complexity $O(D \log^3 D + Dn \log^2 n)$ and an online complexity of $O(2DE \log D + E^3)$ [23], where $D = \sum_{i=0}^{\deg(h)} \binom{N}{i}$ and $E = \sum_{i=0}^{\deg(g)} \binom{N}{i}$.

Let $\mathbb{F}_{2^n}$ denote a finite field with 2^n elements. It can be viewed as an n-dimensional vector space over its subfield $\mathbb{F}_2$. Every function $f : \mathbb{F}_{2^n} \to \mathbb{F}_{2^n}$ can be uniquely represented as a polynomial $\sum_{i=0}^{2^n-1} a_i x^i$, where $a_i \in \mathbb{F}_{2^n}$, and f is a Boolean function if and only if $\sum_{i=0}^{2^n-1} a_i x^i \in \mathbb{F}_2$ for any $x \in \mathbb{F}_{2^n}$. Given a basis $(\beta_1, \beta_2, \cdots, \beta_n)$, we can identify any element $x = \sum_{i=1}^{n} x_i \beta_i \in \mathbb{F}_{2^n}$ with the n-tuple of its coordinates $(x_1, x_2, \cdots, x_n) \in \mathbb{F}_2^n$, and f can then be represented as an n-variable polynomial over $\mathbb{F}_2$.

3   A Bound between Fast Algebraic Immunity and Higher Order Nonlinearity

Let f be any Boolean function. If there are functions g of low degree and h of reasonable degree such that $fg = h$, then f is considered to be weak against fast algebraic attacks. Moreover, if g is a nonzero low degree annihilator, then the algebraic attack using g is more efficient and it is a particular case of the fast algebraic attack. Therefore, the notion of fast algebraic immunity was introduced by [26] to assess the resistance of f to fast algebraic attacks as follows:

Definition 1. *The fast algebraic immunity of an n-variable Boolean function f, denoted by $\mathcal{FAI}(f)$, is defined as*

$$\mathcal{FAI}(f) = \min_{g \in B_n} \{2\mathcal{AI}(f), \deg g + \deg(fg)\},$$

where $1 \leq \deg g < \mathcal{AI}(f)$.

It is known that $\mathcal{FAI}(f) \leq n$ [26,27]. To resist fast algebraic attacks, the Boolean function f should have high $\mathcal{FAI}$ and the optimum case is $\mathcal{FAI}(f) = n$. In [7], an $f \in B_9$ with $\mathcal{FAI}(f) = 9$ was observed, and the authors believed that the class of functions they introduced had good fast algebraic immunity. Given a class of functions f, it may be hard to compute $\mathcal{FAI}(f)$. However, we show that we can assess it by higher order nonlinearities, and in fact, it is sometimes easy to prove bad higher order nonlinearity.

Theorem 1. *Let $f \in B_n$ and d be a positive integer. If $nl_r(f) < \sum_{i=0}^{d} \binom{n}{i}$, then $\mathcal{FAI}(f) \leq r + 2d$. In other words,*

$$nl_r(f) \geq \sum_{i=0}^{\lfloor \frac{\mathcal{FAI}(f)-r}{2} \rfloor} \binom{n}{i}.$$

Proof. Let f_1 be a function of degree at most r such that $nl_r(f) = wt(f + f_1)$. Since $wt(f + f_1) < \sum_{i=0}^{d} \binom{n}{i}$, there exists g of degree at most d such that $(f + f_1)g = 0$. In fact, let

$$g(x_1, ..., x_n) = \sum_{\substack{K \subseteq \{1,2,...,n\} \\ |K| \leq d}} a_K \prod_{k \in K} x_k.$$

Clearly, $(f + f_1)g = 0$ if and only if $(f + f_1)(x) = 1$ implies $g(x) = 0$. Hence the coefficients of g satisfy the system of homogeneous linear equations. Since we have $\sum_{i=0}^{d} \binom{n}{i}$ number of variables and $wt(f + f_1)$ number of equations, there exists at least one nonzero solution. Therefore, $fg = f_1 g$ and $\deg g + \deg(fg) \leq r + 2d$. □

From the theorem, we can find that the r-order nonlinearity of the Boolean function f should be high to resist fast algebraic attacks, at least for reasonable r.

Remark 1: In particular, if $nl_r(f) < \sum_{i=0}^{\lceil \frac{n-r}{2} \rceil - 1} \binom{n}{i}$, then

$$\mathcal{FAI}(f) \leq \begin{cases} n - 1 & \text{if } n - r \text{ odd} \\ n - 2 & \text{if } n - r \text{ even.} \end{cases}$$

Therefore, to achieve the optimum fast algebraic immunity, it is necessary for f to satisfy

$$nl_r(f) \geq \sum_{i=0}^{\lceil \frac{n-r}{2} \rceil - 1} \binom{n}{i}.$$

When the order is low, the best known lower bound on the r-order nonlinearity of n-variable Boolean functions with optimum algebraic immunity is [19]:

$$\sum_{i=0}^{\lceil \frac{n}{2} \rceil - r - 1} \binom{n}{i} + \sum_{i=\lceil \frac{n}{2} \rceil - 2r}^{\lceil \frac{n}{2} \rceil - r - 1} \binom{n - r}{i}.$$

When r is large, the best known bound is $\max_{r' \leq n}(min(\lambda_{r'}, \mu_{r'}))$ [14], where

$$\lambda_{r'} = 2 \max(\sum_{i=0}^{r'-1} \binom{n}{i}, \sum_{i=0}^{\lceil \frac{n}{2} \rceil - r - 1} \binom{n - r}{i}) \text{ if } r' \leq \lceil \frac{n}{2} \rceil - r - 1,$$

$$= 2 \sum_{i=0}^{\lceil \frac{n}{2} \rceil - r - 1} \binom{n}{i} \text{ if } r' > \lceil \frac{n}{2} \rceil - r - 1,$$

$$\mu_{r'} = \sum_{i=0}^{\lceil \frac{n}{2} \rceil - r - 1} \binom{n - r}{i} + \sum_{i=0}^{\lceil \frac{n}{2} \rceil - r'} \binom{n - r' + 1}{i}.$$

Clearly, for $r > 2$, these bounds are much less than $\sum_{i=0}^{\lceil \frac{n-r}{2} \rceil - 1} \binom{n}{i}$, especially for r close to $\lceil \frac{n}{2} \rceil$.

Remark 2: It is known that the highest possible algebraic degree of a $2k$-variable bent function is k. Therefore, to achieve a good fast algebraic immunity, a Boolean function f should have large distance to bent functions. Otherwise, there exists a small d such that $nl_k(f) < \sum_{i=0}^{d} \binom{2k}{i}$, and then $\mathcal{FAI}(f) \leq k + 2d$. To resist fast correlation attacks, a Boolean function should have high nonlinearity. However, bent functions have the maximum nonlinearity and many functions with high nonlinearities may have small distances to bent functions and therefore have bad fast algebraic immunities. It may be hard to construct a class of functions which have high nonlinearity and can also behave well against fast algebraic attacks. It is interesting to investigate the relation between $nl(f)$ and $\mathcal{FAI}(f)$, which we leave as an open problem.

Example 1: Braeken introduced a 16-variable symmetric Boolean function f with optimum algebraic immunity 8 in her PhD thesis,

$$f(x) = \sigma_1^{(16)} + \sigma_2^{(16)} + \sigma_3^{(16)} + \sigma_4^{(16)} + \sigma_5^{(16)} + \sigma_6^{(16)} + \sigma_7^{(16)} + \sigma_{16}^{(16)},$$

where $\sigma_i^{(16)}$ denotes the 16-variable homogeneous symmetric Boolean function which contains all terms of degree i. It is known that $\deg(f) = 16$ and $nl(f) = 26333$ [20], which is much better than the worst nonlinearity 19898 of a 16-variable function with optimum algebraic immunity 8 [30]. However, $nl_7(f) = 1 < \sum_{i=0}^{1} \binom{16}{i}$, and hence its fast algebraic immunity is not good. In fact,

$$f(x)(x_1 + 1) = (\sigma_1^{(16)} + \sigma_2^{(16)} + \sigma_3^{(16)} + \sigma_4^{(16)} + \sigma_5^{(16)} + \sigma_6^{(16)} + \sigma_7^{(16)})(x_1 + 1),$$

and $\mathcal{FAI}(f) \leq 9$. This is the worst case for the resistance to fast algebraic attacks of a 16-variable function with algebraic immunity 8.

4   On Repairing the Tu-Deng Functions

The Tu-Deng function $t \in B_{2k}$ is constructed as follows [8].

Let α be a primitive element of the field $\mathbb{F}_{2^k}$ and $g : \mathbb{F}_{2^k} \to \mathbb{F}_2$ satisfy

$$1_g = \{\alpha^s, \alpha^{s+1}, ..., \alpha^{s+2^{k-1}-1}\},$$

where $0 \leq s < 2^k - 1$. The Tu-Deng function $t : \mathbb{F}_{2^k} \times \mathbb{F}_{2^k} \to \mathbb{F}_2$ is defined as

$$t(x, y) = \begin{cases} g(\frac{x}{y}), & \text{if } xy \neq 0, \\ 1, & \text{if } x = 0, \ y \in \Delta, \\ 0, & \text{otherwise}, \end{cases}$$

where $\Delta = \{\alpha^i | i = 2^{k-1} - 1, 2^{k-1}, ..., 2^k - 2\}$.

The Tu-Deng function t has optimum algebraic degree, optimum algebraic immunity and a very good nonlinearity. However, it is vulnerable to fast algebraic attacks [9]. In fact, let

$$b(x,y) = \begin{cases} g(\frac{x}{y}), & \text{if } xy \neq 0, \\ 0, & \text{otherwise.} \end{cases}$$

It is a bent function and belongs to the PSap Dillon's class of hyperbent functions (see [9, 33]). It has algebraic degree exactly k (see [8]). Clearly, t differs from b only when $x = 0$. Therefore, for any linear Boolean function l over $\mathbb{F}_{2^k}$, we have $l(x)t(x,y) = l(x)b(x,y)$, which has algebraic degree at most $k + 1$. This is almost the worst case for the resistance to fast algebraic attacks of a $2k$-variable function with algebraic immunity k. Carlet found this weakness and gave a repair as follows [9].

Define

$$c(x,y) = b(x,y) + 1_E(x,y),$$

where 1_E is the indicator function of the set

$$E = \{(0, u_\phi)\} \cup \{(\alpha^i u_i, u_i) : i \notin \{s, ..., s + 2^{k-1} - 1\}\},$$

spanning the whole vector space $\mathbb{F}_{2^k}^2$ and such that, for every vector e, the set $e + E$ spans $\mathbb{F}_{2^k}^2$ as well, where $u_\phi \in \mathbb{F}_{2^k}$ and $0 \neq u_i \in \mathbb{F}_{2^k}$ are chosen suitably.

The function $c(x,y) \in B_{2k}$ (if it exists) is balanced and has optimum algebraic immunity. The nonlinearity of c satisfies $nl(c) \geq 2^{2k-1} - 2^k$ and perhaps even better for clever choices of E. Since $c(x,y)$ differs from $b(x,y)$ on any affine hyperplane of $\mathbb{F}_{2^k}^2$, there exists no linear function l over $\mathbb{F}_{2^k}$ such that $l(x)c(x,y) = l(x)b(x,y)$, which is better than the Tu-Deng function $t(x,y)$. Carlet mentioned in [9] that they were making investigations to check if $c(x,y)$ can have an optimum algebraic degree and behave well against fast algebraic attacks.

In fact, $c(x,y) \in B_{2k}$ may not exist for some k, something that is explained in Remark 3. For a suitably large k, since there are many choices of E, it may be easy to find a function $c(x,y)$ of optimum algebraic degree. However, no matter how much effort we use, we cannot find a function $c(x,y)$ such that it behaves well against fast algebraic attacks, which can be seen from the following arguments.

Lemma 1. $\binom{2k}{k/4} > 2^{k-1}$, where $k \geq 20$ and $4|k$.

Proof. we will prove this by induction. Clearly, $\binom{40}{5} = 658008 > 524288 = 2^{19}$. Now assume that for some m we have $\binom{2m}{m/4} > 2^{m-1}$, where $m \geq 20$ and $4|m$. Then

$$\binom{2(m+4)}{(m+4)/4} = \binom{2m}{m/4} 8 \prod_{i=1}^{7} \frac{2m+i}{\frac{7}{4}m+i}$$

$$\geq \binom{2m}{m/4} 8 \prod_{i=1}^{7} \frac{40+i}{35+i}$$

$$> 16\binom{2m}{m/4} > 2^{m+4-1}.$$

Hence the result follows by induction. □

Lemma 2. $\binom{2k}{0} + \binom{2k}{1} + \ldots + \binom{2k}{\lceil k/4 \rceil} > 2^{k-1}$, where $k \geq 1$.

Proof. For $k \geq 20$, similar to the proof of Lemma 1, we have $\binom{2k}{\lceil k/4 \rceil} > 2^{k-1}$. For $1 \leq k < 20$, we can verify the inequality by computer, and the result follows. □

Theorem 2. Let $c'(x,y) = b'(x,y) + 1_{E'}(x,y)$, where $b'(x,y) \in B_{2k}$, $\deg(b'(x,y)) \leq k$ and $1_{E'}$ is the indicator function of a set with 2^{k-1} elements. Then $\mathcal{FAI}(c'(x,y)) \leq k + 2\lceil k/4 \rceil$.

Proof. We have $nl_k(c') \leq wt(c' + b') = 2^{k-1}$. By Theorem 1 and Lemma 2, we deduce the result. □

Remark 3: Taking $b'(x,y) = b(x,y)$ and $E' = E$, we deduce that the fast algebraic immunity of the repaired function $c(x,y)$ is at most $k + 2\lceil k/4 \rceil$, which is not a good case for the resistance to fast algebraic attacks. In fact, there exists an $h(x,y)$ of degree at most $\lceil k/4 \rceil$ such that $c(x,y)h(x,y)$ has degree at most $k + \lceil k/4 \rceil$. By using $\prod_{wt(j) = \lceil k/4 \rceil + 1}^{k + \lceil k/4 \rceil}(x + \alpha^j)$ bits of keystream, we can cancel the terms with degree more than $\lceil k/4 \rceil$ of $c(x,y)h(x,y)$, and an equation of degree at most $\lceil k/4 \rceil$ is obtained (see [31]). Then, if the function is used in a filter generator, we can recover the initial state by solving equations of degree at most $\lceil k/4 \rceil$. For example, when $k = 4$, $c(x,y) \in B_8$ (if it exists) and there is a function $h(x,y)$ of degree 1 such that $c(x,y)h(x,y)$ is of degree at most 5. This is almost the worst case for the resistance to fast algebraic attacks of a 8-variable function with algebraic immunity 4. In fact, in this case, we cannot find a set E spanning the whole vector space $\mathbb{F}_{2^k}^2$ and such that, for every vector e, the set $e + E$ spans $\mathbb{F}_{2^k}^2$ as well. That is, for any choice of E, we can find a linear function h such that $1_E * h = 0$ and there exists no $c(x,y) \in B_8$. Assume that a filter generator consists of a length N linear feedback shift register and the Boolean function $c(x,y)$ that taps bits from $2k < N$ positions in the register. Then the fast algebraic attack has a pre-computation step of complexity $O(E_1 \log^3 E_1)$ and an online complexity of $O(D_1^3 + 2D_1 E_1 \log E_1)$, where $D_1 = \sum_{i=0}^{\deg(h)} \binom{N}{i} \leq \sum_{i=0}^{\lceil k/4 \rceil} \binom{N}{i}$ and $E_1 = \sum_{i=0}^{\deg(c*h)} \binom{N}{i} \leq \sum_{i=0}^{k + \lceil k/4 \rceil} \binom{N}{i}$. As a comparison, the time complexity of the standard algebraic attack is roughly $O(D_2^3)$, where $D_2 = \sum_{i=0}^{k} \binom{N}{i}$. Clearly, the fast algebraic attack on $c(x,y)$ is more efficient than the standard one. Therefore, the fast algebraic immunity of $c(x,y)$ is not good, though it is better than $t(x,y)$ in most cases. In fact, for a $2k$-variable function f with optimum algebraic immunity k, we have $k+1 \leq \mathcal{FAI}(f) \leq 2k$. $\mathcal{FAI}(c(x,y)) \leq k + 2\lceil k/4 \rceil$ and it is much less than the highest possible fast algebraic immunity $2k$.

Remark 4: $t(x,y)$ and $c(x,y)$ have high nonlinearities since they have small distances to bent functions which also leads to their bad fast algebraic immunities. We may try to repair $t(x,y)$ by other means. However, to assure its high nonlinearity, we might change $t(x,y)$ only on a few points. Then it is still close to bent functions and cannot behave well against fast algebraic attacks.

5   Conclusion

This note deduced a bound between fast algebraic immunity and higher order nonlinearity. We found that no matter how much effort we make, the Tu-Deng functions cannot be repaired to behave well against fast algebraic attacks. Therefore, we should give up repairing this class of Boolean functions and try to find other classes of functions with good cryptographic properties or to prove that the Carlet-Feng function behaves well.

Moreover, it may be hard to construct an infinite class of functions that have high nonlinearity and can also behave well against fast algebraic attacks. It is interesting to investigate the upper bound between $nl(f)$ and $\mathcal{FAI}(f)$, which we leave as an open problem.

References

1. Braeken, A., Preneel, B.: On the algebraic immunity of symmetric Boolean functions. In: Maitra, S., Veni Madhavan, C.E., Venkatesan, R. (eds.) INDOCRYPT 2005. LNCS, vol. 3797, pp. 35–48. Springer, Heidelberg (2005)
2. Carlet, C., Dalai, D.K., Gupta, K.C., Maitra, S.: Algebraic immunity for cryptographically significant Boolean functions: analysis and construction. IEEE Trans. Inf. Theory 52(7), 3105–3121 (2006)
3. Dalai, D.K., Gupta, K.C., Maitra, S.: Cryptographically Significant Boolean Functions: Construction and Analysis in Terms of Algebraic Immunity. In: Gilbert, H., Handschuh, H. (eds.) FSE 2005. LNCS, vol. 3557, pp. 98–111. Springer, Heidelberg (2005)
4. Dalai, D.K., Maitra, S., Sarkar, S.: Basic theory in construction of Boolean functions with maximum possible annihilator immunity. Des. Codes Cryptogr. 40(1), 41–58 (2006)
5. Li, N., Qi, W.-F.: Construction and Analysis of Boolean Functions of $2t+1$ Variables with Maximum Algebraic Immunity. In: Lai, X., Chen, K. (eds.) ASIACRYPT 2006. LNCS, vol. 4284, pp. 84–98. Springer, Heidelberg (2006)
6. Pasalic, E.: Almost Fully Optimized Infinite Classes of Boolean Functions Resistant to (Fast) Algebraic Cryptanalysis. In: Lee, P.J., Cheon, J.H. (eds.) ICISC 2008. LNCS, vol. 5461, pp. 399–414. Springer, Heidelberg (2009)
7. Carlet, C., Feng, K.: An infinite class of balanced functions with optimal algebraic immunity, good immunity to fast algebraic attacks and good nonlinearity. In: Pieprzyk, J. (ed.) ASIACRYPT 2008. LNCS, vol. 5350, pp. 425–440. Springer, Heidelberg (2008)
8. Tu, Z., Deng, Y.: A Conjecture on Binary String and its Application on constructing Boolean Functions of Optimal Algebraic Immunity. Des. Codes Cryptogr., Online First Articles. doi: 10.1007/s10623-010-9413-9 (2010)
9. Carlet, C.: On a weakness of the Tu-Deng function and its repair. Cryptology ePrint Archive, 2009/606, http://eprint.iacr.org/
10. Courtois, N.T.: Higher order correlation attacks,XL algorithm and cryptanalysis of toyocrypt. In: Lee, P.J., Lim, C.H. (eds.) ICISC 2002. LNCS, vol. 2587, pp. 182–199. Springer, Heidelberg (2003)
11. Golić, J.D.: Fast low order approximation of cryptographic functions. In: Maurer, U.M. (ed.) EUROCRYPT 1996. LNCS, vol. 1070, pp. 268–282. Springer, Heidelberg (1996)

12. Knudsen, L.R., Robshaw, M.J.B.: Non-linear approximations in linear cryptanalysis. In: Maurer, U.M. (ed.) EUROCRYPT 1996. LNCS, vol. 1070, pp. 224–236. Springer, Heidelberg (1996)

13. Iwata, T., Kurosawa, K.: Probabilistic higher order differential attack and higher order bent functions. In: Lam, K.-Y., Okamoto, E., Xing, C. (eds.) ASIACRYPT 1999. LNCS, vol. 1716, pp. 62–74. Springer, Heidelberg (1999)

14. Carlet, C.: On the higher order nonlinearities of algebraic immune functions. In: Dwork, C. (ed.) CRYPTO 2006. LNCS, vol. 4117, pp. 584–601. Springer, Heidelberg (2006)

15. Carlet, C., Mesnager, S.: Improving the Upper Bounds on the Covering Radii of Binary Reed-Muller Codes. IEEE Trans. Inf. Theory 53(1), 162–173 (2007)

16. Carlet, C.: Recursive Lower Bounds on the Nonlinearity Profile of Boolean Functions and Their Applications. IEEE Trans. Inf. Theory 54(3), 1262–1272 (2008)

17. Lobanov, M.S.: Tight bounds between algebraic immunity and nonlinearities of high orders. Cryptology ePrint Archive 2007/444, http://eprint.iacr.org/

18. Carlet, C.: On the Higher Order Nonlinearities of Boolean Functions and S-Boxes, and Their Generalizations. In: Golomb, S.W., Parker, M.G., Pott, A., Winterhof, A. (eds.) SETA 2008. LNCS, vol. 5203, pp. 345–367. Springer, Heidelberg (2008)

19. Mesnager, S.: Improving the Lower Bound on the Higher Order Nonlinearity of Boolean Functions With Prescribed Algebraic Immunity. IEEE Trans. Inf. Theory 54(8), 3656–3662 (2008)

20. Braeken, A.: Cryptographic properties of Boolean functions and S-boxes. Ph. D. thesis, Katholieke Universiteit Leuven, Belgium (2006), http://www.cosic.esat.kuleuven.be/publications/thesis-129.pdf

21. Meier, W., Staffelbach, O.: Fast correlation attacks on stream ciphers. In: Günther, C.G. (ed.) EUROCRYPT 1988. LNCS, vol. 330, pp. 301–314. Springer, Heidelberg (1988)

22. Johansson, T., Jönsson, F.: Fast Correlation Attacks through Reconstruction of Linear Polynomials. In: Bellare, M. (ed.) CRYPTO 2000. LNCS, vol. 1880, pp. 300–315. Springer, Heidelberg (2000)

23. Hawkes, P., Rose, G.G.: Rewriting Variables: The Complexity of Fast Algebraic Attacks on Stream Ciphers. In: Franklin, M. (ed.) CRYPTO 2004. LNCS, vol. 3152, pp. 390–406. Springer, Heidelberg (2004)

24. Rothaus, O.S.: On bent functions. J. Comb. Theory A20(3), 300–305 (1976)

25. Courtois, N., Meier, W.: Algebraic attacks on stream ciphers with linear feedback. In: Biham, E. (ed.) EUROCRYPT 2003. LNCS, vol. 2656, pp. 345–359. Springer, Heidelberg (2003)

26. Liu, M., Lin, D.: Fast Algebraic Attacks and Decomposition of Symmetric Boolean Functions. ArXiv: 0910.4632v1 [cs.CR]

27. Courtois, N.: Fast Algebraic attacks on stream ciphers with linear feedback. In: Boneh, D. (ed.) CRYPTO 2003. LNCS, vol. 2729, pp. 176–194. Springer, Heidelberg (2003)

28. Cusick, T.W., Li, Y., Stanica, P.: On a combinatoric conjectur. Cryptology ePrint Archive, 2009/554, http://eprint.iacr.org/

29. Flori, J.P., Randriambololona, H., Cohen, G., Mesnager, S.: On a conjecture about binary strings distribution. Cryptology ePrint Archive, 2010/170, http://eprint.iacr.org/

30. Lobanov, M.S.: Tight bound between nonlinearity and algebraic immunity. Cryptology ePrint Archive, 2005/441, http://eprint.iacr.org/

31. Rønjom, S., Helleseth, T.: A New Attack on the Filter Generator. IEEE Trans. Inf. Theory 53(5), 1752–1758 (2007)
32. Wang, Q., Peng, J., Kan, H., Xue, X.: Constructions of Cryptographically Significant Boolean Functions Using Primitive Polynomials. IEEE Trans. Inf. Theory 56(6), 3048–3053 (2010)
33. Carlet, C.: Boolean Functions for Cryptography and Error Correcting Codes. In: Chapter of the Monography "Boolean Models and Methods in Mathematics, Computer Science, and Engineering, pp. 257–397. Cambridge University Press, Cambridge (2010), http://www-roc.inria.fr/secret/Claude.Carlet/pubs.html

Comments and Improvements on Key-Exposure Free Chameleon Hashing Based on Factoring*

Xiaofeng Chen[1], Haibo Tian[2], Fangguo Zhang[2], and Yong Ding[3]

[1] Key Laboratory of Computer Networks and Information Security,
Ministry of Education, Xidian University, Xi'an 710071, P.R. China
xfchen@xidian.edu.cn
[2] School of Information Science and Technology,
Sun Yat-sen University, Guangzhou 510275, P.R. China
[3] School of Mathematics and Computational Science,
Guilin University of Electronic Technology, Guilin 541004, P.R. China

Abstract. Chameleon signatures simultaneously provide the properties of non-repudiation and non-transferability for the signed message. However, the initial constructions of chameleon signatures suffer from the key exposure problem of chameleon hashing. This creates a strong disincentive for the recipient to forge signatures, partially undermining the concept of non-transferability. Recently, some specific constructions of key-exposure free chameleon hashing based on various assumptions are presented.

In this paper, we present some security flaws of the key-exposure free chameleon hash scheme based on factoring [10]. Besides, we propose an improved chameleon hash scheme without key exposure based on factoring which enjoys all the desired security notions of chameleon hashing.

Keywords: Chameleon hashing, Factoring problem, Key exposure.

1 Introduction

Chameleon signatures, introduced by Krawczyk and Rabin [13], are based on well established hash-and-sign paradigm, where a chameleon hash function is used to compute the cryptographic message digest. A chameleon hash function is a trapdoor one-way hash function, which prevents everyone except the holder of the trapdoor information from computing the collisions for a randomly given input. Chameleon signatures simultaneously provide non-repudiation and non-transferability for the signed message as undeniable signatures [4] do, but the former allows for simpler and more efficient realization than the latter. In

---

* This work is supported by the National Natural Science Foundation of China (No. 60970144, 60773202, 61003244, 60963024), Guangdong Natural Science Foundation (No. 8451027501001508), Program of the Science and Technology of Guangzhou, China (No. 2008J1-C231-2), and the Fundamental Research Funds for the Central Universities (No. K50510010003).

X. Lai, M. Yung, and D. Lin (Eds.): Inscrypt 2010, LNCS 6584, pp. 415–426, 2011.

particular, chameleon signatures are non-interactive and less complicated. Besides, since the chameleon signatures are based on well established hash-and-sign paradigm, it provides more generic and flexible constructions.

One limitation of the original chameleon signature scheme is that signature forgery results in the signer recovering the recipient's trapdoor information, *i.e.*, the private key. The signer then can use this information to deny other signatures given to the recipient. Ateniese and de Mederious [1] firstly addressed the key exposure problem of chameleon hashing and introduced the idea of identity-based chameleon hashing to solve this problem. Due to the distinguishing property of identity-based system, the signer can sign a message to an intended recipient, without having to first retrieve the recipient's certificate. Moreover, the signer uses a different public key (corresponding a different private key) for each transaction with a recipient, so that signature forgery only results in the signer recovering the trapdoor information associated to a single transaction. Therefore, the signer will not be capable of denying signatures on any message in other transactions. We argue that this idea only provides a partial solution for the problem of key exposure since the recipient's public key is changed for each transaction.

Chen et al. [6] proposed the first full construction of a key-exposure free chameleon hash function in the gap Diffie-Hellman (GDH) groups with bilinear pairings. Ateniese and de Mederious [2] then presented three key-exposure free chameleon hash schemes, two based on the RSA assumption, as well as a new construction based on pairings. Recently, Gao et al. [11] claimed to present a key-exposure free chameleon hash scheme based on the Schnorr signature. However, it requires an interactive protocol between the signer and the recipient and thus violates the basic definition of chameleon hashing and signatures. Chen et al. [7] proposed the first discrete-logarithm-based key-exposure free chameleon hashing without using the GDH groups. Besides, Gao, Wang and Xie [10] proposed a factoring-based chameleon hash scheme without key exposure, which we call Gao-Wang-Xie's chameleon hash scheme. Independently, Kurosawa et al. [12] proposed a double-trapdoor commitment scheme based on factoring. Since any commitment scheme with a non-interactive commitment phase induces a chameleon hash function and vice versa, these two schemes are actually equivalent to each other. Also, we argue that they are both closely related to the presentation problem of factoring [9].

It seems that the single-trapdoor commitment schemes are not sufficient for the construction of key-exposure free chameleon hashing. All of the existing key-exposure free chameleon hash schemes [2,6,10] are based on the double-trapdoor mechanism, where a master trapdoor can be used to compute an ephemeral trapdoor for each specific transaction. On the other hand, as pointed out by Ateniese and de Medeiros [2], the double-trapdoor mechanism can be used to construct either an identity-based chameleon hash scheme or a key-exposure free one, but not both. Very recently, Chen et al. [8] firstly proposed an identity-based chameleon hash scheme without key exposure based on the three-trapdoor mechanism.

Our Contribution. In this paper, we give a comment on Gao-Wang-Xie's chameleon hash scheme and point out some security flaws of the scheme. We also propose an improved chameleon hash scheme based on factoring which achieves all the desired security notions of chameleon hashing.

Organization. The rest of the paper is organized as follows: Some preliminaries are given in Section 2. Gao-Wang-Xie's chameleon hash scheme is introduced in Section 3. The comment on Gao-Wang-Xie's chameleon hash scheme is given in Section 4. The improved key-exposure free chameleon hashing based on factoring is proposed in Section 5. Finally, conclusions will be made in Section 6.

2 Preliminaries

In this section, we first introduce the formal definitions and security requirements of chameleon hash schemes [1,2], and then introduce a variant Rabin signature scheme [10].

2.1 Chameleon Hashing

A chameleon hash function is a trapdoor collision-resistant hash function, which is associated with a trapdoor/hash key pair (TK, HK). Anyone who knows the public key HK can efficiently compute the hash value for each input. However, there exists no efficient algorithm for anyone except the holder of the secret key TK, to find collisions for every given input. In the following, we present a formal definition of a chameleon hash scheme.

Definition 1. *A chameleon hash scheme consists of four efficient algorithms* (**GenKey, Hash, UForge, IForge**):

- **GenKey:** *A probabilistic polynomial-time algorithm that, on input a security parameter k, outputs a trapdoor/hash key pair (TK, HK).*
- **Hash:** *A probabilistic polynomial-time algorithm that, on input the hash key HK, a label L, a message m, and a random string r, outputs the hashed value $h = \text{Hash}(HK, L, m, r)$. Note that h does not depend on TK.*
- **UForge:** *(universal forge) A deterministic polynomial-time algorithm $\mathcal{F}$ that, on input the trapdoor key TK, a label L, a message m, a random string r, and another message $m' \neq m$, outputs a string r' that satisfies*

$$\text{Hash}(HK, L, m', r') = \text{Hash}(HK, L, m, r).$$

  Moreover, if r is uniformly distributed in a finite space $\mathcal{R}$, then the distribution of r' is computationally indistinguishable from uniform in $\mathcal{R}$.
- **IForge:** *(instance forge) A deterministic polynomial-time algorithm that, on input a tuple (HK, L, m, r, m', r') such that $h = \text{Hash}(HK, L, m', r') = \text{Hash}(HK, L, m, r)$, outputs a new collision (m'', r'') that also satisfies $h = \text{Hash}(HK, L, m'', r'')$.*

A secure chameleon hashing scheme satisfies the following properties:

- **Collision resistance:** Without the knowledge of trapdoor key TK, there exists no efficient algorithm that, on input a message m, a random string r, and another message m', outputs a string r' that satisfy $Hash(HK, L, m', r') = Hash(HK, L, m, r)$, with non-negligible probability.
- **Semantic security:** For all pairs of messages m and m', the probability distributions of the random values $Hash(HK, L, m', r)$ and $Hash(HK, L, m, r)$ are computationally indistinguishable. In formal terms, let $H[X]$ denote the entropy of a random variable X, and $H[X|Y]$ the entropy of the variable X given the value of a random function Y of X. Semantic security is the statement that the conditional entropy $H[m|h]$ of the message given its chameleon hash value h equals the total entropy $H[m]$ of the message space.
- **Message hiding:** Given a collision (m', r') and (m, r) of the chameleon hash scheme, i.e., $h = Hash(HK, L, m', r') = Hash(HK, L, m, r)$. Then the sender can successfully contest this invalid claim by releasing a third pair (m'', r'') such that $h = Hash(HK, L, m'', r'')$, without having to reveal the original signed message m.
- **Key exposure freeness:** If a recipient has never computed a collision under a label L, then there is no efficient algorithm for an adversary to find a collision for a given chameleon hash value $Hash(HK, L, m, r)$. This must remain true even if the adversary has oracle access to $\mathcal{F}$ and is allowed polynomially many queries on triples (L_j, m_j, r_j) of his choice, except that L_j is not allowed to equal the challenge L.

2.2   A Variant of Rabin Signature Scheme

Let $N = pq$ is a Blum integer, where p, q are two random primes such that $p = q = 3 \mod 4$. Denote by QR_N the set of all quadratic residue modulo N, we know that either $m \in QR_N$ or $-m \in QR_N$ if the Jacobi symbol $(\frac{m}{N}) = +1$. Note that the Jacobi symbol can be calculated without knowledge of the factorization of N. Also, for a Blum integer, squaring is a permutation on the group of quadratic residues QR_N. Trivially, it can be extended to 2^l-th power for any positive integer l.

Define a cryptographic hash function $H : \{0, 1\}^* \to \mathbb{Z}_N^*[+1]$, where $\mathbb{Z}_N^*[+1] = \{a | a \in \mathbb{Z}_N^*, (\frac{m}{N}) = +1\}$ is the set of elements of $\mathbb{Z}_N^*$ with Jacobi symbol is $+1$. Constructions of the hash function H can be found in [5,10]. A variant Rabin signature scheme based on factoring assumption is given as follows:

- **Sign:** Given a message m, compute the signature $\sigma = |H(m)|^{\frac{1}{2}} \mod N$, where $|H(m)| = H(m)$ if $H(m) \in QR_N$; $|H(m)| = -H(m)$ otherwise.
- **Verify:** Given a pair (m, σ), if either $\sigma^2 = H(m) \mod N$ or $\sigma^2 = -H(m) \mod N$ holds, then σ is a valid signature for message m.

3   Gao-Wang-Xie's Chameleon Hashing

In this section, we introduce Gao-Wang-Xie's chameleon hash scheme without key exposure based on factoring [10], which consists of the following efficient algorithms.

-   **GenKey:** Given a security parameter k, let $N = pq$ where p, q are two distinct odd primes with the same length such that $p = q = 3 \mod 4$. Define a cryptographic hash function $H : \{0,1\}^* \to \mathbb{Z}_N^*[+1]$. The public key is N and the secret key is (p, q). Additionally, we restrict the considered message space of the chameleon hash is $\{0,1\}^{f(k)}$ where $f(k)$ is super-logarithmic in k, i.e., $0 \le m \le 2^{f(k)} - 1$. Trivially, the case of the message space of $\{0,1\}^*$ can be easily extended by using a collision-resistant hash function from $\{0,1\}^*$ to $\{0,1\}^{f(k)}$.
-   **Hash:** Given the public key N, a label L, and a message $m \in \{0,1\}^{f(k)}$, firstly choose a random string $r \in \mathbb{Z}_N$ and compute the hash value

$$h = \text{Hash}(N, L, m, r) = bJ^m r^{2^{f(k)}} \quad \mod N,$$

where $J = H(L)$, $b \in \{+1, -1\}$.
-   **Uforge:** Given the secret key p, q, the original input (m, r), another message $m' \neq m$, first compute the ephemeral trapdoor $B = |H(L)|^{\frac{1}{2^{f(k)}}} \mod N$ for the label L, here $|H(L)| = H(L)$ if $H(L) \in QR_N$; $|H(L)| = -H(L)$ otherwise. Then compute the corresponding random string $r' = rB^{m-m'} \mod N$. Note that

$$
\begin{aligned}
\text{Hash}(N, L, m', r') &= \pm H(L)^{m'} r'^{2^{f(k)}} \\
&= \pm H(L)^{m'} (rB^{m-m'})^{2^{f(k)}} \\
&= \pm H(L)^{m'} |H(L)|^{m-m'} r^{2^{f(k)}} \\
&= \pm H(L)^m r^{2^{f(k)}} \\
&= \pm \text{Hash}(N, L, m, r)
\end{aligned}
$$

Since the only difference between $\text{Hash}(N, L, m, r)$ and $\text{Hash}(N, L, m', r')$ is $\pm$, (m, r) and (m', r') are viewed as a valid collision of the chameleon hash function.
-   **IForge:** Given a valid collision (m, r) and (m', r'), we have $\text{Hash}(N, L, m, r) = \pm \text{Hash}(N, L, m', r') \mod N$, i.e., $|H(L)|^{m-m'} = (r'/r)^{2^{f(k)}} \mod N$. Similar to the technique in [9], we can compute a square root θ of $J' = |H(L)|$ as follows:
    Let $2^s = \gcd(m - m', 2^{f(k)})$, where $0 \le s < f(k)$. Compute $u, v \in \mathbb{Z}$ such that $u(m - m') + v2^{f(k)} = 2^s$ and then compute

$$
\begin{aligned}
J'^{2^s} &= J'^{u(m-m') + v2^{f(k)}} \\
&= (J'^{m-m'})^u (J'^v)^{2^{f(k)}} \\
&= ((r'/r)^u J'^v)^{2^{f(k)}} \quad \mod N
\end{aligned}
$$

Let $\theta = ((r'/r)^u J'^v)^{2^{f(k)-s-1}}$, we have $J'^{2^s} = (\theta^2)^{2^s}$. Since $J', \theta \in QR_N$ and square is a permutation of the group QR_N, we have $J' = \theta^2 \mod N$.

Now if $m' \geq 2^{f(k)-1}$, let $m'' = m' - 2^{f(k)-1}$ and $r'' = r'\theta \mod N$; if $m' < 2^{f(k)-1}$, let $m'' = m' + 2^{f(k)-1}$ and $r'' = r'/\theta \mod N$. We can verify that $\text{Hash}(N, L, m'', r'') = \pm\text{Hash}(N, L, m', r') \mod N$.

Theorem 1. *[10] The above chameleon hash scheme enjoys the properties of collision resistance, message hiding, semantic security, and key-exposure freeness.*

Proof. – Collision Resistance: Exposing a collision allows anybody to compute a variant Rabin signature $|H(L)|^{\frac{1}{2}}$ on message L. Since the variant Rabin signature is existentially unforgeable under the factoring assumption, the proposed chameleon hash function is collision resistance.

– Message Hiding: Given a collision (m, r) and (m', r'), we can use the algorithm **IForge** to compute another pair (m'', r'').

– Semantic Security: For each message m, the hash value $h = \text{Hash}(N, L, m, r)$ is uniquely determined by the value $r^{2^{f(k)}}$ with ignoring $\pm$, and vice versa. So, the conditional probability taken over the message space $\mu(m|h)=\mu(m|r^{2^{f(k)}})$. Also, $\mu(m|r^{2^{f(k)}}) = \mu(m)$ since m and r are independent variables. So, $\mu(m|h) = \mu(m)$, i.e., the chameleon hash value h discloses no information about m.

– Key-exposure Freeness: If an attacker $\mathcal{A}_1$ against the above chameleon hash scheme can be successful with respect to the property of key-exposure freeness, then we can use it to construct an attacker $\mathcal{A}_2$ of type *uf-ecma* against the above variant Rabin signature as follows: First $\mathcal{A}_2$ is given the public parameters $(N, H, f(k))$ of the variant Rabin signature, and $\mathcal{A}_2$ passes them to $\mathcal{A}_1$. Then when $\mathcal{A}_1$ makes a query (L_i, m_i, r_i) to the oracle **UForge**, $\mathcal{A}_2$ can get the ephemeral trapdoor $|H(L)|^{\frac{1}{2^{f(k)}}} \mod N$ from its own oracle access and further compute a collision (m_i', r_i') as in **UForge** and return it. At last, $\mathcal{A}_1$ returns a collision (m, r) and (m', r') and a never queried label L such that $\text{Hash}(N, L, m', r') = \text{Hash}(N, L, m, r)$, $\mathcal{A}_2$ can compute $|H(L)|^{\frac{1}{2}} \mod N$ as in **IForge**, which is the variant Rabin signature for message L.

4 Comments on Gao-Wang-Xie's Chameleon Hashing

In this section, we present some disadvantages of Gao-Wang-Xie's chameleon hash scheme. More precisely, there are mainly three security flaws in their hash scheme.

1. The definition of the chameleon hashing

Firstly, we point out that the definition of Gao-Wang-Xie's chameleon hashing is not rigorous. For a given input, the hash value h is a random variable dependent on the random bit b. This is considered to be a main trick to design key-exposure free chameleon hashing based on factoring. For more details, please refer to the remark 2 of [10]. Also, (m, r) and (m', r') is a valid collision if $\text{Hash}(N, L, m', r') = \pm\text{Hash}(N, L, m, r)$ holds. This strongly violates the original definition of chameleon hashing and the collisions. The reason for this paradoxical definition is that anyone without the information of p, q can not know whether $H(L)$ is a quadratic residue. We present a solution to this problem as follows:

Define the chameleon hash function $h = \text{Hash}(N, L, m, r) = H(L)^m r^{2^{f(k)}}$ mod N. We consider the following situations:

- If $H(L) \in QR_N$, the receiver with the trapdoor $H(L)^{1/2^{f(k)}}$ to compute a pair (m', r') such that $h = H(L)^{m'} r'^{2^{f(k)}}$.
- If $H(L) \notin QR_N$, then $-H(L) \in QR_N$.
  - If m is an even, then $h = H(L)^m r^{2^{f(k)}} = (-H(L))^m r^{2^{f(k)}}$ mod N, the receiver can use the trapdoor $(-H(L))^{1/2^{f(k)}}$ to compute a collision (m', r') where m' is also an even.
  - If m is an odd, then $h = H(L)^m r^{2^{f(k)}} = -(-H(L))^m r^{2^{f(k)}}$ mod N, the receiver can use the trapdoor $(-H(L))^{1/2^{f(k)}}$ to compute a collision (m', r') where m' is also an odd.

Therefore, we can always define $h = \text{Hash}(N, L, m, r) = H(L)^m r^{2^{f(k)}}$ mod N. This makes the chameleon hash scheme very simple and easily to be understand. In the section 5, we present another solution which still uses the random bit b to fix this problem.

2. The proof of key-exposure freeness

The second security flaw is the proof for key-exposure freeness. When $\mathcal{A}_1$ makes queries (L_i, m_i, r_i) to **Uforge**, can $\mathcal{A}_2$ always know the information $|H(L_i)|^{1/2^{f(k)}}$? Note that $\mathcal{A}_2$ cannot know the master trapdoor (p, q).

Let us consider **IForge** more carefully: Given a collision (m, r) and (m', r') for L, we have $|H(L)|^{m-m'} = (r'/r)^{2^{f(k)}}$. Define $\gcd(m - m', 2^{f(k)}) = 2^s$, here $0 \leq s < f(k)$ (note that the message space of the chameleon hash is $0 \leq m \leq 2^{f(k)} - 1$). Compute (u, v) such that $u(m - m') + v2^{f(k)} = 2^s$, so we have $((r'/r)^u |H(L)|^v)^{2^k} = |H(L)|^{2^s}$.

Trivially, $\theta = ((r'/r)^u |H(L)|^v)^{2^{f(k)-s-1}} = |H(L)|^{\frac{1}{2}}$ mod N (this is the result of [10]). On the other hand, if we define $\theta' = (r'/r)^u |H(L)|^v$, then we have $\theta' = |H(L)|^{\frac{1}{2^{f(k)-s}}}$ mod N. Of course, if we know θ', we can compute θ easily. However, for any integer $s > 0$, it is difficult to compute $|H(L)|^{\frac{1}{2^{f(k)}}}$.

In the proof for key-exposure freeness of Gao-Wang-Xie's chameleon hash scheme, the attacker $\mathcal{A}_2$ can always obtain the ephemeral trapdoor key $|H(L)|^{\frac{1}{2^{f(k)}}}$ mod N from its own oracle access. This requires that the variant Rabin signature is still existentially unforgeable against the so-called uf-ecma attacker under the factoring assumption. The uf-ecma attacker is more powerful than the traditional adaptively chosen message attacker because uf-ecma attacker can always access to an oracle to obtain $|H(L)|^{\frac{1}{2^{f(k)}}}$ mod N. This seems to be a much stronger assumption to prove the security of the variant Rabin signature, *i.e.*, it is much more difficult to prove the unforgeability of the variant Rabin signature. The authors [10] do not provide the complete proof. Actually, observe that $|H(L)|^{\frac{1}{2^l}}$ is $f(k)$ consecutive trapdoors, where $1 \le l \le f(k)$. A higher trapdoor $|H(L)|^{\frac{1}{2^l}}$ can be used to compute a lower trapdoor $|H(L)|^{\frac{1}{2^{l-1}}}$. In the random oracle model, we argue that it is enough to compute a collision of the chameleon hash scheme with the trapdoor $|H(L)|^{\frac{1}{2}}$. Therefore, it only requires that the variant Rabin signature is existentially unforgeable against the traditional adaptively chosen message attacker, which can be easily proven based on the technique [3]. We will present the details in the section 5.

3. The collision computation in **IForge**

Finally, the collision (m'', r'') is a fixed pair in **IForge** of Gao-Wang-Xie's chameleon hash scheme. Actually, we can provide plenty of other collisions since the real ephemeral trapdoor is not $H(L)^{\frac{1}{2}}$, but $|H(L)|^{\frac{1}{2^{f(k)-s}}}$ as discussed above. Therefore, for any message m'' such that $2^s | m' - m''$, we can compute the corresponding r'' as a collision. Only when $s = f(k) - 1$, the pair (m'', r'') is unique determined. For more details, please refer to section 5.

5   Improved Chameleon Hashing Based on Factoring

In this section, we present an improved chameleon hashing without key exposure based on factoring. Our chameleon hash scheme is defined as

$$h = \text{Hash}(N, L, m, r, b) = bJ^m r^{2^{f(k)}} \mod N,$$

where $J = H(L)$, $b \in \{+1, -1\}$.

Though we also use a random bit b, it is viewed as a part of the input of the chameleon hash scheme. This modification makes the chameleon hash value h is a constant for a given input. Also, (m, r, b) and (m', r', b') is a valid collision if $\text{Hash}(N, L, m', r', b') = \text{Hash}(N, L, m, r, b)$ holds. This consists with the original definition of the collisions since we avoid the notation " $\pm$ ".

The improved chameleon hash scheme based on factoring consists of the following efficient algorithms:

- **GenKey:** The system parameters are the same as that of Gao-Wang-Xie's chameleon hash scheme.
- **Hash:** Given the public key N, a label L, and a message $m \in \{0,1\}^{f(k)}$, firstly choose a random string $r \in \mathbb{Z}_N$ and a random bit $b \in \{+1, -1\}$, compute the hash value

$$h = \text{Hash}(N, L, m, r, b) = bJ^m r^{2^{f(k)}} \mod N,$$

where $J = H(L)$.
- **Uforge:** Given the secret key (p, q), the original input (m, r, b), another message $m' \ne m$, first compute the trapdoor $B = |H(L)|^{\frac{1}{2^{f(k)}}} \mod N$ for the

label L, here $|H(L)| = H(L)$ if $H(L) \in QR_N$; $|H(L)| = -H(L)$ otherwise. Then the corresponding collision (r', b') can be given as follows:

$$r' = rB^{m-m'} \mod N,$$

$$b' = \begin{cases} b, & \text{if } H(L) \in QR_N \\ b(-1)^{m-m'}, & \text{Otherwise} \end{cases}$$

Note that

$$\begin{aligned}
\text{Hash}(N, L, m', r', b') &= b'J^{m'}r'^{2^{f(k)}} \\
&= b'H(L)^{m'}(rB^{m-m'})^{2^{f(k)}} \\
&= b'H(L)^{m'}|H(L)|^{m-m'}r^{2^{f(k)}} \\
&= bH(L)^{m}r^{2^{f(k)}} \\
&= \text{Hash}(N, L, m, r, b)
\end{aligned}$$

Therefore, the forgery is successful. Moreover, if (r,b) is uniformly distributed, then the distribution of (r', b') is computationally indistinguishable from uniform.

- **IForge:** Given a collision (m, r, b) and (m', r', b'), we have $\text{Hash}(N, L, m, r, b)$ = $\text{Hash}(N, L, m', r', b') \mod N$, i.e., $|H(L)|^{m-m'} = (r'/r)^{2^{f(k)}} \mod N$. Let $2^s = \gcd(m - m', 2^{f(k)})$, where $0 \le s < f(k)$. Compute $u, v \in \mathbb{Z}$ such that $u(m - m') + v2^{f(k)} = 2^s$. Similarly, we can compute $\theta = (r'/r)^u |H(L)|^v = |H(L)|^{\frac{1}{2^{f(k)-s}}} \mod N$. Trivially, we can compute $|H(L)|^{\frac{1}{2}} \mod N$. Moreover, if $\theta^{2^{f(k)-s}} = H(L)$, then $H(L) \in QR_N$; else, $-H(L) \in QR_N$. That is, it is efficient to check whether $H(L)$ is a quadratic residue modulo N.

For any message m'' such that $0 \le m'' \le 2^{f(k)} - 1$ and $2^s | m' - m''$, the corresponding collision (r'', b'') can be given as follows:

$$r'' = r'\theta^{2^{-s}(m'-m'')} \mod N,$$

$$b'' = \begin{cases} b', & \text{if } H(L) \in QR_N \\ b'(-1)^{m'-m''}, & \text{Otherwise} \end{cases}$$

Actually, note that

$$\begin{aligned}
\text{Hash}(N, L, m'', r'', b'') &= b''J^{m''}r''^{2^{f(k)}} \\
&= b''H(L)^{m''}(r'\theta^{2^{-s}(m'-m'')})^{2^{f(k)}} \\
&= b''H(L)^{m''}\theta^{2^{(f(k)-s)(m'-m'')}}r'^{2^{f(k)}} \\
&= b''H(L)^{m''}|H(L)|^{m'-m''}r'^{2^{f(k)}} \\
&= b'H(L)^{m'}r'^{2^{f(k)}} \\
&= \text{Hash}(N, L, m', r', b')
\end{aligned}$$

Thus, the instance forgery is successful.

Theorem 2. *The proposed chameleon hash scheme enjoys the properties of collision resistance, message hiding, semantic security, and key-exposure freeness.*

Proof. We prove that the proposed chameleon hash scheme satisfies all the desired security properties.

- Collision Resistance: Given two pairs (m, r) and (m', r') with the label L such that $\text{Hash}(N, L, m', r', b') = \text{Hash}(N, L, m, r, b)$, then as in **IForge** the trapdoor $|H(L)|^{\frac{1}{2^{f(k)-s}}} \mod N$ is revealed, which allows anybody to compute a variant Rabin signature $|H(L)|^{\frac{1}{2}}$ on message L. Since the variant Rabin signature is existentially unforgeable under the factoring assumption, the proposed chameleon hash function is collision resistance.
- Message Hiding: Given a collision (m, r) and (m', r'), we can use **IForge** to compute another pair (m'', r'').
- Semantic Security: For each message m, the chameleon hash value $h = \text{Hash}(N, L, m, r, b)$ is uniquely determined by the value $(r^{2^{f(k)}}, b)$, and vice versa. Therefore, the conditional probability $\mu(m|h)$ equals to $\mu(m|(r^{2^{f(k)}}, b))$. Also, $\mu(m|(r^{2^{f(k)}}, b)) = \mu(m)$ since m and (r, b) are independent variables. So, $\mu(m|h) = \mu(m)$. Then, we can prove that the conditional entropy $H[m|\mathcal{H}]$ equals the entropy $H[m]$ as follows:

$$H[m|h] = -\sum_m \sum_h \mu(m, h) \log(\mu(m|h)) = -\sum_m \sum_h \mu(m, h) \log(\mu(m))$$
$$= -\sum_m \mu(m) \log(\mu(m)) = H[m].$$

Therefore, the chameleon hash value h discloses no information about m.
- Key-exposure Freeness: If an attacker $\mathcal{A}_1$ against the above chameleon hash scheme can be successful with respect to the property of key-exposure freeness, then we can use it to construct an adaptive chosen message attacker $\mathcal{A}_2$ against the above variant Rabin signature.

  Suppose $\mathcal{A}_2$ is given the public parameters $(N, H, f(k))$ of the variant Rabin signature, and $\mathcal{A}_2$ is allowed to makes queries to the H oracle and **Sign** oracle of the variant Rabin signature scheme. $\mathcal{A}_2$ passes $(N, \text{Hash}(), H, f(k))$ to $\mathcal{A}_1$, where $\text{Hash}()$ is the proposed chameleon hash scheme. Similar to [10], the security analysis will view H as a random oracle. When $\mathcal{A}_1$ makes a query (L_i, m_i, r_i, b_i) to the oracle **UForge**, $\mathcal{A}_2$ firstly makes a query L_i to the H oracle and **Sign** oracle to get a pair $(H(L_i), \sigma_i = |H(L_i)|^{\frac{1}{2}} \mod N)$, and then uses the trapdoor σ_i to compute a collision (m'_i, r'_i, b'_i) as follows:

  Let $s = f(k) - 1$ in **IForge**, we have $m_i - m'_i = \pm 2^{f(k)-1}$. Therefore, if $m_i \geq 2^{f(k)-1}$, then the collision is $(m_i - 2^{f(k)-1}, r_i\sigma_i, b_i)$; if $m_i < 2^{f(k)-1}$, then the collision is $(m_i + 2^{f(k)-1}, r_i/\sigma_i, b_i)$. $\mathcal{A}_2$ sends $H(L_i)$ and the collision (m'_i, r'_i, b'_i) to $\mathcal{A}_1$. At the end of the game, the output of $\mathcal{A}_1$ is a collision (m, r, b) and (m', r', b') for a never queried label $L \neq L_i$ such that $\text{Hash}(N, L, m', r', b') = \text{Hash}(N, L, m, r, b)$. Then $\mathcal{A}_2$ can compute $|H(L)|^{\frac{1}{2}}$

mod N as in **IForge**, which is the variant Rabin signature for message L. Since the variant Rabin signature is existentially unforgeable against the adaptively chosen message attacker in the random oracle model, the proposed chameleon hash scheme is key-exposure free. So, it is unnecessary to prove that the variant Rabin signature is still existentially unforgeable against the so-called uf-ecma attacker in the random oracle model (even the claim is true).

6 Conclusions

Chameleon signatures simultaneously provide the properties of non-repudiation and non-transferability for the signed message. However, the initial constructions of chameleon signatures suffer from the problem of key exposure. This creates a strong disincentive for the recipient to forge signatures, partially undermining the concept of non-transferability. Recently, some constructions of chameleon hashing and signatures without key exposure are presented based on different mathematical assumptions.

In this paper, we present some security flaws and disadvantages of the key-exposure free chameleon hash scheme based on factoring [10]. Moreover, we propose an improved chameleon hash scheme without key exposure based on factoring which enjoys all the desired security notions of chameleon hashing.

Acknowledgement

The first author would like to thank Wei Gao for his valuable comments. Moreover, we are grateful to the anonymous referees of Inscrypt 2010 for their invaluable suggestions for improving this paper.

References

1. Ateniese, G., de Medeiros, B.: Identity-based chameleon hash and applications. In: Juels, A. (ed.) FC 2004. LNCS, vol. 3110, pp. 164–180. Springer, Heidelberg (2004)
2. Ateniese, G., de Medeiros, B.: On the key exposure problem in chameleon hashes. In: Blundo, C., Cimato, S. (eds.) SCN 2004. LNCS, vol. 3352, pp. 165–179. Springer, Heidelberg (2005)
3. Bellare, M., Rogaway, P.: The Exact Security of Digital Signatures - How to Sign with RSA and Rabin. In: Maurer, U.M. (ed.) EUROCRYPT 1996. LNCS, vol. 1070, pp. 399–416. Springer, Heidelberg (1996)
4. Chaum, D., van Antwerpen, H.: Undeniable signatures. In: Brassard, G. (ed.) CRYPTO 1989. LNCS, vol. 435, pp. 212–216. Springer, Heidelberg (1990)
5. Cocks, C.: An identity based encryption scheme based on quadratic residues. In: Honary, B. (ed.) Cryptography and Coding 2001. LNCS, vol. 2260, pp. 360–363. Springer, Heidelberg (2001)
6. Chen, X., Zhang, F., Kim, K.: Chameleon hashing without key exposure. In: Zhang, K., Zheng, Y. (eds.) ISC 2004. LNCS, vol. 3225, pp. 87–98. Springer, Heidelberg (2004)

7. Chen, X., Zhang, F., Susilo, W., Mu, Y., Lee, H., Kim, K.: Key-exposure free chameleon hashing and signatures based on discrete logarithm systems, http://eprint.iacr.org/2009/035
8. Chen, X., Zhang, F., Susilo, W., Tian, H., Li, J., Kim, K.: Identity-based chameleon hash scheme without key exposure. In: Steinfeld, R., Hawkes, P. (eds.) ACISP 2010. LNCS, vol. 6168, pp. 200–215. Springer, Heidelberg (2010)
9. Fischlin, M., Fischlin, R.: The representation problem based on factoring. In: Preneel, B. (ed.) CT-RSA 2002. LNCS, vol. 2271, pp. 96–113. Springer, Heidelberg (2002)
10. Gao, W., Wang, X., Xie, D.: Chameleon hashes without key exposure based on factoring. Journal of Computer Science and Technology 22(1), 109–113 (2007)
11. Gao, W., Li, F., Wang, X.: Chameleon hash without key exposure based on Schnorr signature. Computer Standards and Interfaces 31, 282–285 (2009)
12. Kurosawa, K., Schmidt-Samoa, K.: New online/offline signature schemes without random oracles. In: Yung, M., Dodis, Y., Kiayias, A., Malkin, T. (eds.) PKC 2006. LNCS, vol. 3958, pp. 330–346. Springer, Heidelberg (2006)
13. Krawczyk, H., Rabin, T.: Chameleon hashing and signatures. In: Proc. of NDSS 2000, pp. 143–154 (2000)

Quasi-Linear Cryptanalysis of a Secure RFID Ultralightweight Authentication Protocol

Pedro Peris-Lopez[1], Julio Cesar Hernandez-Castro[2], Raphael C.-W. Phan[3],
Juan M.E. Tapiador[4], and Tieyan Li[5]

[1] Security & Privacy Lab, Faculty of EEMCS, Delft University of Technology
[2] School of Computing, University of Portsmouth
[3] Department of Electronic and Electrical Engineering, Loughborough University
[4] Department of Computer Science, University of York
[5] Institute for Infocomm Research, A*STAR Singapore

Abstract. In 2010, Yeh, Lo and Winata [1] proposed a process-oriented ultralightweight RFID authentication protocol. This protocol is claimed to provide strong security and robust privacy protection, while at the same time the usage of resources on tags is optimized. Nevertheless, in this paper we show how the protocol does not achieve any of its intended security objectives; the main result is that the most valuable information stored on the tag, that is, the static identifier ID, is easily recovered even by a completely passive attacker in a number of ways. More precisely, we start by presenting a traceability attack on the protocol that allows tags to be traced. This essentially exploits the fact that the protocol messages leak out at least one bit of the static identifier. We then present a passive attack (named Norwegian attack) that discloses $\lfloor \log_2 L \rfloor$ bits of the ID, after observing roughly $O(L)$ authentication sessions. Although this attack may seem less feasible in retrieving the full 96-bits of the ID due to the large number of eavesdropped sessions involved, it is already powerful enough to serve as a basis for a very effective traceability attack. Finally, our last attack represents a step forward in the use of a recent cryptanalysis technique (called Tango attack [2]), which allows for an extremely efficient full disclosure attack, capable of revealing the value of the whole ID after eavesdropping only a very small number of sessions.

Keywords: RFID, Cryptanalysis, Ultralightweight, Authentication.

1 Introduction

In the RFID context, some researchers have dealt with the stimulating challenge of designing secure RFID protocols based only on simple bitwise logical or arithmetic operations such as bitwise XOR, OR, AND and modular addition. This type of RFID protocols are categorized as ultralightweight protocols, and are intended for very low-cost tags. In 2006, the UMAP family of protocols [3,4,5] was introduced and attracted certain attention of the research community. After some rounds of cryptanalysis of these schemes, many (if not all) of its security objectives were circumvented, e.g. with active attacks [7,8] and later with passive

X. Lai, M. Yung, and D. Lin (Eds.): Inscrypt 2010, LNCS 6584, pp. 427–442, 2011.
© Springer-Verlag Berlin Heidelberg 2011

attacks [9,10]. They served, however, as interesting thought-provoking proposals that influenced later ultralightweight RFID designs. In 2007, Chien proposed the SASI protocol [11], which aims to provide a better security margin and requires only a tiny footprint. The main contribution was the addition of the bitwise rotations to the set of operations supported on tag. Despite this twist in the design of the protocol, some attacks were subsequently published [6,12,13,14]. In 2008, Peris-Lopez et al. introduced a new protocol, named Gossamer inspired by both the UMAP family and SASI. The operations on tags are limited in this case to bitwise XOR, addition and left rotation. A key factor in the design of Gossamer is the inclusion of the $MixBits$ function. This is a very lightweight function with highly non-linear relations between inputs and outputs (see the original paper for details [15]). A desynchronization attack [16] conducted by an active attacker is, to the best of our knowledge, the only attack to date proposed against Gossamer. As an alternative to Gossamer, Yeh, Lo and Winata recently presented a new ultralightweight authentication protocol [1]. The protocol is claimed to provide strong security, and to optimize the use of the tag memory in comparison with Gossamer.

This paper presents various cryptanalytic results on the Yeh-Lo-Winata protocol. All the attacks can be mounted by passive adversaries, and thus are highly feasible. The organization of the paper is as follows. In Section 2, the protocol is briefly introduced. Then in subsequent sections, three passive attacks are presented, the last two being able to disclose the static identifier ID, thus breaking tag privacy (i.e. information and location). The reader should note that it is commonly assumed that ultralightweight RFID protocols should be resistant against passive attacks, but not necessarily to active ones. Section 3 presents a traceability attack that shows how the protocol messages leak at least one bit of information on the static identifier ID. In Section 4 we present a Norwegian attack [6] that allows to disclose $\lfloor \log_2 L \rfloor$ bits of the ID, after observing roughly $O(L)$ authentication sessions. While the number of sessions that the adversary has to eavesdrop may be large, nevertheless the attack is quite effective when only the knowledge of some bits is needed to guarantee a successful attack, e.g. in a traceability attack. In Section 5, a much more powerful and efficient full disclosure attack (the Tango attack [2]) is introduced and discussed. More precisely, the adversary listens to a small number of legitimate sessions and the protected ID is almost fully disclosed. Finally, we draw some conclusions and end with some recommendations on the design of future ultralightweight protocols.

2   Yeh et al. Protocol

Yeh et al. proposed a process-oriented ($flag = 0$ or $flag = 1$) ultralightweight RFID authentication protocol for very low-cost RFID tags. Simple bitwise operations such as AND, OR, XOR, addition mod 2^m and circular shift rotations[1]

---

[1] We confirmed by personal communication with one of the authors that the most common definition of rotation is used. That is, $Rot(X, Y) = X \lll (Y \bmod m)$, where m is the bit length of the variables.

are the set of operations assumed to be supported on-chip by tags. The authors assume that m is the bit length of all the variables in the scheme[2]. Both backward and forward channels are exposed to passive attacks. On the other hand, the communication channel between the reader and the back-end database is assumed to be secure.

In the initialization process, three values are stored in the tag's memory: 1) an authentication key K_t; 2) index-pseudonym IDS_t; and 3) an unique static identifier ID_t. Correspondingly, the back-end database maintains four values: 1) an authentication key K_{tr}; 2-3) two index pseudonyms to avoid desynchronization attacks $\{IDS_{tr_{old}}, IDS_{tr_{new}}\}$; 4) a static identifier ID_{tr}.

The protocol considers two different situations depending on the success/fail of completion of the previous protocol session ($flag = 0$ / $flag = 1$). The protocol works as follows:

$Reader \rightarrow Tag : Hello$ The reader sends to the tag a request message.
$Tag \rightarrow Reader : IDS_t$ The tag replies to the reader with its index-pseudonym.
$Reader \rightarrow Tag : A||B||C||flag$ The reader uses the received IDS_t as a search index to allocate all the information linked to an specific tag. The authentication key of the current session is set depending on the succesful/failed completion of the previous session:

$$\begin{cases} \text{if } (IDS = IDS_{tr_{new}}) & K = K_{tr} & \text{and} & flag = 0 \\ \text{if } (IDS = IDS_{tr_{old}}) & K = ID_{tr} & \text{and} & flag = 1 \end{cases} \quad (1)$$

The reader generates two nonces $\{n_1, n_2\}$, computes messages $\{A, B, C\}$ and sends this tuple to the tag. Messages $\{A, B, C\}$ are defined by:

$$\text{Compute:} \quad A = (IDS \oplus K) \oplus n_1 \quad (2)$$
$$B = (IDS \vee K) \oplus n_2 \quad (3)$$
$$C = (\overline{K} \oplus n_1) + n_2 \quad (4)$$
$$\overline{K} = Rot(K \oplus n_2, n_1) \quad (5)$$

$Tag \rightarrow Reader : D$ Upon receiving the tuple $\{A||B||C||flag\}$, the tag sets the value D depending on the flag. It extracts the nonces $\{n_1, n_2\}$ from A and B. Then, the correctness of C is checked:

$$\begin{cases} \text{if } (flag = 0) & K = K_t \\ \text{if } (flag = 1) & K = ID_t \end{cases} \quad (6)$$

$$\text{Compute:} \quad \overline{K} = Rot(K \oplus n_2, n_1) \quad (7)$$
$$\overline{C} = (\overline{K} \oplus n_1) + n_2 \quad (8)$$
$$\text{Verify:} \quad \overline{C} = C \quad (9)$$

---

[2] In our experimentation, we assume that the bit length of the variables used in the protocol is 96 ($m = 96$). If fact this is one of the most common bit length values for the static identifier ID of a tag (e.g GID-96, SGTIN-96, GIAI-96, etc. [17]).

If the reader is authenticated ($\overline{C} = C$), the tag computes the values $\{\overline{K'}, D\}$ and sends message D to the reader.

$$\overline{K'} = Rot(K \oplus n_1, n_2) \tag{10}$$
$$D = (\overline{K'} \oplus n_2) + n_1 \tag{11}$$

Reader Updating. On receiving D, the reader checks its correctness. If so, the tag is authenticated and the reader updates its internal values:

$$\text{Compute:} \quad \overline{K'} = Rot(K \oplus n_1, n_2) \tag{12}$$
$$\overline{D} = (\overline{K'} \oplus n_2) + n_1 \tag{13}$$
$$\text{Verify:} \quad \overline{D} = D \tag{14}$$

Updating phase:

$$\text{If } \overline{D} = D, \text{ compute:} \quad IDS_{tr_{old}} = IDS \tag{15}$$
$$IDS_{tr_{new}} = (IDS + (ID \oplus \overline{K'})) \oplus$$
$$n_1 \oplus n_2 \tag{16}$$
$$K_{tr} = \overline{K} \tag{17}$$

Otherwise, the protocol is aborted.

Finally, the reader sends an *Update command* to the tag.

Tag Updating. Upon receiving the *Update command*, the update phase of the internal values is executed:

$$\text{Compute:} \quad IDS = (IDS + (ID \oplus \overline{K'})) \oplus n_1 \oplus n_2 \tag{18}$$
$$K_t = \overline{K} \tag{19}$$

3   Traceability Attack

Within the untraceability (UNT) model [14], tags ($\mathcal{T}$) and readers ($\mathcal{R}$) interact in protocol sessions, while the adversary ($\mathcal{A}$) is assumed to control the communications between all parties. In order to model $\mathcal{A}$'s capabilities, the following oracle queries are defined:

-   Execute($\mathcal{R}, \mathcal{T}, i$) query. This models a passive attacker. $\mathcal{A}$ eavesdrops on the channel, and gets read access to the exchanged messages between $\mathcal{R}$ and $\mathcal{T}$ in session i of a genuine protocol execution.
-   Test($i, \mathcal{T}_0, \mathcal{T}_1$) query. This is defined to simplify the modelling of the untraceability notion. When this query is invoked for test session i, a random bit is generated $b \in \{0, 1\}$. Then, a pseudonym IDS^i corresponding to either of $\{ID^{\mathcal{T}_0}, ID^{\mathcal{T}_1}\}$ depending on the bit b is given to $\mathcal{A}$.

The untraceability (UNT) notion is then defined as a game $\mathcal{G}$ comprising three phases:

Phase 1 (Learning): $\mathcal{A}$ can make any number of Execute queries, which model the eavesdropping of exchanged messages, i.e. a passive attack, over the insecure radio channel.

Phase 2 (Challenge): $\mathcal{A}$ chooses two fresh tags whose associated identifiers are $ID^{\mathcal{T}_0}$ and $ID^{\mathcal{T}_1}$. Then he sends a Test(i, $\mathcal{T}_0$, $\mathcal{T}_1$) query. As result, $\mathcal{A}$ is given a pseudonym IDS^i corresponding to either of $\{ID^{\mathcal{T}_0}, ID^{\mathcal{T}_1}\}$ depending on a randomly chosen bit $b \in \{0, 1\}$.

Phase 3 (Guessing): $\mathcal{A}$ ends the game and outputs a bit $\tilde{b} \in \{0, 1\}$ as its guess of the value of b.

$\mathcal{A}$'s success in winning $\mathcal{G}$ is equivalent to the success of breaking the untraceability property offered by the protocol. Thus the advantage of $\mathcal{A}$ in distinguishing whether the pseudonym corresponds to $\mathcal{T}_0$ or $\mathcal{T}_1$ is defined below, where t is a security parameter (i.e. the bit length of the key shared between the tag and the reader) and r is the number of times $\mathcal{A}$ runs an Execute query.

$$Adv_{\mathcal{A}}^{\mathsf{UNT}}(t, r) = |Pr[\tilde{b} = b] - \frac{1}{2}| \qquad (20)$$

So, an RFID protocol offers resistance against traceability if $Adv_{\mathcal{A}}^{\mathsf{UNT}}(t, r) < \varepsilon(t, r)$, where $\varepsilon(\cdot, \cdot)$ symbolizes some negligible function.

We now show that the RFID authentication protocol by Yeh et al. does not achieve untraceability (UNT). The adversary mounts the attack as follows:

Phase 1 (Learning): $\mathcal{A}$ issues an Execute($\mathcal{R}$, $\mathcal{T}_0$, i) query, thereby obtaining $\langle IDS^i, A^i, B^i, C^i, flag^i, D^i \rangle$.

Phase 2 (Challenge): $\mathcal{A}$ chooses two fresh tags whose associated identifiers are $ID^{\mathcal{T}_0}$ and $ID^{\mathcal{T}_1}$, where $\mathsf{lsb}(ID^{\mathcal{T}_1}) = \neg\mathsf{lsb}(ID^{\mathcal{T}_0})$, $\mathsf{lsb}(\cdot)$ denotes the least significant bit and $\neg x$ symbolizes the bitwise NOT of x. Then he sends a Test($i + 1$, $\mathcal{T}_0$, $\mathcal{T}_1$) query. As result, $\mathcal{A}$ is given a new pseudonym IDS^{i+1} corresponding to either of $\{ID^{\mathcal{T}_0}, ID^{\mathcal{T}_1}\}$ depending on a chosen random bit $b \in \{0, 1\}$.

Phase 3 (Guessing): $\mathcal{A}$ computes $d = \mathsf{lsb}(IDS^{i+1} \oplus IDS^i \oplus D^i)$. It sets $\tilde{b} = 0$ if $d = \mathsf{lsb}(ID^{\mathcal{T}_0})$; else $\tilde{b} = 1$. Then $\mathcal{A}$ ends $\mathcal{G}$ and outputs a bit $\tilde{b}$ as its guess of the value b.

We now analyze the success probability of the adversary in winning the game. The adversary computes a bit d which is the least significant bit (lsb) of the value

$$IDS^{i+1} \oplus IDS^i \oplus D^i = ((IDS^i + (ID \oplus \overline{K'}^i)) \oplus n_1^i \oplus n_2^i) \oplus IDS^i \oplus (\overline{K'}^i \oplus n_2^i + n_1^i) \qquad (21)$$

Since we are dealing only with the lsb, thus XOR equals addition ($+$), so equation (21) becomes

$$\mathsf{lsb}(IDS^{i+1} \oplus IDS^i \oplus D^i) = \mathsf{lsb}(((IDS^i \oplus ID \oplus \overline{K'}^i) \oplus n_1^i \oplus n_2^i) \oplus$$
$$IDS^i \oplus (\overline{K'}^i \oplus n_2^i \oplus n_1^i))$$
$$= \mathsf{lsb}(ID), \qquad (22)$$

and thus we have

$$d = \mathsf{lsb}(ID), \tag{23}$$

where ID is the static identifier which is either of $\{ID^{T_0}, ID^{T_1}\}$ depending on the bit b. So the adversary just checks the $\mathsf{lsb}(IDS^{i+1} \oplus IDS^i \oplus D^i)$ to determine if it is ID^{T_0} or ID^{T_1}, thus it wins the game with probability 1.

Hence we have

$$Adv_{\mathcal{A}}^{\mathsf{UNT}}(t, 1) = |Pr[\tilde{b} = b] - \frac{1}{2}| = 1 - \frac{1}{2} = \frac{1}{2} > \varepsilon. \tag{24}$$

4   Full Disclosure Norwegian Attack

RFID tags have a static identifier ID that facilitates the unequivocally identification of labeled items. RFID protocols should transmit this value in a secure way (e.g. after an unilateral or mutual authentication protocol) to avoid traceability attacks. In this section, we present a passive attack able of recovering $\lfloor \log_2 L \rfloor$ bits of the ID after eavesdropping $O(L)$ legitimate authentication sessions.

In Yeh et al.'s protocol, the authors use two random numbers $\{n_1, n_2\}$ to guarantee the freshness of each session – among other security objectives. Nevertheless, the proposed protocol slightly abuses the usage it makes of these nonces, and misuses how these are computed. We can analyze what happens to the protocol when these two nonces happen to have the same value module L, i.e.:

$$n_1 \mod L = n_2 \mod L \tag{25}$$

Here L should be a power of two. However, we will later show that all these equations probabilistically hold for any positive integer. (We shall provide some guidelines regarding how to choose L later on this section.) Under the assumption that equation 25 holds, we can probabilistically greatly simplify the index-pseudonym updating equation (Equation 16). More precisely, the least significant bits of the last two terms are canceled out ($n_1 \oplus n_2 \mod L = 0$):

$$IDS_{tr_{new}} \mod L = (IDS + (ID \oplus \overline{K'})) \oplus n_1 \oplus n_2 \mod L \tag{26}$$
$$= (IDS + (ID \oplus \overline{K'})) \mod L$$

If, on the other hand, the public message D is examined and we approximate addition by XOR:

$$D \mod L = (\overline{K'} \oplus n_2) + n_1 \mod L \tag{27}$$
$$\simeq \overline{K'} \oplus n_2 \oplus n_1 \mod L = \overline{K'} \mod L$$

Combining Equations 26 and 27, and working out the value of ID, we get an approximation where only public messages transmitted on the insecure radio channel are involved:

$$ID \mod L = (IDS_{tr_{new}} - IDS) \oplus D \mod L \tag{28}$$

The only remaining question is how to recognize when the condition $n_1 \mod L = n_2 \mod L$ holds, since $\{n_1, n_2\}$ are secret values. From Equations 5 and 10, it is relatively straightforward to deduce that the above mentioned condition implies $\overline{K} \mod L = \overline{K'} \mod L$. The next step is the correlation of this condition with some values or test on the public exchanged messages transmitted over the channel. Specifically, we can use the approximation of the sum by the XOR operation in messages C and D, and finally compare these values:

$$C \mod L = (\overline{K} \oplus n_1) + n_2 \mod L \simeq \overline{K} \oplus n_1 \oplus n_2 \mod L \qquad (29)$$
$$\simeq \overline{K} \mod L$$
$$D \mod L = (\overline{K'} \oplus n_1) + n_2 \mod L \simeq \overline{K'} \oplus n_1 \oplus n_2 \mod L$$
$$\simeq \overline{K'} \mod L \qquad (30)$$

So, by comparing the values of public messages C and D $(mod\ L)$, we are able to probabilistically detect the condition that opens the door to the disclosure of the static identifier of the tag by passively eavesdropping on the channel. However, our testing condition $C \mod L = D \mod L$ may hold just by pure chance while $n_1 \mod L \neq n_2 \mod L$ does not. As a consequence of this, we have to filter and analyze the results to obtain the pursued value of $ID \mod L$. Basically, we repeat this process many times to obtain different candidates for the $ID \mod L$ value, we count the number of times each of these values is observed and pick the maximum as our guess of the static identifier. We sketch the steps of the Norwegian attack below:

---

1. For $i = 0$ to L
2. $Observations[i] = 0$
3. Repeat a sufficiently high number of times N the following steps:
4.   Observe an authentication session and get IDS, A, B, C and D
5.   Check if for these values it holds that $C \mod L = D \mod L$
6.   If this is not the case, go to step 4.
7.   Perform the following tasks:
8.   Wait for the authentication session to finish.
9.   Send to the tag a "Hello" message to obtain $IDS_{tr_{new}}$.
10.   Compute $ID_{estimated} \mod L = (IDS_{tr_{new}} - IDS) \oplus D \mod L$
11.   Increment $Observations[ID_{estimated}]$
12. Filter: find $ID_{conjecture}$, the maximum of the values in $Observations[i]$.
13. Guess that $ID_{conjecture} = ID \mod L$.

To further clarify the Norwegian attack, in Appendix A (Figure 2) we display an example of the $Observations$ vector obtained for $L = 128$ and $N = 2^{18}$.

Finally, in Appendix B (Figure 3) we can observe, for several values of L, the adversary's success probability depending on the number of eavesdropped sessions. Although the attack just presented can be run independently for any value of L, it is highly recommended to select one which is a power of 2 (the probabilistic equations presented before hold with greater probabilities) in order to have a higher success probability and to minimize the number of snooped sessions. An interesting point of the Norwegian attack is its success regardless of the rotation definition used. In other words, the attack is feasible even if the Hamming weight based rotation[3] is used.

The main drawback of the proposed attack in that the number of eaves-dropped sessions needed to recover the whole value of the ID may be excessive. Nevertheless, the knowledge of some bits of the static identifier is informative enough to conduct a successful traceability attack. In fact, only one bit is required in the formal privacy model introduced in [14]. In case that we need to recover the whole ID, the attack described in the following Section 5 is much more convenient.

5   Full Disclosure Tango Attack

In [2], a new technique reminiscent of Linear Cryptanalysis, named Tango attack, is introduced. In this section, we present a very efficient passive attack against Yeh et al.'s scheme, based on Tango cryptanalysis principles. We emphasize here that despite of residing in the same bases, we need an extra twist in the aforementioned technique to success in our attack. More precisely, we use a non-linear approach instead of the completely linear approach used in [2].

The proposed attack reveals the most valuable information stored on the tags memory, the static identifier ID, which is the information the protocol was built to protect. The main singularity of the Tango attack compared with the Norwegian attack presented in the previous section is its much higher efficiency and devastating consequences – from a security point of view – for Yeh et al.'s protocol. The eavesdropping of a very small number of authentication sessions in this case is enough to reveal the complete ID.

Before presenting the inner details of our attack, we first sketch its general approach. Variables can be represented in a m-dimensional space instead of considering them as numerical values. Recall that m is the bit length of variables used in the protocol. More precisely, if a variable z is represented in binary format, the coefficients a_i are the values of the vector Z in each dimension:

$$z = \sum_{i=0}^{m-1} a_i \cdot 2^i, \ a_i \in \{0, 1\} \tag{31}$$

$$Z = [a_0 \ a_1 \cdots a_{m-1}]$$

The attacker follows some simple steps. Firstly, she eavesdrops an authentication session, computes an approximation of the static identifier as a function of the observed messages, and stores this vector:

$$ID_{approx} = f(IDS(k), A, B, C, D, IDS(k+1)) \tag{32}$$

---

[3] $Rot(X, Y) = X << wt(Y)$, where $wt(Y)$ stands for the Hamming weight of vector Y.

The above step is repeated during N eavesdropped sessions. Then, the attacker combines (in our proposal, he simply adds up) all the vectors obtained in this way, and an average value of this resulting vector becomes the conjectured static identifier $ID_{conjecture}$. We provide a numerical example for clarification purposes. For simplicity, we set $m = 8$ in the example.

- **Session k:**
  Eavesdropping of vectors $\{IDS(k), A, B, C, D, IDS(k+1)\}$
  Computing of an approximation: i.e. $ID_{approx}(1) = [0\ 1\ 0\ 1\ 1\ 1\ 1\ 1]$
- **Session $k + 1$:**
  Eavesdropping of vectors $\{IDS(k+1), A', B', C', D', IDS(k+2)\}$
  Computing of an approximation: i.e. $ID_{approx}(2) = [0\ 1\ 0\ 1\ 0\ 1\ 0\ 0]$
- **Session $k + 2$:**
  Eavesdropping of vectors $\{IDS(k+2), A'', B'', C'', D'', IDS(k+3)\}$
  Computing of an approximation: i.e. $ID_{approx}(3) = [0\ 1\ 1\ 0\ 0\ 1\ 0\ 1]$
- **Conjecture ID:**

$$
\begin{array}{ll}
\text{Sum of the vectors:} & [0\ 1\ 0\ 1\ 1\ 1\ 1\ 1] \\
& [0\ 1\ 0\ 1\ 0\ 1\ 0\ 0] \\
& [0\ 1\ 1\ 0\ 0\ 1\ 0\ 1] \\
+ & \overline{} \\
ID_{approx} = & [0\ 3\ 1\ 2\ 1\ 3\ 1\ 2]
\end{array}
$$

$$
\text{Average value:} \quad
\begin{cases}
\text{if } (id_i^{approx} \geq \gamma) & id_i^{conjecture} = 1 \\
\text{if } (id_i^{approx} < \gamma) & id_i^{conjecture} = 0
\end{cases}
$$

i.e. If $\gamma = 1.5$ \qquad $ID_{conjecture} = [0\ 1\ 0\ 1\ 0\ 1\ 0\ 1]$

Conjecture: \qquad $ID_{conjecture}(base\,10) = 85$

Of course, much more complex combinations of the different approximations, and more elaborate filters are possible, but for the protocol at hand this approach works exceedingly well so we do not feel justified to introduce any additional complexity into the attack.

Now, we provide the details of the Tango based attack. We start with the search of good approximations to the static identifier ID. Basically, the attacker captures all the public messages exchanged over the insecure radio channel and combines these values to compute approximations for ID. Of course, not all combinations produce good results. Only those that are closer (on average) to the static identifier are useful. The Hamming weight can be used as an effective (but not the only) metric to evaluate the quality of an approximation. More precisely, if the average Hamming weight between an approximation X and the target value ID is below $\frac{m}{2}$, X is a good approximation:

$$
\begin{cases}
\text{if } \langle wt(X, ID) \rangle < m/2 & X \text{ is a good approximation} \\
\text{if } \langle wt(\neg X, ID) \rangle < m/2 & \neg X \text{ is a good approximation} \\
\text{Otherwise} & X \text{ is ruled out}
\end{cases}
$$

where $\langle \cdot \rangle$ denotes the average value and $\neg x$ symbolizes the bitwise NOT of x. In Appendix C (Table 1) we summarize the results obtained by all possible combinations of the public exchanged messages as approximations of the ID. Unfortunately, none of these approximations – contrary to what happens in [2] – constitutes a good approximation of the static identifier. In all cases, the Hamming weight obtained is so close to the optimal value (i.e. $m/2 = 48$) that the alternate hypothesis (the approximation under scrutiny does not leak any useful information about the ID) cannot be rejected. This seems to be quite a powerful result in showing that the protocol is well though-off and not easy to crack by any linear approximation. One can easily be tempted to believe that there is no information leakage in the public messages as Yeh et al. claim themselves. Nevertheless, an additional twist can shed more light on this issue. We have to carefully analyze the updating equation for the index-pseudonym:

$$IDS_{tr_{new}} = (IDS + (ID \oplus \overline{K'})) \oplus n_1 \oplus n_2 \qquad (33)$$

This is the only message in which the ID takes part. We can work out this variable from the above equation,

$$ID = ((IDS_{tr_{new}} \oplus n_1 \oplus n_2) - IDS) \oplus \overline{K'} \qquad (34)$$

In a slightly more elaborate approach to the problem, we can try to approximate individually the different unknown components of the above equation, instead of doing all globally in a single step. IDS and $IDS_{tr_{new}}$ are the current index-pseudonym and the potential new index-pseudonym. If the adversary eavesdrops two consecutive legitimate sessions, these values are thus known since they are transmitted in the clear on the channel. So, the adversary has to find good approximations for $n_1 \oplus n_2$ and K'. By combining messages A and B a good approximation of the XOR between the nonces n_1 and n_2 can be obtained as shown below. K' can be approximated by using the above equation and the public message $D = (\overline{K'} \oplus n_2) + n_1$.

$$n1 \oplus n2 \simeq A \oplus B \qquad \langle wt(A \oplus B, n1 \oplus n2) \rangle = 23.9411 \pm 4.2505$$
$$\overline{K'} \simeq \neg(D + (A \oplus B)) \qquad \langle wt(\neg(D + (A \oplus B)), \overline{K'}) \rangle = 40.4185 \pm 5.2096$$

From all the above, we have an approximation for the ID value which only involves public values:

$$ID_{approx} = ((IDS_{tr_{new}} \oplus A \oplus B) - IDS) \oplus (\neg(D + (A \oplus B))) \qquad (35)$$

This is enough to mount a powerful Tango attack. From here on, the attacker simply eavesdrops a session and the new index-pseudonym of the new session, computes an approximation of $ID_{approx}(i)$ using Equation 35 and finally stores this vector. Once the adversary has eavesdropped N sessions, the sum of all the approximations is computed:

$$ID_{approx} = \sum_{i=1}^{N} ID_{approx}(i) \qquad (36)$$

The only remaining question is to obtain the average value of the above vector (i.e. $ID_{conjecture} = g(ID_{approx})$). We propose using the following g function which is simple but entirely effective. The components of the input and output vector in each axis are denoted by id_i^{approx} and $id_i^{conjecture}$, respectively. The parameter γ is set to $\frac{N}{2}$.

$$For\ i = 0, m - 1 \begin{cases} \text{if } (id_i^{approx} \geq \gamma) & id_i^{conjecture} = 1 \\ \text{if } (id_i^{approx} < \gamma) & id_i^{conjecture} = 0 \end{cases} \qquad (37)$$

Finally, the attacker concludes $ID_{conjecture} = \sum_{i=0}^{m-1} id_i^{conjecture} \cdot 2^i$ as its conjecture of the static identifier ID.

To evaluate the effectiveness of our Tango attack, we have ran several simulations. First, we randomly initialize the secret values $\{K, ID, IDS_{old}, IDS_{new}\}$ stored in the tag and the back-end database. Then, we simulate N sessions of the protocol and follow the algorithm just described. To measure the adversary's success, we compare the conjecture value $ID_{conjecture}$ with the real value of the target ID. For each value of N, we repeat the experiment $10,000$ times[4].

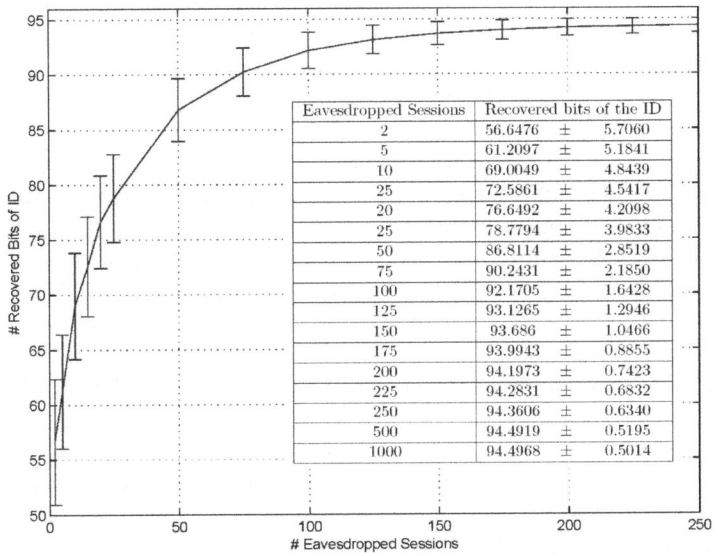

Eavesdropped Sessions	Recovered bits of the ID		
2	56.6476	±	5.7060
5	61.2097	±	5.1841
10	69.0049	±	4.8439
25	72.5861	±	4.5417
20	76.6492	±	4.2098
25	78.7794	±	3.9833
50	86.8114	±	2.8519
75	90.2431	±	2.1850
100	92.1705	±	1.6428
125	93.1265	±	1.2946
150	93.686	±	1.0466
175	93.9943	±	0.8855
200	94.1973	±	0.7423
225	94.2831	±	0.6832
250	94.3606	±	0.6340
500	94.4919	±	0.5195
1000	94.4968	±	0.5014

Fig. 1. Adversary success in recovering ID

In Figure 1, we display the mean and standard deviation of the number of bits successfully recovered for various values of eavesdropped sessions. The attack is quite effective and only a low number of eavesdropped sessions are required to disclosure a significant part of the static identifier. More precisely, if the attacker eavesdrops $\{2, 15, 50, 100\}$ sessions, $\{50, 75, 90, 95\}\%$ of the 96-bits ID are

---

[4] The code of this attack can be downloaded from:
http://www.lightweightcryptography.com/research/ywl/ywl.html

disclosed. The threshold of our attack is the recovery of 94 bits of the static identifier. The two least significant bits of the static identifer are not obtained by the adversary, even for very high values of eavesdropped sessions. Nevertheless, the attacker has reduced the search of the static identifier from 2^{96} to 2^2 candidates. Additionally, we can use the Norwegian attack *in parallel* as described before in this same article for recovering these two bits very efficiently (in less than 100 sessions).

6   Conclusions

At the start of 2010, Yeh, Lo and Winata proposed a new ultralightweight authentication protocol. The security analysis carried out by the designers was mainly based on evaluating the randomness of the messages exchanged over the insecure radio channel. Basically, once the internal secret values of the tag (and back-end database) are randomly initialized, the execution of the protocol is simulated for a large number of sessions. The generated messages $\{IDS, A, B, C, D\}$ during each session are stored in a file. Finally, this file is exposed to a battery of statistical tests (i.e. NIST test suite). Yeh et al. concluded that messages looked sufficiently random since the file passed all the test at hand. This randomness based study is certainly an interesting analysis, but unfortunately randomness of the exchanged messages is neither a sufficient nor necessary condition for protocol security.

In this paper we explicitly show that a good degree of randomness in the public messages does not guarantee by itself the security of the protocol. In fact, we show how even a passive attacker is able to disclose the full static identifier of the tag by simply combining wisely some public messages – passed over the insecure radio channel – and using both the Norwegian and the Tango attack.

Apart from the cryptanalytic results on the Yeh et al. protocol, we believe that the Tango attack can be very useful for the analysis and design of new ultra lightweight protocols, as we have shown it is quite powerful and efficient. The only almost negligible limitation of not being able to retrieve the full ID but only 94 out of 96 bits instead can easily be solved by its combined utilization together with the Norwegian attack (i.e. with $L = 4$), thus becoming nicely complementary attacks.

If we had to point out the design mistakes that led the Yeh et al. protocol to this full disclosure attack we should say that, as already shown in the literature [6], Hamming weight based rotations seem to generally provide more secure proposals. So choosing circular shift rotations instead, while not being a major mistake can certainly be considered suboptimal. Nevertheless, the Tango attack introduced in this paper is independent of the definition of rotation used (e.g. hamming weight or circular shift rotations). Additionally, the key K is too exposed in messages A and B, which have a striking similitude that almost completely leaks out the value of $n_1 \oplus n_2$. The value of $\overline{K'}$ should probably depend on that of K' (not of K only) to increase its strength. And again, while being aesthetically pleasing the construction of messages D and C are so symmetric that, as we have shown, they leak too much information.

As future work, we will continue to analyze new proposals in the light of these cryptanalysis techniques, and use them to motivate new design criteria.

References

1. Yeh, K.-H., Lo, N.W., Winata, E.: An Efficient Ultralightweight Authentication Protocol for RFID Systems. In: Proc. of RFIDSec Asia 2010. Cryptology and Information Security Series, vol. 4, pp. 49–60. IOS Press, Amsterdam (2010)
2. Hernandez-Castro, J.C., Peris-Lopez, P., Phan, R.C.-W., Tapiador, J.M.E.: Cryptanalysis of the David-Prasad RFID Ultralightweight Authentication Protocol. In: Proc. of Workshop on RFID Security 2010 (2010)
3. Peris-Lopez, P., Hernandez-Castro, J.C., Estevez-Tapiador, J.M., Ribagorda, A.: LMAP: A real lightweight mutual authentication protocol for low-cost RFID tags. In: Hand. of Workshop on RFID and Lightweight Crypto (2006)
4. Peris-Lopez, P., Hernandez-Castro, J.C., Estevez-Tapiador, J.M., Ribagorda, A.: M2AP: A minimalist mutual-authentication protocol for low-cost RFID tags. In: Ma, J., Jin, H., Yang, L.T., Tsai, J.J.-P. (eds.) UIC 2006. LNCS, vol. 4159, pp. 912–923. Springer, Heidelberg (2006)
5. Peris-Lopez, P., Hernandez-Castro, J.C., Estevez-Tapiador, J.M., Ribagorda, A.: EMAP: An efficient mutual-authentication protocol for low-cost RFID tags. In: Meersman, R., Tari, Z., Herrero, P. (eds.) OTM 2006 Workshops. LNCS, vol. 4277, pp. 352–361. Springer, Heidelberg (2006)
6. Hernandez-Castro, J.C., Tapiador, J.E., Peris, P., Li, T., Quisquater, J.-J.: Cryptanalysis of the SASI Ultralightweight RFID Authentication Protocol with Modular Rotations. In: Proc. of WCC 2009, May 10-15 (2009)
7. Li, T., Wang, G.: Security analysis of two ultra-lightweight RFID authentication protocols. In: Proc. of IFIP-SEC 2007 (2007)
8. Chien, H.Y., Huang, C.-W.: Security of ultra-lightweight RFID authentication protocols and its improvements. SIGOPS Oper. Syst. Rev. 41(4), 83–86 (2007)
9. Bárász, M., Boros, B., Ligeti, P., Lója, K., Nagy, D.: Breaking LMAP. In: Proc. of RFIDSec 2007 (2007)
10. Bárász, M., Boros, B., Ligeti, P., Lója, K., Nagy, D.: Passive attack against the M2AP mutual authentication protocol for RFID tags. In: Proc. of First International EURASIP Workshop on RFID Technology (2007)
11. Chien, H.-Y.: SASI: A new ultralightweight RFID authentication protocol providing strong authentication and strong integrity. IEEE Transactions on Dependable and Secure Computing 4(4), 337–340 (2007)
12. Cao, T., Bertino, E., Lei, H.: Security Analysis of the SASI Protocol. IEEE Transactions on Dependable and Secure Computing 6(1), 73–77 (2009)
13. D'Arco, P., De Santis, A.: Weaknesses in a Recent Ultra-Lightweight RFID Authentication Protocol. In: Vaudenay, S. (ed.) AFRICACRYPT 2008. LNCS, vol. 5023, pp. 27–39. Springer, Heidelberg (2008)
14. Phan, R.: Cryptanalysis of a new ultralightweight RFID authentication protocol - SASI. IEEE Transactions on Dependable and Secure Computing 6(4), 316–320 (2009)
15. Peris-Lopez, P., Hernandez-Castro, J.C., Tapiador, J.M.E., Ribagorda, A.: Advances in Ultralightweight Cryptography for Low-Cost RFID Tags: Gossamer Protocol. In: Chung, K.-I., Sohn, K., Yung, M. (eds.) WISA 2008. LNCS, vol. 5379, pp. 56–68. Springer, Heidelberg (2009)

16. Yeh, K.-H., Lo, N.W.: Improvement of Two Lightweight RFID Authentication Protocols. Information Assurance and Security Letters (2010) (in press)
17. GS1 EPCglobal. EPCglobal Tag Data Standards Version 1.4, http://www.epcglobalinc.org/standards/ (ratified on June 2008)

Appendix

A   Algorithm – Norwegian Attack

In Figure 2, we display an example of the *Observations* vector obtained for $L = 128$ and $N = 2^{18}$. By simply inspection of the above figure, we can easily detect a pick and correctly conjecture this value is the target value – in the example $ID \mod L = ID_{conjecture} \mod L = 21$. It is interesting to observe that half of the times the *Observations* vector has a zero value, and that most of the other peaks occur at values that share the least significant bits with the real value (i.e. $21 + 64 = 85$, $21 + 64 + 32 = 117$).

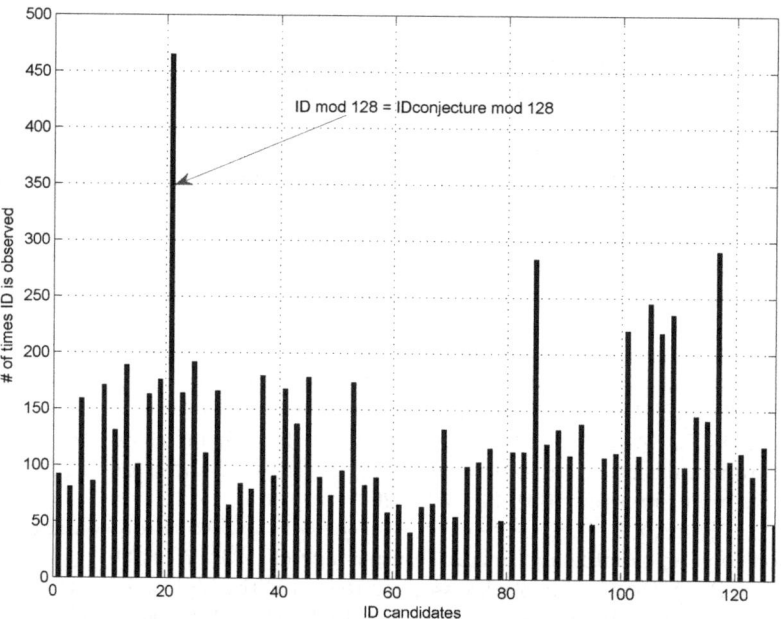

Fig. 2. Histogram of ID candidates ($L = 128$, $N = 2^{18}$)

B   Adversary Success's Probability – Norwegian Attack

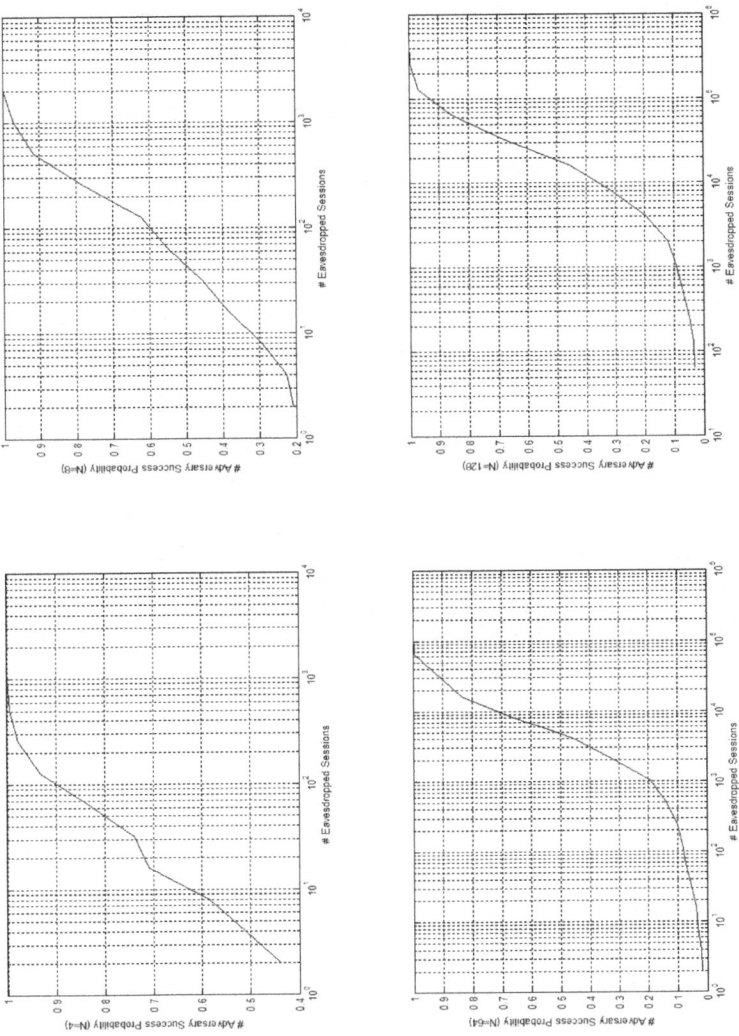

Fig. 3. Adversary success probability for various values of L ($L = \{4, 8, 64, 128\}$)

C   Approximations to the ID − 10.000 Experiments

X	wt(X ⊕ ID)	X	$\overline{\text{wt}}$(X ⊕ ID)
A	47.9473 ± 4.9481	$B \oplus C \oplus IDS_{tr_{old}}$	47.9726 ± 4.8819
B	48.0286 ± 4.9290	$B \oplus C \oplus IDS_{tr_{new}}$	47.9550 ± 4.9445
C	47.9155 ± 4.9111	$B \oplus D \oplus IDS_{tr_{old}}$	48.0133 ± 4.9098
D	47.8964 ± 4.8949	$B \oplus D \oplus IDS_{tr_{new}}$	47.9009 ± 4.8951
$IDS_{tr_{old}}$	48.0107 ± 4.9459	$B \oplus IDS_{tr_{old}} \oplus IDS_{tr_{new}}$	48.0706 ± 4.9132
$IDS_{tr_{new}}$	48.0115 ± 4.9452	$C \oplus D \oplus IDS_{tr_{old}}$	48.0520 ± 4.9140
$A \oplus B$	47.9671 ± 4.8567	$C \oplus D \oplus IDS_{tr_{new}}$	47.9936 ± 4.9111
$A \oplus C$	48.0044 ± 4.9504	$C \oplus IDS_{tr_{old}} \oplus IDS_{tr_{new}}$	47.9995 ± 4.8690
$A \oplus D$	48.0557 ± 4.8726	$D \oplus IDS_{tr_{old}} \oplus IDS_{tr_{new}}$	47.2532 ± 6.2162
$A \oplus IDS_{tr_{old}}$	47.9872 ± 4.9812	$A \oplus B \oplus C \oplus D$	48.0122 ± 4.8277
$A \oplus IDS_{tr_{new}}$	48.0166 ± 4.9565	$A \oplus B \oplus C \oplus IDS_{tr_{old}}$	47.9755 ± 4.9338
$B \oplus C$	47.9951 ± 4.8832	$A \oplus B \oplus C \oplus IDS_{tr_{new}}$	47.9941 ± 4.8607
$B \oplus D$	48.0074 ± 4.9196	$A \oplus B \oplus D \oplus IDS_{tr_{old}}$	47.9482 ± 4.9107
$B \oplus IDS_{tr_{old}}$	48.0009 ± 4.8799	$A \oplus B \oplus D \oplus IDS_{tr_{new}}$	48.0028 ± 4.8607
$B \oplus IDS_{tr_{new}}$	47.9677 ± 4.9498	$A \oplus B \oplus IDS_{tr_{old}} \oplus IDS_{tr_{new}}$	48.0869 ± 4.8411
$C \oplus D$	47.9513 ± 4.9492	$A \oplus C \oplus D \oplus IDS_{tr_{old}}$	48.0133 ± 4.8971
$C \oplus IDS_{tr_{old}}$	47.9710 ± 4.8698	$A \oplus C \oplus D \oplus IDS_{tr_{new}}$	47.9855 ± 4.9035
$C \oplus IDS_{tr_{new}}$	47.9370 ± 4.8724	$A \oplus D \oplus IDS_{tr_{old}} \oplus IDS_{tr_{new}}$	48.0503 ± 4.9134
$D \oplus IDS_{tr_{old}}$	47.9303 ± 4.9247	$B \oplus C \oplus D \oplus IDS_{tr_{old}}$	48.0292 ± 4.8694
$D \oplus IDS_{tr_{new}}$	48.0183 ± 4.8454	$B \oplus C \oplus D \oplus IDS_{tr_{new}}$	48.0808 ± 4.8879
$IDS_{tr_{old}} \oplus IDS_{tr_{new}}$	47.9936 ± 4.9573	$B \oplus C \oplus IDS_{tr_{old}} \oplus IDS_{tr_{new}}$	47.9523 ± 4.8812
$A \oplus B \oplus C$	48.0768 ± 4.8960	$B \oplus D \oplus IDS_{tr_{old}} \oplus IDS_{tr_{new}}$	48.0086 ± 4.9228
$A \oplus B \oplus D$	48.0815 ± 4.9432	$C \oplus D \oplus IDS_{tr_{old}} \oplus IDS_{tr_{new}}$	48.0069 ± 4.8666
$A \oplus B \oplus IDS_{tr_{old}}$	47.9438 ± 4.8561	$A \oplus D \oplus IDS_{tr_{old}} \oplus IDS_{tr_{new}}$	48.0170 ± 4.9237
$A \oplus B \oplus IDS_{tr_{new}}$	48.0544 ± 4.9069	$A \oplus B \oplus C \oplus D \oplus IDS_{tr_{old}}$	48.0317 ± 4.9723
$A \oplus C \oplus D$	48.0350 ± 4.9326	$A \oplus B \oplus C \oplus D \oplus IDS_{tr_{new}}$	47.9339 ± 4.9490
$A \oplus C \oplus IDS_{tr_{old}}$	47.9515 ± 4.9163	$A \oplus B \oplus C \oplus IDS_{tr_{old}} \oplus IDS_{tr_{new}}$	48.0242 ± 4.8784
$A \oplus C \oplus IDS_{tr_{new}}$	47.9745 ± 4.8637	$A \oplus B \oplus D \oplus IDS_{tr_{old}} \oplus IDS_{tr_{new}}$	48.0149 ± 4.8631
$A \oplus D \oplus IDS_{tr_{old}}$	47.9592 ± 4.8990	$A \oplus C \oplus D \oplus IDS_{tr_{old}} \oplus IDS_{tr_{new}}$	47.9792 ± 4.9179
$A \oplus D \oplus IDS_{tr_{new}}$	48.0550 ± 4.9093	$B \oplus C \oplus D \oplus IDS_{tr_{old}} \oplus IDS_{tr_{new}}$	48.0441 ± 4.9483
$A \oplus IDS_{tr_{old}} \oplus IDS_{tr_{new}}$	47.9939 ± 4.9177	$A \oplus B \oplus C \oplus D \oplus IDS_{tr_{old}} \oplus IDS_{tr_{new}}$	48.0488 ± 4.9018
$B \oplus C \oplus D$	47.9697 ± 4.8648		

Dwork-Naor ZAP and Its Application in Deniable Authentication, *Revisited*

Shaoquan Jiang

School of Computer Science and Engineering
University of Electronic Science and Technology of China
shaoquan.jiang@gmail.com

Abstract. A zap is a two-round public coin witness indistinguishable proof system, where the first round is a random string from the verifier to the prover. This notion is proposed by Dwork and Naor. They constructed a zap for NP from any non-interactive zero-knowledge (NIZK) proof which has many applications in the literature. In this note, we start with a more explicit proof of their soundness through enumeration. Based on this proof view point, we further show that if NIZK used in their zap has an adaptive soundness, then the zap soundness error can be reduced by a factor of $2^{|x|}$, where $|x|$ is the length of the $\mathcal{NP}$-statement and is fixed before the protocol starts (but x itself can be chosen adaptively). Our improved bound is optimal in the sense that for any $\mathcal{NP}$-language L, there exists a NIZK that asymptotically achieves this bound. Finally, we investigate their deniable authentication protocol from this zap. We show that this protocol in fact can be simplified without a zap.

1 Introduction

A zap is a two-round public coin witness-indistinguishable protocol, in which the first round message is a random string from the verifier to the prover. It has been initiated by Dwork and Naor [4,5], where they constructed a zap, based on any non-interactive zero-knowledge (NIZK) protocol. Dwork and Naor also showed that zaps can be used to construct *adaptive* non-interactive zero-knowledge protocol, where the prover can choose the theorem to prove after the common random string is fixed. Zaps are also used by them to construct verifiable pseudorandom generators, oblivious transfer, concurrent zero-knowledge and deniable authentication. Dwork-Naor ZAP has a very important impact to other research topics. Specifically, [2] used this protocol to construct efficient ring signatures; Barak et al. [1] used it to show the existence of resettably-sound proof that is resettable witness indistinguishable; Pass [10] used it to prove the existence of two round interactive argument with certain properties.

1.1 Contribution

In this paper, we start with a more explicit proof for the soundness of Dwork-Naor zap by enumerating bad randomness. Based on this proof view point, we

X. Lai, M. Yung, and D. Lin (Eds.): Inscrypt 2010, LNCS 6584, pp. 443–454, 2011.
© Springer-Verlag Berlin Heidelberg 2011

further show that if NIZK in their zap has an adaptive soundness, then the probability bound for soundness error can be reduced by a factor of $2^{|x|}$, where $|x|$ is the length of the theorem to be proven. We show that the reduced bound is optimal in the sense that for any $0 < \epsilon < 1$, there exists NIZK with adaptive soundness error ϵ such that the zap from it has a soundness error asymptotically achieving this bound. One might wish to use NIZK with perfect soundness (i.e., $\epsilon = 0$) in this protocol. However, we show that such NIZK in the common *random* string model (as required in their zap) does not exist for a language outside $\mathcal{BPP}$. We stress that this impossibility result does not contradict the existence of NIZK in the common *reference* string model in the literature, where the random string model requires that the shared string is a uniformly random string while the common reference string is not necessarily random. Finally, we investigate their application of zap to deniable authentication. We find that their protocol can be significantly improved without a zap. A sender in our protocol only has a cost of one encryption, one timed-commitment and one adaptive sound NIZK proof while a receiver only has a cost of one decryption and one verification of adaptive sound NIZK proof. Zhao [12] also considered an improvement on Dwor-Naor's authentication protocol. His main contribution is to remove the dependency of the first round message on the message to be authenticated. Compared with the original protocol, their protocol still needs two zaps, two encryptions and two timed commitments and hence is less efficient than ours.

Notations. For a set S, $x \leftarrow S$ samples x from S randomly; $A \circ B$ means A concatenating with B. We use $negl : \mathbb{N} \to \mathbb{R}$ to denote a *negligible* function: for any polynomial $p(x)$, $\lim_{n \to \infty} negl(n)p(n) = 0$. Algorithm A (e.g., encryption or commitment) with input m and randomness r is written as $A(m; r)$. When r is unspecified, simply write it as $A(m)$. $x \leftarrow A(m)$ denotes the random output of A with input m and unspecified randomness.

2   Definitions

zap is a special two-round public coin witness-indistinguishable proof system and is formally defined as follows. The following definition follows from [5].

Definition 1. *A* zap *is a 2-round protocol for proving membership of* $x \in L$, *where* L *is a* $\mathcal{NP}$ *language. The first round message* ρ *is from the verifier to the prover and the second round message* π *is from the prover to the verifier, satisfying the following.*

- **Public Coins.** ρ *has a length of a fixed polynomial* $k(|x|)$, *where* $|x|$ *is fixed before the protocol starts but* x *itself can be chosen by prover after receiving* ρ. *The verifier's final decision is deterministic in* x, ρ *and* π.
- **Completeness.**   *Given* ρ, x *and its witness* w, *the prover, following the protocol, can generate a proof* π *that will always be accepted by the verifier. This is called* perfect completeness *and can be relaxed by allowing a negligible probability of* failure.

- **Soundness.** *Over the distribution of ρ, the probability of the existence of (x', π) such that $x' \notin L$ and that the verifier accepts (x', ρ, π), is negligible.*
- **Indistinguishability.** *Let w and w' be two witnesses for $x \in L$. Then, given ρ, the distribution (ρ, x, π) when the prover has input (x, w) and the distribution (ρ, x, π) when the prover has input (x, w'), are indistinguishable even if the distinguisher are given w' and w.*

The following is the definition of non-interactive zero-knowledge protocol in the common random string model, where the public string shared between the prover and the verifier are uniformly random. We follows from [5]. This is the single-theorem version of NIZK and it suffices for our purpose in this work. One can consult [6] for the multi-theorem case. Common random string model is different from the common reference string model [7]. Especially, Groth [7] that showed NIZK with perfect soundness exists in the latter setting while we show that it does not exist in the common random string model. In this paper, without a special mention, by NIZK, we always mean that it is in the common random string model.

Definition 2. *A pair of probabilistic polynomial time machines (P, V) with a common random string σ is a* non-interactive zero-knowledge (NIZK) *proof system for an $\mathcal{NP}$-language L if the following holds.*

- **Completeness.** *For any $x \in L$ with witness w, P, with input (x, w, σ), produces a proof π that will be accepted by V except for a negligible probability, where the probability is over the choices of σ and coins of P.*
- **Soundness.** *For any $x \notin L$, the probability that there exists $\pi \in \{0,1\}^*$ such that V accepts (σ, x, π) is negligible, where the probability is over the choices of σ.*
- **Zero-knowledge.** *For any $x \in L$ with witness w, there exists a probabilistic polynomial time machine Sim (called simulator) that takes x as input and produces (σ, π) such that (σ, π) is indistinguishable from that produced in the real execution between (P, V). Here the distinguisher is given (σ, π, x, w) and probability is over the choices of σ and the coins of Sim and P.*

For the soundness, if we allow the instance x to be chosen after σ is fixed, NIZK *is said to have* **adaptive soundness.** *In other words,* NIZK *is adaptive sound if over the choices of σ, the probability of the existence of (π, x) such that the verifier accepts (σ, x, π), is negligible.*

Adaptive Zero Knowledge. *Adaptive zero knowledge requires that the following two adversary views are indistinguishable, where $\mathcal{A}$ is any non-uniform probabilistic polynomial time adversary.*

- Take common random string $\sigma \leftarrow \{0,1\}^\ell$; $(x, w) \leftarrow \mathcal{A}(\sigma)$ s.t. w is a witness for $x \in L$; compute proof π from (x, w, σ). Adversary view is (σ, π, r), where r is the random tape of $\mathcal{A}$.
- Simulator $\mathcal{SIM}$ simulates a common random string σ with a trapdoor τ; then, $\mathcal{A}(\sigma)$ outputs x; $\mathcal{SIM}$ simulates a proof π from x and trapdoor τ. The adversary view is (σ, π, r), where r is again the random tape of $\mathcal{A}$.

Our adaptive zero knowledge definition follows from Sahai [11] with a slight but equivalent change. In his definition, the adversary consists of two parts: $\mathcal{A}_1$ and $\mathcal{A}_2$, corresponding to $\mathcal{A}$ and distinguisher in the above definition. He lets $\mathcal{A}_1$ forward a state information to $\mathcal{A}_2$ (instead of random tape r and σ in our definition). These two definitions are equivalent since τ is determined by (r, σ) and also one can define $\tau = (r, \sigma)$. We prefer this change since it seems more convenient for our security proof later.

The following is the definition of language $\mathcal{BPP}$ and can be found in almost every complexity book. It essentially means that a language can be decided by a probabilistic polynomial time machine with a good probability.

Definition 3. *A language L is in $\mathcal{BPP}$ if there exists a probabilistic polynomial time Turing machine D satisfying the following two conditions.*

- *For any $x \in L$, $\Pr[D(x) = \text{``accept''}] > 2/3$;*
- *For any $x \notin L$, $\Pr[D(x) = \text{``accept''}] < 1/3$.*

It is known that NIZK proof system exists with some adaptive soundness error $\delta < 1$. For arbitrarily small ϵ, one can use parallel repetitions of this NIZK to obtain a new proof which has a soundness error no more than ϵ, where it should be noted that in each repetition the common random string σ_i must be taken independently. This is clear by a hybrid argument.

Fact 1. *For any $\epsilon > 0$, there exists an NIZK with adaptive soundness error ϵ.*
However, we show that the perfect sound NIZK for a non-trivial language does not exist, where the soundness of this NIZK may or may not be adaptive.

Lemma 1. *If there exists a NIZK proof system in the common random string model with (adaptive) perfect soundness for a language L, then $L \in \mathcal{BPP}$.*

Proof. It suffices to consider the non-adaptive case only. Assume $\langle P, V \rangle$ is a NIZK proof system for L. Then, for any $x \in L$, there exists a simulator $\mathcal{SIM}$ outputting a string (x, σ, π) that is indistinguishable from the real transcript (note the definition allows the distinguisher to get the witness of x and the indistinguishability holds of course when the witness is not given). Now a decider $\mathcal{D}$ for L is as follows. Upon x, $\mathcal{D}$ runs $\mathcal{SIM}$ to obtain (x, σ, π). It accepts if it is accepted by the algorithm V; reject otherwise. If $x \in L$, by zero knowledge property, algorithm V will reject the simulated (x, σ, π) with probability at most $\epsilon_c + negl(n)$, where ϵ_c is the completeness error probability and is negligible. If $x \notin L$, then V will reject; otherwise, a cheating prover P^* with positive soundness error can be designed as follows. Given x and common random string σ, P^* runs $\mathcal{SIM}(x)$ to generate a transcript (x, σ', π') and sends (x, σ, π') to V. If $\sigma = \sigma'$, then by assumption, V will accept with probability $\epsilon > 0$. Since $\mathcal{SIM}(x)$ is independent of σ, $\Pr[\sigma = \sigma'] = 2^{-|\sigma|}$. Hence, P^* convinces V for $x \notin L$ with probability $\epsilon \cdot 2^{-|\sigma|} > 0$, contradicting the perfect soundness of NIZK. Hence, when $x \notin L$, $\mathcal{D}$ always rejects x. ∎

Remark. In this paper, NIZK is defined in the common random string model, instead of common reference string model. In the latter case, the proof in the above lemma does not work since it is possible that $\Pr[\sigma = \sigma'] = 0$. I.e., $\mathcal{SIM}$ never generates a valid reference string. Hence, (x, σ, π') sent by P^* for $x \notin L$ could never be accepted. So we can not reach the contradiction to the perfect soundness of NIZK. In fact, Groth [7] constructed a NIZK with perfect soundness in the common reference string model.

Timed Commitment.   Timed commitment essentially is a special commitment whose security holds only within a fixed period of time and beyond that, one might be able to open it using a moderate hard work. Boneh and Naor [3] proposed this notion and provided an efficient construction. Formally, (T, t, ϵ)-timed commitment consists of three phases, where S is the committer and R is the receiver.

Commit phase: To commit to a string $w \in \{0,1\}^n$, S and R execute a protocol and the final output of R is a commitment α for w.

Open phase: In the open phase, S sends the string w to R. They then execute a protocol, at the end of which R obtains a proof that w is the committed value.

Forced open phase: If S refuses to execute the *open phase*, there exists an algorithm F-Open that takes α and outputs w, where w is the commitment in α. The runtime of F-Open is bounded by T.

Definition 4. *A* **timed commitment** *is secure with parameters* (T, t, ϵ) *if it satisfies:*
Completeness: *When R accepts in the commitment phase, then α is a commitment for some $w \in \{0,1\}^n$ and* F-Open(α) *will result in the same w.*
Binding: *In the open phase, S can not convince R that α is a commitment of $w' \neq w$. This holds even if S has an infinite power.*
Soundness: *In the forced open phase,* F-Open(α) *outputs w in time T.*
Privacy: *For any adversary $\mathcal{A}$ of time $t < T$, the following holds:*

$$|\Pr[\mathcal{A}(tr, w) = 1] - \Pr[\mathcal{A}(tr, w') = 1]| \leq \epsilon, \tag{1}$$

where the probability is over coins of S and R in the commitment phase and tr is the transcript in that phase.

Deniable Authentication. Deniable authentication essentially means that one can authentically send a message to a receiver while on the other hand he can later deny the fact of communication. The public-key deniable authentication considers the setting where the sender has a public key and private key pair while the receiver does not have a secret key. Following the formulation in [5] (seemingly weaker than [8]), it should satisfy the following.

Completeness.   For any message m, if both a sender S and a receiver R follow the protocol specification without an attacker involved in, then R accepts.

Soundness.   It is unforgeable against a concurrent chosen-message attack: an adversary $\mathcal{A}$ plays the role of a receiver adaptively and concurrently schedules S to authenticate a sequence of messages $m_1, m_2, \cdots$. $\mathcal{A}$ is successful if he can authenticate a new message $m \neq m_i$ to a receiver R. The soundness requires that any probabilistic polynomial time adversary $\mathcal{A}$ can succeed with at most negligible probability only.

Deniability. This property essentially means that the sender's action can be simulated without his private key. More formally, for any adversarial receiver $\mathcal{A}$, there exists a simulator that, given the public key, simulates the authentication transcript that is indistinguishable from the real one.

3   Dwork-Naor ZAP from NIZK

In this section, we review Dwork-Naor's NIZK-based ZAP. Let $x \in L$ be an $\mathcal{NP}$-statement to be proved to the verifier. $|x|$ is fixed before the protocol starts but x can be chosen adaptively by the prover. Let w be the witness of x. Use $\pi \leftarrow D(x, w, \sigma)$ to denote the distribution of the NIZK proof with input x, auxiliary input w and the common random string σ. Assume σ has a length $\ell(n, |x|)$, where n is a security parameter. The ZAP protocol is as follows.

First Round: $P \longleftarrow V$:   Verifier V takes $B_i \leftarrow \{0, 1\}^\ell, i = 1, \cdots, m$ and sends them to P.

Second Round: $P \longrightarrow V$:   Prover P takes $C \leftarrow \{0, 1\}^\ell$ and computes $\sigma_j = B_j \oplus C$ (i.e., bit-wise exclusive-OR). Then, he computes $\pi_j \leftarrow D(x, w, \sigma_j)$ for $j = 1, \cdots, m$ and sends $x, C, \{\pi_j\}_{j=1}^m$ to V.

Final Check: V :   For $j = 1, \cdots, m$, V computes $\sigma_j = B_j \oplus C$ and checks whether (π_j, x, σ_j) is accepted by a verifier in NIZK. If all are valid, accept the zap; otherwise, reject.

4   Soundness

In [5], the above protocol is proven to be sound and witness-indistinguishable and hence it is a secure zap. We show that if NIZK used here has an adaptive soundness, then their soundness error bound can be significantly improved. Toward this, we first provide a more explicit proof of their original soundness (i.e., when NIZK is not necessarily adaptively sound). Our new proof uses the enumeration of bad common random strings for NIZKs and seems more clear to verify and follow than the original one, where the latter studied some probabilistic independence between different NIZK instances. Based on our proof view point, we improve the soundness bound for the adaptive sound NIZK case, by a factor of $2^{|x|}$. We also show that this improved bound is optimal.

Theorem 1. *If* NIZK *has a soundness error ϵ, then the* Dwork-Naor *zap has a soundness error $2^{\ell+|x|}\epsilon^m$.*

Proof. NIZK has a soundness error ϵ. Let A_x be the set of common random string σ in NIZK such that there exists π such that (σ, x, π) convinces V. Then, $|A_x| \cdot 2^{-\ell} \leq \epsilon$, since σ has a uniform distribution over $\{0, 1\}^\ell$. Use C_ρ to denote

C taken by the prover of the zap when the first message is $\rho = B_1 \cdots B_m$. In the zap, the verifier accepts if and only if all π_j are consistent. Hence, to construct a consistent proof for some $x \notin L \cap \{0,1\}^{|x|}$ (a prover can choose this 'some x' after receiving ρ), it must hold that $B_j \oplus C_\rho \in A_x$ for all j. We now count the number of such ρ (called bad ρ). Fix x first. For fixed B_1, there are $|A_x|$ possible choices for C such that $B_1 \oplus C \in A_x$. For each fixed such C and $i > 1$, there are $|A_x|$ possible B_i such that $B_i \oplus C \in A_x$. So in total there are at most $2^\ell \cdot |A_x| \cdot |A_x|^{m-1} = 2^\ell \cdot |A_x|^m$ possible choices of bad ρ for fixed x. Hence, the soundness error can occur to this x with probability bounded by $2^{-m\ell} \sum_{\text{bad } \rho} 1 = 2^\ell \cdot \epsilon^m$. There are total $2^{|x|}$ choices of x. The soundness error for zap is thus bounded by $2^{\ell+|x|} \epsilon^m$.   ∎

In the above proof, we saw that the *adaptive* soundness of zap is obtained by adding together the soundness error of every $x \in L$. Conceivably, if NIZK has *adaptive* soundness, this addition is not necessary since it is handled by the adaptive soundness of NIZK. In the following, we carefully implement this intuition and show that the factor $2^{|x|}$ can be dropped.

Theorem 2. *If* NIZK *has an* **adaptive** *soundness error ϵ, then* Dwork-Naor zap *has a soundness error at most $2^\ell \epsilon^m$. This bound is optimal in the sense that there exists a* NIZK *with soundness error ϵ such that the zap has a soundness error at least $2^\ell \epsilon^m - o(2^\ell \epsilon^m)$. In addition, if $2^\ell \epsilon^m < 1$, there must exist a $\rho^* = B_1^* \cdots B_m^* \in \{0,1\}^{m\ell}$ for the first round message such that the zap has perfect soundness.*

Proof. For $\sigma \in \{0,1\}^\ell$, let S_σ be the set of $x \notin L$ such that, when the common random string in NIZK is σ, $\exists \pi$ s.t. (x, σ, π) convinces the verifier. Let $A = \{\sigma \mid S_\sigma \neq \emptyset\}$. Therefore, when $\sigma \notin A$, the soundness error will never occur; when $\sigma \in A$, a cheating prover can search for $x \notin L$ and proof π such that (σ, x, π) convinces the verifier. Hence, the adaptive soundness of NIZK is $|A| \cdot 2^{-\ell}$. Now we consider the soundness of zap. When the first message is $B_1, \cdots, B_m$ and the prover takes C, there exists $x' \notin L$ and $(\pi_1, \cdots, \pi_m)$ that convinces the verifier only if $S_{B_1 \oplus C} \cap \cdots \cap S_{B_m \oplus C} \neq \emptyset$ (to guarantee all proofs use a common 'bad' x). Therefore, the soundness of zap is

$$\left| \left\{ (B_1, \cdots, B_m) \mid \exists C \text{ s.t. } \cap_{i=1}^m S_{B_i \oplus C} \neq \emptyset \right\} \right| \cdot 2^{-m\ell}$$
$$\leq \left| \left\{ (B_1, \cdots, B_m) \mid \exists C \text{ s.t. } S_{B_i \oplus C} \neq \emptyset, i = 1, \cdots, m \right\} \right| \cdot 2^{-m\ell}$$
$$= \left| \left\{ (B_1, \cdots, B_m) \mid \exists C \text{ s.t. } B_i \oplus C \in A, i = 1, \cdots, m \right\} \right| \cdot 2^{-m\ell}$$
$$= 2^\ell \cdot |A|^m \cdot 2^{-m\ell}$$
$$\leq 2^\ell \cdot \epsilon^m.$$

This completes the bound proof.

To construct a protocol approximately achieving this bound, we first construct a NIZK Γ_1 for L from a known NIZK Γ_2 where the latter has a small (to be specified later) exact soundness error ϵ_2. Let $\epsilon = \epsilon_2 + N/2^\ell + \delta'/2^\ell$ for some $N \in \mathbb{N}$ and $0 \leq \delta' < 1$. Γ_1 only modifies the verifier as follows. When the common random string $\sigma < N$, then the verifier directly accepts; otherwise, it proceeds as in Γ_2 normally. As before, define S'_σ in Γ_2 to be the set of $x \notin L$ that has a convincing proof. In Γ_1, we have that $S_\sigma = \{0,1\}^{|x|} \backslash L$ for $\sigma < N$ and $S_\sigma = S'_\sigma$ for $\sigma \geq N$. Hence, as long as $L \cap \{0,1\}^{|x|} \neq \{0,1\}^{|x|}$, Γ_1 has an exact soundness error $\epsilon_1 = N/2^\ell + \delta$ for some $\delta \leq \epsilon_2$. Hence, $\epsilon_1 \leq \epsilon$. Applying Γ_1 into the zap, we have

$$
\left| \left\{ (B_1, \cdots, B_m) \mid \exists\, C \ s.t. \ \cap_{i=1}^m S_{B_i \oplus C} \neq \emptyset \right\} \right| \cdot 2^{-m\ell}
$$
$$
\geq \left| \left\{ (B_1, \cdots, B_m) \mid \exists\, C \ s.t. \ B_i \oplus C < N, i = 1, \cdots, m \right\} \right| \cdot 2^{-m\ell}
$$
$$
= 2^\ell \cdot N^m \cdot 2^{-m\ell}
$$
$$
= 2^\ell (\epsilon - \epsilon_2^*)^m, \quad \text{where } \epsilon_2^* = \epsilon_2 + \delta'/2^\ell
$$
$$
\geq 2^\ell \epsilon^m - 2^\ell \epsilon^{m-1} \epsilon_2^*, \ \text{since } \binom{m}{i} \epsilon^{m-i} \epsilon_2^{*i} \geq \binom{m}{i+1} \epsilon^{m-i-1} \epsilon_2^{*i+1} \text{ for all } i \text{ if } \epsilon \geq m\epsilon_2^*,
$$

which is $2^\ell \epsilon^m - o(2^\ell \epsilon^m)$ as long as $\epsilon_2 = o(\epsilon)$, which can be satisfied since NIZK with arbitrary small soundness error exists by Lemma 1.

The soundness error of zap is the number of bad tuples $(B_1, \cdots, B_m)$ (i.e., tuples for which a cheating prover can find $x \notin L$ with a consistent proof π), divided by $2^{-m\ell}$. As the soundness error is bounded by $2^\ell \epsilon^m$. So if $2^\ell \epsilon^m < 1$, there must exist $(B_1^*, \cdots, B_m^*)$ such that for all x there is no soundness error. That is, it admits perfect soundness. ∎

Note in the above proof, we construct Γ_1 from Γ_2 with small soundness error ϵ_2. As seen in Lemma 1, we can not hope to construct Γ_1 using a perfect sound Γ_2 since a perfect sound NIZK does not exist for L outside $\mathcal{BPP}$.

5   Improving Dwork-Naor's ZAP-Based Timed Deniable Authentication

Based on ZAP, Dwork and Naor present a timed deniable authentication protocol. Their idea is to let a receiver encrypt a random number r together with a message m, compute two timed commitments on two random numbers ρ_1, ρ_2 and attach a zap proving that one of two timed commitments is valid. The sender replies with an encryption η of r and an encryption δ of a random number s, together with a zap proving that either η is an encryption of r or δ is an encryption of $s = \rho_1$ or ρ_2. The authentication is guaranteed since normally the sender does not know ρ_1, ρ_2 and has to be able to compute η by first decrypting r. This protocol invokes each of CCA2 encryptions, timed commitment and zap proof for two times and hence not efficient. In the following, we show that this protocol can be naturally improved using only one encryption and one timed commitment and one adaptive NIZK. Our construction does not require the common reference string for NIZK to be random. It is very simple and intuitive.

Let E be a public key of an encryption scheme with private key D and ρ be a common random string for a non-interactive zero knowledge protocol $\mathcal{P}$. (E, ρ) is set as the public key. T is a timed commitment scheme. Let m be the message that the sender S wish to authenticate to the receiver R. Our idea is to let R encrypt a random number r together with m, compute a timed commitment of r and generate a NIZK proof that the encryption and commitment are done properly. The sender S will reply with r decrypted using his private key. R will accept r only if it is received within a reasonable period of time ϕ_1 (e.g., 1 minute) from his sending out the previous message. Intuitively, the authentication is guaranteed since no one can decrypt the encryption without a private key or can decommit r in time ϕ_1 (T will have this assumption); the protocol is also deniable since any one can obtain r using a forced-decommitment in some moderate longer time T (e.g., 1 days). The decryption and decommitment are consistent by the soundness of NIZK. This protocol is formally described as follows, which we denote by t-Auth.

- R takes $r \leftarrow \{0,1\}^\ell$ and $s_1, s_2 \leftarrow \{0,1\}^*$. He computes $\alpha = E(m \circ r; s_1)$ and $\beta = T(r; s_2)$ and uses ρ as common random string to compute a non-interactive zero-knowledge proof $\pi = \mathcal{P}(\rho, m, \alpha, \beta; r, s_1, s_2)$ that α and β have the said format. R sends (α, β, m, π) to S.
- Receiving (α, β, m, π), S computes $m' \circ r' = D(\alpha)$, and checks if $m' = m$ and π is valid. If yes, send r' to R. Otherwise, reject.
- Receiving r', R checks if it is within a timely fashion (see below) and if $r' = r$. If yes, accept; reject otherwise.

Time Constraint. S's second round message r' must arrive at R within time ϕ_1 from the time the latter sends out the first round message to S. Let ϕ_2 be the upper bound on the time to compute α and π. ϕ_1 is defined such that $\phi_1 + \phi_2 < t$, where t is the time bound below which the timed commitment is secure.

Remark. Although a time constraint is used in the protocol (in the same way as in Dwork-Naor protocol), this time constraint only requires the sender to send back r as soon as possible (i.e., within time ϕ_1). Hence, it does not artificially cause a communication delay. But we have to set ϕ_1 properly. If it is too small, a normal network delay might unexpectedly cause the receiver to reject.

In the following, we show that the t-Auth protocol is a deniable authentication protocol.

Theorem 3. $\mathcal{P}$ *is an adaptive non-interactive zero-knowledge proof with negligible soundness error and perfect completeness.* (E, D) *is a CCA2 secure public key encryption and T is a secure timed commitment (as in Definition 4). Then, t-Auth is a deniable authentication protocol.*

Proof. *Completeness.*   When S and R follows the protocol without an attacker, S will accept R's first round message, due to the perfect completeness of NIZK. In addition, r' produced by S equals r taken by R, due to the completeness of (E, D). The completeness for t-Auth follows.

Soundness.   We need to show that any probabilistic polynomial time adversary $\mathcal{A}$, after interacting with the sender S to receive authenticated messages $m_1, m_2, \cdots$, can not authenticate a new message $m \neq m_i$ to a receiver R. $\mathcal{A}$

can concurrently schedule the message events to both S and R. We use the sequence of game strategy. Denote the success of $\mathcal{A}$ in authenticating such m by **Succ** and assume it has a probability p_s. Denote the real game with $\mathcal{A}$ against it, by Γ_0. We modify Γ_0 to Γ_1 with the only change: ρ is simulated and π^* in the session of receiving m by R is simulated too (using a trapdoor τ of ρ). By reducing to the adaptive zero knowledge property of NIZK, we have that $\Pr[\mathbf{Succ}(\mathcal{A}, \Gamma_1)] > p_s - \epsilon_4$ (since adversary view between Γ_1 and Γ_0 has a gap at most ϵ_4 and **Succ** is implied in adversary view), where ϵ_4 is the distinguishing gap for the simulated zero knowledge proof. Then, we modify Γ_1 to Γ_2 with the only change: in the session to receive m, R generates $\alpha = E(m \circ r')$ for $r' \leftarrow \{0,1\}^\ell$ (instead of r committed in β). By reducing to the CCA2 security of E, we will show that $\Pr[\mathbf{Succ}(\mathcal{A}, \Gamma_2)] \geq p_s - \epsilon_4 - \epsilon_3$, where ϵ_3 is the advantage to break E (note for simplicity we do not mention the attack time but it can be easily calculated from the reduction below). Given E, an attacker $\mathcal{D}$ generates ρ together with its trapdoor τ and then simulates S and R normally, except
(1) when R (simulated by $\mathcal{D}$) is asked to receive an 'authenticated' m which S never sent, he computes $r_0, r_1 \leftarrow \{0,1\}^\ell$ and uses $(m \circ r_0, m \circ r_1)$ as his plaintext challenge pair. He will receive $\alpha^* = E(m \circ r_b)$ for some $b \leftarrow \{0,1\}$. He then computes $\beta^* = \mathtt{T}(r_0)$ and simulates π^* using τ.
(2) whenever S (simulated by $\mathcal{D}$) is authenticating m_i and needs to decrypt α using D, $\mathcal{D}$ asks his decryption oracle to compute it unless $\alpha = \alpha^*$. In this case, he directly rejects (this decision is correct as by assumption S never authenticates m encrypted in α^*).

Finally, when $\mathcal{A}$ replies $r^* = r_{b'}$ in the session of authenticating m, $\mathcal{D}$ outputs b' directly; otherwise, output $b' = 1$. Note when $b = 0$, the simulated game is Γ_1; when $b = 1$, the simulated game is Γ_2. Hence, $\epsilon_3 \geq |\Pr[\mathcal{D}(E(m \circ r_0)) = 0] - \Pr[\mathcal{D}(E(m \circ r_1)) = 0]| = |\Pr[\mathbf{Succ}^*(\mathcal{A}, \Gamma_1)] - \Pr[\mathbf{Succ}^*(\mathcal{A}, \Gamma_2)]|$, where $\Pr[\mathbf{Succ}^*(\mathcal{A}, \Gamma)]$ is the probability that $\mathcal{A}$ successfully outputs r_0 committed in β^*. Note that in Γ_1, r encoded in β^* and α^* is identical (it is r_0 in the reduction). Therefore, $\mathbf{Succ}(\mathcal{A}, \Gamma_1) = \mathbf{Succ}^*(\mathcal{A}, \Gamma_1)$. Next, we show that $\Pr[\mathbf{Succ}^*(\mathcal{A}, \Gamma_2)]| \leq \epsilon_2$, where ϵ_2 is the success probability for an adversary of time t to break $\mathtt{T}$ (see Definition 4). This is done by reducing to the privacy of $\mathtt{T}$. To see this, notice that the time for R to receive the second round message $r^* = r_0$ must be within α from the time of R's sending the first round message and that the time to prepare α^* and π^* is at most γ, where $\alpha + \gamma < t$. Hence, we have that $p_s - \epsilon_4 - \epsilon_3 \leq \epsilon_2$. That is, $p_s \leq \epsilon_4 + \epsilon_3 + \epsilon_2$.

Deniability.   In order to prove that the protocol is deniable, we need to construct a simulator $\mathcal{SIM}$ that simulates the protocol execution with $\mathcal{A}$ without using D such that the view of $\mathcal{A}$ is indistinguishable from that in the real world. Initially, $\mathcal{SIM}$ and $\mathcal{A}$ receive (E, ρ). Then, to authenticate any message m, $\mathcal{SIM}$ can simulate S with $\mathcal{A}$ as follows.

★   When S receives (α, β, π), it verifies if π is consistent with (m, α, β). If not, reject; otherwise, he pauses $\mathcal{A}$ and computes r in β using $\mathtt{F\text{-}Open}$, after which he frees $\mathcal{A}$ and sends out r.

Review the above code, the view of $\mathcal{A}$ in the simulation is different from the real execution only when (α, β) is not consistent with m, r but π is verified successfully. However, this occurs only if the soundness of NIZK is broken, which has a probability of at most ϵ_2.   ∎

Remark. Our protocol requires that an adversary should not be able to construct (α, β) with inconsistent r. This is guaranteed by the adaptive soundness of NIZK. A careful reader might notice that in our authentication proof, Γ_2 computes (α^*, β^*) with an inconsistent r but a simulated proof π^* in the challenge session. This requires that given such information, an adversary should not be able to construct a (α, β) with an inconsistent r but a consistent proof. It seems only one-time simulation sound NIZK [9] can guarantee this. However, in our protocol, such a strong condition is not used. We only use a NIZK with an adaptive soundness. The idea is that the real game (and Γ_1) does not allow an adversary to construct such a consistent proof of a false statement, simply due to the soundness of NIZK. Γ_2 and Γ_1 have a negligible gap on such events, due to a reduction to CCA2 security of (E, D).

Acknowledgements. This work is supported by National Science Foundation of China (No. 60973161) and UESTC Young Faculty Plans.

References

1. Barak, B., Goldreich, O., Goldwasser, S., Lindell, Y.: Resettably-Sound Zero-Knowledge and its Applications. In: Proceedings of the 42nd Annual Symposium on Foundations of Computer Science, FOCS 2001, Las Vegas, Nevada, USA, October 14-17, pp. 116–125. IEEE Computer Society, Los Alamitos (2001)
2. Bender, A., Katz, J., Morselli, R.: Ring Signatures: Stronger Definitions, and Constructions without Random Oracles. J. Cryptology 22(1), 114–138 (2009)
3. Boneh, D., Naor, M.: Timed Commitments and applications. In: Bellare, M. (ed.) CRYPTO 2000. LNCS, vol. 1880, pp. 236–254. Springer, Heidelberg (2000)
4. Dwork, C., Naor, M.: Zaps and Their Applications. In: Proceedings of the 41st Annual Symposium on Foundations of Computer Science, FOCS 2000, Redondo Beach, California, USA, November 12-14, pp. 283–293. IEEE Computer Society, Los Alamitos (2000)
5. Dwork, C., Naor, M.: Zaps and Their Applications. SIAM Journal on Computing 36(6), 1513–1543 (2007)
6. Goldreich, O.: Foundations of Cryptography: Basic Tools. Cambridge University Press, Cambridge (2001)
7. Groth, J.: Simulation-Sound NIZK Proofs for a Practical Language and Constant Size Group Signatures. In: Lai, X., Chen, K. (eds.) ASIACRYPT 2006. LNCS, vol. 4284, pp. 444–459. Springer, Heidelberg (2006)
8. Jiang, S.: Deniable Authentication on the Internet. In: Pei, D., Yung, M., Lin, D., Wu, C. (eds.) Inscrypt 2007. LNCS, vol. 4990, pp. 298–312. Springer, Heidelberg (2008)
9. Lindell, Y.: A Simpler Construction of CCA2-Secure Public-Key Encryption Under General Assumptions. Journal of Cryptology 19(3), 359–377 (2006)

10. Pass, R.: Simulation in Quasi-Polynomial Time, and Its Application to Protocol Composition. In: Biham, E. (ed.) EUROCRYPT 2003. LNCS, vol. 2656, pp. 160–176. Springer, Heidelberg (2003)
11. Sahai, A.: Non-malleable Non-Interactive Zero Knowledge and Adaptive Chosen-Ciphertext Security. In: Proceedings of the 40th Annual Symposium on Foundations of Computer Science, FOCS 1999, New York, NY, USA, October 17-18, pp. 243–353. IEEE Computer Society, Los Alamitos (1999)
12. Zhao, Y.: A note on the Dwork-Naor timed deniable authentication. Information Processing Letters 100(2006), 1–7 (2006)

Efficient Online/Offline Signatures with Computational Leakage Resilience in Online Phase

Fuchun Guo, Yi Mu, and Willy Susilo

Centre for Computer and Information Security Research
School of Computer Science and Software Engineering
University of Wollongong, Wollongong NSW2522, Australia
{fg278,ymu,wsusilo}@uow.edu.au

Abstract. An online/offline signature scheme allows separation of its signing algorithm into *offline* phase and *online* phase. There have been many constructions in the literature, and they are provably secure under chosen-message attacks. However, it has recently been shown that this security notion is insufficient due to *side-channel attacks*, where an adversary can exploit leakage of information from the implementation of the signing algorithm. Regarding the implementation of online/offline signatures, we found that the online phase is much more critical than the offline phase. In this paper, we propose two efficient online/offline signature schemes. Our online phase is secure with unbounded leakage resilience as long as the assumption that only computation leaks information holds. Our constructions offer a very *short* signature length and they are efficient in the online phase with modular additions only.

Keywords: Online/Offline Signatures, Computational Leakage Resilience.

1 Introduction

The notion of online/offline signatures was first introduced by Even, Goldreich and Micali [9]. The signing process of an online/offline signature scheme is separated into two phases, *online* and *offline*. In the offline phase, all costly computations are conducted in absence of messages. In the online phase, the message to be signed is provided and the computation is typically very efficient. Online/offline signatures offer many useful applications. One of them is smart card application, assuming the computational power of a smart card is very weak. We can assume that all heavy computations are accomplished in the offline phase with the aid of a powerful device, while only a light computation is required on a smart card in the online phase.

There have been many online/offline signature schemes (e.g., [9,23,7,13]), which are provably unforgeable against chosen-message attacks [12]. This standard security notion captures many *computational* attacks, but it is usually insufficient when *side-channel attacks* are considered. In practice, an adversary

X. Lai, M. Yung, and D. Lin (Eds.): Inscrypt 2010, LNCS 6584, pp. 455–470, 2011.
© Springer-Verlag Berlin Heidelberg 2011

is allowed to launch side-channel attacks on the implementation of the signing algorithm. The examples of these attacks include timing analysis [16], power consumption [17], electromagnetic radiation [22] and fault detection [4]. Side-channel attacks are powerful attacks. An adversary can exploit leakage information (e.g., signing key) from a side-channel attack. Unfortunately, the standard security notion does not capture information leakage from side-channel attacks.

Due to insufficiency of standard security model, a notion of *leakage resilience* was recently proposed [8] to model side-channel attacks. In this new security model, an adversary is allowed to make queries on signatures and leakages. The leakage queries are associated with a serial of *leakage functions* $f_i : \{0,1\}^* \to \{0,1\}^{\lambda_i}$ specified by the adversary. Many new constructions [20,8,21,15,10] are provably leakage-resilient but different in terms of the restrictions placed on these leakage functions. We refer the reader to [15,10] for concrete restrictions.

In presence of side-channel attacks, online/offline signatures should be also leakage-resilient, especially in the online phase. The signing algorithm of online/offline signature scheme is divided into two phases. Both of them could suffer from side-channel attacks. However, we demonstrate that in some applications, the online phase is much more critical than the offline phase. Smart card applications can be considered as an example that falls into this situation. The offline phase can be accomplished during the production of smart cards in a safe place. On the other hand, the online phase is conducted within a smart card, where it requires a smart card reader, which might not be trusted. Side-channel attacks could be lunched when a smart card is used in practice.

Our Contributions
In this paper, we construct two efficient online/offline signature schemes, such that the online phase is leakage-resilient. It is actually not hard to realize leakage resilience in the online phase without considering its efficiency. Note that online/offline signatures with leakage resilience in the online phase can be realized [9] using leakage-resilient one-time signatures [15,10], a modification of Lamport' scheme [18], and the Merkle's scheme [19]. However, these one-time signatures have a large signature size and therefore are not practical. We shall not utilize one-time signatures with a long signature length in our scheme.

Two online/offline signature schemes are proposed in this paper. Our generic construction is based on Shamir-Tauman signature scheme [23] and a specific construction is modified from Hofheinz-Kiltz short signature scheme [14]. We prove that our online/offline signature schemes are secure with computational leakage resilience in the online phase. The leakage function f we use is the same as in [10]. Precisely, the leakage function can be *arbitrary* with *unbounded* information leakage as long as the input to this leakage function are those accessed secret states in computation. Further discussion of this restriction on the leakage function f can be found in [20,8].

Our schemes offer a very short signature length and an efficient computation in the online phase. Our generic construction has the same signature size as the original scheme, which can be 320 bits for 80-bit security. The signature of our specific construction requires 390 bits, but it can be shortened to 230 bits. Both of schemes require modular additions only in the online phase. Under the same restrictions on leakage functions, we found that two previous schemes [9,13] are naturally resilient to computational leakage in the online phase. However, they do not offer a good efficiency due to a large signature size. We give a comparison in Section 5 to show that our schemes outperform these schemes in terms of signature size.

Roadmap

The rest of this paper is organized as follows. In Section 2, we present definitions and preliminaries. We present our two online/offline signature schemes in Section 3 and Section 4, respectively. In Section 5, we compare the efficiency of schemes with other schemes. In Section 6, we conclude this paper.

2 Definitions

In this section, we present the preliminaries of our work, and define the security model for online/offline signatures with computational leakage resilience in the online phase.

2.1 Online/Offline Signature

An online/offline signature scheme is composed of the following four algorithms.

KGen: On input a security parameter 1^k, the algorithm returns a public key pk and a signing key sk.

Sign: The algorithm is divided into two phases.

- Offline Phase: On input the signing key sk, the algorithm OffSign returns an offline parameter Pa, which is stored for online computation.

- Online Phase: On input the message m, the parameter Pa and the signing key sk, the algorithm OnSign returns the signature $\Sigma_{sk}[m]$.

Vrfy: On input the message-signature $(m, \Sigma_{sk}[m])$ and the public key pk, the algorithm returns *accept* or *reject*.

2.2 Security Model

We first revisit the standard security notion. The standard security notion of online/offline signature schemes is the same as digital signature schemes. It says that signatures should be existentially unforgeable under (adaptively) chosen-message attacks (CMA) [12]. We slightly change the description of security notion for online/offline signatures. The security notion is defined using a game between a challenger and an adversary as follows.

Setup: The challenger runs the algorithm KGen to obtain a pair of public key and signing key (pk, sk). The public key pk is forwarded to the adversary.

Queries: Before the query phase, the challenger uses the algorithm OffSign to compute offline parameters $Pa_1, Pa_2, \cdots, Pa_q$. The adversary makes the ith signature query on m_i. Upon receiving the query, the challenger responds by using Pa_i and the algorithm OnSign to compute the signature $\Sigma_{sk}[m_i]$ and sending it to the adversary.

Forgery: $\mathcal{A}$ outputs a forged message-signature $(m^*, \Sigma_{sk}[m^*])$ and wins the game if $\mathcal{A}$ did not make a signature query on m^* and $\Sigma_{sk}[m^*]$ is a valid signature on m^* signed with sk.

In the query phase, we separate the signing algorithm into OffSign and OnSign. Before the query phase, all offline parameters $Pa_1, Pa_2, \cdots, Pa_q$ have been generated. Upon receiving the ith signature query on m_i, the challenger uses Pa_i instead of the signing key sk to compute the signature $\Sigma_{sk}[m_i]$. However, in the proof for simulation, the challenger might use the signing key to respond the signature query. That is, upon receiving a signature query, the challenger first generates Pa_i and then uses it to compute the signature $\Sigma_{sk}[m_i]$. This is indistinguishable if the adversary receives the signature only. We emphasize this difference to introduce the simulation for the leakage-resilient model simpler.

Definition 1. *An online/offline signature scheme is (t, q, ϵ)-secure against CMA if no adversary (t, q, ϵ)-breaks it in t time at most, making q queries at most and winning the game with advantage ϵ at least.*

We now introduce our security model with leakage resilience in the online phase. In this model, an adversary is allowed to specify leakage functions $f_i : \{0, 1\}^* \to \{0, 1\}^{\lambda_i}$ and makes leakage queries to the challenger. Being the same as [10], we assume that only a computation leaks information, and use the notion Pa_i^+ to denote the part of the internal secret state that has been accessed during computing a signature on m_i using Pa_i. Hence, the adversary can only make a leakage query after it made a signature query. Since we require the online phase to be secure with unbounded leakage resilience, we can directly treat that the output of the leakage function is the secret state Pa_i^+. Here, we assume that the algorithm OnSign is a deterministic algorithm without sampling random coins [10].

The new security model requires the signature scheme to be existentially unforgeable under chosen-message attacks and computational-leakage attacks (online phase only), denoted by CMA&CLA for short. The security notion is defined as follows.

Setup: The same as the standard security notion.

Queries: Before the query phase, the challenger uses the algorithm OffSign to compute offline parameters $Pa_1, Pa_2, \cdots, Pa_q$.

- The adversary makes the ith signature query on m_i. Upon receiving the query, the challenger responds by using Pa_i and the algorithm OnSign to compute the signature $\Sigma_{sk}[m_i]$ and sending it to the adversary.

- The adversary makes the ith leakage query. Upon receiving the query, if the adversary never made the ith signature query, the challenger rejects any output; otherwise, it responds by sending Pa_i^+ to the adversary.

Forgery: The same as the standard security notion.

Definition 2. *An online/offline signature scheme is (t, q, ϵ)-secure against CMA & CLA if no adversary (t, q, ϵ)-breaks it in t time at most, making q signature queries at most and winning the game with advantage ϵ at least.*

2.3 Bilinear Pairing

Let $\mathbb{PG} = (\mathbb{G}, \mathbb{G}_T, g, p, e)$ be a symmetric pairing. More precisely, $\mathbb{G}, \mathbb{G}_T$ are two groups with prime order p and g is a generator of $\mathbb{G}$. $e : \mathbb{G} \times \mathbb{G} \to \mathbb{G}_T$ is the bilinear map and it satisfies the following properties.

- For all $u, v \in \mathbb{G}$ and $a, b \in \mathbb{Z}_p$, we have $e(u^a, v^b) = e(u, v)^{ab}$;
- If g be a generator of $\mathbb{G}$, then $e(g, g)$ is a generator of $\mathbb{G}_T$.

Similarly, an asymmetric pairing is defined as $\mathbb{PG} = (\mathbb{G}_1, \mathbb{G}_2, \mathbb{G}_T, g_1, g_2, p, e)$. Here, $\mathbb{G}_1, \mathbb{G}_2, \mathbb{G}_T$ are groups with prime order p, g_1 is a generator of $\mathbb{G}_1$, g_2 is a generator of $\mathbb{G}_2$. $e : \mathbb{G}_1 \times \mathbb{G}_2 \to \mathbb{G}_T$ is the bilinear map and it satisfies the following properties.

- For all $u \in \mathbb{G}_1, v \in \mathbb{G}_2$ and $a, b \in \mathbb{Z}_p$, we have $e(u^a, v^b) = e(u, v)^{ab}$.
- If g_1 generates $\mathbb{G}_1$ and g_2 generates $\mathbb{G}_2$, then $e(g, g)$ generates $\mathbb{G}_T$.

An asymmetric pairing is used to construct shortest possible signatures. As noted in [5,3], when the bilinear pairing is selected from some special curves, elements of $\mathbb{G}_1$ have shorter representations than those elements of $\mathbb{G}_2$. For example, the group size of $\mathbb{G}_1$ can be 160 bits only for 80-bit security. Many schemes [3,24,11] have successfully utilized this property to build short signatures. In this paper, we simply use the symmetric pairing to describe our constructions. There is no doubt that they can be replaced with an asymmetric pairing for a shorter signature length.

2.4 Complexity

The Shamir-Tauman scheme [23] depends on the security of traditional signature scheme and the hardness of discrete log problem. The Hofheinz-Kiltz scheme [14] is based on the hardness of q-SDH problem [3]. We revisit these assumptions associated with the original schemes.

Definition 3 (DL Problem). *Given an instance $g, g^a, g^b \in \mathbb{G}$ for over random choice of $g \in \mathbb{G}$ and $a \in \mathbb{Z}_p$, the DL problem is to compute $g^{ab} \in \mathbb{G}$.*

Definition 4 (q-SDH Problem). *Given an instance $g, g^a, g^{a^2}, \cdots, g^{a^q} \in \mathbb{G}$ for over random choice of $g \in \mathbb{G}$ and $a \in \mathbb{Z}_p$, the q-SDH problem is to compute any pair $(c, g^{1/(a+c)}) \in \mathbb{Z}_p \times \mathbb{G}$ for a freely chosen $c \in \mathbb{Z}_p/\{-a\}$.*

Definition 5 (DL Assumption). *The DL problem stated in the group $\mathbb{G}$ is a (t, ϵ)-hard assumption if there exists no adversary who can solve it in t-polynomial time with non-negligible probability ϵ.*

Definition 6 (q-SDH Assumption). *The q-SDH problem stated in the group $\mathbb{G}$ is a (t, ϵ)-hard assumption if there exists no adversary who can solve it in t-polynomial time with non-negligible probability ϵ.*

3   Generic Construction

Shamir and Tauman [23] proposed a generic construction of online/offline signature scheme using hash-sign-switch paradigm. Their constructions are very efficient with modular multiplications only in the online phase. We first revisit their scheme and then improve their construction with computational leakage resilience in the online phase by changing their signing algorithm.

3.1   Shamir-Tauman Signature Scheme

Let (G, S, V) be a secure signature scheme, where G, S, V denote the algorithm of key generation, message signing and signature verification respectively. Let $(\mathsf{KGen}^\dagger, \mathsf{Sign}^\dagger, \mathsf{Vrfy}^\dagger)$ be the original scheme proposed by Shamir and Tauman. The online/offline signature scheme using our notion is described as follows.

$\mathsf{KGen}^\dagger$: Use the algorithm G to generate a key pair (pk', sk'). Let g be an element of the pairing group $\mathbb{G}$. Choose α at random from $\mathbb{Z}_p$ and compute $h = g^\alpha \in \mathbb{G}$. The public/signing key of online/offline signature scheme is

$$pk = (pk', \mathbb{G}, p, g, h), \ sk = (sk', \alpha).$$

$\mathsf{Sign}^\dagger$: The signing algorithm is divided into the following two phases.

- Offline Phase: Randomly choose $x \in \mathbb{Z}_p$ and compute $\sigma = \Sigma_{sk'}[g^x]$ using the algorithm S and sk'. Store the offline parameter $\mathsf{Pa} = (\sigma, x)$.

- Online Phase: On input a message $m \in \mathbb{Z}_p$ to be signed, compute

$$r = x - \alpha m \pmod{p}.$$

The signature $\Sigma_{sk}[m]$ on m is (σ, r).

$\mathsf{Vrfy}^\dagger$: On input a message-signature $(m, \Sigma_{sk}[m])$, let $\Sigma_{sk}[m]$ be (σ, r). Compute $h^m g^r$, and verify that σ is a correct signature on $h^m g^r$ using the algorithm V and pk'.

Theorem 1 ([23]). *The online/offline signature scheme is secure against CMA assuming that the traditional signature scheme is secure against CMA and the discrete loq assumption holds.*

The security proof for Theorem 1 is completed in the assumption that no additional information except signatures are learnt by the adversary. In the online phase, the signer is to compute $r = x - \alpha m \pmod{p}$, and this computation could leak α in presence of side-channel attacks. It is easy to verify that the scheme is no longer secure when the adversary knows α. Therefore, the security of Shamir-Tauman signature scheme is insufficient when an adversary can exploit leakage.

3.2 Our Scheme

Based on the Shamir-Tauman signature scheme, we now propose our online/offline signature scheme that is resilient to the leakage of computing $x - \alpha m$ $\pmod{p}$. Let (G, S, V) be the secure signature scheme. The message in our scheme is represented with n-bit string for some n such that $2^n < p < 2^{n+1}$. Here p is the order of the group $\mathbb{G}$. The message space can be naturally extended into an arbitrary string using a collision-resistant hash function $H : \{0,1\}^* \rightarrow \{0,1\}^n$. A generic construction of online/offline signature scheme secure against CMA&CLA is described as follows.

KGen: Use the algorithm G to generate a public key pk' and its signing key sk'. Let g be an element of $\mathbb{G}$. Randomly choose $\alpha \in \mathbb{Z}_p$ and set $h = g^\alpha \in \mathbb{G}$. The public/signing key of online/offline signature scheme is

$$pk = (pk', \mathbb{G}, p, g, h), \ sk = (sk', \alpha).$$

Sign: The signing algorithm is divided into the following two phases.

- Offline Phase:
  - Randomly choose $x, y_1, y_2, \cdots, y_{n-1} \in \mathbb{Z}_p$ and let y_n be

  $$y_n = -(y_1 + y_2 + \cdots + y_{n-1}) \pmod{p}.$$

  - Compute $\sigma = \Sigma_{sk'}[g^x]$ using the algorithm S and sk', and generate the matrix Z

  $$Z = \begin{pmatrix} z_{0,1} & z_{0,2} & \cdots & z_{0,n} \\ z_{1,1} & z_{1,2} & \cdots & z_{1,n} \end{pmatrix},$$

  where $z_{j,i}$ for all $j = 0, 1, i = 1, 2, \cdots, n$ are computed as

  $$z_{j,i} = \frac{x}{n} - j \cdot \alpha \cdot 2^{n-i} + y_i \pmod{p}.$$

  - Store the offline parameter $\mathsf{Pa} = (\sigma, Z)$.
- Online Phase: On input a message $m \in \{0,1\}^n$ to be signed, let $m[i]$ be the ith bit for the message $m = m[1]m[2] \cdots m[n]$. Access $z_{m[i],i}$ for all $i = 1, 2, \cdots, n$ and compute

$$r = z_{m[1],1} + z_{m[2],2} + \cdots + z_{m[n],n} \pmod{p}.$$

The signature $\Sigma_{sk}[m]$ on m is (σ, r).

Vrfy: On input a message-signature $(m, \Sigma_{sk}[m])$ and let $\Sigma_{sk}[m]$ be (σ, r). Compute $h^m g^r$, and verify that σ is a correct signature on $h^m g^r$ using the algorithm V and pk'.

The verification is correct since we have

$$m = m[1]m[2]m[3]\cdots m[n]$$

$$= \sum_{i=1}^{n} m[i] \cdot 2^{n-i}$$

$$m\alpha + r = m\alpha + z_{m[1],1} + z_{m[2],2} + \cdots + z_{m[n],n}$$

$$= m\alpha + \sum_{i=1}^{n}(\frac{x}{n} - m[i] \cdot \alpha \cdot 2^{n-i} + y_i)$$

$$= m\alpha + x - \alpha \sum_{i=1}^{n}(m[i]2^{n-i}) + \sum_{i=1}^{n} y_i$$

$$= m\alpha + x - \alpha \cdot m$$

$$= x$$

$$h^m g^r = g^{\alpha m + r} = g^x.$$

3.3   Main Features

We describe our generic construction using the pairing group $\mathbb{G}$. Actually, it can be any cyclic group in realization [23]. However, the schemes in [5,3] show that we can construct short signatures if the signature scheme is defined in the asymmetric pairing group $\mathbb{G}_1$. In particular, the size of the traditional signature $\Sigma_{sk'}[g^x]$ can be as short as 160 bits for 80-bit security. More discussions can be found in [23,5,3].

The main difference of our construction compared to the original scheme [23] is the signing algorithm. The algorithms KGen and Vrfy are identical. The computation cost in the offline phase is mainly dominated by the exponentiation g^x and the signature generation $\Sigma_{sk'}[g^x]$, the same as [23]. In the online phase, computing the value r requires only n modular additions and is faster than modular multiplications for n-bit strings in [23].

Our construction requires a large storage, compared to the original scheme. Suppose 80-bit security is required in applications, we have $|p| = 160$ and $n = 160$. The storage in the offline phase is mainly dominated by the matrix Z, which has about $2n \cdot |z_{j,i}| \approx 6.4$KB (Kilobyte). Therefore, if a device has a storage capacity of 10MB (Megabyte), we can use it to store about 1,500 different offline parameters Pa to generate the same number of signatures.

3.4   Security

Theorem 2. *Our online/offline signature scheme is (t, q, ϵ)-secure against CMA & CLA assuming that the original signature scheme is (t', q, ϵ)-secure against CMA for $t' \approx t$.*

Proof. Suppose there exists an adversary $\mathcal{A}$ who can (t, q, ϵ)-break our scheme in the CMA&CLA model. We construct an algorithm $\mathcal{B}$ that breaks the Shamir-Tauman signature scheme in the CMA model. The algorithm $\mathcal{B}$ is given a public key pk of the Shamir-Tauman signature scheme $(\mathsf{KGen}^\dagger, \mathsf{Sign}^\dagger, \mathsf{Vrfy}^\dagger)$, and the target is to forge a valid signature with the aid of $\mathcal{A}$'s forged signature. The interaction between the adversary $\mathcal{A}$ and the algorithm $\mathcal{B}$ is defined as follows.

Setup: $\mathcal{B}$ sets pk as its public key and sends it to the adversary $\mathcal{A}$.

Queries:

- The adversary makes the ith signature query on m_i. Upon receiving the query, the algorithm $\mathcal{B}$ makes the signature query on m_i to $\mathsf{Sign}^\dagger$. Let the response from $\mathsf{Sign}^\dagger$ be $\Sigma_{sk}[m_i] = (\sigma_i, r_i) = (\Sigma_{sk'}[g^{x_i}], x_i - m_i\alpha)$, $\mathcal{B}$ sends $\Sigma_{sk}[m_i]$ to the adversary. Note that our signature format is identical to the Shamir-Tauman signature, and therefore $\mathcal{B}$ performs a perfect simulation.

- The adversary makes the ith leakage query. Upon receiving the query, if the adversary never made the ith signature query, the challenger rejects any output; otherwise, let $m_i = m[1]m[2]\cdots m[n]$ and $\Sigma_{sk}[m_i] = (\sigma_i, r_i)$, the algorithm $\mathcal{B}$ randomly chooses $y_1', y_2', \cdots, y_{n-1}' \in \mathbb{Z}_p$ and sets

$$z_{m[i],i} = y_i' \text{ for } i = 1, 2, \cdots, n-1$$

$$z_{m[n],n} = r_i - \sum_{i=1}^{n-1} y_i'.$$

We have that $\mathsf{Pa}_i^+ = (\sigma_i, z_{m[1],1}, z_{m[2],2}, \cdots, z_{m[n],n})$ is known to $\mathcal{B}$, and $\mathcal{B}$ forwards Pa_i^+ to the adversary. The simulation on Pa_i^+ is perfect because there exists universally random and independent $y_1, y_2, \cdots, y_{n-1} \in \mathbb{Z}_p$ and $y_n = -\sum_{i=1}^{n-1} y_i$ such that

$$z_{m[i],i} = y_i' = \frac{x_i}{n} - m[i] \cdot \alpha \cdot 2^{n-i} + y_i, \text{for all } i = 1, 2, \cdots, n-1$$

$$z_{m[n],n} = r_i - \sum_{i=1}^{n-1} y_i' = x_i - m_i\alpha - \sum_{i=1}^{n-1} y_i'$$

$$= x_i - \alpha \sum_{i=1}^{n} (m[i]2^{n-i}) - \sum_{i=1}^{n-1} y_i'$$

$$= \frac{x_i}{n} - m[n] \cdot \alpha \cdot 2^0 + y_n.$$

Forgery: $\mathcal{A}$ outputs a forged message-signature $(m^*, \Sigma_{sk}[m^*])$ and $\mathcal{B}$ also outputs $(m^*, \Sigma_{sk}[m^*])$ as the solution to breaking the security of $(\mathsf{KGen}^\dagger, \mathsf{Sign}^\dagger, \mathsf{Vrfy}^\dagger)$.

This completes our simulation. The time cost in simulation is one modular computation of $z_{m[n],n}$. As the modular computation is negligible compared to other signing cost, the simulation time is nearly the same as the simulation time of the original scheme. The number of signature query to $\mathsf{Sign}^\dagger$ is the same as the query number from the adversary. The algorithm $\mathcal{B}$ can always use the forged signature from the adversary to break $(\mathsf{KGen}^\dagger, \mathsf{Sign}^\dagger, \mathsf{Vrfy}^\dagger)$. Therefore, we yield the Theorem 2 and this completes our proof.   □

4   The Second Construction

In this section, we present our online/offline signature scheme based on Hofheinz-Kiltz short signature scheme [14]. We build our construction based on their work since their signature is 230 bits only for 80-bit security and is provably secure without random oracles [2,6]. Although our signature size for communication is larger than 230 bits, it can be reduced to 230 bits for storage.

4.1   Our Scheme

The message space of our scheme is $\{0,1\}^n$. It can be extended to an arbitrary length using a collision-resistant hash function $H : \{0,1\}^* \rightarrow \{0,1\}^n$. Our online/offline signature scheme secure against CMA&CLA is described as follows.

KGen: Select a bilinear pairing $\mathbb{PG} = (\mathbb{G}, \mathbb{G}_T, g, p, e)$. Randomly choose $n+2$ elements $\alpha_0, \alpha_1, \cdots, \alpha_n, \beta$ from $\mathbb{Z}_p$, and set $g_i = g^{\alpha_i}, h = g^\beta \in \mathbb{G}$ for all $i = 0, 1, \cdots, n$. The public/signing key of online/offline signature scheme is

$$pk = (\mathbb{PG}, g_0, g_1, \cdots, g_n, h), \quad sk = (\alpha_0, \alpha_1, \cdots, \alpha_n, \beta).$$

Sign: The signing algorithm is divided into the following two phases.

– Offline Phase:
  • Randomly choose $s \in \{0,1\}^\eta$ and $x, y_1, y_2, \cdots, y_{n-1} \in \mathbb{Z}_p$. Here, η is a parameter will be defined later. Let y_n be

$$y_n = -(y_1 + y_2 + \cdots + y_n) \pmod{p}.$$

  • Compute $\sigma = g^{\frac{x}{\beta+s}} \in \mathbb{G}$ and the matrix Z

$$Z = \begin{pmatrix} z_{0,1} & z_{0,2} & \cdots & z_{0,n} \\ z_{1,1} & z_{1,2} & \cdots & z_{1,n} \end{pmatrix},$$

  where $z_{j,i}$ for all $j = 0, 1, i = 1, 2, \cdots, n$ are computed as

$$z_{j,i} = \frac{j \cdot \alpha_i + y_i + \frac{\alpha_0}{n}}{x} \pmod{p}.$$

  • Store the offline parameter $\mathsf{Pa} = (s, \sigma, Z)$.

– Online Phase: On input a message $m \in \{0,1\}^n$ to be signed. Let $m[i]$ be the ith bit for the message $m = m[1]m[2] \cdots m[n]$. Access $z_{m[i],i}$ for all $i = 1, 2, \cdots, n$ and compute

$$r = z_{m[1],1} + z_{m[2],2} + \cdots + z_{m[n],n} \pmod{p}.$$

The signature $\Sigma_{sk}[m]$ on m is (s, σ, r).

Vrfy: On input a message-signature $(m, \Sigma_{sk}[m])$, let $\Sigma_{sk}[m]$ be (s, σ, r). Compute σ^r, and check that s is a η-bit string and that

$$e\left(\sigma^r, hg^s\right) = e\left(g_0 \prod_{i=1}^{n} g_i^{m[i]}, g\right).$$

The verification is correct since we have

$$r = z_{m[1],1} + z_{m[2],2} + \cdots + z_{m[n],n}$$
$$= \sum_{i=1}^{n} \frac{m[i] \cdot \alpha_i + y_i + \frac{\alpha_0}{n}}{x}$$
$$= \frac{\alpha_0 + m[1]\alpha_1 + \cdots + m[n]\alpha_n + \sum_{i=1}^{n} y_i}{x}$$
$$= \frac{\alpha_0 + m[1]\alpha_1 + \cdots + m[n]\alpha_n}{x}$$

$$\sigma^r = \left(g^{\frac{x}{\beta+s}}\right)^{\frac{\alpha_0 + m[1]\alpha_1 + \cdots + m[n]\alpha_n}{x}}$$
$$= \left(g^{\alpha_o + m[1]\alpha_1 + \cdots + m[n]\alpha_n}\right)^{\frac{1}{\beta+s}}$$
$$= \left(g_0 \prod_{i=1}^{n} g_i^{m[i]}\right)^{\frac{1}{\beta+s}}.$$

4.2   Main Features

The features of efficiency and storage is similar to our first construction. Considering the length of signature, the signature recipient can store (s, σ^r) as the signature on m instead of (s, σ, r). According to the original scheme ([14], Appendix), we can choose $|\eta| = 70$ for 80-bit security. An asymmetric pairing will further shorten the size σ^r to 160 bits. Therefore, we obtain that the signature is 390 bits and the signature (s, σ^r) stored by the recipient is 230 bits in length.

We observe that batch verification [1] can be utilized. When all signatures are signed by a single signer, we show that only two pairings are required for verifying l different signatures. Our batch verification utilizes small exponent, which was first introduced in [1]. Let Bvrfy be the algorithm of bath verification, it can be described as follows.

Bvrfy: On input l pairs of message-signatures $(m_i, \Sigma_{sk}[m_i])$ for all $i = 1, 2, \cdots, l$. Let the ith message and signature be

$$m_i = m^i[1]m^i[2] \cdots m^i[n], \ \Sigma_{sk}[m_i] = (s_i, \sigma_i, r_i).$$

The signature recipients does the following.

- Choose at random ω-bit strings $t_1, t_2, \cdots, t_l \in \{0, 1\}^{\omega}$;

- Compute B_1, B_2, B_3 defined as

$$B_1 = \sum_{i=1}^{l} (\sigma_i)^{r_i \cdot t_i}, \ B_2 = \sum_{i=1}^{l} (\sigma_i)^{s_i r_i \cdot t_i}, \ B_3 = g_0^l \prod_{j=1}^{n} g_j^{\sum_{i=1}^{l} m^i[j] t_i};$$

- Check that $e(B_1, h) = e(B_2/B_3, g)$.

The computational cost are three multi-exponentiations and two pairings. This is definitely smaller than verifying l signatures one by one. We can choose $|\omega| = 40$ so that the probability of accepting invalid signatures is $1/2^{40}$ only. We give the proof of its correctness as follows.

Theorem 3. *The probability of accepting invalid signature(s) is $1/2^\omega$.*

Proof. Let (s, σ, r) be a valid signature on m, an invalid/fake signature on m can be denoted by

$$\left(s, \sigma \cdot g^{\frac{d}{r}}, r \right)$$

for some unknown $d \in \mathbb{Z}_p/\{0\}$. On input l pairs of message-signatures $(m_i, \Sigma'_{sk}[m_i])$ for all $i = 1, 2, \cdots, l$. Let the ith message and signature be

$$m_i = m^i[1]m^i[2] \cdots m^i[n]$$

$$\Sigma'_{sk}[m_i] = \left(s_i, \sigma_i \cdot g^{\frac{d_i}{r_i}}, r_i \right).$$

Suppose one of them is invalid, without loss of generality, let $d_1 \neq 0$. We obtain $s_1 \neq \beta$; otherwise, the signature scheme is not secure. When they are passed though the bath verification, we deduce from the pairing equation that

$$e\left(g^{t_1 d_1 + t_2 d_2 + \cdots + t_n d_n}, h \right) = e\left(g^{s_1 t_1 d_1 + s_2 t_2 d_2 + \cdots + s_n t_n d_n}, g \right)$$

and that

$$t_1 = \frac{\sum_{i=2}^{n} t_i d_i (s_i - \beta)}{d_1 (\beta - s_1)}.$$

That is, invalid signature(s) will be rejected except that the above equation holds. However, t_1 is universally random and independent chosen from $\{0,1\}^\omega$, such that t_1 happens to be $\frac{\sum_{i=2}^{n} t_i d_i (s_i - \beta)}{d_1 (\beta - s_1)}$ with probability $1/2^\omega$ only. This completes our proof. □

4.3   Security

Theorem 4. *Our online/offline signature scheme is (t, q, ϵ)-secure against CMA & CLA assuming that the original signature scheme is (t', q, ϵ) secure against CMA for $t' \approx t$.*

Proof. The proof is similar to Theorem 2. We only give an intuitive description. To respond a signature query on m_i from the adversary, $\mathcal{B}$ queries and receives $\Sigma_{sk}[m_i] = (s_i, \sigma_i)$ from $\mathsf{Sign}^\dagger$. It then randomly chooses $r_i' \in \mathbb{Z}_p$ and responds the signature query with $(s_i, \sigma_i^{1/r_i'}, r_i')$. It is not hard to verify that $\mathcal{B}$ performs a perfect signature simulation. To respond the ith leakage query, $\mathcal{B}$ randomly chooses $y_1', y_2', \cdots, y_{n-1}' \in \mathbb{Z}_p$ and sets

$$\mathsf{Pa}_i^+ = \left(s_i, \sigma_i^{1/r_i'}, y_1', y_2', \cdots, y_{n-1}', r_i' - \sum_{i=1}^{n-1} y_i' \right).$$

The simulation on Pa_i^+ is also perfect with the same analysis as Theorem 2. $\square$

5   Comparisons

In our leakage-resilient model, we assume that only computation leaks information. The input to leakage functions are restricted in those accessed secret states for computation in the online phase. Our constructions are secure with unbounded leakage resilience since all accessed states (i.e., Pa_i^+) can be publicly known to the adversary. There are two existing online/offline signature schemes [9,13] that are naturally resilient to computational leakage in the online phase.

When Even, Goldreich and Micali [9] first proposed the notion of online/offline signatures, they also proposed a generic construction from one-time signatures. In particular, the generic construction can be realized using Lamport's one-time signature scheme [18] or its improvement by Merkle [19]. This generic construction is naturally resilient to computational leakage in the online phase since no secret computation is required. However, generic constructions based on these one-time signatures have a large signature size. For 80-bit security, the construction based on Merkle's one-time signature [19] roughly requires 6.7 KB for storing offline parameters and 5 KB for each signature. The size is larger when the scheme is based on the Lamport's one-time signature scheme.

The second online/offline signature scheme with the same computational leakage resilience as our construction is proposed in [13]. The basic idea of their construction is similar to the Lamport's work. Whereas their signature can be shortened to 40 bytes by the signature recipient, the signature for communication is still as large as 3.2 KB. We note that their signature can be reduced to 40 bytes by the signer before transmission. However, the online computation will have to add n group multiplications. This will definitely slow down the signing operation in the online phase.

We provide some comparisons in the following table. The comparison is under the same security parameter of 80-bit security and we assume that the message space is $\{0,1\}^n$. Each element in a signature is 20 bytes in length. We use $\mathsf{Signature}^C$ to denote the signature size for communication and $\mathsf{Signature}^S$ to denote the signature size for storage. The comparison shows that our construction is shorter in signature length.

Table 1. Comparisons with the same security level of 80-bit security. We use Ours 1 to denote our generic construction and Ours 2 to denote our second construction.

Scheme	Offline Storage	Online Computation	Signature^C	Signature^S
[18]	12.8KB	Nil	9.6KB	9.6KB
[19]	6.7KB	Nil	5KB	5KB
[13]	6.4KB	Nil	3.2KB	40B
Ours 1	6.4KB	Modular Additions	40B	40B
Ours 2	6.4KB	Modular Additions	49B	29B

6 Conclusion

The traditional security proof for online/offline signature schemes is insufficient due to side-channel attacks. Whereas there exist some online/offline signature schemes with leakage resilience in the online phase, they are impractical due to a long signature length. We proposed two efficient online/offline signature schemes. The online phase is provably secure with unbounded leakage resilience as long as only computation leaks information. Our schemes offer a short signature length and a very efficient computation in the online phase.

Acknowledgement. The authors would like to thank the anonymous reviewers for their insightful comments to improve this work.

References

1. Bellare, M., Garay, J.A., Rabin, T.: Fast batch verification for modular exponentiation and digital signatures. In: Nyberg, K. (ed.) EUROCRYPT 1998. LNCS, vol. 1403, pp. 236–250. Springer, Heidelberg (1998)
2. Bellare, M., Rogaway, P.: Random oracles are practical: A paradigm for designing efficient protocols. In: ACM CCS 1993. pp. 62–73. ACM (1993)
3. Boneh, D., Boyen, X.: Short signatures without random oracles. In: Cachin, C., Camenisch, J. (eds.) EUROCRYPT 2004. LNCS, vol. 3027, pp. 56–73. Springer, Heidelberg (2004)
4. Boneh, D., DeMillo, R.A., Lipton, R.J.: On the importance of checking cryptographic protocols for faults (extended abstract). In: Fumy, W. (ed.) EUROCRYPT 1997. LNCS, vol. 1233, pp. 37–51. Springer, Heidelberg (1997)
5. Boneh, D., Lynn, B., Shacham, H.: Short signatures from the weil pairing. J. Cryptology 17(4), 297–319 (2004)
6. Canetti, R., Goldreich, O., Halevi, S.: The random oracle methodology, revisited (preliminary version). In: STOC 1998. pp. 209–218. ACM (1998)
7. Chen, X., Zhang, F., Susilo, W., Mu, Y.: Efficient generic on-line/off-line signatures without key exposure. In: Katz, J., Yung, M. (eds.) ACNS 2007. LNCS, vol. 4521, pp. 18–30. Springer, Heidelberg (2007)
8. Dziembowski, S., Pietrzak, K.: Leakage-resilient cryptography. In: FOCS 2008. pp. 293–302. IEEE Computer Society (2008)
9. Even, S., Goldreich, O., Micali, S.: On-line/off-line digital schemes. In: Brassard, G. (ed.) CRYPTO 1989. LNCS, vol. 435, pp. 263–275. Springer, Heidelberg (1990)

10. Faust, S., Kiltz, E., Pietrzak, K., Rothblum, G.N.: Leakage-resilient signatures. In: Micciancio, D. (ed.) TCC 2010. LNCS, vol. 5978, pp. 343–360. Springer, Heidelberg (2010)

11. Gentry, C.: Practical identity-based encryption without random oracles. In: Vaudenay, S. (ed.) EUROCRYPT 2006. LNCS, vol. 4004, pp. 445–464. Springer, Heidelberg (2006)

12. Goldwasser, S., Micali, S., Rivest, R.L.: A digital signature scheme secure against adaptive chosen-message attacks. SIAM J. Comput. 17(2), 281–308 (1988)

13. Guo, F., Mu, Y.: Optimal online/offline signature: How to sign a message without online computation. In: Baek, J., Bao, F., Chen, K., Lai, X. (eds.) ProvSec 2008. LNCS, vol. 5324, pp. 98–111. Springer, Heidelberg (2008)

14. Hofheinz, D., Kiltz, E.: Programmable hash functions and their applications. In: Wagner, D. (ed.) CRYPTO 2008. LNCS, vol. 5157, pp. 21–38. Springer, Heidelberg (2008)

15. Katz, J., Vaikuntanathan, V.: Signature schemes with bounded leakage resilience. In: Matsui, M. (ed.) ASIACRYPT 2009. LNCS, vol. 5912, pp. 703–720. Springer, Heidelberg (2009)

16. Kocher, P.C.: Timing attacks on implementations of diffie-hellman, rsa, dss, and other systems. In: Koblitz, N. (ed.) CRYPTO 1996. LNCS, vol. 1109, pp. 104–113. Springer, Heidelberg (1996)

17. Kocher, P.C., Jaffe, J., Jun, B.: Differential power analysis. In: Wiener, M.J. (ed.) CRYPTO 1999. LNCS, vol. 1666, pp. 388–397. Springer, Heidelberg (1999)

18. Lamport, L.: Constructing digital signatures from a one-way function. Tech. rep., SRI-CSL-98, SRI International Computer Science Laboratory (1979)

19. Merkle, R.C.: A digital signature based on a conventional encryption function. In: Pomerance, C. (ed.) CRYPTO 1987. LNCS, vol. 293, pp. 369–378. Springer, Heidelberg (1987)

20. Micali, S., Reyzin, L.: Physically observable cryptography (extended abstract). In: Naor, M. (ed.) TCC 2004. LNCS, vol. 2951, pp. 278–296. Springer, Heidelberg (2004)

21. Naor, M., Segev, G.: Public-key cryptosystems resilient to key leakage. In: Halevi, S. (ed.) CRYPTO 2009. LNCS, vol. 5677, pp. 18–35. Springer, Heidelberg (2009)

22. Quisquater, J.J., Samyde, D.: Electromagnetic analysis (ema): Measures and counter-measures for smart cards. In: Attali, I., Jensen, T.P. (eds.) E-smart 2001. LNCS, vol. 2140, pp. 200–210. Springer, Heidelberg (2001)

23. Shamir, A., Tauman, Y.: Improved online/offline signature schemes. In: Kilian, J. (ed.) CRYPTO 2001. LNCS, vol. 2139, pp. 355–367. Springer, Heidelberg (2001)

24. Waters, B.: Efficient identity-based encryption without random oracles. In: Cramer, R. (ed.) EUROCRYPT 2005. LNCS, vol. 3494, pp. 114–127. Springer, Heidelberg (2005)

Hofheinz-Kiltz Signature Scheme

Let $(\mathsf{KGen}^\dagger, \mathsf{Sign}^\dagger, \mathsf{Vrfy}^\dagger)$ be the original scheme proposed by Hofheinz and Kiltz [14]. The short signature scheme using our notion is described as follows.

$\mathsf{KGen}^\dagger$: Select a bilinear pairing $\mathbb{PG} = (\mathbb{G}, \mathbb{G}_T, g, p, e)$. Randomly choose $\beta \in \mathbb{Z}_p, g_0, g_1 \cdots, g_n \in \mathbb{G}$ and set $h = g^\beta$. The public/signing key of the original scheme is

$$pk = (\mathbb{PG}, g_0, g_1, \cdots, g_n, h), \ \ sk = \beta.$$

$\mathsf{Sign}^\dagger$: On input a message $m \in \{0,1\}^n$ to be signed, let $m[i]$ be the ith bit for the message $m = m[1]m[2] \cdots m[n]$. Randomly choose a η-bit string $s \in \{0,1\}^\eta$ and compute

$$\sigma = \left(g_0 \sum_{i=1}^{n} g_i^{m[i]} \right)^{\frac{1}{\beta+s}}.$$

The signature $\Sigma_{sk}[m]$ on m is (s, σ).

$\mathsf{Vrfy}^\dagger$: On input a message-signature $(m, \sigma_{sk}[m])$, let $\Sigma_{sk}[m]$ be (s, σ). Check that s is a η-bit string and that

$$e\left(\sigma, hg^s \right) = e\left(g_0 \prod_{i=1}^{n} g_i^{m[i]}, g \right).$$

Theorem 5 ([14]). *The signature scheme is secure against CMA assuming assuming that the q-SDH assumption holds in $\mathbb{G}$.*

Characterization of the Electromagnetic Side Channel in Frequency Domain

Olivier Meynard[1,2], Denis Réal[2,4], Sylvain Guilley[1,3],
Florent Flament[1], Jean-Luc Danger[1,3], and Frédéric Valette[2]

[1] Institut TELECOM / TELECOM ParisTech, CNRS LTCI (UMR 5141)
Département COMELEC, 46 rue Barrault, 75 634 Paris Cedex 13, France
{meynard,guilley,fflament,danger}@TELECOM-ParisTech.fr
[2] DGA/MI (CELAR), La Roche Marguerite, 35 174 Bruz, France
{denis.real,frederic.valette}@dga.defense.gouv.fr
[3] Secure-IC S.A.S., 37/39 rue Dareau, 75 014 Paris, France
[4] INSA/IETR, 20 av. des buttes de Coësmes, 35 708 Rennes, France

Abstract. In this article, we propose a new approach to characterize the
EM leakage of electronic devices by identifying and focusing on the signals' frequencies leaking the most information. We introduce a set of tests
based on cryptanalysis methods that will help vendors and users of sensitive devices to estimate the security risks due to leakage through electromagnetic emanations. We propose two approaches: an empirical one and
another based on information theory. Both provide a characterization of
the leakage *i.e.* the frequencies and the bandwidths where information is
contained. These techniques are low cost, automatic, and fast as they can
be performed with an oscilloscope and some softwares for the characterization. Such evaluation could also be carried out with TEMPEST. But
TEMPEST evaluations require dedicated apparatus and time consuming step work that consists in scanning all the spectrum frequencies. Our
approach does not substitute to regulatory TEMPEST evaluation, but
nonetheless can identify the leakage with high confidence. To illustrate
the relevance of our approach, we show that an online software filtering
at some identified frequencies allows us to recover a key stroked in one
measurement at the distance of 5 meters from the keyboard.

Keywords: Side Channel Analysis (SCA), TEMPEST, Mutual Information Analysis (MIA), Correlation Power Analysis (CPA), Principal
Component Analysis (PCA), software demodulation, hardware demodulation, Differential Frequency Analysis (DFA).

1 Introduction

Electronic devices radiate an electromagnetic (EM) field that can compromise
sensitive information handled internally. For instance, since the 60's, TEMPEST
(Telecommunications Electronic Material Protected from Emanating Spurious
Transmissions) tests are used by government agencies in order to measure the
amount of compromising EM signals. With the declassification in the 90's of a

X. Lai, M. Yung, and D. Lin (Eds.): Inscrypt 2010, LNCS 6584, pp. 471–486, 2011.
© Springer-Verlag Berlin Heidelberg 2011

portion of the US TEMPEST standards, the civilian and academic researchers began to explore this topic. Van Eck published in [6] the first unclassified technical analysis of the security risks of emanations from computer monitors. Later Kuhn brought new elements into this area in [14], with eavesdropping experiments on CRT screens. In [13], he shows how to create a covert channel conveyed by a crafted TV program. Academic research teams have applied those methods to intercept keystroke signals [21]. They are able to reconstruct the signal data at a distance up to 20 meters even through walls. Concretely they find out the password that has been entered on a PS/2 keyboard with a bi-conical antenna, by tunning the receiver at the frequency carrying the most information. Because of the complexity of EM compromising signals, their evaluation requires expensive test equipments, advanced skills and time.

EM radiations arise as a consequence of current flowing through diverse parts of the device. Each component affects the other components' emanations due to coupling. This coupling highly depends on the device geometry. Therefore it is sometimes easier to extract information from signals unintentionally modulated at high frequencies, which are not necessarily related to the clock frequency, than baseband signals also referred to as direct emanations.

The characterization of the frequencies that modulate the leakage is a scientific challenge, since as of today no relevant tool allows to distinguish which frequency actually contains the sensitive information. For this reason, we propose a methodology based on an empirical approach, that we contrast with another one based on information theory. Our methodology enable attacks that can be lead without an expensive TEMPEST receiver. Electronic device constructors are legally required to conduct genuine TEMPEST evaluations. For them, our evaluation can give a first idea of the robustness of their devices. Also it can be seen as a preliminary to a TEMPEST evaluation, which is time consuming and expensive.

The rest of the paper is organised as follows: in section 2 we start by describing our test bench and the signal leaking on the EM channel. In section 3 we propose three distinguisher derived from state of the art side channel analysis, that allow to identify leaking frequencies. These methods are based on the CPA [3], the mutual information [9], and the principal components analysis [2]. Then, in section 4, we validate each of the three techniques by checking the demodulated signals at the predicted frequencies with a TEMPEST receiver. In the same section we devise a band-pass filtering method that is able to recover the shape of the compromising signal, using a single EM interception. The conclusion is in section 5.

2   Experimental Setup

To illustrate our experiments we consider a keyboard operating the PS/2 protocol.

2.1   The PS/2 Protocol

The PS/2 protocol is a bidirectional serial communication based on four wires (data, clock, ground, power supply). The data and clock lines are open-collectors and have two possible states: low and high states. If no data are transmitted the data and clock lines are in the high state. We say the bus is "Idle"; the keyboard is allowed to begin transmitting data. The PS/2 protocol transmits data in a frame, consisting of 11 bits. These bits are

- 1 start bit, always at 0,
- 8 data bits, least significant bit first, $(d_i, i \in [0, 7])$,
- 1 optional parity bit (odd parity, equal to $\bigoplus_{i=0}^{7} d_i$),
- 1 stop bit, always at 1.

Data sent from the keyboard to the computer is read on the falling edge of the clock signal as shown in Fig. 1. When a frame is sent, the clock is activated at a frequency specific to each keyboard, typically between 10 kHz and 16.7 kHz. The

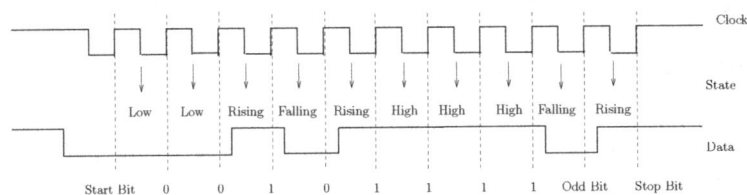

Fig. 1. PS/2 protocol, involved in the keyboard to computer communication

state of sensitive data can be reconstructed thanks to the falling edge of both clock and data. Indeed because these signals are open-collectors, their low state consumes much more power than their high state. This property has already been noticed by Kuhn in [7]. The combination of the falling edge of the clock and the falling edge of the data helps the attacker in guessing the data. In fact a falling edge of the clock is always synchronized with the data start bit, contrarily to the data's falling edges whose positions depend of the keystroke. The eavesdropper can first of all build a dictionary with the positions of data's falling edges as a function of the key stroked.

2.2   Test Bench

Usually in a TEMPEST secure system the "Red/Black" separation principle must be followed, as explained by Kuhn in [14]. The "Red" equipment, which handles sensitive data, has to be isolated from the "Black" equipment that transmits ciphered data. For a TEMPEST protected equipment, the black signal shall not reveal any sensitive information. However in our case we use a commercial keyboard without any countermeasure. As shown in Fig 2 we place a bi-conical antenna at 10 meters from a keyboard connected to a laptop by a PS/2 cable as in [21]. In our case, we name the data signal the red signal and the signal intercepted from the antenna, the black signal. To be sure that the radiated emission are produced only by the keyboard, the experimental test bench is placed in Faraday cage. The attack consists in recovering the red signal from

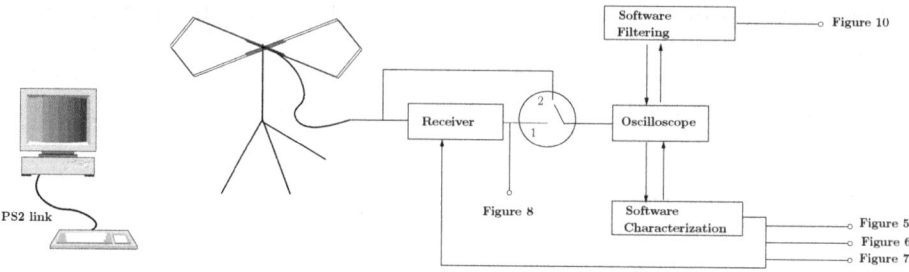

Fig. 2. Setup used for the keyboard eavesdropping

one interception of the black signal. Ideally an efficient attack can be led if the eavesdropper is able to use an antenna adapted to the frequency of the signal on which the receiver is set.

2.3   Hardware vs. Software Setup

To speed up the attack, the attacker needs an essential information concerning the signal: the carrier frequency and the bandwidth of the signal. The carrier frequency is introduced as the crosstalk effect is equivalent to a modulation with close or strong signals like the clock. Indeed this phenomenon introduces a few carrier frequencies as modeled by Li *et al* in [16].

To provide these elements, we propose two possibilities.

On the one hand we can implement the state of the art methodology as used in [1]. It is based on the use of the spectrum analyser/TEMPEST receiver like during a TEMPEST evaluation. Hardware frequency scanning takes advantage of the receiver's dynamic which is often far better than the Analog to Digital converter involved in an oscilloscope. Moreover these receivers offer a large panel of configurations. For example the range of frequencies is $[0, 20]$ GHz and the maximum bandwidth can reach 500 MHz. They are equipped with pre-amplifiers that enhance the dynamic range with a low noise figure. To conduct a TEMPEST evaluation, the evaluator must scan the whole range of frequencies with a spectrum analyser and meanwhile check visually the demodulated signal in order to find sensitive information. The TEMPEST receiver can be tunned continuously between 100 Hz and 10 GHz, with a variable bandwidth. This work is time consuming and irksome, and depends on the evaluator's acuity and background.

On the other hand, we propose to use exclusively a digital oscilloscope, instead of a TEMPEST receiver or more largely a receiver/spectral analyser. By accumulating measurements, we improve the traces accuracy. This helps to achieve an accuracy comparable to that of the receiver. A large number of traces of the signal radiated from the PS/2 cable are recorded. This black signal is divided into parts corresponding to the state level of the red signal. Those parts are Fourier transformed. They highlight consequently different frequency ranges where the compromising signal is potentially present. This methodology can produce the first coarse elements of a TEMPEST evaluation, and allows to avoid the time consuming phase of scanning the whole range of frequencies. We introduce software methods to analyse and characterize the compromising signal. For this paper we used a digital oscilloscope sampling at 1 GigaSample per second. A receiver as in [14] can be used to check our results.

3   Frequency Distinguisher

The phenomena of compromising signal has different origins such as radiation emitted by the clock, crosstalk or coupling. Traditionally, we differentiate the direct emanations and the indirect or unintentional emanations. The first ones can be considered at a very short distance and requires the use of special filters to minimize interference with baseband noise. The direct emanations come from short bursts of current and are observable over a wide frequency band. On contrary, indirect emanations are present in high frequencies. According to Agrawal [1] these emanations are caused by electromagnetic and electrical coupling between components in close proximity. Often ignored by circuits designers, these emanations are produced by a modulation. The source of the modulation carrier can be the clock signal or other sources, including communication related signals. Li *et al* provides in [16] a model to explain such kind of modulation.

In [21], authors use standard techniques, such as Short Time Fourier Transform (STFT) and compute spectrum to detect compromising emanations. The STFT provides a 3D signal with time frequency and amplitude. Another approach is traditionally done by using a spectral analyser to detect signal carriers. Thus the whole frequency range of the receiver is scanned and at each potential frequency of interest the signal is demodulated by the evaluator and manually checked for a presence of red signal.

We lack a lot of information about the TEMPEST tests, which remain classified. Nevertheless, Fig. 3 lets us think that the tools employed for this kind of evaluation are not only based on the spectrum analysers commonly used in standard electromagnetic compatibility (EMC) and radio frequency interference (RFI) testing. As shown in figure 3, the signal in the frequency domain becomes exploitable beyond 15.0 MHz, which is coherent with our equipements' specifications. The bi-conical antenna is amplified with low-noise amplifier of 60.0 dB and

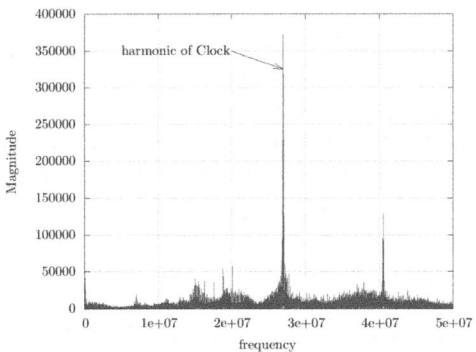

Fig. 3. Spectrum of the black signal

has an approximative bandwidth of 30.0 MHz to 300.0 MHz. Consequently we cannot observe the low frequencies of the signal data, but we observe a high peak at 28.0 MHz. This peak could correspond to some odd harmonic of the internal keyboard microcontroller, for instance the seventh (7.0 × 4.0 MHz) for a microcontroller inside the keyboard running at a frequency of 4.0 MHz, depending on the device constructor, as described in [10, 11].

Hence the indirect emanations are also caused in our case by the cross-talk and the coupling among the internal frequency clock of the keyboard's microcontroller, the data and the clock frequency signal of the PS/2 line. Besides the FFT applied on the whole black signal does not provide us every leaking frequencies.

Therefore we propose in the sequel an approach based on the correlation between the red signal measured directly from the target system and the black signal, noisy and distorted, received from antenna proposed. We can distinguish the keystroke by the position of the falling edges of the data signal. We propose to gather a large number of measurements with the same keystroke. Each pair is composed of a red signal related to the data and a black signal from the antenna as shown in Fig. 4. Then after acquisition the black signal is cut according to the data, represented by the red signal.

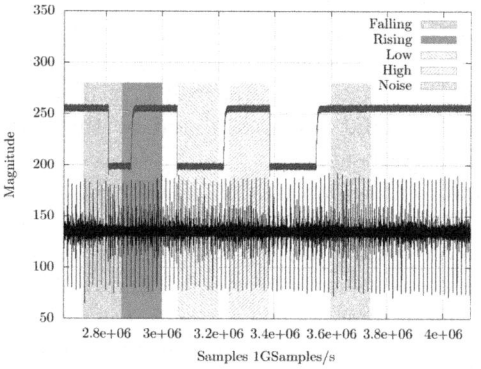

Fig. 4. Red/Black signals

The parts of the black signal correspond respectively to the low state, high state, falling edge and rising edge of the red signal, and an additional part corresponding to the ambient noise. When no data are transmitted by the PS/2 link, the bus line is in the "Idle" state (*see Section 2.1*). This technique is also used in [18]. After this windowing phase we perform a FFT for each part of the measure. Each section of the signal is equal in term of number of samples. Then we calculate an average spectrum and the variance for each part of the signal. It is noticeable that the results do not change with the size of the window. Firstly we introduce a technique inspired from the Correlation Power Analysis.

An approach based on the correlation between the red signal measured directly from the target system and the black signal, noisy and distorted, received from antenna is appropriate. As we will see in the next section, we can attribute to each part of the signal a specific spectral signature. We propose in Section 3.1 an empirical approach.

3.1   First Approach Based on the CPA

We use an approach derived from CPA, introduced in [3]. However we process the signal in frequency domain, as already shown in these papers [8, 18]. They introduced the DFA, *i.e.* the Differential Fourier Analysis. In this technique, the FFT (*Fast Fourier Transform*) is used to avoid synchronization problems. In [17], the FFT is used to mitigate randomization countermeasures like shuffling. Here the FFT is used in order to select the frequencies which are carrying sensitive information and their bandwidth for characterizing the EM side channel. It is a profiling stage in the frequency domain that allows to learn details about the frequencies that depend of the red signal state. Therefore we compute the difference between

- the mean of the spectrum related to a specific state and
- the mean of the noise spectrum (*i.e.* when nothing occurs on the PS/2 link).

Then we divide this difference by the variance of the noise. It is suggested in [15] that in some cases the normalization factor induces a high noise level in CPA signal; to avoid this artifact, it is recommended to add a small positive constant ϵ to the denominator.

Thus we obtained four vectors in frequency domain by computing:

$$\rho(f, State) = \frac{E(f, State) - E(f, N)}{\sigma(f, N) + \epsilon} \quad ,$$

where $E(f, State)$ and $E(f, N)$ represent the averaged spectrum curve obtained respectively for one state and for the noise. $\sigma(f, N)$ stands for the variance of the noise for every frequency f. State is a state from the StateSet set, defined as the set containing all the possible configurations of the red signal: $StateSet = \{High, Low, Falling, Rising\}$. The four frequency vectors corresponding to each state are plotted in Fig. 5. From these curves, we can deduce the range of frequencies that characterize each state.

The "correlation" level in $\rho(f, Falling)$ is higher and contains a lot of frequency peaks compared to the other frequency domains traces. We notice three ranges of relevant frequencies:

- between 14.0 and 20.0 MHz,
- between 24.0 and 32.0 MHz,
- between 40.0 and 49.0 MHz.

3.2   Approach Based on Mutual Information Analysis

In Sec. 3.1, we highlighted a range of frequencies that can possibly carry information about the red signal. Now we adopt an information theory viewpoint. In

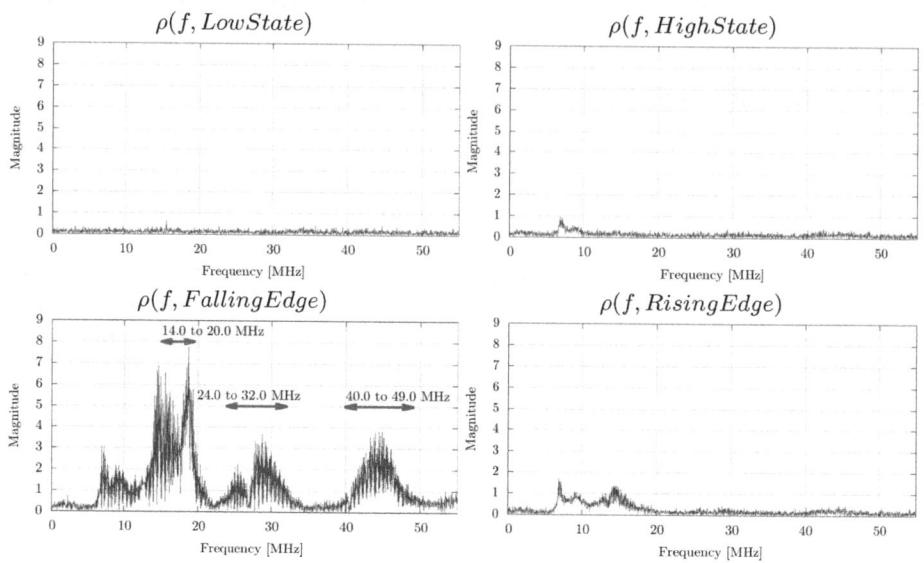

Fig. 5. Results of the Correlation for every state

previous work [20], Tanaka used the calculation of the channel capacity (using information theory) for evaluating the success rate of spied images reconstruction. The author calculates the amount of information per pixel in the reconstructed image and estimates a threshold from which it is effective. In our case, it is also interesting to adopt a method based on the information theory, in order to retrieve the relevant frequencies and to bring evidence that the information is not necessarily carried by the clock frequency and its harmonics such as specified by Carlier *et al.* in [4,5].

In 2008, Gierlichs introduced in [9] the Mutual Information Analysis. This tool is traditionally used to predict the dependence between a leakage model and observations (*or Measurements*). Therefore we can use it as a metric that gives an indicator on carriers frequencies. To do so, we compute for each frequency the Mutual Information (MI) $I(O_f; State)$ between Observations O_f and *State* that corresponds to the state of the red signal. Thereby, if $I(O_f; State)$ is close to zero for one frequency, we can say that this frequency does not carry significant information. On the contrary, if $I(O_f; State)$ is high, the sensitive data and the frequency are bound. If we filter the black signal around this frequency, we can retrieve a significant part of the red signal. The MI is computed as:

$$I(O_f; State) = H(O_f) - H(O_f|State) \ , \tag{1}$$

where $H(O_f)$ and $H(O_f|State)$ are the entropies respectively of all the observations and of the observations in frequency domain knowing the *State*. Both these entropies can be obtained according to:

$$\mathrm{H}(O_f) = - \int_{-\infty}^{+\infty} \mathrm{Pr}(O_f)(x) \log_2 \mathrm{Pr}(O_f)(x)\, \mathrm{d}x \ ,$$

$$\mathrm{H}(O_f|State) = \sum_{s \in State} \mathrm{Pr}(s)\mathrm{H}(O_f|s) \ .$$

with

$$\mathrm{H}(O_f|s) = - \int_{-\infty}^{+\infty} \mathrm{Pr}((O_f)(x)|s) \log_2 \mathrm{Pr}((O_f)(x)|s)\, \mathrm{d}x \ ,$$

where $\mathrm{Pr}(O_f)$ denotes the probability law of observations at frequency f. The random variable O_f takes its values x on $\mathbb{R}$, and $\mathrm{Pr}(O_f)(x)\,\mathrm{d}x$ is the probability that O_f belongs to $[x, x + \mathrm{d}x]$. Besides we consider that the states configuration are equi-probable events therefore $\forall s \in State$, $\mathrm{Pr}(s) = \frac{1}{4}$. And the distribution is assumed to be normal $\sim N(\mu, \sigma^2)$ of mean μ and variance σ^2, given by:

$$\mathrm{Pr}(O_f)(x) = \frac{1}{\sqrt{2\pi\sigma^2}} \exp\left(-\frac{(x-\mu)^2}{2\sigma^2}\right) \ ,$$

we call a parametric model. We approximate this model by a parametric estimation, and we use the differential entropy defined for a 1-dimensional normal random variable O_f of mean μ and standard deviation σ as the analytical expression: $H(O_f) = \log_2(\sigma\sqrt{2\pi e})$. From this value, the Mutual Information defined in Eqn. (1) can be derived, by combining for each state the differential entropy:

$$\mathrm{I}(O_f; State) = \mathrm{H}(O_f) - \frac{1}{4}(\mathrm{H}(f|High) + \mathrm{H}(f|Low) + \mathrm{H}(f|Rising) + \mathrm{H}(f|Falling)) \ ,$$

that can be simplified as:

$$\mathrm{I}(O_f; State) = \frac{1}{4} \log_2 \frac{\sigma_{O_f}^4}{\sigma_{O_f,High} \times \sigma_{O_f,Low} \times \sigma_{O_f,Rising} \times \sigma_{O_f,Falling}} \ . \qquad (2)$$

The figure 6 represents the result of Eqn. (2).

The result of the MIA are similar to that of $\rho(f, FallingEdge)$: we obtain the same ranges of relevant frequencies. In this respect, we confirm that some frequencies radiate more information than the others. As this method provides a result with a quantity expressed in bit, the leakage frequencies are easy to interpret. Consequently we are now able to fairly compare the level of compromising signal emanated by different keyboards or electronic devices. Such MI metric also allow to quantify the level of protection against TEMPEST attacks. In addition to the CPA approach, it is worthwhile to underline that MI considers the non linear dependencies; this metric is able to capture any coupling, such as cross-talk, that occurs when keys are pressed on a PS/2 keyboard.

3.3   Frequency Distinguisher in Principal Subspaces

The identification of relevant frequencies can also benefit from the PCA (Principal Component Analysis). The PCA has been applied to side-channel analysis

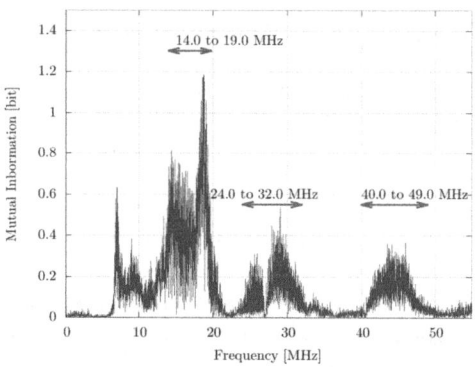

Fig. 6. Result of Mutual Information Metric I(f; *State*)

by Archambeau *et al.* in [2] and Standaert *et al.* in [19] in the case of template attacks. In order to investigate the benefit of PCA, we have adapted it to our topic. In this approach, we use the same partitioning as defined previously in section 3. The observations of black signal in frequency domain are classified according to the state of the data signal, in order to build the covariance matrix. We denote by $\mu_j(f)$ the average of the observations corresponding to a state j, and by $\mu(f)$ the average of all the observations: $\mu(f) = \sum_{j \in StateSet} \mu_j(f)$. The attacker also computes the covariance matrix Σ_o, as:

$$\Sigma_o = \frac{1}{4} \sum_{j \in StateSet} (\mu_j(f) - \mu(f))(\mu_j(f) - \mu(f))^\mathsf{T}. \tag{3}$$

The PCA gives us four main components, which are linear combinations of the four per state black signals averages in frequency domain. These components form a basis, which characterizes four modalities of compromise. The main leakage modality is given by PCA as the eigenvector corresponding to the largest eigenvalue. The four eigenvectors are plotted in Fig. 7.

On the first eigenvector, the three frequencies ranges identified by CPA and MI are visible. Nonetheless, the ranges [24.0, 32.0] MHz and [40.0, 49.0] MHz have a small amplitude and are noisy. Additionally, one narrow peak appears at $f = 27$ MHz, that can be bound to the frequency of the keyboards' microcontroller. The second eigenvector is very similar to the first one. Anyway the ratio between the largest eigenvalue and the second one is greater than five orders of magnitude. This means that the first direction contains an overwhelming quantity of information. The fourth eigenvalue is theoritically null, but because the covariance matrix is badly conditioned the numerical computation yields value 2×10^7 this indicates that the eigenvector corresponding to small eigenvalue are very approximative, thus untrustworthy. Therefore the two last ones carry mostly noise information. However the PCA does not consider the non-linear dependencies.

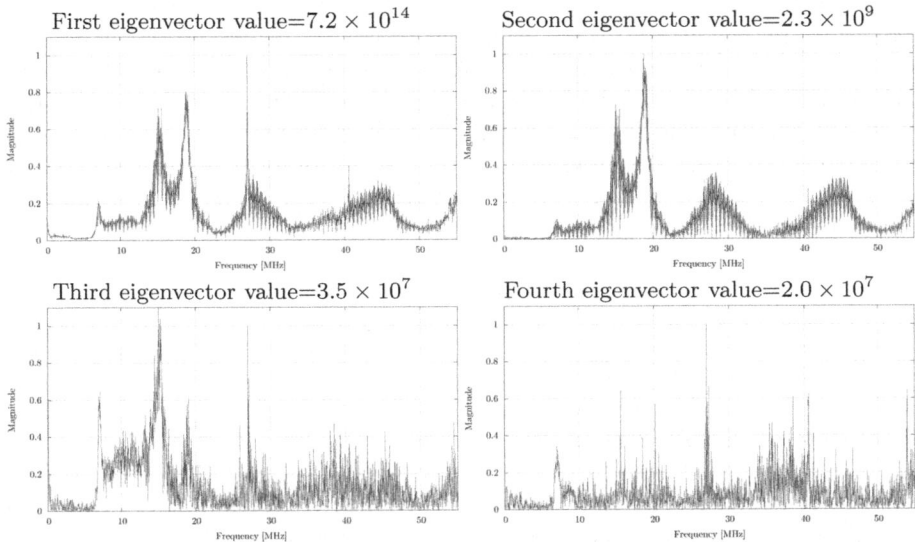

Fig. 7. The four eigenvectors obtained by PCA

Table 1. Drawbacks and advantages of the three analyzed distinguishers

Distinguisher	Advantages	Drawbacks
CPA	⋆ Easiest method.	⋆ Empirical methods. ⋆ Four curves results. ⋆ Hard to compare two implementations. ⋆ Only linear dependencies considered.
MIA	⋆ Based on information theory. ⋆ Single curve result. ⋆ Commensurable results (Mutual Information values are expressed in bits). ⋆ Non-linear dependencies considered.	
PCA		⋆ Hard to compare two implementations. ⋆ Results are not only on first eigenvector. ⋆ Spurious peaks appear. ⋆ Only linear dependencies considered.

To summarize, in Tab. 1 we establish a comparison between the different methods.

To check the results obtained with the three previous methods, two ways can be followed. The first one consists in using a hardware receiver, as described by Agrawal in [1] and Kuhn in [7]. The second one consists in software demodulation thanks to an appropriate filtering.

4   Extraction of the Compromising Signal.

4.1   Confirmation of the Results with a Hardware Receiver.

Different types of hardware receivers exist. We can cite receivers such as described by Agrawal in [1] or Kuhn in [7]. Typically, Kuhn presents in his PhD thesis the R-1250 produced by *Dynamics Sciences*. Those receivers are super-heterodyne and wide-band. They offer a large panel of configurations. For example, they can be tuned continuously between 100 Hz and 1 GHz and they offers the selection of 21 intermediate frequency bandwidths from 50 Hz to 200 MHz. They switch automatically between different pre selection filters and mixers depending on the selected tuning frequency. Therefore those devices are quite expensive and uncommon. These devices are usually used to receive an Amplitude Modulated narrow-band signal:

$$s(t) = A \cdot \cos\left(2\pi f_c t\right) \cdot [1 + m \cdot v(t)] \ ,$$

where f_c is the carrier frequency, $v(t)$ is the broadcast signal, A is the carrier's amplitude and m is the modulator's amplitude.

With such a device, we successfully demodulate the black signal at various frequencies, as shown in Fig. 8. We focus on a range of frequencies between 0.0 and 50.0 MHz, and demodulate at the frequencies exhibited by the previous methods (PCA, MIA and PCA), at 17.0 MHz, 27.0 MHz and 41.0 MHz with a bandwidth of 1 MHz. Each time, the demodulated signal shows a peculiarity that allows to distinguish clearly the state of the red signal. More precisely, the falling edge of the red signal is indicated by a clear peak. This concurs with the observation about the "falling edge transition technique" explained by Vuagnoux in [21]. Also, it is consistent with observations from Section 2.1.

Moreover the data are read on the falling edge of the clock. Consequently the falling edge of the clock occurs just after the falling edge of the data, as already shown in Fig. 1. We see on the demodulated signal that the energy at dates corresponding to the clock falling edges is not constant. Empirically, clock peaks have more energy when the state of data signal is high, and are doubled by falling transitions of the signal data. This is another leakage that can be used to recover the red signal.

During these experiments we noticed an other kind of compromising signal not based on the "Falling edge Transition Technique". As shown in Fig. 8, at the frequency 36.0 MHz, only the signal related to data (falling edge) appears, whereas the peaks bound to the clock completely disappear. This compromising signal is not very obvious to characterize, and requires some care to find the adequate frequency of demodulation. In this case, the TEMPEST receiver definitely provides us the setup to pinpoint this compromising frequency.

4.2 Software Filtering

To estimate the part of the sensitive signal contained in our measurements, and also to find the compromising signal, we devise a software band-pass filter by using MATLAB. We perform bandpass filtering within the range frequencies identified during the leaking frequencies characterization stage.

We propose to realize a filter based on the zero padding technique in frequency domain: its frequency response is sketched in Fig. 9. The complete software demodulation consists of:

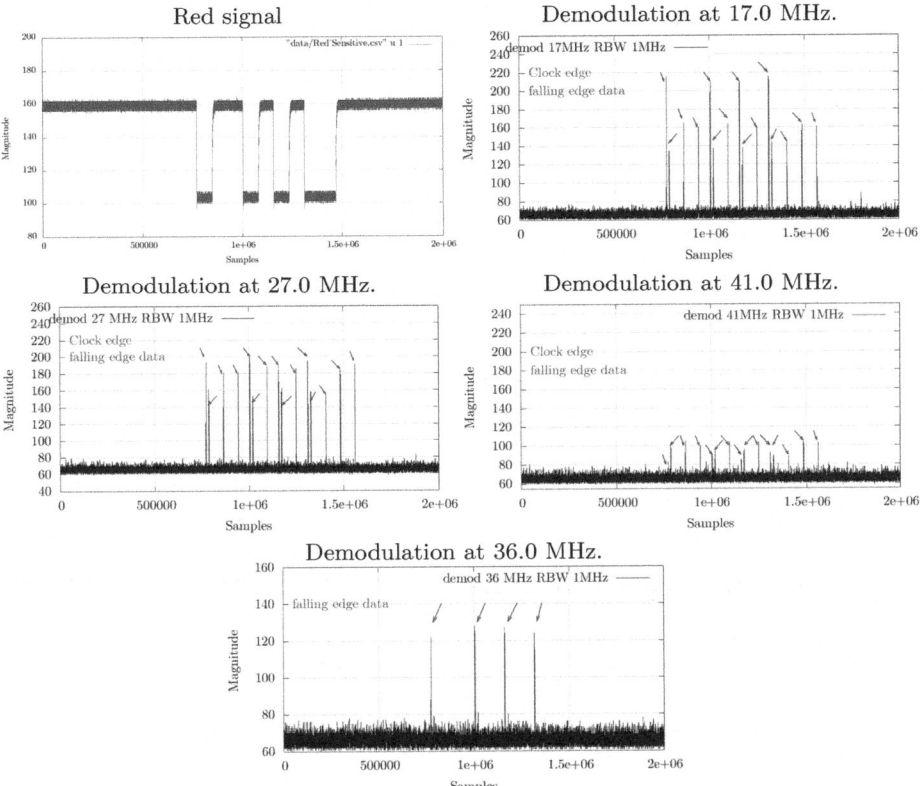

Fig. 8. Results of demodulation (red signal, and black signal demodulated at 17.0 MHz, 27.0 MHz,41.0 MHz and 36.0 MHz)

- converting the black signal from the time to the frequency domain thanks to an FFT,
- multiplying this signal with our pass-band filter,
- converting back the signal from the frequency to the time domain thanks to an IFFT.

This process allows to obtain the approximative shape of the demodulated signal, from which we are hopefully able to extract the key that was pressed.

The figure 10 shows the result of a single black curve demodulated by this software approach. We can distinguish the compromising signal, *i.e.* the falling edge of the data line. Furthermore, the levels of the compromising signal related to PS/2 clock do not have the same amplitude: it is directly linked to that of the red signal's state.

Those observations do match those obtained with the hardware demodulator. Thus the software filtering process offers the possibility to have a coarse idea of the compromising signal shape.

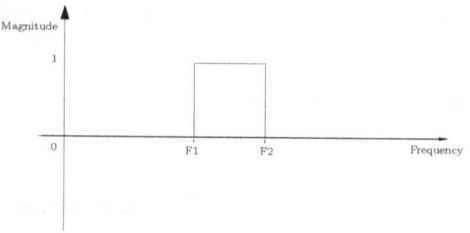

Fig. 9. Design of bandpass filter

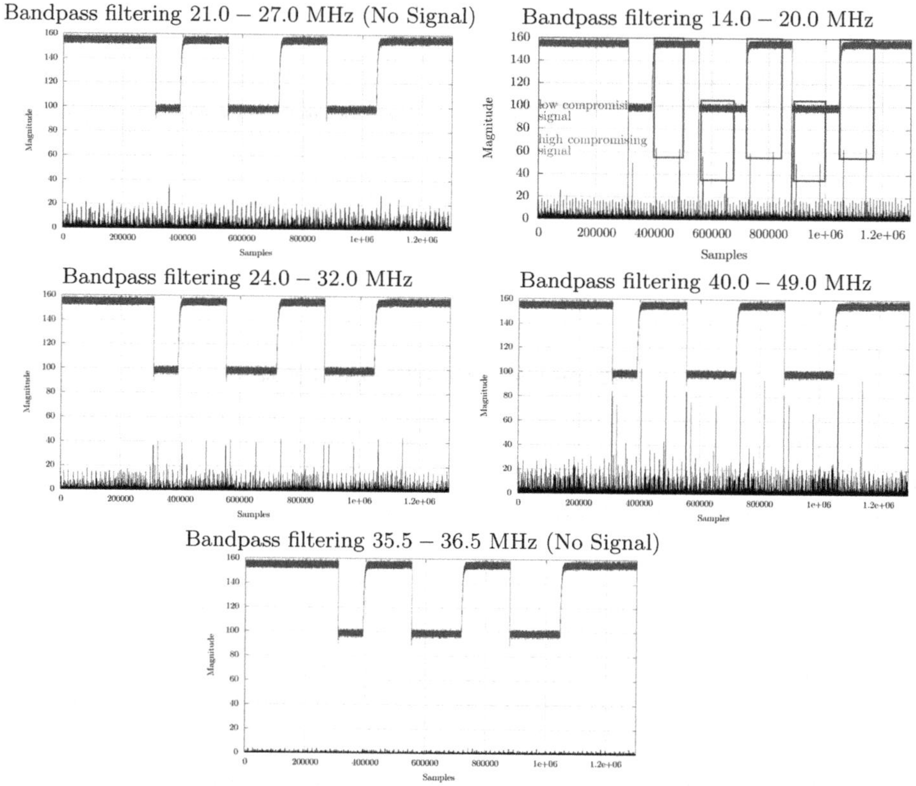

Bandpass filtering 21.0 − 27.0 MHz (No Signal)

Bandpass filtering 14.0 − 20.0 MHz

Bandpass filtering 24.0 − 32.0 MHz

Bandpass filtering 40.0 − 49.0 MHz

Bandpass filtering 35.5 − 36.5 MHz (No Signal)

Fig. 10. Results of software demodulation

Nevertheless with this tool we do not have the advantage of hardware demodulation:

- the bandwidth of the software filter is larger: it cannot be set that narrow as the 1 MHz of the hardware receivers;
- the compromising signal at 36 MHz spotted by the hardware receiver is not visible with the software filtering: no compromising signal is visible.

5   Conclusion

We introduce a new set of techniques to extract the leakage frequencies of the black signal providing information about the red signal. They have successfully been tested on the electromagnetic emissions of a PS/2 keyboard intercepted at a distance of 5 meters. By the help of side channel analysis methods applied in frequency domain, we are able to distinguish the frequencies that are more leaking sensitive information and their bandwidth. Thanks to these tools (inspired from CPA, MIA and PCA), we demonstrate that we are in position to give quick diagnostics about EM leakage.

Our experiments show that the leakage is carried by some frequencies that are not necessarily the harmonics of the clock frequency. This confirms the observations previously done in the work of M. Hutter *et al.* [12]. We also notice that our three methods retrieve the same compromising spectrum shape, and consequently the same leakage frequencies. CPA and MIA yield clearly the most accurate results. Some frequencies that leak more sensitive information than others might result from intermodulation. We show that the red signal can be recovered from the demodulation of the black signal, either with a hardware receiver or by a software band-pass filtering technique, which consists merely in selecting frequencies of interest from the FFT of the black signal. Despite its simplicity, this filter enables an identification of the leakage in time domain. We could successfully characterize the leaking frequencies from our black signal using our methods. This allows us to recover the secret information which is the red signal in this case. However, these generic methods could also be applied in different contexts, for instance RSA recovering key problematics. Indeed in asymmetric cryptography, the sequence of operations are secret dependant. Someone able to find out square and multiply operation sequences occurring during an RSA encryption is able to recover the private exponent. A possible extension to this work could consist in applying our methodology to a confidential sequence of operations.

References

1. Agrawal, D., Archambeault, B., Rao, J.R., Rohatgi, P.: The EM Side–Channel(s). In: Kaliski Jr., B.S., Koç, Ç.K., Paar, C. (eds.) CHES 2002. LNCS, vol. 2523, pp. 29–45. Springer, Heidelberg (2003)
2. Archambeau, C., Peeters, É., Standaert, F.-X., Quisquater, J.-J.: Template attacks in principal subspaces. In: Goubin, L., Matsui, M. (eds.) CHES 2006. LNCS, vol. 4249, pp. 1–14. Springer, Heidelberg (2006)
3. Brier, É., Clavier, C., Olivier, F.: Correlation power analysis with a leakage model. In: Joye, M., Quisquater, J.-J. (eds.) CHES 2004. LNCS, vol. 3156, pp. 16–29. Springer, Heidelberg (2004)
4. Carlier, V., Chabanne, H., Dottax, E., Pelletier, H.: Electromagnetic Side Channels of an FPGA Implementation of AES. Cryptology ePrint Archive, Report 2004/145 (2004), http://eprint.iacr.org/

5. Carlier, V., Chabanne, H., Dottax, E., Pelletier, H.: Generalizing Square Attack using Side-Channels of an AES Implementation on an FPGA. In: Rissa, T., Wilton, S.J.E., Leong, P.H.W. (eds.) FPL, pp. 433–437. IEEE, Los Alamitos (2005)
6. Van Eck, W.: Electromagnetic Radiation from Video Display Units: An Eavesdropping Risk? In: Computers Secutity (1985)
7. Kuhn, M.G.: Compromising Emanations: Eavesdropping risks of computer Displays. In Technical Report UCAM-CL-TR-577
8. Gebotys, C.H., Ho, S., Tiu, C.C.: EM Analysis of Rijndael and ECC on a Wireless Java-Based PDA. In: Rao, J.R., Sunar, B. (eds.) CHES 2005. LNCS, vol. 3659, pp. 250–264. Springer, Heidelberg (2005)
9. Gierlichs, B., Batina, L., Tuyls, P., Preneel, B.: Mutual Information Analysis. In: Oswald, E., Rohatgi, P. (eds.) CHES 2008. LNCS, vol. 5154, pp. 426–442. Springer, Heidelberg (2008)
10. http://www.beyondlogic.org/keyboard/keybrd.htm
11. http://www.computer-engineering.org/ps2keyboard/
12. Hutter, M., Mangard, S., Feldhofer, M.: Power and EM Attacks on Passive $13.56 MHz$ RFID Devices. In: Paillier, P., Verbauwhede, I. (eds.) CHES 2007. LNCS, vol. 4727, pp. 320–333. Springer, Heidelberg (2007)
13. Kuhn, M.G.: Security Limits for Compromising Emanations. In: Rao, J.R., Sunar, B. (eds.) CHES 2005. LNCS, vol. 3659, pp. 265–279. Springer, Heidelberg (2005)
14. Kuhn, M.G., Anderson, R.J.: Soft Tempest: Hidden Data Transmission Using Electromagnetic Emanations. In: Aucsmith, D. (ed.) IH 1998. LNCS, vol. 1525, pp. 124–142. Springer, Heidelberg (1998)
15. Le, T.-H., Clédière, J., Canovas, C., Robisson, B., Servière, C., Lacoume, J.-L.: A Proposition for Correlation Power Analysis Enhancement. In: Goubin, L., Matsui, M. (eds.) CHES 2006. LNCS, vol. 4249, pp. 174–186. Springer, Heidelberg (2006)
16. Li, H., Markettos, A.T., Moore, S.: Security Evaluation Against Electromagnetic Analysis at Design Time. In: Rao, J.R., Sunar, B. (eds.) CHES 2005. LNCS, vol. 3659, pp. 280–292. Springer, Heidelberg (2005)
17. Plos, T., Hutter, M., Feldhofer, M.: Evaluation of Side-Channel Preprocessing Techniques on Cryptographic-Enabled HF and UHF RFID-Tag Prototypes. In: Dominikus, S. (ed.) Workshop on RFID Security 2008, Budapest, Hungary, July 9-11, pp. 114–127 (2008)
18. Schimmel, O., Duplys, P., Boehl, E., Hayek, J., Rosenstiel, W.: Correlation power analysis in frequency domain. In: COSADE, February 4-5, pp. 1–3 (2010)
19. Standaert, F.-X., Archambeau, C.: Using subspace-based template attacks to compare and combine power and electromagnetic information leakages. In: Oswald, E., Rohatgi, P. (eds.) CHES 2008. LNCS, vol. 5154, pp. 411–425. Springer, Heidelberg (2008)
20. Tanaka, H.: Information leakage via electromagnetic emanations and evaluation of tempest countermeasures. In: McDaniel, P., Gupta, S.K. (eds.) ICISS 2007. LNCS, vol. 4812, pp. 167–179. Springer, Heidelberg (2007)
21. Vuagnoux, M., Pasini, S.: Compromising Electromagnetic Emanations of Wired and Wireless Keyboards. In: Proceedings of the 18th USENIX Security Symposium. USENIX Association (2009)

On Obfuscating Programs with Tamper-proof Hardware*

Ning Ding and Dawu Gu

Department of Computer Science and Engineering
Shanghai Jiao Tong University
Shanghai, 200240, China
{dingning,dwgu}@sjtu.edu.cn

Abstract. In recent years, theoretical cryptography community has focused on a fascinating research line of obfuscating programs (circuits). Loosely speaking, obfuscating a program P is to construct a new program which can preserve P's functionality, but its code is fully "unintelligent". No adversary can understand the obfuscated program or reverse-engineering it.

In TCC'10, Goyal et al. showed how to obfuscate any circuit (program) with tamer-proof (stateless) hardware. In their construction, the hardware executes most computation and the software executes a few, and the software needs to interact with the hardware $\Theta(z)$ times if the original circuit is of size z. Thus if a user wants to gain the outputs of the obfuscated circuit on different inputs, he cannot fast the computation by running multiple instances of the obfuscated circuit concurrently well.

In this paper we propose an alternative construction of obfuscating circuits (programs) with tamper-proof hardware. The notable characters of our construction are that the required hardware is still universal in obfuscating circuits and that for a specific circuit the computation on the instantiated hardware is independent of the size of the circuit. When a user runs multiple instances of the obfuscated circuit with different inputs concurrently, the software and hardware have reasonable computation load and thus the entire computation can run almost in parallel and thus be fasten.

Keywords: Obfuscation, Tamper-proof Hardware.

1 Introduction

In recent years, theoretical cryptography community has focused on a fascinating research line of obfuscating programs (circuits). Loosely speaking, obfuscating a program P is to construct a new program which can preserve the functionality of P, but its code is fully "unintelligent". Any adversary can only use the functionality of P and cannot learn anything more than this, i.e. cannot reverse-engineering nor understand it. In other words, an obfuscated program should not

---

* This work was supported by the Specialized Research Fund for the Doctoral Program of Higher Education of China (No. 200802480019).

X. Lai, M. Yung, and D. Lin (Eds.): Inscrypt 2010, LNCS 6584, pp. 487–502, 2011.

reveal anything useful beyond executing it. This highlights a way of designing reverse-engineering resistent software or cryptographic hardware (chips) which can resist against white-box (grey-box) cryptanalysis, e.g. physical attacks and side channel attacks, in a provable manner.

Barak et al. [5] formalized the definition of obfuscation through a simulation-based definition called the virtual black-box property, which says that every adversary has a corresponding simulator that emulates the output of the adversary given oracle (i.e., black-box) access to the same functionality being obfuscated. Following [5], many works focused on how to obfuscate different cryptographic functionalities. Among them, there are some negative results, e.g. [5,18]. [5] showed there doesn't exist any general obfuscation method for all programs. [18] showed many natural cryptographic functionalities cannot be obfuscated. On the other hand, there exist some positive results, e.g. [8,12,10,22,23,27,24]. Among these positive results, [22,24] demonstrated how to securely obfuscate the two complicated functionalities in cryptography, i.e. re-encryption and encrypted signature, while others focused on a very basic and simple primitive, i.e. (multiple-bit) point functions, traditionally used in some password based identification systems.

Though we have achieved a few positive results on obfuscation, these positive results are insufficient to provide solutions for many interesting problems in cryptography. On the other hand, a number of works (e.g. [31,14,30,17,25,9,29,13,19]) have investigated using tamper-proof hardware tokens as tools to achieve a variety of cryptographic goals, including obfuscation. In this research line, Goldwasser et al. [19] proposed using a simple hardware to construct one-time programs which can only be run once and what an adversary can learn from the description of a program as well as a pair of input-output is also computable from oracle access to the program once. Recently, Goyal et al. [21] showed how to construct an obfuscation for any program/circuit based on some stateless hardware. By stateless, we mean the hardware doesn't keep any state after finishing one computation. (Contrary to this, stateful hardware can store the state in one computation and may use it in the next computation. It can be seen the tamper-proof stateful assumption is stronger than the tamper-proof stateless assumption for hardware. In this paper hardware always refers to stateless hardware.)

Goyal et al.'s construction [21] assumed that the hardware token can execute a non-malleable symmetric encryption scheme and a MAC scheme and a pseudorandom function in a black-box way. For a circuit C, its obfuscated version consists of a software part and a hardware token, in which the software part contains ciphertexts of all bits of C (represented as a string) and ciphertexts of all gates and all output wires of C. When a user needs to run the obfuscated circuit on input x, he needs to first compute ciphertexts of all bits of x and then compute values of all internal wires gate by gate. During this computing, all encryption/decryption and MAC operations are performed by the hardware token, while the software part only executes a few computation. Further, if C is of size z, then the software part needs to interact with the hardware token $\Theta(z)$ times.

Consider such a scenario, in which the user wants to execute the obfuscated program/circuit on different inputs. To fast the computation, he is willing to run multiple instances of the obfuscated circuit concurrently on these inputs. Since the software part of the obfuscated circuit can be copied and executed in an arbitrary manner, the user can invoke the multiple instances of the software part on different inputs. But since there is only one hardware token, these instances need to interact with this unique hardware token concurrently. If most computation are performed by the hardware token, the possible situation will be that the hardware token is over-loaded while the instances of the software part are usually idle. Thus the user cannot fast the computation by adopting the concurrent executions.

Thus a problem arises whether or not we can transfer much computation from the hardware token to the software part. That is, can we propose an alternative approach of obfuscating circuits with tamper-proof hardware in which the software part performs most computation while the hardware token performs a few. If we can, then when the user runs multiple instances of the software part to interact with the hardware token, these instances can run concurrently and interact with the unique hardware token. So, in the concurrent computation all parties have reasonable computation load and thus the entire computation can run almost in parallel and thus be fasten. In this paper, we are interested in this problem and attempt to provide a solution to it.

1.1   Our Result

We present an alternative construction of obfuscating polynomial-size circuits. In this construction the software part admits most computation load while the hardware token admits a few and its running-time is a fixed polynomial no matter how large the size of C is (but related to the number of C's output wires). Thus when multiple instances of the software part are invoked to interact with the only hardware token, all parties have balance load and the bad situation mentioned previously will not occur. Thus the concurrent executions can fast the entire computation.

The required hardware token in this construction is universal, like the one in [21], in obfuscating circuits. This means we don't need to design different hardware for different circuits. Our construction requires the tamper-proof hardware token can execute encryption and decryption of a fully homomorphic encryption scheme (without running Evaluate) (e.g. the one in [15]) and a MAC scheme etc. In an execution of the obfuscated circuit, the software part and the hardware token only need constant-round interaction, and the computation on the hardware is independent of the size of the circuit.

Our Technique. Our technique can be briefly sketched as follows. First of all, our basic idea is to use a fully homomorphic encryption scheme as a main ingredient, as shown in [16] (Sect 1.8) which mentioned some applications of fully homomorphic encryption by using this basic idea, to construct the obfuscation in which most computation can be transferred from the hardware token to the software part. Very briefly, the software part contains a ciphertext of the circuit

C. When the user needs to compute $C(x)$, the software part first sends x to the hardware token and obtains a ciphertext of x and then runs algorithm Evaluate to generate the ciphertext of $U(x, C)$ where U is the universal circuit satisfying $U(x, C) = C(x)$. Lastly, he sends this ciphertext to the hardware token to obtain the plaintext, which is $C(x)$. Moreover, we adopt the idea in constructing the universal argument in [4] (based on [26]) which employs a PCP system and a random-access hashing scheme (i.e. tree hashing) in the construction, which can further make the hardware universal, i.e. the hardware can handle any circuit. Further we adopt a MAC scheme, as shown in [21], to prevent adversaries to send fake messages to stateless hardware. Combining these techniques, we can achieve all the desired goals.

1.2   Organizations

The rest of the paper is arranged as follows. Section 2 presents preliminaries this paper needs. Section 3 presents our construction of obfuscating circuits. Section 4 concludes this paper.

2   Preliminaries

This section contains some basic notations and definitions of random-access hashing, obfuscation, MAC, fully homomorphic encryption, probabilistically checkable proofs (PCP) and universal arguments.

2.1   Basic Notions

A function $\mu(\cdot)$, where $\mu : \mathbb{N} \rightarrow [0, 1]$ is called negligible if $\mu(n) = n^{-\omega(1)}$ (i.e., $\mu(n) < \frac{1}{p(n)}$ for all polynomial $p(\cdot)$ and large enough n's). We will sometimes use neg to denote an unspecified negligible function.

In this paper "PPT" machines always refer to non-uniform probabilistic polynomial-time machines unless explicitly stated. We say that two probability ensembles $\{X_n\}_{n \in \mathbb{N}}$ and $\{Y_n\}_{n \in \mathbb{N}}$ are computationally indistinguishable if for every PPT distinguisher D it holds that $|\Pr[D(X_n) = 1] - \Pr[D(Y_n) = 1]| =$ neg(n). We will sometimes abuse notation and say that the two random variables X_n and Y_n are computationally indistinguishable when each of them is a part of a probability ensemble such that these ensembles $\{X_n\}_{n \in \mathbb{N}}$ and $\{Y_n\}_{n \in \mathbb{N}}$ are computationally indistinguishable. We will also sometimes drop the index n from a random variable if it can be inferred from the context. In most of these cases, the index n will be the security parameter.

2.2   Hashing and Tree Hashing

Definition 1. *An efficiently computable function ensemble* $\{h_\alpha\}_{\alpha \in \{0,1\}^*}$*, where* $h_\alpha : \{0,1\}^* \rightarrow \{0,1\}^{|\alpha|}$ *is called collision resistant hash functions if for every PPT A,* $\Pr_{\alpha \leftarrow_R \{0,1\}^n}[A(\alpha) = \langle x, y \rangle \text{ s.t. } x \neq y \text{ and } h_\alpha(x) = h_\alpha(y)] < $ neg(n)

Definition 2. *A random-access hash scheme is an ensemble* $\{\langle h_\alpha, \mathsf{cert}_\alpha \rangle\}_{\alpha \in \{0,1\}^*}$ *of a pairs of efficiently computable functions, where* $h_\alpha : \{0,1\}^* \to \{0,1\}^{|\alpha|}$ *and* cert_α *takes two inputs* x, i, *where* $x \in \{0,1\}^*$ *and* $|i| = log|x|$, *and a polynomial-time algorithm* V *that satisfy the following properties:*

Efficiency: $|\mathsf{cert}_\alpha(x,i)| = poly(|\alpha|, log|x|)$

Completeness: *For every* $\alpha, x, V_{\alpha, h_\alpha(x)}(i, x_i, \mathsf{cert}_\alpha(x,i)) = 1.$

Binding (Soundness): *For every polynomial-sized circuit family* $\{C_n\}_{n \in \mathbb{N}}$, $\Pr_{\alpha \leftarrow_R \{0,1\}^n}[C_n(\alpha) = \langle y, i, \sigma_0, \sigma_1 \rangle \; s.t. \; V_{\alpha, y}(i, 0, \sigma_0) = 1 \; and \; V_{\alpha, y}(i, 1, \sigma_1) = 1] < neg(n)$

Constructing a random-access hashing scheme using hash trees. There is a well known construction due to Merkle of a random-access hash scheme based on any collision-resistant hash function ensemble [28].

2.3 Obfuscation

We adopt the following definition of obfuscation with respect to circuits explicitly, which strengthes the virtual black-box property presented in [8,7,32]. In [8,7,32], the virtual black-box property only requires for each D, p there exists a S such that $|\Pr[D(\mathcal{O}(f)) = 1] - \Pr[D(S^{f(\cdot)}) = 1]| < 1/p(n)$, while we require a universal S satisfying for each D, $|\Pr[D(\mathcal{O}(f)) = 1] - \Pr[D(S^{f(\cdot)}) = 1]| = neg(n)$. We adopt this stronger definition since our construction can satisfy it.

Definition 3. *Let* $\mathcal{F}_n$ *be a family of polynomial-size circuits in which each is of size* $z(n)$ *and* n *input wires and* $l(n)$ *output wires. Let* $\mathcal{O}$ *be a uniform PPT algorithm which maps (description of) each circuit* $f \in \mathcal{F}_n$ *to a circuit* $\mathcal{O}(f)$. *We say that* $\mathcal{O}$ *is an obfuscator iff the following holds:*

Functionality: *for all* $n \in \mathbb{N}$, *all* $f \in \mathcal{F}_n$, *and all* $O = \mathcal{O}(f)$, *we have that* O *computes the same function as* f. *That is, for every* $x \in \{0,1\}^n$, $O(x) = f(x)$.

Virtual black-box property: *There is a uniform PPT simulator* S *such that for each PPT* D *and each* $f \in \mathcal{F}_n$ $|\Pr[D(\mathcal{O}(f)) = 1] - \Pr[D(S^{f(\cdot)}(z(n), l(n), 1^n)) = 1]| = neg(n).$

2.4 Message Authentication Codes

We use the following standard definition of message authentication codes.

Definition 4. *A message authentication code (MAC)* $\mathsf{MAC} = (G; Sig; Ver)$ *consists of the three uniform PPT algorithms with the following semantics:*

1. *The key generation algorithm* G *samples a key* k.
2. *The signature algorithm* Sig *signs a message* $M \in \{0,1\}^*$ *and produces a MAC* σ. *We write* $\sigma \leftarrow Sig(k; M)$.
3. *The verification algorithm* Ver *verifies a MAC* σ *for a message* M. *We write* $ver \leftarrow Ver(k; \sigma; M)$, *where* $ver \in \{0,1\}$.

We require perfect correctness, i.e., $Ver(k; Sig(k; M); M) = 1$ *for all* M *and all possible* k.

Security of MAC. In this paper, we demand that MACs possess the security of strong unforgeability under chosen message attack (SUF-CMA) in the sense defined in [6]. That is, the forged message does not have to be new as long as the MAC was not previously attached to this message by the legitimate parties.

2.5 Fully Homomorphic Encryption

We introduce the following definition of fully homomorphic encryption schemes (FHES) presented in [15].

Definition 5. *The scheme* FHES = (Gen; Enc; Dec; Evaluate) *consists of the four uniform PPT algorithms with the following semantics:*
1. *(Gen; Enc; Dec) constitutes an ordinary public-key encryption scheme.*
2. *For a given t-input circuit C, for any $m_1, \cdots, m_t$, and any ciphertexts $c_1, \cdots, c_t$ with $c_i \leftarrow$ Enc$(pk; m_i)$, it is the case that* Dec$(sk;$ Evaluate$(pk; C; c_1, \cdots, c_t)) = C(m_1, \cdots, m_t)$.
3. *There exists a fixed polynomial f such that, for every value of the security parameter n, the decryption algorithm can be expressed as a circuit of size at most $f(n)$. (It is required that the number of C's output wires is fixed in advance, say 1 output wire. Then this condition means ciphertext size and decryption time to be upper bounded independently of C. If C is of many output wires, let* Evaluate *compute a ciphertext for each output and then all the ciphertexts are viewed as the ciphertext of C's whole output.)*

Security of FHES. We demand FHES possesses the security of IND-CPA as shown in [15].

2.6 PCP and Universal Arguments

PCP systems are probabilistic proof systems for deciding languages in Ntime(t) where t can be a super polynomial. A PCP system for a language $L \in$ Ntime(t) refers to a pair of machines, denoted $(P_{\text{PCP}}, V_{\text{PCP}})$, where for a public input $x \in L$ P_{PCP} generates a proof π from the witness for x and V_{PCP} on oracle access to the proof π accepts or rejects the input x. The notable character of PCP systems is that the verifier V_{PCP} can be a uniform PPT machine.

The standard definition of the PCP refers to two recourses of the verifier, i.e. the numbers of coin tosses and positions in π V_{PCP} needs to access. Since our paper will not refer to the two recourses explicitly, we omit presenting the rigorous definition of the PCP, which can be found in [1,2]. Further, in this paper we always require perfect completeness and negligible soundness error probability for PCP systems.

[26] showed how to use the PCP system for any language $L \in$ NEXP, e.g. [3], together with a random-access hashing scheme (tree hashing) to construct an argument in which the communication complexity can be dramatically decreased and the verifier runs in a fixed polynomial-time. In this construction, verifier first sends a random hash function to prover. Then prover sends the root of the hash tree of the PCP proof π using the tree hashing scheme. Third, verifier chooses a

random challenge. Lastly, prover sends the values of the positions in π decided by the challenge as well as the certificates and verifier verifies if the certificates are valid and then runs V_{PCP} to verify if the values are correct and accepts the public input iff V_{PCP} accepts.

[4] called this argument the universal argument and showed a weak proof of knowledge property, i.e. if prover can convince verifier that $x \in L$ where $L \in \mathsf{Ntime}(t)$ with non-negligible probability, then there exists a polynomial-time extractor which on oracle access to this prover, can output an implicit witness for x with non-negligible probability and then runs the implicit witness within $t^{O(1)}$ steps to obtain an explicit witness.

3   Our Result

In this section we present our construction of obfuscation for polynomial-size circuits (polynomial-time programs). In Section 3.1 we present our obfuscation as well as illustrating some obvious properties, e.g., the universal property of the hardware token, and lastly present a theorem that claims that our construction is indeed an obfuscation for circuits. In Section 3.2 we present the proof of the theorem and thus finish the description of our result.

3.1   The Construction

Assume the circuit we need to obfuscate is C of size $z(n)$ and n input wires and $l(n)$ output wires where $z(n)$ and $l(n)$ are publicly known. (If we need to obfuscate a program P with running-time T, we can first construct a circuit ensemble in which the nth one is equivalent to P's computation on all n-bit inputs.) Let $\{U_n\}_{n\in\mathbb{N}}$ be a universal circuit ensemble in which U_n on two inputs $\mathsf{Input} \in \{0,1\}^n$, $\mathsf{Circuit} \in \{0,1\}^{z(n)}$ where $\mathsf{Circuit}$ is the description of a circuit of n input wires and $l(n)$ output wires, outputs $\mathsf{Circuit}(\mathsf{Input})$ (note that for different $z(n)$ and $l(n)$, $\{U_n\}_{n\in\mathbb{N}}$ is different).

Assume $\mathsf{FHES} = (\mathsf{Gen}; \mathsf{Enc}; \mathsf{Dec}; \mathsf{Evaluate})$ is a fully homomorphic encryption scheme with security of IND-CPA, and $\mathsf{MAC} = (\mathsf{G}; \mathsf{Sig}; \mathsf{Ver})$ is a SUF-CMA MAC scheme. Note that in FHES, the algorithms $\mathsf{Gen}, \mathsf{Enc}, \mathsf{Dec}$ run in fixed polynomial-time, while the running-time of $\mathsf{Evaluate}$ is mainly decided by the second parameter, i.e. the description of a circuit (refer to Definition 5). Thus the running-time of $\mathsf{Evaluate}$ cannot be bounded by any fixed polynomial since the circuit can be arbitrarily large.

Define an $\mathsf{Ntime}(n^{\log\log n})$ language Λ in which each instance can be parsed as (c, H, V) and possesses a witness $(\mathsf{EncInput}, \mathsf{EncCircuit}, pk, U_n, h, r)$ such that $c = \mathsf{Evaluate}_r(pk; U_n; \mathsf{EncInput}, \mathsf{EncCircuit})$ and $H = h(\mathsf{EncCircuit})$ and $V = h(U_n)$, where h is a hash function of a tree hashing scheme, and $\mathsf{EncInput}$ and $\mathsf{EncCircuit}$ are promised being two ciphertexts ($\mathsf{EncInput}$ and $\mathsf{EncCircuit}$ will be ciphertexts of Input and $\mathsf{Circuit}$ in our construction). We assume the collision resistance of the hash functions holds for all $n^{O(\log\log n)}$-time (non-uniform) machines.

We comment that if we only need to design the hardware for obfuscating C, we can define Λ as an NP language. But since we want to make the hardware universal for obfuscating any polynomial-size circuit which size cannot be bounded in advance. So we relax Λ to be a language in $\mathsf{Ntime}(n^{\log\log n})$. Let $(P_{\mathsf{PCP}}, V_{\mathsf{PCP}})$ be a PCP system for Λ with negligible soundness error, e.g. the one in [3], in which P_{PCP} is relatively efficiently, i.e., its running-time is a polynomial in the time of verifying Λ, and it has a weak proof of knowledge property (refer to [4]).

Requirements on hardware. We require that the tamper-proof hardware token can execute Enc and Dec of FHES (without running $\mathsf{Evaluate}$) and MAC etc.

Construction. We now turn to describe the obfuscation of C. We first describe the idea underlying the construction. Denote by sender the party who prepares the obfuscated circuit and by receiver the party who uses the circuit. The obfuscated circuit consists of a software part and a hardware token. Our goal is to reduce the computation on the hardware token and reduce the interaction times to constant.

Briefly, the sender first generates the following information, i.e. the public key and secret key of FHES, the key of MAC and the random hash function. Then encrypt C (represented as a string) and hash the ciphertext. Lastly, choose the appropriate universal circuit U_n and hash it. Thus, the public key, the ciphertext of C, U_n, the hash function and the hashing values represent the software part of the obfuscated circuit. Then the sender constructs the hardware token which can execute FHES (without executing $\mathsf{Evaluate}$) and MAC. When obtaining the obfuscated circuit and starting to execute the circuit with an input x, the receiver first obtains a ciphertext of x by access to the hardware token. Then he runs $\mathsf{Evaluate}$ of FHES to compute a ciphertext of $U_n(x; C)$ (note that he possesses the ciphertexts of x and C). Lastly, he queries the hardware token for decrypting this ciphertext to obtain the plaintext, which is $U_n(x, C) = C(x)$.

From the above description, we can see the computation on the hardware token is independent of the size of C, while the heavy computation (i.e., running $\mathsf{Evaluate}$ and P_{PCP} of the PCP system) is performed by the software part. In the following we present the strategies of the sender and receiver in detail.

The sender. The sender runs Gen of FHES to gain (pk, sk) and G of MAC to obtain the key s and chooses randomly a hash function h on security parameter n. Then compute a ciphertext $c_0 \leftarrow \mathsf{Enc}(pk; C)$ and $H \leftarrow h(c_0)$ and $V \leftarrow h(U_n)$. (pk, h, c_0, H, V, U_n) represents the software part of the obfuscated circuit. Then the sender constructs the hardware token $\mathcal{T}$ which possesses (sk, pk, s, h, H, V). Notice that (sk, pk, s, h, H, V) is independent of the size of C. The software part and $\mathcal{T}$ constitute the obfuscated circuit, denoted $\mathcal{OBC}$.

The receiver. On obtaining the obfuscated circuit $\mathcal{OBC}$, the receiver runs the software part and $\mathcal{T}$ of $\mathcal{OBC}$ on an input $x \in \{0,1\}^n$ as follows:

1. **Software.** The software part sends x with query type 1 to the token $\mathcal{T}$.

2. **Hardware.** On receiving the query x of type 1, $\mathcal{T}$ computes $c_1 \leftarrow \mathsf{Enc}(pk; x)$ and $\mathsf{MAC}_1 \leftarrow \mathsf{Sig}(s; c_1)$. Output (x, c_1, MAC_1). (If the query is not of the required form, respond $\perp$. Similarly for queries of types 2, 3 and 4.)

3. **Software.** On receiving (x, c_1, MAC_1), the software part computes $c_2 \leftarrow$ Evaluate$(pk; U_n; c_1; c_0)$. Then employ P_{PCP}'s strategy of the PCP system to compute the PCP proof π from the witness for $(c_2, H, V) \in \Lambda$. Send $(c_1, \mathsf{MAC}_1, c_2)$ with query type 2 to $\mathcal{T}$.

4. **Hardware.** On receiving the query $(c_1, \mathsf{MAC}_1, c_2)$ of type 2, $\mathcal{T}$ verifies if MAC_1 is a MAC of c_1, output $\bot$ if not. Else, $\mathcal{T}$ randomly chooses a hash function h^* of the tree hashing scheme, and computes $c_3 \leftarrow \mathsf{Enc}(pk; h^*||c_1||c_2)$ and $\mathsf{MAC}_3 \leftarrow \mathsf{Sig}(s; c_3)$, where "$||$" denotes concatenation operation. Output $(h^*, c_3, \mathsf{MAC}_3)$.

5. **Software.** On receiving $(h^*, c_3, \mathsf{MAC}_3)$, the software part uses h^* to compute the root value of π according to the tree hash scheme, i.e. root $\leftarrow h^*(\pi)$, and sends $(c_3, \mathsf{MAC}_3, \mathsf{root})$ with query type 3 to $\mathcal{T}$. (Note that we don't need to make the PCP proof zero-knowledge or satisfy some other security since $\mathcal{T}$ is always honest and that using the PCP system together with the tree hashing scheme aims to make $\mathcal{T}$ universal in obfuscating any C.)

6. **Hardware.** On receiving the query $(c_3, \mathsf{MAC}_3, \mathsf{root})$ of type 3, $\mathcal{T}$ verifies if MAC_3 is a MAC of c_3, output $\bot$ if not. Else, choose a poly-bit random challenge ch and compute $c_4 \leftarrow \mathsf{Enc}(pk; ch||\mathsf{root}||c_3)$ and $\mathsf{MAC}_4 \leftarrow \mathsf{Sig}(s; c_4)$. Output $(ch, c_4, \mathsf{MAC}_4)$.

7. **Software.** On receiving the response $(ch, c_4, \mathsf{MAC}_4)$, the software part gathers those values of the desired positions in π determined by ch as well as the certificates in tree hashing using h^*, denoted v. Send (v, c_4, MAC_4) with query type 4 to $\mathcal{T}$.

8. **Hardware.** On receiving the query (v, c_4, MAC_4) of type 4, $\mathcal{T}$ verifies the following conditions and if any one is not satisfied, output $\bot$:

   (a) Verify if MAC_4 is a MAC of c_4.

   (b) Decrypt c_4 to obtain (ch, root, c_3) and decrypt c_3 to obtain (c_1, c_2, h^*).

   (c) Verify if v is consistent with ch, h^*, root and adopt V_{PCP}'s strategy to verify if the values of the desired positions determined by ch in v is valid for (c_2, H, V) in Λ.

   If all these conditions are satisfied, decrypt c_2 and output the plaintext.
   (It can be seen that if we are oblivious of MAC, the usage of the PCP system together with the tree hashing scheme in this obfuscation is essentially the same as that in the universal argument in [4]. Thus if a malicious software part can convince the hardware that $(c_2, H, V) \in \Lambda$ with non-negligible probability, then there is an extractor which on oracle access to the software part, can output the original witness within $n^{O(\log \log n)}$ time.)

9. **Software.** The software part outputs this plaintext as the final output.

So far we have completed the description of $\mathcal{OBC}$. Obviously, the software part and $\mathcal{T}$ are polynomial-time strategies for polynomial-size C and only interact constant times in a honest execution. It can be seen that $\mathcal{T}$ is universal since its strategy is independent of C and even if input/instantiated with

(sk, pk, s, h, H, V), its computation is still independent of the size of C (it is related to $l(n)$), while the software part admits the heavy computation, i.e. running Evaluate and P_{PCP}. Thus all that is left is to show $\mathcal{OBC}$ is indeed an obfuscation of C, as the following theorem states.

Theorem 1. *$\mathcal{OBC}$ is an obfuscation of C.*

In the next subsection we will present the proof of this theorem.

3.2   Proof of the Theorem

In this subsection we prove Theorem 1. To this end, we need to show the functionality and virtual black-box properties can be satisfied, as Definition 3 requires.

Functionality. Since the plaintexts of c_1, c_0 are x and C respectively and $c_2 =$ Evaluate$(pk; U_n; c_1; c_0)$, we have c_2's plaintext is $U_n(x, C) = C(x)$. Thus when honestly running $\mathcal{OBC}$, $\mathcal{OBC}(x) = C(x)$ for each $x \in \{0,1\}^n$.

Virtual black-box property. To show this, we need to prove there is a uniform PPT simulator Sim, such that for any distinguisher D, D cannot distinguish $\mathcal{OBC}$ from $Sim^{C(\cdot)}(z(n), l(n), 1^n)$. In the following we first present the construction of Sim and then show the indistinguishability.

Construction of Sim. Sim first prepares the following fake information: It independently runs Gen of FHES to obtain (pk', sk') and G of MAC to obtain s' and chooses a dummy circuit C' of size $z(n)$ and n input wires and $l(n)$ output wires, and a random hash function h'. Then compute a ciphertext $c_0' \leftarrow$ Enc$(pk'; C')$ and $H' \leftarrow h'(c_0')$ and $V' \leftarrow h'(U_n)$. $(pk', h', c_0', H', V', U_n)$ represents the software part of the fake obfuscated circuit, denoted $\mathcal{OBC}'$. (Actually, Sim only generates the software part and emulates the hardware token with the fake parameters in answering queries). Then Sim puts the software part of the fake obfuscated circuit as input to D and runs S (a part of Sim) with the fake parameters to emulate $\mathcal{T}$ to answer D's oracle queries. In answering queries, S basically follows $\mathcal{T}$'s strategies described previously except that S records all D's queries and the responses and organizes them in trees as the following shows:

1. When it receives a query of type 1 (if the query is not of the required form, respond $\perp$. Similarly for queries of types 2, 3 and 4), denoted q_1, S thinks this is a new execution of the obfuscated circuit and creates a new tree for this execution, even if there already exist some queries of type 1 which has the same content with q_1. Follow $\mathcal{T}$'s strategy to output the response, denoted res_1. Let (q_1, res_1) be the root of this tree.

2. When it receives a query of type 2, which can be parsed as $(c_1, \mathsf{MAC}_1, c_2)$, S traces roots (i.e. level 1) of all trees and checks if there exists a root in which the response contains (c_1, MAC_1). If not, respond $\perp$. Else, w.l.o.g. denote this root by (q_1, res_1). (If there are more than one trees satisfying the search requirement, choose an arbitrary one, e.g. the first one, and proceed.) Denote this query $(c_1, \mathsf{MAC}_1, c_2)$ by q_{1k}. Then S follows $\mathcal{T}$'s strategy to generate and output the response, denoted res_{1k}. Insert (q_{1k}, res_{1k}) to the tree as the kth

son of (q_1, res_1), where assume there already exist $k - 1$ sons of (q_1, res_1) (note that D can re-compute or replay a query to the stateless $\mathcal{T}$).

3. When it receives a query of type 3, which can be parsed as $(c_3, \mathsf{MAC}_3, \text{root})$, S traces all trees and checks if there exists a node in level 2 in some tree in which the response contains (c_3, MAC_3). If not, respond $\perp$. Else, w.l.o.g. denote this node by (q_{1k}, res_{1k}). (If there are more than one nodes in all trees satisfying the search requirement, choose an arbitrary one and proceed.) Then follow $\mathcal{T}$'s strategy to generate the response. W.l.o.g. denote this query $(c_3, \mathsf{MAC}_3, \text{root})$ by q_{1kt} and its response by res_{1kt}. Insert (q_{1kt}, res_{1kt}) to the tree as the tth son of (q_{1k}, res_{1k}), where assume there already exist $t - 1$ sons of (q_{1k}, res_{1k}).

4. When it receives a query of type 4, which can be parsed as (v, c_4, MAC_4), S traces all trees and checks if there exists a node in level 3 in some tree in which the response contains (c_4, MAC_4). If not, respond $\perp$. Else, w.l.o.g. denote this node by (q_{1kt}, res_{1kt}). (If there are more than one nodes in all trees satisfying the search requirement, choose an arbitrary one and proceed.) Then follow $\mathcal{T}$'s strategy to verify the 3 conditions. If verification fails, respond $\perp$. Else, S retrieves the input x from the root in the tree this node belongs to. Send this input to the oracle $C(\cdot)$ and lastly respond what C outputs. W.l.o.g. denote this query (v, c_4, MAC_4) by q_{1ktj} and its response by res_{1ktj}. Insert (q_{1ktj}, res_{1ktj}) to the tree as the jth son of (q_{1kt}, res_{1kt}), where assume there already exist $j - 1$ sons of (q_{1kt}, res_{1kt}). Note that the node containing (q_{1ktj}, res_{1ktj}) is also a leaf of the tree.

Now we adopt a game-based technique to show for each PPT distinguisher D, $|\Pr[D(\mathcal{OBC}) = 1] - \Pr[D(Sim^{C(\cdot)}(z(n), l(n), 1^n)) = 1]| = \mathsf{neg}(n)$.

Game 0. Let Game 0 denote the computation of $D(\mathcal{OBC})$ (note that D can only access $\mathcal{T}$ in the oracle manner). Let out_0 denote D's output.

Game 1. Game 1 is identical to Game 0 except that $\mathcal{T}$ is emulated by S_1 with all the true information (i.e. (sk, pk, s, h, H, V), in this proof the true information doesn't contain the description of C), where S_1 is identical to S except that in answering each query of type 4, S_1 doesn't retrieve x from the root in the tree this query belongs to. Instead, it decrypts c_2 and outputs c_2's plaintext. Let out_1 denote D's output. We now show that $|\Pr[out_0 = 1] - \Pr[out_1 = 1]| = \mathsf{neg}(n)$.

Let bad denote the event that in the two games D sends a query of type i $(1 < i \le 4)$ satisfying that the pair of ciphertext-MAC contained in this query can pass $\mathcal{T}$'s or S_1's verification but it was not output by $\mathcal{T}$ or S_1. It can be seen that on the occurrence of $\neg$bad, Game 0 and Game 1 proceed identically, i.e. $\Pr[out_0 = 1|\neg\text{bad}] = \Pr[out_1 = 1|\neg\text{bad}]$. We show $\Pr[\text{bad}] = \mathsf{neg}(n)$. In fact, the occurrence of bad means D can forge a MAC. By the unforgeability of MAC, we have $\Pr[\text{bad}] = \mathsf{neg}(n)$. Thus, combining $\Pr[out_0 = 1|\neg\text{bad}] = \Pr[out_1 = 1|\neg\text{bad}]$ with $\Pr[\neg\text{bad}] = 1 - \mathsf{neg}(n)$, we have $|\Pr[out_0 = 1] - \Pr[out_1 = 1]| = \mathsf{neg}(n)$.

Game 2. Game 2 is identical to Game 1 except that S_1 is replaced by S (with the true information and oracle access to $C(\cdot)$). Let out_2 denote D's output. We now show $|\Pr[out_1 = 1] - \Pr[out_2 = 1]| = \mathsf{neg}(n)$.

It can be seen that Game 2 differs from Game 1 in S's strategy after verification passes in answering queries of type 4. Let bad_1 denote the event that in the two games there exists a query of type 4 which can pass the verification but in answering this query c_2's plaintext is not equal to $C(x)$ where x is the query content in the root of the tree this query belongs to. It can be seen that on the occurrence of $\neg\mathsf{bad}_1$, Game 1 and Game 2 proceed identically. Thus to show the two games are indistinguishable, we only need to show $\Pr[\mathsf{bad}_1] = \mathsf{neg}(n)$.

Suppose, on the contrary, $\Pr[\mathsf{bad}_1]$ is non-negligible. Then at least in one of the two games, this bad event occurs with non-negligible probability. W.l.o.g. assume in Game 1, there exists a query of type 4 which can pass the verification but c_2's plaintext is not equal to $C(x)$ with non-negligible probability. Thus we can show the collision resistance of h would not hold. Details follows.

Since S_1 at most creates polynomial trees in the execution of Game 1, we have there exists a number j_1 satisfying with non-negligible probability, the j_1th tree (ordered in an arbitrary way) contains a leaf such that the query of type 4 in this leaf can pass the verification but in answering it c_2's plaintext is not equal to $C(x)$. We now construct a PPT D_1 which only sends out the queries of the execution of the j_1th tree. D_1 runs as follows: it has D hardwired and adopts the sender's strategy to generate the true information. Then run D internally and adopt S_1's strategy with the true information to answer D's queries except for the queries of the j_1th tree. For the execution of the j_1th tree, D_1 sends out D's queries of this tree to S_1 and transmits S_1's responses to D and proceeds. Thus from the view of outside, D_1 only takes part in the execution of one tree. By our assumption, in the interaction between D_1 and S_1, D_1 can generate a c_2 and convince S_1 that $(c_2, H, V) \in \Lambda$ and c_2's plaintext is not $C(x)$ with non-negligible probability.

Since there are at most polynomial paths (from the root to a leaf) in this tree (i.e. the j_1th tree), we have there exists a number j_2 satisfying D_1 can generate a c_2 and convince S_1 that $(c_2, H, V) \in \Lambda$ and c_2's plaintext is not $C(x)$ in the j_2th path (ordered in an arbitrary way) with non-negligible probability. Denote this probability by ε. Then we construct a PPT D_2 which only sends out the queries of the j_2th path and proceeds consecutively. D_2 runs as follows: it has D_1 hardwired and runs D_1 to obtain the required true information and adopts S_1's strategy to answer D_1's queries except for the j_2th path. For the execution of the j_2th path, if D_1 has sent out a query of type i, $1 \leq i \leq 4$, D_2 adopts S_1's strategy to respond all later D_1's queries of type i. Otherwise, D_2 sends out this query to S_1 and transmits S_1's response to D_1 and proceeds. Thus from the view of outside, D_2 only takes part in one path and proceeds consecutively in the interaction. Thus we have D_2 can generate a c_2 and convince S_1 that $(c_2, H, V) \in \Lambda$ and c_2's plaintext is not $C(x)$ with probability ε.

Thus for at least $\frac{\varepsilon}{2}$ fraction of the true information and the coin tosses of the joint computation of D_2 and S_1 prior to S_1's answering the query of type

2, D_2 can convince S_1 that $(c_2, H, V) \in \Lambda$ and c_2's plaintext is not $C(x)$ with probability at least $\frac{\varepsilon}{2}$. Thus fixing any choice of the true information and the coins in this $\frac{\varepsilon}{2}$ fraction (c_2 and thus the public input to the PCP system are fixed), D_2 can convince S_1 that $(c_2, H, V) \in \Lambda$ and c_2's plaintext is not $C(x)$ with probability at least $\frac{\varepsilon}{2}$.

By the soundness of the PCP system as well as the tree hashing scheme, we have except negligible probability, for this (c_2, H, V) there exists a witness $(c_1, c_0, pk, U_n, h, r)$ such that $c_2 = \mathsf{Evaluate}_r(pk; U_n; c_1, c_0)$ and $h(c_0) = H$ and $h(U_n) = V$. Since D_2 can convince S_1 that $(c_2, H, V) \in \Lambda$ with probability $\frac{\varepsilon}{2}$, by the weak proof of knowledge property of the PCP system, we can adopt the strategy of the knowledge extractor of the PCP system on oracle access to D_2 to output a witness for $(c_2, H, V) \in \Lambda$ within $n^{O(\log \log n)}$ time with non-negligible probability. Thus if the c_0 and U_n in this extracted witness are identical to their counterpoints in the software part, we have c_2's plaintext is $C(x)$. However, by our assumption, it is the case that at least one of c_0 and U_n in the witness is not identical to its counterpoint in the software part. Thus this one and its counterpoint constitute a collision of h with non-negligible probability. This is a contradiction.

Thus $\Pr[\mathsf{bad}_1] = \mathsf{neg}(n)$, and $|\Pr[out_1 = 1] - \Pr[out_2 = 1]| = \mathsf{neg}(n)$.

Game 3. Game 3 is identical to Game 2 except that S is replaced by a new S_2, which is identical to S except that S_2 doesn't have the oracle $C(\cdot)$ to access and the true information for it doesn't contain the secret key sk, but it has the description of C hardwired. When answering each query of type 4, denoted (v, c_4, MAC_4), S_2 first verifies condition (a) and then goes to condition (b). At this time S_2 doesn't decrypt c_4, c_3 to obtain $(ch, \mathsf{root}, c_1, c_2, h^*)$ in condition (b) (since it doesn't know sk). Instead, it retrieves $(ch, \mathsf{root}, c_1, c_2, h^*)$ along the path from the node this query belongs to to the root in the corresponding tree and then verifies condition (c). If the verification passes, S_2 retrieves x from the root of the tree and runs $C(x)$ and responds to D what C outputs.

Let out_3 denote D's output. It can be seen by S_2's strategy, the information $(ch, \mathsf{root}, c_1, c_2, h^*)$ S_2 retrieves from that path is identical to that from the decryption S_2 would perform in condition (b) if it knew sk. Thus $\Pr[out_2 = 1] = \Pr[out_3 = 1]$.

Game 4. Game 4 is identical to Game 3 except that c_0 in the obfuscated circuit is now changed into a ciphertext of the dummy circuit Sim chooses instead of a ciphertext of C (thus H is the hashing value of this c_0). Let out_4 denote D's output. We show $|\Pr[out_3 = 1] - \Pr[out_4 = 1]| = \mathsf{neg}(n)$.

It can be seen Game 4 differs from Game 3 only in c_0 which is either a ciphertext of C or a ciphertext of the dummy circuit. Thus if D can distinguish Game 3 from Game 4, we can construct a PPT algorithm B which can distinguish the two ciphertexts of C and the dummy circuit. We sketch B's construction: B on input c_0, a ciphertext either of C or of the dummy circuit, and the public key pk of FHES, adopts the sender's strategy to generate the remainder parameters (s, h, H, V, U_n). Then it invokes D and S_2 with the required inputs (note that D

and S_2 don't have sk as input) and lastly outputs what D outputs. Note that here B knows the description of C since S_2 has it hardwired.

Notice that for encryption, IND-CPA means for every two plaintexts of same length any (non-uniform) PPT algorithm cannot distinguish their ciphertexts even the algorithm knows the plaintexts. Thus by the security of IND-CPA of FHES, we conclude that B, though it knows the description C, cannot distinguish the two ciphertexts of C and the dummy circuit. Thus $|\Pr[out_3 = 1] - \Pr[out_4 = 1]| = \mathsf{neg}(n)$.

Game 5. Game 5 is identical to Game 4 except that we first run Sim to generate all fake information, and then replace all required true parameters in Game 4 by the corresponding fake parameters (the true information doesn't include the description of C. Namely, S_2 still has the description of C hardwired in this game). Let out_5 denote D's output. Since all the fake information is identically distributed to the true information, $\Pr[out_4 = 1] = \Pr[out_5 = 1]$.

Game 6. Game 6 is identical to Game 5 except that we resume S to substitute S_2, where S doesn't have the description of C hardwired but can access oracle $C(\cdot)$ and its input contains a more parameter sk'. Let out_6 denote D's output, which is indeed $D(Sim^{C(\cdot)}(z(n), l(n), 1^n))$. Using the same analysis presented in Game 3, we conclude $\Pr[out_5 = 1] = \Pr[out_6 = 1]$.

Taking all the results above, we conclude that $|\Pr[out_0 = 1] - \Pr[out_6 = 1]| = \mathsf{neg}(n)$. Thus the theorem follows.

4   Conclusions

In this paper we investigate an important issue of theoretical cryptography, i.e., how to obfuscate any circuit/program with tamper-proof hardware. The previous work by Goyal et al. [21] has provided a solution to this issue. However, we think their construction cannot fast concurrent executions of multiple instances of the obfuscated circuits well. Thus we present an alternative obfuscation in which the software part admits most computation and the hardware admits a few. Thus when a user invokes multiple instances of the software part to interact with the unique hardware token, although the software part admits most computation, these instances of the software part can run almost in parallel and thus the entire computation can be fasten.

Acknowledgments

We thank the anonymous reviewers of INSCRYPT 2010 for their useful comments and suggestions.

References

1. Arora, S., Lund, C., Motwani, R., Sudan, M., Szegedy, M.: Proof verification and hardness of approximation problems. Journal of the ACM 45(3), 501–555 (1998)
2. Arora, S., Safra, S.: Probabilistic checking of proofs: a new characterization of NP. Journal of the ACM 45(1), 70–122 (1998)

3. Babai, L., Fortnow, L., Levin, L.A., Szegedy, M.: Checking computations in polylogarithmic time. In: Proc. 22nd STOC, pp. 21–31. ACM, New York (1991)
4. Barak, B., Goldreich, O.: Universal arguments and their applications. Cryptology ePrint Archive, Report 2001/105 (2001); Extended abstract appeared in CCC 2002
5. Barak, B., Goldreich, O., Impagliazzo, R., Rudich, S., Sahai, A., Vadhan, S., Yang, K.: On the (im)possibility of obfuscating programs. In: Kilian, J. (ed.) CRYPTO 2001. LNCS, vol. 2139, pp. 1–18. Springer, Heidelberg (2001)
6. Bellare, M., Namprempre, C.: Authenticated encryption: relations among notions and analysis of the generic composition paradigm. In: Okamoto, T. (ed.) ASIACRYPT 2000. LNCS, vol. 1976, pp. 531–545. Springer, Heidelberg (2000)
7. Canetti, R.: Towards realizing random oracles: hash functions that hide all partial information. In: Kaliski Jr., B.S. (ed.) CRYPTO 1997. LNCS, vol. 1294, pp. 455–469. Springer, Heidelberg (1997)
8. Canetti, R., Dakdouk, R.R.: Obfuscating point functions with multibit output. In: Smart, N.P. (ed.) EUROCRYPT 2008. LNCS, vol. 4965, pp. 489–508. Springer, Heidelberg (2008)
9. Chandran, N., Goyal, V., Sahai, A.: New Constructions for UC Secure Computation Using Tamper-Proof Hardware. In: Smart, N.P. (ed.) EUROCRYPT 2008. LNCS, vol. 4965, pp. 545–562. Springer, Heidelberg (2008)
10. Canetti, R., Tauman Kalai, Y., Varia, M., Wichs, D.: On symmetric encryption and point obfuscation. In: Micciancio, D. (ed.) TCC 2010. LNCS, vol. 5978, pp. 52–71. Springer, Heidelberg (2010)
11. Canetti, R., Varia, M.: Non-malleable obfuscation. In: Reingold, O. (ed.) TCC 2009. LNCS, vol. 5444, pp. 73–90. Springer, Heidelberg (2009)
12. Canetti, R., Rothblum, G.N., Varia, M.: Obfuscation of hyperplane membership. In: Micciancio, D. (ed.) TCC 2010. LNCS, vol. 5978, pp. 72–89. Springer, Heidelberg (2010)
13. Damgård, I.B., Nielsen, J.B., Wichs, D.: Isolated Proofs of Knowledge and Isolated Zero Knowledge. In: Smart, N.P. (ed.) EUROCRYPT 2008. LNCS, vol. 4965, pp. 509–526. Springer, Heidelberg (2008)
14. Desmedt, Y.G., Quisquater, J.-J.: Public key systems based on the difficulty of tampering (Is there a difference between DES and RSA?). In: Odlyzko, A.M. (ed.) CRYPTO 1986. LNCS, vol. 263, pp. 111–117. Springer, Heidelberg (1987)
15. Gentry, C.: Fully homomorphic encryption using ideal lattices. In: Proc. STOC 2009, pp. 169–178 (2009)
16. Gentry, C.: A fully homomorphic encryption scheme. PhD dissertation, Stanford University (2009)
17. Goldreich, O., Ostrovsky, R.: Software protection and simulation on oblivious rams. J. ACM 43(3), 431–473 (1996)
18. Goldwasser, S., Kalai, Y.T.: On the impossibility of obfuscation with auxiliary input. In: Proc. FOCS 2005, pp. 553–562 (2005)
19. Goldwasser, S., Kalai, Y.T., Rothblum, G.N.: One-Time Programs. In: Wagner, D. (ed.) CRYPTO 2008. LNCS, vol. 5157, pp. 39–56. Springer, Heidelberg (2008)
20. Goldwasser, S., Rothblum, G.N.: On best-possible obfuscation. In: Vadhan, S.P. (ed.) TCC 2007. LNCS, vol. 4392, pp. 194–213. Springer, Heidelberg (2007)
21. Goyal, V., Ishai, Y., Sahai, A., Venkatesan, R., Wadia, A.: Founding Cryptography on Tamper-Proof Hardware Tokens. In: Micciancio, D. (ed.) TCC 2010. LNCS, vol. 5978, pp. 308–326. Springer, Heidelberg (2010)
22. Hada, S.: Secure obfuscation for encrypted signatures. In: Gilbert, H. (ed.) EUROCRYPT 2010. LNCS, vol. 6110, pp. 92–112. Springer, Heidelberg (2010)

23. Hofheinz, D., Malone-Lee, J., Stam, M.: Obfuscation for cryptographic purposes. Journal of Cryptology 23(1), 121–168 (2010)
24. Hohenberger, S., Rothblum, G.N., Shelat, A., Vaikuntanathan, V.: Securely Obfuscating Re-encryption. In: Vadhan, S.P. (ed.) TCC 2007. LNCS, vol. 4392, pp. 233–252. Springer, Heidelberg (2007)
25. Katz, J.: Universally composable multi-party computation using tamper-proof hardware. In: Naor, M. (ed.) EUROCRYPT 2007. LNCS, vol. 4515, pp. 115–128. Springer, Heidelberg (2007)
26. Kilian, J.: A note on efficient zero-knowledge proofs and arguments. In: Proceedings of 24th STOC, pp. 723–732. ACM, New York (1992)
27. Lynn, B., Prabhakaran, M., Sahai, A.: Positive results and techniques for obfuscation. In: Cachin, C., Camenisch, J.L. (eds.) EUROCRYPT 2004. LNCS, vol. 3027, pp. 20–39. Springer, Heidelberg (2004)
28. Merkle, R.C.: A certified digital signature. In: Brassard, G. (ed.) CRYPTO 1989. LNCS, vol. 435, pp. 218–238. Springer, Heidelberg (1990)
29. Moran, T., Segev, G.: David and Goliath Commitments: UC Computation for Asymmetric Parties Using Tamper-Proof Hardware. In: Smart, N.P. (ed.) EUROCRYPT 2008. LNCS, vol. 4965, pp. 527–544. Springer, Heidelberg (2008)
30. Quisquater, J.-J.: Secret Distribution of Keys for Public Key Systems. In: Pomerance, C. (ed.) CRYPTO 1987. LNCS, vol. 293, pp. 203–208. Springer, Heidelberg (1988)
31. Smid, M.E.: Integrating the data encryption standard into computer networks. IEEE Tr. Commun. 29(6), 762–772 (1981)
32. Wee, H.: On obfuscating point functions. In: Proceedings of the 37th ACM Symposium on Theory of Computing, pp. 523–532 (2005)

DepSim: A Dependency-Based Malware Similarity Comparison System[*]

Yang Yi[1,2], Ying Lingyun[1,3], Wang Rui[2], Su Purui[1], and Feng Dengguo[1,2]

[1] State Key Laboratory of Information Security, Institute of Software, Chinese Academy of Sciences, Beijing 100190, China
[2] State Key Laboratory of Information Security, Graduate University of Chinese Academy of Sciences, Beijing 100049, China
[3] National Engineering Research Center for Information Security, Beijing 100190, China
{yangyi,yly,wangrui,supurui,feng}@is.iscas.ac.cn

Abstract. It is important for malware analysis that comparing unknown files to previously-known malicious samples to quickly characterize the type of behavior and generate signatures. Malware writers often use obfuscation, such as packing, junk-insertion and other means of techniques to thwart traditional similarity comparison methods. In this paper, we introduce DepSim, a novel technique for finding dependency similarities between malicious binary programs. DepSim constructs dependency graphs of control flow and data flow of the program by taint analysis, and then conducts similarity analysis using a new graph isomorphism technique. In order to promote the accuracy and anti-interference capability, we reduce redundant loops and remove junk actions at the dependency graph pre-processing phase, which can also greatly improve the performance of our comparison algorithm. We implemented a prototype of DepSim and evaluated it to malware in the wild. Our prototype system successfully identified some semantic similarities between malware and revealed their inner similarity in program logic and behavior. The results demonstrate that our technique is accurate.

Keywords: Malware Analysis; Similarity Analysis; Dynamic Taint Analysis.

1 Introduction

Malware, software with malicious intent, such as viruses, worms, Trojans, and backdoors has emerged as a widely-spread thread to system security. According to a Microsoft report [3], in the first half of 2009, as many as 39,328,515 computers around the world have been infected by malware. It is difficult to detect and stop malware spreading reliably because new and polymorphic malware programs appear rapidly. For example, AgoBot [10] has more than 580 variants since it first come into view in 2002.

---

[*] Supported by the National Natural Science Foundation of China under Grant No. 60703076, 61073179; the National High-Tech Research and Development Plan of China under Grant No. 2007AA01Z451, 2009AA01Z435.

X. Lai, M. Yung, and D. Lin (Eds.): Inscrypt 2010, LNCS 6584, pp. 503–522, 2011.

One of the main factors driving this explosion of variety is that malware authors usually reuse their old programs because of the cost of developing a new malware [18]. To address this dilemma and fast analyze malicious code, researchers would like to re-use stale behavior profile information from a prior malware sample by using similarity comparison to identify and analyze the malicious code variants. The problem of finding similarities in programs has been a central problem in malware analysis.

Previous efforts to automatically analyze and compare malware focused primarily on two types of comparisons, comparison of program structure and comparison of program behavior. Several program structure comparison methods have been proposed [1] [2] [7] [9] [13] [20]. For all these structural comparison approaches, successfully disassembling of malware is a pre-condition; malware writers usually use obfuscations to hinder traditional malware similarity comparison system, such as packing, encryption and instruction permutation, as these transformations can obviously change the content-based signatures of code. Without the precondition of successfully disassembling of malware, it is hard to deal with obfuscated malware with structural comparison. Previous behavioral comparison methods [8] [10] [11] [12] [15] mainly depend on behavior sequences, which could be changed easily by function-reordering, junk-insertion and other means of techniques. In addition, both two types of comparison methods use text distance or weighted text distance to measure the difference. These ways ignore the logical relations among system calls and focused primarily on sequence-based signatures that could be obfuscated easily and significantly. In summary, malware writers use various obfuscation techniques to transform their malware to make it hard to analyze. The means for traditional analysis are not sufficient to alleviate a threat posed by so many obfuscated malware variants.

To address the limitations of existing binary similarity comparison tools, we proposed and evaluated a novel technique, called DepSim, to find behavioral similarity. Unlike existing systems [11] [12], DepSim's similarity comparison algorithm does not operate directly on system call sequences. We have implemented a proof-of-concept system of DepSim based on Wookon [29], our dynamic analysis system that monitors the execution of a malware in a controlled environment. DepSim first uses taint analysis and backtracking techniques to construct extended control dependency graphs and extended data dependency graphs. Then, at dependency graphs preprocessing phrase, we remove junk calls, reduce loops and take other normalization measures to convert them to a normalized form. At last, a customized graph isomorphism algorithm is used to find the best matches between dependency graphs.

In order to evaluate our system, we have implemented our prototype system and conducted experiments on collected wild malware. The experimental results demonstrate that our malware analysis techniques and semantic similarity comparison algorithms are more accurate than previous techniques used in binary similarity analysis, especially in dealing with obfuscated malware. Summarizing, this paper makes the following contributions:

- We present a novel, precise approach to describe malware behaviors and relations between them by extending CDG (Control Dependency Graph) and DDG (Data Dependency Graph) with Virtual Vertex and behavior profile.
- We propose a new semantic similarity comparison algorithm. The isomorphism algorithm depends on extended dependency graphs and is more accurate than previous techniques.

● We evaluate our system on amount of real-world malware and their variants. Our experimental results demonstrate that our technique has obvious advantages in accuracy comparing to previous methods of similarity comparison.

This paper is organized as follows: Section 2 describes the problem of semantic similarity analysis and the architecture of our system. We present our dynamic taint analysis method and dependency graph construction method in Section 3, pre-processing algorithm and dependency graph isomorphism in Section 4. Our detailed evaluation is shown in Section 5. We present performance and overhead in Section 6, related work in Section 7. Limitations and future directions are discussed in Section 8.

2 Overview of Our Approach

There are two types of similarity between two malware, syntactic and semantic. Syntactic similarity refers to same instructions, same basic blocks and same system calls, whereas semantic similarity refers to similarity between system call sequences and their relations. The target of our work is to find the semantic matching between functions from the two binary files.

At most time, it is possible that a syntactic difference is not semantic. Syntactic can be easily changed without changing the program behavior and semantic while losing textual, lexical and structural similarities comparing to the original. We show original

```
1:  char fbuff[512];                                       1:  char fbuff[128];
2:  ...                                                    2:  ...
3:  fh = InternetOpenUrl(internetHandle, dl.url, NULL,     3:  f = CreateFile(dl.dest, GENERIC_WRITE, 0, NULL, CREATE_ALWAYS, 0, 0);
    0, 0, 0);                                              4:  hFileMapping=CreateFileMapping(f,NULL,PAGE_READWRITE,0,0,NULL);
4:  if (fh != NULL){                                       5:  pCurrentPointer=MapViewOfFile(hFileMapping,FILE_MAP_WRITE,0,0,0);
5:     f = CreateFile(dl.dest, GENERIC_WRITE, 0, NULL,     6:  temp=CreateFile("C:\\test.txt",GENERIC_READ,0,
       CREATE_ALWAYS, 0, 0);                                              OPEN_EXISTING,FILE_ATTRIBUTE_NORMAL,0);
6:     if (f < (HANDLE)1){                                 7:  if (f < (HANDLE)1){
7:        return 0;                                        8:     return 0;
8:     }                                                   9:  }else{
9:     total = 1;                                          10: fh = InternetOpenUrl(internetHandle, dl.url, NULL, 0, 0, 0);
10:    start = GetTickCount();                             11: if (fh == NULL){
11:    do{                                                 12:    return 0;
12:       memset(fbuff, 0, sizeof(fbuff));                 13: }
13:       InternetReadFile(fh, fbuff, sizeof(fbuff), &r);  14: total = 1;
14:       WriteFile(f, fbuff, r, &d, NULL);                15: start = GetTickCount();
15:       total = total + r;                               16: do{
16:       if (dl.update != 1)                              17:    ReadFile(temp,fbuff,sizeof(fbuff),&r);
17:          sprintf(threadDescriptions[dl.threadnum],     18:    memset(fbuff, 0, sizeof(fbuff));
           "file download (%s - %dkb transferred)", dl.url, total / 1024);  19:    InternetReadFile(fh, fbuff, sizeof(fbuff), &r);
18:       else                                             20:    memcpy(pCurrentPointer,fbuff,r);
19:          sprintf(threadDescriptions[dl.threadnum],     21:    pCurrentPointer=(void*)((DWORD)pCurrentPointer+r);
           "update (%s - %dkb transferred)", dl.url, total / 1024);  22:    total = total + r;
20:    } while (r > 0);                                    23     CreateFile("d:\\command.txt",GENERIC_READ,0,
21:    speed = total / (((GetTickCount() - start) / 1000) + 1);              OPEN_EXISTING,FILE_ATTRIBUTE_NORMAL,0);
22:    CloseHandle(f);                                     24:    if (dl.update == 1)
23:}                                                       25:       sprintf(threadDescriptions[dl.threadnum],
                                                             "update (%s - %dkb transferred)", dl.url, total / 1024);
                                                          26:    else
                                                          27:       sprintf(threadDescriptions[dl.threadnum],
                                                             "file download (%s - %dkb transferred)", dl.url, total / 1024);
                                                          28:    }while(r>0);
                                                          29:    speed = total / (((GetTickCount() - start) / 1000) + 1);
                                                          30:    CloseHandle(f);
                                                          31:}while (r > 0);
```

(a) Original code segment   (b) Obfuscated code segment

Fig. 1. Original and obfuscated code segment of SDBot

malware source code and obfuscated code of a variant of SDBot in Fig. 1. The code fragment in Fig. 1 prepares to download a file from a defined IP address or website into local Windows file system. After applying junk-insertion and instruction-reordering to codes in Fig. 1.(a), malware writer could obtain the code in Fig. 1.(b).

The result of the obfuscation is that syntactic signatures such as basic blocks and behavior sequences changed greatly. Under such circumstances, previous efforts to compare their similarity will no longer get the right match and thus the malware writers make the analysis more complex and time-consuming.

We noticed that while the syntactic signatures of malware changing rapidly, the dependency, namely relationship between behaviors, remains stable. And the set of dependency graphs of the program is an "interpretation" for the semantics, making it an attractive feature for finding semantic similarities. To achieve this target, we proposed DepSim to find the semantic similarities between two malware based on dependency graphs.

Fig. 2 shows the overall system architecture. As is shown in Fig. 2, DepSim consists of four components. The binary files are first executed in a front-end system emulator with taint analysis engine, which outputs an execution trace and taint propagation traces. These data are then used to dependence analysis, where the output is extended dependency graphs. Next, the extended dependency graphs are normalized by our pre-processing algorithm. At the same time, extensive profile data is collected for each extended dependency graph. In the last step, extended graphs and behavior profiles of two binary files are passed to our graph isomorphism engine to find semantic matches between them.

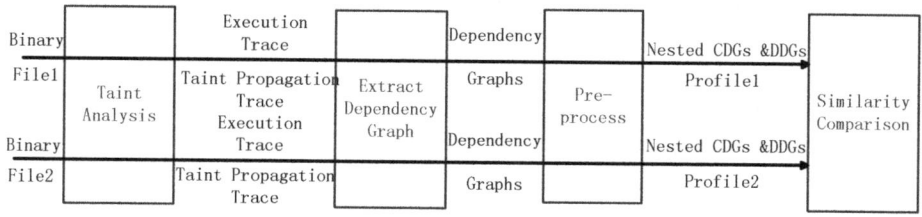

Fig. 2. System overview

The output of our similarity comparison system is the similarity degree of samples. We represent similarity degree in terms of the percentage of similar behaviors and dependency relations compared to average behaviors and relations. We briefly introduce these four components as below:

- Dynamic Taint Analysis
  In order to construct dependency graphs, we developed DepSim, based on QEMU [6], a whole-system emulator for PCs and the Intel x86 architecture, to actually execute samples in a controlled environment and observe their persistent actions to specify the relationship between behaviors. We monitor the behavior of the sample and analyze its information accessing and processing behavior with respect to the taint data with our pre-defined taint analysis rules.

- Constructing Dependency Graphs
  We build extended control dependency graph (ECDG) and extended data dependency graph (EDDG) to represent the functionality of malware. We do this during the dynamic taint analysis phrase. We follow the taint propagation procedure to

infer relations between system calls and instructions. Depend on the information, we backtrack through taint propagation path and construct dependency graphs.

- Pre-processing of Dependency Graphs
  Since malware are usually obfuscated, changes of instructions and behaviors may not correspond to changes in functionality. We proposed a pre-processing algorithm targeting the most common obfuscations in malware-generation libraries found in wild [27] to normalize the dependency graphs before similarity comparison. In the procedure we delete junk calls, reduce loops, replace special instructions and system calls, and make up behavior profile for each dependency graph.

- Comparing ECDGs and EDDGs
  The last step of DepSim is to compare dependency graphs to find semantic matches between vertices and edges. This can be conceptualized as the maximum common subgraph isomorphism problem. Since that maximum common subgraph isomorphism is NP-complete, and the most important factor of the comparison efficiency is the sequence in which graphs and vertices are examined for possible matches, we introduce a new graph isomorphism algorithm based on ECDG and EDDG. In order to firstly try graphs which have higher matching probability, we take measures to quickly tell the algorithm how similar two graphs are.

3 Dynamic Taint Analysis and Dependency Graph Construction

To address the limitations of existing automated classification and analysis tools, we propose a new description technique that describes malware behavior in terms of extended dependency graphs. The extended dependency graphs are constructed according to the following two phrases.

3.1 Process-Aware Taint Analysis

Firstly, we perform process-based, fine-grained taint tracking to monitor how tainted data propagates throughout the application. All critical functions' return value and out-parameters are marked as taint sources. Critical functions stand for functions which can change the status of system, including file operation functions, registry operation functions and network operation functions. We use Shadow Memory to store the taint status of each byte of the process virtual memory, emulated CPU registers and EFLAGS register. We denote taint data set as T_{taint}, each taint byte in T_{taint} is associated with a data structure recording the taint source and other status information. Process virtual memory and emulated CPU registers can be treated similarly in the spirit of previous system [5], whereas the EFLAGS register is special because it can affect the control flow and be changed by side-efforts of instructions.

After marking taint source, we monitor each CPU instruction and system call in order to determine how tainted data propagates. To this end, we intercept system calls and force process in analysis to execute in single step mode by adding hidden single-step flag to the QEMU code translation engine. System calls are intercepted by comparing EIP of the emulated CPU with system call entries recorded in a pre-defined address table. We read parameters from stack and investigate how taint information propagates through system calls. We also add a disassemble engine [18] to parse each instruction during execution. Since Intel x86 platform has a very complicated instruction set, under some circumstances, it is hard to perform taint propagating at instruction level, for example, environment switching from user mode to kernel mode. This situation happens frequently, especially in system calls. To make our analysis more efficient and accurate, as is shown in Table 1, we consider system calls as a special type of instructions and divide Intel x86 instruction sets into five groups. Taint analyzing rules are defined to each group of instructions.

Table 1. Taint Analyzing Rules

Instruction Type	Taint Analyzing Rule	Example
Data Transfer	$OP_1 \in Taint \Rightarrow OP_2 \in Taint$	mov op1, op2
Calculation	$(OP_1 \in Taint) \vee (OP_2 \in Taint)$ $\Rightarrow (OP_1, EFLAGS) \in Taint$	add/and op1, op2
Comparison	$(OP_1 \in Taint) \vee (OP_2 \in Taint) \Rightarrow EFLAGS \in Taint$	cmp op1, op2
Control Flow	$EFLAGS \in Taint \Rightarrow ControlDependency$	jnz addr
System Call	$Param_{in} \in Taint \Rightarrow (Result, Param_{out}) \in Taint$	$Result$=CreateFile($Param_{in}$,...)

There are two types of relations which we are interested in, control dependence and data dependence. In taint analysis, control dependence presents as the tainted EFLAGS register affecting the control flow direction. In this paper, we focus on the condition that system call result affects the control flow. That is, we have to identify the control flow decisions that involve data obtained via critical functions. To do this, we mark critical functions' return value, out-parameters and EFLAGS register as tainted to trace their propagation path. Data dependence can be drawn when the tainted data propagates between functions.

Intuitively, there are two situations we should stop taint analysis. One is taint bleaching, that is, taint data is overwritten by non-taint data. The other is the process exiting. In particular, there are some malware that never stop running unless they receive commands to destroy themselves, such as Trojans and botnets. To address this problem, we defined Time Out, denoted as T_{out}. Whenever the running time of process is beyond T_{out}, we will stop taint analysis.

3.2   Constructing Dependency Graphs

Based on the taint propagation information collected from dynamic taint analysis at instruction level, we can infer dependences between system calls and generate extended control dependency graphs and extended data dependency graphs. Extended dependency graphs are represented as follows:

Extended Control Dependency Graph (ECDG):

$$G_{cd} = \{ V_{cd}, E_{cd}, VV_{cd}, Entry_{cd}, Type_{cd}, Count_{Type} \}$$

In the ECDG, V_{cd} is the set of normal vertices; E_{cd} stands for control dependency edges; VV_{cd} is the set of virtual vertices; $Entry_{cd}$ is the entry point of the graph; $Type_{cd}$ stands for the system call types in the dependency graph; $Count_{Type}$ stands for the quantity of each type of system call.

Extended Data Dependency Graph (EDDG):

$$G_{dd} = \{ V_{dd}, E_{dd}, Entry_{dd}, Type_{dd}, Count_{Type} \}$$

In the Extended DDG, V_{dd} is the set of normal vertices; E_{dd} is the set of data dependency edges; $Entry_{dd}$ is the entry point; $Type_{dd}$ stands for the system call types in the dependency graph; $Count_{Type}$ is the quantity of each type of system call. We define system call type set as $Type \in \{Network, File, Registry, Process\}$.

We generate extended dependency graphs while the taint analysis is processing. First, we construct control dependency graph set and denote it as T_c. Once a critical system call is invoked, we mark the result as taint source and generate the first dependency graph $G_1 \in T_c$ with current function as $Entry_{cd} \in G_1$. During the program's run-time, we compute the taint propagating trace to generate new vertices and edges by means of resolving instructions and intercepted system calls. Since it is difficult to recognize taint control range, we solve this problem by computing the dominators with the algorithm mentioned in [14]. For this, when the tainted EFLAGS register affects a control flow instruction, we have to follow both two candidate flows to disassemble instructions that are going to be executed. Subsequent system calls invoked within the control range will be added as new vertices into current graph and we'll link a directed edge from the taint source to the newly added vertex by backtracking through the taint propagation trace.

We construct data dependency graph set T_d at the same time as T_c. Similar to control dependency graph, when the first critical system call is invoked, a vertex will be insert into the graph as entry and taint source is marked. Since data dependency can be identified even without computing dominators and the access of taint data intuitively reflects the data dependence between behaviors, it is easier to construct data dependency graph than to construct control dependency graph. We consider system calls as a special type of instruction and define taint propagation rules for instructions within them as a whole. For example, *ReadFile* has two in-parameters, one return value and three out-parameters. If any of the two in-parameters has been tainted, we will mark the return value and out-parameter as tainted and insert a new vertex into dependency graph. We backtrack following the taint propagation trace and draw a directed edge from the entity corresponding to taint source to the entity corresponding to the taint propagated system call. Both the two construction procedures continue until the end of taint analysis.

At last, we insert virtual vertices into control dependency graph. Virtual vertices stand for system calls that can be reordered to evolve the control dependency range of functions without changing the functionality. For example, in Fig. 1.(a) *CreateFile* and subsequent system calls depend on *InternetOpenUrl*. After swapping *CreateFile* and *InternetOpenUrl* in Fig. 1.(b), the *InternetOpenUrl* and following system calls depend on *CreateFile*. This type of obfuscation can change our control dependency graph without affecting the functionality of the code fragment. We define a virtual vertex to replace this type of swappable system calls. If two system calls *A* and *B* has no data dependence between them and *A* is in the control range of *B*, we define *A* and *B* as swappable system calls. Once we add a new virtual vertex, we will link the original vertices corresponding to swappable system calls to the virtual vertex and move all the edges from the original vertices to the virtual vertex.

4   Comparing ECDGs and EDDGs

4.1   Pre-processing of Dependency Graphs

The critical part of our system is the comparison algorithm. It contains two procedures, pre-processing procedure and extended graph comparison. The pre-processing procedure targets on junk calls insertion, equal behaviors replacement and changing operation size in loop, it will undo the obfuscations and reduce the complexity of our CDGs and DDGs. It consists of four steps.

First, we remove junk system calls. A system call in a program is a junk call if its removal from the program does not change the behavior of the program. This condition can be expressed, equivalently, in terms of program behaviors that never change the system state. In our taint analysis, if a system call generates a new taint source but it never propagates, or the propagation of the taint source never leads to change of system status, the system call will be consider as a junk call and removed from the graph. To this end, we defined the set of functions which will change system status as

$$Func_{change} = \{ \, WriteFile, CopyFile, DeleteFile, RegSetValueEx, ... \, \}$$

If a system call sequence in propagation path L obeys $Func_i \notin Func_{change}$ and

$Func_i \in L$. We consider it as junk call sequence and remove the corresponding edges and vertices from CDGs and DDGs.

Secondly, we identify and replace some special instructions and system calls, which could be replaced by equivalent system call or sequences without changing the functionality. This type of code is widely used in malware obfuscation such as code replacement. To get rid of the interference of these codes, we have to convert the replaceable instructions and system calls to uniform expressions. To this end, we divide functional equivalent instructions and system call sequences into several groups and choose one from each group as the delegate. Then we construct a DFA

(Deterministic Finite Automaton) for each equal sequence. If a taint propagation path in graph can lead one of the DFAs to its final stage, the sequence should be replaced with the delegate of matched group. For example, code in Fig. 1 replaced traditional file reading operation by mapping file into memory. After matching *CreateFile*, *CreateFileMapping* and *MapViewOfFile* with DFA, we replace the sequence of *CreateFile*, *CreateFileMapping*, *MapViewOfFile* with *CreateFile*, the subsequent *memcpy* is replaced by *ReadFile*.

Thirdly, we reduce loops, because the redundant data brought by loops, such as repeated system calls may widen the difference of behavior profile to thwart our analysis. We identify loops by tracking instruction trace in dynamic taint analysis. If an instruction switches control flow to an already existed instruction, we consider it as a loop. We attach description information of taint data to each vertex in graph as $\{StartAddress, TaintLength\}$. *StartAddress* stands for the virtual address of taint data and *TaintLength* for its length in byte. Once a loop is identified, we compare the instructions and calls within the loop range by their virtual address. If the instructions and system calls in loop which have the same virtual address are equal, we will merge taint operation in loop as a whole. In formal, we compute taint trace L, $Loop \subset L$, $N_{prior} \in L$ and $N_{current} \in L$. If

$$N_{current}.StartAddress = N_{prior}.StartAddress + N_{prior}.Length$$

We will reduce the loops as one and remove the repeat instructions as

$$Taint_{loop}.StartAddress = N_{head}.StartAddress$$

$$Taint_{loop}.Length = \sum_{i=1}^{n} N_i.Length$$

Fourthly, we identify dispatch functions. Malware, such as Trojans and botnets, always have a function to parse control protocol and do corresponding actions. We consider it more important than other functions because it decides the core functionality of malware. Since text-based protocols such as IRC, are widely used in botnets [28], we identify dispatch functions by analyzing the taint propagation path with sequences of string operations. If there are five or more string operation functions in the path, we consider it as a dispatch function. The threshold here is defined manually; we can also use other techniques to refine it, for example, using the method mentioned in paper [26].

Finally, to improve efficiency of the isomorphism algorithm, extensive profile data is collected. We capture the operations of a program at a higher level of abstraction and characterize dependency graphs' behavior in form of system call types and quantities. We first divide system call set into four types which denote as $FunctionType = \{FILE, NETWORK, REGISTRY, PROCESS\}$. Then, we enumerate vertices in graph to record its type in extended $Type$ record, and the quantity in the $Count_{Type}$ counter.

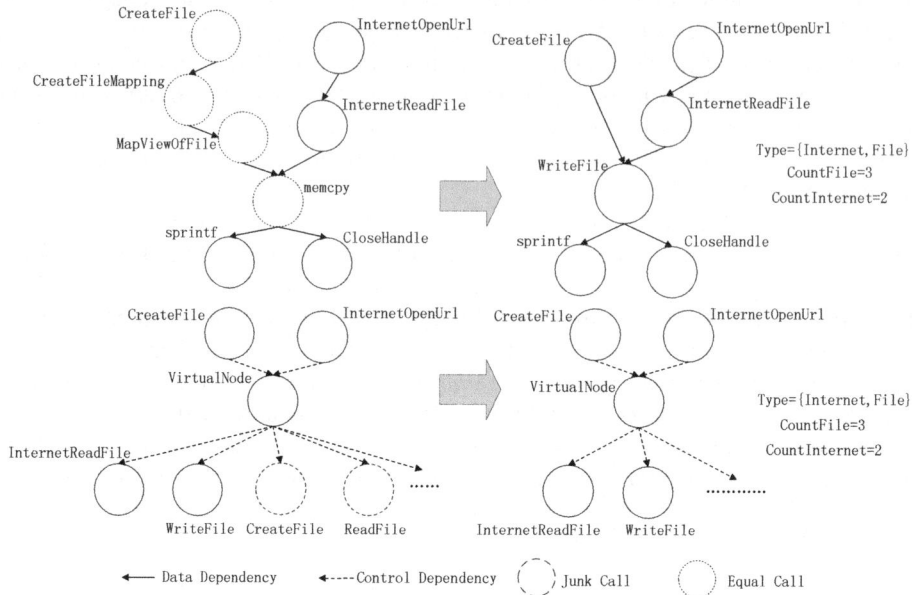

Fig. 3. Pre-processing procedure

4.2 Dependency Graph Comparison

Similarity measurement between dependency graphs can be achieved by identifying the maximum common subgraph. We discuss the algorithmic details of the key steps in our comparison algorithm in the following paragraphs.

We compare ECDGs before EDDGs. The comparison starts from the entry points of the two graphs. The factor that our dependency graphs are made from a certain taint source determines two similar graphs should have equal entry points. Therefore, the precondition of comparing adjacent vertices connected to entry points is whether the entry vertices of the candidate graphs are the same, otherwise, we have to select another ECDG to compare. Sometimes, we may encounter the situation that there are multi-taint sources. If so, we try to compare each pair of entry points made by the taint sources, to make sure that the entry points could be matched. After comparing entry points, we follow the edges connected to current vertex to compare related vertices in recursive order. Vertices stand for system calls, which may have a variety of parameters. At most time, it is time-consuming to compare all the parameters and usually we are interested in only a small part of them. So, we defined rules for each system call to compare the fields we are interested in. For example, to compare *CreateFile*, we have to compare its *FileName* and *OpenType*, other fields such as *dwShareMode* or *dwFlagsAndAttributes* will be ignored unless they contain taint data. Edges stand for control dependency relations between behaviors. For edge E_1 directs

Algorithm 1: Control Dependency Graph Comparison Algorithm

```
------------------------------------------------------------------------------------
if( IsEqualVertices( G_{c1}.Entry , G_{c2}.Entry )){    //Compare control dependency graph
    return    False;
}else{
    VN_1 = TopologicalGetAllVirtualVertices( G_{c1} );
    VN_2 = TopologicalGetAllVirtualVertices( G_{c2} );
    foreach( N ∈ VV_1 && V ∉ MachedVertices ){   //Compare Virtual Vertices
        foreach( N' ∈ VV_1 && N' ∉ MachedVertices ){
            CompareVertices( N, N' );
            CompareInEdges( N, N' );
            CompareInEdgeNodes( N, N' );
        }
        MarkMaxSimVerticesAsMatched( N, N );
        MarkSimEdges( N , N' );
    }
    while( HaveUnMatchedVertices(G_{c1}, G_{c2}) ){
        N_1=SelectSourceVertexFromMatchedVertices( G_{c1} ); //Optimized select function
        N_1'=SelectDestVertexFromMatchedVertices( G_{c2} );
        If( IsEqualVertices( N_1 , N_1' ) == true ){
            MarkVerticesAsMatched( N_1, N_1' );
            CompareEdgesConnectedToCurrentVertex( N_1, N_1' );    //Compare edges
            CompareVerticesConnectToCurrentVertex( N_1, N_1' );//Compare nodes
        }
    }
}
```

Fig. 4. Control dependency graph comparison algorithm

Algorithm 2: Data Dependency Graph Comparison Algorithm

```
------------------------------------------------------------------------------------
if( IsEqualVertices( G_{d1}.Entry , G_{c2}.Entry )){              //Compare data dependency graph
    return    False;
}else{
    while( HaveUnMatchedVertices(G_{d1}, G_{d2}) ){
        N_1=SelectSourceVertexFromMatchedVertices( G_{d1} ); //Optimized select function
        N_1'=SelectDestVertexFromMatchedVertices( G_{d2} );
        If( IsEqualVertices( N_1 , N_1' ) == true ){
            MarkVerticesAsMatched( N_1 , N_1' );
            CompareEdgesConnectedToCurrentVertex( N, N' ); //Compare edges
            CompareVerticesConnectToCurrentVertex( N, N' );  //Compare nodes
        }
    }
}
```

Fig. 5. Data dependency graph comparison algorithm

from V_2 to V_1, and E_2 directs from V_2' to V_1', if V_1 matches V_1' and V_2 matches V_2', E_1 and E_2 will be considered as matched and denoted as $E_1 \equiv E_2$. What makes the comparison of ECDGs special is that they contain virtual vertices, which have to be considered and compared as data sets. When the comparison procedure reaches virtual vertices, we first compare their inner vertices because they stand for swappable system calls without considering their order. For example, virtual vertex V_1 has *Create-File* and *RegCreateKey* while V_2 has *RegCreateKey* and *CreateFile*. We will consider V_1 and V_2 as matched. Otherwise, we will record the matched function count and unmatched function count. Then, we compare adjacent vertices and edges connected to current matched virtual vertices. The adjacent vertices and connected edges are compared by using the same method as comparing normal vertices and edges. We mark each compared vertex and edge as visited, and the recursive algorithm will continue until all vertices and edges are visited. At last, we record the equal vertex count and equal edge count with corresponding counters.

After comparing ECDGs, we will compare EDDGs. We compare EDDGs using comparison method similar to that was mentioned above. Since there are no virtual vertices, it is easier to compare EDDGs than to compare ECDGs. We compare EDDGs in a recursive manner from entry point. We track the edges connected to current compared vertex to follow the data dependency relations between system calls. Vertices are compared by their behavior information, whereas edges are compared by their connected vertices and direction. Once each round of comparison finished, we mark each vertex and edge as visited. The stop condition of our algorithm is one of the two graphs has no unvisited vertices or edges. Finally, when the whole comparison is done, we increase the counter of equal vertices and equal edges.

The target of our comparison method is to find semantic behavior differences between two malware binary files. We choose a sample as the baseline and compare left sample with it. After comparing ECDGs and EDDGs, we will get matched vertex count and matched edge count. First we compute the average vertex count and edge count of the two matched graphs. Then, we measure the similarity as the ratio of matched vertex count and edge count comparing to the average count computed before.

4.3 Customized to Promote Efficiency

Since graph isomorphism is a NP-complete problem, we need to propose an efficient and practical optimal algorithm when dealing with real problems. As the isomorphism algorithm needs to enumerate all possible matches, its efficiency highly depends on the sequence in which graphs are compared with each other. Our target can be achieved by comparing high matching probability graphs with high priority. It is achieved by taking following measures.

First, we try to compare dispatch functions. Identifying dispatch function is one of the quick methods to get a clue of our comparison. We compare dispatch functions first from their entry points. The entry point is compared only by its type, that is, such as a network function used to receive data from a remote server, we will not consider its remote address and port. The reason is that the semantic of received data is determined by subsequent functions that operate on the data rather than the function receives the data. We assume that the control protocol is text-based and it is accessed by string operation functions since this type of Trojans and botnets are widespread. The string operation functions are compared with function name, destination string and return value. That is, for two functions, if their destination strings and return value are equal, we will mark them as matched.

Secondly, we use behavior profile of graphs to promote the efficiency of our algorithm. Profile consists of system call types and quantity of each type in the graph. By quickly comparing the profiles to tell whether two graphs present the same action, we arrange the comparison order of graphs by their function type and count, so we can promote the efficiency. There are two factors to determine the priority of comparison. One is the difference of function type, while the other is the difference of function count. The priority of graphs to be compared is in descending order and is decided first by function type difference from large to small. That is, the priority of function type is higher than that of function count. Only if two graphs have the same function type, we will arrange their comparison order by their function count difference in the order large-to-small.

Finally, we use the known knowledge of the previously compared graphs to guide our subsequent comparison. We consider graphs that have corresponding vertices to already matched graphs as higher priority to compare. Corresponding vertices is judged by their addresses. We compare vertices that have the same function address corresponding to previously matched graphs before other vertices. In our algorithm, we use ECDG comparison results as clue to guide EDDG comparison. For example, if G_1 and G_2 are matched graphs, and functions $F_1 \in G_1$, $F_2 \in G_2$, and $F_1 \equiv F_2$. When selecting candidate graphs, we consider graphs G' and G'' which have F_1' and F_2' correspondingly, as high priority to be compared.

5 Evaluation

To verify the effectiveness of our approach, we implemented a system with the above mentioned components and techniques, and used our system to analyze malware samples in the wild. Our collection of malware samples used for comparison was obtained from VXHeavens [16]. We describe the details on the experimental evaluation of our prototype system in this section. Our evaluation consisted of three parts. First, we took Bagle worm variants as samples to monitor their behaviors and compare their similarity. Secondly, we chose backdoor NetSky to discover the similarities between them. At last, we measure DepSim's performance by monitoring its analyzing time and comparing it with other similarity comparison methods. In all our experiments, we ran the DepSim prototype system on a Linux machine with a 3.2 GHz dual-core Pentium 4 CPU, 160 GB hard disk and 2 GB RAM. We install Windows XP SP2 Professional as guest operation system on top of DepSim.

Bagle and NetSky are real world samples. As mentioned before, it is hard to get source code of malware, so they are analyzed without any addition information except for binary files and we manually analyze these samples to prove the correctness of analysis results of DepSim. In order to compare DepSim with other methods in terms of accuracy and efficiency, we also implemented the structure-based similarity comparison and behavior-based similarity comparison methods. The details of our experiments are described below.

5.1 Bagle

Bagle is a mass-mailing and self-encrypting computer worm written in pure assembly and infects all versions of Microsoft Windows. It contains a homemade SMTP engine to mass-mail itself as an attachment to mail addresses gathered from the victim computer. Since the first sample of Bagle was captured in 2004, in less than a year, there are over 80 variants had appeared in the wild. We use Bagle as first sample in our experiment to test our algorithm in real world condition.

Table 2. Analysis result of Bagle

Name	Packer	Record Size	CDG count	DDG count	Junk Call Count	Running Time
Bagle.a*	None	87MB	28	29	0	7m31s
Bagle.b	UPX	99MB	51	29	25	6m20s
Bagle.e*	PeX	130MB	16	2	8	7m11s
Bagle.f	PeX	160MB	16	2	8	6m22s
Bagle.g	PeX	137MB	13	2	2	5m49s

We show experiment details of Bagle in Table 2. In this table, all the samples marked with * are selected as baseline, and other samples are compared with it. We noticed that the samples, except for Bagle.a, are all packed and obfuscated. This factor made the traditional comparison techniques hard to analyze these samples. In our experiment, the longest analysis time of Bagle samples is 7 minutes and 31 seconds. The largest size of record file is 160 MB, it is acceptable considering nowadays hard disk volume. See the matter from our results, Bagle.a is similar to Bagle.b, whereas Bagle.e, Bagle.f and Bagle.g are grouped as a family. The similarity between these two groups is not obvious. We proved this by hand analyzing experiment records of these samples and find that Bagle.e did more operations than Bagle.a. For example, Bagle.e creates *C:\WINDOWS\system32\godo.exe* and *C:\WINDOWS\system32\ii455nj4.exe* in our system, while Bagle.a only creates *bbeagle.exe*. The results also show that the structure of Balge.e is not similar to that of

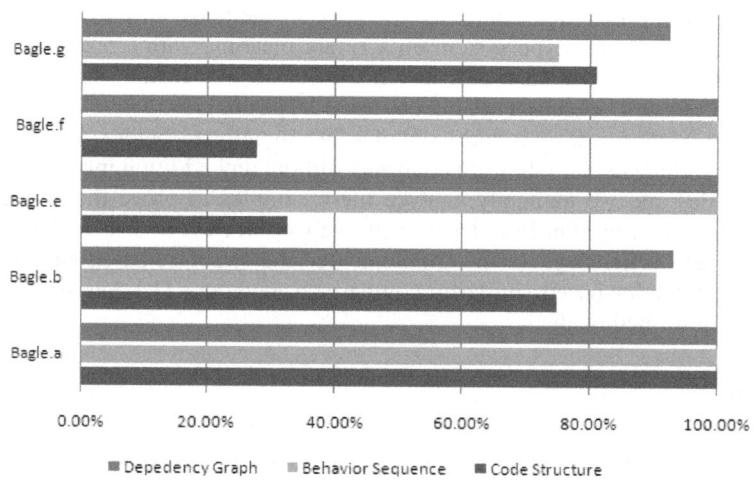

Fig. 6. Result of similarity comparison on Bagle samples

Bagle.f. We check these samples manually and find that their basic blocks and instructions are different indeed because they are changed largely at variant transformation phrase.

When analyzing Bagle samples, we find that Bagle implements some system calls by hand. It uses mapping files into memory instead of using traditional *CreateFile* approach, and writes functions by hand to replace system calls such as *strcmp, strcpy*. As showed in the experiment result, this type of confusion doesn't make big trouble to our algorithm. If malware writers rewrite most of system calls by hand, it can disturb our system call match method. And it is our future work to research the comparison method in instruction level semantics.

5.2 NetSky

NetSky is a prolific family of backdoors that can infect all versions of Windows. The first variant appeared on Monday, February 16, 2004 [25]. It can spread by email or net shares. We chose NetSky.ad as baseline because it is not packed or obfuscated. We noticed that the record size of NetSky.aa and NetSky.t is larger than other samples'. The reason is that both these two samples use loop to copy themselves to system directory, this procedure brought us much superfluous data. For example, NetSky.aa copied itself to system directory as *Jammer2nd.exe* through 973 times Read/Write operations, while NetSky.t copied itself to a file named *base64.tmp* as 4229 adjacent blocks. Since NetSky is more complex than Bagle, the analysis time is longer and record file size is much bigger than those of Bagle.

Table 3. Analysis result of NetSky

Name	Packer	Record Size	CDG count	DDG count	Junk Call Count	Running Time
NetSky.ad*	None	291MB	20	16	0	9m53s
NetSky.aa	UPX	1071MB	17	11	0	10m7s
NetSky.c	Petite	727MB	23	16	3	8m3s
NetSky.f	PE-Pack	222MB	15	16	4	7m36s
NetSky.r	Petite	253MB	17	10	0	7m52s
NetSky.t	UPX	1319MB	18	5	0	10m20s

Then we evaluated the accuracy of our system, we use each group of samples to compare with each other, and their similarity degrees are all zero. We also compare these samples with some normal applications such as *iexplore.exe, calc.exe, winhelp32.exe* and *explore.exe*. The highest level of similarity degree is 12.35%. It is because malware is usually written for certain purpose while normal programs are designed for common functionality which can be shared with each other. The results demonstrate that the general level of false positive rate of our algorithm is very low.

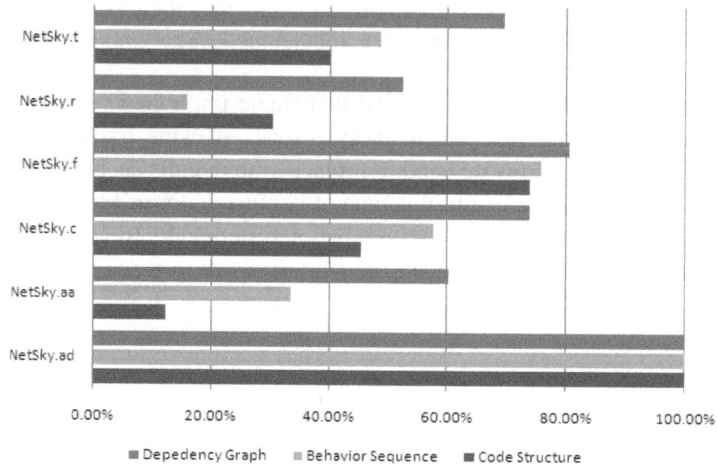

Fig. 7. Result of similarity comparison on NetSky samples

6 Performance Overhead

In our experiment, running time of Bagle samples in real world is less than 2 seconds, while average running time of all samples is more than 6 minutes and 30 seconds. It is 200 times of the running time in real computer. And compared to other analysis method, the time complexity of our algorithm is higher. The comparison method based on system call sequences and code structure cost range from 20 percent to half of running time. Because our system is mainly used to analyze malware

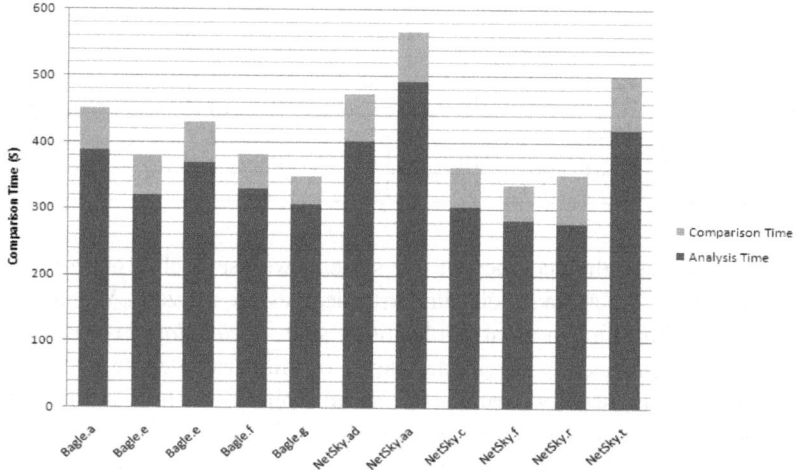

Fig. 8. Time Overhead

samples off-line, there is no restrict time limitation, and we also noticed that, as is shown in Fig. 9, most of DepSim' runtime is consumed at the phrase of executing malware in controlled environment, not in our analysis engine. It gives us a clue that we can improve DepSim by updating its hardware and optimizing efficiency of our algorithm. In addition, our technique has the highest accuracy and it is an automated analysis system. Based on the reasons mentioned above, our system and similarity finding algorithm are practical.

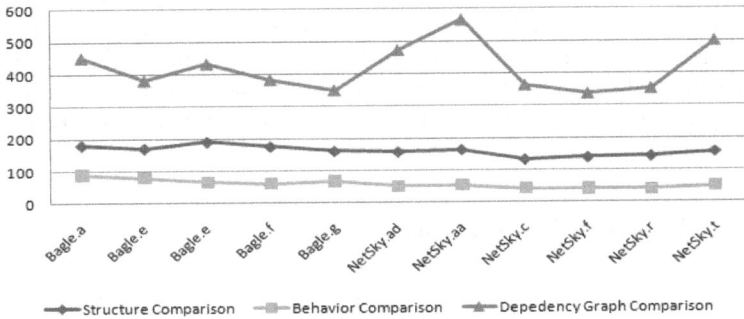

Fig. 9. Time complexity comparison

7 Related Work

There are two types of malicious code similarity comparison method, one is structural comparison, and the other is behavioral comparison. structural comparison treats malware as basic blocks, and requires an accurate disassembler to convert binary code into instruction lines to constructs control flow graphs (CFGs) for each function and call graphs (CGs) for the entire binary file. Most of this research base on basic block as the smallest comparison unit and use a customized graph isomorphism algorithm to find the best matches between functions and basic blocks, such as [7] [9] [13]. Z. Wang [2] proposed a binary file comparison method by treating the entire file as call graphs and control flow graphs to compare code and data in the binary file. D. Song proposed BinHunt [1], a binary file semantic difference finder by using symbolic execution and theorem proving to promote the accuracy of matching basic blocks. There are many disadvantages of static comparison. First, to construct control flow graph requires an accurate disassembly procedure, which was easy to be obstructed by using obfuscation techniques to hide the realistic code and behavior of the malware. Second, there are many cases that are hard to determine whether two basic blocks are similar, because of the confusion of semantic made by obfuscation. Therefore, similarity comparison of the structural approach is easy to achieve but hard to get good result and has great limitations susceptible to interference from a variety of code protection technology.

Behavioral comparison is another way to get malware similarity information. It is able to analysis polymorphic and metamorphic malware as a result of it has the advantage of not affected by obfuscated code. The comparison requires behavior information generated by analysis system. To get behavior information, many dynamic analysis tools have been proposed such as CWSandBox [22], Norman SandBox [24], ANUBIS [23] and Panorama [5]. Previous behavioral comparison techniques, such as [8] [9] [10] [11] [15], focused primarily on sequence-based system calls fragments, called behavior sequences, generated that aim to support a comparison in syntactic. Since behavior sequence is easy to transform by reordering functions, inserting junk-calls and other means of obfuscations, it is hard to accurately find matches when dealing with obfuscated malware. Bayer [12] presented a scalable cluster algorithm, they use taint analysis and symbolic execution to trace code relationship and compare the relations between system calls. Their way promoted the efficiency and accuracy by comparing behaviors at an abstract level. But, if the malware insert junk calls, that using the tainted data without changing system status in the taint propagation path, it is hard to get accurate result that without the help of normalization operations.

8 Conclusions and Limitations

In this paper, we introduced a novel similarity comparison technique, DepSim, based on control dependency and data dependency analysis. We compared DepSim with previous techniques; the result shows that DepSim is able to accurately find the semantic similarities even deal with packed or obfuscated malware.

Essentially, each vertex in our dependency graph is a user mode system call; if malware (such as rootkits) that doesn't operate in user mode, our taint analysis will not work properly. We will solve this problem by analyzing and describing behaviors at kernel level upon system objects. Since the DepSim use dynamic taint analysis, our system shares common weaknesses associated with dynamic analysis. It can only analyze one path at a time. In future works, we will try to use symbolic execution and concept proving to explore more paths.

References

1. Gao, D., Reiter, M., Song, D.: Binhunt: Automatically Finding Semantic Differences in Binary Programs. In: Proceedings of the International Conference on Information and Communications Security, pp. 238–255 (2008)
2. Wang, Z., Pierce, K., McFarling, S.: BMAT – a binary matching tool for stale profile propagation. The Journal of Instruction-Level Parallelism 2 (May 2000)
3. Microsoft Security Intelligence Report (January through June 2009),
   http://www.microsoft.com/downloads/details.aspx?FamilyID=037f3771-330e-4457-a52c-5b085dc0a4cd&displaylang=en
4. Bayer, U., Kruegel, C., Kirda, E.: TTAnalyze: A Tool for Analyzing Malware. In: Proc. of the 15th European Institute for Computer Antivirus Research Annual Conference (April 2006)
5. Yin, H., Song, D., Egele, M., Kruegel, C., Kirda, E.: Panorama: capturing system-wide information flow for malware detection and analysis. In: Proceedings of the 14th ACM Conference on Computer and Communications Security, Virginia, USA, Alexandria, October 28-31 (2007)

6. Bellard, F.: QEMU, a fast and portable dynamic translator. In: In Proc. of the USENIX Annual Technical Conference, pp. 41–46 (April 2005)
7. Dullien, T., Rolles, R.: Graph-based comparison of executable objects. In: Proceedings of SSTIC 2005 (2005)
8. Kolter, J.Z., Maloof, M.A.: Learning to detect malicious executables in the wild. In: Proceedings of the Tenth ACM SIGKDD International Conference on Knowledge Discovery and Data Mining, Seattle, WA, USA, August 22-25 (2004)
9. Bilar, D.: Statistical Structures: Tolerant Fingerprinting for Classification and Analysis given at BH 2006, Las Vegas, NV. Blackhat Briefings, USA (August 2006)
10. Bailey, M., Oberheide, J., Andersen, J., Mao, Z.M., Jahanian, F., Nazario, J.: Automated classification and analysis of internet malware. In: Kruegel, C., Lippmann, R., Clark, A. (eds.) RAID 2007. LNCS, vol. 4637, pp. 178–197. Springer, Heidelberg (2007)
11. Lee, T., Mody, J.J.: Behavioral classification (2006), http://www.microsoft.com/downloads/details.aspx?FamilyID=7b5d8cc8-b336-4091-abb5-2cc500a6c41a&displaylang=en
12. Bayer, U., Comparetti, P.M., Hlauscheck, C., Kruegel, C., Kirda, E.: Scalable, behavior-based malware clustering. In: Network and Distributed System Security Symposium, NDSS (2009)
13. Baker, B.S., Manber, U.: Deducing Similarities in Java Sources from Bytecodes, pp. 179–190 (1998)
14. Sreedhar, V.C., Gao, G.R., Lee, Y.-F.: Identifying loops using DJ graphs. ACM Transactions on Programming Languages and Systems (TOPLAS) 18(6), 649–658 (1996)
15. Christodorescu, M., Jha, S., Kruegel, C.: Mining specifications of malicious behavior. In: Proceedings of the 6th Joint Meeting of the European Software Engineering Conference and the ACM SIGSOFT Symposium on The Foundations of Software Engineering, Dubrovnik, Croatia, September 03-07 (2007)
16. VXHeavens, http://www.netlux.org
17. Lee, W., Stolfo, S.: Data mining approaches for intrusion detection. In: Proceedings of the 7th USENIX Security Symposium (1998)
18. Udis86, http://udis86.sourceforge.net/
19. Christodorescu, M., Kinder, J., Jha, S., Katzenbeisser, S., Veith, H.: Malware normalization. Technical Report 1539, University of Wisconsin, Madison, Wisconsin, USA (November 2005)
20. Walenstein, A., Venable, M., Hayes, M., Thompson, C., Lakhotia, A.: Exploiting similarity between variants to defeat malware: "Vilo" method for comparing and searching binary programs. In: Proceedings of BlackHat, DC 2007 (2007)
21. Newsome, J., Song, D.: Dynamic taint analysis for automatic detection, analysis, and signature generation of exploits on commodity software. In: Proceedings of NDSS 2005, San Diego, California, USA (February 2005)
22. Willems, C., Holz, T., Freiling, F.: CWSandbox: Towards automated dynamic binary analysis. IEEE Security and Privacy 5(2) (2007)
23. Anubis: Analyzing Unknown Binaries, http://anubis.iseclab.org/
24. Norman SandBox, http://www.norman.com/enterprise/all_products/malware_analyzer/norman_sandbox_analyzer/no
25. NetSky Wiki, http://en.wikipedia.org/wiki/Netsky_%28computer_worm%29
26. Lee, W., Stolfo, S.: Data mining approaches for intrusion detection. In: Proceedings of the 7th USENIX Security Symposium (1998)

27. Jordan, M.: Dealing with metamorphism. Virus Bulletin, 4–6 (October 2002)
28. Zhuge, J., Holz, T., Han, X., Guo, J., Zou, W.: Characterizing the IRC-based Botnet Phenomenon, Reihe Informatik Technical Report TR-2007-010 (December 2007)
29. Lingyun, Y., Purui, S., Dengguo, F., Xianggen, W., Yi, Y., Yu, L.: ReconBin: Reconstructing Binary File from Execution for Software Analysis. In: Proceedings of the 2009 Third IEEE International Conference on Secure Software Integration and Reliability Improvement, pp. 222–229 (2009)

Author Index